T0334782

IN ASIAN WATERS

In Asian Waters

OCEANIC WORLDS
FROM YEMEN TO YOKOHAMA

ERIC TAGLIACOZZO

PRINCETON UNIVERSITY PRESS

PRINCETON & OXFORD

Published by Princeton University Press
41 William Street, Princeton, New Jersey 08540
6 Oxford Street, Woodstock, Oxfordshire OX20 1TR

press.princeton.edu

All Rights Reserved

Library of Congress Cataloging-in-Publication Data

Names: Tagliacozzo, Eric, author.
Title: In Asian waters : oceanic worlds from Yemen to Yokohama / Eric Tagliacozzo.
Other titles: Oceanic worlds from Yemen to Yokohama
Description: Princeton : Princeton University Press, 2022. | Includes bibliographical references and index.
Identifiers: LCCN 2021041745 (print) | LCCN 2021041746 (ebook) |
    ISBN 9780691146829 (hardback) | ISBN 9780691235646 (ebook)
Subjects: LCSH: Ocean and civilization. | Seas—Asia—History. | Navigation—Asia—History. | Asia—Relations—Africa, East. | Africa, East—Relations—Asia. | BISAC: HISTORY / Asia / General | HISTORY / Africa / East
Classification: LCC CB465 .T34 2022 (print) | LCC CB465 (ebook) |
    DDC 909/.0962—dc23/eng/20211022
LC record available at https://lccn.loc.gov/2021041745
LC ebook record available at https://lccn.loc.gov/2021041746

British Library Cataloging-in-Publication Data is available

Editorial: Priya Nelson, Abigail Johnson, and Barbara Shi
Production Editorial: Natalie Baan
Jacket Design: Lauren Smith
Production: Danielle Amatucci
Publicity: Kate Farquhar-Thomson Alyssa Sanford

Jacket art: Zhang Hongnian, *China's Greatest Armada*, 2004

This book has been composed in Arno

Printed on acid-free paper. ∞

Printed in the United States of America

10 9 8 7 6 5 4 3 2 1

CONTENTS

List of Illustrations   vii

Acknowledgments   xi

A Note on Languages   xix

1 South from Nagasaki, West from Hormuz   1

PART I. MARITIME CONNECTIONS

Preface: In Asian Waters   21

2 From China to Africa: Prolegomenon   25

3 Vietnam's Maritime Trade Orbit   52

PART II. BODIES OF WATER

Preface: The Imbricated Histories of Two Seas   75

4 Smuggling in the South China Sea: Illicit Histories   79

5 The Center and Its Margins: How the Indian
   Ocean Became "British"   103

PART III. RELIGION ON THE TIDES

Preface: Buddhism, Hinduism, Islam, and Christianity in Asian Waters 141

6 Passage of Amulets: Hindu-Buddhist Transmissions
   in the Bay of Bengal   145

7 Zamboanga, Mindanao: Islam and Christianity
   at the End of the World   167

PART IV. CITIES AND THE SEA

Preface: Urbanism Connects: The Life of Asian Cities　191

8　The Morphogenesis of Port Cities in "Greater Southeast Asia"　195

9　From Aden to Bombay, from Singapore to Pusan:
Colonial Circuits　224

PART V. THE BOUNTY OF THE OCEANS

Preface: The Environmental History of Asian Seas　251

10　Fins, Slugs, Pearls: Marine Products and Sino-Southeast Asia　255

11　On the Docks: How India's Southern Coasts
Became "Spice Central"　282

PART VI. TECHNOLOGIES OF THE SEA

*Preface: The Technological Imperative in the Maritime
History of Asia*　309

12　Foucault's Other Panopticon, or Lighting Colonial
Southeast Asia　313

13　Of Maps and Men: Hydrography and Empire　344

14　If China Rules the Waves　369

Appendix A: Base Chronologies for Asia's Seas　391
Appendix B: Written-Down Oral Histories of the Swahili Coasts　395
Appendix C: Fieldwork Excerpt from Sana'a: An Arab Herbalist　397
Appendix D: Indian Spice Traders in India and Malaysia　399
Appendix E: Dutch East Indies Regulations with Local Maritime States　401
Appendix F: Chinese Marine Goods Traders in East and Southeast Asia　403
*Appendix G: Chinese Marine Products Newspaper Clipping,
Taipei, Taiwan*　409
Bibliography　411
Index　475

ILLUSTRATIONS

Figures

2.1 Acacia Trees and Dhows on the Swahili Coasts   30

2.2 Zheng He's Treasure Ship and the *Wu Bei Zhi* Charts   42–43

2.3 *The Yong-Le Giraffe Brought Back to China,* 1415 CE   45

2.4 Coxinga's African Guard   50

3.1 Vietnamese "Ave Maria"   59

3.2 Vietnamese Bronze/Copper Coin   61

3.3 Topography of Vietnam's North Coasts   70

4.1 Qingping Market, Guangzhou: Baboons, Sea Horses   84

4.2 Qingping Market, Guangzhou: Oryx Horns, Monkey Feet   85

4.3 Dutch Blockade Runners, 1947   90–91

4.4 Burmese Smugglers in Penang, Malaysia   99

4.5 Thai Illegal Fishing Vessels, Songkhla   100

5.1 Indian Stevedore, Cochin, Kerala   120

6.1 Stone Votive Figures, Southern Siam   161

6.2 Bay of Bengal Sculpture: Avalokitesvara   163

7.1 Zamboanga, Mindanao: Cannon and Mosque   173

8.1 *Singapore Harbor Shortly after Its Founding*   204

9.1 Istanbul   228

9.2 Puccini's *Madama Butterfly*   245

10.1 Turtle Shell   263

10.2 Pearls   263

10.3 Trepang (Edible Sea Cucumber)   264

11.1 Cinnamon from Sri Lanka   291

11.2 Malabar Coast Landscape   292

12.1 The Panopticon: Karimata Strait   333

12.2 Screw-Pile Lights and Dioptric Lenses   337

13.1 Colonial Dutch Reef Notices   353

13.2 The Ajax Shoal   360

13.3 Dutch Hydrography in the Netherlands Indies   363

Tables

3.1 The Open Cadence of Maritime Vietnam at the Turn of
the 19th Century   69

4.1 Smuggling Statistics for the South China Sea   95

6.1 Underwater Archaeological Ceramic Data   157

9.1 Japanese Open-Port Additions and Port/Vessel Tonnages,
1898/1899   246

11.1 Singapore Manufacturer's Association Spice Statistics, 1989   303

13.1 Hydrographic Mapping of the Dutch East Indies   356

Maps

1.1 Maritime Asia: South from Nagasaki, West from Hormuz   3

2.1 From China to Africa by Sea   28

2.2 East African Coastal Cities   33

2.3 Monsoon Patterns in the Western Indian Ocean   35

3.1 Vietnam's Maritime Trade Orbit   54

4.1 The South China Sea   82

5.1 The Indian Ocean   106

6.1 The Bay of Bengal   147

7.1 The Sulu Sea   168

8.1 Maritime Southeast Asian Ports   197

9.1 Colonial Oceanic Circuits   226

10.1 Sino-Southeast Asia   269

11.1 South Asian Waters: The Malabar and Coromandel Coasts   283

12.1 An Arena of Lights   315

13.1 Hydrographic Waters   347

14.1 Competing Claims in the South China Sea   372

ACKNOWLEDGMENTS

Often when historians write on a larger canvas than their own patch of academic turf they are trying to get across a "big idea." This might be a statement as to how they see the world, or some segment of it, in centuries past. That's admirable, in my view—but it's not really the case here. In truth, this book has very modest ambitions. Though both the geographies and the temporalities on offer in this volume are large, the main thing I hoped to do was simple. I wanted to see how looking through a series of different windows might tell us something interesting about the role the sea has played in Asian history. Those windows show us a variety of vantages on the sea and its importance in this part of the world—through the prisms of distance (part I), region (part II), religion (part III), urbanism (part IV), the environment (part V), and technology (part VI). It seemed to me that by looking through these different apertures we might see Asian history in somewhat more connected ways than we normally do, as parts of this region are distributed throughout various area studies rubrics in the academy, each assigned a "place" all their own. My feelings on this are perhaps to some extent also born out of my own middle age. I have spent a lot of time now moving between many of these places, despite their supposed separateness as "objects of study," and the fact that I often asked myself if I hadn't already seen something somewhere else resonated with me after a while. That uneasy feeling of recognition was one of the reasons I pursued this project. Another was that as the world gets smaller—at least to our perceptions—the linkages between things start to become clearer and more pronounced. I wanted to record those sentiments as they became more manifest to me over time.

Going beyond one's comfort zone also necessitates relying on the expert advice of others. I'm very glad and grateful for the comments and critique I received not only from Princeton's reviewers, who read the whole manuscript, but from twenty-five colleagues and friends who agreed to read specific chapters pertaining to their own expertise. For chapter 2, on China and Africa's early connections, I thank Tansen Sen (NYU/Shanghai) and Geoff Wade (formerly ARI/Singapore) for their input and corrections. For chapter 3, on Vietnam's coasts, I thank Nhung Tran (University of Toronto) and Li Tana (formerly ANU/Canberra). For chapter 4, on illicit pathways in the South China Sea, I thank Robert Antony (University of Macau) and Yangwen Zhang (University of Manchester). For chapter 5, on the Indian Ocean, equal thanks go to Fahad Bishara (University of Virginia) and Isabel Hofmeyr (University of the Witwatersrand in South Africa). For chapter 6, on Buddhist amulets in the Bay of Bengal, I thank Anne Blackburn (Cornell) and Justin McDaniel (Penn). For chapter 7, on Islam and Christianity in Zamboanga, I thank Jojo Abinales (University of Hawai'i), Michael Laffan (Princeton), and Noelle Rodriguez (formerly Ateneo de Manila) for their considered commentaries. For chapter 8, on urbanism in "greater" Southeast Asia, thanks go to Michael Leaf (UBC) and Su Lin Lewis (Bristol). For chapter 9, on colonial circuits, I thank Rachel Leow (Cambridge) and Remco Raben (University of Amsterdam). For chapter 10, on marine goods products, thanks go to Pedro Machado (Indiana University) and Edyta Roszko (Bergen University). For chapter 11, on examining spices in the Bay of Bengal, I thank Prasenjit Duara (Duke) and Sebastian Prange (UBC). For chapter 12, on the lighting of Asian seas, I thank Peter Cunich (HKU) and Robert Elson (formerly University of Queensland). Finally, for chapter 13, on hydrography, thanks go to John Butcher (Murdoch University) and Suzanne Moon (University of Nebraska).

A larger number of people have been part of conversations about the sea together for many years now. Most important here have been Seema Alavi, Sunil Amrith, Sugata Bose, and Kerry Ward, all of whom have deeply shaped my own thinking—on the sea, and on life. Likewise, a group of other scholars have also been vital vis-à-vis educating me on the sea, including David Biggs, Jenny Gaynor, John Guy, Takeshi Hamashita, Tim Harper, Robert Hellyer, Eng Seng Ho, Isabel Hofmeyr, Celia Lowe, Matt Matsuda, Dilip Menon, Atsushi Ota, Ronald Po, Tony Reid, Tansen Sen, Singgih Sulistiyono, Heather Sutherland, Nancy Um, and Jim Warren. An even larger coterie of scholars in the academy have spoken with me at one point or another on some of the larger ideas appearing in this book: for doing so, I wish to thank Barbara Watson Andaya, Leonard Andaya, Maitrii Aung-Thwin, Tim Barnard, Zvi Ben-Dor, Leonard Blusse, Shelly Chan, Adam Clulow, Robert Cribb, Dhiravat na Pombejra, Don Emmerson, Michael Feener, Anne Gerritsen, Valerie Hansen, Robert Hellyer, David Henley, Matt Hopper, Naomi Hosoda, Diana Kim, Dorothy Ko, Michael Laffan, Eugenia Lean, Rachel Leow, Vic Lieberman, Mandana Limbert, Mona Lohanda, David Ludden, Fouad Makki, Rachel

McDermott, Arnout van der Meer, Rudolf Mrazek, Oona Paredes, Lorraine Paterson, Peter Perdue, James Pickett, Ken Pomeranz, Jeremy Prestholdt, Geoff Robinson, James Rush, Danilyn Rutherford, Yoon-hwan Shin, Takashi Shiraishi, John Sidel, Megan Thomas, Jing Tsu, Wu Xiao-an, Wen-hsin Yeh, Charles Wheeler, Bin Yang, and Peter Zinoman. Helen Siu and Angela Leung unite both of these lists: their support and friendship over the years crosses both seas and ideas. Holding "office hours" together in the sea off Zanzibar is still one of my favorite memories of the last thirty years. The above list is likely missing a fair number of people, but I hope it goes at least some way toward paying my intellectual debts. All these debts started in one place, however—in graduate school. I still owe my teachers from Yale an enormous amount: Ben Kiernan, Jim Scott, and Jonathan Spence helped set me on a path.

I wish to thank seven roughly same-age colleagues here in a bit more depth; these "fellow travelers" have really helped me in one way or another over the years, and I want to acknowledge that here. None of them are historians, and as a result all of them opened new worlds to me. Joshua Barker (Anthropology, University of Toronto) has been my partner in crime editing the journal *Indonesia* for fifteen-plus years now. I cannot think of a better person to do this with; he is a model citizen in all manner of ways, which I hope he knows. Siddharth Chandra (Economics, Michigan State) has also been important to me, mostly through the AIFIS hat that he wears, but in terms of real intellectual fellowship too, which I hope he knows as well. Wen-Chin Chang (Anthropology, Academia Sinica) and I have edited two books together—but it's the time that we have spent laughing about everything else that really means a lot to me. Her fearlessness has been inspirational to those of us who mostly write books from behind a desk. Carol Hau (Literature, Kyoto) has a grace that speaks volumes to me; especially important was one tea we shared together in Kyoto, which allowed me to understand her better. She is an inspiration to me in many ways. Natasha Reichle (Art History, San Francisco Museum of Asian Art) has been a great friend since our time at Advanced Indonesian SEASSI together in Seattle. Her warmth and quiet wisdom has been a bicoastal feature of my adult life, and all to the good. Ronit Ricci (Religion, Hebrew University) has also been a very important interlocutor to me. But more than that, she has been a great listener—a friend "over the ocean," though often the oceans changed. Finally, Andrew Willford (Anthropology, Cornell) has been a guiding presence in my life for twenty-plus years. Try doing a book together with Andrew to see how little you really know; his intellect and more so his moral compass always teach me in surprising and wonderful ways. His is the best CB presence one could hope for, until the founding of CBU becomes an actuality.

My teaching in Ithaca has informed this book quite a lot. I have taught a class on the Indian Ocean at Cornell for many years, as well as a more general course called "Ocean: The Sea in Human History." About six or seven years ago I began to teach a new class, called "The Pacific Horizon," with my friend and Latin Americanist colleague Ray Craib. That course eventually led to my being on a number of PhD committees together with Professors Craib and Ernesto Bassi, where I was always the general "oceans person" for a group of (mostly) Latin America–focused students. I have fulfilled much the same role (for the Indian Ocean) on South Asia PhD committees together with Durba Ghosh and Robert Travers. Those committees led me to think more generally about some of the issues that have ended up in this book. Finally, a last course—the "History of Exploration," which I was able to co-teach with Carl Sagan's replacement at Cornell, the astronomer Steve Squyres (before he left to become Jeff Bezos's chief engineer at the latter's space-start-up, Blue Origin)—inspired me to think about some of these patterns on an even larger scale. I taught about the history of exploration by land and especially by sea, while Professor Squyres covered everything that lifted up and off the planet. This course provided yet another perspective to what appears here. The graduate students and indeed some of the undergraduates I've been lucky enough to teach at Cornell made me think about these issues in a much more focused way than I ever would have, had I not had them in my classes. I owe all of these Cornell constituents for what they have taught me over the years.

My department colleagues in History have also been very important in this regard. My Asia-focused colleagues are wonderful, representing different generations. I've also been lucky to be part of a similar-age departmental cohort, give or take a few years to either side, who have shared time and space together in Ithaca. In this sense, I wish to record my gratitude to Ed Baptist, Ernesto Bassi, Judi Byfield, Derek Chang, Ray Craib, Paul Friedland, Maria Cristina Garcia, Durba Ghosh, Larry Glickman, TJ Hinrichs, Tamara Loos (Southeast Asia co-conspirator extraordinaire), Mostafa Minawi, Russell Rickford, Barry Strauss, Robert Travers, and Claudia Verhoeven. I want to include my new colleague Sun Peidong here as well; her example teaches us what courage looks like in its most basic form. A number of these folks are not only my colleagues but good friends as well; they know who they are. I've also worn a number of hats at Cornell, where I inevitably learned more than I taught from the people involved in these initiatives. In this regard, directing the Comparative Muslim

Societies Program has been particularly important; so too has been running Cornell's Modern Indonesia Project. I also put in this category editing the journal *Indonesia*, which I inherited (again, with Joshua Barker) from Benedict Anderson and Jim Siegel. A few years ago another rubric was added to this, when I was asked to co-helm the Migrations Initiative on campus. This huge initiative, with its broad sweep and emphasis on people in movement, has also had a direct impact on the thinking that went into this book. The fellow-leaders of the Migrations orbit here have been fantastic to work with; Shannon Gleeson, Gunisha Kaur, Steve Yale-Loehr, Rachel Riedl, and Wendy Wolford have taught me an enormous amount about how to work together in a group. Their perspectives on how to see a world in motion have definitely affected how I see the world too, from the locus of the various disciplines they represent (sociology, medicine, law, political science, and geography).

A number of my Cornell colleagues have departed in recent years, and I wish to name a few of them as well, for the importance they have had in my life, intellectual and otherwise. Lindy Williams just retired, and her presence at Cornell's Southeast Asia Program will be sorely missed. In my own department, Holly Case decamped to Brown but is still here with us in Ithaca in spirit, no matter where her corporeal self now resides. Itsie Hull retired some years ago but remains an example (to me and everyone else) of the kind of scholar one hopes to be, through her integrity and good humor. Larry Moore is now also gone but is not forgotten—I miss the lunches we had over the years, for their fun and conviviality. Larry was only the most important of a number of senior Americanists who treated me with great kindness after I got here, something I have never forgotten. In a related vein, I still remember writing lectures until 1 a.m. in McGraw Hall and going up to get my mail before returning home; Walt LeFeber would show up then, getting set to work for a while. I remember thinking: "Jesus, if Walt is here at 1, I had better be here until 3," but it was just indicative of the dedication of this group of Americanists, an example that has stayed in my mind for twenty years. Most important of all, however, has been Sherm Cochran, who retired several years ago but who still remains an outsized influence in my life. Sherm is a model in all ways; his example suggests how to attempt a life well-lived, in both scholarly and other terms. The road-trip we took together to visit our common teacher at Yale, Jonathan Spence, on his eightieth birthday is still one of the great moments of my adult life. Would we have enough to talk about for twelve hours in the car, there and back, I wondered? I remember pulling back into his driveway when we returned, and looking across at him after all of that driving. "Vegas?" I said, putting the key back in the ignition. Sherm is a teacher in the full sense of the term. I hope he knows this, though I suspect his modesty won't allow him to fully understand the effect he has had on my life.

A series of editors and editorial assistants (mostly at Princeton) greatly helped this book on its way. Brigitta van Rheinberg signed on the project; Eric Crahan shepherded it through reviewing; and Priya Nelson brought the proj-ect home—I'm very grateful to all three of them. My production editor, Nata-lie Baan, also very much helped this book see the light of day, and Anne Cherry was a rigorous copy-editor. Thalia Leaf and Abigail Johnson made sure all got done when it needed to and guided me along the way. Abby Kleiman contrib-uted some vital editorial work. Several venues allowed me to publish revised materials here that appeared in earlier versions elsewhere. Thanks on this count to *Critical Asian Studies* 34, no. 2 (2002): 193–220 (for chapter 4); *Itin-erario* 26, no. 1 (2002): 75–106 (for chapter 5); the *Journal of Urban History* 33, no. 6 (2007): 911–32 (for chapter 8); my chapter in my and Wen-Chin Chang's 2011 edited volume for Duke University Press, *Chinese Circulations* (for chap-ter 10); *Technology and Culture* 46, no. 2 (2005): 306–28 (for chapter 12); and *Archipel* 65 (2003): 89–107 (for chapter 13). A large number of institutions in North America and Europe allowed me to test these notions in invited lec-tures, and I sincerely thank these universities. But I particularly appreciated the chance to speak on the ideas taking shape in this book in venues along the routes themselves. Many thanks therefore to Kyoto University's Southeast Asia Program; to the Hong Kong Institute for Humanities and Social Sciences (HKU); to the Academia Sinica in Taipei; to ARI/Singapore; to the Universiti Kebangsaan Malaysia; to the E & O (Penang); to USINDO (Jakarta); to the Netaji Institute (Kolkata); to Cornell Medical School (Doha); to Yale's "China/Africa" conference in Nairobi; and finally to the Yale/HKIHSS work-shop in Zanzibar. The HKIHSS (Hong Kong) and the Academia Sinica (Tai-pei) also gave me fellowships to sit and write, for which I am extremely grate-ful. The faculty and staff in both of these places are wonderful and really made me feel welcome. Finally, I wish to thank the following scholars for checking my translations: Tineke Hellwig for antiquated Malay; Michela Baraldi for Italian; and Leon Sachs and Phi Van Nguyen for French. Thanks also to Thuy Tranviet for assistance with Vietnamese diacritic marks. Translations from Chinese oral history interviewing and from Dutch sources are my own.

A disparate group of friends has been with me for a long time now, in dif-ferent guises; these folks deserve a mention as well for the role they have played in my life's arc over the years. Park Bun Soon in Seoul has been my

Korean "older brother" for some thirty years now; I still marvel at the longevity of our friendship. Ming-chi Chen in Taipei has also become an important friend, especially in the times that I have been in Taiwan; he and his family remind me of what grace looks like under trying circumstances. In Germany, both Birte Saager and Peter and Sabia Schwarzer, though unknown to each other, have been stalwarts in my consciousness for many years now—and all of this from a single year's initial friendship, which grew into one of decades in both cases, spanning several continents. My college friends Morgan Hall, John Heller, and Mike Steinberger remain important touchstones in my life, and blessedly so. The untimely passing of two close graduate-school friends, John Jones and Bruce McKim, has served to remind me that life is fragile. The only inadvertent blessing that came of that was my holding on just a bit tighter to several other friends from Yale days with whom I had mostly lost touch—especially Felipe Hernandez, Joanne Rim, and Joel Seltzer, dear old friends all. The oldest friendships of all, though, are still those shared with my Bronx High School of Science crew—all of us friends for forty years, and some of us for even longer than that, going back to elementary school. In Jon Auerbach, Eric Baron, Tom Crowe, Marc DeLeeuw, Sheesh Gonzales, Sang Ho Kim, Dick Lau, Mark Mokryn, James O'Shea, Peter Stefanopolous, Tom Stepniewski—and most especially, Robert Yacoub—I have life-long friendships. Very possibly the only good thing to have come out of the entire Covid pandemic was the advent of Zoom, which has gotten the lot of us together on screen every Thursday and Sunday for the past two years. The craft-beer companies made out like bandits.

Finally, my family is deeply responsible for this book as well. My wife, Katherine Peipu Lee, and our children, Clara and Luca, bear the brunt of my being away from the collective when I disappear to do these books. Clara was only a baby when my first book was published, and Luca was not yet even born; both are now teenagers, and Clara has one foot out the door. This whispers ominously to me about the passing of time. My sister and her family also make me understand how lucky I've been to have kinship of this sort in my life. Many years ago, my father passed away suddenly and unexpectedly before he turned fifty; my first monograph was dedicated to him. My second book was dedicated to my family here in Ithaca. This book is dedicated to my mother, who picked up the pieces for all of us after my dad's passing. My sister and I were still teenagers then—I was nineteen and a sophomore in college, and my sister was almost seventeen and just finishing high school. Our mother let me stay away in the years following, and let my sister head off to university too, despite the grievous loss to all of us at that time. I knew that was difficult for her, but perhaps I didn't realize quite how difficult until now, when my own kids are getting set to leave. After I graduated from college I departed on an even longer journey, disappearing onto the ocean routes of Asia to interview spice and marine goods merchants on a fellowship, much of it spent traveling by ship. For over a year I was simply "out there"—there was no internet then— somewhere on the Indian Ocean rim, or crisscrossing the South China Sea. My mother let us start our lives, though that must have taken a great deal of will and must have come at a great sense of loss to herself. This book is dedicated to her in thanks for letting me head out to sea, and into the waiting arms of the world.

A NOTE ON LANGUAGES

This book required the use of a number of languages, both in consulting various libraries and archives on several continents, and in the conduct of fieldwork. All translations from Chinese (in interviewing), and Indonesian/Malay, Dutch, French, and Italian are my own, unless otherwise stated. I have endeavored to keep spellings as systematized as possible—though when the sources themselves are speaking, I follow period usages.

IN ASIAN WATERS

1

South from Nagasaki, West from Hormuz

Suddenly the full long wail of a ship's horn surged through the open window and flooded the dim room . . . burdened with all the passion of the tides, the memory of voyages beyond counting.

—YUKIO MISHIMA, *THE SAILOR WHO FELL FROM GRACE WITH THE SEA*

WHEN I ARRIVED IN NAGASAKI, the first thing I did was to climb into the hills. These hills ring the port on almost all sides, leaving a narrow basin of water below, where the ships come in from the sea. Four hundred years ago, as these vessels began to bring in more and more "things," including strange commodities and strange, foreign ideas, the local ruler of Nagasaki decided that enough was enough. He had better act before he lost his kingdom. The sea was dangerous; its gifts were equally dangerous. He rounded up several dozen Christians, those who had converted to the new religion that had come through the port, along with a few foreign Christians, and he held them captive. Then he ordered his men to crucify them on wooden posts ringing Nagasaki harbor. Within full view of the docking ships, the strangers who had come by sea—and their impressionable Japanese audiences, some of whom had dared to believe their teachings—were told in no uncertain terms who ruled this place. Dejima (Deshima), the little island settlement in the bay where the foreign ships were quarantined so as to take advantage of their trade, but not their dangerous notions, fell into disrepair for a while after this. As an act of terror the local *daimyo*, or chief, had done his work well—the maritime "foreign" had been intimidated into acquiescence. But only for a while. Soon Deshima's commerce picked up again, and over the next two centuries, while

1

Japan tried to some extent to isolate itself from the currents of the maritime world, a trickle of influence still came in through the port. Guns came, and were adopted quickly, though with much angst, moral hand-wringing, and discussion. Clocks came too, as did Western calendars, and more ideas. But the shadow of those executions can still be felt in the hills of the port city even now, some half a millennium away.[1] One wonders if the martyred believers felt their sacrifice was worth it, to bring gifts from the sea to a place that so clearly did not want such offerings.[2]

On the seacoast of Oman, in a town called Sur, I walked in the huge, sprawling fish market until I was weary. Sur is on the coast of Oman jutting out into the Arabian Sea; farther west along those shores, the waterway bends into the Gulf of Hormuz, and then sweeps into the Persian Gulf. From the Omani coastline farther up the strand, on a clear day, you can barely make out the dust-pink shimmer of Iran across the water. I had been walking in that fish market for hours, writing down the names of the fish that I could recognize, though there were many species that I did not know. But all of nature's plenty was there—huge sharks whose fins had been sliced off, destined for the Chinese market; tiny reef fish, neon red and orange and magenta-blue. A manta ray as big as a motorcycle sat in its own blood on the grimy concrete floor, its rattail pointing out to the sea like a beckoning, spindly arm. Here, too, as in Nagasaki, lay evidence of the foreign, and the distant—in addition to the shark

1. For a sense of Catholic missionary interactions with Japan in the early centuries of contact, and voyages in both directions, see G. O. Schurhammer, "Il contributo dei missionary cattolici nei secoli XVI e XVII alla conoscenza del Giappone," in *Le missioni cattoliche e la cultura dell'Oriente. Conferenze 'Massimo Piccinini'* (Rome: Istituto italiano per il Medio ed Estremo Oriente, 1943), 115–17; G. Berchet, *Le antiche ambasciate giapponesi in Italia: Saggio storico con documenti* (Venice 1877), 53–54; "Ragionamento I che contiene la partenza dall'Isole Filippine a quelle del Giappone ed altre cose notabili di quel paese," in *Ragionamenti di Francesco Carletti fiorentino sopra le cose da lui vedute ne'suoi viaggi si dell'Indie Occidentali, e Orientali come d'altri paesi. All'Illustriss. Sig. Marchese Cosimo da Castiglione gentiluomo della Camera del Serenissimo Granduca di Toscana* (Florence 1701), part II: *Ragionamenti . . . sopra le cose da lui vedute ne' suoi viaggi dell'Indie Orientali, e d'altri paesi,* 35–36.

2. For the big-picture view on these interactions, see Matsukata Fuyoko, "From the Threat of Roman Catholicism to the Shadow of Western Imperialism," in *Large and Broad: The Dutch Impact on Early Modern Asia,* ed. Yoko Nagazumi (Tokyo: Toyo Bunko, 2010); Adam Clulow, *The Company and the Shogun: The Dutch Encounters with Tokugawa Japan* (New York: Columbia University, 2013); Robert Hellyer, *Defining Engagement: Japan and Global Contexts, 1640–1868* (Cambridge: Harvard University Asia Center, 2009); and Leonard Blussé, *Visible Cities* (Cambridge: Harvard University Press, 2008).

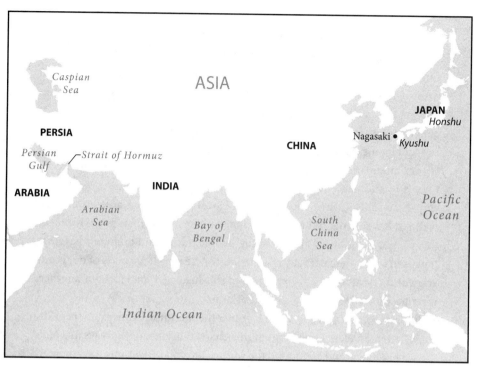

MAP 1.1. Maritime Asia: South from Nagasaki, West from Hormuz

fins, a small café advertised its connections with Indonesia. A sign in Bahasa told visitors—likely construction crewmen from the polar opposite side of the Indian Ocean—that they could come here to make phone calls back to Jakarta, as well as grab snacks that they missed from home. Fins and coffee; Christianity and quiet ships, moored on the tide. These ports on the opposite ends of Asia had much in common, and yet nothing in common. Arabic could be heard in one, and Japanese was spoken in the other, in both cases by gnarled, suntanned men on the docks. But the murmur of connection between these places was unmistakable. One didn't even need to listen; one simply had to watch. As several dhows headed out to sea from Sur, pulling east with the monsoon winds toward the open waters of the Indian Ocean, I asked myself, "Haven't I seen all of this before?" When I couldn't answer that question to my own satisfaction, I started taking notes in preparation for writing this book.

When one drinks coffee in the morning, it is partly because of the sea routes of Asia. If one hears Chinese being spoken on one's way to work in the Western world, it is partly because of the sea routes of Asia. If a call center in Mumbai approved your credit card purchase today (and it probably did), this was partly because of the sea routes of Asia as well. How can this be so? How can maritime pathways that have existed for centuries be partially responsible for so many of the day-to-day realities of our lived existence?[3] It seems counterintuitive, yet this observation is true. The slow-moving, elegant ships that brought coffee to the world from early modern Yemen; the quiet sailing vessels that brought Chinese immigrants to all of the planet's shores; the growth of industry and population along India's arid outstretched coasts—all are interconnected phenomena. All of these circumfusing actors have in common the single crucial element of the sea linking local places to far larger, translocal realities. It would not be an exaggeration, perhaps, to say that the sea routes of this part of the globe—and all of the people, ideas, and materiel that have traversed them—are partially responsible for creating large parts of our modern world.[4] Most of us are connected to this history in one form or another, whether we realize this on a daily basis or not.

In Asian Waters attempts to tie together the maritime history of Asia into a single, interconnected web. The volume charts out some of the ways in which the sea has linked and connected the various littorals of Asia into a segmented and (at the same time) a unitary circuit over roughly the past five hundred

3. There has been a small renaissance, lately, in looking at the sea for big-picture ideas on history; see, for example, Lincoln Paine, The Sea and Civilization: A Maritime History of the World (New York: Alfred Knopf, 2013); Philip de Souza, Seafaring and Civilization: Maritime Perspectives on World History (London: Profile Books, 2001); Jerry Bentley, Renate Bridenthal, and Kären Wigen, eds., Seascapes: Maritime Histories, Littoral Cultures, and Transoceanic Exchanges (Honolulu: University of Hawai'i Press, 2007); Kären Wigen, "Oceans of History," American Historical Review, 111, no. 3 (2006): 717–21; Barry Cunliffe, By Steppe, Desert, and Ocean: The Birth of Eurasia (Oxford: Oxford University Press, 2015); Tsukaya Mizushima, George Souza, and Dennis Flynn, eds., Hinterlands and Commodities: Place, Space, Time and the Political Economic Development of Asia over the Long Eighteenth Century (Leiden: Brill, 2015); Lin Yu-ju and Madeleine Zelin, eds., Merchant Communities in Asia, 1600–1800 (London: Routledge, 2016); Alain Forest, "L'Asie du sud-est continentale vue de la mer," in Commerce et navigation en Asie du sud-est (XIVe–XIXe siècles), ed. Nguyễn Thế Anh and Yoshiaki Ishizawa, 7–30 (Paris: L'Harmattan, 1999); and Geoffrey Gunn, History without Borders: The Making of an Asian World Region, 1000–1800 (Hong Kong: Hong Kong University Press, 2011).

4. See Martin Lewis and Kären Wigen, The Myth of Continents: A Critique of Metageography (Berkeley: University of California Press, 1997); see also Lauren Benton and Nathan Perl-Rosenthal, eds., A World at Sea: Maritime Practices and Global History (Philadelphia: University of Pennsylvania Press, 2020).

years, since the so-called contact age initiated a quickening of patterns and engagement that had already begun.[5] As such, it is part and parcel of the new transnational history now being written widely across the discipline; this is a history that makes the broad sweep, both of geography and of time, the center of the narrative. Janet Abu-Lughod famously said of Asia in the time period just before this book takes place: "In a system, it is the connections between the parts that must be studied. When these strengthen and reticulate, the system may be said to 'rise'; when they fray, the system declines, although it may later undergo reorganization and revitalization."[6] This book integrates transnational history à la Abu-Lughod with other avenues of historical vision that are now being used more and more by scholars, such as environmental history, science and technology studies, subalternity, and the critical history of empire. How these approaches fit together provides a window into the working gears of the globe as we know it.

I argue in this volume that by looking at the half-millennium "grand curve" of Asia's seas, a number of important themes that ultimately helped forge our common, modern world come to the fore. The creeping advance of external power, and indigenous action and agency in dealing with this phenomenon, form one of these themes. The regional and eventually global trade in a wide variety of objects, both sea-related and non-sea-centered, but passing through the region on thousands of ships, is another. Finally, the maritime movement of religion and concomitant political challenges to earlier forms of entrenched authority are but some of these ideas. These notions—power; trade; the oscillation of empires; diaspora; and religion-in-transit—are among the main linking themes of the book. *In Asian Waters* tries to connect these disparate notions into a single study through a series of topical windows, and asks how our vision of the world's largest continent and its history might vary if we see this vast expanse of territory not by land, but rather from the sea, as part of a unitary story.[7] How does that shift in cadence change our collective historical vision?

5. Parts of the narrative go even further back in time, where I think a more extended timeline is useful; see particularly chapters 2, 6, and 8.

6. Janet Abu-Lughod, *Before European Hegemony: The World System AD 1250–1350* (New York: Oxford University Press, 1989), 368.

7. Some scholars have already been moving in this direction; I am by no means the first. I outline many of these studies in the notes of the pages that follow here in the introduction, but for a useful overview of the issues, see Markus Vink, "Indian Ocean Studies and the New Thalassology," *Journal of Global History* 2, 2007: 41–62.

Writing histories of large bodies of water is not new; not all explanations of the past are geochronometric in character.[8] Among the first historians to do this was the great Fernand Braudel, whose two-volume study of the Mediterranean world in the early modern age became the gold standard for a generation of historians following in his wake.[9] Instead of studying Europe per se or even any of its nation-states, Braudel unified the history of southern Europe and North Africa's Maghreb into one story. The results made great sense to the profession, who saw in his books new ways of approaching history generally. Bernard Bailyn did something along the same lines for the Atlantic, when he refused the disaggregated approaches of "European" and "American" history and instead sewed the two other in his own work, forming a single, coherent world.[10] This approach also ensnared many admirers, and different takes on

8. For just a limited sense of some of the possibilities, see David Armitage, Alison Bashford, and Sujit Sivasundaram, eds., Oceanic Histories (New York: Cambridge University Press, 2017); Jerry H. Bentley, "Sea and Ocean Basins as Frameworks of Historical Analysis," Geographical Review 89, no. 2 (April 1999), 215–24; Beernhard Klein and Gesa Mackenthun, eds., Sea Changes: Historicizing the Ocean (New York: Routledge, 2004); Martin Lewis, "Dividing the Ocean Sea," Geographical Review 89, no. 2 (April 1999): 188–214; Philip E. Steinberg, The Social Construction of the Ocean (New York: Cambridge University Press, 2001); Daniel Finamore, ed., Maritime History As World History (Gainesville: University Press of Florida, 2004); Jennifer L. Gaynor, "Maritime Ideologies and Ethnic Anomalies: Sea Space and the Structure of Subalternality in the Southeast Asian Littoral," in Seascapes: Maritime Histories, Littoral Cultures, and Transoceanic Exchanges, ed. Jerry H. Bentley, Renate Bridenthal, and Kären Wigen, 53–68 (Honolulu: University of Hawai'i Press, 2007); and Bernhard Klein and Gesa Mackenthun, eds., Sea Changes: Historicizing the Ocean (London and New York: Routledge, 2004).

9. Fernand Braudel, The Mediterranean and the Mediterranean World in the Age of Phillip II (Berkeley: University of California Press Reprints, 1996), 2 vols.

10. Bernard Bailyn, The Ideological Origins of the American Revolution (Cambridge, MA: Harvard University Press, 1967); Bernard Bailyn, The Peopling of British North America (New York: Vintage Press, 1988); and Bernard Bailyn, Voyagers to the West: A Passage in the Peopling of America on the Eve of the Revolution (New York: Vintage Press, 1988). For some of the intellectual descendants of Bailyn, see Jorge Cañizares-Esguerra and Erik R. Seeman, eds., The Atlantic in Global History, 1500–2000, 2nd. ed. (New York: Routledge, 2018); Jack P. Greene and Philip D. Morgan, eds., Atlantic History: A Critical Appraisal (New York: Oxford University Press, 2009); Michael Pye, The Edge of the World: A Cultural History of the North Sea and the Transformation of Europe (New York: Pegasus Books, 2014); Daviken Studnicki-Gizbert, A Nation upon the Ocean Sea: Portugal's Atlantic Diaspora and the Crisis of the Spanish Empire, 1492–1640 (New York: Oxford University Press, 2007); Julius S. Scott, The Common Wind: Afro-American

"Atlantic history" eventually became very popular. Perhaps this was no more so than in the well-received (and often imitated) study of the "Black Atlantic" by Paul Gilroy. If Braudel brought the worlds of Christianity and Islam together through trade and the environment of the Mediterranean, then Bailyn brought what used to be called the "old" and the "new" worlds together through migration, and the exchange of revolutionary ideas across the North Atlantic. Gilroy added race into this potent mixture, and when triangle trades, the genesis of capitalism, and new forms of cultural history were grafted in as well, the study of the sea showed all kinds of new possibilities.[11] Historians of the Left, too, found fecund possibilities here; Marcus Rediker and others then moved the paradigm forward in the Caribbean, with studies of piracy, class, and the advent of shipborne democracies as part of this evolution. Indeed, the Caribbean, much like the Mediterranean on the other side of the Atlantic, has become a complicated site of historical experimentation, especially when it comes to looking at transgression and innovation in history as regards race, class, and the rise of the modern state.[12]

The Pacific has not been as popular a site for this sort of experimentation, at least until fairly recently. Significantly larger than the Atlantic and also less obviously connected in terms of the kinds of sources that could illustrate such ties, it has only been in the past several decades that Pacific history has caught up to the Atlantic paradigm. Thick, somewhat popular-tinged volumes were published, and these look at the vast ambit of this ocean, from Tierra del Fuego north to the Aleutians, and the Kamchatka Peninsula down to Tasmania and New Zealand.[13] Here again themes abound: the importance of whaling in the

---

Currents in the Age of the Haitian Revolution (New York: Verso, 2020); John Thornton, *Africa and Africans in the Making of the Atlantic World, 1400–1800*, 2nd. ed. (New York: Cambridge University Press, 1998); Jace Weaver, *The Red Atlantic: American Indigenes and the Making of the Modern World, 1000–1927* (Chapel Hill: The University of North Carolina Press, 2014).

11. Paul Gilroy, *The Black Atlantic: Modernity and Double Consciousness* (Cambridge, MA: Harvard University Press, 1993).

12. Marcus Rediker, *Between the Devil and the Deep Blue Sea: Merchant Seamen, Pirates, and the Anglo-American Maritime World, 1700–1750* (Cambridge: Cambridge University Press, 1989); and (with Peter Linebaugh), *The Many-Headed Hydra: Sailors, Slaves, Commoners, and the Hidden History of the Revolutionary Atlantic* (New York: Beacon Press, 2013); Lance Grahn, *The Political Economy of Smuggling: Regional Informal Economies in Early Bourbon New Granada* (Boulder, CO: Westview Press, 1997); and see Ernesto Bassi, *An Aqueous Territory: Sailor Geographies and New Granada's Transimperial Greater Caribbean World* (Durham: Duke University Press, 2016).

13. Frank Sherry, *Pacific Passions: The European Struggle for Power in the Great Ocean in the Age of Exploration* (New York: William Morrow, 1994); and Walter McDougall, *Let the Sea Make*

Pacific interocean economy, for example, or the diaspora of indigenous peoples who were seeded through the ocean via ethno-astronomy and outrigger canoes, outfitted for epic, long-distance journeys. Only recently, however, have there been more sophisticated attempts to define and tabulate what all of this movement has meant.[14] The injection of indigenous perspectives into this dialogue by scholars such as Epeli Hauʻofa and Kealani Cook has been of crucial importance, both by writers of Pacific heritage themselves, and sometimes by non-indigenes, who have nonetheless been sympathetic to the decades-long writing of local people out of Pacific History by earlier practitioners of the genre.[15] It has been through these more recent studies by Matt Matsuda and others that Pacific History has taken on a new sophistication, and also a mooring of sorts within the larger global histories that are now being written.[16] The history of the polar seas, for example, does not yet show much evidence of this sort of incorporation or evolution, focused as it still is on narratives of heroic exploration. The first Europeans who penetrated the polar seas certainly did not lack courage. But their stories are still for the most part told in isolation

---

a Noise: Four Hundred Years of Cataclysm, Conquest, War and Folly in the North Pacific (New York: Avon Books, 1993).

14. Two early exceptions to this rule were Greg Dening, *Islands and Beaches: Discourse on a Silent Land; Marquesas 1774–1880* (Chicago: Dorsey Press, 1980); and David A. Chappell, *Double Ghosts: Oceanian Voyagers on Euroamerican Ships* (New York: M. E. Sharpe, 1997). For a range of newer and more inclusive approaches, see Stuart Banner, *Possessing the Pacific: Lands, Settlers, and Indigenous People from Australia to Alaska* (Cambridge: Harvard University Press, 2007); David Igler, *The Great Ocean: Pacific Worlds from Captain Cook to the Gold Rush* (New York: Oxford University Press, 2013); Rainer F. Buschmann, Edward R. Slack Jr., and James B. Tueller, *Navigating the Spanish Lake: The Pacific in the Iberian World, 1521–1898* (Honolulu: University of Hawaiʻi Press, 2014); and David A. Chang, *The World and All the Things upon It: Native Hawaiian Geographies of Exploration* (Minneapolis: University of Minnesota Press, 2016).

15. See, for example, Epeli Hauʻofa, *We Are the Ocean: Selected Works* (Honolulu: University of Hawaiʻi Press), 2008; Epeli Hauʻofa, "Our Sea of Islands," *The Contemporary Pacific* 6, no. 1 (1994); and K. R. Howe, *Nature, Culture and History: The "Knowing" of Oceania* (Honolulu: University of Hawaiʻi Press, 2000). Also see Kealani Cook, *Return to Kahiki: Native Hawaiians in Oceania* (New York: Cambridge University Press, 2018).

16. Matt Matsuda, *Pacific Worlds: A History of Seas, Peoples, and Cultures* (New York: Cambridge University Press, 2012); Lorenz Gonschor, *A Power in the World: The Hawaiian Kingdom in Oceania* (Honolulu: University of Hawaiʻi Press, 2019); Ricardo Padrón, *The Indies of the Setting Sun: How Early Modern Spain Mapped the Far East as the Transpacific West* (Chicago: University of Chicago Press, 2020); and Nicholas Thomas, *Islanders: The Pacific in the Age of Empire* (New Haven: Yale University Press, 2010).

from local communities, as the exploits of "great men" who conquered nature, as if no one else was standing on the ice with them in their travels.

With only one recent exception, in the work of Sunil Amrith, there has not really been a single study looking at Asia's seas through a broad macro-lens, and that is a lacuna that the present book hopes to fill.[17] But that does not mean that scholars have not looked at maritime issues in Asia in novel and interesting ways. For East Asia, and the seas that have abutted and fed into the South China Sea as a sort of middle body of water, binding the region proper, comparatively few authors have staked out claims. The ones who have done so have often been very, very good, however. Andre Gunder Frank is one of these scholars, and his remarkable *ReOrient*—though not a maritime history in its constitution—laid down the gauntlet to others.[18] *ReOrient* asks us to try to reconceptualize both space and the histories of those who have flowed through such spaces in novel and fascinating ways. Asians are at the center of his world history, and not (as has almost always been the case) figures upon whom history solely has acted, mainly through the expansion of Europeans. This was a real shift in lenses, and the production of Gunder Frank's book led to new ways of thinking about Asian History as constituting its own motor for transformative events in the world over the last several centuries.[19] Takeshi Hamashita has been more centrally located in the maritime paradigm, and his studies of the South China Sea (from the Ryukyu Kingdom of Okinawa down to Southeast Asia) have given us new impetus in thinking about the connections between China and the Sinicized countries of Northeast Asia in powerful ways.[20]

17. The closest thing we have is Amrith's wonderful study. This is a very different kind of work than the present one, however, as it looks at water in all forms, and it is primarily geared toward the Indian Ocean. See Sunil Amrith, *Unruly Waters: How Rains, Rivers, Coasts, and Seas Have Shaped Asia's History* (New York: Basic Books, 2018).

18. Andre Gunder Frank, *ReOrient: Global Economy in the Asian Age* (Berkeley: University of California Press, 1998).

19. For a more comparative approach, and equally excellent, see Kenneth Pomeranz, *The Great Divergence: China, Europe, and the Making of the Modern World Economy* (Princeton: Princeton University Press, 2000).

20. Takeshi Hamashita, *China, East Asia, and the Global Economy: Regional and Historical Perspectives* (New York: Routledge, 2013); Takeshi Hamashita, "The Tribute Trade System and Modern Asia," trans. Neil Burton and Christian Daniels, in Takeshi Hamashita, *China, East Asia, and the Global Economy: Regional and Historical Perspectives*, eds. Linda Grove and Mark Selden, 12–26 (London and New York: Routledge, 2008); Takeshi Hamashita, "The Intra-regional System in East Asia in Modern Times," in *Network Power: Japan and Asia*, ed. Peter J. Katzenstein and Takashi Shiraishi, 113–35 (Ithaca, NY: Cornell University Press, 1997).

Hamashita has led this charge, though there have been other important figures more recently in this movement, too.[21] But his work is based on the painstaking accumulation of many other scholars' findings as well, so that he is in conversation with many Chinese and Japanese researchers whose data might not otherwise have been seen by English-speaking reading publics. Finally, Dian Murray has also been important in this context, with her pioneering *Pirates of the South China Coasts* also breaking new ground, in at least two ways. First, the book brought China and Sinicized Southeast Asia into one frame, to be discussed as equals in the maritime history that flowed between them. Second, her book also introduced gender to this debate in ways that had not previously been tried. Her monograph has become a classic of sorts in both of these senses, and is regularly cited not just by historians of a transnational bent but by scholars who are receptive to gender analyses in the drive of history as well.[22]

In the lower latitudes of the South China Sea, and into maritime Southeast Asia itself, the history of the sea has also been a topic for vigorous debate.[23] In this area, the "lands beneath the winds," the ocean has been a necessary format for writing history for quite some time. Indonesia is the world's largest archipelago, with some seventeen thousand islands, and when the Philippines and Malaysia and other regional cultures are thrown in, one can easily see why

21. For just a few, see Giovanni Arrighi, Takeshi Hamashita, and Mark Selden, "Introduction: The Rise of East Asia in Regional and World Historical Perspective," in *The Resurgence of East Asia: 500, 150 and 50 Year Perspectives*, ed. Arrighi et al., 1–16 (London and New York: Routledge, 2003); and Angela Schottenhammer, ed., *The East Asian Maritime World 1400–1800: Its Fabrics of Power and Dynamics of Exchanges* (Wiesbaden: Harrassowitz Verlag, 2007); John E. Wills, "Maritime Asia 1500–1800: The Interactive Emergence of European Domination," *American Historical Review* 98, no. 1 (1993): 83–105; Charlotte von Verschuer, *Across the Perilous Sea: Japanese Trade with China and Korea from the Seventh to the Sixteenth Centuries*, trans. Kristen Lee Hunter (Ithaca, NY: Cornell University Press, 2006); and William D. Wray, "The Seventeenth-century Japanese Diaspora: Questions of Boundary and Policy," in *Diaspora Entrepreneurial Networks: Four Centuries of History*, ed. Ina Baghdiantz McCabe, Gelina Harlaftis, and Ioanna Pepelasis Minoglu, 73–79 (Oxford and New York: Berg, 2005).

22. Dian Murray, *Pirates of the South China Coast, 1790–1810* (Palo Alto: Stanford University Press, 1987).

23. See Derek Heng, "Trans-Regionalism and Economic Co-dependency in the South China Sea: The Case of China and the Malay Region (Tenth to Fourteenth Centuries AD)," *International History Review* 35, no. 3 (2013): 486–510; David C. Kang, *East Asia before the West: Five Centuries of Trade and Tribute* (New York: Columbia University Press, 2010); and Geoffrey C. Gunn, *History without Borders: The Making of an Asian World Region, 1000–1800* (Hong Kong: Hong Kong University Press, 2011).

lucid conceptualizations of maritime history become immediately necessary in this part of the world. The touchstone study here has been Anthony Reid's two-volume *Southeast Asia in the Age of Commerce*, which bound the early modern history of Southeast Asia—and especially insular Southeast Asia—into one coherent story.[24] Reid took on how all of these seemingly separate societies in fact had much in common, attributes often transmitted or shared by maritime means. Though some of his assertions were later challenged by scholars such as Victor Lieberman and Barbara Watson Andaya, the core assumptions seem to have been largely right, even if the farther one goes from island Southeast Asia up and onto the mainland (or as one takes gender more centrally into account), several of his points may lose some valence.[25] But Reid's was only the largest and most ambitious study to try to encircle the region's seas, and to spin a narrative out of local waters that he saw as connecting cultures more than separating them. On a slightly smaller scale, the great French scholar Denys Lombard tried much the same thing with his remarkable *Le Carrefour Javanais*, and in the Southern Philippines James Francis Warren also moved along these intrepid lines in his path-breaking *The Sulu Zone*.[26] In eastern Indonesia, Roy Ellen, too, did this for what he called the Banda Zone, and on the opposite side of the archipelago Dianne Lewis and later Leonard Andaya sought similar results from marking off the Melaka Straits.[27] Clearly the notion of bodies of water hit home in Southeast Asian History, expanding the sea as a unit of analysis that could then tell us new things about historical patterns as a whole.[28]

24. Anthony Reid, *Southeast Asia in the Age of Commerce: The Lands beneath the Winds* (New Haven: Yale University Press, 1993 and 1998).

25. Two important revisionist critiques have come from Victor Lieberman, *Strange Parallels* (Cambridge: Cambridge University Press, 2003), and Barbara Watson Andaya, *The Flaming Womb: Repositioning Women in Early Modern Southeast Asian History* (Honolulu: University of Hawai'i Press, 2006).

26. Denys Lombard, *Le carrefour javanais: Essai d'histoire globale* (Paris: École Hautes Études en Sciences Sociales, 1990); James Francis Warren, *The Sulu Zone* (Singapore; Singapore University Press, 1981).

27. Roy Ellen, *On the Edge of the Banda Zone: Past and Present in the Social Organization of a Moluccan Trading Network* (Honolulu: University of Hawai'i Press, 2003); Dianne Lewis, *Jan Compagnie in the Straits of Malacca* (Columbus: Ohio University Press, 1995); Leonard Andaya, *Leaves from the Same Tree: Trade and Ethnicity in the Straits of Melaka* (Honolulu: University of Hawai'i Press, 2008).

28. See, in addition, Alain Forest, "L'Asie du Sud-est continentale vue de la mer," in *Commerce et navigation*, ed. Nguyễn and Ishizawa, 7–30; and Peter Boomgaard, ed., *A World of Water: Rain, Rivers, and Seas in Southeast Asian Histories* (Leiden: KITLV Press, 2007.

Yet if moves have been made in these directions over the past several decades for Southeast Asia, the site of the most frenetic intellectual exchange vis-à-vis Asia's seas has undoubtedly been the Indian Ocean. It has been here, more than anywhere else in the region, that historiographical battle lines have been drawn, and in the starkest terms. K. N. Chaudhuri was undoubtedly the *pater nostrum* of this scholarship, with his *Trade and Civilisation in the Indian Ocean* making him the intellectual counterpart of Braudel and Bailyn for this part of the world. The level of synthesis of his study of the Indian Ocean was formative, and he managed to combine analysis of the monsoons, the environment, trade, and human actors all into one seamless web.[29] His monograph was followed by others', with Ashin Das Gupta, Sanjay Subrahmanyam, Michael Pearson, Sugata Bose, Kerry Ward, and others all contributing studies that made the level of complexity and detail of Indian Ocean Studies quite something to behold.[30] Engseng Ho, Clare Anderson, Michael Laffan, Isabel Hofmeyer, Ronit Ricci, Sebouh Aslanian, and Gwyn Campbell (among many others) have only deepened the evolving picture in the last twenty years.[31]

29. K. N. Chaudhuri, *Trade and Civilisation in the Indian Ocean: An Economic History from the Rise of Islam to 1750* (Cambridge: Cambridge University Press, 1985).

30. Ashin Das Gupta, *Merchants of Maritime India: Collected Studies, 1500–1800* (Ashgate: Variorum, 1994); Sanjay Subrahmanyam, *The Political Economy of Commerce: Southern India 1500–1650* (Cambridge: Cambridge University Press, 2002); Michael Pearson, *The Indian Ocean* (New York: Routledge, 2003); Sugata Bose, *A Hundred Horizons: The Indian Ocean in the Age of Global Empire* (Cambridge: Harvard University Press, 2006); and Kerry Ward, *Networks of Empire: Forced Migration in the Dutch East India Company* (New York: Cambridge University Press, 2009).

31. See Engseng Ho, *The Graves of Tarim: Genealogy and Mobility across the Indian Ocean* (Berkeley: University of California Press, 2006); Engseng Ho, "Empire through Diasporic Eyes: A View from the Other Boat," *Comparative Studies in Society and History* 46, no. 2 (Apr. 2004); Clare Anderson, *Subaltern Lives: Biographies of Colonialism in the Indian Ocean World, 1790–1920* (Cambridge: Cambridge University Press, 2012); Michael Laffan, *The Makings of Indonesian Islam: Orientalism and the Narraiton of a Sufi Past* (Princeton: Princeton University Press, 2011) Isabel Hofmeyer, "The Complicating Sea: The Indian Ocean as Method," *Comparative Studies of South Asia, Africa and the Middle East* 32, no. 3 (2012): 584–90; Ronit Ricci, *Islam Translated* (Chicago: University of Chicago Press, 2011); Sebouh Aslanian, *From the Indian Ocean to the Mediterranean: The Global Trade Networks of Armenian Merchants from New Julfa* (Berkeley: University of California Press, 2011); and Gwyn Campbell, *Africa and the Indian Ocean World from Early Times to circa 1900* (Cambridge: Cambridge University Press, 2019). See also, in a slightly more specialized vein, Robert Harms, Bernard K. Freamon, and David W. Blight, eds. *Indian Ocean Slavery in the Age of Abolition* (New Haven: Yale University Press, 2013); and, for more of a wide-angled approach, see Thomas Metcalf, *Imperial Connections: India in the Indian*

There are now Indian Ocean study centers in places as distant from one another as Montreal and Perth, and Cambridge University Press has commissioned a two-volume history of the ocean, while classes are taught on the region in universities worldwide. There are even now excellent studies of regional avatars of the Indian Ocean, such as René Barendse's *The Arabian Seas* and Sunil Amrith's *Crossing the Bay of Bengal*.[32] This is a kind of rude health for the examination of an ocean that few could have imagined when the study of such seas was just in its infancy and questions were being asked whether this kind of history could (or should) be done at all. It is being done, and more and more PhDs are being minted in the large research institutions who take this sort of vantage as their own, rather than relying on land-based geographies. That more than anything else may be a clue as to where the profession is going, as new knowledge is produced and the scale of analysis is brought closer and closer to the ground (or to the sea, in this case).

Yet, perhaps a better index of how important Indian Ocean Studies has become as a kind of vanguard of maritime scholarship might be in the phalanx of smaller, topic-specific studies that are now out there to be used by researchers. A number of large, syncretic studies have now been done (as above), and these will doubtless be challenged in the years to come by others, who will focus on highlighting differing themes. But we can now rely on literally shelves of smaller studies that allow us to focus down on Indian Ocean ontologies that can come only from painstaking, small-scale research. It is in this vein that we have scholarship on the archaeology of individual ports, as well as on cyclones, mangroves, and the tidal basins of historical harbors.[33] The histories of the large East India companies are known, but we are also learning about the Danes, the Armenians, and others in this respect, and the parts they played in

Ocean Arena, 1860–1920 (Berkeley and Los Angeles: University of California Press, 2007); and Leila Tarazi Fawaz and C. A. Bayly, eds., *Modernity and Culture: From the Mediterranean to the Indian Ocean* (New York: Columbia University Press, 2002).

32. René J. Barendse, *The Arabian Seas: The Indian Ocean World of the Seventeenth Century* (New York: Routledge, 2014); Sunil Amrith, *Crossing the Bay of Bengal: The Furies of Nature and the Fortunes of Migrants* (Cambridge, MA: Harvard University Press, 2013).

33. See S. Z. Qasim, "Concepts of Tides, Navigation and Trade in Ancient India," *Journal of Indian Ocean Studies* 8, nos. 1/2 (2000): 97–102; T. S. S. Rao and Ray Griffiths, *Understanding the Indian Ocean: Perspectives on Oceanography* (Paris: UNESCO, 1998), 21–60; Zahoor Qasim, "The Indian Ocean and Cyclones," *Journal of Indian Ocean Studies* 1, no. 2 (1994): 30–40; and Zahoor Qasim, "The Indian Ocean and Mangroves," *Journal of Indian Ocean Studies* 2, no. 1 (1994): 1–10.

the ocean's contact and commerce.[34] We are now able even to get to the roots of interaction on India's seacoasts century by century, in micro-histories (often written by indigenous authors) that tell us details from the sixteenth century period of open trade to the imposition of British control in the late imperial age.[35] When we add this all together, the benefits are clear. Writing histories of maritime Asia is easier now than ever before; many people have put in the hard, local work to make this so, whether in the archives, in the field, or on the ocean itself, collecting data. This is so from Hokkaido all the way to Aden, and in all the stretches of Asia's seas in between. It will be the task of this volume to reveal some of these connections through a series of topical windows, which in turn can show us the unity and relatedness of these seas as the centuries have slowly swept by.

––––––

The book is organized into fourteen chapters. Two of these are an introduction and a conclusion with wide vantages on the importance of the oceans, as seen

34. Martin Krieger, "Danish Country Trade on the Indian Ocean in the 17th and 18th Centuries," in ed., *Indian Ocean and Cultural Interaction, 1400–1800*, ed. K. S. Mathew, 122–29 (Pondicherry: Pondicherry University, 1996); Vahe Baladouni and Margaret Makepeace, eds., *Armenian Merchants of the Early Seventeenth and Early Eighteenth Centuries* (Philadelphia: American Philosophical Society, 1998); and Charles Borges, "Intercultural Movements in the Indian Ocean Region: Churchmen, Travelers, and Chroniclers in Voyage and in Action," in *Indian Ocean and Cultural Interaction*, ed. Mathew, 21–34.

35. For the sixteenth century, for example, see K. S. Mathew, "Trade in the Indian Ocean During the Sixteenth Century and the Portuguese," in *Studies in Maritime History*, ed. K. S. Mathew (Pondicherry: Pondicherry University, 1990): 13–28; Sanjay Subrahmanyam, "Profit at the Apostle's Feet: The Portuguese Settlement of Mylapur in the Sixteenth Century," in Sanjay Subrahmanyam, *Improvising Empire: Portuguese Trade and Settlement in the Bay of Bengal* (Delhi: Oxford University Press, 1990): 47–67; Syed Hasan Askarai, "Mughal Naval Weakness and Aurangzeb's Attitude Towards the Traders and Pirates on the Western Coast," *Journal of Indian Ocean Studies* 2, no. 3 (1995): 236–42. For the seventeenth century, see Shireen Moosvi, "The Gujurat Ports and Their Hinterland: The Economic Relationship," in *Ports and Their Hinterlands in India, 1700–1950*, ed. Indu Banga (Delhi: Manohar, 1992), 121–30; and Aniruddha Ray, "Cambay and Its Hinterland: The Early Eighteenth Century," in *Ports and Their Hinterlands*, ed. Banga, 131–52. For the eighteenth century, see Lakshmi Subramanian, "Western India in the Eighteenth Century: Ports, Inland Towns, and States" in *Ports and Their Hinterlands*, ed. Banga, 153–80; and Rajat Datta, "Merchants and Peasants: A Study of the Structure of Local Trade in Grain in Late Eighteenth Century Bengal," in *Merchants, Markets, and the State in Early Modern India*, ed. Sanjay Subrahmanyam, 139–62 (Delhi: Oxford University Press, 1990).

from Japan and the Middle East at the volume's start (the two geographic poles of this study), and China at the book's end. The remaining twelve chapters are evenly subdivided into six rubrics, each dealing with a particular theme that has been crucial to the history of these seas. Each of the six parts of the book has a short preface so that readers are given background into the rubric at hand. The two thematically linked chapters following then serve (in juxtaposition) as broad yet detailed windows into the dynamics of these large, ocean-related topics. As such, they function like an accordion that can be compressed or expanded, with one of the two chapters moving in each direction—as apertures—one widening, and one narrowing toward the theme at hand. Together, the essays span the waters between Pacific Russia and Japan on the one hand and eastern Arabia and the Red Sea on the other, making stops along the way in China, Southeast Asia, the Indian subcontinent and the Middle East, all through a variety of analytical windows. Southeast Asia forms the "center" of the volume in some senses. This is both because I am a card-carrying Southeast Asianist by trade, and also because this region was the geographic center of these routes, in many ways. This is history on a continental scale, therefore, and the book attempts to reach out to scholars, students, and the interested reading public along the width and breadth of these sea lanes. It is explicitly *not* a history of every ship that has ever set sail in Asia over the past centuries. It *is*, however, a way of looking at all of these ships—encapsulated into thematic form—so that these voyages and the people who made them can be thought about in one, expansive sweep. I do not see any of the human populations referred to in this book as static, either, in "ethnic composition." Rather, I agree with some of the formative scholarship on ethnicity in Asia that all of the people chronicled here passed in and out of evolving "categories" as they connected to the routes.[36] Each of the six thematic rubrics in the book mixes approaches to the sea and its histories by using a number of different methodologies: archival history, anthropology, archaeology, art history, and geography/resource studies. I have spent time on the ground in all of the regions that I write about here over the past thirty years, and there is a mixture in the source bases between history and lived experience, usually in the form of interviewing and oral history reportage for the latter.

---

36. See Edmund Leach, *Political Systems of Highland Burma: A Study of Kachin Social Structure* (Cambridge, MA: Harvard University Press, 1954); Renato Rosaldo, *Ilongot Headhunting* (Palo Alto: Stanford University Press, 1980); Eric Wolf, *Europe and the People without History* (Berkeley: University of California Press, 1982).

Wherever possible I have tried to allow local people to speak into the record themselves, so that their own voices are heard.[37] This happens through ethnographic work done in the markets and ports of many of these places: a variety of harbors in Indonesia and the Philippines, for example, as well as interviews with merchants of spices and marine goods throughout Hong Kong, Taiwan, and southern China, as well as Singapore, Malaysia, and southern India. Travels in the Arabian Sea, the Persian Gulf, the Red Sea, and coastal East Africa also informed this book. I have been fortunate to live or work in Asia for roughly ten of the past thirty years, cumulatively, and the rubrics of the book reflect these experiences. The languages of the sources and interviewing used in these chapters include Indonesian/Malay, Chinese, Dutch, French, and Italian (as well as English), so a wide mixture of reporting has been possible. *In Asian Waters* is a book that connects a large swath of geography and a large temporal frame at the same time, but it is a story that is indeed connected, and one that must be seen in its breadth to be appreciated for its coherence. Asia is the world's most dynamic region, but beyond the neon of Tokyo harbor, the factories of southern China, and the seaside villages surrounding Mumbai there is the story of how these worlds fit together. Merchants—indigenous and foreign—once sailed between all of these ports in sleek, elegant ships. They still do, though the vessels now might carry huge cargo containers, the corrugated-iron descendants of this maritime past.

The first part of this book looks at "maritime connections." Chapter 2, "From China to Africa," does this by adopting the widest possible lens in Asian waters—looking at the long, though little discussed, history of connection between China and East Africa. The ties between these places, improbable as they are, go back many centuries, and are discernible through chronicles and histories, as well as through archaeology and DNA. Trade contacts between these two poles of Asian waters (the Indian Ocean after all washes up against East Africa's shores) have existed for a long time. We do know that this connection persisted over the ages, and that at one moment at least—during the famed Zheng He voyages of the early fifteenth century—Africa was very much on the minds of the Chinese court. At that time, a live giraffe was brought back from one of the Zheng He expeditions, and was paraded through the streets of Nanjing. One can only imagine what local Chinese must have thought,

---

37. For a terrific new book that accomplishes this across much of Asia in the fin-de-siècle period, see Tim Harper, *Underground Asia: Global Revolutionaries and the Overthrow of Europe's Empires in the East* (London: Allen Lane, 2019).

looking up at this strange beast for the first time. Chapter 3, "Vietnam's Maritime Trade Orbit," also looks at maritime connections, but instead of adopting a "tie the endpoints together" approach, as in chapter 2, proceeds with the opposite logic, discussing the ties between one place—the outstretched coasts of Vietnam during the early modern period—and the wider maritime world. During this time, as Vietnam began to coalesce into something more than a collection of small polities, the country began trading with an extraordinary range of distant peoples by sea. This chapter analyzes that trade, and asks what its conduct can tell us about the gradual opening up of a centuries-old polity to the new possibilities of the international routes. Vietnam, of course, traded with other places before this time, but during these centuries maritime commerce took on an importance that had been generally more muted before.

The second part of the monograph focuses down on "bodies of water," of which two are of paramount importance in Asia. Chapter 4, "Smuggling in the South China Sea," takes a *longue-durée* approach, focusing specifically on smuggling patterns and subaltern movement. It questions how strong states try to control nonstate spaces such as the South China Sea, and asks how local populations have resisted these enforced realities, often by voting with their feet to move trade and commerce outside of officially sanctioned channels. The chapter is both historical and concerned with the present in the relationship between China and Southeast Asia as "macro-regions." Chapter 5, "The Center and Its Margins," then looks at the Indian Ocean over a three-hundred-year period, from roughly 1600 to 1900 CE. It problematizes currents of exchange that were taking place over this huge geography, as Asian contact with European companies phased toward colonial domination over a broad sweep of time. The chapter catalogues these changes partially through the ideas of thinkers such as Adam Smith and Karl Marx who witnessed them in their own lifetimes, but also through close studies of events on the ground, and on several different rims of this vast ocean.

The third part of the book looks at "religion on the tides," its two chapters showing first the transmission of early Indian religions overseas, and then how global religions have been incorporated into a single out-if-the-way place in the Philippines. Chapter 6, "Passage of Amulets," analyzes the transit of Buddhism from South Asia (southern India and Sri Lanka) to mainland Southeast Asia and back. It takes the Bay of Bengal as a single sphere of study, and asks how this space became worn with the tracks of ships carrying Buddhist monks, who eventually proselytized their faith into the majority religion of this region. The chapter relies on studies of Buddhist canonical scripture, material culture (including the archaeology of amulets and statuary), as well as anthropology in sketching out this complicated and fascinating history of transmission, especially to southern Siam. Chapter 7 examines one remarkably understudied city: Zamboanga, the main port of southwestern Mindanao in the southern Philippines. Zamboanga has had a Spanish fort and Spanish cannon trying to control local Muslim populations for many hundreds of years. It also has a thriving Muslim secessionist presence, replete with men with more guns in the streets, and a splinter group of Al-Qaeda in the form of Abu Sayyaf. Yet Zamboanga also has a large Catholic community, and a history of remarkable tolerance, too. This chapter scrutinizes these two opposing trends, and asks how the port is both representative of Asia's maritime roots and anomalous at the same time.

The fourth part of the book then queries what Asia's "cities and the sea" mean for this huge sweep of geography along the trade routes. Chapter 8 looks at the history of coastal cities in "greater Southeast Asia," but this description is a very loose one, as it incorporates ports now lying at some distance from what most now consider to be this region, including Canton (Guangzhou) and Hong Kong. The chapter asks how coastal cities became important on the Asian trade routes, when this happened, why, and in what eventual formations of urbanism alongside the edge of the sea. A wide lens is employed in order to examine these patterns over a broad stretch of geography, and an equally large cross-section of time. Chapter 9 then ties the even larger maritime geography of (mainly British) empire together in Asia: from Aden (in Yemen) to Bombay in India; from Singapore in Southeast Asia up to Pusan in colonial Korea. The chapter looks at the "circuits" of travel, movement, and ideas along this thoroughfare, both of colonial officials and administrators, and of Asians who both served the empire and eventually challenged it in the desire for their own postcolonial states. The chapter uses a range of reporting from predominantly British civil servants that bind these entwined histories together into a single, complex story.

The fifth part of our story then moves into greener, less urban directions, taking in the ecological sweep and "bounty of the oceans." Chapter 10, "Fins, Slugs, Pearls," dives literally into the sea: under scrutiny here is the (lived) history of marine-goods transport, all along the trade routes that have connected East and Southeast Asia for the past several hundred years. The high point of this commerce, in many ways, was the late eighteenth and early nineteenth centuries, when sea produce helped fuel the "opening of China," both to global commerce and to opium addiction (opium and sea produce were two of the main commercial products exchanged for Chinese tea, porcelain, and silk). But the chapter is half ethnographic as well, looking at how these Sino-Southeast Asian marine trades operate now, in our own time. Chapter 11, "On the Docks," queries how the coasts of southern India became "central" to the passage of spices across the Indian Ocean. This happened on the wider shipping routes of the great companies (the East India Co, the VOC, etc.) before the region was later backwatered to some extent by the main oceanic steamship lines (the P & O, Rotterdamsche Lloyd, etc.). Since antiquity the Malabar and Coromandel coasts have had a number of ports that connected Asia to the wider world in fascinating ways (mostly through spices). But the opening of Suez in 1869 significantly changed these patterns, and also changed the nature of the commerce carried out on these ancient slipways. This chapter (which, like the previous one, is historical but also anthropological at the same time, both of them making use of fieldwork and interviewing), explores these processes, particularly vis-à-vis connections with Southeast Asia.

The sixth part of the book takes on "technologies of the sea" as a theme of Asian interconnectivity. Chapter 12, "Foucault's Other Panopticon, or Lighting Colonial Southeast Asia," is an analysis of one maritime-specific technology among many: the history of lighthouses in the area, stretching from Aceh in North Sumatra all the way to New Guinea and the fluid borders of Oceania. Lighthouses were critical structures in maintaining the safety of ships and commerce, yet they were also appropriated by burgeoning colonial states to "herd" and surveille Asian shipping into pathways deemed acceptable by imperial regimes. Chapter 13, "Of Maps and Men," presents the history of another vital technology in the history of Asia's oceans: sea-mapping, or hydrography, as it was called in colonial times. The mapping of the sea in this part of the world was at least as important as any land-based cartography, and this was so starting from the earliest European voyages to the region, around the turn of the sixteenth century. Mapping out shoals, reefs, and other dangers of the sea allowed European colonial projects to get off the ground with less and less loss of life. It also eventually gave rise (in Foucault's terms) to a conjuncture between power and knowledge that eventually swung the way of the numerically inferior visitors from the West.

Chapter 14, "If China Rules the Waves," concludes the book by looking both toward the past and toward the future. The primary locus of this final chapter is the China coasts—the place that many observers, both "expert" and casual, seem to think will be the engine of the world economy in the coming century. This last chapter looks at this assumption from the standpoint of history, asking how reasonable this hypothesis might be, given past and present conditions. Some two thousand years ago, in the Han Dynasty, deceased Chinese courtiers were found with cloves buried in their mouths. Since at that time cloves only grew thousands of kilometers away in eastern Indonesia, off the outstretched coasts of New Guinea, we can see how powerful the maritime trade impulse was for much of human history. On those same Chinese coasts now, some two millennia later, newer Chinese ships are setting sail every day, their holds full of cargo for the outside world. What will happen if China becomes master of the sea? Will this be a peaceful process, as it was when the Han were looking for cloves to freshen the breath of their princes for the afterlife? Or will it be an altogether different approach to the wider world, whereby the sea becomes an avenue less of trade and connection, but one of conquest, recalling other (Western) histories of landings on distant shores, when the "contact age" began? This chapter asks these questions. It also leaves us with some historical perspective on the hyping of the world's newest superpower, one that we are told is destined to rule the waves.

PART I

Maritime Connections

Preface: In Asian Waters

TRYING TO MAP OUT the trade routes of Asia as they have existed in historical time is a challenging, nigh impossible task. The routes stretched everywhere; they also changed radically in shape. How can one impose a Linnaean, taxonomic order to such undulating pathways as these, as they have displayed themselves over the course of the centuries? The geography of Asia's maritime circuits over time has been breathtaking in its diversity, and still is, even in our own age. In Eastern Indonesia, traders moved east into Malinowski's famous kula networks of Oceania, while also maintaining ties with Filipino peoples to the north, and with a succession of Javanese and Java-based empires to the west. They even went south to Australia, as we will see later on in this book. In Korea, turtle ships scuttled to China, carrying back paper and Buddhism from the Chinese sphere. But then they also headed east to Japan, where the same things were redeposited among Japanese populations from a very early date. In India, Bengali merchants ended up facilitating imperial rice circuits between emerging British colonies, while also helping to build imperial railways in East Africa, at the westernmost terminus of the Indian Ocean's shores. Yemeni traders traveled even farther, seeding the ports of Southeast Asia with Hadhrami communities that survive to this day. We are back in Indonesia now again, whence we started this geographic tour earlier in this paragraph. One can see the power of these routes. Much of Asia has seemed to be in motion, and the sea was the easiest and cheapest way to connect. It still is, in some ways, even in the age of jet travel. Most of the world's cargo—as it nearly always has, in this part of the world—in fact still travels by sea.

Thinking about maritime connections in Asia requires us to keep a number of themes in mind. The weather vis-à-vis monsoon timetables is one of these themes; these cycles ruled nearly all travel, at least for most of recorded time. To try to sail against the monsoons was not only foolish but almost impossible—one had to go where the winds pointed, and at the time of year this was allowed. This reality helped to forge maritime pathways to some extent, and conditioned the circuits and their geographies. Sailing directly from Asia to Africa, for example, directly across the Indian Ocean, was viable only through the use of Pritcher's Current, an invisible slipstream in the middle latitudes of that body of water. Many interesting connections were made in this way, but it would only be much later, in the "contact age," that shipping and nautical techniques could fathom these kinds of journeys outside of such known pathways. Similarly, knowledge of the routes was cumulative, and aggregated over time. Arab geographers tabulated and stored this knowledge in classical Arabic texts, which was then used by large, oceangoing dhows in their journeys. The Chinese did much the same thing for larger vessels (and for other ships referred to in the West as "junks," an identifiable class of vessels) over time. By the time European state-making projects entered the Indian Ocean and South China Sea, this project of knowledge production of the routes was well advanced, and getting more sophisticated all the time. The routes changed over time, for sure, but they were also now entered into ledgers and log books and *portolans*, and even trade circuits that withered could be reinvigorated or stimulated, to meet new market demands. Profitable crops were replanted, and this process changed the outline of the routes again. It is clear, therefore, that these maritime connections were not ossified or fossilized; they were not ontologically constant as the centuries wore on.

Part I of this book looks at all of these possibilities through two different approaches. Chapter 2 takes the long view of the routes as a type of maritime connection. This chapter examines the near entirety of the Asian trade pathways on water, stretching from the North China coasts all the way to the westernmost stretches of the Indian Ocean, astride Africa. Here we take these maritime connections as a conversation between poles, very distant in their location, and ask how the two were joined through trade over time. This is not a well-known history, but it is one that is becoming more interesting to both specialists and lay readers alike, as China now invests heavily in Africa. These contemporary links are often trumpeted as a relatively new development, a refashioning of old geographies to meet contemporary, global geopolitics. Yet, as this chapter shows, these connections are actually quite old, and stretch back into some antiquity. They were never constant, nor were they facilitated on a regular basis, but the episodic pull between Asia and Africa by sea brought a number of important gifts in both directions. That history is in turn explored here. Chapter 3 takes the exact opposite tack. Instead of looking at the endpoints of a transnational and indeed transregional trade, it proceeds from one place—the Vietnamese coasts themselves—and asks how power, politics, and commerce all spilled inward and outward from those same shores. From the early modern period forward, Vietnam's court found itself in quiet conversation with the outside world, and most of that contact occurred by sea. The Annamite Cordillera, with its craggy precipices and near-vertical drops, made land-based connection more difficult in most places. Vietnam's coasts, to the contrary, skirted much of the South China Sea's existing trade routes, even the very distant ones connecting the Middle East and India with T'ang Dynasty China. Vietnam became an interesting way station of sorts along these pathways, part of a larger system but also bargaining and trading for items on its own terms. Together, these two chapters show the possibilities of using a historical zoom lens both in its widest and in its narrowest forms, to tell us more about how maritime connections along Asia's trade routes evolved and were maintained over time.

2

From China to Africa

PROLEGOMENON

(Africa) is in the sea to the south-west. . . . There are usually great birds
(there), which so mask the sun in their flight that the shade of the sun-dial
is shifted.

—ZHAO RU GUA, PORTMASTER OF QUAN-ZHOU, 1225 CE[1]

IT IS QUITE DIFFICULT to think of two entities that seem farther apart in
history than China and Africa; no thread of connection seems to suggest itself
for most of the passage of the centuries, until we get to very modern times. Yet
this is of course untrue. Even some of the most distant parts of the planet, we
now know, had concourse between them in strange and wonderful ways in the
centuries before the "contact age" (c. 1500 CE) really began. China and Africa
are no different in this respect than some other parts of the world that are
now turning up as "connected," when previously we'd thought such bonds
of travel were impossible.[2] In this chapter, some of the current evidence is
presented for Sino-African maritime contact, as well as knowledge of each
other's places in the world in the centuries predating our own. This is done

1. In Frederick Hirth and W. W. Rockhill, *Chau Ju Kua: His Work on the Chinese and Arab
Trade in the 12th and 13th Centuries, Entitled Chu Fan Chï* (New York: Paragon Book Reprint Co.,
1966), 149.

2. For a good start at looking at these connections, see Helen Siu and Mike McGovern,
"China-Africa Encounters: Historical Legacies and Contemporary Realities," *Annual Review of
Anthropology* 46 (2017): 337–55; and Dorian Fuller, Nicole Boivin, et al., "Across the Indian
Ocean: The Prehistoric Movement of Plants and Animals," *Antiquity* (June 2011): 544–58.

especially vis-à-vis monsoon Asia, which can be seen as a sort of "central pivot" in connecting these two places through a number of different ways. The story put together here is archaeological, linguistic, geographical, and textual in nature; it is also continually evolving, as we learn new things and develop new techniques to decipher the patterns of the past. It is a fascinating story, but also an incomplete one, or one that can still only be put together in fragments. Future historians and practitioners of related disciplines will no doubt be able to flesh out this narrative even more, as new evidence makes itself available in the years to come.

We start our inquiry by looking at some of the DNA evidence that has been put together that helps us to connect East Africa and "Asia" across the centuries, as well as across thousands of miles of open water. The genetic forays of scientists are very recent, and still incomplete, but are very suggestive in what they tell us about the nature of these early contacts. From there we move on to ethnolinguistic evidence, which has a much longer and more documented history, as explorers in this part of the world saw a connection between Malagasy (the language of Madagascar) and insular Southeast Asian languages at a very early date. Some of this history is analyzed here, as well as hypotheses about the early Asian "raft sailors" who made trans–Indian Ocean voyages over a thousand years ago. We also will look at East Africa's urban coastal tradition, and how this began to be augmented by trade with various parts of Asia as well during the early centuries of the second millennium CE. Chinese ceramics and the archaeology of these commodities play a large role in deciphering this story. Finally, we will turn to the Chinese materials in earnest, both of the material kind just mentioned, and those of a more textual nature, in what they show us about such oceanic connections over the *longue durée*. These expeditions culminated in the voyages of the Chinese admiral Zheng He in the early fifteenth century, which are well known. Yet it is clear that Africans were moving east across the Indian Ocean during the early modern period as well, and into Asian seas. This chapter argues that these journeys were part of a larger (and longer) conversation between the maritime poles of Asia, from the South China Sea to the western Indian Ocean.

The Earliest Evidence of African-Asian Connections

If we go back to the "beginning," whenever the "beginning" may be, we know that East Africa was in conversation with what we now think of "Asia" from a very early date. The jury is still out on exactly when these conversations started, but it is certain that seafarers from what we now term Indonesia sailed across the Indian Ocean in "rafts" (lash-lugged or planked-craft) to East Africa in the first millennium CE, or even earlier.[3] We know that they brought certain things with them—like rice and bananas, both of which transplanted well in Africa[4]—and that they also brought their genes. Many people living on the eastern seaboard of Madagascar today have noticeably "Asian" facial features, for example, and look quite different from many of the populations on the western side of the island, who are genetically more Bantu in origin. The DNA structure/genomes of people living in Madagascar has now been studied, but this is only a very recent phenomenon, so interpretations of the data are still being constructed. The genetic evidence points toward Asia for the provenance of people on the eastern side of the island—and geneticists are able to pinpoint the evidence even more precisely. With some certainty, it seems clear that a major genetic marker of people living in Madagascar comes from southeastern Borneo, in the region around Banjarmasin.[5] There is also another subgroup of people who seem to have roots near Kota Kinabalu, on the northwestern part of Borneo (in contemporary Sabah, Malaysia).[6] All but two genetic lineages (these are single chromosomes belonging to haplogroups L* and R1b. Haplogroup L*) come from either the East African mainland or from Southeast Asia. This seems to be definitive proof of very early contact taking place between "Asia" writ large and East Africa, almost certainly based on

3. For the prehistory of Southeast Asia, and voyaging as part of that history, see Peter Bellwood, *Prehistory of the Indo-Malaysian Archipelago* (Honolulu: University of Hawai'i Press, 1997); Robert Blust, "The Prehistory of the Austronesian-Speaking Peoples: A View from Language," *Journal of World Prehistory* 9, no. 4 (1995): 453–510; and J. Dars, "Les jonques chinoises de haute mer sous les Song et les Yuan," *Archipel* 18 (1979): 41–56.

4. Michel Mollat [du Jourdin], "Les contacts historiques de l'Afrique et de Madagascar avec l'Asie du sud et du sud-est: Le rôle de l'Océan indien," *Archipel* 21 (1981): 37.

5. See Tatiana M. Karafet et al., "Major East-West Division Underlines Y Chromosome Stratification across Indonesia," *Molecular Biology and Evolution* 27–28 (2010): 1833–1844; Mark Lipson et al., "Reconstruction Austronesian Population History in Island Southeast Asia," *Nature Communications* 19 August 2014 (5:4689; DOI 10.1038/ncomms 5689; see also Gabriel Ferrand, "Les voyages des Javanais à Madagascar," *Journal Asiatique*, series 10, no. 15 (1910), 281–330.

6. For the place of Borneo in some of these hypotheses and arguments, see K. Alexander Adelaar, "Borneo as a Cross-Roads for Comparative Austronesian Linguistics," in *The Austronesians: Historical and Comparative Perspectives*, ed. Peter Bellwood, James Fox, and Darrell Tryon, 75–95 (Canberra: Department of Anthropology, Research School of Pacific and Asian Studies, Australian National University, 1995).

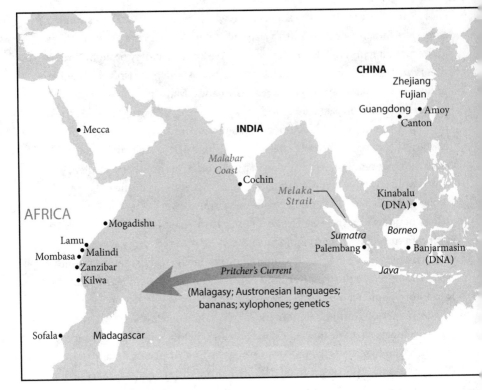

MAP 2.1. From China to Africa by Sea

celestial navigation of the Indian Ocean and an evolving knowledge of the seasonal monsoons.[7] Sailors from what we now term "Indonesia" literally began this conversation of connection between "Asia" and Africa, therefore, likely well over a thousand years ago.

Linguistically, too, and not just genetically, this "smoking gun" of connection, Asia to Africa, is fairly certain by now. Malagasy (spoken primarily in eastern Madagascar) is part of the Austronesian language group. This linguistic family stretches from Madagascar off the eastern coast of Africa through the Indonesian archipelago, and then farther east to Hawai'i in the mid-Pacific.[8]

7. M. E. Hurles, B. C. Sykes, M. A. Jobling, and P. Forster, "The Dual Origin of the Malagasy in Island Southeast Asia and East Africa: Evidence from Maternal and Paternal Lineages," *American Journal of Human Genetics* 76 (2005:): 894–901.

8. For an overview of the linguistic evidence on Southeast Asia, see Roger Blench, "Was There an Austroasiatic Presence in Island Southeast Asia Prior to the Austronesian Expansion?,"

Malaysia and parts of the Philippines are also covered.[9] Unlike the genetic evidence supplied by DNA, the linguistic connections of Malagasy to Asian languages of maritime Southeast Asia has been known for some time.[10] The early Dutch voyager Cornelis de Houtman (one of the European "discoverers" of Java) published a very limited vocabulary of words common to the two languages (Malay and Malagasy) in 1598, and five years later, in 1603, his brother Frederick de Houtman put out a much larger one of close to three thousand words. A dictionary of Malagasy was published by Flacourt a half century later, with subsequent word lists coming out in 1729 and 1773. Unpublished works by Barthélémy Huet de Froberville were compiled during this time, too, and treatises on Malagasy grammar were also produced by Flageollet and Chapelier.

Yet the first definitive notice of a connection between Malay and Malagasy was made earlier by the Portuguese Luis Mariano in 1613–14. He surmised that Madagascar's people must have originally sailed from Melaka. The seventeenth-century naturalist Engelbert Kaempfer references other works as having pointed out that the language spoken by Madagascar's peoples is full of Javanese and Malay loanwords.[11] All of this helped, but the first scholar to put out an actual side-by-side analysis between Malagasy and Malay was the Dutchman Adriaan Reland, in 1708;[12] a century later, William Marsden, the famous

---

Bulletin of the Indo-Pacific Prehistory Association 30 (2010): 133–44; Cristian Capelli et al., "A Predominantly Indigenous Paternal Heritage for the Austronesian-Speaking Peoples of Insular Southeast Asia and Oceania," *American Journal of Human Genetics* 68, no. 2 (2001): 432–43; and Mark Donohue and Tim Denham, "Farming and Language in Island Southeast Asia: Reframing Austronesian History," *Current Anthropology* 51, no. 2 (2010): 223–56.

9. See Mark Lipson, Po-Ru Loh, Nick Patterson, Priya Moorjani, Ying-Chin Ko, Mark Stoneking, Bonnie Berger, and David Reich, "Reconstructing Austronesian Population History in Island Southeast Asia," *Nature Communications* 19 (August 2014): 4, no. 5: 4689; DOI: 10.1038/ncomms5689.

10. See the evidence presented in Alexander Adelaar, "The Indonesian Migrations to Madagascar: Making Sense of the Multidisciplinary Evidence," in *Austronesian Diaspora and the Ethnogenesis of People in Indonesian Archipelago: Proceedings of the International Symposium,* ed. Truman Simanjuntak, Ingrid H. E. Pojoh, and Muhammad Hisyam, 1 and passim (Jakarta: LIPI Press: 2006). Adelaar gives one of the most convincing accounts of how the connections between these two world regions can be conceptualized, especially through linguistic evidence.

11. Engelbert Kaempfer, *The History of Japan, Together with a Description of the Kingdom of Siam* (Richmond, Surrey: Curzon Press, 1993; reprint of 1906 edition), 194.

12. Parts of these two paragraphs are abstracted from Ann Kumar, "'The Single Most Astonishing Fact of Human Geography': Indonesia's Far West Colony," *Indonesia* 92 (2011): 59–95.

FIGURE 2.1. Acacia Trees and Dhows on the Swahili Coasts (author's photo)

English traveler and scholar of Southeast Asia, stated that the relationship of Malagasy with Malay was one of the most astonishing linguistic relationships in the history of language.

The actual route of these premodern Asians who sailed to initiate contact with Africa is still unknown, but very likely was along Pritcher's Current, a strong mid-Indian Ocean ribbon of fast-moving water that cuts directly across the middle latitudes of that ocean.[13] The Southeast Asian sailors who accomplished these incredible feats of navigation were called the Waq-Waqs, and though their story has been known for some time in academic circles, the more scientific details of their passage are only now coming to light.[14] If we think of Bronislaw Malinowski's epic 1922 study, *Argonauts of the Western Pacific*, there is a fair case to be made that in the Indian Ocean, these argonauts were perhaps more akin to astronauts—almost those kinds of open-ocean distances were traversed in comparison to the (still amazing) island hopping of the South-Western Pacific that made Malinowski famous.[15] The most important thing to take away from these voyages, however, and the fascinating mix of evidence that they present (linguistic, genetic, crop-based, etc.) is that East Africa was known to Southeast Asia from a very early date, and vice versa.[16] When Chinese begin to show up in the records as being part of these exchanges, there had already been links in place between "Asia" and Africa for a number of centuries.

The Place of Urbanism and the Chinese in Early East African History

Chinese do not show up in this story until far after the Austronesian Waq-Waqs, but they do appear much earlier in Indian Ocean history than most people surmise. It is well known that coastal East African society began to

13. See Michel Mollat [du Jourdin], "Les contacts historiques de l'Afrique et de Madagascar avec l'Asie du sud et du sud-est: Le rôle de l'Océan indien," *Archipel* 21 (1981): 35–54.

14. See Peter Bellwood, *Prehistory of the Indo-Malaysian Archipelago.*

15. Branislaw Malinowski, *Argonauts of the Western Pacific* (London: Routledge & Kegan Paul, 1922).

16. Indonesian peoples such as the Bugis also traveled in premodern times to Australia, in search of edible sea cucumbers (holothurians); see A. A. Cense, "Makassarsche- Boeginese paruwvaart op Noord-Australië," *Bijdragen tot de Taal- Land-en Volkenkunde* 108 (1952): 248–65; and D. Soelaiman, "Selayang pandang pelayaran di Indonesia," *Suluh Nautika* 9, no. 3 (1959): 40–43.

become more and more urban and complex in the early second millennium CE; coastal towns such as Kilwa, Pate, and Mombasa became cosmopolitan centers in the fourteenth and fifteenth centuries, replete with traveling populations and well-built walls.[17] There seems to have been a continual conversation up and down the coasts, as Islam spread and Swahili became the main language of exchange between traders and religious scholars who moved between the ports. This was part of a pattern of the diffusion of Islam along the trade routes, bringing distant places such as Aceh, Melaka, the coast of Java (or *pasisir*) and eventually large parts of coastal Southeast Asia into a connected orbit. In Africa, Sofala (in modern-day Mozambique) represented the far south of these exchanges, as it was here that gold mines were found that sent quantities of the mineral up and into these Indian Ocean circuits of exchange. Kilwa (in modern-day Tanzania) was the epicenter for a while of these connections; the archaeology of Kilwa is very well studied, as some of the formative digs on the East African coast were done here, often by British scientists in the early decades of independence. Moving farther north, the stone town on the island of Zanzibar became important only after 1699, when it was brought into Omani political history, but sites such as Pemba, Mombasa, Malindi, and Lamu, all the way up to Mogadishu on the Somali coast, were a ribbon of cities in conversation with each other, and with other parts of the trading world that the sea brought to their door. Eventually these conversations stretched east across parts of the Arabian Sea as well, to places such as Oman, the Hadhramaut in Yemen, and even India.

Existing primary sources on the East African littoral for the premodern period, though fragmentary, stretch all the way back into antiquity. Ptolemy wrote of the riches of the East African coast in the first century CE when he composed the *Periplus of the Erythraean Sea* in Alexandria, so if the Greeks and Romans had an idea of these geographies and their products and peoples, perhaps it should not surprise us that another apex civilization, even one as far away as China, might also have had access to a trickle of information.[18] In 525 CE, Cosmas Indicopleustes, a Greek merchant, wrote on the Kingdom of

---

17. Neville Chittick, *Kilwa: An Islamic Trading City on the East African Coast* (Nairobi: British Institute in Eastern Africa, 1974).

18. G. S. P. Freeman-Grenville, *The East African Coast: Select Documents from the First to the Earlier Nineteenth Century* (Oxford: Clarendon Press, 1962), 1–4. Freeman-Grenville's corpus is extremely useful in bringing together in one place much of the earliest evidence on the cosmopolitan nature of the East African coast.

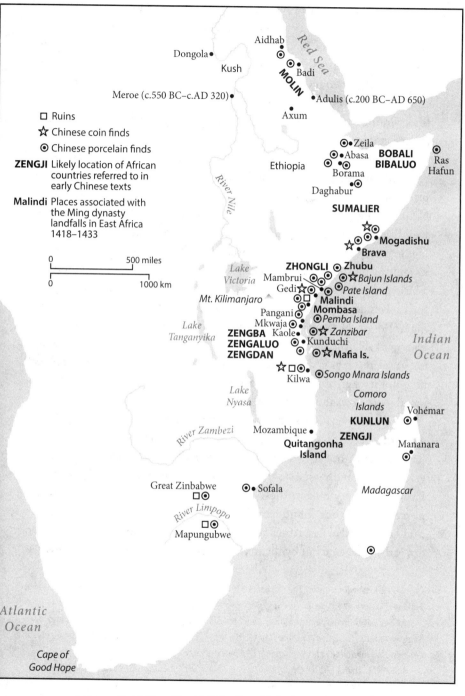

MAP 2.2. East African Coastal Cities. From Philip Snow, *The Star Raft*
(Ithaca: Cornell University Press, 1988), Map 1, p. 7

Axum in contemporary Eritrea, showing knowledge of these coasts as well.[19] Abu al-Fida was only one of a number of Arab geographers who continued to write on the "coast of Zanj," as this shoreline was described in the Arabic-speaking world; his own account of the early 1300s was followed by further information by men such as the famous Ibn Battuta (himself from Morocco), and slightly later by Abu al-Mashasin, who wrote from Mecca in 1441.[20] All of these writings were part and parcel of Arab geographers describing the world at large at this time, even as far away as the distant spice islands in Indonesia, whose position they noted in their texts. Of course Marco Polo also knew of—and admired—the riches of the East African coast; he never visited the place, having traveled by ship through Southeast Asia on his return to Europe, but it became part of this narrative of the strange and wonderful things in the world, very few of which escaped his gaze.[21] Before we look at Chinese writings in more detail as part of the chronicling of these distant coasts, however, it would be helpful first to look at the passage of one surviving commodity that whispers to us of a Chinese presence, before we even examine what Chinese themselves had to say about East Africa from their locus on the other side of the world. As the theorist Arjun Appadurai has told us in the introduction to his remarkable *The Social Life of Things*: "in and through economic exchange . . . the value of things is determined reciprocally. . . . Thus, the economic object does not have an absolute value as a result of the demand for it, but the demand . . . endows the object with value."[22]

Asian-export ceramics (including Chinese ones) became nearly omnipresent in these coastal port towns, described above. Some came from the Middle East and Persia, but large numbers came from farther away, including from the great kilns of Southeast Asia at Sawankhalok/Si Satchanalai and Sukhothai in Siam, and from Vietnam. These kilns churned out large quantities of export porcelain, and they found markets not only in Southeast Asia but in the Middle East and in East Africa as well. We know that Asian ceramics were used not just by the elite but by the middle classes of a number of these towns at

19. See J. W. McCrindle, *The Christian Topography of Cosmas, an Egyptian Monk* (London: Hakluyt Society, 1897), 37–40, 51–4.

20. See M. Reinaud, *Géographie d'Aboul-feda* (Paris, 1848), 206–8; C. Defrémery and B. R. Sanguinetti, *Les voyages d'Ibn Batoutah* (Paris, 1854), 2:179–96; and M. Guillain, *Documents sur l'histoire, la géographie et le commerce de l'Afrique orientale* (Paris, 1856), 1:299–300.

21. R. E. Latham, *The Travels of Marco Polo* (New York: Penguin Books, 1958), 275–77.

22. Arjun Appadurai, ed., *The Social Life of Things* (Cambridge: Cambridge University Press, 1986), 2–3.

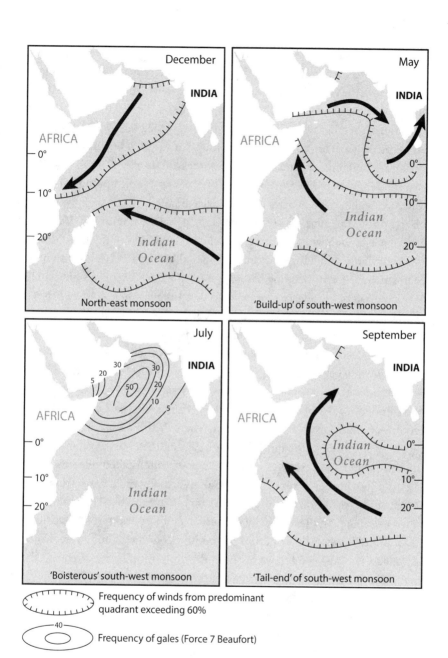

December — INDIA — AFRICA — 0° — 10° — 20° — Indian Ocean — North-east monsoon

May — INDIA — AFRICA — 0° — 10° — Indian Ocean — 20° — 'Build-up' of south-west monsoon

July — INDIA — AFRICA — 0° — 10° — 20° — Indian Ocean — 30 — 20 — 30 — 5 — 50 — 20 — 10 — 5 — 'Boisterous' south-west monsoon

September — INDIA — AFRICA — Indian Ocean — 0° — 10° — 20° — 'Tail-end' of south-west monsoon

Frequency of winds from predominant
quadrant exceeding 60%

—40—
Frequency of gales (Force 7 Beaufort)

MAP 2.3. Monsoon Patterns in the Western Indian Ocean
(Meteorological Office, 1943, 1949)

specific periods in history. Fine pieces of Chinese porcelain were often used as adornments on top of pillar tombs built for Swahili royalty—a single niche would adorn the top of some of these structures, in which would be placed an elegant ceramic of fine quality. Niches in mosques show that this practice was also known for religious buildings, and not just for the grave markers of kings. Other pieces were broken and could be found in a kind of bricolage adorning important buildings, a pattern seen in Southeast Asia as well, such as at Wat Arun in Bangkok, and in some mosques on the Javanese *pasisir*. Indeed, if one walks along the beach in parts of East Africa today, you can still cut your feet on shards of Ming blue-and-white porcelain, if you are not careful. I had this experience in 1990 when I had a chance to sail in dhows up the East African coasts of Kenya and Tanzania, conducting oral history interviews with merchants there (this foot-cutting has happened to me with broken porcelain in Maluku, Eastern Indonesia, as well). This detritus gives an idea of how much porcelain must have been around at the heyday of this trade, if it is still washing up now six hundred years later. Chinese coins have also been discovered in places such as Mogadishu and Kilwa, so we know there was other material culture moving between China and Africa via Southeast Asia as well.

The trade ceramics coming all the way from Asia to East Africa seem to have been predominantly of four types. We can get a sense of these classes of commodities from the excavations at Shanga, where British excavator Mark Horton completed one of the most thorough digs on the entire Swahili coast.[23] There he found green wares of very good quality (often called celadons), dating from the thirteenth century. These pieces actually run a range from dark to pale green, even to white; in the art history literature they are often designated as Longquan pieces. Many of these extant jars and plates have floral decorations. A second class of the commodities found was stoneware, which included Changsha painted wares (from the ninth century forward) and the later Dusun and Martaban jars from Southeast Asia; very large, heavy specimens most famously known from their Bornean and Burmese varieties, as implied by the names. Whitewares came slightly later; from the tenth century onward at Shanga, but more commonly from the twelfth and thirteenth centuries elsewhere on the East African coast. Many of these pieces were Qingbai glazed wares, white with a ghostly blue tinge to them, and often eerily beautiful

23. Mark Horton, *Shanga* (London: British Institute in Eastern Africa, 1996), 303–10.

in appearance. Chinese porcelains (that is to say, "true porcelains") were also found, of the blue-on-white variety and in several other appearances as well.[24] These are well known from the Indian Ocean networks of trade, and reached all the way to East Africa across the width and breadth of the Indian Ocean. Though Horton's excavations were important in setting a tone for the diversity and breadth of ceramics that were found on these coasts, the British were by no means the only ones either digging up or interpreting these histories, nor the connections they represent. Italians have also been important in teasing out these histories and looking at Chinese porcelains in funerary contexts (such as the Swahili pillars tombs pictured in this chapter), up and down the coasts.[25] French journals have also been involved, even though most French contact with Africa has been in the north (Maghreb) and west of the continent; nevertheless French academia has contributed in these debates (vis-à-vis Indian Ocean ceramic pathways) as well.[26] But perhaps most welcome has been the fact that Chinese archaeologists and scholars have also begun to contribute to this expanding field of knowledge, and have helped push forward the boundaries of what is understood with their own long histories of tabulating and classifying Chinese wares from the other side of the routes. Work by Zhao Bing and Qin Dashu, among others, helps us to see exactly which pieces traveled, when, and why, in the larger export tradition of Chinese ceramics moving south over the centuries.[27] Africa was one of the farthest destinations for these items of material culture, but it was just part of the larger maritime circuit where these commodities turned up, from China all the way west to East Africa and even Europe.

24. Timothy Insoll, *The Archaeology of Islam in Sub-Saharan Africa* (Cambridge: Cambridge University Press, 2003), 188.

25. Andrea Montella, "Chinese Porcelain as a Symbol of Power on the East African Coast from the 14th Century Onward," *Ming Qing Yanjiu* 20, no. 1 (2016): 74–93.

26. Zhao Bing, "La céramique chinoise importée en Afrique orientale (IXe–XVIe siècles): Un cas de changement de valeur marchande et symbolique dans le commerce global," *Afrique: Débats, méthodes et terrains d'histoire*, https://doi.org/10.4000/afriques.1836.

27. Zhao Bing, "Global Trade and Swahili Cosmopolitan Material Culture: Chinese-Style Ceramic Shards from Sanje ya Kati and Songo Mnara (Kilwa, Tanzania)," *Journal of World History* 23, no. 1 (2012): 41–85; Dashu Qin, "Archaeological Investigations of Chinese Ceramics Excavated from Kenya," in *Ancient Silk Trade Routes: Selected Works from Symposium on Cross Cultural Exchanges and Their Legacies in Asia*, ed. Qin Dashu and Jian Yuan, chapter 4 (World Scientific, 2015).

Chinese Texts and Chinese Knowledge on East Africa

In terms of texts, it has been mentioned by Philip Snow, the author of perhaps the most famous book on Sino-African historical relations, *The Star Raft*, that notices of Africa may date back to the Han Dynasty. These would not have been direct contacts with Africa, but rather notices through a series of third parties of the existence of places and people that the Chinese identified as Africa, albeit in regional guises.[28] More reliable accounts of Africa come from the T'ang Dynasty (618–907 CE), when both the *Ching-hsing Chi* [Record of Travels] and the *Yu-yang Tsa-tsu* [Assorted Dishes from Yu-yang] were written. In the Song Dynasty (960–1279 CE), a trove of information comes from the great record of contact with foreign lands, the *Zhu-fan-zhih* [Gazetteer of Foreigners] (1226 CE) of Zhao Ru Gua, who was the portmaster of Quanzhou along China's southeastern coast. His descriptions there mention products and peoples of Africa as part of an exegesis of trade contacts extending south and west from China during the beginning ages of concentrated sail.[29] Zhao Ru Gua spent the most ink pinpointing many places in Southeast Asia, and the various kinds of trade goods that could be found from the Philippines to Eastern Indonesia to the coasts of distant Burma.[30] Yet portions of this narrative concerns the commodities that might be garnered in Africa as well, as Zhao Ru Gua was a port official, after all, and someone who was keenly interested in commerce. A number of these passages are anthropological in nature as well, and show what some of China's earliest impressions of Africa may have been. To wit, and perhaps describing bride-price negotiations which still today are not unknown in some rural parts of East Africa: "Their women are clean and well-behaved. The people of the country themselves kidnap them

28. Philip Snow, *The Star Raft: China's Encounter with Africa* (New York: Weidenfeld & Nicholson, 1988), 2.

29. See Chen Dasheng and Denys Lombard, "Foreign Merchants in Maritime Trade in Quanzhou ('Zaitun'): Thirteenth and Fourteenth Centuries," in *Asian Merchants and Businessmen in the Indian Ocean and the China Sea*, ed. Denys Lombard and Jan Aubin (Oxford: Oxford University Press, 2000); and Michel Cartier, "The Chinese Perspective on Trade in the Indian Ocean," in *Asian Merchants and Businessmen*, ed. Lombard and Aubin.

30. See Chen Dasheng and Denys Lombard, "Foreign Merchants in Maritime Trade"; and Michel Cartier, "The Chinese Perspective on Trade in the Indian Ocean," in *Asian Merchants and Businessmen*, ed. Lombard and Aubin.

and sell them to strangers at prices many times more than they would have fetched at home."[31]

During the Ming Dynasty (1368–1644), the main texts became the so-called *Wu-Bei-Zhi* [Notes on Military Preparedness], alongside *Xing-cha Sheng-lag* [The Triumphant Vision of the Starry Raft], as well as the actual "Ming History" itself, or the *Ming Shi,* alongside the *Ying-yai Shen-lan.*[32] All of these gave an idea of Africa in Chinese circles during the course of the Ming, a time (at least at the beginning of the dynasty) when China opened up to exploring the world like it had at no other point in its history. We can start by this time to infer something of a worldview vis-à-vis China and Africa, though in reality Africa probably stretched as part and parcel of an assemblage of lands that were now known, but so distant to China as to be almost on the other side of the world.[33] The *Wu-Bei-Zhi* charts are especially instructive because they give us a glimpse of Chinese navigational science at the time of China's first real engagement with Africa in the fifteenth century, even though the text itself of the charts (a fragment of which is reproduced in Figure 2.2) is from 1621, reproducing knowledge from some two centuries earlier. Most Chinese voyages at the time were going to Southeast Asia, but Africa was not unknown to early Ming rulers.[34] Bearings were taken by compass, and the altitudes of stars near the horizon were recorded to figure out latitudes over the course of seaborne travel. These stellar diagrams took in the position of Polaris, the pole star, and of various constellations. Reckonings were often counted in the widths of fingers when looking out at the sky, and above the imaginary

31. G. S. P. Freeman-Grenville, *The East African Coast* (Oxford: Oxford University Press, 1962), 8; see also Michel Cartier, "La vision chinoise des étrangers: Réflexions sur la constitution d'une pensée anthropologique," in *Asia Maritima: Images et réalité: Bilder und Wirklichkeit 1200–1800,* ed. Denys Lombard and Roderich Ptak (Wiesbaden: Harrassowitz Verlag, 1994).

32. John Shen, "New Thoughts on the Use of Chinese Documents in the Reconstruction of Early Swahili History," *History in Africa* 22 (1995), 349–58.

33. Paul Wheatley, "Analecta Sino-Africana Recensa," in *East Africa and the Orient,* ed. H. Neville Chittick and Robert Rotberg, 76–114 (New York, 1975).

34. See Michel Cartier, "La vision chinoise du monde, Taiwan dans la littérature géographique ancienne," in *Actes du IIIe colloque international de sinologie, Chantilly 1980,* 1–12 (Paris: Les Belles Lettres, 1983); Charles Le Blanc et Rémi Mathieu, "Voir à ce propos Rémi Mathieu, *Étude sur la mythologie et l'ethnologie de la Chine ancienne: Traduction annotée du Shan-haijng* (Paris, 1983); and Rémi Mathieu, "L'inquiétante étrangeté," in *Mythe et philosophie à l'aube de la Chine impériale: Études sur le Huainan zi,* 15–26 (Montreal and Paris, 1992).

plane of the horizon line.[35] Africa may have been "on the other side of the world" when it came to China, but the Chinese at least were doing their best at this time in trying to figure out how to get there via southern Asia's intervening seas.[36]

Scholars have been fascinated by the complexities of these Chinese maritime voyages for a long time. As early as 1938, contributions started to be made in the literature about the nature of these journeys, being published in specialized geographic journals which were linked with Europe's colonial presence in the world.[37] After World War II and decolonization, this kind of scholarship became more purely "academic" in its slant, and was pushed forward not just by the "major" Western powers but also by smaller countries with lesser footprints in the carving up of the world, such as the Italians.[38] Yet Chinese authors also began to publish more and more on this topic, often utilizing Chinese-language sources that were easier for them to access than scholars in the West, especially after the mid-1960s.[39] The crowning achievement in many ways was Joseph Needham's much-talked-about history of science and civilization in China, which had an entire, dense volume just on the topic on nautics, and which discussed the era of Chinese premodern voyages in great detail.[40] Yet the study of such nautical feats of engineering and of seamanship have not lost their luster, and this is still a growth industry among scholars of our own time,

35. Louise Levathes, *When China Ruled the Seas: The Treasure Fleet of the Dragon Throne, 1405–1433* (New York: Oxford University Press, 1994), 97. See also Edward J. Dreyer, *Zheng He: China and the Oceans in the Early Ming Dynasty, 1405–1433* (New York: Pearson Longman, 2007).

36. See Li Kangying, *The Ming Maritime Trade Policy in Transition, 1368 to 1567* (Wiesbaden: Harrassowitz Verlag, 2010); Roderich Ptak, "Ming Maritime Trade to Southeast Asia, 1368–1567: Visions of a 'System,'" in *From the Mediterranean to the China Sea: Miscellaneous Notes,* ed. Claude Guillot, Denys Lombard, and Roderich Ptak (Wiesbaden: Harrassowitz Verlag, 1998), 157–91; and Pierre-Yves Manguin, "Trading Ships of the South China Sea: Shipbuilding Techniques and Their Role in the History of the Development of Asian Trade Networks," *JESHO* 36, no. 2 (1993), 253–80.

37. E. H. L. Schwarz. "The Chinese Connection with Africa," *Journal of Bengal Branch, Royal Asiatic Society, Letters* 4 (1938): 175–93.

38. Teobaldo Filesi, "I viaggi dei Cinesi in Africa nel medioevo" [The voyages of the Chinese in Africa in the medieval period], *Africa: Rivista trimestrale di studi e documentazione dell'Istituto italiano per l'Africa e l'Oriente* 16, no. 6 (1961): 275–88.

39. Kuei-sheng Chang, "The Ming Maritime Enterprise and China's Knowledge of Africa prior to the Age of Great Discoveries," *Terrae Incognitae* 3, no. 1 (1971): 33–44.

40. Joseph Needham, ed., *Science and Civilisation in China* (Cambridge: Cambridge University Press, 1971), vol. 4, part 3.

who have gradually been able to put together a corpus of knowledge on Asian seafaring traditions during this period that help us to better understand how voyages of this scale could actually work.[41]

This feeling of distance—metaphorical and actual—was palpable in China's production of knowledge about Africa, but at one famous premodern moment China actually came to the latter continent, and set foot on East African shores for a short space of time. This of course was during one of the renowned Zheng He voyages (1405–33), when the great eunuch admiral (a Chinese Muslim, whose family hailed from Yunnan Province) led seven expeditions away from China, and down to monsoon Asia. At least several of the voyages made it into the Indian Ocean, and at least one of them to Africa. These were fleets of enormous size and complexity; the ships were built on the eastern coasts of China near the capital of Nanjing over many years, and when they were finally assembled and the voyages began, tens of thousands of souls sailed on them, many of them soldiers but also sailors, merchants, diplomats, concubines, priests, and a variety of other people, all collected together for the trips. The ships brought huge amounts of treasure to distribute as presents to the no doubt "shocked and awed" inhabitants of the world that they encountered. It was a public-relations coup of the highest order. Dozens of societies along the maritime Asian littorals were treated to a glimpse of the ascendant Ming Dynasty and its power, fresh from the liberation of China from the Mongols who had been in power not just in China (1279 to 1368 CE) but across the expanse of Eurasia for nearly one hundred years. A contemporary line drawing of the (estimated) comparative sizes of Zheng He's command ship and Columbus's *Santa Maria*, which sailed seventy years later to "discover" the New World, gives us an idea of scale. The Iberians were discovering the world in rowboats, essentially, next to the Chinese equivalent of aircraft carriers of the age.[42]

Alas, the official records of the voyages are thought to have been destroyed in 1480, after this age of exploration came to a halt, so the majority of our

41. Here the work of Pierre-Yves Manguin is paramount. His oeuvre is extensive, but for the present purposes, see Pierre-Yves Manguin, "Trading Ships of the South China Sea: Shipbuilding Techniques and Their Role in the Development of Asian Trade Networks," *Journal of the Economic and Social History of the Orient* 36: 253–80.

42. Levathes, *When China Ruled the Seas*, 21. See also Sally Church and others on the matter of comparative size; we are still unsure of the exact dimensions, but it is clear that the Chinese ships were far larger than their European counterparts. See also Christopher Wake, "The Myth of Zheng He's Great Treasure Ships," *International Journal of Maritime History* 16, no. 1 (2004), 59–75.

FIGURE 2.2. Zheng He's Treasure Ship and the *Wu Bei Zhi* Charts. Courtesy Jan Adkins; and J. V. G. Mills, trans., *Ying-yai Sheng-lan: The Overall Survey of the Ocean's Shores, by Ma Huan* (London: Haklyut Society, 1970), Appendix 6

knowledge about them comes from the surviving narrative of Ma Huan, who traveled on several of the seven expeditions. On the fourth voyage (1413–15 CE) Ma Huan made it through Southeast Asia (to the north coast of Java, or the *pasisir* in Malay), through the Strait of Melaka, up to Bengal and Sri Lanka and the Malabar Coast in South Asia, and even to Hormuz in Persia and to Aden (and the environs of Mecca), astride the Red Sea. He likely saw the coast of northeast Africa (the Horn) at Somalia, Eritrea, and Djibouti on this last part of the trip. Ma Huan, himself a Chinese Muslim, went aboard as an Arabic/Chinese translator of documents, and as a young man (thirty-two at the time of the voyage) he already read and spoke Arabic with great fluency. Ma Huan's account is one of only three surviving records of the voyages that were written at the time that the ships went out to sea and participated in China's "discovery of the world." He described the nobility of Chinese personages on board the ships, as well as giving an anthropological account of many of the peoples encountered on shore all through the long course of travels. He described the sea and its infinite variations, and made careful observations on the mountains and forests that he spied from the deck of his ship, as well as from land when

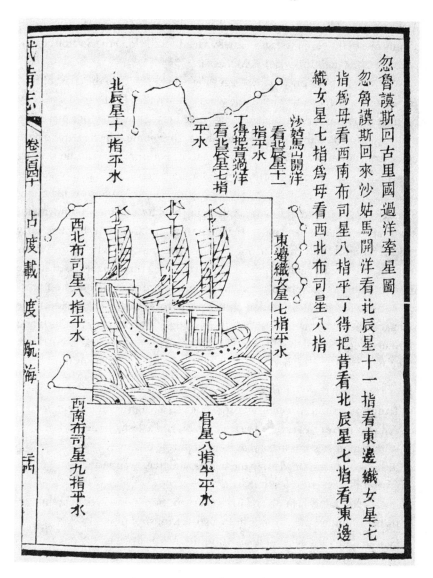

忽魯謨斯回古里國過洋牽星圖

FIGURE 2.2. (*continued*)

able to go ashore. He was particularly interested in the occasional Chinese satellite communities that were discovered out in the world, almost all of them in Southeast Asian coastal cities, where Chinese were engaged in making a living as merchants, artisans, and advisers in a variety of places. Ma Huan's descriptions are almost certainly the oldest surviving Chinese narrations of

Africa and the Middle East.[43] Yet he may not have set foot in Africa himself, as only one of the seven voyages actually sailed south along the Swahili coasts, possibly as far (latitude-wise) as Madagascar.[44]

We know that this one, farthest-traveling fleet lingered on the coast of East Africa for a while, awaiting favorable winds. When they finally did leave, they brought a live giraffe with them, which—together with another one picked up in Bengal—made it all the way back to China. This giraffe, which seems to have come from either Malindi in modern-day Kenya or from Somalia, depending on which modern-day historiography is to be believed, was painted in the court of the Yongle emperor in 1415 CE by the Hanlin Academy calligrapher Shen Du. He depicted the giant giraffe being held by a Chinese retainer with a rope around his face and neck. The Chinese man stares up at the huge, lofty head of the animal, and one can only wonder what the crowds lining the streets from the port to the capital must have thought when this amiable beast strode by. The date was 20 September 1414—a little more than six hundred years ago.[45] Shen Du was also asked to write a poem for the occasion, to adorn the official painting that memorialized the meeting of the emperor of China and this huge beast, which the Chinese thought was a *qilin*, a mythical animal from their own mythological bestiary. His poem is preserved, and runs thus:

> In a corner of the western seas, in the stagnant waters of a great morass,
> Truly was produced a *qilin*, whose shape was as high as fifteen feet.
> With the body of a deer and the tail of an ox, and a fleshy, boneless, horn,
> With luminous spots like a red cloud or purple mist.
> Its hooves do not tread on living beings, and in its wanderings,
> It carefully selects its ground.
> It walks in stately fashion and in its every motion it observes a rhythm,
> Its harmonious voice sounds like a bell or a musical tube.
> Gentle is this animal, that in all Antiquity, has been seen only once.
> The manifestation of the divine spirit rises up to Heaven's abode.[46]

Some of the scholarship on the "Ming moment" of the Zheng He voyages began to change in the first decade of the 2000s, especially through the

---

43. See J. V. G. Mills, trans., *Ying-yai Sheng-lan: The Overall Survey of the Ocean's Shores*, by *Ma Huan* (London: Haklyut Society, 1970).

44. Stewart Gordon, *When Asia Was the World* (Philadelphia: Da Capo, 2008), 117–37.

45. Ibid., facing p. 113.

46. Ibid., 141–42.

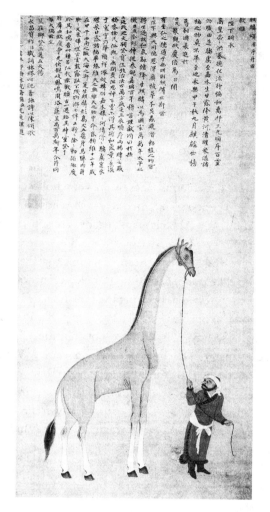

FIGURE 2.3. *The Yong-Le Giraffe Brought Back to China,*
1415 CE (Philadelphia Museum of Art)

auspices of two historians with impeccable language skills. One of these was
Geoff Wade, whose *Southeast Asia and the Ming Shi-lu* (2005) must be rightly
seen as one of the great advances in our knowledge about early modern China
in any way, shape, or form.[47] This open-access source allows scholars anywhere

47. Geoffrey Wade, *Southeast Asia in the Ming Shi-lu: An Open Access Resource* (Singapore:
Asia Research Institute and the Singapore E-Press, National University of Singapore, http://
epress.nus.edu.sg/msl.

in the world to comb through the Ming dynastic records by keyword to find anything they need—including notices of various places along the sea routes; the various and sundry episodes of different reign periods; and the location and contributions of individual historical people, all organized digitally (and for free). On top of this, Wade was also beginning to publish a series of essays reassessing the Zheng He voyages as a state-sponsored project, and asking whether the voyages were as benevolent as many historians had continuously maintained in Chinese historiography.[48] By roughly a decade later, the first questionings of this "official narrative" were no longer tentative, and were stated in much more direct terms. These works of scholarship have acted to enrich the debate in a period six hundred years ago, whose sources are largely lost to us in the modern world but whose echoes are still very much felt in contemporary geopolitics.[49]

A second scholar who has been crucial in putting together these histories is Tansen Sen, who (like Wade) has a strong Sinological background, but who also has been very interested in bringing the Indian Ocean further in these discussions. Starting in roughly 2006, Sen began to publish a series of articles on how the changing seaways of Asia looked, not only from China's standpoint but also from the vantage of the Indian Ocean as a whole.[50] What started out as episodic "interactions" early on, ultimately began to morph into qualitatively different experiences of contact as the years wore on in this "middle period" of civilizational discourse. Some of these conversations were religious in nature, and involved the movement of Buddhism and Buddhist texts between these civilizations.[51] But some of the expeditions were more military in character, and though there was a diplomatic tinge to them as well, it seems clear that the Chinese Empire was figuring out what might be done in these

48. Geoffrey Wade, "The Zheng He Voyages: A Reassessment," *Journal of the Malaysian Branch of the Royal Asiatic Society* 78, no. 1 (2005): 37–58; and Geoffrey Wade, "Engaging the South: Ming China and Southeast Asia in the Fifteenth Century," *Journal of the Economic and Social History of the Orient* 51, no. 4 (2008): 578–638.

49. Geoffrey Wade, "Ming China's Violence against Neighboring Polities and Its Representation in Chinese Historiography," in *Asian Encounters: Exploring Connected Histories*, ed. Upinder Singh and Parul Dhar, 20–41 (New Delhi: Oxford University Press, 2014).

50. Tansen Sen, "The Formation of Chinese Maritime Networks to Southern Asia, 1200–1450," *Journal of the Social and Economic History of the Orient* 49, no. 4 (2006): 421–53.

51. Tansen Sen, "Diplomacy, Trade, and the Quest for the Buddha's Tooth: The Yongle Emperor and Ming China's South Asian Frontier," in *Ming China: Courts and Contacts, 1400–1450*, ed. Craig Clunas, Jessica Harrison-Hall, and Luk Yu-Ping (London: British Museum, 2016).

monsoon waters by way of influence (and possibly) ultimately conquest as well.[52] In this sense, then, the Zheng He expeditions can be seen to be important not just for what they tell us about the "open cadence" of the early Ming court but also in the ramifications of these voyages thousands of miles away, where Ming politics were affecting the seaways of an entire continent.[53]

Africans Going East: Africa toward China

Interest in Chinese exposure to the sea and its long histories has been in vogue now for a short time, but we can end by giving just a very short description of contact working in the *opposite* direction, from Africa moving toward China.[54] This is a less well-known story, and one that is still being unpacked even as this book is written, as new materials become available and scholars search for new texts. The major book on this topic was published some years ago by Don Wyatt under the rather plain title of *The Blacks of Premodern China*.[55] In it, Wyatt argues that a killing in 684 CE—in the early part of the T'ang Dynasty— represents the first time that an African is mentioned in Chinese history. We can only summarize very briefly here, but by following the term *kunlun*—a person whom Wyatt says the Chinese found to be "utterly unlike themselves," and ethnically African, in his estimation—he posits that Black Africans were

52. Tansen Sen, "Maritime Interactions between China and India: Coastal India and the Ascendancy of Chinese Maritime Power in the Indian Ocean," *Journal of Central Eurasian Studies* 2 (2011): 41–82.

53. Tansen Sen, "The Impact of Zheng He's Expeditions on Indian Ocean Interactions," *Bulletin of the School of Oriental and African Studies* 79, no. 3 (2016): 609–36.

54. For several good texts on the "Chinese looking south" paradigm, see Zhang Yangwen, *China on the Sea: How the Maritime World Shaped Modern China* (Leiden: Brill, 2012); Xing Hang, *Conflict and Commerce in Maritime East Asia: The Zheng Family and the Shaping of the Modern World, 1620–1720* (Cambridge: Cambridge University Press, 2016); Xing Hang and Tonio Andrade, eds., *Sea Rovers, Silver, and Samurai: Maritime East Asia in Global History, 1550– 1700* (Honolulu: University of Hawai'i Press, 2016); Ronald Po, *The Blue Frontier: Maritime Vision and Power in the Qing Empire* (Cambridge: Cambridge University Press, 2018); Geoffrey Wade, "The Southern Chinese Borders in History" in G. Evans, C. Hutton, and K. E. Kuah, eds., *Where China Meets Southeast Asia: Social and Cultural Change in the Border Regions* (Singapore; ISEAS Press, 2000), 28–50; and Geoffrey Wade, "Engaging the South: Ming China and Southeast Asia in the Fifteenth Century," *JESHO* 51 (2008): 578–638.

55. Don Wyatt, *The Blacks of Premodern China* (Philadelphia: University of Pennsylvania Press, 2010).

not unknown to China before Zhao Ru Gua in the Song Dynasty, and before Zheng He in the Ming.

By tracing a series of incidents and descriptions of Guangzhou port, he makes an interesting (but to this point untested) case that Africans were coming to southeast China with the trade winds for centuries, as part of the general flow of maritime commerce. Wyatt is careful to point out that the term *kunlun* probably encompassed over time a number of tellurian peoples with dark skin, and that it was likely flexible in designation. Therefore Australian aborigines, Malay tribal people from the interior of the Malay Peninsula (Orang Asli), and Tamils from South India, if any of them ever found their way to T'ang China, could all have been subsumed under this designation. All had very dark skin. Crucially, all had likely darker skin than most Chinese would have seen in their normative tributary-trade contacts with darker-skinned peoples than themselves across the wide stretch of Southeast Asia. Gwyn Campbell tells us that by the Mongol period (1260–1368), aristocratic Chinese families found it fashionable to try to possess African manservants—so much so that in 1382, the Javanese court dispatched more than a hundred such men as a tributary gift to the Chinese court.[56]

This broad definition on Wyatt's part as to the term *kunlun* seems prudent. And he is also clear that Black Africans certainly did turn up on the China coasts as part of the traffic of Europeans, who landed with some of these people in tow from the sixteenth century onward.[57] Indeed, by the seventeenth century and the famous Coxinga period of Fujian and Taiwan, at the end of the Ming, it is well established that there were Africans serving a variety of roles on the China coasts, often as bodyguards and soldiers, but likely in other iterations as well. All or nearly all of these Africans would have passed through Southeast Asia, likely on European ships. Coxinga himself seems to have had a very feared and loyal inner circle of mercenary-soldiers attendant upon him at all times called the Black Guard. These were men from Africa who had come via Portuguese slave ships, and who had settled into a niche on the South China coasts. Most Chinese avoided them, not having seen any humans

56. Gwyn Campbell, *Africa and the Indian Ocean World from Early Times to Circa 1900* (Cambridge: Cambridge University Press, 2019), 261.

57. For some context, see P. M. D'Elia, *Galileo in Cina: Relazioni attraverso il Collegio Romano tra Galileo e i gesuiti scienziati missionari in Cina (1610–1640)* (Rome: 1947), 21; and, by the same author, *Fonti Ricciane: Documenti originali concernenti Matteo Ricci e la storia delle prime relazioni tra l'Europa e la Cina (1579–1615)*, ed. P.M. D'Elia, (Rome, 1942), I:259 n. 310.

like them, apparently, and they were regarded with some suspicion and fear by local Chinese inhabitants, who seem to have called them "demons."[58]

Because Coxinga himself (Chen Chen-gong) was so important in the early modern history of China, the fame of these Black Africans—even though they were likely fairly small in number—has been amplified. Coxinga's father was one of the most important men designated as "pirates" by the state in the roiling South China Sea of the seventeenth century, and his mother (amazingly) was a samurai, showing his dual ethnic heritage in this osmotic part of the world. People moved back and forth on the seaways between China, Japan, Korea, and Southeast Asia, and Coxinga was no exception. He had been classically trained in the traditions of Chinese elite culture, and some of that training seems to have really stayed with him, in that he—unlike many others when the Ming dynasty fell and was subsumed into the ethnically Manchu Qing—refused to give up on his former dynastic masters. His loyalty was not for sale. This despite the words of the Manchus, who were in the process of taking over China as their own: "In the counties, districts, and locales that we pass through, all those who are able to shave their heads and surrender, opening their gates to welcome us, will be given rank and reward, retaining their wealth and their nobility for generations. But if there are those who resist us, then . . . the stones themselves will be set ablaze, and everyone will be massacred."[59]

It makes perfect sense in this "waterworld" of the seventeenth century that a contingent of Africans from very far away on the sea routes would find a home in Coxinga's care, acting as his inner cadre of protectors in a milieu where treachery and the changing of sides was commonplace. These men were too far from home to have local ties that compromised them, we might assume. And these Africans guards were not the only such companies of men from that distant continent who found employment in such circumstances. Other Africans were known to have wound up as archers on the coasts of early modern India, and they may well turn up in still other places, as more research is done. The publication of Wyatt's book will likely set off others on this trail too, which promises to open other doors as to how long and how old the communion between China and Africa really may be.

58. John Clements, *Coxinga and the Fall of the Ming Dynasty* (Phoenix Mill: Sutton Publishing, 2005), 17, 79.

59. Frederic Wakeman, *The Great Enterprise* (Berkeley: University of California Press, 1985), 317.

FIGURE 2.4. Coxinga's African Guard (Olfert Dapper,
1670, *Gedenkwaerdig bedryf der Nederlandsche
Oost-Indische Maetschappye*, Lilly Library,
University of Indiana)

Conclusion

It is clear that the relationship between China and Africa via maritime South-east Asia goes back some way into the distant past. This is not just a story of modern-day contacts based on economic aid and political maneuvering but rather, an ancient story, with deep roots in the past. From Chinese records it is clear that Africa was known from a very early time, at least the Song Dynasty, though what kinds of knowledge (other than those involving the provenances of commodities) might have existed is difficult to discern.[60] Though some

---

60. See Donatella Guida, "Immagini del Nanyang: Realtà e stereotipi nella storiografia ci-nese verso la fine della dinastia Ming (Naples: Istituto Universitario Orientale di Napoli, 1991);

fairly recent scholarship has posited links going all the way back to the T'ang, at this point at least these references are indeterminate, though it should not surprise us if a few Africans did somehow manage to make it to Canton, even as far back as the first millennium. By the Song Dynasty this knowledge was growing. But it was only in Ming times that it was really concretized, and deepened with actual contacts recorded by Chinese travelers. These were mariners sailing all the way across the Indian Ocean, from starting points in Southeast Asia. The Zheng He voyages were undoubtedly the highlight of these processes. But Chinese knowledge of Africa was already clearly inscribed by this time, with Islam and thickening sea-lanes aiding the passage of information along vast and distant oceanic networks. Black Africans also seem to have started moving in the opposite direction, at least from this moment, though quite possibly earlier than this. The fact that the Ming loyalist Coxinga possessed a bodyguard of Africans with him in the seventeenth century as he fled the Ching to Taiwan offers a nice symmetry to this story. If the Ming reached out furthest to Africa during this era, Africa also seems to have reached out farthest to China during these years as well. Both transits required the monsoon regions of maritime Southeast Asia as a "middle ground." In coming decades, as archival research deepens and the archaeological (and genomic) record divulges more of its secrets, we may be astounded to find that Sino-African contacts have been going on for longer than we all think—and in ways that continue to amaze us.

---

and Denys Lombard and Roderich Ptak, eds., *Asia Maritima: Images et réalité: Bilder und Wirklichkeit 1200–1800* (Wiesbaden: Harrassowitz Verlag, 1994).

3

Vietnam's Maritime Trade Orbit

Centuries of human existence . . .
Mulberry trees turned into open sea.

—*TRUYỆN KIỀU* [TALE OF KIỀU] (NGUYỄN DU, 1769–1820)

VIETNAM IS NOT USUALLY mentioned in the same breath with several other countries—most notably China, Japan, and India—when the maritime trading world of early modern Asia is described.[1] Neither Vietnam's commercial infrastructure nor its incorporation into the mercantile orbit of the time has been judged sufficient to place the country on an even par with many of its larger neighbors. Yet, while this judgment remains essentially valid, Vietnam did have an important role to play in the maritime economic life of Asia during

1. Visits to Saigon and Huế in 2009, and Hanoi in 2009 and 2016, contributed to this chapter. For some useful descriptions of this world, more or less in chronological order, see Momoki Shiro, "Dai Viet and the South China Sea Trade from the 10th to the 15th Century," *Crossroads*, 12, no. 1 (1998): 1–34; Patrizia Carioti, "The Zheng's Maritime Power in the International Context of the Seventeenth Century Far Eastern Seas: The Rise of a 'Centralized Piratical Organization' and Its Gradual Development into an Informal State," *Ming Qing Yanjiu* (Napoli, 1996): 29–67; Tonio Andrade, "The Company's Chinese Pirates: How the Dutch East India Company Tried to Lead a Coalition of Pirates to War against China, 1621–1662," *Journal of World History* 15, no. 4 (2004), pp. 415–44; Timothy Brook, "Trade and Conflict in the South China Sea: Portugal and China, 1514–23," in *A Global History of Trade and Conflict since 1500*, ed. Lucia Coppolaro and Francine McKenzie, 20, 37 (Basingstoke: Palgrave Macmillan, 2013); William S. Atwill, "Ming China and the Emerging World Economy, c.1470–1650," in *The Cambridge History of China*, vol. 8: *The Ming Dynasty, 1368–1644, Part 2*, eds. Denis Twitchett and Frederick Mote, 376–416 (Cambridge: Cambridge University Press, 1998); and Robert Antony, *Like Froth Floating on the Sea: The World of Pirates and Seafarers in Late Imperial China* (Berkeley: Institute for East Asian Studies, 2003).

this time.[2] This chapter attempts to chronicle this role, which entwined the lands of the Nguyễn and the Trịnh with Europeans and other Asians for more than three centuries. By examining these ongoing interactions, we will link tribute-trade, laissez-faire economics, and politics into one coherent narrative. The major argument that emerges from this analysis is a realization that the Vietnamese coasts provided an important subsidiary trading milieu to a host of merchants linked within the greater "China trade" of the region.[3] However, before characterizing the nature of this complementarity, we must first quickly outline the internal socioeconomic matrix of Vietnam itself, in order to provide a background to the enormous changes attendant to this age.[4]

2. Useful here is Charles Wheeler, "Re-thinking the Sea in Vietnamese History: The Littoral Integration of Thuận-Quảng, Seventeenth-Eighteenth Centuries," *Journal of Southeast Asian Studies* 17, no. 1 (Feb. 2006): 123–53; and Charlotte Pham, "The Vietnamese Coastline: A Maritime Cultural Landscape," in *The Sea, Identity and History: From the Bay of Bengal to the South China Sea*, ed. Satish Chandra and Himanshu Prabha Ray, 137–67 (Delhi: Society for Indian Ocean Studies, 2013).

3. For a helpful characterization of the southward passage of humans in this trade, see G. William Skinner, "Creolized Chinese Societies in Southeast Asia," in *Sojourners and Settlers: Histories of Southeast Asia and the Chinese*, ed. Anthony Reid, 51–93 (Honolulu: University of Hawai'i Press, 2001). For a longer history of Sino/Vietnamese contact, see Dian Murray, *Conflict and Coexistence: The Sino-Vietnamese Maritime Boundaries in Historical Perspective* (Madison: Center for Southeast Asian Studies, University of Wisconsin, 1988); and Jamie Anderson, "Slipping through Holes: The Late Tenth and Early Eleventh Century Sino-Vietnamese Coastal Frontier as a Subaltern Trade Network" in Nola Cooke, Tana Li, and Jamie Anderson, eds., *The Tongking Gulf through History* (Philadelphia; University of Pennsylvania Press, 2011), 87–100, for the early period. For the *longue durée*, see Niu Junkai and Li Qingxin, "Chinese 'Political Pirates' in the Seventeenth-Century Gulf of Tongking," in *The Tongking Gulf*, ed. Cooke, Li, and Anderson, 133–42; Vu Duong Luan and Nola Cooke, "Chinese Merchants and Mariners in Nineteenth-Century Tongking," in *The Tongking Gulf*, ed. Cooke, Tana, and Anderson, 143–59; James Kong Chin, "The Junk Trade between South China and Nguyen Vietnam in the Late Eighteenth and Early Nineteenth Centuries," in *Water Frontier: Commerce and the Chinese in the Lower Mekong Region, 1750–1880*, ed. Nola Cooke and Tana Li, 53–70 (Lanham, MD: Rowman & Littlefield, 2004); and Choi Byung Wook, "The Nguyen Dynasty's Policy toward Chinese on the Water Frontier in the First Half of the Nineteenth Century," in *Water Frontier*, ed. Cooke and Tana, 85–100.

4. Milton Osborne, in his preface to John White's 1824 work *A Voyage to Cochin China* (Kuala Lumpur, Oxford University Press Historical Reprints 1972), xv, points out that the history of foreign trade in Vietnam may be one of the few areas where English language accounts are of equal or greater value than the French. Most pre-1860s French literature on Vietnam was written by or about missionaries, with very little attention to matters of

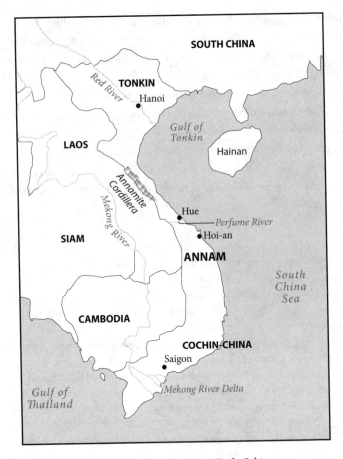

MAP 3.1. Vietnam's Maritime Trade Orbit

There are very clear and practical reasons in the historical record why a "commercial revolution" in Vietnam was a more difficult and gradual process than it was for some of its neighbors. The dissolution of the Lê Dynasty from an initially united realm into a land ruled by essentially two (and at one point, three) fiefdoms created an atmosphere where political power among the Trịnh and the Nguyễn was maintained essentially through *sui juris* allegiance of their

---

economics and trade. Englishmen came to the country with a different vision, and as part of a different project. Another obvious example where this linguistic distinction would hold true was the Vietnam War.

respective elites.[5] Local landowners wielded considerable leverage in the court-based clan systems of these two great families; they also maintained a strong grip on their local constituencies (farms, villages, and village economies). With the ascension of the Nguyễn Dynasty in 1802, therefore, it was decidedly in these aristocrats' own interest to dissuade any sort of sustained mercantile activity that would strengthen the power of the state (or create a wealthy new merchant class), over and against these elites' own local benefit. The sea and its potential benefits were often regarded with suspicion in the past several centuries of Vietnamese history, therefore, though there were moments—as we will see below—when this paradigm was essentially untrue, or even turned on its head.

The Evolution of an Economy

This fundamental conflict of interest was one reason why Vietnam's economy rose relatively slowly out of the village domain, and in fits and starts, despite the fact that vast tracts of new land were coming under dominion in the south.[6] In fact, even in the face of the French imperial project from the mid-nineteenth century onward, large landowners resisted change in this system of local and court patronage power, though the inevitable result for this rigidity was a relative economic stasis countrywide and (at least tangentially) a diminished ability to cope with European penetration. The Nguyễn of the South may have been slightly more amenable to allowing change in these basic

5. See Keith W. Taylor, "Regional Conflicts among the Viêt People between the 13th and 19th Centuries," in *Guerre et paix en Asie du sud-est*, ed. Nguyễn Thế Anh and Alain Forest, 109–33 (Paris: L'Harmattan, 1998); see also Keith W. Taylor, "The Literati Revival in Seventeenth-Century Vietnam," *Journal of Southeast Asian Studies*, 18, no. 1 (1997): 1–23. See also Khac Thuan, Dinh, "Contribution à l'histoire de la Dynastie des Mac au Viet Nam," PhD thesis, Université de Paris, 2002.

6. On the importance of this southernmost region of Vietnam, see Christopher Borri, "An Account of Cochin-China," in *A Collection of the Best and Most Interesting Voyages and Travels in All Parts of the World*, ed. John Pinkerton, vol. 11 (London 1811); Anthony Reid, "The End of Dutch Relations with the Nguyen State, 1651–2: Excerpts Translated by Anthony Reid," in *Southern Vietnam under the Nguyen: Documents on the Economic History of Cochin China (Dang Trong), 1602–1777*. Singapore: ISEAS, 1993; and Yang Baoyun, *Contribution à l'histoire de la principauté des Nguyen au Vietnam méridional (1600–1775)* (Geneva: Éditions Olizane, 1992). Also see Joseph Buttinger, *The Smaller Dragon* (New York: Praeger, 1958), 171. Such an incredible growth in territory may have been singularly responsible for controlling Vietnam's population explosion at this time, notes the last author.

patterns than the Trịnh, as with the former a frontier society prevailed, and older ways of doing things were sometimes thrown out in favor of local solutions.[7] A practical ramification of this ideology could even be seen in simple indices such as the local markets, where Cochin-Chinese bazaars were overflowing with exotic new goods, while their northern counterparts were much more local (that is to say, agricultural) in character.[8]

It was into this warring world of princes and rival courts that the first Europeans arrived in the sixteenth century.[9] Only twenty-five years after the Portuguese storming of Melaka in 1511, one of de Albuquerque's captains, Dom Antonio da Faria, built a trading station at Faifo (Hội An), along the Bay of Tourane.[10] This was followed by an English attempt to do the same through the East India Company's representative in Japan, Richard Cocks, but the

7. John Adams and Nancy Hancock, "Land and Economy in Traditional Vietnam," *JSEAS* 1, no. 2 (1970, n. 90. For some useful research on Tonkin in the North during this era, see Nguyễn Thúa Hy, *Economic History of Hanoi in the 17th, 18th and 19th Centuries* (Hanoi: ST Publisher, 2002); David E. Cartwright, "Tonkin Tides Revisited," *The Royal Society*, 57, no. 2 (2003); and P. W. Klein, "De Tonkinees-Japanse zijdehandel van de Vereenigde Oost-indische Compagine en het inter-Aziatische verkeer in de 17e eeuw," in *Bewogen en bewegen: Dehistoricus in het spanningsveld tussen economie and cultuur*, ed. W. Frijhoff and M. Hiemstra (Tilburg: Gianotten, 1986). For primary/period accounts, see Samuel Baron, "A Description of the Kingdom of Tonqueen," in *A Collection of the Best and Most Interesting Voyages and Travels in All Parts of the World*, vol. IX, ed. John Pinkerton (London, 1811); J. M. Dixon, "Voyage of the Dutch Ship 'Groll' from Hirado to Tongking," *Transactions of the Asiatic Society of Japan* XI (Yokohama, 1883); and C. C. van der Plas, *Tonkin 1644/45, Journal van de Reis van Anthonio Brouckhorst* (Amsterdam: Koninklijk Instituut voor de Trompen, Mededeling No. CXVII, 1995).

8. P. J. B. Truong-Vinh-Ky, trans. P. J. Honey, *Voyage to Tanking in the Year 1876* (London: SOAS, 1982), 94. For interesting discussions on regionalism in Vietnamese history, see Iioka Naoko, "The Trading Environment and the Failure of Tongking's Mid-Seventeenth-century Commercial Resurgence," in *The Tongking Gulf*, ed. Cooke, Li, and Anderson, 117–32; and Choi Byung Wook, "The Nguyen Dynasty's Policy toward Chinese on the Water Frontier in the First Half of the Nineteenth Century," in *Water Frontier*, ed. Cooke and Li, 85–100 (Lanham, MD: Rowman & Littlefield, 2004).

9. On Europeans in Vietnam generally, from earliest evidence, see Pierre-Yves Manguin, *Les portugais sur les côtes du Viet-Nam et du Campa: Étude sur les routes maritimes et les relations commercialistes, d'après les sources portugaises (XVIe, XVIIe, XVIIIe siècles)* (Paris: EFEO, 1972); and, more generally, Frédéric Mantienne, "Indochinese Societies and European Traders: Different Worlds of Trade?" in *Commerce et navigation en Asia du sud-est (XIV–XIX Siècle)*, ed. Nguyễn Thế Anh and Yoshiaki Ishizawa, 113–26 (Paris: L'Harmattan, 1999).

10. On the Portuguese in Vietnam, see Manguin, *Les portugais sur les côtes du Viêt-Nam et du Campã*; and George B. Souza, *The Survival of Empire: Portuguese Trade and Society in China and the South China Sea 1930–1754* (Cambridge: Cambridge University Press, 1986); Pierre-Yves

mission failed, and the envoy and his interpreter were killed by the local inhabitants in 1613.[11] The Dutch then sent a factor (trade representative) farther
north into Trịnh lands in 1636, while the English finally succeeded in establishing a factory in 1672, with the French close behind in 1680.[12] By 1700, however,
all of these initial European trading ventures to Vietnam were in disarray. The
Trịnh and the Nguyễn traded with these new strangers, buying armaments and
munitions from the Dutch and the Portuguese respectively, but a several decades peace by the turn of the century obviated the practical need for such
contacts, and the majority of the merchants were (at least officially) expelled.
The Trịnh court intoned to the Dutch:

> You complained that I had not replied to your letter last year. It was neither
> because I was displeased with you nor because I disrespected you. . . .
> While all foreign merchants had to reside outside the capital Thăng Long,
> your people were allowed to live inside. They were even allowed to build a
> stone factory. These favors are evidence that I always favored your people
> above other foreigners. You complained about my strictness towards your

Manguin, *Les Nguyễn, Macau et la Portugal: Aspects politiques et commerciaux d'une relation privilégiée en Mer de Chine, 1773–1802* (Paris: École française d'Extrême-Orient, 1984).

11. Narratives on the earliest English intercourse with Vietnam can be found in C. B. Maybon,
"Une factorerie anglaise au Tonkin au XVIIe siècle (1672–1697)," *BEFEO* 10 (1910); and A. Lamb,
*The Mandarin Road to Old Hué: Narratives of Anglo-Vietnamese Diplomacy from the 17th Century
to the Eve of the French Conquest* (London: Chatto & Windus, 1970).

12. Buttinger, *The Smaller Dragon*, 200. For good primary sources on the Dutch in Vietnam,
see L. C. D. van Dijk, *Neerlands vroegste betrekkingen met Borneo, den Solo Archipel, Cambodja,
Siam en Cochinchina* (Amsterdam: J. H. Scheltema, 1862); and *The Deshima Dagregisters* XI
(1641–50) and XII (1651–60), ed. Cynthia Viallé and Leonard Blussé (Leiden: Intercontinenta
Nos. 23 and 25, 2001 and 2005). On the VOC in particular, see W. J. M. Buch, "La Compagnie
des Indes Néerlandaises et l'Indochine," *BEFEO* 36 (1936) and 37 (1937); and W. J. M. Buch, "De
Oost-Indische Compagine en Quinam: De betrekkingen der Nederlanders met Annam in de XVIIe
eeuw" (Amsterdam/Paris, 1929). For neighboring Laos and Cambodia, see H. P. N. Muller, *De
Oost-Indische Compagnie in Cambodja en Laos* (The Hague: Martinus Nijhoff, 1917). The Dutch
role in Asian trade was crucial, from an overarching point of view; see Leonard Blussé, "No
Boats to China: The Dutch East India Company and the Changing Pattern of the China Sea
Trade, 1635–1690," *Modern Asian Studies* 30, no. 1 (1996); Femme Gaastra, *The Dutch East India
Company, Expansion and Decline* (Zutphen: Walburg Pers, 2003); Femme Gaastra, "Geld tegen
goederen: Een structurele verandering in het Nederlands-Aziatisch handelsverkeer," *Bijdragen
en Mededelingen Betreffende de Geschiedenis der Nederlanden* 91, no. 2 (1976); and Els M. Jacobs,
Koopman in Azië: De handel van de Vernigde Oost-Indische Companie tijdens de 18de eeuw (Zutphen:
Walburg Pers, 2000).

people. I accept that truth. But your people caused all such strictures. Anyone who lives in my country has to obey the local laws; as those living in your country should obey your laws. The Dutch forgot this. They often declared only half of the cargoes they shipped to my country. This caused me great losses. I do not oppose the decision to recall your people and abandon your trade in my country.[13]

Only a small number of Portuguese connected to the China trade at Macao were allowed by the authorities to remain. Yet a fair number of French and Portuguese missionaries continued to temper Vietnam's connections to the West until the turn of the nineteenth century. There was still some amount of Catholic missionization attempted from this time forward, with texts translated into Western languages, and catechisms translated in the reverse direction.[14] But Confucianization was still relatively evident across parts of the Vietnamese coasts at this point in time.

This state of affairs, however, did not mean that Vietnam's doors were closed to trade. Some revisionist work of early dogmas on this topic suggest just the opposite. Whitmore has shown how fully Vietnam came to be incorporated into the *Asian* trade nexus as an *alternative* to European trade, receiving most of what the country needed from much closer shores than the distant West.[15] His analysis of precious metals flowing through Vietnam in this period is a case in point, but only one of several studies that might have been done on a variety of commodities.[16] Both the Trịnh and the Nguyễn decided to make Chinese copper cash the currency of their realms, conforming to the overall East Asian pattern of using this metal for monetization, as opposed to gold and silver (which were traded instead as commodities well into the eighteenth century). In this respect, the Vietnamese followed the policy decisions of

13. Hoàng Anh Tuấn, *Silk for Silver: Dutch-Vietnamese Relations, 1637–1700* (Leiden: Brill, 2007), 123.

14. For a convincing rendering of this world, see George Dutton, *A Vietnamese Moses: Philippe Binh and the Geographies of Early Modern Capitalism* (Berkeley: University of California Press, 2016).

15. John Whitmore, *Vietnam and the Precious Metals in the Later Medieval and Early Modern Worlds* (Durham, NC: Carolina Academic Press, 1983); John Whitmore, "Vietnam and the Monetary Flow of Asia, 13–18th Centuries," in *Precious Metals in the Later Medieval and Early Modern Worlds*, ed. J. F. Richards, 363–96 (Durham, NC: Carolina Academic Press, 1983).

16. On this topic, also see Ryuto Shimada, *The Intra-Asian Trade in Japanese Copper by the Dutch East India Company during the Eighteenth Century* (Leiden: Brill, 2005).

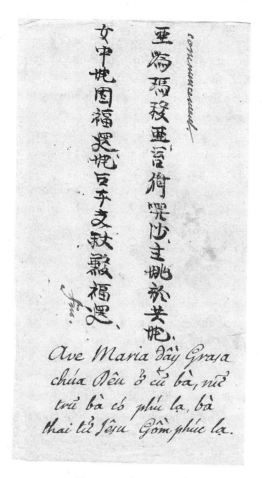

FIGURE 3.1. Vietnamese "Ave Maria" (Dominique
Erster, 1773, in Chu Nom and Quoc Ngu)

Majapahit, Srivijaya, and Melaka at their zeniths, as noted by several Chinese
authors.[17]

It's clear that Vietnam was in fact part of the greater East Asian maritime
trade routes during the late sixteenth century, and all the way into the eighteenth century, albeit not (perhaps) one of the top-tier players. The increasing

17. See, for example, Zhao Ru Gua's (1225) writings, as well as Ma Huan's (1433), in Whitmore, "Vietnam and the Monetary Flow," at 363–64.

commerce centering around Canton and other ports of the South China coasts, and also the development of Spanish Manila as a transshipment center for products in circulation between Japan, China, and parts of Southeast Asia, was important in Vietnam, too, however.[18] Some of the commodities being traded were of the bulk variety, such as rice, but many of them were more specialized, such as environmental products of the "South Seas" and the precious metals discussed above. Chinese merchants were particularly important in ferrying these goods from place to place, but a range of other actors were also involved, and the East Asian routes were nothing if not cosmopolitan at this time.[19] Japanese scholars have been especially important in showing how this early modern system carried on into the eighteenth century, delineating the lines of a trading milieu that evolved within the structural changes of Asian economies at this time, and before imperialism washed over the region more thoroughly later in the nineteenth century, across many of the societies of the extended South China Sea.[20]

Interestingly enough, however, in returning to precious metals, Vietnam harbored substantial quantities of gold and silver, which were exported to Southeast Asia and China in return for "exotica goods" and copper cash respectively.[21] The reasons for such a macroeconomic decision are still not entirely clear, but it is probable that the Vietnamese thought they would receive more revenue from selling their gold and silver on the open market than by converting it into their own coinage. Contemporary records reveal an ongoing mining industry in operation north of the Red River delta,

18. See Birgit Tremml-Werner, ed., *Spain, China, and Japan in Manila, 1571–1644* (Amsterdam University Press, 2015), 124, 191, 304.

19. Lin Yu-ju and Madeleine Zelin, eds., *Merchant Communities in Asia, 1600–1980* (Brookfield: Pickering & Chatto, 2015), especially chapters 3 and 4.

20. Ryoto Shimada, "Hinterlands and Port Cities in Southeast Asia's Economic Development in the Eighteenth Century" in *Hinterlands and Commodities: Place, Space, Time and the Political Economic Development of Asia over the Long Eighteenth Century*, ed. Tsukasa Mizushima, George Bryan Souza, and Dennis Flynn (Leiden: Brill, 2015): 197–214; and Ei Murakami, "Trade and Crisis: China's Hinterlands in the Eighteenth Century," in *Hinterlands and Commodities*, ed. Mizushima, Souza, and Flynn, 215–34.

21. See Claudine Salmon, "Regards de quelques voyageurs chinois sur le Viêtnam du XVIIe siècle," in *Asia Maritima: Images et réalité: Bilder und Wirklichkeit 1200–1800*, ed. Denys Lombard and Roderich Ptak (Wiesbaden: Harrassowitz Verlag, 1994).

which smelted copper, gold, silver, and zinc throughout the tenure of the Lê.[22] Yet whether or not this policy, in the long run, was truly beneficial for the Vietnamese economy is still open to question: by the eighteenth century the government was decentralizing these operations, in a desperate effort to alleviate chronic cash shortages. Even counterfeiting was tolerated, though the official injunction of capital punishment was still on the books for this type of crime.

FIGURE 3.2. Vietnamese Bronze/Copper Coin (from the Reign of Tu Duc, 19th c.)

New Linkages

What is less open to question is the fact that such monetary linkages tied Vietnam into the early modern Asian economy as never before.[23] The movement of metal was only one artery in this much larger circulating system of extraordinary size and complexity that we have described, from silver to the trade in books.[24] Vietnamese trade with Okinawa and Japan was a case in point. A Portuguese priest who visited the Red River delta in the 1570s saw little evidence of an established international trade, but he would have been shocked to see the port of Hội An a mere thirty years later, several hundred miles down the coast.[25] The Ming Promulgation of 1567, which banned the export of copper from China, was a boon to the Japanese: from this date

22. Eighteenth-century Vietnam possessed eight copper mines, two gold, two silver, one zinc, and one tin mine, the latter used to help forge tutenague, a zinc-tin mixture used as a secondary coinage. See Whitmore, "Vietnam and the Monetary Flow," 372.

23. See Angela Schottenhammer, "The 'China Seas' in World History: A General Outline of the Role of Chinese and East Asian Maritime Space from Its Origin to c. 1800," *Journal of Marine and Island Culture* 1 (2012): 63–89; and Nhung Tuyet Tran and Anthony J. S. Reid, eds., *Việt Nam: Borderless Histories* (Madison: University of Wisconsin Press, 2006).

24. See Nguyễn Thế Anh, "Trade Relations between Vietnam and the Countries of the Southern Seas in the First Half of the Nineteenth Century," in *Commerce et navigation*, ed. Nguyễn and Ishizawa, 171–85; Momoki Shiro, "Was Dai Viet a Rival of Ryukyu within the Tributary Trade System of the Ming during the Early Le Period, 1428–1527?" in *Commerce et navigation*, ed. Nguyễn and Ishizawa, 101–12; Geoff Wade, "A Maritime Route in the Vietnamese Text 'Xiem-la-quoc lo-trinh tap-luc' (1810)," in *Commerce et navigation*, ed. Nguyễn and Ishizawa, 137–70.

25. C. R. Boxer, *South China in the 16th Century* (London: Crown Press, 1953), 73.

onward Japanese syndicates built fortunes on bringing their own copper supplies to Vietnam, exchanging them for sugar and silk on the docks of that same city. By the first decades of the seventeenth century, two-thirds of all Japanese ships heading to mainland Southeast Asia were en route to this port,[26] and the market in these two particular Vietnamese products was almost completely monopolized by Japan. Silver was also brought from Honshu, but it was primarily strings of copper cash that paid for these items, as well as for precious woods, ceramics, and the skins of deer and rays.[27] Port charges levied by the Nguyễn on Japanese craft were 4,000 strings to arrive, a further 400 to depart. Hội An grew in correspondence with the trade.[28] It would only be in the 1640s, after the Portuguese Expulsion edicts in Japan, that Japanese commerce with Hội An would wane, as that country retreated into relative isolation for the next two hundred years.

Hoàng Anh Tuấn has also looked carefully at the Dutch role in keeping Vietnam active in Asia's maritime routes, connecting them through Dutch shipping to other, regional economies. As Japan began to close itself off (relatively, at least in comparison to earlier decades when its ports had been quite open), the Dutch stepped in to help market Vietnamese goods to the rest of this maritime world. The Ming/Ch'ing transition in China at this time (1644), just after the majority of the Japanese expulsion edicts between 1623 and 1651, suddenly allowed northern Vietnam a space in the market that up to this point had been occupied much more fully by Chinese and Japanese concerns. The Dutch helped to push Tonkinese commodities along during these decades of crisis, and for a time silk production in particular in the Red River delta became of regional importance, both in quality and in the bulk amounts needed to drive a thriving transregional carrying trade. The Trịnh court in the North also asked the VOC to help them against their southern Vietnamese neighbors, as part of these interactions:

> My country Tonkin lies at the center [of the region]. Kings and lords from the East, West, and North come to pay their respects to me with the

---

26. A. Lamb, *The Mandarin Road to Old Hué* (London: Chatto & Windus, 1970), 21.

27. On ceramics, particularly, see Christian Jorg and Michael Flecker, *Porcelain from the Vung Tau Wreck* (London: Sun Tree Publishing, 2001); and Aoyagi Yoji, "Production and Trade of Champa Ceramics in the Fifteenth Century" in *Commerce et navigation*, ed. Nguyễn and Ishizawa, 91–100.

28. See Charles Wheeler, "One Region, Two Histories: Cham Precedents in the History of Hoi An Region," in *Việt Nam: Borderless Histories*, ed. Tran and Reid, 163–93.

exception of the South (Quinam). The people there are country folk whose lives and contacts are weak, and who carry out all good and laudable things in a wrong way. They rely on and comfort themselves in unusual ways and do not obey me. If I want to war against them at seas with galleys, then the passage thence is too far for me, and the billows too high and the wind and the rain disadvantageous. Therefore I cannot achieve this by this means, which leads these wicked people to persist even more in their wrongful ways and behavior; which pleases them. These are the reasons why I have planned to seek the help from the Dutch. Should your majesty be willing to agree, then I shall ally my country forever with your country. Could you supply me with three ships and 200 excellent men who can handle ordinance well and send them to Tonkin?[29]

Most scholars learn French in order to be able to contribute to Vietnamese history, but in this case the miles upon miles of Dutch documents in the VOC archives allowed Hoàng Anh Tuấn to show what had been largely obscured, previously. At least in terms of Europeans, it was the Dutch, not the French, who were of primary importance in these connections of the early modern period. Vietnamese merchants traded with whomever they could, but they seem to have had a very active agency in making these decisions, and also in choosing different partners as exigencies allowed.

Despite these discoveries, over the *longue durée* of the early modern period it was the sustained trade with Chinese merchants that really vaulted a number of Vietnamese ports (such as Hội An) into regional commercial sites by the early seventeenth century. These traders came from China proper, but also from most other countries in the *Nanyang* (South Seas) to participate in the thriving transit trade between the South China coasts, Japan, and Spanish Manila. Silver transported from the Americas was the Chinese objective here, and Hội An was drawn into this complex grid as a secondary city for exchanging valued goods.[30] The Chinese junks brought silk, copper cash (illegally after 1567), and *tutenague* for these transactions, taking Japanese silver (also illegal in China after 1600) and Southeast Asian exotica products such as camphor, pepper, and aromatics in the bargain.[31] Although Chinese traders were

---

29. Tuấn, *Silk for Silver*, 72.

30. William Schurz, *The Manila Galleon* (New York, 1939), 26–27.

31. See the figures provided in William Atwell, "Notes on Silver, Foreign Trade, and the Late Ming Economy," *Ch'ing Shih Wen-t'i* 3 (1977): 2–3; Seiichi Iwao, "Japanese Foreign Trade in the

paramount in the ports, many may have conscripted ethnically Vietnamese merchants to procure goods for them in the inland polities of Cambodia and Laos.[32] Even the transition mentioned above from a Han-Chinese Dynasty (the Ming) to a Jurchen one (the Ch'ing, in 1644) did not substantially alter these patterns for the long term, despite real instabilities at the time. Ming loyalists continued to trade to Hội An from Fujian until the 1660s, and from Taiwan until the island's conquest in the 1680s. Nguyễn duties on these merchants were substantially lower than on the Japanese: 2,000 strings of cash for Chinese of the Nanyang (and 200 to leave); 3,000 strings for those direct from China (and a further 300 to depart). By the 1830s Chinese merchants in Vietnam were even helping to facilitate massive silver shipments back to China, financing British opium and its addiction upon the native populace.[33]

European traders could only look upon this thriving commerce with a mixture of frustration and envy.[34] From 1700 until almost the end of the century, the tiny contingent of Macao Portuguese "official" traders continued their small-scale commerce with Vietnam, while other missionaries attempted to Christianize the populace.[35] Some inroads were made here, but in general the eyes of the French and English governments were more firmly fashioned on

---

16th and 17th Centuries," *Acta Asiatica* 30 (1976): 10; and John Wills, *Pepper, Guns, and Parleys* (Cambridge: Harvard University Press, 1974), 9–10, 20.

32. William Skinner, *Chinese Society in Thailand* (Ithaca: Cornell University Press), 1957, 7–13.

33. Alexander Woodside, *Vietnam and the Chinese Model* (Cambridge: Harvard University Press, 1971), 276–78. For more on the complicated economy of the South China Sea, and Vietnam's place in that economy over the centuries, see Shiro, "Dai Viet and the South China Sea Trade; G. V. Scammell, "European Exiles, Renegades and Outlaws and the Maritime Economy of Asia, c. 1500–1750," *Modern Asian Studies* 26, no. 4 (1992): 641–61; and Yoneo Ishii, ed., *The Junk Trade from Southeast Asia: Translations from the Tosen Fusetsu-gaki, 1674–1723* (Canberra: Research School of Pacific and Asian Studies, Australian National University, and Singapore: ISEAS, 1998).

34. See two interesting takes on these separate but combining worlds; Frédéric Mantienne, "Indochinese Societies and European Traders: Different Worlds of Trade? (17th–18th Centuries)," in *Commerce et navigation*, ed. Nguyễn and Ishizawa; and Nguyễn Thế Anh, "Ambivalence and Ambiguity: Traditional Vietnam's Incorporation of External Cultural and Technical Contributions," *East Asian Science* 40, no. 4 (2003): 94–113.

35. On the role of missionaries, see Alain Forest, *Les missionaires français au Tonkin et au Siam, XVIIe-XVIIIe siècles: Analyse comparée d'un relatif succès et d'un total échec,* vol. 2: *Histoires du Tonkin* (Paris: l'Harmattan, 1998); and Patrick Tuck, *French Colonial Missionaries and the Politics of Imperialism in Vietnam, 1857–1914: A Documentary Survey* (Liverpool: Liverpool University Press, 1987).

the struggle for India, with its wealth of land and produce, than on Vietnam. French merchants, in particular, continually badgered the authorities in Paris to try to open a more lucrative trade, but their pleas were consistently ignored. In 1686 a French East India Company employee actually met with some royal interest when his plan to occupy Pulao Condore (an island off the mouth of the Mekong) was put before the Crown, but British forces beat the French ashore, though the occupation ended in disaster.[36] Only with the settling of the Treaty of Paris in 1763, whereby France lost nearly all of her Indian possessions, and the outbreak of the Tây Sơn Rebellion in 1772 (with the possibilities this presented in terms of favorable instability) did Europeans once more look toward Vietnam with renewed interest.[37] Charts began to be published reexamining the geography and coastline of the country.[38] Emperor Gia-long (Nguyễn Ánh), upon his ascension, was judged to be amenable—or at least "benevolently neutral," an improvement upon his forebears—toward trade. New missions were therefore sent to Vietnam.

It is through these late-eighteenth- and early-nineteenth-century missions, each of which failed in its overall purpose to open a much wider trade between Vietnam and the West, that we receive a detailed portrait of what inroads international commerce had made into precolonial Vietnam.[39] The men who reported on these conditions, in particular John Barrow (who accompanied the Macartney Mission of 1793), John White (a lieutenant on the US brig *Franklin* in 1819), and John Crawfurd (a British envoy in 1822), were looking carefully at what Vietnam had to offer, both at the time of their visits and in a prospective trading future. Indeed, a recurring theme in all of these narratives

36. Buttinger, *The Smaller Dragon*, 225 n. 60. The contingent left by the British to hold the island, consisting mostly of Makassarese troops, massacred their British officers in 1705 when payment and supplies proved to be in arears. The East India Company abandoned Pulao Condore soon after that.

37. See George Dutton, *The Tay Son Uprising: Society and Rebellion in Eighteenth-Century Vietnam* (Honolulu: University of Hawai'i Press, 2006).

38. The 1793 survey published by Alastair Lamb in his "British Missions to Cochin China 1778–1882," *JMBRAS* 34, Pts. 3, 4 (1961), following page 98 and titled "A Chart of Part of the Coast of Cochin China Including Turon Harbor and the Island of Callao," is an interesting example. The map shows how little was known of Vietnam before the mid-19th-century: some depth soundings, a vague impression of coastal hills, rivers that disappear into a blank white interior, and the existence of some "curious marble rocks."

39. For an exception to this, see the work on trade in the South and in Saigon in the eighteenth century by Claudine Ang, *Poetic Transformations: Eighteenth Century Cultural Projects on the Mekong Plains* (Cambridge: Harvard East Asia Monographs, 2019).

is a plea for the respective home governments to take seriously the idea of acquiring a port in the region.[40] The intensity of trade, in combination with the richness of Vietnamese resources, served as the basis for this advice. In addition to the aforementioned precious metals, a host of other valuables was in circulation via Vietnam: odoriferous woods (eagle, rose, sappan, etc.), dammar, porcelain,[41] cinnamon, cardamom, indigo, and raw silk, to name just a few. Ivory, gold dust, rhinoceros horn, and rice were also traded out of the country, the property of a royal monopoly. Nutmegs, cloves, and pepper could be found (the legacy of transshipment networks to Indonesia), as well as trepang and birds' nests on the offshore islands. In return for these goods the Chinese junks brought vermilion, drugs, old clothes, and borax, while the occasional Portuguese craft traded ironmongery, looking-glasses, opium, and mathematical instruments.[42]

The descriptions of local interest in certain unusual goods (like bottled English mustard) have an almost fantastic quality to them, and are certainly revealing of a two-sided dynamic. White records an episode in which a representative of Gia-long came on board the *Franklin* and, after tea and betel were presented, proceeded to produce an empty mustard bottle with the coat of arms of the king of England on its side. The label read "Best Durham Mustard," and a piece of paper with some "dried, black, tasteless, smell-less, apothecary-plaster-like substance" (the mustard) was shown to the crew. The emissary asked White if he had any more of the substance, which Gia-long had grown "extravagantly fond-of." As the same incident had happened the year before, White had taken the precaution in the interim of buying a stock of the mustard

40. See especially John Barrow, *A Voyage to Cochin China* (Kuala Lumpur: Oxford University Press, 1975 [orig. 1806]), 342.

41. This item was particularly important; see Louise Allison Cort, "Vietnamese Ceramics in Japanese Contexts," in *Vietnamese Ceramics: A Separate Tradition*, ed. John Stevenson and John Guy (Michigan: Art Media Resources, 1994; repr. Chicago: Art Media Resources, 1997); John Guy, "Vietnamese Ceramics in International Trade," in *Vietnamese Ceramics*, ed. Stevenson and Guy; John Guy, "Vietnamese Ceramics in International Trade," in *Vietnamese Ceramics*, ed. Stevenson and Guy; Nguyen Long Kerry, "Vietnamese Ceramic Trade to the Philippines in the Seventeenth Century," *Journal of Southeast Asian Studies* 30, no. 1 (1999); John Stevenson, "The Evolution of Vietnamese Ceramics," in *Vietnamese Ceramics*, ed. Stevenson and Guy, 22–45; and more generally, Bennet Bronson, "Export Porcelain in Economic Perspective: The Asian Ceramic Trade in the 17th Century," in *Ancient Ceramic Kiln Technology in Asia*, ed. Ho Chumei (Hong Kong: University of Hong Kong, 1990).

42. John Stevenson, "The Evolution of Vietnamese Ceramics," In *Vietnamese Ceramics*, ed. Stevenson and Guy, 22–45.

from some wholesalers in Manila. The new bottles were presented to the emissary. Taken in microcosm, it was this sort of event, it seems—and these sorts of rather mundane products, which took on new valences in local trade—that might episodically make or break trading missions in Southeast Asia.[43]

European Notices

The actual process of trade also begins to be described in detail for among the first times with the arrival of Europeans. Vessels desiring to trade in Saigon first had to contract through the local "Mandarin" a fisherman as river pilot, who guided the craft safely up through the shoals and sandbars at the mouth of the river. This same Mandarin, however, also had to be induced to provide these services by means of a few gifts: hats, lengths of red or blue cloth, and bottles of sweet wine were deemed the most appropriate items.[44] This process of "oiling the wheels of commerce" would have to be continued even up to the walls of the palace, with eunuchs receiving bribes for advancement all along the way. The language of commerce between these tepidly accepted Europeans of the Tây Sơn and Gia-long era and the local populace was "Indian Portuguese," a dialect of the mother-language spoken among traders in Eastern seas. Almost every person in Asia, regardless of nationality, had at least one hand on board who could converse in this market patois. Ships finally reaching Saigon would anchor at the Great China Bazaar three miles south of the city, where the king's warehouses were located, and where the craft's tonnage could be measured for exactions, length by breadth by keel. *Sepecks* were the local coinage (fashioned out of *tutenague*, an alloy), as well as the ubiquitous copper cash, while the Cochin Chinese *catty* (measuring one and a half English pounds) was the accepted unit of weight.[45] All of the narrators warned extensively of thieves, who permeated the marketplace in every shape and disguise, apparently.

Yet it is from these European accounts that we also receive a different kind of information, less commercially oriented but nevertheless significant within Vietnam's orbit of trade. One of these subjects was piracy. Mendes Pinto was already supplying harrowing tales of pirates off the Vietnamese coasts in the

---

43. See White, *A Voyage to Cochin China*, 244.

44. Milburn, *Oriental Commerce*, II:450–51. Firearms, docks, sabers, and velvet were also acceptable presents.

45. White, *A Voyage to Cochin China*, 257–59.

sixteenth century, men who commonly "squeezed the brains out of their Portuguese victims with a crossbar" as a punishment for their Christian faith.[46] The fact that a small "pirate" *prahu* captured by Pinto off these same coasts consisted of a mixed crew of Achenese, Turks, and other Muslims seemed to justify, in his eyes, the same treatment meted out to his prisoners as had befallen those earlier Portuguese. Later accounts verified the Vietnamese coasts as a natural chokepoint for corsairs, preying on shipping pulling into local havens, as well as the long-distance craft of the international trade routes. John White cautioned his readers that *ladrones* (pirates) infested Vietnam's estuaries, offering them a perfectly tangled topographical environment in which to run and hide.[47] Edward Brown, in his *Seaman's Narrative of His Adventures during a Captivity among Chinese Pirates on the Coasts of Cochin-China* (1861) repeated the injunction, detailing the rape of women on passing junks and various grim depredations (massacres, torture, and decapitations) from his own grisly experiences.[48]

Not all of these observations were as violence ridden, however, and some concerned more mundane topics, like the position of women in Vietnamese commerce. Barrow pointed to the wide gulf between Chinese and Vietnamese women in their respective societies, the former "secreted indoors, never to be seen by even most of their male relatives,"[49] while the latter, by contrast, played an active role in daily economic life. Though this observation needs to be tempered by the role of class, Vietnamese women seemed indeed to form a crucial economic link in the exchange of goods between foreigners and the local population, so much so, in fact, that Milburn went so far as to call them "the principal merchants of Vietnamese society."[50] While this appraisal is still debatable, especially within the sphere of cross-cultural contact, all the chroniclers noted their acumen and savvy. White complained of their tendency to

---

46. Mendes Pinto, *The Travels of Mendes Pinto*, trans. Rebecca Catz (University of Chicago Press, 1990), 71. Of course, Pinto's account has not been universally accepted as factual, so care must be taken in seeing his descriptions as definitively "real" events.

47. Ibid., 190.

48. Edward Brown, *A Seaman's Narrative of His Adventures during a Captivity among Chinese Pirates on the Coast of Cochin China* (London: Charles Westerton, 1861), 66; 74–76. See also Charles Wheeler, "Placing the 'Chinese Pirates' of the Gulf of Tonking at the End of the Eighteenth Century," in *Asia Inside Out: Connected Places*, ed. Eric Tagliacozzo, Helen F. Siu, and Peter C. Perdue, 30–63 (Cambridge, MA: Harvard University Press, 2015).

49. Barrow, *Voyage to Cochin China*, 305.

50. Milburn, *Oriental Commerce*, II:455.

TABLE 3.1. The Open Cadence of Maritime Vietnam at the Turn of the Nineteenth Century

Ethnic Minorities in the Vietnamese Court, 1780–1820[a]
Siamese officials/military officers
Malay officials
Cambodian officials/military officers
Chinese officials/military officers/"pirates"
Portuguese officials/traders/Jesuit missionaries
Spanish officials/mercenaries/missionaries
French officials/traders/missionaries
(Also traces of English, Irish, Dutch, and Javanese presences)

Tay-son Era Trading and Raiding Fleets in Vietnam, Circa 1805[b]
Fleet "A": 5 boats, 489 people, 100 cannon, 500 catties gunpowder, 883 miscellaneous hand
   weapons/guns
Fleet "B": 10 boats, 669 people, 127 cannon, 500 catties powder, 789 miscellaneous hand
   weapons/guns
Fleet "C": 36 junks, 1,422 men, 2016 cannon, 1,207 miscellaneous hand weapons/guns
Fleet "D": 11 junks, 301 men, with an arsenal as follows:

6 iron cannon	30 t'iao tao knives
55 turtledove cannon	180 long-handled knives
1 wooden cannon	134 short knives
40 lead shells	28 rattan shields
27 catties iron bullets	10 iron chains
55 catties old lead/iron	36 catties gunpowder

[a] Abstracted from Wynn Wilcox, "Transnationalism and Multiethnicity in the Early Gia Long Era," in *Việt Nam: Borderless Histories*, edited by Nhung Tuyet Tran and Anthony Reid, 194–218, especially pp. 194–200 (Madison: University of Wisconsin Press, 2006).

[b] Abstracted from Dian Murray, *Pirates of the South China Coast (1790–1810)* (Stanford: Stanford University Press, 1987.), 97–98.

overcharge once they knew which goods the Europeans valued, while Milburn instructed prospective merchants to take them on as housekeepers, in order to better facilitate local transactions.[51] However, while their business sense seems never to have been questioned, their physical appearance in these market exchanges certainly was. This was especially so in terms of their teeth, which were "straggling fangs, blackened with areca and betel."[52]

51. See White, *A Voyage to Cochin China*, 246; and Milburn, *Oriental Commerce*, II:455. Milburn advised the best choice to be a "Chinaman's widow."

52. White, *A Voyage to Cochin China*, 268. For a very useful corrective to these European visions of what life was like for Vietnamese women leading up to this period in the early nineteenth century, see Nhung Tran, *Familial Properties: Gender, State, and Society in Early Modern Vietnam, 1463–1778* (Honolulu: University of Hawai'i Press, 2018).

FIGURE 3.3. Topography of Vietnam's North Coasts (author's photo)

Finally, the role of ethnic Chinese in Vietnamese commerce was once again touched upon by these authors, continuing the observations of Europeans several centuries earlier. By the turn of the nineteenth century, Chinese had entered almost every crevice of Vietnamese economic life imaginable: they were butchers, tailors, bankers, and peddlers, as well as moneylenders and wholesalers, to name just a few pursuits.[53] Chinese entrepreneurs ran the new privatized mining concessions, importing advanced technology and management techniques from their own country; they also owned and sailed the ships of many Southeast Asian polities, such as the Malay States and Siam. Most of Vietnam's durable goods were even produced in China, so that one period sailor could only "watch in envy at their good fortune" as Chinese ships sailed

53. For background, see Baoyum Yang, *Contribution à l'histoire de la principauté des Nguyên au Vietnam méridional (1600–1775)* (Geneva, 1992), 123.

past him with cargoes of clothing, porcelain, and utensils bound for Saigon.[54] By 1750, Hội An was handling up to eighty Chinese junks a year, its Sinic population double that of only fifty years previously.[55] Meanwhile, Crawfurd reported rather startling population statistics of 1822 to be approximately 25,000 Chinese engaged in mining throughout the country, five hundred at Huế (the capital), a thousand at Cachao, two thousand at Hội An, and a further five thousand in Saigon.[56] Such a preponderance of men described as "aliens," however, was also clearly starting to make the Nguyễn government nervous. As Crawfurd noted in his account (with some amount of prescience for other areas of Southeast Asia), there were grumblings in Saigon that the Chinese controlled too much of Vietnam's business.

On the long, outstretched coasts of the country, however, at least to some degree—Vietnamese interactions with the sea continued on as they had for many centuries. Chinese traders and middlemen in Hanoi, Huế, and Saigon may have gained a larger commercial share than previously of the urban life of the ports, but out and along the coasts themselves, where fish were caught, and where marine produce was gathered, most of the people still doing these tasks were Chams or ethnic Vietnamese. Sensitive ethnohistorical work done by anthropologist Edyta Roszko in some of these villages shows us how long these patterns have existed—as far into collective village memory as such stories can go, and that means many generations, including into these early times.[57] The coasts have always been a part of this world, but the rhythms changed more slowly here in terms of the frequency and intensity of connection, except at certain moments (such as during the Tây Sơn Rebellion, but there were other moments as well). Vietnam's relationship with the commercial world of the sea fluctuated in a softer register here, less obvious perhaps than in the country's bustling ports, but in important ways nonetheless.

54. Ibid., 261.

55. Whitmore, "Precious Metals," 385.

56. John Crawfurd, *Journal of an Embassy to the Courts of Siam and Cochin China* [orig. 1822] (Kuala Lumpur: Oxford University Press, 1967), 470.

57. See, for example, Edyta Roszko, "Fishers and Territorial Anxieties in China and Vietnam: Narratives of the South China Sea Beyond the Frame of the Nation," *Cross-Currents: East Asian History and Culture Review* 21 (2016): 19–46; Edyta Roszko, "Geographies of Connection and Disconnection: Narratives of Seafaring in Ly Son," in *Connected and Disconnected in Vietnam: Remaking Social Relationships in a Post-Socialist Nation*, ed. Philip Taylor, 347–77 (Canberra: Australian National University Press, 2016).

Conclusion

The relative spate of hopeful writings on maritime trade in Vietnam at the turn of the nineteenth century would prove to be a short-lived phenomenon. The turbulence of the Tây Sơn Rebellion and Gia-long's neutral stance on foreign trade covered a period of nearly half a century of "possibility." After this, however, and especially with the ascension of Minh-Mạng in 1820, Vietnam tried much harder to insulate itself from the outside world.[58] It has been suggested that Gia-long deliberately chose the xenophobic Minh-Mạng as his successor, knowing full well that Vietnam's only chance for cultural survival lay in staying above the fray of European competition, as Siam was managing to do next door.[59] Merchant guilds were starting to diminish in importance. Something altogether larger—capitalism, and the power to harness it by modernizing states—was on the not-too-distant horizon in these seas.[60] It would be a stretch to say that the Vietnamese emperors fully understood the nature of these storm clouds, but they did certainly understand the dangers of an open coastline in very turbulent times.

Within this Vietnamese worldview, very limited trade might be more prudent than expansive trade, a fact attested to by the arrival of only three Chinese

---

58. For the long lead-up to this, the most important scholar is Tana Li; see her "An alternative Vietnam? The Nguyen Kingdom in the Seventeenth and Eighteenth Centuries," *Journal of Southeast Asian Studies* 29, no. 1 (1998); also Tana Li, *Nguyun Cochinchina: Southern Vietnam in the Seventeenth and Eighteenth Centuries* (Ithaca: SEAP, 1998); Tana Li, "A View from the Sea: Perspectives on the Northern and Central Vietnam Coast," *Journal of Southeast Asian Studies* 37, no. 1 (2006); and Tana Li and Anthony Reid, eds., *Southern Vietnam under the Nguyen: Documents on the Economic History of Cochin China (Dang Trong), 1602–1777* (Singapore: ISEAS, 1993).

59. For an interesting account of contacts between the two Southeast Asia countries as Europeans came to the region, see Christopher E. Goscha, "La présence vietnamienne au royaume du Siam du XVIIéme siècle: Vers une perspective péninsulaire," in *Guerre et paix en Asie du sud-est*, ed. Nguyễn Thế Anh and Alain Forest (Paris: L'Harmattan, 1998). For the ongoing trade relationship between Vietnam and its Mainland Southeast Asian neighbors, see Pierre-Bernard Lafont, ed., *Les frontières du Vietnam: Histoires et frontières de la péninsule indochinoise*, (Paris: Éditions l'Harmattan, 1989); and Rungwasdisab Puangthong, "Siam and the Control of the Trans-Mekong Trading Networks," in *Water Frontier*, ed. Cooke and Li, 101–18.

60. See Claudio J. Katz, "Karl Marx on the Transition from Feudalism to Capitalism," *Theory and Society* 22 (1993); Avner Greif, Paul Milgrom, and Barry R. Weingast, "Coordination, Commitment, and Enforcement: The Case of the Merchant Guild," *Journal of Political Economy* 102, no. 4 (1994): 745–76; and Avner Greif, *Institutions and the Path to the Modern Economy: Lessons from Medieval Trade* (Stanford: Stanford University Press, 2006).

junks to Saigon in 1819, as opposed to twelve much larger ones in 1805.[61] Roughly half a century later, with the French about to begin the consolidation of their hold over the entire country from 1859 onward, such a policy may have proved to be a short-sighted one, rooted more perhaps in a fairly rigid Confucianism than in an acute appraisal or engagement with impending realities. But at the time of the closing of this chapter, in 1825, Vietnam's decision to close its doors to trade was having the desired effect on foreign maritime trade. As one Western merchant would bitterly lament in his 1824 narrative:

> As long as these practices exist, Cochin China is rendered the least desirable country for mercantile adventures [in the world]. These causes have made the Japanese relinquish the trade; they have driven the Macao Portuguese from the country, and are yearly and rapidly lessening their intercourse with China and Siam. The philanthropist, the man of enterprise, and the civilized world in general can see in the present miserable state of this naturally fine country no other than a source of deep regret and commiseration.[62]

61. White, *A Voyage to Cochin China*, 259. This is despite the fact that the Vietnamese populace, at least in certain places, still attached great value to the sea. For just one example of a well-researched, historical example, see Nguyen Quoc-Thanh, *Le culte de la baleine: Un héritage multiculturel du Vietnam maritime* (Aix: Presses Universitaires de Provence, 2017); Charles Macdonald, "Le culte de la baleine, une exception vietnamienne?" *Aseanie* 12 (2003): 123–36; Nguyen Quoc Thanh, "The Whaler Cult in Central Vietnam: A Multicultural Heritage in Southeast Asia," in *Memory and Knowledge of the Sea in Southeast Asia*, ed. Danny Wong Tze Kin, 77–95 (Kuala Lumpur: Institute of Ocean and Earth Sciences, University of Malaya, 2008); Truong Van Mon, "The Raja Praong Ritual: A Memory of the Sea in Cham-Malay Relations," in *Memory and Knowledge*, ed. Kin, 97–111.

62. White, *A Voyage to Cochin China*, 247.

PART II

Bodies of Water

Preface: The Imbricated Histories of Two Seas

ASIA'S WATERS FLOW across an impressive spread of geography. To the north, the seas are frigid, connecting the Russian Far East and the great peninsulas or island chains such as Kamchatka and the Kuriles, with Hokkaido and the Sea of Japan. To the south, the oceans are tropical and spill across a number of marked-off seas: the Banda Sea, the Ceram Sea, the Sulu Sea, and the Java Sea, among several others. Here the waters tend to be protected by land out of sight on all sides, and also by the shallow bottom of the Sunda Shelf, which makes this region a haven for shipping. Trade courses easily in this part of the world, in other words; it is Asia's Mediterranean, to use a commonly referenced analogy. Farther to the west, there is the more open maritime terrain of the Indian Ocean, which is separated into a number of "spaces," including the Arabian Sea, the Bay of Bengal, and—at the lower latitudes of the sea—the open ocean itself. But even here there are further subdivisions. The Bay of Bengal has the Andaman Sea and the Straits of Melaka as part of its ambit, and the Arabian Sea flows into both the Persian Gulf and into the Red Sea, and from the latter on to Europe via Suez. These scattered geographies of maritime Asia are important: they show the diversity of what at first sight appears to be merely thousands of kilometers of interconnected water, a flat field of blue. But the realities of all that water are inconstant, and continually susceptible to change. Climate change has raised and lowered seas, and the silting of great rivers has also continually raised and backwatered a succession of Asian ports. The sea has been and still is alive in this sense; it expands and contracts with consequences for human populations, and for human history. This part of the book looks at two of the largest and most important maritime spaces in Asia—the South China Sea and the Indian Ocean—and

75

asks what we can learn about the oceanic history of this region by looking at each as a separate system.

Here again, as with part I, "Maritime Connections," there are a number of themes that come forward. Thinking about both of these large bodies of water as systems requires certain tools. The South China Sea has seen a relative paucity of this sort of analysis, and not many historians have tried to link this sea's histories together in historical time. The reasons for this may be institutional, to some extent: the northern reaches of the South China Sea belong to "East Asia," while the southern reaches of the same body of water are primarily located in "Southeast Asia." Since area studies programs have largely split academic expertise between these two places, there haven't been many scholars willing to "jump the aisle" and tread on their neighbors' ground, or in this case, in their neighbors' waters. This is a shame because more holistic thinking about what this body of water means can and likely should be done by doing just that. Language competencies have also meant that Sinologists and Southeast Asianists have not often combined their respective archives, using the linguistic traditions of both places to write more unified histories of this sea. In the Indian Ocean, a different paradigm has existed. Here, analysis from nearly the beginning of such studies has indeed focused on this ocean as a system, from K. N. Chaudhuri's pioneering work on forward. Yet the themes that have connected Indian Ocean societies into one broad grid across the three populated littorals of this sea seem to be strangely missing from the literature. Almost every scholarly analysis of the Indian Ocean tries to bundle a huge package of themes—the kind of "total history" of which Fernand Braudel would certainly have approved—into their respective books. Trade, environment, diaspora, politics—all get included in the mix. This is admirable and instructive, because it means that scholars are trying to be holistic from the outset in thinking about this particular sea. But it leaves less space in some ways to choose individual themes and then to follow them in greater detail, to see where they may lead.

That more modest and limited approach is what I have attempted in the two chapters presented here. Part II, "Bodies of Water" follows two specific histories of these two largest of Asian seas. In chapter 4, I analyze the history and roughly contemporary dimensions of smuggling in the South China Sea. For me, this includes looking at both East and Southeast Asia in one frame, with the ports and populations of South China, for example (Fujian, Guangdong, and to some extent maritime Taiwan as well) in the same field of vision as the "lands beneath the winds." Doing this allows us to see several wider patterns of interaction, some of which have existed for quite some time; others are only now coming to the fore. Human populations crisscrossed this space for many centuries, and brought a wide range of commodities with them. Some of these goods were and still are "illicit," as defined by nation-states and their governments, the regimes that get to make such definitions in our own time. Chapter 4 looks at some of these patterns, and asks how we might see the South China Sea as a trans-Asian system that links geographies that are separate in academic circles, yet are anything but separated in the passage of ships bearing contraband. Chapter 5 then takes on another theme to look at the outstretched waters of the Indian Ocean. Though most scholars have examined the Indian Ocean in holistic, multi-theme ways, I have chosen only one current to run through the chapter presented here: How did the Indian Ocean, from Cape Town up to India, and then down again to Singapore and Perth, become so dominated by British interests, and British power? One can go to any of the geographically disparate societies I just mentioned, and find bureaucrats today speaking English in the conduct of their daily work. How did that happen? Why did this not end up being Arabic or Dutch or French or Portuguese? Chapter 5 traces the evolution of British influence over this arena over the course of several centuries, from the sixteenth into the nineteenth centuries and during the years in between. What started out as a relative free-for-all in terms of trade and competition eventually became a mismatch. There was only one winner when the dust settled on who would rule these seas, not so much politically, but in terms of of the power of economic might. In tracking trade routes and mobile populations, Chapter 5 shows how one Asian maritime system evolved over time and became a vast British sphere of influence as we entered the High Imperial age.

4

Smuggling in the South China Sea

ILLICIT HISTORIES

It has gotten harder and harder to move things. The government has
many eyes.

—ANONYMOUS CHINESE TRADER, TAIPEI, TAIWAN[1]

THERE ARE VERY FEW maritime environments in the world that are in the
news as much as the South China Sea. In the past, this space has been an
important crossroads, funneling trade, migration, and the flow of ideas between East and Southeast Asia for at least two millennia. In our own modern
world, it still provides all of these functions, but also has taken on renewed
geopolitical importance in the contest for resources and power between independent nation-states. The South China Sea touches upon many different polities, and it both connects and fragments at least a dozen countries in Asia, as
well as the shipping of other nations whose vessels transect its open waters.
Few bodies of water loom as large in considerations of environmental, strategic, and economic calculations. It is not an exaggeration at all to say that this
is one of the most "watched" spaces on the planet, both by academics and by
those who formulate government policies.[2] In terms of both scholarship and

1. Author's fieldwork notes, January 2012 [translation: E. Tagliacozzo].
2. For a recent overview, see Eric Tagliacozzo, "The South China Sea," in *Oceanic Histories*,
ed. David Armitage, Alison Bashford, and Sujit Sivasundaram, 113–33 (Cambridge: Cambridge
University Press, 2018).

in terms of policy and praxis, this is currently perhaps the most carefully studied maritime arena in the world.[3]

This chapter examines both historical and contemporary dimensions of this broad aquatic space through one lens: that of smuggling, or illicit trade. In the first portion of the chapter, building on the work of Ronald Po, Robert Antony, Paul van Dyke, Tonio Andrade, Philip Thai, and others, I show how contrabanding in this arena has been intimately linked to the development and evolution of regional maritime worlds in the nineteenth century.[4] I then catalogue the place of Chinese "smugglers" in these activities, before examining the (state-defined) illegal "swirl of commodities" passing through this space in the last two centuries.[5] The second half of the chapter, based on fieldwork, interviewing, and documentary research completed in the late 1990s, analyzes the more recent scope of smuggling in the South China Sea, around the turn of the millennium. I question the forces that both forge and fragment authority in the region, before studying the passage of illegal inanimate objects and the trafficking of humans in the last part of the chapter. I argue that both vantages of vision—historical and contemporary—are necessary and interdependent in piecing together the importance of this vast body of water to Asian maritime

3. Humphrey Hawksley, *Asian Waters: The Struggle over the South China Sea and the Strategy of Chinese Expansion* (New York: Abrams, 2018).

4. These exchanges have a long history—for the early modern background to this story, see Tonio Andrade, *The Gunpowder Age: China, Military Innovation, and the Rise of the West in World History* (Princeton University Press, 2016). Also see Ronald Po, *The Blue Frontier: Maritime Vision and Power in the Qing Empire* (Cambridge: Cambridge University Press, 2018); Robert Antony, *Unruly People: Crime, Community and State in Late Imperial South China* (Hong Kong: Hong Kong University Press, 2016); Robert Antony, ed., *Elusive Pirates, Pervasive Smugglers: Violence and Clandestine Trade in the Greater China Seas* (Hong Kong University Press, 2010); Robert Antony, *Like Froth Floating on the Sea: The World of Pirates and Seafarers in Late Imperial South China* (Berkeley: UC Institute of East Asian Studies, 2003); Paul Van Dyke, *Merchants of Canton and Macao: Politics and Strategies in Eighteenth Century Chinese Trade* (Hong Kong University Press, 2011); Paul Van Dyke, *The Canton Trade: Life and Enterprise on the China Coast, 1700–1845* (Hong Kong University Press, 2007); Philip Thai, *China's War on Smuggling: Law, Economic Life, and the Making of the Modern State* (New York: Columbia University Press, 2018).

5. This history has some real longevity; see Pin-tsun Chang. "Maritime China in Historical Perspective," *International Journal of Maritime History* 4, no. 2 (1992), 239–55; Hugh R. Clark, "Frontier Discourse and China's Maritime Frontier: China's Frontiers and the Encounter with the Sea through Early Imperial History," *Journal of World History* 20, no. 1 (2009), 1–33; James Chin, "Merchants, Smugglers, and Pirates: Multinational Clandestine Trade on the South China Coast, 1520–50," in *Elusive Pirates, Pervasive Smugglers: Violence and Clandestine Trade in the Greater China Seas*, ed. Robert J. Antony, 43–57 (Hong Kong University Press, 2010).

worlds, over the past two hundred years.[6] A number of themes become clear in such a comparison, even if there are also differences manifested by the ongoing passage of time.

Contrabanding Pasts

Not many places in the world have experienced as immense an expansion in shipping and sea traffic as the South China Sea did in the later nineteenth century. Seamen's guides to navigation of the waterways of the area were published often, outlining the winds, storms, and currents of the region for the merchantmen of many nations. Selling nautical charts became a large publishing industry on its own, with maps available at ever smaller scale.[7] The result was an overall shipping milieu where Asians as well as Europeans were highly involved in area commerce. Vessels ran west to Suez and the Indian Ocean, north to China and Japan, and even south to the expanding ports of British Australia. The South China Sea became a kind of patchwork of maritime activity that was akin, in spirit and praxis, perhaps, to the dynamics and patterns of the ancient Mediterranean in the classical period.

Expanded European control, however, eventually gave way to new rules; the Western powers began to decree that certain commodities and certain geographies were off-limits to trade. "Contraband" as a category grew in state ledgers and archives at this time. Who was involved in smuggling commodities in this vast maritime domain of the South China Sea, from Okinawa south to Southeast Asia? European "country traders" were one such community, and they commissioned specialized ships, some of which were small and fleet-winged to better smuggle opium.[8] A thriving business sprouted around Batavia for Chinese opium runners, for example, looking to purchase the illegal product. Country traders entered the shallow harbor, paid the requisite bribe to

6. For a map-based approach to some of the themes discussed in this chapter, see Pierre-Arnoud Chouvy, *An Atlas of Trafficking in Southeast Asia: The Illegal Trade in Arms, Drugs, People, Counterfeit Goods, and Natural Resources in Mainland Southeast Asia* (London: Bloomsbury, 2013).

7. See, for example, [Anon.], *Catalogue of the Latest and Most Approved Charts, Pilots, and Navigation Books Sold or Purchased* (London: James Imray and Sons, 1866).

8. W. H. Coates, *The Old Country Trade of the East Indies* (London: Imray, Laurie, Nurie, and Wilson, 1911), 58–59; Robert Kubicek, "The Role of Shallow-Draft Steamboats in the Expansion of the British Empire, 1820–1914," *International Journal of Maritime History* VI (June 1994), 86 and passim.

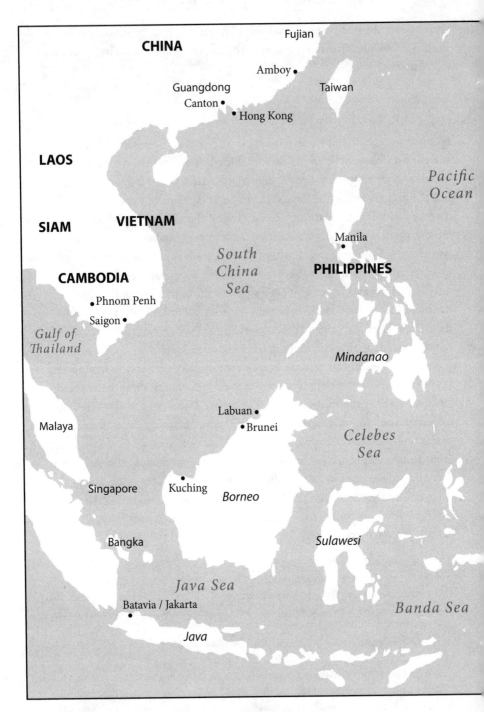

MAP 4.1. The South China Sea

crooked Dutch officials, and were then told where to pick up contraband cargoes of ocean produce and the inlets frequented by the junks.[9] In this way, valuable local products found their way up to Canton. The country traders could thus continue their coasting trade in Southeast Asia, picking up more commodities while their original cargoes sped north on consignment.[10] W. H. Coates has helpfully published a letter of a Parsee shipowner to his captain, instructing him on how to avoid customs patrols and war junks cruising around Whampoa.[11] These sorts of actions seem to have been quite common.

Many craft of the class that European observers would call "junks" sailed south from coastal China into the South China Sea to participate in this commerce, in addition to the ships of European country traders. Chinese shipping was a complicated endeavor requiring a large cast of actors and their concomitant skills—merchants, capitalists, seamen, and navigators all came together to share in the venture. Syndicates called *bang* were set up in Guangdong, Zhejiang, and Fujian to defray costs and share in the risks, as construction fees on the junks alone often reached into the tens of thousands of gold cash.[12] John Crawfurd noted the state of affairs in the 1820s by observing that "the cargo of Chinese junks is not the property of an individual but of many—the proprietors merely have their own compartments in the vessel."[13] Plenty of people stood ready to invest despite the risks involved. The profit margin on junks sailing across the South China Sea to Sulu in the Southern Philippines ranged between 30 and 300 percent, with certain marine products commanding 100 percent profits back home, and mother-of-pearl three times that amount.[14] Amoy (Xiamen) in Fujian served as the main base for the fleets, although ships

9. C. Northcote Parkinson, *Trade in the Eastern Seas (1793–1813)* (Cambridge University Press, 1937), 351; for scandals involving Chinese payoffs to an incumbent governor general, see also F. de Haan, *Oud Batavia* (Batavia: Kolff, 1922), I:498.

10. See Paul Van Dyke, *Americans and Macao: Trade, Smuggling and Diplomacy on the South China Coast* (Hong Kong: Hong Kong University Press, 2012).

11. Coates, *The Old Country Trade*, 81–82.

12. Sarasin Viraphol, *Tribute and Profit: Sino-Siamese Trade 1652–1853* (Cambridge: Harvard University Press, 1977), 124; see also Yen-Ping Hao, *The Commercial Revolution in Nineteenth Century China: The Rise of Sino-Western Capitalism* (Berkeley, University of California Press, 1986).

13. John Crawfurd, *Journal of an Embassy from the Governor General of India to the Courts of Siam and Cochin-China* (Oxford Historical reprints, 1967 [orig. London: Henry Colburn, 1828]), 160–61.

14. James Francis Warren, *The Sulu Zone* (Singapore University Press, 1981), 8.

FIGURE 4.1. Qingping Market, Guangzhou: Baboons, Sea Horses (author's photo)

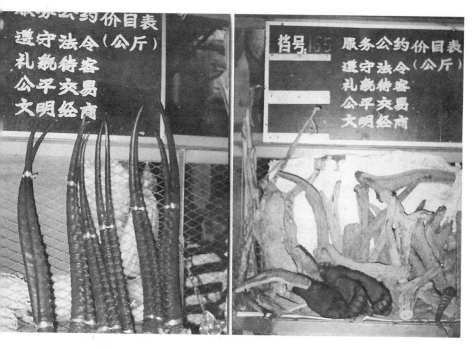

FIGURE 4.2. Qingping Market, Guangzhou: Oryx Horns, Monkey Feet (author's photo)

departed from as far north as Shanghai and as far south as Hainan. Most arrived in Southeast Asia in January and early February, having left China during the beginning of the northeast monsoon.[15]

The (often) very trying circumstances surrounding such ventures produced this penchant for tightly coordinated cooperation. Overseas trade was continually restricted on an on-again, off-again basis by the Ch'ing, and bankruptcy in such a dangerous endeavor as transoceanic shipping was only as far away as the nearest pirate or squall. Yet by far the most difficult hurdle in making these ventures a success was the degree of official "propitiation" needed to oil the machine. Sarasin Viraphol estimates that 20 to 40 percent of total costs during this period was earmarked for the local *yamens* to serve as "protection."[16] Chinese viceroys and customs officials were not necessarily opposed to such

15. Anthony Reid, "The Unthreatening Alternative: Chinese Shipping in Southeast Asia 1567–1842," *RIMA* 27, nos. 1–2 (1993): 2.

16. Sarasin Viraphol, *Tribute and Profit: Sino-Siamese Trade 1652–1853* (Cambridge: Harvard University Press, 1977), 127. Pirate confederations also demanded such fees when they could; Paul van Dyke has written on this, as have others.

journeys. They merely wanted their cut. Such graft and inefficiency did take its toll, however. Official outlets for overseas goods were often ignored by many junk captains, who preferred to put into Chinese ports where such exactions could be minimized. There separate deals could be cut with local coastal authorities, and if the price was not right the captain could simply move on.[17] In these places, arrangements could be made with local officials, and if the local "taxes" were too high, there were always more ports to visit down the coast.

As Western imperial power grew, this complex system was deemed more and more of a problem. The illicit and unrecorded trades of many Chinese networks in particular worried colonial regimes, as many Chinese traded a broad range of products outside the vision and reach of these states. Several of these products were eventually designated as officially illegal, such as unfarmed opium and firearms.[18] A single Dutch report from Bangka in 1879 demonstrates some of these dimensions very well. A study tour of these remote coasts yielded an unwelcome shock to Batavia; Chinese vessels were shuttling goods literally everywhere along these shores, from Pahid and Rangam to Roemah Batoe and Tandjong Nioer. The epicenter of these trades seems to have been Tandjoeng Tedoeng, funneling opium and textiles across the Bangka Straits by way of a string of ethnic Chinese villages along the shore. The report noted that voyages of this type were absurdly easy to undertake from the majority of these villages. Smugglers had strong business ties to Singapore in particular, and state supervision was almost nonexistent in the area.[19]

Both the Dutch and the British, the two major Western powers in this arena, were exasperated at times about how to deal with Chinese traders in the South China Sea, and their illegal commerce in the years leading up to the fin de siècle. This, however, was a policy problem that would not ever be fully solved. All along the South China Sea basin these patterns of ascribed "illegality" continued unabated, with Chinese merchants figuring out ways to sidestep the growing proscriptions of the state. Such movements happened in peripheral, outlying areas, away from the coercive "eye" and reach of the

17. For a provocative take on how much freedom Chinese merchants really had in Late Imperial China, see Madeleine Zelin, "Economic Freedom in Late Imperial China," in *Realms of Freedom in Modern China*, ed. William Kirby (Palo Alto: Stanford University Press, 2004).

18. For a broad new study on the former across Southeast Asia, see Diana Kim, *Empires of Vice: The Rise of Opium Prohibition across Southeast Asia* (Princeton: Princeton University Press, 2020).

19. See ANRI, Maandrapport der Residentie Banka 1879 (Banka no. 105).

center.[20] Yet these transactions also happened right in the laps of colonial cit-ies, as Chinese used the expanding size of these centers to lose themselves in the chaos and complexity of colonial capitals.[21] The movements, feints, and connections of overseas Chinese in Southeast Asia thus leapfrogged all crystal-lizing boundaries. It was the clear impunity with which Chinese merchants conducted state-sanctioned "illegal" commercial practices that caused such consternation to both colonial regimes into the twentieth century.

By the early 1900s, however, this same impunity of Chinese smugglers in the lower reaches of the South China Sea was being severely tested by newly determined colonial governments in the region. Everywhere attempts were being made to eradicate any transgressive powers that such smugglers might have, especially those which could be used to compete with the coercive abili-ties of the state. Anthropometric identity proofs were being experimented with in Java, with an eye toward documenting all "Foreign Asians" (*Vreemde Oosterlingen*) in the Indies a few years later.[22] Dutch and British governments also tightened restrictions on Chinese "secret societies" (*hui*). One legal amendment, for instance, introduced flogging as a punishment for secret so-ciety participation in North Borneo. Western regimes were letting the *hui* know in no uncertain terms that smuggling was now under attack by increas-ingly assertive colonial administrations.[23]

Yet exactly which sorts of items were being trafficked across the reaches of the South China Sea during this period? Although a huge spectrum of items might be examined, the shadowy trade in spirits and narcotics make for an instructive window. From as early as the 1850s, ports such as Labuan, off the western coast of Borneo, farmed out licenses to sell spirits in order to raise revenues for the colony's exchequer. Almost as quickly, smuggling syndicates sprang up to challenge these monopolies, necessitating constant changes in

20. See "Mr. Everett's Journal at Papar, 1879–80, 5 December, 1879, Volume 73," in PRO/CO/874/Boxes 67–77, Resident's Diaries. Robert Antony reports that the Spratly Islands were one such place where these movements happened; not a small irony, given the importance of these islands right now.

21. For Batavia, see "Jualan Chandu Gelap Dalam Betawi," *Utusan Malayu* (2 February 1909): 2; for Singapore, see *Bintang Timur*, 4 January 1895, p. 2.

22. See the deliberations, discussions, and legislation of the Bertillon system as outlined in ARA, 1892, MR no. 1144; 1896, MR no. 743; 1898, MR no. 379.

23. See the "Secret Societies Amendment Proclamation of 1913," as declared by the Governor of British North Borneo on 9 August 1913, in PRO/CO/874/Box 803, "Secret Societies."

the laws to fight these attacks on diminishing government profits.[24] Liquor was also contrabanded elsewhere in the British possessions, such as on the Malay Peninsula, while Malay-language newspapers from the 1890s make clear that even the seat of English power (Singapore) was never fully immune to these problems.[25] Spirits such as gin, brandy, whiskey, and even homemade arrack all poured across the border and into the Dutch Indies as well.[26] This happened in places such as West Borneo, where smugglers brought small batches of European liquor in at a time to circumvent the regulations of the local monopoly.[27] Attempts to ban the transit of alcohol altogether as part of a moral crusade were doomed to failure because of the huge profits traders reaped by these sales. Only at the turn of the twentieth century were larger, more systemic efforts made to stanch these commodity flows in arenas like the Sulu basin, where help from the Spanish was deemed to be forthcoming.[28]

The most important commodity being moved illegally was opium. By the nineteenth century, opium had been circulating in the South China Sea for a very long time. Though notices of opium use reach back far into the past, it was only in the seventeenth century that detailed records started to be written documenting its production and passage. Dutch traders used Southeast Asia as a conduit to ferry small amounts of opium to Taiwan; from there it was traded to the vast interior market of China, often on the sly. Though opium was sold freely in much of Southeast Asia, many local rulers tried to forbid or inhibit its sale because of the drug's adverse effects on local populations. European traders and many Chinese, Armenian, and other merchant classes that

24. Officer of the Committee of the Privy Council for Trade to Herman Merivale, Esq., 17 June 1850, in CO 144/6; Extracts from the Minutes of the Legislative Council of Labuan, 3 January 1853, in CO 144/11; Gov Labuan to CO, 9 January 1872, no. 2, in CO 144/36; CO Jacket (Mr. Fairfield, and Mr. Wingfield), 21 May 1896, in CO 144/70; Gov Labuan to BNB HQ, London, 13 November 1896, in CO 144/70.

25. See Enactment no. 6 of 1915, Malay States; also *Bintang Timor*, 6 December 1894, p. 2.

26. *Straits Settlements Blue Books* (Singapore: Spirit Imports and Exports, 1873), 329, 379–80.

27. ANRI, Politiek Verslag Residentie West Borneo 1872 (no. 2/10); ARA, Extract Uit het Register der Besluiten, GGNEI, 2 January 1881, no. 7, in 1881, MR no. 18.

28. ARA, First Government Secretary to Director of Finances, 6 November 1889, no. 2585, in 1889, MR no. 773; also First Government Secretary to Resident Timor, 8 March 1892, no. 600, in 1892, MR no. 217; ARA, Dutch Consul, Manila to MvBZ, 5 April 1897, no. 32; MvBZ to MvK, 24 May 1897, no. 5768, both in (MvBZ/A Dossiers/223/A.111/"Verbod Invoer Wapens en Alcohol"); ARA, Dutch Consul, London to MvBZ, 28 Jan 1893, no. 37, and GGNEI to MvK, 27 Nov 1892, no. 2268/14, both in (MvBZ/A Dossiers/223/A.111/"Still Zuidzee").

were gradually subsumed under European power sold the opium anyway. Other local rulers saw the economic benefits in participating in this commerce themselves, as opium had a high resale value, especially in its retail form, known as *chandu*. As European trading companies and indigenous Southeast Asian state-making projects evolved during the nineteenth century, however, different actors tried to corner the market in drugs for their own long-term profits. States and private speculators competed, therefore, in selling opium over large expanses of the South China Sea. This paradigm would continue into the early years of the 1900s without abatement.[29] We can see this from Malay newspaper notices from the period:

> ... banyak Chandu dijualan. ... Didalam Tanjong Periok dilabohan Betawi. ... Harga jualan lebih sembilan kali daripada harga belinya ... Chandu dating dari Singapura dan China.[30]

> ... much chandu is sold ... in Tanjong Priok harbor in Batavia ... the price of selling is more than nine times the price of buying (there) ... the chandu comes from Singapore and China.

The contrabanding of drugs in the late nineteenth century South China Sea region, thus, was complex. Colonial states took measures to directly control the opium trade, yet with only ambiguous results vis-à-vis smuggling. Top European officials acknowledged as much in reports back to the colonial metropoles.[31] Smuggling seems to have risen by the turn of the twentieth century, partially because prices on legalized chandu were raised, and partially because the now out-of-work farmers often used their specialized knowledge on smuggling mechanisms to practice it themselves.[32] In insular Southeast

29. In addition to Diana Kim's recent book, two excellent monographs on the history of opium in nineteenth-century Southeast Asia are Carl Trocki's *Opium, Empire, and the Global Political Economy* (London: Routledge, 1999), and James Rush, *Opium to Java: Revenue Farming and Chinese Enterprise in Colonial Indonesia, 1800–1910* (Ithaca: Cornell University Press, 1990). See also sections of James Warren, *The Sulu Zone, 1768–1898: The Dynamics of External Trade, Slavery, and Ethnicity in the Transformation of a Southeast Asian Maritime State* (National University of Singapore Press, 1981), and Eric Tagliacozzo, "Kettle on a Slow Boil: Batavia's Threat Perceptions in the Indies' Outer Islands," *Journal of Southeast Asian Studies* 31, no. 1 (2000), 70–100.

30. *Utusan Malayu*, 2 February 1909, 2 [translation: E. Tagliacozzo].

31. ARA, Chief Inspector of the Opium Regie to Gov Gen NEI, 30 Oct 1903, no. 3017/R in Verbaal 13 Jan 1904, no. 34.

32. To discourage opium abuse, prices were raised as part of the moral argument for the government taking over the trade.

FIGURE 4.3. Dutch Blockade Runners, 1947 (KITLV Collection, Leiden, #14092/#14093)

FIGURE 4.3. (*continued*)

Asia, the vast labyrinth of narcotics legislation and its uneven application to various territories and people also ensured continuity in smuggling. In the years in and around 1910, separate rules were drawn up for various British dependencies in the area, but were also written internally, within each polity. In the Federated Malay States (FMS), for example, legislation drew distinctions on the acceptability of narcotics use by race, occupation, and even by coastal or interior habitation.[33] The sheer complexity of the system, and the colonial state's inability to enforce this complexity across all of its dominions, guaranteed that narcotics contrabanding in this region survived well into the early twentieth century. Similar patterns vis-à-vis opium were eventually taken up by the Japanese Empire, too, as Tokyo commenced its own program of aggression in Asia.[34]

33. CO/882 Eastern, 9, no. 114 gives some of these stipulations for the Malay Peninsula. There were different laws depending on whether coastal or inland areas were in question, while racially only male Chinese over the age of twenty-one were allowed to smoke opium on licensed premises, etc. This document gives a good overview of the scope and complexity of narcotics legislation.

34. See, for example, John Jennings, *The Opium Empire: Japanese Imperialism and Drug Trafficking in Asia, 1895–1945* (Westport: Praeger, 1997); and Carl Trocki, *Opium, Empire, and the Global Political Economy: A Study of the Asian Opium Trade* (New York: Routledge, 1999).

The Contrabanding Present

So much for the past; in what ways do these patterns of historical smuggling in the South China Sea make themselves manifest now, in our own contemporary world? In the southernmost regions of this vast maritime basin, the islands and coastlines of Southeast Asia have a very open cadence to trade which has been distinctive of this part of the world for many centuries. Because the modern territorial conception of borders was alien here and was introduced only forcibly by Europeans, it should not surprise us that goods continue to flow across these demarcations, often without the blessing of the state.[35] Globalization, regional economic blocs, and the growth of subregional economic development "triangles" have only accelerated this trend in recent years, providing new avenues and impetus to a range of traders (acting legally and illegally) to move their cargoes across national boundaries. The establishment of localized, multi-country growth areas in particular has aided this process, with compilations such as the BIMP-EAGA development triangle (centered around the Sulu Sea between the Philippines, Indonesia, and Malaysia) turning out to be particularly amenable to both graft and the evasion of government dictates .[36]

Opening regional commercial flows by administrative fiat has led to a large number of infrastructural projects designed to better connect borders in the South China Sea region. In the above-mentioned BIMP-EAGA development sphere, expanded postal routes now link northern Indonesia and the southern Philippines, for example. A second causeway was added between Malaysia and Singapore; the volume of traffic crossing the original road-bridge was too great for customs officials on either side to check all transiting vehicles for contraband. One Marine Bureau official in Singapore told me, "It's already impossible now to check everything that comes in and out of Singapore; with the second causeway, it becomes even more impossible, but that's the price of increased trade."[37]

Plans have even been announced for the construction of a huge bridge connecting Malaysia and Indonesia across the Straits of Melaka as well, though it

---

35. See discussion in Thongchai Winichakul, *Siam Mapped* (Honolulu: University of Hawai'i Press, 1994). For a theoretical discussion on the nature (and evolution) of borders, see J. R. V. Prescott, *Political Frontiers and Political Boundaries* (London: Allen & Unwin, 1987).

36. "Bersaing Di Langit Terbuka BIMP-EAGA," *Suara Pembaruan*, 25 November 1997, 16; and "Mindanao Bakal Unggul Di Timur ASEAN," *Suara Pembaruan*, 25 January 1997, 17.

37. Anonymous Marine Board Official, Singapore, April 1997 (Author's fieldwork notes).

is yet to be built. Although the specific location of the structure's endpoints has not yet been determined, the agreement calls for railway, gas pipes, and power cables on the bridge, as well as a main connecting section of road.[38] Other connective projects have also been planned. The enormous opening of border facilities and connections along the South China Sea's margins has come at a price, however. Alongside increased legitimate border trade revenues have also flowed goods and problems of another kind. The pursuit of smuggling and the violations of state sovereignty therein have become important points of negotiation in the politics of the region.

Southeast Asian administrations have taken a number of steps to lessen the effects of contrabanding that are part of the boundary liberalization process, because of the salient openness of frontiers in this arena. These efforts have manifested in different forms. One of the ways to do this has been to encourage cooperation of law enforcement agencies across frontiers: the police forces of Singapore and Malaysia have been particularly adept at this, while Vietnam and Cambodia have signed similar accords.[39] Another way has been to map out coasts and terrain with a greater degree of efficiency, both by increasing interdiction forces in these areas and also by producing more accurate charts of difficult terrain. The Philippines added more ships and Malaysia more coastal radar stations along these lines, while Laos is using Global Positioning Systems (GPS) to better map its borders. Indonesia has closed down old markets and opened new ones along its frontiers, trying to influence the terms of regional trade more directly.[40] Finally, better "tagging" is being attempted on human beings who frequently cross borders, so that a more watchful eye may

38. "Pos Pelintas Batas RI-Filipina Ditambah," *Kompas*, 12 October 1997: 8; "Tenaga Willing to Supply Power to Sumatra via Bridge Link," *Straits Times*, 29 June 1997; "Malaysia Undecided Where Bridge to Indonesia Will Begin," *Straits Times*, 26 June 1997. For boundary agreements across the land border in Borneo, see *Laporan Delegasi Republik Indonesia Mengenai Pertemuan Panitia Teknis Bersama Perbatasan Indonesia-Malaysia Yang Ke-12 Tentang Survey dan Penegasan Bersama Perbatasan Darat Antara Indonesia and Malaysia* (Jakarta: Taud ABRI, 1981).

39. "Other ASEAN States Urged to Follow Singapore-KL Joint Approach to Crime," *Straits Times*, 10 June 1997; "Vietnam, Cambodia Police Sign Police Accord," *Weekly Review of the Cambodia Daily*, 3 March 1997, 8; "Lao Police Delegation Back from Interpol Meeting in Beijing," *Vientiane Times*, 3 March 1997, 4.

40. Indonesia has taken to mapping the culture of border peoples in this manner, too; see Suwarsono, *Daerah Perbatasan Kalimantan Barat: Suatu Observasi Terhadap Karekteristik Sosial Budaya Dua Daurah Lintas Batas* (Jakarta: Pusat Penilitian dan Pengembangan Kemasyarakatan dan Kebudayaan [LIPI], 1997). "Eye on Ships," *Straits Times*, 7 June 1997; "Seminar on New Lao Mapping and Survey Network Held in Vientiane," *Vientiane Times*, 11/5–7/97: 4; "Border

be kept on their activities. Indonesia has differentiated the passports which many of its citizens use to travel abroad illegally (sometimes under the guise of undertaking the pilgrimage to Mecca, which requires different documentation than for those who are not making the Hajj), while Kuala Lumpur has introduced electronic security features into Malaysian passports to prevent forgeries. China is doing this as well. All of these steps, it is hoped by governments in the region, will make the increasing porosity of Asia's boundaries more profitable to national exchequers. At the same time, it is hoped by these same regimes that these practical adjustments will limit the abilities of smugglers to bend the circumstances of borders to their own ends.

Consumer goods are a vital subset of commodities that can be analyzed in the tabulation of contrabanding and boundaries in the South Chinas Sea region. This category is representative of a broad spectrum of commodities that are illegally transited: cigarettes, automobiles, compact discs, pornography, even antique sculpture and religious items. In terms of the sheer number of cases, this subbranch of contrabanding is probably the most important in the region. "We can't catch the real smugglers," said one Southeast Asian official to the *Far Eastern Economic Review*, citing the traffickers' mobile phones and faster boats, which render them far better equipped than border guards on frequent occasions.[41] Yet regional administrations have tried to combat contraband syndicates, using measures as diverse as stiff fines and advances in computerized customs services. The results have been disappointing, from the state's viewpoint; smuggling of consumer goods is still booming in the South China Sea arena. The passage of contraband is so widespread in the region, especially in the case of consumer goods, that it is often actually difficult to pick out one border over another in how these patterns work.

Still, a look at just one or two of these locales can provide an idea of how systemic this trafficking has really become, and what is being routed. The Sino-Vietnamese border is a transit area of high volume for contraband. Garments, electric fans, and bicycles are "hot" items, mostly because Hanoi restricts these goods in an effort to protect domestic production. Maritime spaces adjoining the South China Sea should also be mentioned in the Southeast Asian context, however, as there is no shortage of consumer-good smuggling in this realm, either. In interviews I have conducted with Indonesian sailors on Jakarta's

Market to Be Opened," *Jakarta Post*, 10 November 1997, 2; for the other example, mentioned above, see "AFP Waging High-Tech War vs. Abus," *Philippine Daily Inquirer*, 9 April 2001, 2.

41. "Struggle or Smuggle," *Far Eastern Economic Review*, 22 February 1997, 26 and passim.

TABLE 4.1. Smuggling Statistics for the South China Sea

Estimated Black Market Values of Trade, 2014

Global rank	Country	Amount	Global rank	Country	Amount
2	China	$261.00 B USD	42	Taiwan	$2.60 B USD
6	Japan	$108.30 B USD	43	N. Korea	$2.24 B USD
12	S. Korea	$26.20 B USD	44	Burma	$1.70 B USD
13	Indonesia	$23.05 B USD	52	Laos	$0.85 B USD
14	Philippines	$17.27 B USD	53	Vietnam	$0.81 B USD
20	Thailand	$13.95 B USD	56	Cambodia	$0.61 B USD
40	Malaysia	$2.99 B USD	66	Singapore	$0.27 B USD

Selection of Asian Trafficking Statistics, South China Sea Countries

Ivory Price in China, 2010	$750 US/kg.
Ivory Price in China, 2104	$2,100 US/kg.
Pangolins Taken from the Wild, Vietnam	40–60,000/year
Poaching Traps Found in Malaysia, 2008–12	2,377
Thailand Animal Rescues	46,000/year

Contraband Narcotics Prices in the Philippines, 2014/15

Cocaine	$119/gram
Ecstasy	$27.50 per pill
Heroin	$108.80/gram
Marijuana	$.90 per gram
Methamphetamine	$214.10/gram

Sources: All information collected, collated, and adapted from havocscope.com, accessed 16 July 2015. Data is combined from security and intelligence agencies, corporate reports, and other risk assessment programs.

docks, I was told that the passage of goods outside local waters to the country's neighbors could easily be arranged. Meanwhile, Indonesian workers interviewed in Singapore said that almost anything could be ordered from nearby Riau, if one knew how.[42] In the Philippines the situation is much the same; long coastlines and corrupt maritime patrols make for easy on- and off-loading, so the possibilities for smuggling stretch to the horizon for many miles, and in multiple directions.[43]

42. These interviews were conducted with Bugis sailors on Jakarta's Sunda Kelapa docks in August and September of 1998; I cannot give the names of crew members (or their ships) for obvious reasons. These sailors, in fact, spoke of the true "outlaws" in Indonesian waters as being the maritime police—agents who can shake down passing ships with near impunity. Interviews were also conducted with Indonesian laborers (in a variety of occupations) in Singapore.

43. "Believe It or Not," *Far Eastern Economic Review*, 27 October 1997, 23.

As we have already seen in the historical section earlier in this chapter, few inanimate objects travel as quickly or profitably as narcotics. Over the course of the last century, the drug trade in Southeast Asia has evolved and showed certain remarkable continuities with patterns of an earlier age. Though the early decades of the twentieth century saw a concerted effort by colonial administrations to streamline and profit from this commerce, international pressures—mainly from "opium suppression societies" based in the West—also challenged the status quo. Narcotics trading in Asia became increasingly criminalized, and global conferences (such as The Hague Convention in 1912) brought public opinion to bear on the colonial management of drug trafficking. Prices on opium in Southeast Asia were raised until it became difficult for locals to buy the drug legally on a regular, addictive basis.[44] Decolonization changed this dynamic to a degree, as the newly independent states of the region strove to rid themselves of drug addiction, which was often attributed to the evils of imperial domination. Yet the limits of state-building allowed many segments of society, especially elites and minority frontier populations, to continue profiting from narcotics against the dictates of indigenous states. Graft, preexisting networks of ethnic dispersion, and the evolution of long-range communications oiled these gears considerably. The prosecution of the conflict in Vietnam ensured that drugs reached many places, and US troops both aided and thwarted this process (through individual GIs and through the CIA, respectively).[45]

By the late twentieth century, a trade in illegal substances that was both larger and diverse had developed, one that was in fact far broader than the historical commerce, which had once been mainly a transit in imported opium. The South China Sea region now imports *and* exports drugs.[46] Narcotics trafficking in the region is famed via the notorious "Golden Triangle," but in recent years the trade has seeped into nearly every corner of ASEAN, and into all socioeconomic classes. In Southeast Asia, countries outside the Golden Triangle such as Indonesia and the Philippines are beginning to admit that they are no longer just transit nations but consuming "end destinations" as

44. Warren Bailey and Lan Truong, "Opium and Empire: Some Evidence from Colonial-Era Asian Stock and Commodity Markets," *Journal of Southeast Asian Studies* 32 (2001): 173–94, Figure 1.

45. See especially the very detailed exposé in Alfred McCoy, *The Politics of Heroin: CIA Complicity in the Global Drug Trade* (New York: Hill Books, 1991), 193–261.

46. See *Synthetic Drugs in East and Southeast Asia: Latest Developments and Challenges*, 2021 (New York: United Nations Office on Drugs and Crime, 2021).

well.[47] Norodom Ranariddh of Cambodia at one point warned that his country would be paralyzed by international drug-trafficking barons, unless it received substantial outside assistance.[48] Even tiny Brunei, staunchly Muslim and easily patrolled, has acknowledged the beginnings of a serious drug problem.[49] These factors taken together all suggest serious issues for the stability of the region, vis-à-vis regional administrations, international health organizations, and even the UN.

Where does one point fingers in attributing a source for all of this contrabanding? As the spectrum of narcotics and geographies involved are both broad, it should not surprise us that the net of human beings involved is also diverse—politicians, merchants, professional criminals, and even "ordinary folk" all take part in this commerce. One trend that stands out is that narcotics trafficking in the South China Sea region, as in the nineteenth century with Chinese and Armenian trade networks, often still seems to be accomplished along predominantly ethnic lines. Pakistani groups have been caught selling heroin into Indonesia, for example, while Indonesians are regularly caught contrabanding drugs north into Malaysia (perhaps because religious, linguistic, and cultural similarities, all historically based, have facilitated kinship connections and trust). Chinese networks supply the Southeast Asian drug-smuggling nexus by land and by sea. Two Triad groups that have been active in these activities for a long time are the 14K and Bamboo gangs, among others operating out of southern China, Macau, and Hong Kong.[50] These syndicates are contemporary manifestations of much older Chinese organizations, which transited illegal substances such as drugs between the various countries of Asia trans-regionally.[51]

47. "Indonesia Sudah Lama Jadi Pemasaran Narkotika," *Angkatan Bersenjata*, 4 November 1997, 12; "Philippine Police Seize Huge Volume of Drugs This Year," *Vientiane Times*, 29–31 October 1997, 6.

48. "Drugs Blacklist," *Phnom Penh Post*, 16–29 March, 2001, 2; "PM Warns of Takeover by Drug Merchants," *Weekly Review of the Cambodia Daily*, 24 April 1997, 12; "Medellin on the Mekong," *Far Eastern Economic Review*, 7 September 1995, 29–30; "Medellin on the Mekong," *Far Eastern Economic Review*, 23 November 1997, 24–6.

49. "Dadah Musush Utama Masyarakat," *Pelita Brunei*, 2 July 1997, 1.

50. "Pakistanis Tried for Trafficking Heroin," *Jakarta Post*, 1 December 1997, 3; "Drug Bust," *Straits Times*, 26 June 1997; "4 Chinese Nabbed in Drug Swoop," *Philippine Daily Inquirer*, 10 November 1997, 24; "3 Die in Drug Bust," *Philippine Daily Inquirer*, 19 November 1997, 20; "Drug Dealers Find 'Open' Market in Philippines," *Straits Times*, 21 June 1997.

51. For these larger, Asia-wide patterns, see Timothy Brook and Bob Tadashi Wakabayashi, eds., *Opium Regimes: China, Britain, and Japan, 1839–1952* (Berkeley: University of California Press, 2000); and Kathryn Meyer and Terry Parssinen, *Webs of Smoke: Smugglers, Warlords,*

"Biota" (writ large) is another contraband trade that is interesting in drawing a genealogy of historical and contemporary patterns of smuggling in the region. Human trafficking makes up the majority of this commerce, likely, in terms of value.[52] The movement of human beings across boundaries in the South China Sea region, both legally and illegally, also has a long history in this part of the world. Migration theorists have noted that there has been a fundamental, worldwide shift in the nature of population movements in the last two centuries: in the nineteenth century, the majority of migrants were moving from rich to poor countries, while in the twentieth and into the twenty-first century, the tide has clearly reversed.[53] It is clear that the brokered transit of human beings is on the rise globally, and that this is markedly so in the South China Sea region. This human tide of smuggling contributes enormously to modern-day contrabanding in Asia, and also evinces real historical continuities.

There are still large movements today of illegal workers across national boundaries in search of stable livelihoods, just as in ages past.[54] In the late 1990s there were, for example, over 700,000 foreign laborers in Thailand by official figures, 1.2 million in Malaysia, and over 4 million Filipinos working abroad.[55] Trafficked workers, governments argue, pose a threat and are themselves at risk at the same time. They are often accused of bringing crime and disease with them, but such workers are concomitantly at the mercy of gangs who distribute them for the highest price. The places that receive these desperate human flows often need the labor, however, even if trafficking is involved in their passage.[56]

Spies, and the History of the International Drug Trade, (Lanham: Rowman & Littlefield Publishers, 1998).

52. See Michele Ford, Lenore Lyons, and Willem van Schendel, eds. *Labour Migrations and Human Trafficking in Southeast Asia: Critical Perspectives* (London: Routledge, 2014).

53. M. M. Kritz and C. B. Keely, "Introduction," in their edited volume, *Global Trends in Migration: Theory and Research on International Migration Movements* (Staten Island: Center for Migration Studies, 1981): xiii–xiv.

54. See Netsanet Tesfay. *Impact of Livelihood Recovery Initiatives on Reducing Vulnerability to Human Trafficking and Illegal Recruitment: Lessons from Typhoon Haiyan* (Geneva: International Organization for Migration and International Labour Organization, 2015).

55. "Foreign Maids Fight Modern Day Slavery," *Philippine News*, 4 April 2001, 2; "Labour Migration in Southeast Asia: Analysis, Cooperation Needed," *TRENDS* (Singapore: Journal of the Institute of Southeast Asia Studies,), 27 September 1997; "AIDS Time Bomb Ticks Away among Asia's Migrant Labor," *Viet Nam News*, 2 November 1997, 12.

56. "Illegal Workers Dumped Far from Shore," *Straits Times*, 18 November 1997; "Colour-Coded Tags for 1.2 Million Foreign Workers," *New Straits Times* (Malaysia), 27 November 1997, 4;

FIGURE 4.4. Burmese Smugglers in Penang, Malaysia (author's photo)

FIGURE 4.5. Thai Illegal Fishing Vessels, Songkhla (author's photo)

Undocumented labor is not the only avatar of human smuggling prevalent in the region. Prostitution has also been a magnet for the movement of women through the South China Sea, as the poor of various countries have often had few alternatives but to sell their own bodies to make ends meet. In colonial times, the forces that drove prostitution trafficking often started from outside the region: indigent country girls from China and Japan, reacting to famine and underdevelopment in their own countrysides, were sometimes lured by tales of Southeast Asia's burgeoning ports.[57] Others were trafficked unwittingly, or even knowingly chose to sail south because they had few other options. These broad, systemic movements also took place from rural Asian landscapes into the new cities of empire, as well as into colonial barracks, plantations, and mines.[58] The contemporary scene has witnessed an elaboration and expansion of this dynamic, pushing women and children in new

"Foreign Workers May Be Sent to Key Sectors," *New Straits Times* (Malaysia), 8 December 1997, 14.

57. See James Francis Warren, *Ah Ku and Karayuki-san: Prostitution in Singapore (1880–1940)* (Singapore: Oxford University Press, 1993.)

58. For the Dutch Indies/Indonesian case, see for example Terence Hull, Endang Sulistyaningsih, and Gavin Jones, eds., *Pelacuran di Indonesia: Sejarah dan Perkembangannya* (Jakarta: Pusat Sinar Harapan, 1997): 1–17; Hanneke Ming, "Barracks-Concubinage in the Indies,

directions. The sums of money for trafficking women across international borders and into prostitution are simply huge, and seem to grow all the time.[59]

Prostitutes are moved into the major urban centers, but also to relative "backwaters," across Southeast Asia. In urban centers, a syndicate was exposed some years ago that brought Filipina prostitutes into Singapore, secreting them day and night through customs at Changi Airport. Thirty-nine women were ultimately arrested, partially because the traffickers were also importing drugs in the same "shipments" and had thus aroused the surveillance of police. In Malaysia, prostitutes have been run into the country via Chinese networks out of Thailand and Southern China; many have been lied to, and have been told that they have jobs in factories, so that they will readily make the journey.[60] The trade siphons women off even into rural geographies, however, so long as it is felt that there are profits to be made. The "resort island" of Batam off Singapore is one example of this phenomenon, while women are also brought even to Indonesian New Guinea (West Papua), as Thai fishermen spend weeks at a time there, far from their own homes.[61] Even religiously conservative Brunei has seen this kind of trafficking: seven women were arrested at one point who had been trafficked to the sultanate, simply because the strength of the Brunei dollar made the risks worthwhile.[62]

1887–1920," *Indonesia* 35 (1983); and Ann Stoler, *Capitalism and Confrontation in Sumatra's Plantation Belt 1870–1979* (New Haven: Yale University Press, 1986).

59. Several excellent studies of the dynamics of prostitution in Southeast Asia have been published recently; see especially Lisa Law, *Sex Work in Southeast Asia: A Place of Desire in a Time of AIDS* (New York: Routledge, 2000); Lin Leam Lim, *The Sex Sector: The Economic and Social Bases of Prostitution in Southeast Asia* (Geneva: International Labour Office, 1998); Siriporn Skrobanek, *The Traffic in Women: Human Realities of the International Sex Trade* (New York: Zed Books, 1997); and Thanh-Dam Truong, *Sex, Money, and Morality: Prostitution and Tourism in Southeast Asia* (London: Zed Books, 1990).

60. "Ten Foreign Women Held in Anti-Vice Operation," *New Straits Times*, 13 November 2000, 8; "Arrests in Singapore," *Manila Bulletin*, 12 November 1997, 12; "Crackdown on Rings That Bring in Foreign Call Girls," *Straits Times*, 14 July 1997; "First Students, Then Call Girls," *Straits Times*, 22 July 1997.

61. "Banyak Wanita di Bawah Umur Melacur," *Angkatan Bersenjata*, 25 July 1997, 7; "Fishermen Involved in Prostitution," *Jakarta Post*, 29 November 1997, 2; "Banyak Tempat Hiburan Jadi Tempat Prostitutsi," *Angkatan Bersenjata*, 12 November 1997, 6. For a view not from the "periphery" but rather from the center, see Allison Murray's fine ethnography, *No Money, No Honey: A Study of Street Traders and Prostitutes in Jakarta* (Singapore: Oxford University Press, 1991).

62. "Alleged Call Girls Detained," *Borneo Bulletin*, 12 November 1997, 1; "Pimps Jailed, Call Girls Fined," *Borneo Bulletin*, 13 November 1997, 3.

Conclusion

It was asserted earlier in this chapter that the South China Sea acts to both sunder and cohere the societies that surround it over thousands of kilometers. The littoral states of this body of water have traded, raided, and negotiated with each other for at least two thousand years. In the past several centuries, many of these interactions have been recorded in the vernacular languages of the region, as well as in the documents and ledgers of European archives.[63] The activities of smugglers, who were also vital in these binding processes, left far fewer documents, but were nevertheless important in helping to forge this common world. Contrabanders helped cement a unity to this maritime field, and their voyages connected diasporas to area ports and hinterlands, even if their watery tracks are no longer apparent in the evidentiary record. Occasionally these journeys do survive in the archives, however. If their echo does not seem that strange to us as contemporary humans, it is because so many of these voyages are still happen, all along the outstretched margins of the South China Sea.

The capitalist implications of this longevity are apparent into our own age. Domestic economies are influenced by such movements, and the official reporting of trade flows will never fully take into account the crucial importance that such journeys play in the economic development of local societies. Politically, too, the role of smuggling in the South China Sea is of great import, as the transit of a variety of commodities—including weapons, drugs, and trafficked human beings—makes clear immediately, just by mentioning the nature of such transited items. The passage of contraband certainly deserves a place in any serious discussion about the nature and evolution of the South China Sea as an integrated region, simply because it has been so important in both historical and contemporary eras as a medium of human connection.[64] These trends exhibit every evidence of pushing further into the twenty-first century as well, in marking out this maritime space's coherence as an integrated nautical domain.

63. For a *longue durée* look at the issues at stake in who speaks about smuggling, see Simon Harvey, *Smuggling: Seven Centuries of Contraband* (London: Reaktion Books, 2016).

64. For a glimpse of where smuggling fits into larger narratives about the history and present of the South China Sea, see Robert Kaplan, *Asia's Cauldron: The South China Sea and the End of a Stable Pacific* (New York: Random House, 2014).

5

The Center and Its Margins

HOW THE INDIAN OCEAN
BECAME "BRITISH"

... then only will human progress cease to resemble that hideous pagan idol,
who would not drink the nectar but from the skulls of the slain ...

—KARL MARX, "THE FUTURE RESULTS OF
BRITISH RULE IN INDIA"[1]

THE INDIAN OCEAN has been scrutinized from many angles in scholarly ex-
egeses seeking to explain the history of this huge maritime arena.[2] A number
of thinkers have focused on predation as a linking theme, charting how piracy
connected a broad range of actors for centuries in these dangerous waters.[3]
Others have focused on environmental issues, asking how patterns of winds,
currents, and weather allowed trade to flourish on such a vast, oceanic scale.

1. *New York Daily Tribune*, 8 August 1853.

2. For two recent multi-authored surveys, see Angela Schottenhammer, ed., *Early Global
Interconnectivity in the Indian Ocean World* (London: Palgrave Series in the Indian Ocean World,
2019), and Martha Chaiklin, Philip Gooding, and Gwyn Campbell, eds., *Animal Trade Histories
in the Indian Ocean World* (London: Palgrave Series in the Indian Ocean World, 2020).

3. Vijay Lakshmi Labh, "Some Aspects of Piracy in the Indian Ocean during the Early Modern Period," *Journal of Indian Ocean Studies* 2, no. 3 (1995): 259–69; and John Anderson, "Piracy
and World History: An Economic Perspective on Maritime Predation," in C. R. Pennell, *Bandits
at Sea* (New York University Press, 1991), 82–105. See also Sebastian Prange, "Measuring by the
Bushel: Reweighing the Indian Ocean Pepper Trade," *Historical Research* 84, no. 224 (May 2011):
212–35.

These latter historians have appropriated a page out of Braudel and have grafted his approaches to the Mediterranean to fit local, Indian Ocean realities.[4] Still other scholars have used different tacks, following trails of commodities such as pepper or precious metals, or even focusing on far-flung archaeological remains, in an attempt to piece together transregional histories from the detritus that civilizations left behind.[5] All of these epistemological vectors have shed light on the region as a whole, though through different tools and lenses, and via a variety of techniques of inquiry.

In spite of the concentricity of these projects of knowledge, however, we still don't have a broadly accurate reading of when in the last five hundred years trade started to phase toward production on a systemic scale, and the Indian Ocean started to become "modern" in the full sense of the term. Here I mean modernity as described by Eric Wolf: a set of conditions and processes whereby the world became linked through increasingly powerful hierarchies, especially in the past two centuries.[6] Adam Smith, writing in the 1770s, felt that the Indian Ocean was a site of enormous energy and flux: all along its shores, he saw commerce being pushed forward by millions of eager hands, although there were already ominous signs of developing inequalities. Smith

4. T. S. S. Rao and Ray Griffiths, *Understanding the Indian Ocean: Perspectives on Oceanography* (Paris: UNESCO, 1998); Vivian Louis Forbes, *The Maritime Boundaries of the Indian Ocean Region* (Singapore University Press, 1995).

5. M. N. Pearson, *Spices in the Indian Ocean World* (Ashgate: Variorum, 1996); Osmand Bopearachichi, ed., *Origin, Evolution, and Circulation of Foreign Coins in the Indian Ocean* (Delhi: Manohar, 1988); Om Prakash, *Precious Metals and Commerce: The Dutch East India Company and the Indian Ocean Trade* (Ashgate: Variorum, 1994); C. Scholten, *De Munten van de Nederlandsche Gebiedsdeelen Overzee, 1601–1948* (Amsterdam: J. Schulman, 1951); Jeremy Green, "Maritime Aspects of History and Archaeology in the Indian Ocean, Southeast and East Asia," in S. R. Rao, *The Role of Universities and Research Institutes in Marine Archaeology: Proceedings of the Third Indian Conference of Marine Archaeology* (Goa: National Institute of Oceanography 1994); S. R. Rao, ed., *Recent Advances in Marine Archaeology: Proceedings of the Second Indian Conference on Marine Archaeology of the Indian Ocean* (Goa: National Institute of Oceanography 1991); Tom Vosmer, "Maritime Archaeology, Ethnography and History in the Indian Ocean: An Emerging Partnership," in Himanshu Prabha Ray, *Archaeology of Seafaring* (Delhi: Pragati Publications, 1999).

6. See the argument as laid out by Eric Wolf in his *Europe and the People without History* (Berkeley: University of California Press, 1982). Also see in this context Sujit Sivasundaram's exciting new book, *Waves across the South: A New History of Revolution and Empire* (University of Chicago Press, 2020), which argues for the evolving modernity of this outstretched space through the lens of revolution.

felt that this massive trade ultimately ensnared all nations that participated in its conduct, regardless of geographic origins.[7] Karl Marx, thinking about this same arena nearly a century later, saw a different vista unfolding before his eyes. Production was now overtaking mercantilism as the organizing principle of wealth in the region, and England in particular was no longer keen on sharing the rewards of interaction. "In India," he wrote in the third volume of *Capital*, "the English applied their direct political and economic power, as masters and landlords, to destroying these small (indigenous) economic communities."[8] The ideas of these two historical thinkers are used here as broad foils in the pages that follow. Marx's theories and assumptions were indeed taken one step further by Michel Foucault in our own time, who saw in these transvaluations power as a necessary by-product of Europe's expanding knowledge, alongside its expanding markets.[9] Yet how did this happen on such a huge oceanic scale? Why did it happen, and did these changes take place at more or less the same speed in a wide variety of locales? These are some of the queries that will be analyzed in this portion of the book, when we look at the Indian Ocean as a corollary space to some of the patterns we have already identified in the South China Sea.

Ruminating about the past of large global spaces in these ways, whether land-based or oceanic, is not novel, of course. In the introduction of this book we noted that academics have adopted broad-visioned approaches to the Atlantic and Pacific Oceans for decades, to give only two examples. There is already a substantial literature on the Indian Ocean as a system per se, much of which (as stated earlier) was trailblazed by K. N. Chaudhuri's important work several decades ago.[10] Other scholars have followed him with notable success, chronicling the effects of the "contact period" and subsequent centuries from

7. Adam Smith, *An Inquiry into the Nature and Causes of the Wealth of Nations* (Clarendon: Oxford University Press, 1976), I:223–24; Ted Benton, "Adam Smith and the Limits to Growth" in Stephen Copley and Kathryn Sutherland, eds., *Adam Smith's Wealth of Nations: New Interdisciplinary Essays* (Manchester University Press, 1995) 144–70.

8. Karl Marx, *Capital* (New York: International Publishers, 1976), III:451.

9. See Richard Mardsen, *The Nature of Capital: Marx after Foucault* (London: Routledge, 1999). For an interesting critique of Foucault on modernism, see also Thomas Flynn, "Foucault and the Eclipse of Vision," in David Michael Levin, *Modernity and the Hegemony of Vision* (Berkeley: University of California Press, 1993), 273–86, especially 283.

10. K. N. Chaudhuri, *Trade and Civilisation in the Indian Ocean: An Economic History from the Rise of Islam to 1750* (Cambridge University Press, 1985).

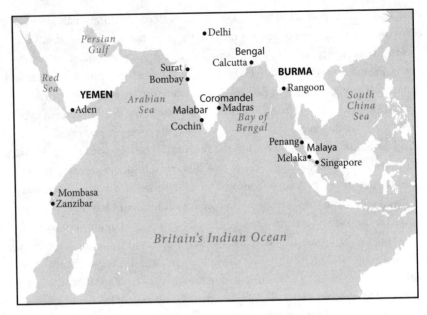

MAP 5.1. The Indian Ocean

economic, political, and social vantages.[11] Certainly religion has been crucial in thinking about the history of this ocean as well, as Buddhism, Islam, and finally Christianity contributed to the diffusion of ideas, ideologies, and people themselves in important ways. Indeed, all of these currents have been part of a larger historiographical attempt, particularly energetic in the last thirty years, to figure out when, where, and how current configurations of the global political economy took shape. Immanuel Wallerstein was a major voice in shaping this debate, and he has been joined by other important contributors, who have wrestled with his theories (and each other) in extremely vigorous ways.[12] Fortunately or unfortunately, the majority of heat and light

11. Denys Lombard and Jean Aubin, eds., *Marchands et hommes d'affaires asiatiques dans l'Océan Indien et la Mer de Chine 13–20 siècles* (Paris: Éditions de l'École des Hautes Études en Sciences Sociales, 1988); Sanjay Surahmanyam, *The Political Economy of Commerce: Southern India, 1500–1650* (Cambridge University Press, 1990); Kenneth McPherson, *The Indian Ocean: A History of People and the Sea* (Delhi: Oxford University Press, 1993).

12. Immanuel Wallerstein, *The Capitalist World-Economy* (Cambridge: Cambridge University Press, 1979), 1–36; Andre Gunder Frank, *ReOrient: Global Economy in the Asian Age* (Berkeley: University of California Press, 1998); David Landes, *The Wealth and Poverty of Nations: Why Some Are So Rich, and Some So Poor* (New York: W. W. Norton, 1998); Kenneth Pomeranz, *The Great Divergence: Europe, China, and the Making of the Modern World Economy* (Princeton

generated from these debates has concerned the ramifications of Europeans penetrating *East* Asian spheres. The Indian Ocean as a locus for examination has trailed behind the western Pacific, though there is no real reason why this state of affairs should be accepted by anyone.

This chapter tries to refocus some of the above-mentioned "heat and light" onto the interlinked shores of the Indian Ocean. It is particularly concerned with mapping out processes of trade and production, as elements of the former slowly started to phase into the latter on regional scales around this ocean's rim. The chapter starts off with an examination of these transvaluations in Southeast Asia, where the initial attention of Europeans was centered because of the wealth and renown of the international spice trade. The analysis then moves on to India, as the subcontinent gradually became the apple of England's eye in particular, replete with mercantile (and ultimately, productive) promise as well. Finally, the case of East Africa, the third major littoral of the Indian Ocean, is also considered, especially from the viewpoint of Zanzibar, where these changes were writ large over the last several centuries.[13] The primary contention of the chapter is that European hegemony in all three of these regions (as scholars increasingly recognize) was only achieved extremely gradually, and often *not* at the point of a gun. Rather, it was the awkward yet ultimately pervasive drive for control over regional means of production that really altered the flow of centuries of Indian Ocean history. What were the mechanics of this process? Where did these changes occur first, and in which forms were they expressed? There were several diasporic competitors implicated in the unfolding of these events, from the Portuguese, Dutch, and French to Indian merchant communities (both Hindu and Muslim) which circled the breadth of these seas. These actors, and several others, all helped mold the shape of things to come. Yet in the end it was only England that had the means to sustain these energies toward productive ends that Marx had predicted. This

---

University Press, 2000); A. J. R. Russell-Wood, "The Expansion of Europe Revisited: The European Impact on World History and Global Interaction, 1450–1800," *Itinerario*, 23, no. 1 (1994): 89–94; and Johan Matthew, *Margins of the Market: Trafficking and Capitalism across the Arabian Sea* (Berkeley: University of California Press, 2016).

13. Arabia, the Red Sea, and the Persian Gulf are not considered as a separate shore of the Indian Ocean in this piece, though they do figure in the narrative on India and especially East Africa. Nevertheless, I have particularly benefited from the work of René J. Barendse; see especially his "Reflections on the Arabian Seas in the Eighteenth Century," *Itinerario* 25, no. 1 (2000): 25–50, and his book *The Arabian Seas: The Indian Ocean World of the Seventeenth Century* (Armonk: M. E. Sharpe, 2002).

task was accomplished differently in different places, however, between the dawn of the seventeenth and the close of the nineteenth centuries. We can start seeing how, by focusing on Southeast Asia first.

The Eastern Rim of the Indian Ocean

The lands and seas now defined as "Southeast Asia" underwent a broad spectrum of transitions between 1600 and 1900, of which many were directly caused by the collision of European and indigenous worlds.[14] The ongoing results of this interface, however, were gradual in nature: hegemony did not arrive with the first Portuguese ships in the early sixteenth century, nor did European political and commercial power begin to gain a true paramountcy in much of the region until nearly 350 years later. Set against this mosaic of intrusion were local patterns of action, agency, and response. Heightened royal absolutism in the early years of contact, marked by indigenous territorial expansion, administrative centralization, and the commercial monopolies of ruling classes, gradually gave way to subsumption and finally incorporation as the European presence solidified. Adam Smith was already critical of what he saw as the deleterious effects of Western interventions in parts of Southeast Asia in the late eighteenth century.[15] Marx was even pithier in his condemnations ninety years later, when he described these regional European initiatives as backward and ultimately self-defeating.[16] Yet what remains to be explained in the unfolding of these processes is the actual place of Western trade as a stimulus for systemic historical change.

One good place to start in answering this question is Anthony Reid's attempt at grafting the *Annales* framework onto Southeast Asian history. He succeeds in charting the beginnings of this inquiry from a range of perspectives.[17] First among these, perhaps, is a broad delineation of what the region's economy looked like during the Age of Mercantilism and encroaching European power. Southeast Asia's population of 20 million traded heavily among themselves, mostly in the larger bulk items of commerce such as rice, dried

---

14. For a snapshot of what this world looked like before this period started, see Kenneth R. Hall, "Multi-Dimensional Networking: Fifteenth-Century Indian Ocean Maritime Diaspora in Southeast Asian Perspective," *JESHO* 49, no. 4 (2006): 454–81.

15. Smith, *Wealth of Nations*, I:91.

16. Marx, *Capital*, III:422.

17. Anthony Reid, *Southeast Asia in the Age of Commerce: The Lands Beneath the Winds* (New Haven: Yale University Press, 1988 and 1993).

fish, and salt. Foreign goods that did enter the nexus of trade in the early European contact period fit into local systems of culture and exchange, with alcohol circulating alongside native arrack, tobacco alongside betel, and Chinese porcelain being incorporated into existing dowry and burial rituals in Borneo and the southern Philippines.[18] The arrival of European ships accelerated the incorporation of a range other goods into the region, however, such as textiles and metals. Most pre–Industrial Age households in Southeast Asia aimed to be at least partially self-sufficient in cloth production, but with increased shipments of textiles from the Coromandel coasts of southeastern India (via Company and country-trade ships) and still higher exports later from British India, foreign cloth became the largest item of luxury expenditure in the region. This, of course, had enormous repercussions on Southeast Asian textile industries, which on the much smaller village scale could produce only on commissioned orders as hedges against inadequate food supply. The increased importation of metals also brought about widespread change, as substances like iron and bronze—used first for war and second for agriculture—penetrated local communities in large quantities for the first time. Fantastic in its potential for profit, but also deadly if turned against Westerners themselves, this trade was however a double-edged sword for Europeans.[19]

A failure to incorporate martial technologies quickly and efficiently could prove immediately fatal, so the military dimension of European arrival also initiated systemic change in Southeast Asian societies. Links with trade here were multifarious. The number of specialized mercenaries in Southeast Asian employ went directly up after the conquest of Melaka in 1511, consisting mostly of foreign traders/adventurers trained in firearms. Standing armies started to

18. Reid's emphasis on bulk commodities took issue with Jacob van Leur's characterization of trade as being "splendid but trifling"; see J. C. van Leur, *Indonesian Trade and Society: Essays in Asian Social and Economic History* (The Hague: W. van Hoeve, 1955). On the role of ceramics, see Barbara Harrison, *Pusaka: Heirloom Jars of Borneo* (Singapore: Oxford University Press, 1986); and Roxanna Brown, *The Ceramics of South-East Asia: Their Dating and Identification* (Singapore: Oxford University Press, 1988), 57–79.

19. A Dutch ship gutted in northeast Java in 1597 was pillaged almost immediately by dozens of local prahu; in 1609 Spanish troops in Mindanao removed all the bolts from one of their own ruined caravels, in the hope that they would not fall into Muslim hands. An interesting corollary to this Southeast Asian metal hunger is that often locals would pay more for certain metals based on cultural indices of value. This happened in the polities of the Javanese *pasisir*, where Sulawesi's high-nickel iron was preferred for manufacturing *krisses* (based on the swirling designs of the nickel etched in the blades) over the cheaper imported iron brought by Europeans and Chinese. See Reid, *Southeast Asia in the Age of Commerce*, I:107, 110.

be employed, rather than courts relying solely on local nobilities, and brick and stone buildings (which Europeans asked to maintain, ostensibly as warehouses resistant to accidental fires) were forbidden, as they could easily be fortified against royal power.[20] If the demographic, court, and even architectural matrices of power could be changed by the rise of European trade in the region, it should come as no surprise that Southeast Asian monarchs used these powers to tighten their control over their own expanding kingdoms. A perfect example exists in the musket expeditions sent by the sultan of Jambi in 1655 to his own hinterlands, enforcing pepper exactions so that the sultan would not default on his spice contracts with the VOC. While the Dutch were complaining that dirt, stones, and pith had now started appearing in large quantities in their pepper shipments, uplanders made clear their dissatisfaction with the new power inequalities by perpetrating such actions on a large scale. Eighteenth-century Sumatran folktales had fathers advising sons to "cut wood or catch fish, rather than become indebted (in the new enforced trade system) to the Raja or the Company."[21]

In fact, it was in the ruthless prosecution of the spice trade that Europeans most closely foreshadowed many changes in trade and production that would sweep over Southeast Asia in a more systemic fashion in subsequent centuries. The Dutch were particularly energetic in their attempts to control not only the commercial radials of spices but production at the source as well. Toward these ends, portions of the indigenous population of Maluku in Eastern Indonesia were tortured, killed, or deported in the seventeenth century, while British competitors were treated little better.[22] Yet the British ultimately regrouped

20. Mercenaries were hired from Japan, Arabia, Holland, France, and Persia; see Dhiravat da Pombejra, "Ayutthaya at the End of the Seventeenth Century: Was There a Shift to Isolation?," in Reid, ed., *Southeast Asia in the Early Modern Era*, 250–72; see also Anthony Reid, "Europe and Southeast Asia: The Military Balance," *James Cook University of North Queensland, Occasional Paper* 16 (Townsville: Queensland University Press, 1982), 1.

21. See Barbara Watson Andaya, "Cash-Cropping and Upstream/Downstream Tensions: The Case of Jambi in the 17th and 18th-Centuries," in Reid, ed., *Southeast Asia in the Early Modern Era*, 108. For a summation of Dutch activities in the Indian Ocean, see Eric Tagliacozzo, "The Dutch in Indian Ocean History," in *The Cambridge History of the Indian Ocean*, ed. Sugata Bose; vol. I, ed. Seema Alavi, Sunil Amrith, and Eric Tagliacozzo (Cambridge: Cambridge University Press, forthcoming.

22. See Leonard Andaya, *The World of Maluku: Eastern Indonesia in the Early Modern Period* (Honolulu: University of Hawai'i Press, 1993); Chris van Frassen, "Ternate, de Molukken and de Indonesische Archipel," PhD thesis, Leiden University, 2 vols., 1987; and the early historical chapters of Patricia Spyers, *The Memory of Trade* (Durham: Duke University Press, 2000).

elsewhere in the region, and started to parallel the Dutch transit system with spices (mainly nutmeg) and other agricultural exports (including pepper and gambier).[23] The important point here is that spices were an important entry point for Westerners into local circuits of commerce, exchange, and (eventually) production. Though there were historic booms and busts to these processes based on demand, competition, and overproduction, Europeans gained a foothold in different parts of the region in order to exploit trade opportunities that gradually phased into opportunities of an altogether more draconian nature.

It also bears saying that the influx of Western traders contributed to major changes in the social arenas of Southeast Asia as well. While male and female spheres of labor did not change drastically in many villages between 1600 and 1900, the relatively high position of women in coastal cities (versus China or India, for example) took a decided turn for the worse after the Age of Commerce. Most of this devolution can be attributed to the "cosmopolitan" nature of the ports, where Southeast Asian values came into conflict with the world religions of foreign traders, which often posited a less egalitarian place for women within the social fabric.[24] In these multiethnic ports, for example, prostitution grew in response to these more recently imported values, which did not sanction the temporary marriages that had been an indigenous hallmark of the early modern period.[25] Indeed, Reid also sees in these polyglot communities the development of nouveau riche commercial classes as well, as conspicuous consumption and an inability to gauge different peoples' hereditary status (exactly because of their foreignness) bred a new transnational clique comprised of people from various cultures. A wide range of data suggests the systemic cultural changes wrought by exploding trade, such as diverging indigenous and European skeleton heights over time (an index of the rising nutrition of the latter population group), indigenous chronicles, East Asian shipping logs, and European eyewitnesses, all discussing the spread of infectious disease.[26]

23. John Bastin, "The Changing Balance of the Southeast Asian Pepper Trade," in M. N. Pearson, *Spices in the Indian Ocean World* (Ashgate: Variorum, 1996), 283–316.

24. Anthony Reid, "Islamization and Christianization in Southeast Asia: The Critical Phase, 1550–1650," in Reid, ed., *Southeast Asia in the Early Modern Era*, 151–79.

25. For a snapshot of gender dynamics in the early modern period ports, see the essays in Barbara Watson Andaya, ed. *Other Pasts: Women, Gender and History in Early Modern Southeast Asia* (Honolulu: University of Hawai'i Press, 2000).

26. Using a time series of measurements, Reid juxtaposes the near-equal 5′2″ heights of Europeans and Filipinos in the seventeenth century (based on Robert Fox's excavations at

The British presence in the region became increasingly amplified in both commercial and geopolitical circles by the eighteenth and nineteenth centuries. Much of this activity centered around the crucial Straits of Melaka. Dianne Lewis has identified the four principal vectors of British movement in this period: a concern to acquire command of the sea-lanes, an attempt at maintaining a favorable balance of power back in Europe, a search for outlets for the nation's new industrial capacity, and a desire to protect the agglomerating territories that were becoming British India.[27] Well into the seventeenth century Southeast Asian rulers on the whole had to be much more concerned with their own internecine struggles than with European rivalry, but by the 1760s Anglo-Dutch competition in the region (punctuated by British demands for free trade and the acquisition of bases like Penang in 1786) launched a new specter of territorial conquest that heretofore had been unseen.[28] The Napoleonic Wars allowed the British to overrun the East Indies and prosecute their own trade, but the archipelago was later ceded to Holland as a means of keeping that country afloat as a buffer between Great Powers in Europe.[29] The resultant 1824 Anglo-Dutch Treaty stood as a watershed in Melaka Strait history: for the first time the Malay-speaking world was split along segmented lines, the islands coming under Dutch sway, and the Malay peninsula under an English sphere of influence. On a more practical level, the new spatial arrangement delineated new economic and political postures based on an agenda of British trade. Tin and other products of the Malay sultanates became more attractive as sources farther south in Indonesia were now closed, and local power connections became vital to maintain influence over

Calatagan), to a Western jump to 5'6" mean male height two centuries later. The cross-referencing on disease outbreaks between *hikayats*, *sejarahs*, Chinese, and Japanese trading accounts and European ship-captains' logs is also impressive. See Robert Fox, "The Calatagan Excavations," *Philippine Studies* 7, no. 3 (1959): 325–90; and Reid, *Southeast Asia in the Age of Commerce*, I:47–8, 61.

27. The Dutch, meanwhile, started to fall behind by the eighteenth century. See Dianne Lewis, *Jan Compagnie in the Straits of Malacca, 1641–1795* (Athens, OH: Ohio University Press, 1995).

28. J. A. de Moor, "'A Very Unpleasant Relationship': Trade and Strategy in the Eastern Seas, Anglo-Dutch Relations in the Nineteenth Century from a Colonial Perspective," in G. J. A Raven and N. A. M Rodger, eds., *Navies and Armies: The Anglo-Dutch Relationship in War and Peace 1688–1988* (Edinburgh: Donald Co., 1990), 46–69.

29. J. H. Zeeman, *De Kustvaart in Nederlandsch-Indië, Bechouwd in Verband met het Londensch Tractaat van 17 Maart 1824* (Amsterdam: Zeeman, 1936).

Terengganu and Johor, both of which were British "hinterlands" in an emerging British empire.[30]

As with Reid's use of skeleton heights in his charting of the larger effects of European trade on the region, Terengganu, in fact, makes for an interesting case study toward larger insights. Nicholas Tarling also succeeds in using various smaller phenomena—which can be refracted up to macrocosm—to illuminate larger processes of the age. The furor that developed over the junk *Kim Eng Seng* is a useful example. In 1851 a Chinese junk out of Singapore destroyed several Malay prahus off the coast of Kelantan; the junk was later chased down by the sultan's gunboats, the crew captured and summarily executed. An inquiry by the Singaporean government revealed that the junk was a trading vessel that was heavily armed, and that based on testimonies of surviving (escaped) crewmen on both sides, each party had probably mistaken the other for pirates. The incident reveals several trends. First, that piracy was rampant along the Malay coasts, and this was particularly so because of the increased volume of British trade, in this case to Singapore. Second, dual roles were developing for traders-cum-pirates (as suggested by the massive ordnance the *Kim Eng Seng* was carrying), as indigenous coastal dwellers were eager to take advantage of *all* avenues of profit: piracy, trade, or an admixture of the two.[31] The *Kim Eng Seng* incident also suggests the increasingly complicated vectors developing between international law, diplomatic strategy, policy, and reparations as an attempt was made to settle the issue. At base, highminded morality was probably not atop the agenda of most British merchants when they complained to the *Singapore Free Press* (16 July 1852): "Our government seems disposed to leave traders sailing out of this port to the tender mercies of the native Rajas who may chuse [*sic*] to appropriate their goods and put them to death on any charge, however unfounded."[32] Yet perhaps even more revealing was the final compensation demanded from the sultan of Trengganu: $11,190, two thousand dollars of which was for loss of life, the

30. For some of the historical context on these processes in Johor, see Leonard Andaya, *The Kingdom of Johor, 1641–1728: A Study of Economic and Political Developments in the Straits of Malacca* (Kuala Lumpur: Oxford University Press, 1975).

31. This mirrors the ambiguity of piracy and trade that exists, to some extent, in these same waters today. A certain percentage of craft that commit piratical acts in the Strait of Melaka do so opportunistically, plying commerce as their primary activity at other moments on their voyages. Tagliacozzo, 1990 fieldwork notes, 239.

32. Nicholas Tarling, *Imperial Britain in Southeast Asia* (Kuala Lumpur: Oxford University Press, 1975) 81.

remainder ($9,090) asked toward appropriation of property. The relative equities of British morality were quite clear.

These valuations are instructive, but we can also follow the effects of English commerce into a time when dominion became more important than free trade. Though there was a continuum of British interest in the region throughout the course of the nineteenth century, the theory and practice of England's overseas empire eventually changed from strict mercantilism to idealized free trade, and finally to imperial land-grabbing. Traditionally, 1870 has been posited as a very rough dividing line for the shift into "High Colonialism" in much of the literature.[33] Before this time, diplomacy was preferred by the Company and the Crown to outright violence, the former a cheaper alternative toward the same goal: ever-expanding markets. Free trade was best because Britain, simply, was best at trade: her factories and mills (in England and India) made the highest-quality exports, and her ships carried goods cheaper and more extensively than any of her rivals. Penang (founded in 1786) grew out of this free-trade philosophy, as did Singapore (founded in 1819); belated Dutch attempts to mimic these policies with free-trade ports of her own (in Riau, Makassar, and Ambon) ultimately failed. Yet, as the nineteenth century wore on, Britain started to lose its competitive advantage to industrial newcomers such as Germany, Japan, and the United States, a process that would have been even more painful *without* her expanding colonial markets. Centralized policies changed: it now became imperative, as Eric Wolf has shown, to take over existing areas of wealth and production (the arable land and ports of Malaya, for example), while hedging on the potential of new domains such as Australia. Those who stood everything to gain by the unfolding of the process were British private traders in Asia, and they inexorably pushed this process along.[34]

During the course of the nineteenth century, Britain's relationship with coastal Burma bears out this hypothesis of phasing politics and trade very well. In the early 1800s, the primary British view of Burma was one predicated on the safety of Bengal: trade was desirable but not imperative, and what commercial possibilities that did exist were judged as paramount in the Chinese transit-trade, not in any innate Burmese potential. A border war in 1824 ceded Arakan and some "breathing room" to the growing Bengal residency, but served more to elucidate the now enormous possibilities of commerce to

33. Eric Hobsbawm, *The Age of Empire 1875–1914* (New York: Pantheon, 1987.)

34. Eric Wolf, *Europe and the People without History*; Anthony Webster, *Gentleman Capitalists: British Imperialism in South East Asia 1770–1890* (London: Tauris, 1998).

Yunnan as described by several British travelers into the interior.[35] Rubies, amber, jade, and teak all lay alongside these routes, not to mention the flourishing carrying trade in cotton, which the British envisioned would clothe 40 million Chinese along that kingdom's southwestern border. Local English merchants based in Arakan, Tenasserim, Singapore, and India did not take long to smell these opportunities, and through a concerted campaign of lobbying (and manipulation of the existing Burmese trade situation to a point where imperial prestige demanded a flexing of muscle to protect the national honor) succeeded in driving London to annex lower Burma in 1852.[36] While the Burmese tried to forestall further disaster through concessions and an amicable pliancy, allowing (though lamenting) extensive British surveying and exploration on Burmese soil, the transition from trade to conquer shifted into high gear toward the end of the century.[37] Upper Burma finally fell in the 1880s, and Britain eyed the possibilities of a "back door to China" and the encroaching French Mekong expeditions with vigilant eyes.

Yet, in keeping with the theme of indigenous agency and response to these shifts in the British trading presence in Southeast Asia, it is perhaps best to end this sketch of cause and effect with a comparative success story, the case of Siam. Here too the familiar pattern of European trade, eventual encroachment, and widening dominion could have been played out, but through the vagaries of geography and with shrewd royal maneuvering such events did not come to pass. As with the Burmese situation, a tension existed all along between London and Calcutta on the one hand (which saw Siam as a potential ally against the Burmese and a valuable buffer state versus the French) and the British trading bloc in Asia (which consistently tried to penetrate Sino/Siamese commerce, and draw Britain in—by force, if necessary—to accomplish these goals). Although all of the elements of gunboat diplomacy were present in

35. Andrew Turton, "Ethnography of Embassy: Anthropological Readings of Records of Diplomatic Encounters Between Britain and Tai States in the Early Nineteenth Century," *South East Asia Research* 5, no. 2 (1997): 175.

36. Many of the "true" initiatives behind the campaign can be seen in small actions committed after the occupation was already accomplished, such as the extension of the new border between Upper and Lower Burma fifty miles north from the line originally agreed upon, to include valuable forests of teak. A.G. Pointon, *The Bombay-Burma Trading Corporation* (Southampton: Milbrook Press, 1964), 12.

37. See the translated Burmese letter (probably from 1876) reproduced in *British Documents on Foreign Affairs: Reports and Papers from the Foreign Office Confidential Print*, vol. E26 (Washington, D.C.: University Press of America, 1995), 104–5.

Siam as they had been in Burma and China, the kingdom managed to avoid direct colonization. The price for this freedom, however, was the decline of its flourishing China trade, and of much of Siam's economic autonomy to Britain as well.[38] King Mongkut's sensitivity (and that of the powerful Bunnag family) to the vastly changing ideological landscape of the European powers surrounding him let him gauge correctly that economic openness—rather than the xenophobia of his neighbors—was the only way toward his kingdom's survival.[39] The voracious British trade interests of Asia received their open markets, and with them, the major rationale for political domination (in this case) disappeared. Europeans of varying nationalities peppered the royal court as advisers, and Siamese rice left Siamese docks on British steamers, but the gilded crown of the kingdom remained atop Chulalongkorn's head during the apex of the age of dominion. This fact, considering the onslaught of almost four centuries of British and European trade, was about as encouraging a situation as any local kingdom could hope for, given the circumstances.

Ocean's Northern Rim

Analyzing the web of commerce and politics between Westerners and indigenous peoples in India complements and metamorphoses these Southeast Asian currents to a considerable degree.[40] How similar, and how different, were these processes in a different Indian Ocean theater? Were the lines of

38. Chinese junks fell from 400 per annum to under 100 within a decade of the Bowring Treaty (1856), while British shipping carried 87 percent of Siamese tonnage by the year 1892. One contemporary Englishman boasted that Siamese brought rice to the mills, but there their part in the economic process ceased: the machinery was British, the jute packing bags were fashioned in Calcutta, the steamers were from London, and the banks and insurers that financed the entire operation were British as well. See D. R. Sardesai, *British Trade and Expansion in Southeast Asia, 1830–1914* (Delhi: Allied Publishers, 1977), 92–93. See also Jennifer Cushman, *Fields from the Sea: Chinese Junk Trade with Siam during the Late 18th and Early 19th Centuries* (Ithaca: Cornell Southeast Asia Program, 1993); and Ian Brown, *The Elite and the Economy in Siam, 1890–1920* (Oxford: Oxford University Press, 1988).

39. Pasuk Phongpaichit and Chris Baker, *Thailand: Economy and Politics* (Kuala Lumpur: Oxford University Press, 1995).

40. For a sense of the international context, see, among others: Sugata Bose, ed., *South Asia and World Capitalism* (Oxford: Oxford University Press, 1991); Nile Green, *Bombay Islam: The Religious Economy of the Western Indian Ocean, 1840–1915* (New York: Cambridge University Press, 2011); Pier Martin Larson, *Ocean of Letters: Language and Creolization in an Indian Ocean Diaspora* (Cambridge: Cambridge University Press, 2009); and Ronit Ricci, *Islam Translated:*

contact, trade, and ultimately coercion analogous or incomparable across these regional arenas? To answer these questions, we need to chart out the broad brushstrokes of historical dynamics along the northern rim of "India's Ocean," chronicling change again from the Braudelian perspective of the *longue durée*. We can then take the equation one step further, examining how the seeds of power, commerce, and dominion came to be intertwined in the early stages of England's arrival. Finally, we need to glance at the changing nature of relations between Indian and Western traders over time, as the latter gradually pushed the former into a subordinated position within the new structures of empire. The sum total of these approaches is a growing portrait of partnership and change, as well as competition and domination—what Adam Smith called the "incurably faulty" evolution of European administration in India.[41] Marx, as with the case of Southeast Asia, described the unfolding of these processes as the destruction of an entire way of life—an even more damning appraisal than what Smith had to offer.[42]

The evolution of trade relations between the subcontinent and the outside world can be analyzed chronologically by individual century, a useful (if rather artificial) mode of analysis. A feeling for trade before the arrival of Europeans can be sketched through several factors. The monsoons were of crucial importance to the international orbit of trade, dictating prices and opportunities based on the timetables of ships' arrivals and departures.[43] Multicultural exchange was already a central fact of life in the region, as seen by the lists of visitors to ports such as Calicut and Cochin in the southwestern reaches of the subcontinent.[44] India's place in commodity specialization was also crucial, with her textiles, spices, and luxuries traveling to port cities all along the shores

---

Literature, Conversion and the Arabic Cosmopolis of South and Southeast Asia (Chicago: University of Chicago Press, 2011).

41. Smith, *Wealth of Nations*, II:638.

42. Karl Marx, *Capital*, III:452.

43. S. Z. Qasim, "Concepts of Tides, Navigation and Trade in Ancient India," *Journal of Indian Ocean Studies* 8, no. 1/2 (2000): 97–102.

44. Arabians, Persians, Syrians, Egyptians, Maghrebis, Sumatrans, people from Pegu, and Chinese are all mentioned as visitors to these cities; evidence of these pre-European communities can still be seen in Cochin, for example, in the synagogue and Jewish community surviving on "Jew Town Road," and the Chinese cantilevered fishing nets (brought by ambassadors of the Great Khan in the thirteenth century) overhanging Cochin harbor. For more on the early maritime relationships of Southwest India, see Haraprasad Ray, "Sino-Indian Historical Relations: Quilon and China," *Journal of Indian Ocean Studies* 8, nos. 1/2 (2000): 116–28.

of this enormous ocean. This was especially true in the Bay of Bengal, where finished cotton cloth left Eastern India for Southeast Asia in huge quantities. The cadence of India's coasts was therefore outward rather than inward: as with most of the other ports of this extended marine region, Indian Ocean littorals often had much more in common with each other than with their own immediate hinterlands. This was particularly so in the realm of religion, as Theravada Buddhism had long since left Sri Lanka for Burma and Siam, and Islam had also departed Gujarat for the Malay Peninsula and Indonesia. The confluence of winds and tides brought ships to India's ports on intermediate stages of their transoceanic journeys, ensuring the subcontinent's importance because of its median geography at the "roof" of the ocean.

We understand now that the sixteenth century, which has been portrayed in older literature as a cataclysmic epoch of Portuguese arrival (with the consequent fire and sword), was often very much less than that.[45] Overall patterns of India's trade and the mechanisms therein did not universally change during this century. While the Portuguese erected their *cartaz* (pass) system the cost to local traders was sometimes minimal: though many Indians did pay the passage fees, those in areas under weaker Portuguese surveillance and policing simply avoided it altogether. The Zamorins of Calicut and the Rajas of Cochin, Cannanore, and Quilon, for example (all on the Malabar coast) continued to trade, incorporating themselves under the umbrella of Portuguese "protection" when they had to, but also ignored the Portuguese at other times and in other places. Yet the majority of early modern Indians, especially under the Mughals, whose revenue came primarily from the land and *not* the sea, were not greatly affected by the Portuguese caravels.[46] The Mughal aphorism, "Wars by sea are merchants' affairs, and are of no concern to the prestige of kings,"

45. For two revisionist histories, see K. S. Mathew, "Trade in the Indian Ocean during the Sixteenth Century and the Portuguese," in K. S. Mathew, ed., *Studies in Maritime History* (Pondicherry: Pondicherry University Press, 1990) 13–28; and Sanjay Subrahmanyam, "Profit at the Apostle's Feet: The Portuguese Settlement of Mylapur in the Sixteenth Century," in Sanjay Subrahmanyam, *Improvising Empire: Portuguese Trade and Settlement in the Bay of Bengal* (Delhi: Oxford University Press, 1990), 47–67.

46. For an early look into the Mughal court by Europeans not beholden to the Portuguese project, see these Italian sources: G. Tucci, "Del supposto architetto del Taj e di altri italiani alla Corte dei Mogul," *Nuova Antologia* CCLXXI (1930), 77–90; G. Tucci, *Pionieri italiani in India*, *Asiatica* 2(1936), 3–11; G. Tucci, *Pionieri italiani in India*, in G. Tucci, *Forme dello spirito asiatico* (Milan and Messina, 1940), 30–49.

operated in the royal court.[47] India's foreign shipping to the Middle East and Southeast Asia remained largely in indigenous hands in the early years of European arrival, despite strenuous Portuguese attempts to the contrary.

The balance of Indian commerce began to change only with the arrival of the seventeenth century, and the far more organized Dutch and British concerns. Yet even here, such change often benefited Indian trade instead of crippling it. Though we need to be mindful of the available sources, the records actually seem to indicate that the arrival of Northern Europeans initially served as a boon for indigenous commerce, providing new capital, shipping, navigational technology, and marketing, all for Indians to use. Thus Gujarati trade extended to Manila in the 1660s, using British ships and navigation routs while Gujarati capital often funded the voyages.[48] The diversity of trade and its actors stood out in this period—by region, religion, and linguistic group— as well as by occupation, as when English pilots sailed Tamil and Bengali ships. Even so, the cluttering presence of Europeans served to augur change in other ways, as when Anglo-Dutch naval rivalries endangered the stability of travel. European patronage hastened the "life cycles" of Indian cities, ascending Surat in favor of Cambay, for example, though such processes had larger international (and even local) causes as well.[49] European bottoms provided greater speed and reliability, by virtue of sturdier ship construction (nails versus sewn

47. M. N. Pearson, "India and the Indian Ocean in the Sixteenth Century," in *India and the Indian Ocean 1500–1800*, ed. Ashin Das Gupta and M. N. Pearson (Calcutta: Oxford University Press, 1987), 71–93, at 79; see also Syed Hasan Askarai, "Mughal Naval Weakness and Aurangzeb's Attitude towards the Traders and Pirates on the Western Coast," *Journal of Indian Ocean Studies* 2, no. 3 (1995): 236–42.

48. For a description of the enduring diversities of this trade to Manila, even a century later, see Thomas and Mary McHale, eds, *The Journal of Nathaniel Bowditch in Manila, 1796* (New Haven: Yale University Southeast Asian Studies, 1962).

49. One can still really feel the effects of this dynamic in Cambay, which is now a quiet "fringe city" compared to the more prosperous Surat: Tagliacozzo, 1990 fieldwork notes, 380. The later Mughal need for a dominant transit port also helped Surat vis-à-vis Cambay, while a rise in pilgrims undertaking the Hajj (and the rising price of coffee as a commodity) vaulted Mocha over Muscat in the seventeenth-century Arabian Peninsula. For some of the permutations of trade in Gujarat, see Shireen Moosvi, "The Gujarat Ports and Their Hinterland: The Economic Relationship," in Indu Banga, ed., *Ports and Their Hinterlands in India, 1700–1950* (Delhi: Manohar, 1992), 121–30; Aniruddha Ray, "Cambay and Its Hinterland: The Early Eighteenth Century," in Banga, ed., *Ports and Their Hinterlands*, 131–52; and Ashin Das Gupta, "The Merchants of Surat," in *Elites in South Asia*, ed. Edmund Leach and S. N. Mukherjee (Cambridge: Cambridge University Press, 1970).

FIGURE 5.1. Indian Stevedore, Cochin, Kerala (author's photo)

planks) and sleeker ship designs, although Indians had to pay for protection more often than before.[50]

From the standpoint of Indian choices, the eighteenth century pushed change in a new direction, which was a negative one. Although European trade did not initially hurt most Indian merchants, Indian shippers suffered a different fate: as more and more of the carrying trade was monopolized by foreign vessels, India's fleets dwindled, shrinking in competition with the new

50. Baldeo Sahai, *Indian Shipping: A Historical Survey* (Delhi: Ministry of Information, 1996), 208–51.

so-called country traders. It was this special-interest bloc, diverse in its own right, that began to nudge the once sizable Gujarati fleets off some of the international trade routes and gradually into the more minor, subsidiary role of small coastal carriers.[51] Yet it was also these Anglo-Indian country traders—some of whom worked for the Company, others of whom were "free traders"—who began to radically alter the "strange Mughal mix of despotism, traditional rights, and equally-traditional freedoms" that was the prevailing system of trade and production in the rural Indian countryside (port merchants to brokers to sub-brokers to headmen to weavers to indigo growers, etc.)[52] We can return to this in a moment, but it is in precisely these mutations that we see Eric Wolf's gradations between kin and capital modes of production beginning to blur. Most always with the help of local merchants, Westerners were able to reorient production away from traditional destinations and into conduits of their own design.[53] Surat, for example, changed from a cloth- and indigo-exporting town (to the Middle East) into a Company entrepôt geared toward China exports.[54] The traditional "Mughal ladder" of production in the countryside was eventually phased out of existence: Indian middlemen lost out to country traders, who hired their own Indian facilitators now as salaried employees. Europeans, but particularly the British, penetrated farther into the Indian countryside, creating new bonds of commercial and productive dependency as the eighteenth century wore on.[55]

51. Savitri Chandra, "Sea and Seafaring as Reflected in Hindi Literary Works During the 15th to 18th Centuries," in Matthew, ed., *Studies in Maritime History*, 84–91; and R. Tirumalai, "A Ship Song of the Late 18th Century in Tamil," in Matthew, ed., *Studies in Maritime History*, 159–64. See also Pedro Machado's recent work, cited elsewhere in this book.

52. Ashin Das Gupta, "India and the Indian Ocean in the Eighteenth Century," in *India and the Indian Ocean*, ed. Gupta and Pearson, 136.

53. On this question broadly, see Sugata Bose, *Peasant Labour and Colonial Capital: Rural Bengal Since 1770* (Cambridge: Cambridge University Press 1993); Kum Kum Banerjee, "Grain Traders and the East India Company: Patna and Its Hinterland in the Late Eighteenth and Early Nineteenth Centuries," in Sanjay Subrahmanyam, ed., *Merchants, Markets, and the State in Early Modern India* (Delhi: Oxford University Press, 1990), 163–89; and Lakshmi Subramanian, "Western India in the Eighteenth Century: Ports, Inland Towns, and States," in *Ports and Their Hinterlands*, ed. Banga, 153–80.

54. Dilbagh Singh and Ashok Rajshirke, "The Merchant Communities in Surat: Trade, Trade Practices, and Institutions in the Late Eighteenth Century," in *Ports and Their Hinterlands*, ed. Banga, 181–98.

55. See Philip Stern, *The Company-State: Corporate Sovereignty and the Early Modern Foundations of the British Empire in India* (New York: Oxford University Press, 2011).

This ripening process of dependence, and the gradual shifts in its evolution, can be explored here with more nuance. Power and politics were also part and parcel of the wider undertaking of British trade. As with the Portuguese, the English did not simply blast their way into dominance by way of their superior firepower and technology; this is important because later on these advantages truly did came to bear for the British. Although we need to acknowledge the general tenets of Europe's "military revolution," the disequilibrium created by such advances, as in Southeast Asia, really had little lasting effect in India until the mid-eighteenth century.[56] There were simply too few Portuguese and Dutch soldiers in the subcontinent ever to force significant changes in trade, and when British armies did appear en masse, it was primarily to counter the French.[57] This was the moment when power and commerce seriously began to fuse, as European rivals were ejected and England found itself in a position for the first time to enforce its programs for trade. India's actions and responses to this evolution were neither static nor unimaginative: armament design was incorporated and European mercenaries adopted, with one Briton observing that "hardly a ship comes [in the 1760s] that does not sell the Indians cannon or small arms."[58] Bloody battles fought by the British against the Nawab of Bengal and the Wazir of Oudh in the 1760s and against Mysore and the Marathas later in the eighteenth century were a testament to this near equilibrium. Local Indian rulers cast about for allies, including to the Ottoman Sultans, and were told that exertions would indeed be made between "brethren Mussalmans according to the obligations of religion and towards defending Hindustan itself."[59] The balance did change, however, and British capabilities

56. Larger armies and navies, heightened specialization, professionalization, higher codes of discipline, and greater control of the state being several of these tenets. See Geoffrey Parker, *The Military Revolution: Military Innovation and the Rise of the West, 1500–1800* (Cambridge: Cambridge University Press, 1996).

57. On the Dutch and French presence in India, see H. K. s' Jacob, "De VOC en de Malabarkust in de 17de eeuw," in M. A. P. Meilink-Roelofsz, ed., *De VOC in Azië* (Bussum: Unieboek, 1976), 85–99; Om Prakash, *The Dutch Factories in India, 1617–1623* (Delhi: Munshiram, 1984); and Indrani Ray, ed., *The French East India Company and the Trade of the Indian Ocean* (Calcutta: Munshiram, 1999).

58. P. J. Marshall, *Trade and Conquest: Studies on the Rise of British Dominance in India* (Aldershot: Variorum, 1993), 27; on mercenaries, see G. V. Scammell, "European Exiles, Renegades and Outlaws and the Maritime Economy of Asia," in Mathew, *Mariners, Merchants, and Oceans,* 121–42.

59. See the letter from Sultan Salim to Tipu Sultan of 20 September 1798 reproduced in Kabir Kausar, compiler, *Secret Correspondence of Tipu Sultan* (New Delhi: Manohar, 1980), 253–65.

to enforce trade and structural change along with it, in the nineteenth century. This was when the costs of shipping troops out to the colonies began to significantly diminish, and when arms production went up in Europe at the same time.

It is clear though that before 1784, any sort of truly integrated British policy toward Indian trade was practically non-existent. Previous to this date, the Company, the home government, and the individual presidencies (Bombay, Bengal, and Madras) all made highly uncoordinated decisions, but by January of that year the London Board of Control and the governor-general of India had been established to streamline control. Coupled with the disintegration of the Mughal polity and the expulsion of the French, the British—with new powers of organization and the manpower to back it up—faced an India radically different from the one they had previously known. While the East India Company still professed that it did not want to absorb territory, significant arms of the organization—the army, navy, and private trade interest *within* the structure of the Company—pushed for just such acquisitions. Coercive power was seen by these interests as the key to stability, enrichment, and the greater good of the empire. Statistically, 1784 seems to serve as a watershed for heightened British investment, as the Company and its agents brought the very real specter of force to their trade negotiations with Indian courts. Private traders collected "donations" for helping to influence local succession struggles, while "presents" were forwarded to Englishmen who helped settle internecine campaigns. These perquisites initially came in grants of revenue production (such as weaving villages, collecting rights, and grants on indigo manufacturing), but increasingly they came in the form of investitures of land.[60] British laissez-faire attitudes toward trade had shifted to a clear favoring of direct administration by the turn of the nineteenth century.

A useful test case of these changing dynamics can be found in the dominions of Oudh. P. J. Marshall has shown how Oudh was first attacked by the British in 1764 and large tracts of its territory annexed in 1801. Yet, before this

---

60. These complicated currents are treated well in the following works: P. J. Marshall, "Private Trade in the Indian Ocean Before 1800," in *India and the Indian Ocean*, ed. Gupta and Pearson, 276–300; S. Arasaratnam, "Weavers, Merchants, and Company: The Handloom Industry in South-Eastern India 1750–1790," in *Merchants, Markets*, ed. Sanjay Subrahmanyam, 190–214; Bruce Watson, "Indian Merchants and English Private Interests: 1659–1760," in *India and the Indian Ocean*, ed. Gupta and Pearson, 301–16; and Ashin Das Gupta, *Merchants of Maritime India, 1500–1800* (Ashgate: Variorum, 1994), chapter 14.

latter date, the mechanics of domination pushed forward in a steady onslaught. Indigo cultivators and cotton weavers in the province were already responding to Calcutta's demands by 1764, but more and more these producers came under the direct (or indirect) British yoke.[61] In 1765 Clive gained the right to station troops in Oudh by restoring the wazir to his throne, with further troop allowances and subsidies demanded soon after that. During that same year, Nabob Nudjum-ul-Dowlah had declared himself "graciously pleased to grant to the English Company the Dewanny of Bengal, Behar [Bihar], and Orissa," in return for annual revenues that paid off all of his expenses.[62] In 1773 a Company Resident was installed into the Oudh government, primarily to facilitate a similar flow of payments here. Meanwhile, the wazir himself was paying for the Company soldiers' salaries, ostensibly as protection against rival territories and polities. Private British capital quickly took advantage of this promising situation. The resident and his successors (against the dictates of the Company) gained a monopoly on the production of saltpeter, while free merchants like John Scott marketed piece goods, built factories, and supplied the Company with textiles under subcontract. There are many other similar stories, but the important aspect here is the pattern: country traders would not submit to the wazir's courts, evaded paying his customs, set up their own local monopolies, and struck their own bargains with local merchants and aristocrats. Whenever they felt their presence threatened, They could always in fact ask for the East India Company's protection, when and if they saw themselves being threatened.

This begs the question, however: How did Indian merchants—who seemingly had the most to lose by these penetrations—respond to the unfolding new parameters of trade?[63] This is an important question. There were enormous possibilities of Anglo-Dutch partnership in the early phase of European arrival, when British and Indian merchants often complemented each other to maximize their respective profits. The earliest country traders simply did

---

61. Bengali textiles sold very well in Europe and America, with the demands for cotton spilling over into Oudh—where its price was cheaper—as well. By 1800 it was said that "every foreign ship importing bullion into Calcutta brings this bullion especially for Oudh piece goods." See Marshall, *Trade and Conquest*, 475–6. See also Joseph Brennig, "Textile Producers and Production in Late Seventeenth Century Coromandel," in *Merchants, Markets*, ed. Subrahmanyam, 66–89.

62. "Agreement between the Nabob Nudjum-ul-Dowlah and the Company, 12 August 1765," in Barbara Harlow and Mia Carter, eds., *Imperialism and Orientalism: A Documentary Sourcebook* (Oxford: Wiley, 1999), 6.

63. On this question generally, see Bose, *Peasant Labour and Colonial Capital*.

not have the necessary resources to trade effectively on their own, and, as the Company took a dim view of any activities that competed with the organization's profit, Englishmen were forced to turn elsewhere for help. Indians were engaged as partners in a variety of roles—investors, managers, agents, and bankers—who directed trade and the flow of commodities toward concerns the Company ignored.[64] These earliest partnerships often existed in the "interstices" of Company trade, where the directors allowed them to flourish as supplementary lines of commerce. Yet as time went on, such sidelights in fact grew enormously in proportion. Men such as the governor of Madras, Elihu Yale, working mostly in association with local Tamil merchants, made huge private fortunes.[65]

We have already explored the growth of this country trade, and the concomitant expansion of British power in the subcontinent that we have already explored, helped change the nature of cooperation in the eighteenth century.[66] Yet "helping" and "causing" are two different things: larger, structural shifts were already disadvantaging Indian trade by the middle decades of the century. British economic pressure in the subcontinent was already meeting with seriously debilitated competition. A prime example here were the new international handicaps experienced by Muslim Indian shippers, as chaos in the Middle East forced huge exactions on traditional Gujarati networks, while many of the main ports of Southeast Asia came under pan-Christian control.[67] The fortunes of British trade at that time were moving in exactly the opposite direction: concessions near Surat (1759) and in Malabar (1790s), Penang (1786), and Bengkulu (1770s) were expanding English markets, instead of causing contraction. Indeed, in India new arteries of trade were also being established *between* British possessions, as opportunities expanded for shipping grain, pulses, saltpeter, and spirits to the burgeoning British armies.

64. S. Arasaratnam, *Maritime India in the Seventeenth Century* (Delhi: Oxford University Press, 1994), chapter 7. This is to say nothing of the gendered partnerships that also occurred; see Durba Ghosh, *Sex and the Family in Colonial India: The Making of Empire* (New York: Cambridge University Press, 2006).

65. Arasaratnam, *Maritime Trade*, chapter 3.

66. On this notion writ large, especially in the realm of ideas, see Robert Travers, *Ideology and Empire in Eighteenth-Century India* (Cambridge: Cambridge University Press, 2009); for a more regional-based examination of this process, see also Andrew Sartori, *Bengal in Global Concept History: Culturalism in the Age of Capital* (Chicago: University of Chicago Press, 2008).

67. Patricia Risso, *Merchants and Faith: Muslim Commerce and Culture in the Indian Ocean* (Boulder: Westview Press, 1995), 77–98.

The changing complexion of ships calling at India's major ports registered these changes.[68] What is harder to register, though it seems no less true, is that English country traders were building up a reservoir of local trade knowledge that they once had to procure from others. No longer considered unconditionally necessary to the success of British ventures, Indian compradorial partners who were once regarded as equals saw their statures diminished.[69]

Writing Indian merchants out of their own commercial history by the mid-eighteenth century would be a serious mistake, however. The active agency of these traders found new ways to survive, even in associations that are sometimes quite surprising. Faced with marginalization on a grand scale, Indians often attached themselves to the one constant they could find: private English greed. The dictates, policies, and laws of the Company and the emerging colonial state were often as burdensome for country traders as they were suffocating for indigenous merchant classes. Herein lay the seeds of a new partnership. Country traders often brought in Indians to maximize their profits *against* the Company they ostensibly served, by colluding over price fixing, underreporting, bribery, and overcharging—a kind of collaborative "weapons of the weak."[70] Private traders also sold safe-conduct passes to Indian merchants on the sly so that they could evade their own rulers' taxes: as their goods were now headed for "Company coffers, the nawabs could not enforce exactions. The levels of cooperation in these ventures spread throughout British India, from the lowest district officer to the Governors of the Presidencies, and were of 'infinite variety, color, and movement.'"[71] It was in this new complexity of

68. By 1777 Calcutta harbor registered a total of 290 private British trading ships in and out of port that year, with only 5 percent of total traffic on ships over 80 tons remaining of (native) Indian registry. See Bruce Watson, *Foundation for Empire: English Trade in India 1659–1760* (New Delhi: Vikas, 1980).

69. Holden Furber, *Private Fortunes and Company Profits in the India Trade in the 18th Century* (Aldershot: Variorum, 1997).

70. The phrase, of course, is James Scott's; see his *Weapons of the Weak: Everyday Forms of Peasant Resistance* (New Haven: Yale University Press, 1985).

71. In Madras, for example, the governor of Fort St. George (Edward Winter) partnered primarily with the merchant Beri Timmanna, while the Surat president, George Oxenden, held his closest ties with Bhinji Parak. In 1721 Hastings was dismissed for his private dealings and his Tamil associate, Khrishnama Venkatapati, was interrogated as well. Indian merchants could grow to be quite connected, and extremely powerful. Adiappa Narayan, *dubash* to Governor Richard Benyon of Madras, transacted for Indian coolies, commodity merchants, other dubashes, artisans, Tamil Chetties, local Indian dignitaries, resident Portuguese, and the high society of British Madras. See Bruce Watson, *Foundation for Empire*: 309–12.

relations in the expanding imperial world that Indian commerce found a revised niche.[72] The traders of indigenous India survived these widespread alterations by evolving, and by adapting to local and translocal rhythms of change: first as partners, then as competitors, and finally (often) as subordinates.

Ocean's Western Rim

The final arena we can touch on in our analysis of European influence on Indian Ocean commerce and politics is the East African littoral.[73] Here, the salient issues of the age were analogous to patterns elsewhere along the Indian Ocean Rim: change in the coastal population centers, the incorporation of increasingly important hinterlands, and the movements of local peoples, whether these were merchants, *banians*, or slaves.[74] Several major trends can be identified as being of primary importance among these phenomena for the East African case, however. Perhaps first and foremost was the rise of Zanzibar, which became an Omani outpost at the end of the seventeenth century and very gradually developed into a commercial empire on its own accord. This vault to prominence was achieved by mercantilist means, but the Zanzibari "empire," once established, underwent fundamental structural changes over the course of the eighteenth and nineteenth centuries.[75] This process, as related

72. For the complexities of these new arrangements, see Om Prakash, "European Corporate Enterprises and the Politics of Trade in India, 1600–1800," in *Politics and Trade in the Indian Ocean World*, ed. R. Mukherjee and L. Subramanian (Delhi: Oxford University Press, 1998), 165–82; and Sanjay Subrahmanyam and C. A. Bayly, "Portfolio Capitalists and the Political Economy of Early Modern India," in Subrahmanyam, ed., *Merchants, Markets*, 242–65.

73. For some recent scholarship, see Gijsbert Oonk, *The Karimjee Jiwanjee Family, Merchant Princes of East Africa, 1800–2000* (Amsterdam: Pallas, 2009); Erik Gilbert, *Dhows and the Colonial Economy of Zanzibar, 1860–1970* (Athens, OH: Ohio University Press, 2004); Jeremy Prestholdt, *Domesticating the World: African Consumerism and the Genealogies of Globalization* (Berkeley: University of California Press, 2008); and Abdul Sheriff, *Dhow Cultures of the Indian Ocean: Cosmopolitanism, Commerce, and Islam* (New York: Columbia University Press, 2010).

74. See Edward Alpers, *The Indian Ocean in World History* (New York: Oxford University Press, 2013); Abdul Sheriff, "The Persian Gulf and the Swahili Coast: A History of Acculturation over the Longue Durée," in Lawrence Potter, ed. *The Persian Gulf in History* (New York: Palgrave Macmillan, 2009): 173–88; and Gwyn Campbell, *Africa and the Indian Ocean World from Early Times to Circa 1900* (Cambridge: Cambridge University Press, 2019).

75. For commentary on Oman and Zanzibar during this time, see René J. Barendse, "Reflections on the Arabian Seas in the Eighteenth Century," *Itinerario* 25, no. 1 (2000): 25–50. On the Swahili civilizations of the East African coast that developed as a result of these trading contacts

both by indigenous accounts (such as "The Ancient History of Dar es-Salaam") and period English documents, was inherently linked to Zanzibar's relations with British India.[76] In greater perspective, these developments were also tied to the evolving world of global capitalism in general, and to the changing institution of slavery in particular. Adam Smith was fascinated by these connections, and wrote voluminously on the outstretched threads of this African web. Smith knew that the future not only of Africa but of the Americas was tied into these questions, and he saw the phenomenon of African slavery as one of the central moral and economic issues of his day.[77]

In the sixteenth and seventeenth centuries, the long, extended coastline of East Africa was an arena of constant warfare and turmoil. More than elsewhere along the rim of the Indian Ocean, the Portuguese presence here proved to be not only fundamentally destabilizing but part of a century-long pattern of violence and reprisal as different actors warred for the riches of coastal trade. Prior to this time, at least according to indigenous Swahili chronicles, there had been relative peace, as the coast was gradually Islamized; Persians seem to have been particularly important in these processes:

"The Ancient History of Kilwa Kisiwani" (Swahili Translation)
... [the Shirazi] disembarked at Kilwa, that is to say, they went to the headman of the country, the Elder Mrimba, and asked for a place in which to settle at Kisiwani. This they obtained. And they gave Mrimba presents of trade goods and beads.

"The Ancient History of Dar es Salaam" (Swahili Translation)
The original name of Dar es Salaam was Mzizima, which means the healthy town. Originally it was bush. Then came people ... who cleared it with axes, hoes, and sickles. They cut down the bush and built large houses. There also came Shirazi who joined up with the Barawa settlers in one place.[78]

Omani Arabs were involved in the more confrontational epoch of the sixteenth and seventeenth centuries, as were the Portuguese themselves and

---

over the centuries, see Mark Horton and John Middleton, *The Swahili: The Social Landscape of a Mercantile Society* (Oxford: Blackwell, 1988), 5–26.

76. For the former, see "The Ancient History of Dar es-Salaam," in G. S. P. Freeman-Grenville, *The East African Coast: Select Documents from the First to the Earlier Nineteenth Century* (Oxford: Oxford University Press, 1962), 233–37.

77. See, for example, Smith, *Wealth of Nations*, II:571, 578, 586–87, 939.

78. From Freeman-Grenville, *The East African Coast*, 221, 234.

African communities on the coast.[79] Initially, Fort Jesus at Mombasa was the focal point of these struggles, and we have good contemporary records (both eyewitness accounts and archaeological remains) that attest to the ferocity of assaults by all parties.[80] Yet, by 1698–99, it was the unobtrusive Omani station at Zanzibar that was emerging as an important new factor in regional trade and diplomacy. As the seventeenth folded into the eighteenth century only a year later, the small port town's influence steadily grew.[81]

Zanzibar's basic productive and social relations changed to accommodate new international realities as the town became more economically and politically incorporated into circuits of exchange. Karl Marx and Friedrich Engels commented on these African transvaluations in the nineteenth century, but these processes had already been occurring for quite some time.[82] Instead of trading on its own behalf, the Zanzibari polity became a "conveyor belt" between African goods and markets and the industrializing West. Dhows and caravans that had once been utilized for predominantly mercantilist purposes were now directed toward different ends: the purchase of slaves, for instance, to populate clove and food-production plantations under Zanzibari rule, and the transit of ivory, which fetched high prices in Europe and America.[83] Such changes in the nature of the empire, of course, also had their reverberations on the peoples of the mainland, as weaker polities were depopulated and stronger ones were reoriented to provide desired primary materials (i.e., ivory, gum copal, etc.) Yet even in the metropole itself (in this case Zanzibar, vis-à-vis its own East African hinterland), changes rearranged the existing social fabric such that new hierarchies developed. Indians, for example, who were important traders under the old mercantilist state (but never predominant ones)

79. See Jean Aubin, "Merchants in the Red Sea and the Persian Gulf at the Turn of the Fifteenth and Sixteenth Centuries," in *Asian Merchants and Businessmen*, ed. Lombard and Aubin.

80. See, for example, the account of Manuel de Faria y Sousa in Zoe Marsh, ed., *East Africa through Contemporary Records* (Cambridge: Cambridge University Press, 1961), 19–22. A visit to this fort and its small museum collection is very instructive.

81. See Michael Pearson, *Port Cities and Intruders: The Swahili Coast, India, and Portugal in the Early Modern Era* (Baltimore: Johns Hopkins University Press, 1998).

82. See Engels, especially, in Marx, *Capital*, III:1047.

83. The purchasing of slaves in East Africa, and in the Indian Ocean generally, had a long pedigree by this point; see S. Arasaratnam, "Slave Trade in the Indian Ocean in the Seventeenth Century," in Mathew, *Mariners, Merchants*, 95–208. The American role on the East African coast also became important, as her merchants brought copious quantities of ivory, gum copal, and other commodities back to Salem and other northeastern ports.

were given vast new advantages by their British associations, clearly to the detriment of ethnically Arab merchants. By the mid-nineteenth century, the Omani rulers of Zanzibar were so dependent on the British military to maintain tribal stability in Oman itself, as well as on the capital that British Indians brought from the Raj, that they could do little to preclude these changes from happening.[84] In 1861 Oman and Zanzibar were formally split under the Canning Award, following internal instabilities in this outstretched maritime polity, and in 1890 Zanzibar was named a protectorate by the British empire.

The complexities of Zanzibar's transformation gloss over these broad brushstrokes. More will be said of the mainland opposite Zanzibar in a moment, but it is useful first to get a sense of how this Wallersteinian "core" was changing, before looking at its tendrils. The two most important currents here were cloves and slaves. In the 1770s the Dutch monopoly on cloves in Maluku was broken, and seedlings were brought to Mauritius off the East African coast. Concurrent with the rise of British influence over the Omani clans both in Zanzibar and the Persian Gulf, clove production was encouraged as its potential in Western markets was still partially unfulfilled.[85] Yet a salient part of this growing British influence was the new campaign to abolish African slavery as well, a movement that some scholars have identified as a "humanitarian guise" for the deeper motive of economic penetration.[86] We know from both European and indigenous sources (such as "The Ancient History of Kilwa Kisiwani") that a substantial percentage of the Zanzibari merchant class made their living on slaving, mostly in the Middle East, where Africans were used

---

84. Iftikhar Ahmad Khan, "Merchant Shipping in the Arabian Sea—First Half of the 19th Century," *Journal of Indian Ocean Studies* 7, nos. 2/3 (2000): 163–73.

85. Primarily because the Dutch exported only a fraction of the cloves that they could have from the Indies, in order to keep prices artificially high.

86. This is one of the places where a nationalist history such as the one forwarded by Abdul Sheriff (in his *Slaves, Spices, and Ivory in Zanzibar: The Integration of an East African Commercial Enterprise into the World Economy 1770–1873* (Athens, OH: Ohio University Press, 1987) seems a bit Manichaean, perhaps. The author sees only machinations in these movements, with clear protagonists (Zanzibaris) and antagonists (Englishmen), rather than more realistic shades of gray. There were Englishmen who believed in the antislavery campaigns because of their religious convictions, or on pure humanitarian grounds, without being involved in British policies of trade and expansion. Likewise, there were East African elites who saw slaving as an avenue toward their own prosperity as well. See also a newer, comprehensive treatment of this subject in Matthew Hopper, *Globalization and Slavery in Arabia in the Age of Empire* (New Haven: Yale University Press, 2015).

as pearl divers; in the army; as servants; and as concubines.[87] British dictates and conventions like the Moresby Treaty of 1822, in which slave trading was prohibited south of Cape Delgado, Tanzania, and east of Diu, India, caught these merchants in a vise. The solution for these men, and for Zanzibar as a whole, was to fuse the two currents of restricted slaving and expanding clove production into a new ideology: "if slaves could not be exported, then the products of their labor could."[88] The result was an explosion in the clove industry on Zanzibar and Pemba proper, a directed agricultural policy that was encouraged by both aristocrats and the Zanzibari state and built upon slavery. Said Sultan himself had enormous plots of land converted to clove production, while his children and concubines followed suit. Overland caravan traders who saved enough after several journeys into the African interior also invested. By 1834, there were over four thousand clove trees in Kizimbani alone, between five and twenty feet tall, with cloves yielding over 1,000 percent profit on the costs of production.[89] The rush toward ownership was so strong in the "core regions" of Pemba and Zanzibar that the former island lost two-thirds of its forest cover in the space of a decade. This was quickly followed by changing demographic and social relations on the island.[90]

87. Compare the narratives of the French slave dealer Monsieur Morice (1776) with that of the Kilwa Kisiwani chronicle, both reproduced in Freeman-Grenville, *The East African Coast*, 191 and 223. Slaving is clearly a desired economic arrangement for both parties here, Europeans (such as Monsieur Morice) and for certain Swahili too. See also Shaikh al-Amin bin 'Ali al Mazru'i, *The History of the Mazru'i Dynasty* (London: Oxford University Press, 1995).

88. Sheriff, *Slaves, Spices, and Ivory*, 48.

89. The small average heights on these trees show how recently—and en masse—they had been planted. By way of comparison, in 1990 I climbed the volcano of Ternate in Northern Maluku to reach Cengkeh Afu, an enormous clove tree described in Portuguese and Dutch accounts of the island in the seventeenth century. The tree still stood in 1990, four centuries later, and can produce 600 kilograms of cloves in a single year's harvest. Tagliacozzo, 1990 fieldwork notes, 451.

90. For two good long-term analyses of these patterns, see Edward Alpers, *Ivory and Slaves: The Changing Pattern of International Trade in East Central Africa to the Later Nineteenth Century* (Berkeley: University of California Press, 1975), and C. S. Nicholls, *The Sawhili Coast: Politics, Diplomacy, and Trade on the East African Littoral, 1798–1856* (London: Allen & Unwin, 1971). The landscape (in all senses, geographic and social) of Pemba completely changed in the 1830s. Pemba at one time was a granary for Mombasa and Arabia, but this changed as the local peasantry were marginalized away from their communally owned lands, and plantations were erected by the Zanzibar elite. Although slaves were brought in by the thousands, the original planters were also conscripted, with Said Sultan attempting to expropriate their labor along traditional tribute lines. In 1834 this was converted to a poll tax, as peasants now produced cloves

On the mainland, working through the connections of Zanzibar, Britain's stimulus toward East African change was also quite important. The rise of coastal feeder ports like Kilwa Kivinge, Bagomoyo, and Pangani, all of which acted as caravan terminuses/docking centers for Zanzibari traders penetrating inland into the East African interior, pushed commerce forward. At the same time, Zanzibar's exactions and political control on the coasts north and south of its own direct hinterland (the Mrima) were relatively loose, based on these regions' abilities to trade elsewhere if they desired. The Zanzibari state encouraged its traders to push into the interior, knowing full well the profits that would accrue from sales—especially of ivory—to Britain and British India.[91] By the late 1850s ivory was already constituting half of the total import values into Zanzibar alone. Ivory's acquisition from the source was further complemented by a gradation system on duties, so that the further afield the island's economic net was cast, the lower Zanzibari taxes became.[92] This encouraged more and more Zanzibari traders into the interior, where many settled to practice agriculture, build great estates, and construct trading posts, all while acquiring women as concubines or wives from local rulers in the process.[93] Their appearance also served, however, to reconfigure local power arrangements, as traditional chiefs—who had gained power in the first place by clearing the bush so that subsistence agriculture might be performed—were replaced by new men, who better organized access to the hard cash of cross-cultural trade. In at least one case, in Unyamwezi, these changes corresponded with a flux from matrilineal to patrilineal organization. This same people, by the 1890s,

---

for cash to pay taxes instituted from the Zanzibar Istana, instead of doing subsistence farming. See Sheriff, *Slaves, Spices, and Ivory*, 55–59.

91. On relations between the coasts and the interior, see Michael Pearson, *Port Cities and Intruders*, 63–100; and Richard Hall, *Empires of the Monsoon: A History of the Indian Ocean and Its Invaders* (London: Harper Collins, 1996), chapters 26 and 50.

92. For the evolution of these processes north of Zanzibar on the Kenya coasts, see Marguerite Ylvisaker, *Lamu in the Nineteenth Century: Land, Trade, and Politics* (Boston: Boston University African Studies Association, 1979); and Sir John Gray, *The British in Mombasa, 1824–1826* (London: MacMillan, 1957).

93. One merchant spent thousands of dollars on his house, which had the characteristic carved doors and rafters of a Zanzibari home. Burton commented that some traders in were receiving harems of two to three hundred women as inducement to bring trade that way. See R. F. Burton, *The Lake Regions of Central Africa* (London, 1860), I:270, 376; and R. F. Burton, *Zanzibar: City, Island and Coast* (London: Tinsely, 1872), II:297. See also Mark Horton and John Middleton, *The Swahili: The Social Landscape of a Mercantile Society* (Oxford: Blackwell, 2000), 103–9.

had also reoriented their productive energies into becoming what Abdul Sheriff calls a "nation of porters." Carrying ivory year-round to the coasts, one-third of all Nyamwezi males were engaged as professional porters (*pagazi*) during that decade.[94]

The position of ethnic Indians also underwent substantial change during these transformations. Though the process was long, drawn out, and very complicated, Zanzibari Indians essentially morphed from allies of the Omani merchant class to become proxies of British influence.[95] *Banians*, as we have already seen in our "India" section, provided a crucial liaison between European and indigenous capital in the eighteenth-century subcontinent. In East Africa this relationship functioned in much the same way, with *banians* (usually Gujaratis of the Vanya merchant caste) gaining an early historical ascendancy, partially because of Portuguese exclusionary practices against Muslim shippers.[96] It was expedient for Omanis to maintain ties with these Asian traders because of their far-flung networks, and "The Ancient History of Dar es-Salaam" tells us that Indians were both taxed and used as emissaries, making them important to ruling elites in all kinds of ways.[97] In the civil wars of the 1720s that brought the Busaidi clan to power, Ahmed bin Said sent reinforcements to East Africa on ships borrowed from *banian* merchants, while a century later the great Said Sultan also used their help, transferring his seat of power from Muscat to Zanzibar with *banians* "providing extra armed ships and manpower in his wars with Mombasa."[98] Both in Zanzibar and Muscat up until the mid-nineteenth century, ethnic Indians who traded in Zanzibar were granted the same

---

94. Sheriff, *Slaves, Spices, and Ivory*, 182. What had once been a seasonal activity developed into local subsistence: 80–100,000 Nyamwezi were making the carrying trek to the coasts in the 1890s. All of these changes, based on production, gender organization, leadership, etc., fit in very well with Eric Wolf's thesis on capitalism's effect on kin-ordered societies. See Eric Wolf, *Europe and the People without History*, 77–100.

95. M. N. Pearson, "Indians in East Africa: The Early Modern Period," in *Politics and Trade in the Indian Ocean World* ed. Mukherjee and Subramanian, 227–49.

96. See, for example, Luis Frederico Dias Antunes, "The Trade Activities of the Banyans in Mozambique: Private Indian Dynamics in the Portuguese State Economy, 1686–1777," in Mathew, *Mariners, Merchants*, 301–32. Compared to India and Southeast Asia, the Portuguese had relative success in these endeavors in the Early Modern East African coast, though here too their influence was ultimately short-lived (except in Mozambique).

97. "The Ancient History of Dar es-Salaam," in Freeman-Grenville, *The East African Coast*, 234.

98. M. Reda Bhacker, *Trade and Empire in Muscat and Zanzibar: Roots of British Domination* (London: Routledge, 1992), 71.

privileges as "pure" Arab Omanis, with several being appointed to the prestigious position of customs master, a highly coveted post.[99]

As Britain exercised its leverage on Zanzibar more thoroughly during the middle of the century, these relationships began to change. The first step was the introduction of legislation that made slaveholding illegal for overseas Indians whose ancestral homes were in parts of the subcontinent now administered by England. These laws on paper handed the plantation sector to the Omani clans in Zanzibar. Faced with such sanctions, many Indians invested their capital more heavily in the ivory and gum copal trade, spurring these networks (which we have already glimpsed in the African mainland) into wider areas of incorporation (many Indians still kept investments in money-lending and the plantation sector, however). Yet as British legislation steadily made more of the transit of slaves illegal on the coasts in the nineteenth century, the predominantly Arab planter class now found their plantations failing, with their mortgages falling to Indian moneylenders.[100] The decline of the slave-based plantation economy, concomitant with the expansion of the Indian share of the African carrying trade to the coasts, vaulted the Indian community to new prominence in a changing Zanzibar.[101] Distrust between the two ethnicities, only one of which had access to the munitions of the state, pushed Indian traders further into the camp of the British, who were the only ones who could guarantee their investments. As Zanzibar's empire was being effectively partitioned at this time anyway, it was in Britain's interest to keep economic and political power as diffuse as possible.[102] While the banians of the 1840s rejected British jurisdiction over their affairs in concert with the local Omanis, by the 1890s they were writing letters of gratitude to His Majesty's Resident. These missives were "for assurances given us as regards the

99. V. S. Sheth, "Dynamics of Indian Diaspora in East and South Africa," *Journal of Indian Ocean Studies*, 8, no. 3 (2000): 217–27.

100. Richard Hall, *Empires of the Monsoon: A History of the Indian Ocean and its Invaders* (London: Harper and Collins, 1996), chapter 52.

101. For this topic generally, see the work of Marina Carter, Alessandor Stanziani, and Patrick Harries. Also see Clare Anderson's very comprehensive scholarship on transportation, slavery, and indenture: Clare Anderson, *Subaltern Lives: Biographies of Colonialism in the Indian Ocean World* (Cambridge: Cambridge University Press, 2012); and Clare Anderson, *Convicts in the Indian Ocean: Transportation from South Asia to Mauritius, 1815–1853* (London: Palgrave, 2000).

102. W. E. F. Ward and L. W. White, *East Africa: A Century of Change 1870–1970* (New York: Africana Publishing Company, 1972).

safety of our life, property, and trade in this foreign territory."[103] This was also a time when many more Indians started coming to East Africa, often to work on the Uganda railway.

It is also fascinating to see how these East African fluctuations changed what in many ways was the region's original metropole, Oman, in keeping with Eric Wolf's global perspective on the effects of nineteenth-century capital penetration. The Gulf Sultanate itself metamorphosed during this period, with many of its most visible changes being traceable to Zanzibar's fortunes. Entire industries developed to accommodate Oman's expanding periphery, which in time outstripped the Sultanate of Muscat in population and productivity.[104] Matrah became an enormous center of weaving in the 1830s, churning out so many turbans, sarongs, and cloaks for export to Africa that an English visitor in 1836 commented that "scarcely a hut doesn't contain a spinning wheel, with females busily employed before it."[105] The embroidered cotton skullcaps known as *kofiyya* became a standout within this industry, and were eventually incorporated into the official national dress of Zanzibar and Pemba.[106] Similarly, blacksmiths in Batina and the Omani interior became famous for the production and export of armaments to East Africa, with the thick, curved *jambiyya* daggers indigenous to the region entering elite Zanzibari society as important markers of status. The indigo dyers of Ibri, Bahla, Firq, and Sur also found a market on the African strand, as did carpenters, sandal makers, and rope makers, who could find orders simply based on Zanzibari population density. This was opposed to the sparse desert communities of the Gulf, where such markets were far smaller.[107]

103. Bhacker, *Trade and Empire*, 178.

104. For the balance between Oman and Zanzibar over the centuries, see Patricia Risso, *Oman and Muscat: An Early Modern History* (New York: St. Martin's Press, 1986).

105. Bhacker, *Trade and Empire*, 133.

106. Nineteenth-century British travelers commented that most Swahili males dressed like Arabs in donning kofiyya, though today these caps are being replaced by cheaper, mass-produced ones from mainland China. In 1990 I was able to take photographs of traditional kofiyya shops in Zanzibar, Mombasa, and Lamu, where local store owners told me that higher-quality Middle Eastern caps were still being sold to Swahilis willing to pay the price. Tagliacozzo, 1990 fieldwork notes, 623.

107. See Fahad Bishara, *A Sea of Debt: Law and Economic Life in the Western Indian Ocean, 1780–1850* (New York: Cambridge University Press, 2017), chapter 7; and Thomas McDow, *Buying Time: Debt and Mobility in the Western Indian Ocean* (Athens, OH: Ohio University Press, 2020).

Finally, the human cost behind many of these transformations was appallingly high; therefore slavery must be touched upon again as well. The East African slave trade has never received as much attention as the West African phenomenon, partly because sources (especially American ones) are so much more detailed about the latter, and partly because the numbers involved for West Africa were higher on aggregate. Nevertheless, between the seventeenth and twentieth centuries a stream of East African slaves left for the Middle East, for the French trading station at Kilwa (especially between 1775 and 1800) and into Zanzibar's own clove plantations.[108] Firsthand accounts such as the one given by a slave named Chengwimbe to the Reverend W. J. Rampley show us just how brutal this trade was on the East African coasts, replete with ambushes, the separation of families, and forced amputations.[109] Indeed, Esmond Bradley Martin has come to a mean figure of 3,000 slaves imported per year into Zanzibar between 1770 and 1800, with the numbers tripling by 1830 and reaching 20,000 per annum by 1860.[110] The export of slaves being sold outside of East Africa remained nearly constant at 3,000 per annum for the entirety of this period, however, showing how slavery itself was transformed in the nineteenth century to a much more local, production-oriented activity. "Blackbirding" was no longer the simple export of human beings as trade "commodities" of value. Britain's encouragement of the clove system under the Zanzibari sultans indirectly fueled this awful commerce, despite London's promulgations against slave trading.

Some scholars have argued that much of the poverty witnessed in twentieth-century East Africa is in fact a continuing legacy of these changes, as polities were depopulated and production phased to plantation monocropping to provide for expanding world markets. While there is certainly room in this equation for other factors (droughts and dictators among them), the assertion is certainly at least partially valid. This is because as Europeans and the new

108. Two of the best studies on the denouement of these processes are Frederick Cooper, *From Slaves to Squatters: Plantation Labor and Agriculture in Zanzibar and Coastal Kenya, 1890–1925* (New Haven: Yale University Press, 1980); and Jonathan Glassman, *Feasts and Riot: Revelry, Rebellion, and Popular Consciousness on the Swahili Coast, 1856–1888* (London: Heinemann, 1995).

109. See Chengwimbe's account in Zoe Marsh, ed., *East Africa through Contemporary Records*, 35–41. Missionary accounts, of course, need to be read carefully however, because of the purposes of the visits to these coasts.

110. Esmond Bradley Martin, *Cargoes of the East: The Ports, Trade, and Culture of the Arabian Seas and Western Indian Ocean* (London: Elm Tree Books, 1978), 29.

hyperaggressive capitalism they championed scythed across the Indian Ocean between 1600 and 1900, Africans (and alongside them South and Southeast Asians, as we have seen) were caught in this storm and grappled to survive.[111] Local livelihoods and indeed entire societies evolved in the unleashing of these energies. Even the narrative of how this story was presented became, for a long while, a European one; that was taken, too. As the great Congolese philosopher V. Y. Mudimbe put it, lamenting this state of affairs but offering some final hope for redress: "Yet one can also say that is in these very discourses that African worlds have been established as realities for knowledge. Only today Africans themselves read, challenge, rewrite these discourses as a way of explicating and defining their culture, history, and being."[112]

Conclusion

The Indian Ocean's temporal evolution in the past several centuries has seen some remarkable changes sweep the region's political economy. Maritime networks that crisscrossed these seas continued to play a crucial role in long-distance commerce, but by the nineteenth century this happened only with the forbearance of certain larger compelling forces. Adam Smith recognized this shift early; in the 1770s Smith was presciently describing the end of oceanic struggles that had already consumed Europeans and indigenous peoples for several centuries.[113] It was clear to Smith, and even clearer to Karl Marx writing almost a century later, that other energies were coming to bear. England's gradual shift into control over the means of production in several strategic ocean littorals changed the commercial playing field enormously by the mid-nineteenth century. The energies of trade had begun to phase into processes altogether more hierarchical in nature. As Marx stated in *Capital*, "it may sound harsh and sad to say so, but in India it is easier to replace a man than an ox."[114] This had not always been so, but the changes wrought by shifting capitalism-in-production brought altered realities to the Indian Ocean.

111. For a discussion of East Africa and the Early Modern world economy, see Michael Pearson, *Port Cities and Intruders: The Swahili Coast, India, and Portugal in the Early Modern Era* (Baltimore: Johns Hopkins University Press, 1998), 101–28.

112. V. Y. Mudimbe, *The Invention of Africa* (Bloomington: Indiana University Press, 1988), introduction.

113. Smith, *Wealth of Nations*, II:631.

114. Marx, *Capital*, II:314.

Regional civilizations no longer traded as equals or near equals, but as actors in an ossifying hierarchy. Only during the middle decades of the twentieth century, with the birth and evolution of a number of independent states, would this hierarchy undergo real and significant change.

However, Western commercial concerns had come into the Indian Ocean in the sixteenth century as only one of many possible trading concerns in regional and transregional circuits. Om Prakash and others have shown, though, that this presence from an early date already contained the seeds of greater, coercive capabilities.[115] The potential for moving from mercantilism to something more permanent, including control or partial control over local means of production, was most fully expressed by the English East India Company, and then by the British Crown as the nineteenth century wore on, in places that now make up parts of modern-day South Asia from Pakistan to Bangladesh, and in other parts of the Indian Ocean as well.[116] Yet the French also attempted this leap at certain times and in certain places, though it would be only in very scattered outposts (such as Réunion, Mauritius, and the Seychelles) that this ever really worked.[117] The Dutch also tried to follow this pattern, though they were ultimately successful only in the large but remote corner of the Indian Ocean today known as Indonesia.[118] Other attempts by smaller enterprises like the Danes were attempted as well, though these endeavors always had lesser chances of getting off the ground.[119] The important thing to note is that it was ultimately only the British who were truly able to

115. Om Prakash, ed., *European Commercial Expansion in Early Modern Asia* (Aldershot: Variorum, 1997).

116. John Keay, *The Honourable Company: A History of the English East India Company* (New York: HarperCollins, 1993).

117. Proceeding backward in time, see Paul Bois et al, *L'ancre et la croix du Sud: La marine française dans l'expansion coloniale en Afrique noire et dans l'Océan Indien, de 1815 à 1900* (Vincennes: Service Historique de la Marine, 1998); Indrani Ray, ed, *The French East India Company and the Trade of the Indian Ocean* (Calcutta: Munshiram, 1999); and Ananda Abeydeera, "Anatomy of an Occupation: The Attempts of the French to Establish a Trading Settlement on the Eastern Coast of Sri Lanka in 1672," in Giorgio Borsa, *Trade and Politics in the Indian Ocean* (Delhi: Manohar, 1990).

118. Again proceeding backward, see J. Steur, *Herstel of Ondergang: De voorstellen tot redres van de VOC, 1740–1795* (Utrecht: H & S Publishers, 1984), 17–27; Harm Stevens, *De VOC in Bedrijf, 1602–1799* (Amsterdam: Walburg, 1998); and Femme Gaastra, *Bewind en Beleid bij de VOC, 1672–1702* (Amsterdam: Walburg, 1989).

119. Martin Krieger, "Danish Country Trade on the Indian Ocean in the 17th and 18th Centuries," in *Indian Ocean and Cultural Interaction*, ed. Mathew.

make the leap from mercantile capitalism to the systemic oceanwide control of capitalism-in-production. In the vast aquatic world of the Indian Ocean, with all of its faraway but integrated radials, this was no mean feat.

This success notwithstanding, it would be an error not to see the British as simply one among many merchant diasporas who ultimately helped shape the imbricated histories of these coasts. There were certainly others, and many of these were emphatically *not* European. Christine Dobbin has demonstrated the reach and breadth of a variety of what she calls "conjoint communities" in articulating these processes—networks of actors who ferried commodities, exchanged ideas, and influenced political economies on a grand scale.[120] Other authors have narrowed their vision onto single diasporic communities (such as the Armenians) in these deliberations, and pointed to the contributions that these populations have made on their own.[121] It has even become possible now, historiographically, to select classes of individuals journeying along these networks, or to chronicle the effects of subsets of travelers such as priests or itinerant scribes, and delineate their roles on the unfolding of these histories.[122] The English may have had the heaviest hand in altering the channels of Indian Ocean trade, but they were by no means the only ones wielding the hammer. A number of hands grasped this handle, and the evolution of Indian Ocean history for four hundred years was shaped by the joint efforts of many of these communities.[123]

120. Christine Dobbin, *Asian Entrepreneurial Minorities: Conjoint Communities in the Making of the World-Economy, 1570–1940* (London: Curzon, 1996).

121. Vahe Baladouni and Margaret Makepeace, eds., *Armenian Merchants of the Early Seventeenth and Early Eighteenth Centuries* (Philadelphia: American Philosophical Society, 1998).

122. Charles Borges, "Intercultural Movements in the Indian Ocean Region: Churchmen, Travelers, and Chroniclers in Voyage and in Action," in *Indian Ocean and Cultural Interaction,* ed. Mathew; Karl Haellquist, ed., *Asian Trade Routes: Continental and Maritime* (London: Curzon Press, 1991).

123. For the prehistory to some of the patterns presented here, see Krish Seetah, ed., *Connecting Continents: Archaeology and History in the Indian Ocean World* (Athens, OH: Ohio University Press, 2018). For the warp and weft of these flows, see Michael Pearson, ed., *Trade, Circulation, and Flow in the Indian Ocean World* (London. Palgrave Series in the Indian Ocean World, 2015).

PART III

Religion on the Tides

Preface: Buddhism, Hinduism, Islam, and Christianity
in Asian Waters

PART III LOOKS at how religions swirled through maritime Asia, often following the trade routes as they wound from place to place. Here again, the geographies that concern this process were vast: we have already mentioned Korean "turtle ships" carrying sects of Buddhism from China to Korea, and then from Korea on to Japan. But the transmission of religious doctrines by sea happened in many other places as well. The conquistadors—and later the Manila galleons, for two hundred fifty years—brought versions of Catholicism and its changing dictates to the Philippines across the vast Pacific for centuries. Buddhism came from Sri Lanka and India to Southeast Asia ensconced in the holds of ships, carried by men who traveled as soldiers, traders, or as priests, making their way across the Bay of Bengal. The religion became the main ideological and eschatological vision of most of mainland Southeast Asia, and still is, as Theravada Buddhism predominates in Burma, Laos, Thailand, and Cambodia. And Islam came as well, initially (it is thought) from Persia and western India, but later on from the Middle East directly, and also likely from China, in at least several well-researched episodes. The religion of the prophet eventually spread on the maritime trade routes from Aceh east to Maluku, and from Mindanao south to Sumba. The legacies of this particular transmission are also still with us today: Indonesia is the world's largest Muslim nation, and this is directly traceable to Islam's passage on the commercial circuits of past centuries. But Islam also spread in the other direction as well, to the western shores of the Indian Ocean, where the religion is now practiced as the majority faith on the "Swahili arc," from Somalia south to northern Mozambique. Asia's trade routes by sea helped facilitate all of this religious travel, and in fact assisted in fashioning the geographies of global belief we see before us today.

How did this all happen? How could religions that started in one place find fecund ground in other locales, often thousands of miles away? And how did the trade routes make this process malleable, when languages, cultural formations, and entrenched interests all seemed to mitigate against religious conversion happening on such a large scale? It seems fair to say that the fact that most of these faiths were likely transmitted by traders helped the process along. Outright missionization would have been seen as distasteful and unwanted in many cases; forcible conversion, at the point of a spear, would likely have been equally unsuccessful in the long term. Merchants bringing Buddhism, Hinduism, Islam, and Christianity would probably have brought a more acceptable message, however. These were successful people, at least in the perception of many locals: they had some measure of demonstrable wealth, new ideas, and also a portability to their lives which likely seemed attractive. Crucially, all brought messages of possibility as well, the idea that one could change one's position in this life (or the next) by adopting a new creed. For elites, too, the concept of being able to ensconce oneself within a larger orbit of similarly affiliated people over the maritime trading horizon brought some real benefits. Networks—religious and otherwise—grew and flourished in this way. People grew rich on their connections. By the later decades of the seventeenth century, for example, fully half of all Southeast Asians had adopted one of the world religions as their practicing faith. This was in contrast to the myriad systems of local, varied belief that would have predominated before the early modern Age. Though Hindu/Buddhism swept through the "lands beneath the winds" in the first millennium CE, Islam and Christianity managed to do exactly the same thing in the next thousand years. The religions carried on the trade routes found success farther afield as well, including on the China coasts, and across the western Indian Ocean to Africa. Faith traveled with trade, and vice versa, for much of recorded history.

Chapter 6 looks at these processes in the Bay of Bengal. Monks and traders seem to have come ashore in peninsular Siam from a very early date, likely close to two thousand years ago. From there, the amalgamated faith that they brought with them, a blend of Hinduism and Buddhism (though sometimes more "pure" strains of one or the other), spread rapidly among Siamese populations. We know this from archaeological evidence, both on land and in the form of shipwrecks, the latter of which are still being found and excavated in both the Andaman Sea and in the Gulf of Thailand. Crucially—statuary, amulets, and votives were left behind, and have withstood the test of time in this wettest of monsoon climates. From this detritus we can see how both of these religions traveled, both in the forms of deities that more or less made the trip in unaltered form from South Asia, and also in new incarnations of the gods that sprang up in Southeast Asian workshops. The evolution of faith is on display, therefore, to those—art historians, archaeologists, and scholars of religion—who know how to read the faded signs of the distant past. Chapter 7 then alters the frame of vision from maritime routes crisscrossing a body of water (the Bay of Bengal) and focuses in on a single port. Zamboanga—a Spanish garrison town at the end of Mindanao, and seemingly (in feel, at least) at the end of known worlds—is a meeting place for religion on the frontiers of three nations. Situated at the very end of the southern Philippines, and at the northernmost point of both Malaysia and Indonesia, this was a place where the dar al-Islam (the world of Islam, stretching west all the way to Morocco) and encroaching Catholicism (bleeding south from Spanish Manila) met in one port. The interface of these religions was not always peaceful, and well into our own time Zamboanga has been a dangerous place. But it is also a place where accommodations have been made, and where local people have learned to get along, despite the ideological and historical conflicts of different faiths. Based on fieldwork and also on historical sources, Chapter 7 asks how religion moved on the tides in one small place. It also asks how this process evolved in both peaceful and incendiary ways over the course of time.

6

Passage of Amulets

HINDU-BUDDHIST TRANSMISSIONS IN THE BAY OF BENGAL

The Buddha (Tathagata) has declared
The cause, and also the cessation
Of the things (Dhamma)
That arise from causes.
Such is the teaching. . . .

—ASJAVIT, COMPANION OF THE BUDDHA[1]

ONLY SELECTED THINGS were valuable enough to move across the wide maritime spaces of the premodern world. Spices and marine products were two of these items, as we will see—they were light enough (and rare enough) still to be profitable moving over vast distances of ocean, from one part of the globe to another.[2] Another thing that traveled was religion, and particularly the symbols of religion in material form, such as votive tablets, small statuary, and amulets.[3] Buddhism was instructive in this sense, and its dissemination

1. From Peter Skilling, "Traces of the Dharma: Preliminary Reports on Some Ye Dhamma and Ye Dharma Inscriptions from Mainland Southeast Asia," *Bulletin de l'École française d'Extrême-Orient* 90/91 (2003/4): 273–87, at 273.

2. Field and museum work in southern Thailand in 1989 and then again in 2006 contributed to this chapter. See Elizabeth Ann Pollard, "Indian Spices and Roman 'Magic' in Imperial and Late Antique Indo-Mediterranean," *Journal of World History* 24, no. 1 (2013): 1–23.

3. "Religion" is a complex term, and one that has to be problematized in the scholarly literature; see, for example, Talal Asad, "Anthropological Conceptions of Religion: Reflections on

connected places such as India/Nepal (the birthplace of the religion) with maritime geographies as far flung from the subcontinent as the distant islands of Japan.[4] The accoutrements of the religion also washed up on other shores en route, however, and eventually changed many of these societies in the process, from Indonesia to landlocked Laos to the outstretched coasts of Vietnam. This can be seen through a number of windows, spanning inscriptions to apparitions to the discourse of political philosophy.[5] Though these processes have been historical, they are also very much still with us today in the lived applications of traveling Buddhism, from social mores in Thailand to material goods in Vietnam to the erection and maintenance of a Cambodian religious clergy.[6] Religion travels on the tides just like commodities. In Asia this happened early and often, and it is possible to trace some of these outcomes over various oceanic distances.

This chapter looks at one of these spaces—the Bay of Bengal—to query how Hindu/Buddhism traveled from the Indian subcontinent to Southeast Asia from the first millennium CE onward. The chapter starts out by discussing some of the important maritime connections that made a transit such as this possible, as the building blocks for large-scale ocean voyaging were set in this region long ago. Nods toward China and the Sinitic world to the north are

Geertz," *Man* 18, no. 2 (1983): 237–59; and Tomoko Masuzawa, *The Invention of World Religions* (Chicago: University of Chicago Press, 2005).

4. James Ford, "Buddhist Materiality: A Cultural History of Objects in Japanese Buddhism," *Journal of Japanese Studies* 35, no. 2 (2009): 368–73. For the big picture, see Tansen Sen, *Buddhism, Diplomacy, and Trade: The Realignment of Sino-Indian Relations, 600–1400* (Honolulu: University of Hawai'i Press, 2003); and Tansen Sen, ed., *Buddhism across Asia: Networks of Material, Cultural and Intellectual Exchange* (Singapore: ISEAS, 2014).

5. See, for example, Arlo Griffiths, "Written Traces of the Buddhist Past: Mantras and Dharais in Indonesian Inscriptions," *Bulletin of the School of Oriental and African Studies* 77, no. 1 (2014): 137–94; Patrice Ladwig, "Haunting the State: Rumours, Spectral Apparitions and the Longing for Buddhist Charisma in Laos," *Asian Studies Review* 37, no. 4 (2013): 509–26; and Nguyễn Thế Anh, "From Indra to Maitreya: Buddhist Influence in Vietnamese Political Thought," *Journal of Southeast Asian Studies* 33, no. 2 (2002): 225–41.

6. Duncan McCargo, "The Politics of Buddhist Identity in Thailand's Deep South: The Demise of Civil Religion" *Journal of Southeast Asian Studies* 40, no. 1 (2009): 11–32; Laurel Kendall, "Popular Religion and the Sacred Life of Material Goods in Contemporary Vietnam," *Asian Ethnology* 67, no. 2 (2008): 177–99; and John Marston, "Death, Memory and Building: The Non-Cremation of a Cambodian Monk," *Journal of Southeast Asian Studies* 37, no. 3 (2006): 491–505.

MAP 6.1. The Bay of Bengal

described, before a fuller account is given of maritime connections being forged in the eastern Indian Ocean, both in terms of trade and religious institutions. The second part of the chapter then argues for the relative centrality of southern Siam and the Malay Peninsula, one early locale where both Hinduism and early Buddhism are generally thought to have "come ashore" in Southeast Asia in the first millennium CE. We will look at state-craft as it emerged in this region at this time, and also at some data of ships and shipwrecks, to tell us something about the frequency and also the density of travelers coming to this vital Asian transit point. Finally, the last part of the chapter will concentrate on the votives and amulets themselves, from both an art historical/archaeological standpoint and also that of Religious Studies. We will map out how Hinduism and early Buddhism spread on the tides of Southeast Asia at this early juncture, and ask how these systems of thought spread, both intellectually and as a means of everyday devotion for common people.

Early Historical Interactions

Though long-distance travel by sea—and the cultural contact that could come with it—sounds romantic, everything we know about such voyages in the premodern period suggests that such endeavors were difficult at best. A sixteenth-century Portuguese poem says in a wonderfully pithy way what most would likely have thought about such voyages, despite Portugal's being portrayed as a quintessentially "maritime country": "Why pass so many storms; And life and times so harsh; forever at death's door? I'd give up pepper without qualms."[7] Sojourning across the oceans was a dangerous business, as a bevy of shipwrecks in Asian waters has made perfectly clear.[8] Yet people did, and in the parts of the world that interest us in this book they seem to have done so from a very early date. Kenneth Hall, in his impressive survey of early Southeast Asia, has suggested segmentary spheres to the maritime trading operations of these early peoples; for the present chapter's purposes, one of these centered around the Bay of Bengal, another around the Isthmus of Kra in southern Siam, and a third operated in the Melaka Strait. Travelers from India often would have made the trip to Southeast Asia rounding the "roof" of the Bay of Bengal, skirting modern Bengal, Bangladesh, and Burma before arriving in Southeast Asia, while some more intrepid souls might have attempted mid-latitude crossings in the same body of water.[9] An entire edifice

7. See Michael Pearson, "Studying the Indian Ocean World: Problems and Opportunities," in *Cross Currents and Community Networks: The History of the the Indian Ocean World*, ed. Himanshu Prabha Ray and Edward Alpers, 22 (New Delhi: Oxford University Press, 2007).

8. For a very good study of just one of these (seminal) wrecks, see John Guy, "The Intan Shipwreck: A Tenth Century Cargo in Southeast Asian Waters," in *Song Ceramics: Art History, Archaeology and Technology*, ed. S. Pearson, 171–92 (London: Percival David Foundation, 2004); see also Justin McDaniel, "This Hindu Holy Man Is a Thai Buddhist," *South East Asia Research* 20, no. 2 (2013): 191–209.

9. Kenneth Hall, *A History of Early Southeast Asia: Maritime Trade and Societal Development, 100–1500* (Lanham, MD: Rowman & Littlefield, 2011), 30, 38, 47. The harrowing sea passage across the Bay of Bengal became a very common trope in Thai murals and in Pali narratives. Shipwrecks in Thai murals and the stories of Manimekkhala and the Bodhisatta Mahajanaka often illustrate this. Thanks to Justin McDaniel for this observation.

of professions began to spring up in the first millennium CE to service these connections: fishermen, sailors, craftsmen, merchants, and ship owners. Diasporas began to connect the outstretched communities, and ports gradually developed, sparingly at first, but then in larger and larger numbers, and increasingly of greater size.[10]

The Bay of Bengal was not the only place where these early interactions were happening. If Southeast Asia exerted a siren-like call to the emerging civilizations of India, then China fulfilled much the same function as India, only farther north and east. It is useful to highlight this concurrent magnetism here for a moment. Geoff Wade and Sun Laichen have shown how varied the influence of China was on Southeast Asia as we entered the early modern age, and China began to extend its influence over the countries of the "Nanyang," or the southern seas.[11] Though these contacts dated back roughly two thousand years, and were already taking form in the first millennium CE, it was really by the Song and Yuan Dynasties—thus, roughly the tenth to the fourteenth centuries—that we see these ties of trade and diplomacy growing across the geographic spread of what we now know as Southeast Asia. Ceramic data and also diplomatic correspondence in the various Chinese annals show us beyond doubt that a civilizational dialogue was well under way by this point.[12] Tribute embassies moved in one direction (north), and Chinese ambassadors and traders headed south, with a range of goods in their holds, some of them ceremonial and others among them intended for actual trade.[13] Cloth, silk, banners, and drums would have made up some of the former items, with a whole range of trading commodities (including metals, ceramics, and other trade goods) the latter. Religion and ideology were brought south, too, though they seem to have stuck less than more material concerns. We know that these long-distance voyages even led to the sharing

10. Kenneth McPherson, "Maritime Communities: An Overview," in *Cross Currents and Community Networks*, ed. Ray and Alpers, 36.

11. See Geoff Wade and Sun Laichen, eds., *Southeast Asia in the Fifteenth Century: The China Factor* (Singapore: NUS Press, 2010). The range of ideas collected in this volume—on Chinese contact vis-à-vis Vietnamese paperwork, Southeast Asian geomancy, Burmese gems, and Chinese silver, to name just a few—is really impressive.

12. See B. Ph. Groslier, "La céramique chinoise en Asie du Sud-est: Quelques points de méthode," *Archipel* 21 (1981): 93–121.

13. Derek Heng, *Sino-Malay Trade and Diplomacy from the Tenth through the Fourteenth Century* (Athens, OH: Ohio University Southeast Asian Studies, 2009).

of shipbuilding technologies and construction types in the South China Sea, as China and Southeast Asia reached out to each other over several hundred years at this time.[14]

Yet, if the South China Sea seems to have imparted mostly materiel to Southeast Asia, at least as far as can be ascertained from the archaeological and epigraphic records, the Indian Ocean was perhaps more varied in its gifts. Already a vast literature—far larger than on the South China Sea—has developed, describing the Indian Ocean as an emerging "system" along the lines of Fernand Braudel's Mediterranean. K. N. Chaudhuri, as referenced earlier in this book, was among the first scholars to attempt this sort of analysis, and his early efforts have been refined over the years by Michael Pearson and others, who have sought to show how this particular body of water came to exist as a maelstrom of unleashed energies, environmental and commercial and ideological, all at the same time.[15] Sugata Bose's inspired *A Hundred Horizons* has been among the latest of these studies, but for our purposes here in this chapter it is a newer study, Sunil Amrith's *Crossing the Bay of Bengal*, which is even more focused for our purposes, in this respect.[16] Amrith lays down the scope of the Bay of Bengal's dimensions, historically, in terms of its monsoon patterns and its climate, as well as the vast emporium of economic lives and trade goods that began to circulate around its shores. Crucially, he also focuses on the pathways of Hinduism and Buddhism as they began to move east, too, and seep into Southeast Asia alongside the commodities in ships, and the men sailing them.[17] In the first millennium CE these patterns were established, and imported religion began to "come ashore" in the easternmost Indian Ocean, the doorway to Southeast Asia proper. Early Southeast Asians already had their own varied

14. Pierre-Yves Manguin, "New Ships for New Networks: Trends in Shipbuilding in the South China Sea in the Fifteenth and Sixteenth Centuries," in *Southeast Asia in the Fifteenth Century*, ed. Wade and Laichen, 333–58.

15. See K. N. Chaudhuri, *Trade and Civilisation in the Indian Ocean: An Economic History from the Rise of Islam to 1750* (Cambridge: Cambridge University Press, 1985); and Michael Pearson, *The Indian Ocean* (London: Routledge, 2003). These are just two of the best examples; there are many more good books to choose from on Indian Ocean history.

16. Sugata Bose, *A Hundred Horizons: The Indian Ocean in the Age of Global Empire* (Cambridge: Harvard University Press, 2006).

17. See Sunil Amrith, *Crossing the Bay of Bengal: The Furies of Nature and the Fortunes of Migrants* (Cambridge, MA: Harvard University Press, 2013). The section in pages 88–101 is particularly instructive for our purposes, where religion is described in transit, but the whole book is very worthwhile.

beliefs and customs, of course. But the messages from India were readily adopted, and transposed alongside—and sometimes on top of—existing religious systems. Inscriptions from Thanjavur (modern Tanjore), South India, from AD 1030 testify to widespread Chola raiding in the region as well:

Sriwijaya (Palembang)	Valaippanadaru (Champ, Vietnam)
Malaiyur (Jambi)	Talaitlakkolam (Kra Isthmus, Thailand)
Mayuradingan (Malay Pen.)	Madalingum (Ligor, Tambralinga, S. Thai)
Ilangosangam (Langkasuka)	Ilamuridesam (N. Sumatra)
Mapppalalam (Pegu Burma)	Kadaram (Kedah)
Mevilimbangan (Ligor, S. Thai)	Mavimbangan (Philippines)[18]

We know from later evidence that temples existed in what seems to have been astonishing numbers along the outstretched coasts of India. In Bengal, for example, the easternmost spur of coastal India facing Southeast Asia, the numbers of historically extant Hindu temples have been tabulated for a number of districts by the Directorate of Archaeology and Museums of Bengal. In Howrah, sixty-four Hindu temples of varying age still exist in forty-two different sites; these date back to at least 1384 CE. In Hooghly, 227 temples in 102 villages and towns, and in Midnapur, 293 temples in 130 villages and towns. In both of these places the structures date back to the thirteenth and fifteenth centuries, respectively. Yet in Burdawan, amazingly, some seven hundred temples exist in seventy villages and towns, also dating back to the thirteenth century.[19] This kind of semireligiose density suggests the kind of volume of ships that may have been launched, as missionaries and priests joined trading expeditions across the Bay of Bengal, looking for souls or profits, respectively, as their intended targets of the voyages. Indeed, Anthony Reid has spoken of a very defined sense of the "western ocean" in his writings about Southeast Asia in the sixteenth and seventeenth centuries, particularly in Aceh, which geographically pointed out into the ocean and took in much of what it encountered, on a civilizational basis. The Ottomans and Persia, as well as India in its many dimensions, both Hindu and Muslim, made up part of this worldview.[20]

18. See Celine Arokiasawang, *Tamil Influences in Malaysia, Indonesia, and the Philippines* (Manila: no publisher; Xerox typescript, Cornell University Library, 2000), 37–41.

19. Ray, "Crossing the Seas," 71.

20. Anthony Reid, "Aceh between Two Worlds: An Intersection of Southeast Asia and the Indian Ocean," in *Cross Currents and Community Networks*, ed. Ray and Alpers, 100–22.

If the numbers of temples is eye-opening, then so is the realization that numerous trading forts also littered the coasts of India, linking vast stretches of coastlines (and their attendant, agricultural interiors) with Southeast Asia farther east.[21] All of these factors made the Bay of Bengal a very fecund place for "influence," both of the commercial and of the religious kind.[22] This state of affairs existed for a long time, and also evolved. We will now turn to see how these influences were received in the place where many of these contacts initially came ashore, in the southern realms of the kingdom of Siam and its attendant dependencies.

The Siamese Case: Southern Siam as Ground Zero for "Contact"

Indian religion did not come to a *tabula rasa* in Southeast Asia—there was no "blank slate," as early European scholarship of the region more or less suggested. Rather, political and religious systems were already in place in a number of parts of Southeast Asia, though these tended to exist on a smaller and less-developed scale than what had already happened in these respects on the Indian subcontinent. In Burma, upland and inward from the mouths of the Irrawaddy River, the great civilization of Bagan existed from the ninth to thirteenth centuries, maintaining a flourishing wet-rice civilization far away from the coasts. In Siam, an analogous kingdom developed at Sukothai, where monumental architecture was also built from 1238 CE to the mid-fifteenth century. Farther to the east of mainland Southeast Asia, other, similar civilizations sprang up, most notably the Khmer empire centered around Angkor Wat (802 to 1431 CE)[23] and also a succession of Vietnamese kingdoms, some of them "Viet" in ethnicity (or Sino-Viet, depending on interpretations), but also some of Austronesian origin, as among the Cham polities of the central Vietnamese coasts. All of these political entities, to one degree or another, actively took on elements of Indian culture and society, whether Hinduism, Buddhism, or a potent admixture of the two. Each refined these borrowings into local

21. Himanshu Prabha Ray, in *Cross Currents and Community Networks*, ed. Ray and Alpers, 6. See also McDaniel, "This Hindu Holy Man Is a Thai Buddhist."

22. See Prapod Assavairulkaharn, *Ascending of the Theravada Buddhism in Southeast Asia* (Bangkok: Silkworm, 1984).

23. See the background provided in B. Ph. Groslier, "Angkor et le Cambodge au XVI siècle," *Annales du Musée Guimet* (Paris, PUF, 1958).

manifestations, but also kept certain hallmarks of the religions that would have been easily recognizable across these mainland cultures. Crucially, this process was an evolving and ongoing one—there was not one wellspring of inspiration that scholars can point to at a certain date or time that began or sparked all of this borrowing. The date of the first vessel touching down on Southeast Asian shores and bringing the Indic religions is not known.[24] But it more helpful to think of this as a process, and a burgeoning set of conversations that took place over a number of centuries. This is likely the most accurate way of decoding a complex set of interactions that took many years to make themselves apparent.[25]

Some of our best evidence suggests that what is today southern Thailand—in and around the Kra Isthmus in what for long periods historically would have been southern Siam—is one of the first places these interactions took place.[26] Indian vessels either crossing the Bay of Bengal outright, or hugging its northern littoral, would have come here with trade goods almost directly from the eastern Indian coastline. They brought ideas with them as well as their cargoes, and it seems clear that some of the first iterations of Hindu/Buddhist images came ashore in Southeast Asia along these coasts. From the first to fifth centuries CE, there were already small polities here—Dunsun at the Kra Isthmus itself, Panpan just south of it, Langkasuka near where modern-day Songkhla lies, the Dvaravati civilization, and Kedah on the Straits of Melaka side, pushing into what is now the northernmost parts of peninsular Malaysia.[27] Two of these polities eventually developed roads connecting the Indian Ocean to the South China Sea across the peninsula, and established kingdoms based on this

24. Some of the most important scholars on the earliest inscriptions of this period are Peter Skilling, Hans Penth, Michael Vickery, and Hiram Woodward; we will explore their work later in this chapter.

25. Kenneth Hall, *A History of Early Southeast Asia: Maritime Trade and Societal Development, 100–1500* (Lanham, MD: Rowman & Littlefield, 2011), chapters 7 and 8. See also Anne Blackburn, "Localizing Lineage: Importing Higher Ordination in Theravadin South and Southeast Asia," in *Constituting Communities: Theravada Buddhism and the Religious Cultures of South and Southeast Asia*, John Clifford Holt, ed. Jacob N. Kinnard and Jonathan S. Walters (Albany: State University of New York Press, 2003), chapter 7.

26. See Guy Lubeigt, "Ancient Transpeninsular Trade Roads and Rivalries over the Tenasserim Coasts," in *Commerce et navigation en Asie du Sud-est (XIV–XIX siècles)*, ed. Nguyễn Thế Anh and Yoshiaki Ishizawa, 47–76 (Paris: L'Harmattan, 1999).

27. See Pattaratorn Chirapravati, *The Votive Tablets in Thailand: Origins, Styles, and Usages* (Oxford: Oxford University Press, 1999).

ability to transship goods between two oceanic worlds. This was Tambralinga just south of the Kra Isthmus, and Langkasuka, which connected modern-day Pattani with Kedah.[28] These two polities might be thought of as the "ground zero" of contact, though that is an overly simplistic statement, when contact likely happened in other places as well. Yet the density of evidence points to at least some early landfalls here, and we will review a bit more of the archaeological evidence in a moment. But the time of the rise of the great mainland kingdoms described in the previous paragraph, this area of the peninsula was gradually coming into ethnically Thai hands. By the fifteenth to sixteenth centuries, and the dawn of the early modern Age in Southeast Asia, all of this area was under Siamese sway, down to the middle latitudes of what is now the nation-state of peninsular Malaysia.[29]

Anthony Reid has spoken of how this period initiated a new age in Southeast Asian history—earlier patterns of trade and contact existed, of course, but by this time the pace of all of this movement and interaction was quickening, and ideas, materiel, and human beings were all in motion much more quickly now, and also in greater volume. As the more inwardly facing Sukothai disintegrated high up the Chao Phraya River, its successor state, Ayutthaya (formed in 1351 CE), maintained much more defined relations with the sea, and a range of peoples ringing it both near and far. For a start Ayutthaya was near modern Bangkok, and within close access of the Gulf of Thailand and all of this accelerating international trade.[30] Reid has shown convincingly through the

28. Paul Michel Munoz, *Early Kingdoms of the Indonesian Archipelago and the Malay Peninsula* (Paris: Éditions Didier Millet, 2006), 85, 100.

29. Charles Higham and Rachanie Thosarat, *Early Thailand: From Prehistory to Sukothai* (Bangkok: River Books, 2012), 223–234, 236–24; Betty Gosling, *Sukothai: Its History, Culture, and Art* (Oxford: Oxford University Press, 1991; Charles Higham and Rachanie Thosarat, *Prehistoric Thailand: From Early Settlement to Sukothai* (Bangkok: River Books, 1998), 187–89; and Paul Michel Munoz, *Early Kingdoms of the Indonesian Archipelago and the Malay Peninsula* (Paris: Éditions Didier Millet, 2006), 197.

30. For an overview, see Dhiravat na Pombejra, "Port, Palace, and Profit: An Overview of Siamese Crown Trade and the European Presence in Siam in the Seventeenth Century," in *Port Cities and Trade in Western Southeast Asia* [Anon.], 65–84 (Bangkok: Institute of Asian Studies, Chulalongkorn University, 1998); U San Nyein, "Trans Peninsular Trade and Cross Regional Warfare between the Maritiem Kingdoms of Ayudhya and Pegu in mid-16th century–mid 17th century" in [Anon.], *Port Cities and Trade*, 55–64; and Barend Ter Weil, "Early Ayyuthaya and Foreign Trade, Some Questions," in *Commerce et navigation*, ed. Nguyễn and Ishizawa, 77–90.

numbers of Siamese tribute missions to China, as well as through Ryukyu (Okinawan) trade contacts and other shipping statistics, how maritime a polity Ayutthaya really was, in all senses of the term. As the Malay peninsula came under Siamese sway, many of the products found there were packed up into crates and sold off into these oceanic networks, winding up thousands of kilometers away. The numbers of Okinawan "red-seal" ships and Chinese junks visiting Siam in the sixteenth and seventeenth centuries would have been impressive enough, but Ayutthaya also traded out west from the Andaman Sea and into the Indian Ocean networks. More contacts with India and Sri Lanka, and especially with Buddhism, came in the wake of these voyages, and Ayutthaya eventually became one of the most recognizably Buddhist of all of the Southeast Asian kingdoms at this time. Diplomacy begat commerce, and commerce stimulated cultural ties, with all of these processes washing over Ayutthaya at once. Though the kingdom became "Buddhist," it was also utterly cosmopolitan in its outlook and human constitution, with Chinese traders, Japanese bodyguards, Persian aristocrats, and even a Greek foreign minister all living within the city's gates.[31] We know from a Dutch account of the kingdom, written about 1630, that women were very much a part of the Buddhist religious mix at this time: "Besides male priests, there are connected with the principal temples many old women, who also have to shave their heads. They are dressed in white linen, and they are present at all sermons, songs, ceremonies, and other occasions connected with the religion. They are not, however, subject to any extraordinary rules and the everything out of religious fervor and free will."[32]

Though we have chronicle-based records for some of these assertions, and Buddhist narratives as well (*tamnan* and *phungsawadan* in Thai), ultimately for the period here archaeological data are crucial in ascertaining the path of commerce and cosmopolitanism in these early Siamese kingdoms.[33] Roxanna Brown's work has been crucial in this respect, giving us an overview of the

31. Anthony Reid, *Charting the Shape of Early Modern Southeast Asian History* (Chiang Mai, Silkworm, 1999), chapter 5; and Anthony Reid, "Hybrid Identities in the Fifteenth-Century Straits," in *Southeast Asia in the Fifteenth Century*, ed. Wade and Laichen, 307–32.

32. Jeremias van Vleet, "Description of the Kingdom of Siam" translated by L.F. van Ravenswaay, *Journal of the Siam Society*, 7, no. 1 (1910): 1–105, at 77.

33. Charnvit Kasetsiri, *The Rise of Ayudhya* (Kuala Lumpur: Oxford University Press, 1976); see also a dissenting voice on the usage of such documents as "History" in Michael Vickery, in "A New Tamnan about Ayudhya," *Journal of the Siam Society* 67, no. 2 (1979).

kinds of ceramics found in various Southeast Asian sites during this entry into the early modern era. She has given a wonderful bird's-eye spread on the kinds of pieces, their dates, and ultimate provenances that highlight the trade contacts that Siam would have been enjoying with the outside world at this time. Though there is indeed land-based evidence for some of this, shipwrecks become increasingly important in the Thai case, as they have left their cargoes in situ, and relatively undisturbed. Ships in Thai waters such as the *Ko Si Chung* II (c. 1405–30), the *Rang Kwien* (c. 1380–1400), the *Ko Khram* (c. 1450), the *Prasae Rayong* (also c. 1450), and the *Ko Si Chang* III (c. 1470–87) all give a sense of the sorts of porcelain and celadons that would have bound these trade contacts together. Indeed, much of the wares for the fifteenth century were indeed celadons and not the more famous blue-and-whites, and this has given rise to a range of theories about a "Ming gap" in exports, as well as more attention to indigenous Southeast Asian pottery industries. The Ming seemingly clamped down down commerce, at least for a while.[34] At least one scholar has looked at these patterns vis-à-vis the Zheng He voyages themselves, and what these epic voyages may have meant over the *longue durée* for the southern-based export of commodities from the Middle Kingdom.[35] It is also possible to look more closely at single wrecks, however, such as at the Kho Kradad wreck off Siam, which has been studied in depth for years now.[36] Either from a macroperspective or from this microperspective described above, we see a dispersion of trade and cultural exchange happening in southern Thai and Burmese waters that was more vigorous than ever before.[37] The importation of Hindu and Buddhist images was part of this matrix, and to that niche in the trade we now turn.

34. Roxanna Brown, "A Ming Gap? Data from Southeast Asian Shipwreck Cargoes," in *Southeast Asia in the Fifteenth Century*, ed. Wade and Laichen, 359–83.

35. John Miksic, "Before and after Zheng He: Comparing Some Southeast Asian Archaeological Sites of the Fourteenth and Fifteenth Centuries," in *Southeast Asia in the Fifteenth Century*, ed. Wade and Laichen, 384–408.

36. Pensak Howitz, *Ceramics from the Sea: Evidence from the Kho Kradad Shipwreck Excavated in 1979* (Bangkok: Archaeology Division of Silpakorn University, 1979); and Jeremy Green, Rosemary Harper, Sayann Prishanchittara, *The Excavation of the Ko Kradat Wrecksite Thailand, 1979–1980* (Perth: Special Publication of the Department of Maritime Archaeology, Western Australian Museum, 1981).

37. See Sunait Chutintaranond, "Mergui and Tenasserim as Leading Port Cities in the Context of Autonomous History," in *Port Cities and Trade*, 1–14, and Khin Maung Myunt, "Pegu as an Urban Commercial Centre for the Mon and Myanmar Kingdoms of Lower Myanmar," in *Port Cities and Trade*, 15–36.

TABLE 6.1. Underwater Archaeological Ceramic Data

Several Ceramic-Bearing Wrecks in Thai Waters

Site	Age of wreck	Ceramic cargoes found
Rang Kwien	c. 1380–1400 CE	dishes; storage jars; brown and green wares
Ko Si Chang II	1405–1424/30	storage jars; Sukothai fish and floral motifs; Sawankhalok green
Prasae Rayong	c. 1450	Singburi wares; Champa ware;
Kho Khram	c. 1450	Sukothai plates; classic celadon;
Ko Si Chang II	c. 1470–87	Burmese and Vietnamese wares

Note: Other wrecks have contained Siamese wares of various types, sometimes in great abundance; see Miksic below for details on this for the same approximate period.
Source: Abstracted from Brown (2010) and Miksic (2010)

Ceramics Found in the Koh Kradad Wreck, 1979–1980 Excavations

Complete		Fragments	
Ceramics from Sawankhalok	Free-glazed wares from Sawankhalok	Glazed wares, other origins	Stone/earthenware Various origins
46 pieces	1,801 pieces	8 pieces	747 pieces

Catalogue of artifacts: Sawankhalok, brown (spotted jarlets; gourd-shaped bottles; eared bottles); Sawankhalok black underglaze jars (pear-shaped; jarlets; bowls); Sawankhalok black underglaze cover boxes (mangosteen lids; lotus lids; plain lids); whitewares; earthenwares; stonewares; Chinese blue-and-white wares; ballast.

Source: Adapted from Jeremy Green, Rosemary Harper, and Sayann Prishanchittara, *The Excavation of the Ko Kradat Wrecksite Thailand, 1979–1980* (Perth: Special Publication of the Department of Maritime Archaeology, Western Australian Museum, 1981); and Pensak C. Howitz, *Ceramics from the Sea: Evidence from the Kho Kradad Shipwreck Excavated in 1979* (Bangkok: Archaeology Division of Silpakorn University, 1979).

A Passage of Amulets

Amulets and votives have a hallowed place in Thai society.[38] Even today, the Buddhist amulet of protection is a trope that any Thai person would understand immediately, from the northern borders with Burma and Laos to the far south along the Malaysian frontier. Anthropologists have studied these amulets for what they tell us about Thai senses of danger in the world, and how Buddhism can help avert disaster when such amulets are worn in protective

38. For a general consideration of how amulets and relics work in Buddhism, see Kevin Trainor, *Relics, Ritual, and Representation* (Cambridge: Cambridge University Press, 1997).

form, or kept in one's house as a propitiation tablet.[39] Chris Baker and Pasuk Phongpaichit have taken this story farther into the past, showing how four-hundred-year-old Thai epics encouraged such philosophies, and how the uses of amulets were gradually incorporated away from canonical texts, and brought into mainstream Thai society through common beliefs.[40] Yet the story goes even further back historically than this. Stanley Tambiah and others have also excavated even older forms of amulet-veneration, often going back to forest-monks (rural ascetics being an important class of mendicant Buddhists in Siam), and the beginnings of the *sangha* in classical times.[41] If we take yet another step back, to the arrival of Buddhism in Thai waters in the first mil-lennium CE, we can see an almost uninterrupted line, therefore, between the ascribed efficacy of amulets and votives and the utility such objects are be-lieved to hold, almost literally from the start of Buddhism's arrival in Siam to its most contemporary expression today. Taxi drivers in Bangkok's streets share this genealogy of knowledge with southern Siamese fisher-folk, the latter of whom were introduced to these images well over a thousand years ago. The passage of amulets holds rare influence and deference as tools of belief, there-fore, in Thai society as a whole.

In the middle and later centuries of the first millennium CE, amulets, votive tablets, and small-scale statuary, both Hindu and Buddhist, began to come ashore in southern Siam from the Indian subcontinent.[42] Many of these pieces washed up in and around the Kra Isthmus, the narrowest point of the peninsula, but others ended up coming into Southeast Asia both north and south of here. Hinduism, of course, had already been well established in

39. Pattana Kitiarsa, *Mediums, Monks, and Amulets: Thai Popular Buddhism Today* (Chiang Mai: Silkworm Books, 2012).

40. Chris Baker and Pasuk Phongpaichit, "Protection and Power in Siam: From Khun Chang Khun Phaen to the Buddhist Amulet," *Southeast Asian Studies* 2, no. 2 (2013): 215–42. See also Chris Baker and Pasuk Phongpaichit, *A History of Ayutthaya: Siam in the Early Modern World* (Cambridge: Cambridge University Press, 2017).

41. Stanley Tambiah, *The Buddhist Saints of the Forest and the Cult of Amulets: A Study in Charisma, Hagiography, Sectarianism, and Millennial Buddhism* (Cambridge: Cambridge Uni-versity Press, 1984); see also James McDermott, "The Buddhist Saints of the Forest and the Cult of the Amulets: A Study in Charisma, Hagiography, Sectarianism, and Millennial Buddhism by Stanley Tambiah," *Journal of the American Oriental Society* 106, no. 2 (1986): 350.

42. For a very good review, see John Guy, *Lost Kingdoms: Hindu-Buddhist Sculpture of Early Southeast Asia* (New York and New Haven: Metropolitan Museum of Art and Yale University Press, 2018).

India by this time; a caste system was developing, many of the great epics had already been written, and Hindu gods and goddesses littered the Indian landscape, often standing in stone splendor in brightly colored temples.[43] The Chola empire in southeastern India (ended 1279 CE) became a great naval power in the region, and eventually brought many of the tenets of Hinduism to Southeast Asia, sometimes in armed ships and among soldiers, but more likely via the scattered efforts of itinerant priests. These men acted both as spiritual helpers to Indian troops who were sent to the region, and also likely as practitioners of sorts when some local peoples adopted various notions of Hinduism. Buddhism also came, having developed in Nepal and the north of India in a series of sites associated with the life of the historical Buddha, Gautama; from there the religion spread by land to Tibet and then farther east to China, Japan, and Korea. But it also spread by sea to Southeast Asia, and came in its Theravada variant, which is now marked off in the latter region most visibly by a *sangha* (or community of monks and nuns) who don brown robes.[44] Buddhism and Hinduism mixed easily as ritual and ascetic systems in Southeast Asia. Many early adopters of versions the two religions worshipped various ideas of both traditions (which were themselves varied traditions under one umbrella name), and freely and easily mingled the ideas of both schools of thought in their own daily lives. It is for this reason that we see Visnaivite and Sivite temples and images in the region (and Surya and Krishna, Murugan, Devi and Harihara, etc.), but also more recognizably "Buddhist" ones; a few miles down the road, other edifices or statuary may have evidence of both religions extant at a single site. Southeast Asia borrowed what it wanted of the proffered traditions and lineages, and mixed and matched constantly, according to local needs or tastes.

We can see these processes at work in the remnants of both religions in southern Siam at this time. In his now classic study *Hindu Gods of Peninsular Siam*, art historian Stanley O'Connor has referred to the South-to-Southeast Asia religious transit as both "bridge and barrier," a pithy but plainly accurate description of the history of religious and intellectual movement between the

---

43. For an explanation of Hinduism historically, see David Lorenzon, "Who Invented Hinduism?" *Comparative Studies in Society and History* 41, no. 4 (1999): 630–59.

44. On Theravada Buddhism, its variants and definitions and evolution, see Anne Blackburn and others in Peter Skilling et al., *How Theravada Is Theravada? Exploring Buddhist Identities* (Seattle: University of Washington Press, 2012); and Juliane Schober et al., *Theravada Encounters with Modernity* (London: Routledge, 2019).

two places since at least the third century CE. Some of the statuary that was found on the Malay Peninsula in southern Siam, like a group of figures he calls "aberrant statues of Vishnu," fit this mold—they are recognizably Visnavite, but altered enough (in this case by conch-shells depicted on their hips) to be different in appearance. Inscriptions in Pali, Pallava, and Sanskrit tie them to the subcontinent, but also mark some of the Nakhon si Thammarat pieces as being "other" in conception. O'Connor makes useful comparisons between the Southeast Asian finds and analogous pieces such as Kusana images from Mathura and Vishnus from Bhinmal, in distant Gujarat, so that we can see the wellsprings of inspiration, but also the extant differences between regions. With a Vishnu statue from Takuapa in southern Siam, he also sees Pallava analogies, and then compares these to other figures found in Sichon, Sating Pra, Petburi, and in Surat Thani Province. The spread of influences from distant Indic sources is unmistakable, but so is the diversity of the Southeast Asian pieces, which show ties to India but also some changes as other figures were morphed to reflect local ideas and tastes. Since most of the forms described below date from roughly the sixth to the eighth centuries, we can see how old these processes are, and how long they have been play in this area of Southeast Asia. We can also see how pieces that form clusters in one "landing spot" of Indic symbols then take on new meanings when their iconographies are later repeated elsewhere, in places such as Angkorian Cambodia and Cham Vietnam.[45]

Hiram Woodward has also been an important interpreter of the detritus of civilizational contact in southern Siam. In his case, he has looked long and hard at Buddhist relics in the region, and has even suggested that some Indian workshops that were initially responsible for producing Hindu statuary and votives that traveled to Southeast Asia eventually turned to producing Buddhist relics as well. Woodward has pointed to the similarities between a number of Buddhist statues that were found in the Thai south: for example, a Lokesvara from Chaiya and a Bodhisattva from Khu Bua (stupa no. 40). Facial modeling, coiffures, the draping of clothing over shoulders in statuary representation, and postures all point to similar provenances of production, or at least of the modeling of iconographic ideas. Some of these (and other statues) are made of limestone, but others were made of bronze, and all of these would have traveled and then withstood the test of time to preserve as artifacts.

---

45. See Stanley O'Connor, *Hindu Gods of Peninsular Siam* (Ascona, Switzerland: Artibus Asiae Publishers, 1972), 11–18, 19, 27, 32–37, 41–48.

FIGURE 6.1. Stone Votive Figure, Southern Siam, 8th–12th c.
(British Museum, AS 107 .40)

Woodward suggests the Deccan Plateau in south-central India as one possible place of inspiration for these figures, but also does not rule out Sri Lanka as another possible site. The area of Chaiya seems to have been a major crossroads of sorts from the eighth to the tenth centuries, and the archaeological record is particularly rich in this area. T'ang Dynasty ceramics have also been found in the area, so that the connection between commercial and spiritual worlds—one from China, shipping porcelain, the other from India, shipping religious images—likely met in and around this place. Traditions collided, and then were incorporated locally, both in terms of gods being worshipped, and the more prosaic concern of eating off of durable plates. In this way we see again the central importance of the southern Thai coasts in bridging these two worlds, the Andaman Sea (and its connections to the wider Indian Ocean) and the Gulf of Thailand, with its connections farther north to China.[46]

A third example might be taken from a recent doctoral dissertation completed by Wannasarn Noonsuk at Cornell. Noonsuk has focused his archaeological and art historical efforts down to one place, the Tambralinga site in southern Siam. While O'Connor, Woodward, and others have been primarily concerned with explaining larger stories of these early connections, Noonsuk levels his gaze down to one site, and then proceeds outward from there, the opposite tack from his predecessors, in some respects. Tambralinga, as explained above, became one of the two most important portage centers on the peninsula during the middle centuries of the first millennium; its roads extended both to the Indian Ocean and to the South China Sea, putting it in material and ideological conversation with distant civilizations. Noonsuk shows the archaeological connections with the rest of Southeast Asia that developed as a consequence of this, but also to India, and eventually to Rome, some ten thousand miles away. On the Gulf of Thailand side of its operations, it was also trading with China, as the scattered detritus on its shores still shows in plain detail. Bronze drums began to show up as these quintessentially Southeast Asian material-culture artifacts began to spread through early Southeast Asia, as did Vishnavite statues, transiting from India. But Noonsuk goes further than this, and explores the geography and environment of the Tambralinga area in great detail, to show how the polity ran in its local comings-and-goings and day-to-day manifestations. Thus the seashore becomes not just a site of exchange with distant civilizations but also a place for gathering food. The coastal plain is not just a dwelling but, in Noonsuk's words, the "granary of the kingdom." The foothills and mountains bring in the exotic wealth of Tambralinga, in terms of forest products and other difficult-to-source items. Finally, the polity is also put into perspective next to the political behemoth of the Srivjaya Empire, which was beginning to grow ominously nearby in the Melaka Strait, from the seventh to twelfth centuries. This kind of geographical analysis helps along our religious queries on influence and transmission, as it shows such questions to be only part and parcel of a larger bundle of societal concerns, from sustenance to luxuries to spiritual objects, sourced from afar.[47]

46. Hiram Woodward, *The Art and Architecture of Thailand from Prehistoric Times through the Thirteenth Century* (Leiden: Brill, 2003), 82–86.

47. Wannasarn Noonsuk, "Archaeology and Cultural Geography of Tambralinga in Peninsular Siam," PhD thesis (Ithaca, NY: Cornell University, History of Art Department, 2012).

FIGURE 6.2. Bay of Bengal Sculpture:
Avalokitesvara (Sri Lanka, circa 750 CE) (Sean Pathasema,
Birmingham Museum of Art)

Peninsular Siam thus appears through all of these studies as a kind of microcosm of connection. It was a place where patterns met, where the tendrils of some societies reaching out to the world either commercially or ideologically were met by the tentative "feelers" of others.[48] In a different publication, O'Connor classified many of these overtures looking at this place as just such a multivariable "site," mixing archaeology, stone pottery finds, early Brahmanical sculpture, Tamil (and even Roman) texts on distant geographical knowledge, and the beginnings of Khmer diplomacy on the eve of the Angkorian

48. A fantastic, very new explication of these patterns can be found in Berenice Bellina, *Khao Sam Kaeo: An Early Port-City Between the Indian Ocean and the South China Sea* (Paris: EFEO, 2017).

empire.[49] One senses that the Kra Isthmus and its environs, now such a "distant," "remote," and "marginal" place, was once very much the opposite of all of these admittedly relativist adjectives. But looking at it in this way allows us to "re-vision" (in the words of art historian Piriya Krairiksh) the pathways of religious movement, and to see it as a site of great civilizational worth.[50] In central-place theory, this was a place that once was central, in both religious and commercial terms, even if it is no longer so. It contained what Julius Baptista has called in a related context the "spirit of things," those things being material objects of great worth in transit, the human beings carrying them, and the ideas brought along for the journey, all in one bundled package.[51] It was in spaces such as this one that some of the earliest long-distance conversations between far-flung societies took place. We may never know the exact composition of such conversations, though there is still a record to be read, mostly in scattered shards and broken statues, even if the textual record is mostly silent. Yet it is there to be read and interpreted by those with the tools who know how to do this. That is encouraging, because such efforts will in fact put us in communion with the pathways of the ancients. We inherited their world, though the footprints on a "trackless sea" are no longer all there to be read.[52]

Conclusion

It is clear that commodities moved across large ocean spaces in the distant past—and sometimes across very large spaces, connecting civilizations that we often think of as being separate and isolated. Textiles, for example, have a long history of connectivity, even binding together places such as ancient Rome and ancient India, though in truth some individual pieces may have traveled even larger distances, wrapping Mediterranean antiquity and ancient

49. Stanley O'Connor, ed., *The Archaeology of Peninsular Siam* (Bangkok: The Siam Society, 1986).

50. Piriya Krairiksh, "Review Article: Re-Visioning Buddhist Art in Thailand," *Journal of Southeast Asian Studies* 45, no. 1: 113–18.

51. Julius Bautista, ed., *The Spirit of Things: Materiality and Religious Diversity in Southeast Asia* (Ithaca, NY: Cornell University Southeast Asia Program, 2012).

52. See O'Connor as quoted in Ronald Bernier, "Review of Hindu Gods of Peninsular Siam by Stanley O'Connor," *Journal of Asian Studies* 33, no. 4 (1974): 732–33.

China into one transcontinental commercial circuit.[53] Outside of commerce, religion may have fulfilled some of the same linking functions, bringing together regions that normally had little reason to exist together in the same spheres of activity. Early Hindu and Buddhist statuary, relics, and amulets were part of this process, and are extremely useful tools in telling us how these places came into communion with each other over long periods of time. Unlike textiles, which unravel and eventually wither in the heat and the humidity of the tropics, stone and metal-based votives still survive, though they are exceedingly rare to find. In their archaeological dispersion and displacement, however, we can spy some of the patterns of the ancient world and how regions were brought together. There is no doubt whatsoever that early trade between the Indian subcontinent (including Sri Lanka) and Southeast Asia was based on trade, often in foodstuffs but in a range of other commodities as well. War and the territorial designs of empires such as the Colas and Srivijaya also contributed to this civilizational conversation. Yet it seems equally beyond doubt now that religion played major roles in these connections, too, and the best way to chart these processes is through analyzing such objects of devotion as they moved from one place to another.

I have argued that by the end of the first millennium CE the eastern half of the Indian Ocean was a fairly well-trafficked space. Contact between the Indic worlds of the subcontinent and the emerging small polities of Southeast Asia had already gathered pace by the end of this period, and several centuries of influence had left the latter region in particular filled with images of the former. Hindu and Buddhist iconography was a large part of this process; as the gods travelled, culture traveled as well, and small kingdoms began to sprout up in numerous places in Southeast Asia based at least partially on Indic models. Small, portable statues of the gods, alongside votive tablets and a more wearable class of amulets, all trickled into the region over the course of several centuries. The lower reaches of peninsular Siam became an especially fecund ground for such interactions, as Indian ships must have disgorged over the centuries literally thousands of sailors, priests, and tradesmen looking to make their fortunes in this "New World," out and across the Bay of Bengal. Where they landed, Hinduism and Buddhism took root. By the end of the first

---

53. See John Peter Wild and Felicity Wild, "Rome and India: Early Indian Cotton Textiles from Berenike, Red Sea Coast of Egypt," in *Textiles in Indian Ocean Societies*, ed. Ruth Barnes, 11–16 (New York: Routledge, 2005); and Himanshu Prabha Ray, "Far-flung Fabrics—Indian Textiles in Ancient Maritime Trade," in *Textiles in Indian Ocean Societies*, ed. Barnes, 17–37.

millennium it is not an exaggeration to say that many middle-class households on the peninsula likely had a votive of the "new" religions, in one form or another. These served as markers—"signposts from the sea," in a way—of the new ideas that had come, and that were still coming on the tides. The beginnings of a religious sermon (delivered as a monologue) eventually became a centuries-long conversation instead. And that conversation still continues today, often with monks and materiel now moving in the other direction as well. Here, as elsewhere, the ocean provided a medium for the exchange of ritual technologies and ethical narrative traditions. The terms of that conversation will gradually be better and better understood over time, as more and more of this passage of amulets is discovered and unearthed in these ancient cities by the sea.

7

Zamboanga, Mindanao

ISLAM AND CHRISTIANITY AT
THE END OF THE WORLD

The Muslims here—their ancestors come from everywhere, actually. For such a remote place, it's actually very central.

—MUSLIM WOMAN, ZAMBOANGA, MINDANAO[1]

ZAMBOANGA, A PORT CITY at the end of Mindanao's southwestern "spider-arm" peninsula—which juts away from the rest of the Philippines like an unwanted appendage—looks and feels like the end of the world. It *is* the end of the world, in some respects. This is the place where the Philippines ends and where the Malay world begins. It is connected to the latter through a history of shared religion (Islam) and shared trade (in ocean products). Yet it is also a frontier town of sorts in other ways, one with its own language (Chavacano, a mix of Spanish and Cebuano and other languages), and with its own distinct "feel" when one walks its streets. It has the aura of old Spain, or perhaps more accurately, the crumbling Spanish empire, replete with rusting, standing cannons, facing out to sea. It also is marked with the symbols of Islam as one sees numerous small, corrugated-tin mosques, a sign of some of the most eastern-most extensions of the religion in the monsoon seas of Southeast Asia. The Catholicism of that most Christian of places, the Philippine archipelago, is certainly present, but it stands equally alongside this presence of diasporic Islam. The two mix peacefully at most times now, though with tension

---

1. Author's fieldwork notes, August 2004.

MAP 7.1. The Sulu Sea

episodically. Once in a long while there is a metaphorical or actual explosion, when the two sides cannot coexist.[2] As frontier towns go, this one is understudied. For certain periods of time it has simply been too dangerous to wander around and ask questions, given the dynamics in play. But Zamboanga is nothing if not fascinating. Though it is the "end of the world" in numerous senses (the end of Philippine Catholicism; the end of the "abode of Islam" (dar al-Islam); the end of several nation-states), it also has its own ontology. In terms of maritime connectivity and the place of religion in the binding of far-flung locales, it is difficult to imagine a more central place.

This chapter looks at Zamboanga as such an ending locale with multiple meanings; I argue that it inhabits these spaces (metaphorical and actual) at

2. This in fact happened right around the time I was there, when Muslim insurgents planted a bomb on the Basilan-to-Zamboanga ferry, killing some thirty people when it went off. Patricio Abinales has told me that Zamboanga is a "cosmoplitan town (Malays, Spanish, Chinese, Tagalogs, Visayans, Indians, Germans, Brits, etc.), but also somewhat an 'isolated' and bealeaguered mini-fortress, surrounded by the country's two largest sultanates—with which it was intermittently at war." Personal correspondence, September 2018.

once and at the same time. The chapter is divided into three roughly equally sized parts. In the first third, "The Flow of History," we look at how this place came to be, from its early origins in the network of Islamic ports dotting Asia's seas (from Kilwa in East Africa all the way to Zamboanga in the east) to the arrival of the Spanish in the sixteenth century.[3] Several centuries of rule by Muslim potentates in the region, culminating in the Sulu Sultanate, were ended by more vigorous Spanish interventions toward the end of the nineteenth century. The arrival of the American imperial project after that, pushing into the twentieth century, continued some of these earlier patterns and began some others, which we will examine. The second part of the chapter, "An Incendiary Time," then looks at the tensions around Zamboanga in the period after Philippine independence, and into our own era. The rise of various Moro Islamic organizations will be touched upon, as well as the national and international context of Muslim-Christian strife, which became the norm in the southern Philippines for several decades. Finally, the last part of the chapter, "In Zamboanga," will chronicle in brief my own wanderings there, when I spent some time in the town and its environs asking questions of local people. I spoke to both Muslims and Christians when I was there, as well as to others (mostly in Manila) who were in a position to comment knowledgeably on the place of Zamboanga in the region's troubles. Their observations and opinions end the chapter because their sentiments should indeed matter most, even if I serve here as the conduit to get to their musings on this city by the sea.

The Flow of History

Southwestern Mindanao became important in the seventeenth century as the seat of the Maguindanao Sultanate, a polity based on what is now Cotabato, but with radials extending in all directions (including to Zamboanga) from that central, administrative center. Sultan Kudarat was the most important personage in the maintenance and growth of this state, and his name still

---

3. For background, see H. Grosset-Grange, "Les procédés arabes de navigation en Océan indien au moment des grandes découvertes," in *Sociétés et compagnies de commerce en Orient et dans l'OcéanIindien*, ed. M. Mollat, 227–46 (Paris: SEVPEN, 1970). For the winder context of Islam in the region, see Michael Laffan, *Islamic Nationhood and Colonial Indonesia: The Umma Below the Winds* (London: Routledge, 2003); Michael Laffan, *The Makings of Indonesian Islam: Orientalism and the Narraiton of a Sufi Past* (Princeton: Princeton University Press, 2011); and Michael Feener and Terenjit Sevea, eds., *Islamic Connections: Muslim Societies in South and Southeast Asia* (Singapore: SIEAS Press, 2009).

appears in many contemporary places as a mark of respect for which his achievements are held. The Maguindanao Sultanate was coastal, but it also relied on heavy traffic with the interior of Mindanao. The Pulangi River (named the Rio Grande de Mindanao by the Spanish in their travels into the center of the island) was the ideal thoroughfare for long-distance contact and commerce, and facilitated the exchange of goods with the various peoples living in the forested highlands. Seasonally the river would flood, leaving a vast lake of irrigated land which could then be harvested with crops for months afterward. Maguindanao flourished on both of these tracks, the one mercantile and movement based, and the other sedentary and agricultural. But one of the key items of commerce over time became human beings, both highland minorities who were then captured or sold down to the lowlands, or people living in small communities on coasts or islands close enough to Maguindanao to come into the ambit of this evolving kingdom. The sultanate became large and powerful enough eventually to be known far outside of Southeast Asia's waters, with representatives of Holland, England, and Spain all mentioning the place in their records.[4]

Of these powers, it was eventually Spain who became most important in this arena, starting from the end of the sixteenth century.[5] The Spanish had of course passed through the middle to lower reaches of the Philippines with the voyages of Magellan, as chronicled by Pigafetta, but the sixteenth century was a time of general Spanish activity in the area, as they built small forts from this arena all the way to the Spice Islands in Eastern Indonesia.[6] Between 1597 and 1599, a Spanish fort was erected in Zamboanga, but it was abandoned after only three years when Spanish Cebu was under threat of English attack, and Madrid decided to move the garrison from the former to the later port in defense. In 1635 the Spanish returned to Zamboanga, and this time a fort made out of stone was erected. Captain Juan de Chavez was the instigator of this expedition, and he brought three hundred Spanish and one thousand Visayan (Central Philippine) troops with him to erect the fortifications. Yet in 1663

---

4. See Eric Casino, *Mindanao Statecraft and Ecology: Moros, Lumads, and Settlers across the Lowland-Highland Continuum* (Cotabato: Notre Dame University, 2000), 2, 6, 20–22.

5. For two recent treatments, see Arturo Giraldez, *The Age of Trade: The Manila Galleons and the Dawn of the Global Economy* (Lanham: Rowman and Littlefield, 2015); and Birgit Tremml-Werner, *Spain, China and Japan in Manila, 1571–1644: Local Comparisons and Global Connections* (Amsterdam: University of Amsterdam Press, 2015).

6. See Ricardo Padron, *The Indies of the Settling Sun: How Early Modern Spain Mapped the Far East and the Transpacific West* (Chicago: University of Chicago Press, 2020).

history repeated itself; a new incursion, this time against Manila itself, was threatened, only this time it was the Ming loyalist forces of Coxinga (Chen Chen-kong) who comprised the threat via Taiwan, rather than an invading European navy. Zamboanga's fort was again abandoned, and it would not be until 1718 that the Spanish would come back once again. By this time the Sulu Sultanate, based just south of Zamboanga, was in full ascendency, and Spain needed a counterweight against the sultanate's growing influence in the area. Of primary importance to the Spanish, hundreds and eventually thousands of escaped slaves eventually made their way to Zamboanga, fleeing the coastal depredations of Sulu as the sultanate's slaving vessels increasingly swept through insular Southeast Asia. In order to facilitate communication, it seems the Chavacano language emerged around this time in Zamboanga, a mix of Spanish and various Visayan tongues used to communicate in the town. Settlements around the fort began to grow in earnest after around 1865, when Jesuits came back to the city after a long absence over the centuries of Spanish decline.[7] Their missionary efforts also brought more people "under the bells," so that Zamboanga began to grow. Among these populations were also various nomadic or seminomadic "sea peoples," such as the Samal, the Yakan, and the Bajau Laut, all of which started to scatter along the coastline of the city.

The Maguindanao Sultanate was the earliest Muslim polity of any size or strength in southwestern Mindanao, but Islam predated its rise, and there is in fact good evidence of the presence of Islam stretching back much farther here than the seventeenth century height of Sultan Kudarat.[8] Cesar Majul, the doyen of scholars working on the Muslim southern Philippines, wrote extensively on this early history, and has done the field a great favor in coordinating the scant bits of various information that have been found. Among these are his studies of early Islamic gravestones, scattered throughout Sulu and parts of Mindanao and reaching back to at least the fifteenth century. These gravestones, elegantly inscribed in Arabic script, are a testament to the push of Islam

7. Noelle Rodriguez, *Zamboanga: A World Between Worlds, Cradle of an Emerging Civilization* (Pasig City: Fundación Santiago, 2003).

8. Some of this influence and lineage, as will see later in the ethnographic part of this chapter, was Persian; for background on these early movements, see Jean Calmard, "The Iranian Merchants: Formation and Rise of a Pressure Group between the Sixteenth and Nineteenth Centuries," in *Asian Merchants and Businessmen in the Indian Ocean and the China Sea*, ed. Denys Lombard and Jan Aubin (Oxford: Oxford University Press, 2000); and Gérard Naulleau, "Islam and Trade: The Case of Some Merchant Families from the Gulf," in *Asian Merchants and Businessmen*, ed. Lombard and Aubin.

east along the trade routes at a very early date, when the religion was in fact just coming to Southeast Asia. The Sulu basin is in fact home to some of the earliest physical remnants of Islam in the region. Majul also went through the Chinese chronicles, and found evidence of proto-state Muslim polities that the Chinese identified in this region in the fourteenth century, during Mongol rule in China.[9] Other scholars, such as Peter Gowing but also others, have also taken a deep and abiding interest in the roots of Islam in this arena, and have laid out typologies of how systems comprising sultans and *datus* (princes) might be approached at a time when larger-scale states had not yet developed in the region.[10] All of these sources point to a thriving Islamic culture in the Sulu basin, one that was vital and actively proselytizing, winning converts in a region now shared by several nation-states at their collective interstices.

Yet the most sophisticated treatment of the meeting of Muslim and Christian actors in the region is undoubtedly that of James Francis Warren, through his now classic monograph *The Sulu Zone: The Dynamics of External Trade, Slavery, and Ethnicity in the Transformation of a Southeast Asian Maritime State.* Some of the patterns already identified with the Maguindanao Sultanate farther to the east on Mindanao proper—namely slave raiding and long-distance trade, as well as diplomatic maneuvering—were perfected by the Sulu Sultanate that Warren describes in his book, after the time of the Maguindanao regime. Sulu, in effect, supplanted the Cotabato regime as the most vibrant Muslim power in the region, and because of this, Jolo (the seat of Sulu's power, just south of Zamboanga in the Sulu archipelago itself) became the nemesis of the expanding Spanish project based in Zamboanga. From the late eighteenth to the late nineteenth century, the Sulu Sultanate sent out slaving and raiding expeditions throughout maritime Southeast Asia, all the way to New Guinea in the east and up through the Straits of Melaka as far as Burma in the west. Hundreds of thousands of captives were taken, usually among lowland coastal populations, many of whom themselves were Muslims. But various so-called sea peoples were also taken (the Orang Laut as a group, but of many

9. Cesar Adib Majul, *Muslims in the Philippines* (Quezon City: University of the Philippines Press, 1973). What Majul started others have then taken up—scholarship on Chinese relations with the early Philippines has become a trendy topic of late.

10. Peter Gowing and Robert McAmis, eds., *The Muslim Filipinos* (Manila; Solidaridad Publishing, 1974). The 1970s became a time of expanded publishing on the Muslim Philippine South, with a cottage industry of sorts developing to help explain rising tensions there under the Marcos regime.

FIGURE 7.1. Zamboanga, Mindanao: Cannon and Mosque (author's photo)

different regional nomenclatures), and all of them were put to work in procuring sea products, which were then shipped off across the South China Sea to feed the insatiable Chinese market. Sulu's *datus* were given river-mouth fiefdoms in Mindanao, Borneo, and other places to extract upcountry forest produce as well, which was shipped alongside the sea products to Canton. The entire system worked for roughly a century, and was only gradually checked by the advent of Spanish gunboats in the region. Spain wanted access to these economic profits, and Manila also wanted to ensure that a flourishing Muslim maritime power was not on its doorstep as Spain's own navies advanced southward through the Philippine archipelago.[11]

By the late nineteenth century Spain's dominance was starting to come to bear in southwestern Mindanao. Spanish cruisers had sailed these waters previously, occasionally engaging with Muslim craft and despoiling them of their cargoes. The material commodities were confiscated, and sold for profit elsewhere, either in Zamboanga or in Manila; the human cargoes were kept locally, and though many became settlers in and around Zamboanga, the reality of many of their lives was just another form of servitude under Europeans, instead of under armed Muslim rulers from the Philippine South. The Tausug

11. James Francis Warren, *The Sulu Zone: The Dynamics of External Trade, Slavery, and Ethnicity in the Transformation of a Southeast Asian Maritime State* (Singapore: Singapore University Press, 1981).

and Iranun peoples who made the Sulu Sultanate run were able to marshal an extraordinary amount of seasonal labor to make these operations work, but in the face of Spanish steamships—now appearing in southwestern Mindanao's waters regularly for the first time, by the late nineteenth century—they were technologically outmatched. This went for the other viable Muslim political force in the region too, Datu Utto of Buayan, who was the inheritor of the Maguindanao Sultanate's power in and around Cotabato from earlier in the seventeenth century. Both Datu Utto and the Sulu Sultanate had wide, outstretched trade contacts and vassalages in the Sulu Sea and southwestern Mindanao, yet neither could compete with Spanish ships when they started to make a concerted campaign of harassing Muslim shipping in the region in the 1860s, '70s, and '80s. Both of these sultanates—representing the last gasp of autonomous Muslim political power in this arena which was already now centuries old—succumbed to the new realities by the end of the 1800s. But it would be the presence of a new imperial power in the region, the Americans, that would solidify these evolving patterns and set up a new status quo as the twentieth century began.[12]

The story of the American conquest of the Philippines from Spain, and then from the indigenous Filipinos themselves, has been well told elsewhere.[13] Suffice it to say that for our purposes, the coming of the United States military to the southwestern corner of Mindanao was a major event, as an older, weak colonial power was now replaced with a younger, much stronger imperial one. Though much of the action of the American advance in the Philippines took place elsewhere, especially in the North (particularly on Luzon), between 1899 and 1903 the majority-Muslim areas of the South, including Mindanao and Sulu, were also conquered. After this, Washington and American Manila undertook a carrot-and-stick policy to convince Muslim Filipinos that it was in their best interests to succumb to United States rule. This only partially worked. The US did build schools and roads, and provided for the means of bettering local agriculture, all things that local Muslims wanted in this part of the archipelago. But General Wood, the American commander in the South, was also a hard-nosed soldier, and went after dissenters with all means at his

12. See Reynaldo Ileto, *Magindanao, 1860–1888: The Career of Datu Utto of Buayan* (Manila: Anvil, 2007).

13. Rey Ileto, *Pasyon and Revolution: Popular Movements in the Philippines, 1840–1910* (Manila: Ateneo de Manila Press, 1997); Glenn May, *The Battle for Batangas: A Philippine Province at War* (New Haven: Yale University Press, 1991).

disposal. Military operations ensued in Cotabato (especially the pursuit of Datu Ali), in Lanao (the so-called Taraca expeditions), and in Sulu, where fighting took place by sea as well as inland on heavily forested islands, such as Jolo and Basilan. By the time General John Pershing assumed command for the period of 1909 to 1913, Muslim resistance to the American imperial project was scattered, and then practically nonexistent. The imperial war of attrition now became a day-to-day reality of colonial occupation.[14]

Pershing, like Wood before him, was a soldier—his policies and also the cadence of his administration of southwestern Mindanao was decidedly military in bearing. Yet after 1913 the Muslim South of the Philippines was being run not as a theater of war but as an arm of government. The Department of Mindanao and Sulu was set up for the period of 1914 to 1920 and was put under the guidance of Frank Carpenter, who was much more a bureaucrat than a soldier. Public order was mostly ensured by this time, and finance, mining, trade, and education all became formalized. The far South of the archipelago took on an air of peaceable normalcy not seen for many decades, if not for several centuries (if we include the raiding incursions of the various maritime and riverine sultanates in our considerations). Still, this was rule by outsiders, and by unwanted, Christian outsiders at that. The Americans diminished the powers of Muslim leaders, and also rendered them toothless, for the most part, in all but religious considerations in terms of their hold on the local populace. Perhaps even more tellingly, Manila—whose policies were run and coordinated by Americans at the highest levels of government—encouraged migration from Christian, northern regions of the Philippines to the Muslim South. Southwestern Mindanao, as was the case with other parts of the southern Philippines, was demographically altered by Catholic settlers in the middle decades of the twentieth century. After independence, in particular, areas of the South that had once seen Muslim majorities now became minorities in the space of a few years. In some areas the resulting imbalances were enormous, so that Benigno Aquino, the former senator of the Philippines, commented that in some coastal areas of Mindanao, Christians now outnumbered Muslims five to one. This was especially so after 1945, and in regions that had previously been majority Muslim in character. With such population imbalances occurring in such a short time, and after decades of war and instability, it seems only natural that this vast maritime theater, stretching from Zamboanga for miles

---

14. See Peter Gowing, *Mandate in Moroland: The American Government of Muslim Filipinos, 1899–1920* (Dillliman: University of the Philippines Press, 1977).

in every direction, came into the post-independence era with dark clouds of strife on the horizon.[15]

An Incendiary Time

After Philippine independence in 1945 there was a succession of challenges to national authority in the country, most of which took place in the north and in the countryside among disaffected groups of varying ideological stripes. In the Muslim South there were also rumblings against Manila, but it was not until the founding of the Moro National Liberation Front (MNLF) in 1969 that this disaffection found any real coherence. Before that time, much of this frisson was interethnic (between and among the Tausug, the Maranao, the Yakan, Samal, Subanon, etc.) Yet in that year Nur Misuari, whom we will discuss at greater length in a moment, rallied the disparate Muslim voices of dissent into one group, and rebellion followed cross a swath of territory in the southern Philippines, from Mindanao to Sulu to small parts of other islands in the South. The MNLF called this emerging territory Bangsamoro Land, and they were eventually able to achieve recognition from important transnational organizations such as the Organization of Islamic Cooperation (OIC). Episodic but occasionally heavy fighting between Muslim insurgents and Philippine national armed forces took place in a number of places, and over several decades, with thousands of people dying in the violence and a general pall of instability hanging over the southern regions of the country. Though the MNLF was open to negotiation with Manila, the emergence of splinter groups such as the Moro Islamic Liberation Front (MILF) under Salamet Hashim; a second group headed by Abul Kahyr Alonto (from a Maranao royal family); and Abu Sayyaf, among others, made the peace process much more difficult. A series of treaties and bilateral agreements were eventually signed from the 1970s into the early twenty-first century, but there is still only an uncertain aura of peace in the region.[16] Violence still punctuates Muslim-Christian relations

15. Ibid.; see also Benigno Aquino, "The Historical Background of the Moro Problem in the Southern Philippines," in [Anon.], *Compilation of Government Pronouncements and Relevant Documents on Peace and Development for Mindanao*, 1–16 (Manila: Office of the Press Secretary, 1988).

16. [Anon.] *Autonomy and Peace Review* (Cotabato: Institute for Autonomy and Governance in Collaboration with the Konrad-Adenauer Stiftung, 2001); Florangel Rosario-Braid, ed., *Muslim and Christian Cultures: In Search of Commonalities* (Manila: Asian Institute of Journalism and Communication, 2002); and Patricio Abinales, *Orthodoxy and History in the Muslim-Mindanao Narrative* (Quezon City: Ateneo de Manila Press, 2010).

on this remote corner of the larger Muslim world, and though daily life more or less proceeds normally, one is never sure when a bomb will go off in a market, or when outsiders will be kidnapped by men in masks.

The various peace agreements signed by Muslim forces in the South with the Philippine government give us some idea of the intractability of the problems. As recently as only a couple of years ago, more of these documents were being finalized between both parties, but in reality the paper trail is decades old, with treaties being signed by a number of Philippine presidents, including Ferdinand Marcos (the 1976 Tripoli Agreement), Corazon Aquino (the 1989 ARMM Organic Act), and Fidel Ramos (the 1994 Joint Ceasefire Ground Rules, as well as the 1996 Final Peace Agreement, which turned out not to be so final after all). The 1976 Tripoli Agreement, brokered by Muammar Gaddafi in Libya, gives an indication of the range of issues on the table for the combatants. Regional autonomy was the number-one prospect being discussed, but the potential foreign policy of any autonomous southern entity was also mooted, as well as the erection of courts, education, administrative systems, economic and financial edifices, and the extraction of natural resources in the region. The brokering of a cease-fire, in a region where so many lives had already been lost, was also difficult business. But the main issue at hand was really autonomy, as was proven by the minutes of various meetings of the Islamic Conference, in Jeddah in 1972, in Benghazi in 1973, in Kuala Lumpur in 1974, in Istanbul in 1976, and in Tripoli itself in 1977. The Moro National Liberation Front appealed to Muslim nation-states for help, and these countries in turn prevailed upon Manila to grant more autonomy to Muslims in the Philippine South. Oil money and Western-Soviet geopolitics played into the mix. A very regional struggle between Muslims and Christians at the end of the geographic world for both global religions, therefore, became something much larger.[17]

The chief agent in all of this has undoubtedly been Nur Misuari, the charismatic leader of the MNLF and its major face both at home in the archipelago and abroad. Misuari has been the one enduring constant in the dialogue between the Muslim South and Manila: his voice is reflected through several decades' worth of Philippine politicians, from Marcos to Cory Aquino, from Ramos to Estrada to Gloria Macapagal-Arroyo. He has outlasted them all. And he also has known and cultivated many heads of state outside of the Philippines,

17. [Anon.], *Selected Documents and Studies for the Conference on the Tripoli Agreement: Problems and Prospects* (Quezon City: International Studies Institute of the Philippines, 1985).

particularly in the Islamic World (as previously mentioned), but not bounded by this grouping, either. Misuari was able to do this—to walk among the high and mighty both home and abroad—but he also has been able to convince many Muslim Filipinos in places like Zamboanga and elsewhere that he represents their interests. He speaks as one of them, a child who had grown up in the palm-fringed villages of the South. He went to prison for his views and for his actions, and he wears this badge with honor, as it engenders respect among his compatriots. Misuari has survived almost the whole life cycle of the modern Muslim rebellion of the South, from the Jabidah Massacre in 1968 to Christian death squads to his own internment. But he has never lost sight of the prize, and as a result has been a force to be reckoned with. He married several times, according to Muslim custom, and extended his influence in this way as well. And though he was not ultimately able to convince all Muslim Filipinos to follow his flag, and his influence has waned somewhat over time—there were indeed splinter groups over the years, as we have seen—he has been the most important face of Muslim rebellion in the Philippines, bar none. He has become a major international figure as well as a larger-than-life local one, and his influence can still be felt in the southern Philippines to this day.[18]

Though Nur Misuari has had an indelible effect on Muslim-Christian relations in this corner of the maritime world, it is clear that various political forces have had different agendas in representing the face of this struggle. The established Philippine political hierarchy, for example, for a long time—especially under Ferdinand Marcos—saw the Muslim insurgents as simply bandits, basically as obstacles to nation-building under the terms of dictatorship. Marcos's opponents, meanwhile, chief among them Senator Benigno Aquino, tried to enlist the Muslim South as allies in the struggle against Marcos's rule, but always with rather mixed effect.[19] Nur Misuari himself, as head of the MNLF, and Sultan Haroun al-Rashid Lucman (chief of the Bangsa Moro Liberation Front), as well as others, had their own agendas, and were not always convinced that teaming together with other disaffected parties was the best way to continue their own struggle. After the toppling of the Marcos dictatorship, subsequent presidents tried harder to make a peace work, and Cory Aquino (among others) lent a more sympathetic ear—even while occasionally rattling

18. Tom Stern, *Nur Misuari: An Authorized Biography* (Manila: Anvil Publishing, 2012).

19. Benigno Aquino, "The Historical Background of the Moro Problem in the Southern Philippines," in [Anon.], *Compilation*, 1–16; Benigno Aquino, "From Negotiations to Concensus-Building: The New Parameters for Peace" in Ibid., 17–21.

the saber of "Philippine unity" at the same time—in dealing with the Muslim South.[20] Still other members of the political elite, such as the powerful Secretary Alfredo Bengzon, strove to instill in all parties the notion that peace had to be achieved in increments. Bengzon pushed an agenda that individuals would have to bring malleability to the table in order to make any real and lasting peace process work over the long term.[21]

Yet for the landed Luzon center to find out what the maritime Mindanao periphery has really wanted in these struggles has been a difficult process, and one that has not yielded answers so easily. One way that attempts have been made to get to Muslim attitudes in the South has been through sociological surveying, whereby questions have been asked in sample sets of what local people in places such as Zamboanga feel about the chances—and choices—of peace. These surveys have yielded a number of interesting results, and they have now started to be done in the kinds of numbers that can give a real glimpse into popular mentalities having to do with these intractable, decades-long problems.[22] Focusing on only one of these surveys here, performed in 1999 among one thousand adults, we can see what Mindanao residents feel, what only Muslim respondents feel, or what people feel as an aggregate, pan-Filipino group about questions having to do with "the troubles." So, for example, Muslim respondents felt considerably more alarmed about the Philippine military denying food to local Mindanao residents than all respondents did, ostensibly as a strategy for trying to "starve out" rebellion in the countryside. They also felt more indignant about the military trying to harm religious or historical monuments than did "all respondents," signifying the symbolic war at play, and not just the actual one being fought with rifles and ammunition.[23] Yet, at the same time, often "Muslim" and "all Mindanao" responses were the same or very similar, numerically as a test group, showing that there were

20. Benigno Aquino, "From Negotiations to Consensus-Building: The New Parameters for Peace," in [Anon.], *Compilation*, 17–21; Corazon Aquino, "ROCC: The Start of a New Kind of Political Involvement" in Ibid., 22–25; Corazon Aquino, "Responsibility to Preserve Unity," in Ibid., 26–28.

21. Alfredo Bengzon, "Now That We Have Freedom, Let Us Seek Peace" in [Anon.], *Compilation*, 29–33; Alfredo Bengzon, "Each of Us Is Really a Peace Commissioner," in Ibid., 34–38.

22. See Al Tyrone B. Dy et al., eds., *SWS Surveybook of Muslim Values, Attitudes, and Opinions, 1995–2000* (Manila: Social Weather Stations, 2000). The titles of some of these surveys are instructive: "What Do Filipino Muslims Think?" (29 May 2000); "Muslims Favor National Unity Too" (24 September 1999); "A Poll on Hostage-Taking" (2 June 2000), etc.

23. Ibid., 53–62.

indeed areas of agreement between varying religious communities based on a shared sense of locale, if not of religious provenance. The state in post-Marcos times has tried to learn from these surveys in gauging more accurately what Muslim Filipinos feel in places like Zamboanga about a whole range of pertinent issues.

Of course, probably the best way to ascertain these answers is to hear from Muslim Filipinos themselves. A small publishing industry of pamphlets, tracts, and books has now come into being, representing these prismatic views by the people who write such documents as a testimony of their sentiments in difficult times. One of the most interesting of these genres of publications has been the periodical called *Moro Kurier*, which carries an amalgam of articles on issues of interest to the Muslim Filipino community, both in Mindanao and outside it (in fact it also has links to the CPP, the Communist Party of the Philippines). Articles can be found in these pages on the launching of community workshops, for example, in order to elevate the choices available to local Muslims in various locales.[24] Other articles detail lectures on Islam for the general public, and the meeting of Moro ulama for discussions within the Muslim community itself on what role the ulama should have within the wider Moro struggle.[25] Poetry in local vernaculars (and with English translations side by side, so anyone can be sure to get the meanings imputed) extol the power and beauty of locales in Muslim dominions of the South, so that a sense of pride in origins is spread to readers who may not get to see all of these places with their own eyes. Reading publics are identified, maintained, and broadened in other words, both in languages seen to be "of the people" and in English—the main communication medium for the entirety of the country itself—so that no one is potentially left out.[26] There are even articles on "Islam as a Liberating Force," and on the role of Moro women in the struggle, both of which pass messages on to the community as a whole.[27] A December 1985 piece even published a "Muslim Declaration of Human Rights," showing both

24. [Anon.], "MPRC Launches CSW," *Moro Kurier* 1, no. 1 (1985): 3.

25. Ibid., 4; [Anon.], "First Ulama Consultation," *Moro Kurier* 1, no. 1 (1985): 4.

26. See [Anon.], "Legacy to the New Generation," *Moro Kurier* 1, no. 1 (1985): 9. Benedict Anderson's ideas on print capitalism and how reading publics are made are useful here; Benedict Anderson, *Imagined Communities: Reflections on the Origins and Spread of Nationalism* (London: Verso, 2006).

27. [Anon.], "Islam as a Liberating Force," *Moro Kurier* 1, no. 1 (1985): 12; [Anon.], "Moro Women Seminar Launched," *Moro Kurier* 1, no. 2 (1985): 4.

a connection to wider, global themes on the topic, and its distinctly local take, as seen through Muslim Filipinos in the far South.[28]

It has become clear that there are more and more efforts under way to try to sew the southern part of the country together again, where before it was rent apart. Though there are still "extremists" on both sides, in the sense that only full Muslim autonomy or full integration would do (in 2013 a MNLF splinter group briefly raised their flag at city hall, and tried to proclaim the Bangsa Moro Republic), a more massive "middle interest" seems to have developed in the past decade or two. In a big, somewhat glossy book called *Dar-ul Salam: A Vision of Peace for Mindanao*, authors Pressia Arifin-Cabo, Joel Dizon, and Khomenie Mantawel assembled the thoughts and words of a number of people from both sides as to how they felt the continuing struggle of the Muslim South could be solved. The book is aspirational, and can't be taken at face value only, but its mere appearance sends a message, as it likely would never have existed in recent decades before its publication in 2008. Though there are quotes from both camps, perhaps we can end with just two here, showing the willingness of actors on both sides of the religious and indeed military fence to let their words be seen by all, and memorialized in print. "A Dar ul-Islam is where people can go to their farm and do their job uninterrupted by the conflict," Major General Raymundo Ferrer says, the commander of the 6th Infantry Division of the Philippine Army. "Of course, this also means that children are going to school with adequate rooms and teachers. People have opportunities to improve themselves."[29] Mohagher Iqbal, the chief negotiator of the MILF Peace Panel, seems to agree. "A Dar ul-Islam is a place where there is real peace and there is justice. Peace does not only mean that if there is no fighting, there is peace. There must be justice before peace can reign on the land."[30]

In Zamboanga

I wanted to see some of these connections myself, the webs that bind a place like Zamboanga to locales and histories and events in other parts of the world. But I am not a scholar of the Philippines, and though I had been to the country

---

28. [Anon.], "New Muslim Declaration on Human Rights," *Moro Kurier* 1, no. 2 (1985): 8.

29. Pressia Arifin-Cabo, Joel Dizon, and Khomenie Mentawel, *Dar-ul Salam: A Vision of Peace for Mindanao* (Cotabato: Kadtuntaya Foundation, 2008), p 112.

30. Ibid., 113.

before, I had no experience in the South. I was anxious about going, and in 2004, when I did my fieldwork there, there was still considerable tension in this part of the country. So I turned first to two Filipino colleagues/friends for knowledge on how to proceed, and they obliged me with their expertise, and their connections. Professor Patricio (Jojo) Abinales writes books on the Philippine South, and particularly on Mindanao—he has studied for some twenty years the patterns of local and translocal power and influence on the island, mainly through the lens of Political Science.[31] Abinales gave me a run-down of what to expect in looking at the Muslim-Christian patterns that interested me, and though he was important in helping me to learn what to ask, he was (in my view, anyway) more important in assisting me to know what I should *not* ask. This was for my safety; asking the wrong questions in a tense place like Mindanao, especially as an American, can get you killed, he told me. Professor Noelle Rodriguez, herself a native of Zamboanga but then teaching at the Ateneo de Manila (and chairing its History Department), one of the best universities in the Philippines, also charted my course.[32] She not only helped on what to ask or not ask, but also gave me contacts, and arranged bona fides for me because I was heading south alone and as an unknown to locals in Zamboanga. Without the help of both of them, I would not have been able to learn anything when I was there.[33] I quite possibly might not have left in one piece, either—and this statement is not an exaggeration.

Since I would have to enter the Philippines in Manila anyway, I was told, it would make sense to speak to some people in the capital region (Manila/Quezon City) all the way north, in Luzon, before I got on a separate domestic flight and headed south to Mindanao. I was advised to speak to both local Filipino academics who were knowledgeable about the ongoing situation in the South, and also to members of Muslim institutions in the capital region, who could pave my way with further bona fides. This kind of advance trust being put into place was invaluable; I had followed similar procedures when doing interviews in the Muslim southern provinces of Thailand, where insurgency,

31. Patricio Abinales, *Making Mindanao: Cotabato and Davao in the Formation of the Philippine Nation State* (Honolulu: University of Hawai'i Press, 2000).

32. Rodriguez, *Zamboanga*.

33. The initial help that Professors Abinales and Rodriguez offered me cannot be underestimated; they really pointed my feet in the right direction, and they helped arm me with the right sorts of questions to ask in complicated, and sometimes dangerous, situations. I am very grateful to both of them.

violence, and secession were also a part of everyday life.[34] I approached several Muslim intellectuals who taught at the University of the Philippines, Dilliman, among other places, and made appointments. Though there were a number of these sessions, I will only mention the advice given by two scholars here, Professor Carmen Abubakar and Professor Julkipli Wadi. Both were cautious upon first meeting me. What did I hope to accomplish with these interviews, I was asked. When I replied that I was interested in Zamboanga as a kind of religious outpost at the end of several overlapping maritime worlds, I was met with silence. But gradually both scholars opened up, and became more and more talkative. Professor Abubakar advised me to speak to members of Nur Misuari's retinue in Zamboanga, if I could. Would that be possible? She was not sure.[35] Professor Wadi, by the end of our discussion, was equally adamant that I should talk to "normal," everyday Muslims in the South, not just to those linked with the larger path to secession or independence.[36] I tried to follow both of these suggested paths, and for the reasons that both of these scholars gave me.[37]

34. In interviewing in Pattani, Narathiwat, and Yala in the Thai South, I found the dynamics of interaction to be quite similar to working in Mindanao. Here, too, a Muslim South with long ties to a wider, maritime Muslim world has been coopted into a non-Muslim-majority nation-state (though in this case the majority is Theravada Buddhist, not Catholic). Many of the daily patterns of life and resistance to cooptation by the majority are the same in both cases, however. I include my indebtedness here to Saroja Dorairajoo (NUS/Sociology), who helped me invaluably while I did such interviews in the Thai Muslim South.

35. Professor Abubakar was noticeably reticent with me when we first met; she had no doubt seen many (often well-intentioned, I imagine) foreign researchers like me before. When I explained that the focus of my research was not really the "troubles" in Mindanao per se, and more the short- and longer-distance ties to other places in the maritime world, she gradually opened up in her answers. I understood (and appreciated) this reticence; Western writing about Islam in the Philippine South has not always been very sympathetic to local causes or local viewpoints.

36. Julkipli Wadi was more expansive in his answers from the beginning. I have written about some of the stories he has told me about his own experiences vis-à-vis Islam in the Philippines, in *The Longest Journey: Southeast Asians and the Pilgrimage to Mecca* (New York: Oxford University Press, 2013), chapter 14.

37. In triangulating a sense of what Islam means in the Philippine South, I think this is really the only way to go. Elite narratives around Nur Misuari and the "movers and shakers" of insurgency and secession certainly are important, and tell us things we need to know in teasing out narratives of difference in this fascinating place. But the observations and sentiments of common people "in the street" are also important to me. They may have less to say about the weighty political issues of this vast maritime region, but their observations on locality in Zamboanga and their place in this evolving dialectic is no less important and no less interesting.

But before leaving Luzon I also paid visits to the offices of several Moro institutions, tasked with looking after the interests of the millions of Muslims who still live predominantly in the Philippine South. I spent the longest time of these several interviews in the Office for Muslim Affairs, in Quezon City. There I met a number of officials who were able to help me, including via long conversations over tea, and also by handing me statistics on a number of issues that touched upon my research. These included mosque construction and the numbers and provenances of Hajjis leaving every year for Mecca. Though I was an American and a stranger, I was treated with great courtesy, and also with (what seemed to me, anyway) a great deal of openness. It was clear to me that some phone calls had gone around, and that they had an idea of who I was and what I wanted to know before I had even arrived. I was told of the Moro perspective on the "troubles" in the South, and why it was important for social justice, schools, and poverty relief to be enacted by the central regime in Manila. I nodded my head. The officials I spoke with were—to a person— knowledgeable. They knew their facts. Numbers and the scales of things (mostly in terms of problems) were laid out easily and with little fuss. In my presence, a phone call was placed to Zamboanga, though I did not catch in the midst of the conversation who was on the other end or what was said about my arrival. I was simply told that I was expected, and that I should get in touch with certain individuals after I arrived there, having flown over the entirety of the Philippine archipelago en route. We stood up to say our goodbyes. I noticed one man's trouser leg was slightly hiked up and had caught on something on his calf. My vision was caught on this peripherally and accidentally, but the man saw my eyes wander to his leg and he smiled. He pulled up his trouser leg further and there, where his calf should have been, was a huge, misshapen knot where an enormous chunk of his flesh was gone. A vast purple-and-black scar had developed in its place. "A government artillery shell took this out of my leg on Basilan. My clothes were on fire as they dragged me out of the village." He lowered his trouser leg and shook my hand, keeping my gaze. He and the others wished me a safe and pleasant journey to the South.[38]

Basilan—a large, mountainous island just south of the port of Zamboanga— stayed on my mind. Some of the fiercest fighting between Muslim and government forces has taken place in the jungle heights of this place, and the cone of the island is a purple, hazy presence when you look out from the corniche of

38. Interviews in Quezon City/Manila included those with veterans of the wars in the South, among others.

Zamboanga. Right around the time that I came to the city, Muslim insurgents had planted a bomb on the Zamboanga-Basilan ferry; there was a very large armed presence of Filipino troops when I arrived, all of them carrying American-made M-16 assault rifles. One of the largest military bases in the country is located right there, at the mouth of the city.[39] I took a few days wandering the place before I made any of my calls, because I wanted to drink in the atmosphere of this remote outpost. Though there were settlements in what is now Zamboanga that go back to the twelfth or thirteenth centuries, the Spanish fort was likely the first building there of any real size or sturdiness. The old Iberian cannons still faced out to sea, black with age but formidable and heavy, showing where the West—and now Filipino Catholicism, and Manila—thought the enemy would come. Basilan in that maritime strip of distance seemed to tower over the flatness of the city. I wandered through the *baranguays* (there are ninety-nine *barrios*, or neighborhoods, in Zamboanga), and just got used to the place a bit before I started to ask any questions. The city itself is dusty, and once you are out of the main center it is really packed-dirt paths for the most part, with palm fronds and banana and other fruit trees separating small, compact homes. Roosters walk these quiet lanes with impunity. You can hear people speaking Chavacano in the shade of their little dwellings, and you can imagine the general scene as looking very similar to this centuries back. Conquistadors would have then ridden these same footpaths with horses.[40]

Though when I was in Zamboanga I was mostly interested in talking to Muslims, who are a distinct minority in the city itself, I ended up staying with the modern iteration of conquistadors, to a degree at least. I bunked down in a room graciously (and gratuitously) provided by the Jesuit fathers who ran the Ateneo de Zamboanga, the city's best university. Father William Kreutz took me under his wing.[41] Though I met Father Kreutz in his office several days after I arrived, that was my only daylight meeting with him, or with any of the

39. This is Camp General Basilio Navarro, the main oeprating base of the Western Mindanao Command. There is also an important air force installation based in Zamboanga.

40. Of all the places the Spanish came to in the Philippines, Zamboanga retains most the air of conquest and local accommodation. The only competing locale in this sense is the Intramuros complex in Manila itself; its walls and rusting cannon have much the same aura of Zamboanga, but the latter's distance and comparative isolation out on the sea routes makes this ambiance and connection to the past much stronger in Mindanao.

41. Father William Kreutz, though now stationed back in Manila, is an almost legendary figure in southwestern Mindanao; he knows the dynamics of the place better than almost anyone, I would say. He first came to the Philippines in 1963, and has been there ever since. His

other Jesuits. The rest of my time there, I saw them only by night. Muslims by day, Jesuits by night—there was an almost Manichean dualism to my interactions with these two (at times) warring factions. Yet the Jesuits were not interested anymore in war with the Moros. These Jesuits, at least, were there to educate, they said; to educate and to serve. That professed desire was clear to me, though missionization does (of course) continue, sometimes in the city but more so in the surrounding areas of the southwestern peninsula and in the central mountains of Mindanao proper. Father Kreutz himself had been in the Philippines for more than thirty years by the time I met him. He had spent nearly his entire adult life in the country. Thousands of students of all denominations had passed through the university under his watch. And the message I received from him seemed (on the face of it, at least) to be a gentle one—that the Jesuits were there to educate and to help both sides coexist, so that some measure of harmony could be enjoyed by an historically troubled locale. It was sometimes difficult not to believe them, as their sentiments and their conversations with me were both so earnest (though theirs, of course, was a particular point of view). The Jesuits put me in touch with various local Muslims, some of whom I already had contacts for, others of whom I didn't. And they wined and dined me—with the emphasis perhaps on the former—at dinners that lasted a couple of hours at a time. There was the scent of history in this too.[42] Zamboanga might be the sixth-largest city in the Philippines, but the pace of mealtimes, if nothing else, certainly did suggest that this was still a frontier town, moving at a frontier pace.

I ended up wandering those dusty lanes for a while, looking up contacts and enjoying quiet conversations with a number of Zamboangueños who agreed to talk with me. In almost every instance I was vouched for by others, so that in the beginning I was riding on contacts from Muslim Manila (those mysterious phone calls!) or from Jesuit Zamboanga itself. But eventually there seemed to be enough of a consensus that I was indeed who I said I was—an American academic—and not a CIA or NSA operative, that people

fifty-plus years of local knowledge on Filipino dynamics and the oscillating social processes between groups is tough to match.

42. The Jesuits were known for their devotion to knowledge, of course, but also for their occasional fondness for richness—richness of churches, richness of books and book learning, and (yes) richness at the table, too, despite the oath Jesuits took to observe poverty as one of the cornerstones of their order. For a good sense of these historical Jesuit encounters in Asia, and especially the sensibilities involved, see Jonathan Spence, *The Memory Palace of Matteo Ricci* (New York: Penguin Books, 1985).

kept re-referring me to others. Entire families wanted me to know how they felt about things, and I was able to start cobbling together a story of connection, of locals feeling *translocal* in this most translocal of maritime places. I heard about cousins and business contacts not just in Basilan but in the rest of the Sulu archipelago; Zamboangueños went back and forth on the ferries, keeping these long-term relations alive on machine-powered vessels, when previously they had been traveling on sailing ships. Others moved to Cotabato, and to other (mostly Muslim) coastal cities of the outstretched Mindanao "mainland," off Zamboanga's spider-arm peninsula. Still others were going to Malaysia (to Sabah) and a few were even transiting now and then to Indonesia, mainly by way of Manado, and eventually to Ternate and eastern Maluku province. The echoes of old kingdoms were in their descriptions, sailing directions that had existed for literally hundreds of years as Muslims tracked back and forth across these shallow seas. Some others were going to Mecca itself, or "Mecca the Blessed" as it was described to me, piercing the "local" networks and making the most distant of journeys imaginable, surely, for such an out-of-the-way place. In each home I was greeted with great hospitality, tea and sweets put out on low tables, and children looking at the proceedings through lattice bamboo walls. Small groups of men sat in circles, their legs carefully folded and spoke with me.[43]

Yet it is a conversation with a woman that I want to end with here. I was invited to a gathering in a private home of several prominent Muslim families in Zamboanga; all in all, some thirty people were there, and there were representatives of a number of Muslim clans in attendance. Noticeable among these people was a group of older women, who clearly had some status and confidence in the way they comported themselves. They spoke with me very openly, and were not shy in engaging me, even in front of the assembled men. And prominent among this group was a woman who was of Sulu royal lineage, and who had, in fact, led the Philippines' Hajj contingent some years ago, the only woman in the world that year who had been given such an honor by her country. She had great stories to tell me about the Philippine pilgrimage, then as

---

43. I learned an awful lot by talking to "everyday" Muslims in Zamboanga. One thing that became clear right away in speaking with Muslims here was how variable the community was, ethnically—very few people were strictly "Moro" in their bloodlines. Some clearly had Chinese blood, others Persian genealogies—these could be seen from their faces and physiognomies. But often people had elaborate genealogical trees to show where some of their ancestors came from, at what time, and from which particular place overseas. Even allowing for exaggeration and/or the present-day malleability of some of these charts, being "Muslim" in Zamboanga was an impressively diverse thing.

now the greatest overseas journey that Filipino Muslims can make as part of their faith.[44] I have some wonderful photographs of us all sitting together, and one can see the diversity of their facial features, and the waves of cultural influence that have swept over these islands "at the end of the world," for centuries upon centuries. Yet toward the end of the gathering I was introduced to a quiet, middle-aged woman who spoke very softly to me, but with bright, shining eyes, and she had a great stillness in her bearing that I felt immediately. It turned out that this was one of Nur Misuari's wives, and she ended up speaking to me for almost two hours about her time in the Hejaz, and the many meanings of Islam, both locally and translocally. She described her personal journey to Mecca, and also nested it in context to what other Filipinos felt about performing the Hajj. But she also laid out a vision of social justice for the functioning of the Philippine South which was temperate and reasonable, and presented with the utmost calm and tranquility. It was impressive and humbling. When I got up to go, she held my gaze for a moment longer than she needed to, making sure I was paying absolute attention. Then she said, "You will tell others now, OK? It's important that they all hear what we have to say."

And I agreed that I would. In that quiet goodbye one could hold out hope that decades of strife—built on a century or more of bloodshed, stretching back to the time of General Wood—might possibly come to an end. The Jesuits and the Moros were in common cause on this, or at least a number of the most influential of them were.[45] I thanked her, and went back to the Ateneo de Zamboanga that night. And I thought a long time about what she said to me, sitting quietly in the Mindanao dark.

Conclusion

Zamboanga is one of those places that lingers in the mind, and in one's memory. I have argued above that though it feels like the end of empire, and indeed is that, it is also the center of its own world, in some ways—a vast, watery

44. Again, please see my *The Longest Journey*, chapter 14, for a longer exegesis.

45. This was the most impressive interview I had in my time doing this research—in Zamboanga, Manila, Quezon City, or anywhere else. Some people know not only how to keep information but how to relate it—and she was one such person. Interestingly, in both her case and Father Kreutz's, one sees the possibility for dialogue most strongly. This is so even though one is married to Nur Misuari himself, and the other is a Jesuit (supposedly the least compromising of the Christian orders, when it comes to doctrine; they were called the "soldiers of Christ" for a reason).

domain, and one that centers on its primacy. Taking in the Sulu archipelago to the south, Palawan to the west, the Visayas to the north, and the mountainous mass of Mindanao to the east, the city rests at the geographic center of its own milieu. Situated between all of these places, all of them reached by sea, Zamboanga built up its connections and its importance over the course of the centuries. Islam was crucial in the story of its beginnings, and the Muslim polities that interacted with it left gravestones and mosques, many of which are still extant in and around the city itself. The Spanish made it an important garrison town, and added cannon and ramparts to the earlier edifices, so that spaces that before were mostly open in cadence now became somewhat closed. Within the walls a cosmopolitan but highly distinct society developed over time, one speaking its own language, though one attuned to the linguistic currents of other places that coursed through its own gate, in the form of traders from many nations. The American imperial presence eventually made these connections much less dynamic, and Zamboanga became more of a sedentary society, looking increasingly inward upon itself rather than across many seas. Though most of the time this process was peaceful, at other times the Muslim and Christian contingents could not get along. Constant conflict followed for a certain period following independence, when Zamboanga again became a fortress to wider instabilities playing out right outside the city's gates.

Manila, though ethnically Filipino run by this latter period, was seen as an imperial bastion by many in Zamboanga, little different than when it had been run by Spain or the United States. Manila's reach and intentions were still seen to be extractive, in ensuring that Zamboanga and the peripheries around it contributed raw materials to the development of the new, Christian nation. This was not the opinion of everyone in the city, but it was the majority sentiment of most of southwestern Mindanao, with Zamboanga serving as its seat. Eventually decades of conflict, coercion, and attempted reform were replaced by negotiations, and a tenuous peace was achieved by Muslims and Christians at this most distant of outposts. That is the aura of the city right now, and one can see women in hijab and Jesuit priests walking past each other in many parts of Zamboanga at the moment. Yet there are still occasionally disruptions to the calm, and it is clear that this port complex at the end of the world still harbors resentments, as well as individuals for whom the status quo will not be enough. Soldiers still patrol the dusty alleys, M-16s in hand, and around the main fulcrum of the port there is a significant state military presence. The island of Basilan looms in the hazy marine distance, still the site of an active resistance movement dedicated to the erection of a Muslim sultanate. One feels all of these presences as one ambles through Zamboanga, the present and the past in uneasy partnership in those same streets. Here—at the end of many known worlds, and the beginnings of others—the past may still be prologue. It is that ambivalent frisson that marks the city, and that makes one understand that this frontier town's future is still very uncertain.

PART IV

Cities and the Sea

Preface: Urbanism Connects: The Life of Asian Cities

ONE OF THE MAIN PLACES that the maritime routes of Asia connected was in the ports; the string of cities astride the oceanic pathways that stretched from Aden on the Red Sea coast all the way to Edo/Tokyo in Japan. Though culture, ideas, and materiel all changed hands in other places, including in protected inlets and bays, on agricultural coastlines bereft of cities, and even occasionally on the high seas themselves, the primary place of exchange was the ports, where merchants from both near and far would congregate to do business. Aden, Muscat, Karachi, Surat, Bombay, Cochin, Madras, Calcutta, Rangoon, Penang, Melaka, Singapore—all of these ran along the rim of the Indian Ocean. Farther east and then up to the north, Batavia, Makassar, Brunei, Ayutthaya, Saigon, Hội An, Manila, Canton, Macau, Hong Kong, Nagasaki, and Yokohama beckoned, among a plethora of smaller, more regional ports. Trade moved in segments, and it was normal for merchants to shuttle between a variety of ports in certain areas, such as the Sea of Japan, the Banda Sea, or the Bay of Bengal, not to mention smaller stretches of exposed coastline.

Yet there were also figures who moved longer distances along the routes, connecting truly distant geographies and making grand journeys at a time when such voyages were quite unusual. Marco Polo was one of these men, if his entire itinerary is to be believed, and though the more famous parts of his journey took place overland, across the Eurasian Steppe to Karakorum, he came back to Europe partially by sea, sailing from coastal China, through Southeast Asia, and coming into the Indian Ocean, before plying caravan routes back to Europe. He passed through a number of port cities on this trip, and left a record of his impressions. So did a traveler coming from farther west, the Moroccan jurist Ibn Battuta, whose own *rihla* (or travel account) proceeded in the opposite direction, taking him to a variety of ports and courts as a Muslim man of letters. Not to be outdone, Zheng He, the Chinese admiral whom we have met already, was also festooned in the monsoon cities of Asia, leaving an account of his journeys through his translator and scribe, Ma Huan. These three famous travelers show us some of the possibilities of urbanism in the premodern Asian world, as all of them were met and greeted in cities along the routes, in different times and at different places. As the medieval period bled into the early modern age, the number of ports acting as substrate for these sorts of contacts only grew, and a number of new urban complexes sprang up to facilitate such conversations.

The development of ports along the maritime routes of Asia was likely the single most important condition for expanded cross-cultural contact as the centuries wore on. Though maritime technologies—as we will see later in this book—were crucial in their own right, sailors, merchants, and statesmen had to have reasons to go, and the burgeoning of major ports along the circuit gave them a purpose for these voyages. Trade needed to happen in a place, and ports agglomerated merchants, their wares, and capital into one locale, with the attendant possibilities of stockpiling those things in one place. Perspicacious rulers all along the routes understood this, and institutions were developed to attract contacts and commerce, much in the same ways that businesses think about these things today. One of these institutions was the office of portmaster, or *shahbandar* (from the Persian); many if not most of the main ports along Asia's oceanic pathways had a person of this description, often (but not always) a foreigner, and someone who could speak many languages. We have already met Zhao Ru Gua, in Song China, but there were many others—in Melaka, Makassar, the Gujarati ports, and elsewhere—who followed this description. These figures took care of the trade of the port, and made sure to try to attract new business at the same time that they maintained and stabilized existing transactions in the harbor. But there were other mechanisms to make the system of urban nodes along the routes work, involving diasporic contacts (communities with representatives in a number of distant ports, all in conversation with one another), and the practice of erecting consulates in numerous places, which then took care of a single flag's commercial interests. Legal representation was important, or at least—in a premodern context—having some sort of connection with local rulers was, so that one's rights would not be trampled upon. All of these institutions were ways to deal with the limitations of premodern communication along huge distances, and to facilitate the working of mercantile gears over long periods of time.

Part IV, "Cities and the Sea," examines this phenomena through two inter-related chapters. Chapter 8 looks at the morphogenesis of port cities in "Greater Southeast Asia," though it takes a wide definition of the latter, and includes material about other cities at some distance from Southeast Asia, though clearly in conversation with it. Canton (Guangzhou), Hong Kong, and some of the ports of the Indian subcontinent therefore are also included, both for what they show us about connections to this part of the world, and also how such places differ in urban morphology from Southeast Asian ports. By looking at the growth and geographic mechanisms of port cities in this region, a template for urban connectivity is sketched out, and problematized over a broad period of time. This chapter deals with past, historical patterns, but also takes up many of these same questions for the modern period in which we all live, to see how these cities have evolved as parts of a larger assemblage of cities along the routes. Chapter 9 then takes an altogether larger perspective on the connections between Asian ports. If Chapter 8 is broad, in that it analyzes Southeast Asian cities within the wider ambit of ports connected to it through commerce across both the Bay of Bengal and the South China Sea, Chapter 9 is even more expansive in its geographical coverage. Starting in Istanbul and tying together a string of ports from the farthest reaches of what is considered to be "Asia" at all, it winds its way slowly across the entire maritime Asian world, from West to South Asia, and then from Southeast Asia up to Korea, Japan, and the Russian Far East. Under scrutiny is the way these ports act as nodes in a larger web of commerce and political representation, especially in the fin-de-siècle period around the turn of the twentieth century. Diplomatic correspondence forms the spine of the examination here, but this is diplomacy that was constantly mixed together with commerce, as we shall see. Connect-ing some ten thousand miles of seaways from Istanbul's minarets to Northeast Asia's snowfalls takes into one sweep the entire orbit of the routes, from where they start to where they end, all in one continent. By concentrating on just a few decades at a particularly unstable time, the chapter shows how trade, do-minion, and communication all came together over vast distances, as the world was becoming "modern" right before one's eyes.

8

The Morphogenesis of Port Cities in "Greater Southeast Asia"

> Before, these borders did not exist. All of these seas were collectively ours.
>
> —PAK ADRIAN LAPIAN, JAKARTA, 2006[1]

MODERN GEOGRAPHIC THEORY has been comparatively slow in recognizing the non-Western city as a discrete unit of enormous importance, vital to the general scheme of the world's economic and political interplay.[2] Perhaps nowhere is this more true than in greater Southeast Asia.[3] The emergence of

---

1. Author's interview notes [translation: E. Tagliacozzo].

2. See, for example, Lewis Mumford's classic *The City in History* (New York: Harcourt, Brace, Jovanovich, 1961; repr. 1989), which describes the nature and evolution of a host of cities over several millennia, but which leaves non-Western cities entirely out of his analysis. Correctives on this lacuna have come fast and furious, but are of uneven quality in describing the mechanics and growth of non-Western cities. For Asia, the most sophisticated study of a regional city is probably William Rowe's two-volume *Hankow* (Stanford: Stanford University Press, 1984 and 1989), which describes this central Chinese city as it entered into the age of modern global capitalism. For Southeast Asia, see the pioneering work of Terry McGee, which set the stage for Southeast Asian urban studies in the 1960s (T. G. McGee, *The Southeast Asian City: A Social Geography of the Primate Cities of Southeast Asia* [London: Bell, 1967]), and then ushered in the new study of urbanism in the region with his recent coedited volume: T. G. McGee and Ira Robinson, eds., *The Mega-Urban Regions of Southeast Asia* (Vancouver: UBC Press, 1995). For an examination of some of the ideas of how to think about "Third World" cities generally, see M. Santos, *The Shared Space: The Two Circuits of the Urban Economy Underdevelopment Concept* (London: Methuen, 1979).

3. By "greater Southeast Asia," I am referring here to the eleven contemporary nation-states of the Association of Southeast Asian Nations (ASEAN), plus parts of the nearby shores of the

several ports as de facto economic capitals of transnational regions in Southeast Asia may be the ongoing product of several hundred years of demographic evolution.[4] Yet it has been only within the past few decades that this process has moved itself into high gear at a scale previously unseen.[5] What has emerged from this process has been the genesis of a number of megacities (many of them coastal or maritime in location) that are in turn re-creating the peripheries that surround them. These cities have helped fashion alternate worlds that have changed the face of the maritime basin between South, East, and Southeast Asia.

Still packed to overflow with the merchandise of its Southeast Asian neighbors, Singapore is the legacy of nineteenth-century Britain's desire for a strategic emporium in the crucial Straits of Melaka. Shipping, warehousing, banking and telecom services abound, situating the city as the focal point of the highly touted Singapore-Batam-Johor Bahru Growth Triangle, which connects the city-state with its Malaysian and Indonesian neighbors. Bangkok, one hub of what was once a greater mainland Southeast Asian network of adjoining polities, receives huge amounts of hydroelectric power from Laotian rivers, funnels gems and teak from the once pariah state of Burma, and acts as a crossroads for Cambodian timber and refugees. Last, Hong Kong—technically outside of Southeast Asia, but part of its greater maritime ambit nonetheless—is still the conduit of southeastern China that it was envisioned to be in the time of the mid-nineteenth-century Opium Wars. The huge markets that once tempted illicit drug-runners now beckon new generations of merchants selling commodities to Southeast Asia from the Guangdong countryside, while domestic workers come from the Nanyang ("Southern Ocean") in the opposite direction. Regional cosmopolises have been born, burgeoning at a rate that no one possibly could have foreseen several centuries ago. In the latter

South China Sea and the Indian Ocean, which have been bound into the history of the region. By "morphogenesis," I mean not only the shape of the city itself (the physical arrangement of institutions, the spatial layout of religious structures and ethnic wards and neighborhoods, functionality, etc.) but also the evolving shape of cities as a whole, with a system of ports along the maritime trade routes.

4. For the beginnings of an attempt to do this, see Geoffrey Gunn, *Overcoming Ptolemy: The Making of an Asian World Region* (Lexington: Rowman and Littlefield, 2018); and Geoffrey Gunn, *History without Borders: The Making of an Asian World Region, 1000–1800* (Hong Kong: Hong Kong University Press, 2011).

5. Hans-Dieter Evers and Rudiger Korff, *Southeast Asian Urbanism: The Meaning and Power of Social Space* (Singapore: ISEAS, 2000).

MAP 8.1. Maritime Southeast Asian Ports

part of the twenty-first century, the projections of a number of demographers place several of the largest cities on the planet as standing on Southeast Asian soil.

It is argued in this chapter that though there are universalizing trends in global urbanization currently taking place across the planet, several Southeast Asian urban hubs will adopt these new frameworks and institutions at least partly within a local model of some antiquity. Particular to the region, this model does not parallel South and East Asia's urban evolutions, the two regions traditionally (and somewhat erroneously) regarded as the wellsprings of Southeast Asian culture. Rather, it contradicts it. The ports of the "lands beneath the winds" have been and will continue to be primarily their own creatures from a variety of vantage points.[6] Yet it is only by first examining the pattern of these cities' evolutions that we can hope to gain any insight into how these urban centers may unfold in the future.[7] In these historical patterns portents lie.[8] It is both in the remote and also in the much closer colonial past that we can search for clues that augur how the new Asian "supercapitals" situated along the ribbon of the equator may transform themselves in the future.

The Siren of the Past

Analyzing the composite of Southeast Asian urban history brings into focus several characteristics as prototypically "regional" in nature.[9] Selected together, the confluence of these factors does much to explain the development

6. The term is Anthony Reid's; see his *Southeast Asia in the Age of Commerce*, 2 vols. (New Haven: Yale University Press, 1988 and 1993), especially vol. II, chapter 2, "The City and Its Commerce," for a picture of the evolution of Southeast Asian cities in the early modern age.

7. It should be stated from the outset that the nature of extant sources helps to determine some of the comparisons put forward in this piece. Sources on premodern and colonial Southeast Asian port cities are relatively abundant in comparison with the surrounding hinterlands; they are also relatively abundant (as a percentage) in comparison with surviving materials on the South and East Asian pasts, where cities were often merely parts of larger political entities. I'm grateful to geographer Michael Leaf for pointing out to me in personal correspondence that "in short, the inland cities reproduced existing cultures while the port cities generated new cultures."

8. Many of the historical cities mentioned in this article were embedded in territorial states. The types of states, the scale of these states, the relations between the various nodal points—which were often simultaneously the capitals of elites and the shifting bases of overlapping mercantile diasporas—differed both by the type of state and longitudinally over time. This overall point needs to be made within the larger schema of the argument.

9. For an interesting discussion of a regional "ethos," see Zaharah binti Haji Mahmud, "The Malay Concept of Tanah Air: The Geographer's Perspective," in *Memory and Knowledge of the Sea in Southeast Asia*, ed. Danny Wong Tze Ken, 5–14 (Kuala Lumpur: Institute of Ocean and

of a large and often-occurring pattern, one that has been dictated by geography but also by cultural and economic forces.[10] These factors are, first, the international orientation of the region; second, the dual workings of harbor and political administration; third, urban adaptation as a mechanism of survival, and fourth, a notable balance of politics moving away from the center, and economics moving in the opposite direction, toward an administrative center. It is important to first understand the workings of these concepts within a historical context, and then we can move forward in time to see how these issues have played out more recently. Several short examples are included here to try to better illustrate these processes, followed by later explanations as to why they may be of use in thinking about "greater Southeast Asia" in our own time.

The material in this chapter covers both the insular world of the region and the mainland, though it is primarily the coasts of the latter that conform to the patterns described here. An interesting and very useful historiographical controversy has played out in the last two decades on whether the *longue durée* trends of the mainland really have corresponded to similar processes in the islands of the region. At issue most centrally have been the ideas of Anthony Reid, whose two-volume *Southeast Asia in the Age of Commerce* significantly changed scholarship on the historical development of the region, including on the growth and function of cities.[11] Reid's interpretation has not stressed significant differences in the evolution of the island and mainland worlds of Southeast Asia in the early modern period. His writings on urban history have generally adhered to an overall contention that—across the width and breadth of territory in the region—there has been a continuity in historical energies and trends.

Victor Lieberman in the first book of his two-volume history of the region, *Strange Parallels*, subsequently challenged this schemata to some

---

Earth Sciences, University of Malaya, 2008). I am indebted to J. K. Wells and John Villiers, eds., *The Southeast Asian Port and Polity: Rise and Demise* (Singapore: Singapore University Press, 1990), and Bennet Bronson, "Exchange at the Upstream and Downstream Ends: Notes toward a Functional Model of the Coastal States in Southeast Asia," in *Economic Exchange and Social Interaction in Southeast Asia: Perspectives from Prehistory, History, and Ethnography*, ed. K. L. Hutterer (Ann Arbor: University of Michigan Southeast Asia Program, 1977) for stimulating some of the discussion in the next few pages.

10. For Southeast Asia within the larger flow of Asia's regional commodity trade, see Mizushima Tsukaya, George Souza, and Dennis Flynn, eds., *Hinterlands and Commodities: Place, Space, Time and the Political Economic Development of Asia over the Long Eighteenth Century* (Leiden: Brill, 2015).

11. Reid, *Southeast Asia in the Age of Commerce*, 2 volumes (1988 and 1993).

degree.[12] Lieberman has contended that many long-term patterns of history in fact are dissimilar between the mainland and the island worlds, and he has argued for a stronger weight to distinctiveness in many areas, including in the genesis and development of urban centers. Tony Day has also weighed in partially along these lines as well, though his input has concerned the processes of state formation more than the actual morphological evolution of cities.[13] Recently Su Lin Lewis has also taken issue with the periodization of a declining "cosmopolitanism" after the seventeenth century.[14] It is good to be mindful here of this ongoing interpretive debate, though some common ground can be found between the Reid and Lieberman approaches by linking the patterns of mainland coastal areas with the larger history of the insular world. The sea connects. Though there are indeed corresponding similarities between certain inland urban complexes and their relationships with their surrounding countrysides, and indeed with other mainland cities, much of the purview of this chapter refers to population centers on the coasts. It is in this manner that some constructive unity can be found in larger patterns, both over time and over the outstretched topographies of Southeast Asia.

Southeast Asia's Trans-Regional Cadence

Southeast Asian cities through the ages have often existed on a lifeblood of international commerce.[15] This is in marked contrast to China, Japan, and the Indian subcontinent, which have, by contrast, often had large cities that

12. Victor Lieberman, *Strange Parallels: Southeast Asia in Global Context, 800–1830,* vol. 1: *Integration on the Mainland* (Cambridge: Cambridge University Press, 2003).

13. Tony Day, *Fluid Iron: State Formation in Southeast Asia* (Honolulu: University of Hawai'i Press, 2002).

14. See Su Lin Lewis, *Cities in Motion: Urban Life and Cosmopolitanism in Southeast Asia, 1920–1940* (Cambridge: Cambridge University Press, 2016). Lewis invokes Milner in fashioning this thesis, and argues that certain realms (such as Burma) discouraged indigenous commerce while welcoming foreign traders.

15. Of course, there were urban centers in classical Southeast Asia that were primarily religious and agricultural in nature, and not dependent on the sea. Angkor, Pagan, and Hanoi are all good examples of these cities, but as a category of "place," they seem to have been outnumbered over the centuries by the combined ports/polities discussed in this essay. For further information on these landlocked cities, see Georges Coedes, *The Indianized States of Southeast Asia* (Honolulu: East-West Press, 1968); and Kenneth Hall and John Whitmore, eds., *Explorations in Early Southeast Asian History: The Origins of Southeast Asian Statecraft* (Ann Arbor: Center for South and Southeast Asian Studies, University of Michigan, 1976).

were primarily inwardly focused and largely self-supporting. Metropolises like Suzhou and Hangzhou in medieval China, Kyoto in Japan, and even Delhi under the Mughals were primarily domestic centers. Their economies and political lives flourished, to be sure, but the great majority of these energies were domestically concerned and oriented, rarely straying too far into the international arena. Southeast Asian cities took on a decidedly different worldview. Extending in nodes along the great trade routes between the South China Sea and the Indian Ocean, these coastal cities welcomed foreign influences, and in fact survived on them. Whole frameworks and institutions were developed to promote trade, and sagacious rulers were constantly on the lookout for ways to advance their commerce, and thus their own political importances further into the international nexus. One such institution deeply embedded in these processes and worthy of a quick mention here was the transregional office of *shahbandar*.

The *shahbandar* (literally, "portmaster" in Persian), a concept we have already discussed briefly in the preface to this section of the book, was often the second-most-important official in most Southeast Asian polities, after the ruler. His main purpose was to attract, manage, and promulgate trade on behalf of the city-state for which he worked. Every metropolis of any size in the region had a shahbandar, usually a foreigner, who was multilingual, and who was a kind of cultural "fixer," someone who understood the locality of his (often adopted) maritime city. There are extant records of nearly every major Southeast Asian city-state possessing a person in this position: from the *I Ching*'s narrative account of (Sumatran) Palembang in the seventh century, to the Portuguese traveler Mendes Pinto's records of (Malaysian) Melaka in the 1500s, to Dutch and British accounts of the trading city of colonial Makassar (in Sulawesi) in the eighteenth century.[16] All of these shahbandar-run ports shared a common thread of outward orientation, receptivity, and a willingness and ability to accommodate outsiders, along with the cross-culturalism that they engendered. One has only to look at late Ming and early Ch'ing dynastic

---

16. O. W. Wolters, *Early Indonesian Commerce: A Study of the Origins of Srivijaya* (Ithaca: Cornell University Press, 1967); Rebecca D. Catz, trans. and ed., *The Travels of Mendes Pinto / Fernão Mendes Pinto* (Chicago: University of Chicago Press, 1989); and Heather Sutherland, "Trepang and Wangkang: The China Trade of Eighteenth Century Makassar," in *Authority and Enterprise among the Peoples of South Sulawesi*, ed. R. Tol, K. van Dijk, and G. Accioli (Leiden: KITLV Press, 2000). See also, in this respect generally, Kenneth Hall, *Maritime Trade and State Development in Early Southeast Asia* (Honolulu: University of Hawai'i Press, 1985); and Paul Wheatley, *The Golden Chersonese: Studies in the Historical Geography of the Malay Peninsula Before AD 1500* (Kuala Lumpur: University of Malaya Press, 1961).

histories or post-1600 documents in Tokugawa Japan to find examples of the generally sterner attitude toward foreigners that these cultures bore in comparison to their Southeast Asian neighbors.[17] In the "Nanyang" the mindset seems to have been quite apart from this, a cultural and urban difference whose echo can be felt even in our own times.

The Twin Functioning of Polis and Harbor

Functionality is another important difference in the normative pattern between Southeast Asian cities and their historical counterparts to the north and west. It has been the case since at least the first millennium CE that both the administrative and economic heart of many traditional Southeast Asian polities has been fused into *one* city. This has been a functional union that is very different from what documents tell us about Classical Chinese, Japanese, and Indian cities, for the most part. In the Tokugawa epoch, while Edo (modern Tokyo) functioned as the political and to some extent cultural center of the Japanese realm, commerce and trade were left to secondary cities: ports such as Nagasaki and what would later become Yokohama.[18] It was here that contacts were first made with the Western world, initially through Portuguese, Dutch, and Spanish traders.[19] Similarly, the fulcrum of Chinese power and authority was kept in Beijing's Forbidden City, funneling trade from the southern coastal cities of Amoy (Xiamen) and Canton (Guangzhou). Yet

17. See David E. Mungello, *The Great Encounter of China and the West, 1500–1800* (Lanham: Rowman & Littlefield Publishers, 1999); and Michael Smitka, *The Japanese Economy in the Tokugawa Era, 1600–1868* (New York: Garland Publishers, 1998). Explications on Chinese and Japanese xenophobia during these periods have been substantially revised in recent decades by the work of John Wills, Jonathan Spence, Joanna Waley-Cohen, Ronald Toby, and Martha Chaiklin. See, for example, John Wills, *Embassies and Illusions: Dutch and Portuguese Envoys to K'ang-hsi, 1666–1687* (Cambridge, MA: Harvard University East Asian Studies, 1984); Jonathan Spence and John Wills, eds., *From Ming to Ch'ing: Conquest, Region, and Continuity in 17th-Century China* (New Haven: Yale University Press, 1979); Joanna Waley-Cohen, *The Sextants of Beijing: Global Currents in Chinese History* (New York: W. W. Norton Press, 1999); Ronald Toby, *State and Diplomacy in Early Modern Japan: Asia in the Development of the Tokugawa Bakufu* (Princeton: Princeton University Press, 1984); and Martha Chaiklin, *Cultural Commerce and Dutch Commercial Culture: The Influence of European Material Culture on Japan, 1700–1850* (Leiden: CNWS, 2003).

18. Edward Seidensticker, *Low City, High City: Tokyo from Edo to the Earthquake; How the Shogun's Ancient Capital Became a Great Modern City, 1867–1923* (Cambridge, MA: Harvard University Press, 1991).

19. Chaiklin, *Cultural Commerce.*

another example of this pattern can be found with landlocked Delhi, and the Indian seaboard cities of the eastern Arabian Sea (Surat, Bharygaza [Bharuch], Bombay, etc.).[20]

In many of the premodern examples of Southeast Asian history that we know, by contrast, political power and mercantilism were concentrated into a single spatial locale. Thus the northern Javanese coastal entrepôts of Tuban, Demak, and Gresik were not only their own political masters but their own bankers as well: the money necessary to prop up the state flowed through the same physical walls that dictated land reform and jurisprudence.[21] Ayutthaya, up the Chao Phraya River from Bangkok and not even physically within view of the sea, followed the same pattern from a riverine perspective, as did Jambi in Sumatra and Mandalay (to some extent) in Burma.[22] Such a decision to concentrate organizational legitimacy and the rewards of an expanding commerce should not be underestimated. Southeast Asian cities largely developed differently from their neighbors because of this syncretism. Because of these initial decisions on placement, there is every indication that they probably will continue to do so in the future as well.

It is clear that colonial Southeast Asian cities continued many of these patterns in their evolution, ones that often were inherited from an earlier time. Manila, for example, continued to be both the economic and political center of the Philippines through both the Spanish and American colonial periods.[23]

20. Chin Keong Ng, *Trade and Society: The Amoy Network on the China Coast* (Singapore: Singapore University Press, 1983; John Keay, *The Honourable Company: A History of the English East India Company* (New York: HarperCollins, 1993).

21. On this point see chapter 1 in Knaap's 1996 book, which lays out the history of the northern Javanese *pasisir* prior to Knapp's discussion of the eighteenth century: Gerrit Knaap, *Shallow Waters, Rising Tide: Shipping and Trade in Java Around 1775* (Leiden: KITLV Press, 1996). See also Atsushi Ota, *Changes of Regime and Social Dynamics in West Java Society, State, and the Outer World of Banten, 1750–1830* (Leiden: Brill, 2006); and Hui Kian Kwee, *The Political Economy of Java's Northeast Coast, 1740–1800* (Leiden: Brill, 2006).

22. Dhiravat na Pombejra, "Ayutthaya at the End of the Seventeenth Century: Was There a Shift to Isolation?" in *Southeast Asia in the Early Modern Era: Trade, Power, and Belief*, ed. Anthony Reid, 250–72 (Ithaca: Cornell University Press, 1993); Barbara Watson Andaya, *To Live as Brothers: Southeast Sumatra in the Seventeenth and Eighteenth Centuries* (Honolulu: University of Hawai'i Press, 1993); Victor Lieberman, "Was the Seventeenth Century a Watershed in Burmese History?" in *Southeast Asia in the Early Modern Era*, ed. Reid, 214–49.

23. The most important theorist on urbanism in the Philippines has been Berkeley geographer Robert Reed, whose publications on Manila and also hill stations further north in Luzon have put Philippine urbanism on the scholarly map.

FIGURE 8.1. *Singapore Harbor Shortly after Its Founding* (painted by Charles Dyce, Singapore, 1842/43)

Batavia/Jakarta followed this logic throughout the length of the Dutch imperial reign in the Indies, and Singapore and Rangoon (Yangon) served as both the principal markets (and economic distribution centers), as well as the political headquarters of the British in these Southeast Asian realms.[24] Though these cities were now becoming situated as colonial capitals over and above their earlier incarnations as local centers, they maintained links to both indigenous hinterlands, and also, increasingly, to regional and global markets

24. For Jakarta, see Zeffry Alkatiri's and Ewald Ebing's work: *Dari Batavia Sampai Jakarta, 1619–1999: Peristiwa Sejarah dan Kebudayaan Betawi-Jakarta Dalam Sajak* (Magelang: IndonesiaTera, 2001); and *Batavia-Jakarta, 1600–2000: A Bibliography* (Leiden: KITLV Press, 2000); and [Anon.], "De haverwerken te Tanjung Priok," *Tijdschrift voor Nederlandsch-Indië* II (1877), 278–87, respectively. For Rangoon, see Adas's classic text on the Burma Delta: Michael Adas, *The Burma Delta: Economic Development and Social Change on an Asian Rice Frontier, 1852–1941* (Madison: University of Wisconsin Press, 1974). For Penang, see Loh Wei Leng, "Visitors to the Straits Port of Penang: British Travel Narratives as Resources for Maritime History," in *Memory and Knowledge of the Sea*, ed. Ken, 23–32.

that the colonial projects presented. They therefore became focal points for the introduction, circulation, and transmission of ideas as well as materiel. As the colonial age matured toward independence, this was also true for larger and larger quantities of people and materiel.

Evolution and Adaptation

Thinking about "modes of adaptation" is also a useful concept in attempting to decipher Southeast Asia's urban past. The existence of this string of independent city-states situated along several thousand miles of trade routes was highly precarious: changes in the flow or direction of commerce could bring fabulous wealth or stagnation with little or no warning.[25] Few of the Southeast Asian polities were endpoints in the transcontinental caravan of trade, "final destinations" like the silk capitals of China or the textile centers of Europe.[26] Almost all were instead median points in an ever-changing nexus. As such, mutations in the trade brought economic life or death, vicissitudes that were sometimes completely out of the hands of the potentate and his or her shahbandar. At other times, a smart ruler might manipulate these processes by adapting the cadence of the port itself, however—if such actions were necessary.

This kind of far-sighted modulation extant in Southeast Asian history can be found through numerous examples, but perhaps none was as successful as the beginnings of Malacca (Melaka) in the early fifteenth century. Founded by the renegade Sumatran prince Parameswara in his flight from Sumatra, Melaka grew in the space of fifty years from what has often been described as a "pirates' nest" into one of the world's great emporia.[27] The city achieved this

25. For the colonial period in particular on this topic, see Anthony Reid, "The Structure of Cities in Southeast Asia, 15th to 17th Centuries," *Journal of Southeast Asian Studies* 11 (1980): 235–50.

26. A notable exception here might be Batavia (contemporary Jakarta), which was used as the Dutch East India Co.'s "mother city" in Asia for two hundred years. On the VOC and its place in these transoceanic urban networks, see H. K. s'Jacob, "De VOC en de Malabarkust in de 17de eeuw," in *De VOC in Azië*, ed. M. A. P. Meilink-Roelofsz, 85–99 (Bussum: Fibula, 1976); Prakash, *The Dutch Factories* (1984); J. Steur, *Herstel of Ondergang: De Voorstellen tot Redres van de VOC, 1740–1795* (Utrecht: HES Uitgevers, 1984), 17–27; Harm Stevens, *De VOC in Bedrijf, 1602–1799* (Amsterdam: Walburg Press, 1998); and Femme Gaastra, *Bewind en Beleid bij de VOC, 1672–1702* (Amsterdam: Walburg Press, 1989).

27. See Mardiana Nordin, "Undang-Undang Laut Melaka: A Note on Malay Maritime Law in the Fifteenth Century," in *Memory and Knowledge of the Sea*, ed. Ken, 15–22.

by essentially reversing the state-policy of its regional antecedent, the Srivi-jayan Empire based in Palembang, Sumatra.[28] Instead of spending an enor-mous percentage of the polity's coffers on building and maintaining a power-ful navy, solely designed to coerce shipping passing through the Straits of Melaka to put into port and to trade on (often) unfavorable terms, Melaka instead *lowered* its duties to such reasonable levels that it simply became bet-ter business to trade there than anywhere else. This was an unprecedented move, and medieval merchants from as far away as East Africa, Egypt, and Okinawa came to understand that they would receive a fair, standardized price for their goods there, and that they could expect the same surveillance (and enforcement) on whatever merchandise they chose to buy as well.[29] The Srivijayan method of monopoly coercion was not wrong. It was simply the best course of action to be taken in appropriate circumstances, that is, a pe-riod of Southeast Asian history predating the emergence of a large number of competing polities (circa 1000 CE). Yet the above example also shows how adaptation and an awareness of geopolitical change in the region could buoy one city's fortunes at the expense of its competitors. This is a lesson that Singapore learned very well in the past two centuries. As discussed further on in this chapter, it is also one that Ho Chi Minh City has been recently contem-plating with great earnestness as well.

Politics Moving "Outward"; Economics Moving "Inward"

A recurring model of economic and political exchange is a fourth and last major attribute of the maritime hub in Southeast Asia that we can mention here. It can be described as a tendency for political entropy to occur in upland, jungle, and outlying areas away from the central metropolis, but for these dis-integrative forces to be checked and balanced to a degree by the cohesive bonds of mercantile exchange.[30] Throughout Southeast Asian history there

28. [Anon.], *Sriwijaya Dalam Perspektif Arkeologi dan Sejarah* (Palembang: Pemerintah Dae-rah Tingkat I Sumatera Selatan, 1993).

29. Kay Kim Khoo, "Melaka: Persepsi Tentang Sejarah dan Masyarakatnya," in *Bajunid Esei-Esei Budaya dan Sejarah Melaka*, ed. Omar Farouk (Kuala Lumpur: Siri Minggu Kesenian As-rama Za'ba, 1989); Kernial Singh Sandhu and Paul Wheatley, eds., *Melaka: The Transformations of a Malay Capital, c. 1400–1980* (Kuala Lumpur: Oxford University Press, 1983).

30. Bennet Bronson, "Exchange at the Upstream and Downstream Ends"; Tania Li, "Mar-ginality, Power, and Production: Analyzing Upland Transformations," in *Transforming the*

are examples of this dialectic at work, and at perhaps no time is it more visible than today. A useful illustration of the pattern can be presented by just briefly recounting the history of forest-product collection in the region, as well as the political implications of this trade.

There have been relatively few instances when the actual metropolis of a given polity—and the primary products over which it held jurisdiction—did not exist in the same approximate place in Southeast Asian history. Much more common has been a central authority center with all the attributes thus far described holding sway over hinterlands that supplied the city with items of international exchange. These relationships usually existed in one of three manifestations. The first would entail primary-product suppliers to live in dense jungle or forest cover reachable only by river craft. This was the case with various inland peoples like the "Dayaks" and Batak of Borneo and Sumatra, who supplied merchants of various polities (often ethnic Chinese) with goods esteemed elsewhere along the trade routes (items such as hornbills, camphor, gold bound for China, etc.).[31] These patterns happened in an arc through the breadth of insular Southeast Asia, from the Straits of Melaka to "central" Indonesia all the way to the east of the archipelago, and up through the Philippines.[32] The second possibility had primary producers living in outlying hills or mountains, such as the various upland minorities of Siam and Burma who participated in an exchange of animal products and other plant-based

Indonesian Uplands: Marginality, Power, and Production, ed. Tania Li, 1–44 (Amsterdam: Harwood Academic Publishers, 1999).

31. James Warren, _The Sulu Zone: The Dynamics of External Trade, Slavery, and Ethnicity in the Transformation of a Southeast Asian Maritime State (1768–1898)_ (Singapore: Singapore University Press, 1981); Eric Tagliacozzo, "Onto the Coast and into the Forest: Ramifications of the China Trade on the History of Northwest Borneo, 900–1900," in _Histories of the Borneo Environment_, ed. Reed Wadley (Leiden: KITLV Press, 2005).

32. See, for example, Leonard Andaya, _Leaves of the Same Tree: Trade and Ethnicity in the Straits of Melaka_ (Honolulu: University of Hawai'i Press, 2008); Leonard Andaya, _The World of Maluku: Eastern Indonesia in the Early Modern Period_ (Honolulu: University of Hawai'i Press, 1993); Heather Sutherland and Gerrit Knaap, _Monsoon Traders: Ships, Skippers and Commodities in Eighteenth Century Makassar_ (Leiden: Brill, 2004); Jennifer Gaynor, _Intertidal History in Island Southeast Asia: Submerged Genealogy and the Legacy of Coastal Capture_ (Ithaca: Cornell Southeast Asia Program, 2016); Adrian Lapian, "Laut Sulawesi: The Celebs Sea, from Center to Peripheries," _Moussons_ 7 (2004): 3–16; and Laura Lee Junker, _Raiding, Trading and Feasting: The Political Economy of Philippine Chiefdoms_ (Honolulu: University of Hawai'i Press, 1999).

medicinals for foodstuffs grown in the lowlands.[33] The last variation placed these "hinterlands" on other islands or island groups altogether. The great Majapahit polity of fourteenth-century Java claimed the Spice Islands (Maluku, or the Moluccas) five hundred miles to the west as dependencies. Yet, in actuality, there wasn't much by way of real administrative links, the connections really being more economic in nature.[34]

The fact that the metropole's jurisdiction over the periphery was much more economic than political was what all of these examples had in common. The authority that was lost over distance or geography was often rebolstered by the benefit accruing to both parties in simply continuing the exchange. Yet a tension that was endemic to this relationship existed as well, stemming from the tendency for either the center to demand too much allegiance (in the form of religious conversion, tribute, or political modifications) or the periphery too much independence (in the form of license to trade these same products to whomever they chose, freedom of lifestyle and belief, etc.). This pattern is evident in the precolonial as well as the colonial period in the region. Once again, this same dialectic is evident in many of Southeast Asia's internal conflicts today, from Burma and Laos to the southern Philippines and parts of "Outer" Indonesia.[35] How these manifestations of traditional maritime hubs have acted themselves out in contemporary Southeast Asia is an interesting question, if we now turn to the modern period.

The Present and the Future

Delineating these patterns has been important because Southeast Asian cities have incorporated many of these same historical elements into their own contemporary realities. It is no accident that while Floridians feel themselves to

---

33. Susan Russell, ed., *Ritual, Power, and Economy: Upland-Lowland Contrasts in Mainland Southeast Asia* (DeKalb: Center for Southeast Asian Studies, 1989); Ann Maxwell Hill, *Merchants and Migrants: Ethnicity and Trade Among Yunnanese in Southeast Asia* (New Haven: Yale University Southeast Asia Studies, 1998): 33–94.

34. Roy Ellen, "Environmental Perturbation, Inter-Island Trade, and the Relocation of Production along the Banda Arc; or, Why Central Places Remain Central," in *Human Ecology of Health and Survival in Asia and the South Pacific*, ed, Tsuguyoshi Suzuki and Ryutaro Ohtsuka, 35–62 (Tokyo: University of Tokyo Press, 1987).

35. On the latter, see Roy Ellen, *On the Edge of the Banda Zone: Past and Present in the Social Organization of a Moluccan Trading Network* (Honolulu: University of Hawai'i Press, 2003); and Patricia Spyer, *The Memory of Trade: Modernity's Entanglements on an Eastern Indonesian Island* (Durham: Duke University Press, 2000).

be a part of the American Union every bit as much as Californians, and that the same holds true for residents of Vladivostok and Muscovites in the Russian Republic, townsmen in Aceh feel little of this kind of allegiance to Indonesia. Villagers in Kawthoolei (on the Thai/Burmese border), Mindanao (in the Southern Philippines), and the "Montagnard highlands" (Annamite Cordillera in Laos and Vietnam) often don't exhibit much of this allegiance either.[36] Why is this? And will these dissatisfactions be tolerated—or steamrolled by centralized government power—in the years to come? How do resources fit into this equation, and how far into the "periphery" will the more traditional cultures of Southeast Asia allow their new supercity "masters" to intrude? Will they have a choice? In short, what are the present and future directions—replete with avant-garde notions like "edge cities," and ancient patterns such as concentric models of exchange—of Southeast Asian harbors, and their environs?[37]

The Global Cadence

It has thus far been clear that the fundamental structure of many premodern and colonial Southeast Asian maritime cities was an openness to trade, international commerce, and foreign ideas. Many urban centers were set up with these designs in mind, as opposed to many examples to the contrary in both East Asia and the Indian subcontinent. There is little reason to suggest that this cadence should not continue in the present and future. In fact, most of Southeast Asia's major cities are admirably placed to compete in the global mercantile orbit of the moment: two of the most important ingredients in the recipe, adequate ports and a vigorous merchant class, are already in place as legacies of the past. The same trade routes that brought porcelains, textiles, and religions also brought waves of Indian, Arab, and Chinese settlers, immigrants who now populate Southeast Asia's trade ties through their family contacts

---

36. Bertil Lintner, *Cross Border Drug Trade in the Golden Triangle* (Durham: International Boundaries Research Unit, 1991); Moshe Yegar, *Between Integration and Succession: The Muslim Communities of the Southern Philippines, Southern Thailand, and Western Burma/Myanmar* (Lanham, MD: Lexington Books, 2002); Hickey, Gerald, *Sons of the Mountains: Ethnohistory of the Vietnamese Central Highlands to 1954* (New Haven: Yale University Press, 1982).

37. The most sophisticated elucidation of traditional Southeast Asian political, religious, and economic concentricities remains Paul Wheatley's *Nagara and Commandary: Origins of the Southeast Asian Urban Traditions* (Chicago: University of Chicago Press, 1983).

and *guanxi* (networks or connections).[38] It is these *guanxi* that often keep business moving in the region, as linkages have been forged throughout the area based on blood, trust, and a shared sense of culture that is centuries old. Naturally, these contacts extend outside of the nexus of Southeast Asian immigrant communities as well, to the source countries of South Asia and China, and increasingly now to the newest immigrant shores of Australia, Europe, and North America.[39] These bonds are likely to grow in importance in the years to come. Westerners and the nouveaux riches of Asia will almost certainly continue to prize the primary products of the region, which used to consist of forest products and medicinal "exotica," but now include petroleum and natural gas. These populations will want to spend their newfound wealth on foreign goods, which will in turn encourage more and more commerce and trade as the nations of ASEAN further industrialize.[40]

The recognizable fact that these cities have been so successful in entering the international fold has also caused real problems, however. The future is not all optimistic. Pollution, highly taxed infrastructures, and overpopulation rank as perhaps the most major issues. The imbalances are worst in the cities least far along the modernization curve: while populations expand quickly in these countries, large numbers of the rural poor migrate to the new cities in search of some sort of employment.[41] The result in these places is tremendous overcrowding, further strain on already overstretched urban resources, and finally a shifting mass of low-income or destitute people who have already begun to ring these cities with little chance for work. Although several indigenous Southeast Asian systems exist that attempt to combat these pressures (such as the poverty-sharing mechanisms identified by anthropologists in western and central Java), the outlook is for the trend to continue. The structure of these cities may mutate therefore to include more and more squatter camps,

38. Kernail Sandhu and A. Mani, eds., *Indian Communities in Southeast Asia* (Singapore: ISEAS/Times Academic Press, 1993); Aiwha Ong, *Flexible Citizenship: The Cultural Logics of Transnationality* (Durham: Duke University Press, 1999).

39. Adam McKeown, *Chinese Migrant Networks and Cultural Change: Peru, Chicago, Hawaii, 1900–1936* (Chicago: The University of Chicago Press, 2001).

40. For a discussion of pan-ASEAN conceptions of a shared culture, including urban culture, see Donald Emmerson, "Security and Community in Southeast Asia: Will the Real ASEAN Please Stand Up?," *International Relations of the Asia-Pacific* (Stanford, CA: Shorenstein Asia-Pacific Research Center, 2005).

41. Gelia Castillo, *Beyond Manila: Philippine Rural Problems in Perspective* (Ottawa: International Development Research Center, 1980).

perennially unemployed populations, and, by implication, greater general poverty.[42] It is when cycles like this truly reach unmanageable proportions that cities once again feel the danger of being bypassed by the international flow of trade. It simply becomes no longer attractive for companies or governments to waste their time and investment dollars on overpressured infrastructures that do not work. Primary cities become secondary cities, and secondary cities devolve into tertiary ones. This process has already occurred in many large cities in Southeast Asia, including Semarang in Java, Nakhon Si Thammarat in Thailand, and to some extent (though the dialectic is more complicated here) Manila in the Philippines.[43] Jakarta will be displaced in the next few years by a new Bornean capital precisely because Indonesian planners have deemed the former city to be "unlivable." Although a natural part of the life cycles of great metropolises, one can also see the possibilities of this pattern on the horizon for several other Southeast Asian cities. Unless concrete and holistic steps are taken sometime soon to begin alleviating these issues, structural problems such as these—exacerbated by climate change—will surely exist into the region's future.[44]

42. Ironically, these are many of the same problems discussed in Clifford Geertz's prescient *Agricultural Involution* (Berkeley: University of California Press, 1963), which dealt with trends in Java one hundred and fifty years ago.

43. On a fieldwork trip to Manila in 1990, I completed interviews with spice merchants in the Binondo and Divisoria warehouse districts of the city. The crumbling infrastructure of these parts of Manila was all too apparent; I had to take hand-pulled rafts across a river strewn with garbage to reach several of my informants' warehouses. Interview notes, Manila, January 1990.

44. Jakarta is an interesting case in this regard, as many of the factors that could potentially backwater it are inherited from colonial times. For this city, see Zeffry Alkatiri, *Dari Batavia Sampai Jakarta, 1619–1999: Peristiwa Sejarah dan Kebudayaan Betawi-Jakarta Dalam Sajak* (Magelang: IndonesiaTera, 2001); and Ewald Ebing et al., *Batavia-Jakarta, 1600–2000: A Bibliography* (Leiden: KITLV Press, 2000). The relationship of Indonesian port cities to their hinterlands and to each other is a fascinating one, given the size and complexity of the Indonesian archipelago. For analysis pertaining to this issue in Sumatra, see Nangsari Ahmad Makmun, F. A. Soetjipto, and Mardanas Safwan, *Kota Palembang sebagai "kota dagang dan industri"* (Jakarta: Departemen Pendidikan dan Kebudayaan, Direktorat Sejarah dan Nilai Tradisional, Proyek Inventarisasi dan Dokumentasi Sejarah Nasional, 1985); *Sejarah Daerah Bengkulu* (Jakarta: Departemen Penilitian dan Pencatatan, Kebudayaan Daerah, Departemen Pendidikan dan Kebudayaan, n.d.); and Mardanas Sofwan, Taher Ishaq, Asnan Gusti, and Syafrizal, *Sejarah Kota Padang* (Jakarta: Departemen Pendidikan dan Kebudayaan, Direktorat Sejarah dan Nilai Tradisional, Proyek Inventarisasi dan Dokumentasi Sejarah Nasional, 1987). For Kalimantan, see Lisyawati Nurcahyani, *Kota Pontianak Sebagai Bandar Dagang di Jalur Sutra* (Jakarta: Departemen Pendidikan dan Kebudayaan, Direktorat Sejarah dan Nilai Tradisional, Proyek

Re-Merging Politics and Economics

This last thought returns us to the concept of what Indonesians call "dwi-fungsi," the concept of dual functionality. As has been shown previously, since their earliest beginnings Southeast Asian polities have displayed little separation between political and economic roles; a pattern that stands in vivid contrast to much of premodern and colonial-era China and India. As a result of this fusion, most Southeast Asian nations today are characterized by a single, predominant metropolis, while several other subsidiary cities (usually ports) tend to make up the balance of the country's trade by complementing the capital as regional feeder-centers for exchange. A *direct corollary* of this history is that instability in the periphery will not usually be as economically based in Southeast Asia as it is in China, for example. Centrifugal forces will always exist in Southeast Asia as they do anywhere else (to be discussed further in a moment), but these tendencies toward factionalism tend to be more weighted by religion and divergent customs than by money. In China, however, the imbalance caused by this system of binary authority—the one economic, the other political—has been coming to a head. To see why, we need only turn to the example of China's southern coasts, which are a useful mirror to the problem in that for well over a thousand years, they have been China's major contact point with maritime Southeast Asia and the world.[45]

The then dean of the UC Berkeley Graduate School of Journalism and prominent China watcher Orville Schell, mentioned in an interview some years ago that there were essentially three avatars of "China": a Socialist North,

Inventarisasi dan Dokumentasi Sejarah Nasional, 1999); for Java, see Susanto Zuhdi, *Cilacap (1830–1942): Bangkit dan Runtuhnya Suatu Pelabuhan di Jawa* (Jakarta: KPG, 2002); for Ciirebon, see [Anon.], "De Cheribonsche havenplannen," *Indisch Bouwkundig Tijdschrijf* (15 August 1917): 256–66; and [Anon.], "De nieuwe haven van Cheribon," *Weekblad voor Indië* 5 (1919): 408–09; and for Eastern Indonesia, see Restu Gunawan, *Ternate Sebagai Bandar Jalur Sutra* (Jakarta: Departemen Pendidikan dan Kebudayaan, Direktorat Sejarah dan Nilai Tradisional, Proyek Inventarisasi dan Dokumentasi Sejarah Nasional, 1999); and G. A. Ohorella, *Ternate Sebagai Bandar di Jalur Sutra* (Jakarta: Departemen Pendidikan dan Kebudayaan, Direktorat Sejarah dan Nilai Tradisional, Proyek Inventarisasi dan Dokumentasi Sejarah Nasional, 1997). Generally, see [Anon.], Departement der Burgerlijke Openbare Weken, *Nederlandsch-Indische Havens Deel I* (Batavia: Departement der Burgerlijke Openbare Werken, 1920).

45. In a trip to Xiamen, Fujian Province, the links and outward cadence of this city with and toward Taiwan, Southeast Asia, and indeed maritime Asia in general were unmistakable. One eye is kept toward Beijing for funding and political purposes, but one eye of Xiamen's government and business is most definitely rooted east and south.

a laissez-faire South, and an Islamic West, increasingly looking across the border to the Central Asian republics.[46] These de facto "polities" are nothing new, he said; they have existed in uneasy juxtaposition under the same rubric of "China" for quite some time.[47] Yet despite the authoritarian present, for how long is geopolitical unity possible under constantly evolving conditions? A global battle-cry for democracy and the right to determine one's own individual economic destiny was never part of the T'ang Dynasty's An Lu Shan rebellion, or the Boxer uprisings of the fin de siècle.[48] China has known many periods of fragmentation in its four millennia of recorded history, from the Warring States Period in 400 BCE to the chaos of competing warlords in the first half of the twentieth century. It is not inconceivable—as is the case in any other country, the United States with its fragmented politics included—to imagine a scenario of the de facto division of the People's Republic, based on the above-mentioned demarcations, at some future point in time. These are secessions and potential recastings that might act themselves out along lines existing everywhere but on the map.

A less radical change of events, albeit one with essentially many of the same characteristics, might be more believable as an interim step, however. Guangdong and Fujian, fueled by Special Economic Zones like Shenzhen and Zhuhai and linkages to capital from Hong Kong, Taiwan, and abroad, may expand the gulf between mainland rich and poor by continuing their campaigns of frenetic modernization (Guangdong alone has at times received up to half of all foreign investment entering into the People's Republic). Because of a fear of aggression from the United States and Taiwan in the two decades immediately following the 1949 revolution, Chinese Central Planning located the majority of the nation's heavy industry *away* from the southern coasts. This is a policy that has reaped rewards for southern populations who now have much less of a vestigial legacy of enormous state-owned inefficiency to bear. Instead

46. Schell stressed that these fractured outlines have been visible for some time now, though it may be decades or even centuries before some kind of pressure or event comes along to split these divisions at the seams. Interview notes, Berkeley, California, May 1992.

47. The idea of "other Chinas" has received attention from John Wills, but before him earlier suggestions to this effect were put forward by G. William Skinner. See his *Marketing and Social Structure in Rural China* (Tucson: University of Arizona Press, 1965) and his edited volume, *The City in Late Imperial China* (Stanford: Stanford University Press, 1977).

48. Valerie Hansen, *The Open Empire: A History of China to 1600* (New York: Norton, 2000), 221–24; Joseph Esherick, *The Origins of the Boxer Uprising* (Berkeley: University of California Press, 1987).

of working within this archaic structure, industrial, commercial, and service industries are being built in Guangdong and Fujian from the bottom up. For a while at least, this was accomplished often with the very non-socialist know-how of these same Hong Kong and Taiwanese businessmen, who (although Chinese) developed their business practices differently than their counter-parts on the mainland. A merchant I spoke to in Xiamen, Fujian, said it best, perhaps: "We look more toward Taipei here, and Hong Kong, than to Beijing. Beijing is very far away."[49]

Something close to a traditional polity is developing in southeastern China, one with its own customs and bylaws and whose ways of exchange are often opposed to a distant authority center, one thousand miles to the north. The linkages within the polity—linguistic, cultural, and now increasingly monetary—are real: they are also part of a larger historical continuum predat-ing even Marco Polo's descriptions of "Zaitun's" harbor (the contemporary Ch'uan-zhou/Quanzhou).[50] If Beijing does not continue bringing the rest of the country up to this same standard of living across the board, or dampen down this brand of hypercapitalism before it spins out of their control, further instabilities could conceivably be in the wings. We are already witnessing this process on a near-daily level in contemporary news cycles. The same situation holds true in Vietnam, where a similar history of binary authority in politics and exchange is also demonstrative of some of the qualitative difference be-tween Hanoi and the flourishing Mekong Delta.[51] In each case, the resultant southern polities would be strong, mercantilist-minded dynamos, while their northern counterparts would have a much more difficult time competing, for reasons *that are as much historical as they are economic*. The long arc of what we are witnessing today is the germination of a centuries-old process, yet one

---

49. Anonymous merchant, Xiamen, Fujian, South China. Fieldwork notes, June 2014 [trans-lation: E. Tagliacozzo].

50. Marco Polo, *The Travels of Marco Polo*, edited and revised from William Marsden's trans-lation by Manuel Komroff (New York: Modern Library, 2001); Frederick Hirth and W. W. Rockhill, *Chau Ju Kua: His Work on the Chinese and Arab Trade in the 12th and 13th Centuries, Entitled Chu Fan Chï* (New York: Paragon Book Reprint Co., 1966).

51. For three excellent comparative essays on this, see Michael Leaf, "Periurban Asia: A Commentary on Becoming Urban," *Pacific Affairs* 84, no. 3: 525–34; Michael Leaf, "A Tale of Two Villages: Globalization and Peri-Urban Change in China and Vietnam," *Cities* 19, no. 1: 23–32; and Michael Leaf, "New Urban Frontiers: Periurbanization and Retentionalization in Southeast Asia," in *The Design of Frontier Spaces: Control and Ambiguity*, ed. Carolyn S. Loeb and Andreas Loescher, 193–212 (Burlington: Ashgate, 2015).

(aided by technology and virtual communication) that potentially has more of a chance to succeed in the future, perhaps, than in decades previously. The current situation in Hong Kong may in fact only be a blip, if we think in these *longue-durée* terms. In either scenario, Hong Kong/Shenzhen might then become the cosmopolis of a new regional polity servicing and being served by the cities of the South China Sea, and by maritime Southeast Asia in general.[52] Whether this will occur under a Chinese-socialist or a Western-capitalist rubric is still uncertain. We all watch our screens at the speed of these events occurring every day.

Urban Evolution and Urban Competition

When we think about how certain Southeast Asian polities have been able to strategically adapt to circumstances in order to survive, the fifteenth-century Melaka Sultanate was held up earlier in this chapter as a good example. Through its policies of low commercial tariffs and its rigid enforcement of weights and measures, Melaka received a global reputation as a singular place to transact fair and profitable business. As a result of these initiatives, the city grew in the late 1400s to become one of the largest emporia in the world.[53] Contemporary Southeast Asia also boasts such success stories, as well as new cosmopolises that are now positioning themselves to become even larger polities in the future. However, it is also interesting to analyze at least one port that has struggled in the past two decades, and that is only recently re-emerging into international orbits of trade.

Once called the "Venice of Asia" by breathless European visitors, that city is Saigon (now officially called "Ho Chi Minh City"). Saigon's outstretched canals, bustling commerce, and Gallic mien made it a crossroads for mercantile traffic proceeding between China and Southeast Asia. Vietnamese merchants, especially from the Chinese neighborhood of Saigon known as Cholon, were famous in the region as hard-driving bargainers, middlemen, and as a living conduit between disparate worlds. Many in fact spoke and read Chinese fluently because of their at least partially Chinese roots, while simultaneously bearing Southeast Asian cultural sensibilities.[54] Then came the

52. Frank Welsh, *A Borrowed Place: The History of Hong Kong* (New York: Kodansha, 1993).

53. Mohamed Jamil bin Mukmin, *Melaka Pusat Penyebaran Islam di Nusantara* (Kuala Lumpur: Nurin Enterprise, 1994).

54. Dian Murray, *Pirates of the South China Coast* (Stanford: Stanford University Press, 1987).

Vietnam War, and when the war was over, Saigon/Ho Chi Minh City found itself quickly passed by the international nexus. When I was doing interviewing in Southeast Asia some years ago, I spoke to many informants who used to have widespread family contacts in Vietnam, but whose *guanxi* had subsequently dried up as ideological purity became more important to rulers in Hanoi than advancing the material well-being of their own populations.[55] Saigon literally receded from the Southeast Asian mercantile orbit in the space of five years. The first Western reporters allowed back into the city after the fall of Saigon were astonished at the changes that had taken place: people had begun to live on next to nothing, and the standard of living as a whole had plummeted to abysmal proportions. US-led sanctions for twenty years helped this process along. Of course, Hanoi's ideological purity has now thawed considerably, and every attempt is being made to reverse a generation of economic hibernation, including via investment from the outside world. But the damage was done. It is only relatively recently that Ho Chi Minh City has become more fully a part of the colonial-era conduits within which it used to thrive as an important port .[56]

Then there is Singapore. Completely on the opposite side of the spectrum has been this city-state, now formally two hundred–plus years old, whose political raison d'être since its "official" founding in 1819 has been and continues to be an attempt to remain just slightly ahead of its neighbors.[57] This is the mechanic of selective adaptation—so important to Southeast Asian ports and their politics throughout history—taken to its fullest proportions. Singapore has been the principal feeder/collecting/warehousing center of Southeast Asia for so long now that its wealth has often been resented by its ethnically Malay neighbors.[58] However, up until this point at least, its efficacy as a transit

---

55. These conversations took place with Chinese merchants in several parts of Southeast Asia. Echoing the political-speak of the American government in the 1950s, '60s, and '70s, many of these merchants saw Vietnam as "lost" to them, especially in familial and economic terms. Interview notes, Singapore (October 1989); Kuala Lumpur (November 1989); and Bangkok (February 1990).

56. See Erik Harms, *Saigon's Edge: On the Margins of Ho Chi Minh City* (Minneapolis: University of Minneapolis Press, 2011); and Erik Harms, *Luxury and Rubble: Civility and Dispossession in the New Saigon* (Berkeley: University of California Press, 2016).

57. Ernest Chew, and Edwin Lee, eds, *A History of Singapore* (Singapore: Oxford University Press, 1991).

58. For the unfolding of this particular dialectic of the city-state as the object of anger and envy by surrounding polities, see Robert Griffith and Carol Thomas, eds., *The City-State in Five Cultures* (Santa Barbara: ABC-Clio, 1981).

and trade metropolis to these very same neighbors has outweighed its role as an economic syphon drawing off many of the profits to be had in the region. Singapore is looking to extend this lifeline by any means possible.[59] Announcements of enormous tax incentives to multinational companies looking for a regional headquarters in the area and advancements in establishing a statewide "computer net" that will track all capital on the island are moves toward enhancing this edge. So is the completion of the last stages in completely interlinking the island through rapid mass transit, which has somewhat abated decades of horrendous traffic problems. These are not cosmetic orchestrations, designed merely to convince outside investors that Chinese Singapore is still an "intelligent island" in what has been sometimes crassly (and unfairly) advertised as a "backward" Muslim sea. Rather, the Singaporean Planning Board has been trying to ensure that the structural and economic geography of the island keeps pace with the newest advances in global organization. This is so that Singapore manages to modulate itself into a viable geopolitical future. With few natural advantages of its own and plenty of dangerous Achilles' heels (including water supply, underpopulation, and the perceived regional Muslim resentment mentioned earlier), the city-state has made clear that it has few choices in this.

Which other urban centers might accompany Singapore in successfully adapting to this pattern of Southeast Asian morphogenesis, into the modern age? While for the near term no other port in the region will be able to match the city-state in terms of sheer technology and levels of organization, certain centers are moving toward these ends faster than others. We see this through a combination of informal urban growth, medium-scale industrialization, and the movement of wealth and power to the (expanding) suburbs of a number of cities. Bangkok, with its monumental expenditure on updating telecommunications in the kingdom, is one such possibility. Increasing amounts of capital being spent on upgrading and modernizing the Gulf of Thailand seaboard between Bangkok and Chonburi will go a long way toward realizing greater efficiency, as will the ascension of Laem Chabang port, which has largely replaced the older, more dilapidated Klong Toey harbor. Kuala Lumpur is also becoming significantly more important, especially as it exhibits the qualities of Western "edge city" planning to a far greater extent than any of its

59. See Chua Beng Huat, "Singapore as Model: Planning Innovations, Knowledge Experts," in *Worlding Cities: Asian Experiments and the Art of Being Global*, ed. Ananya Roy and Aihwa Ong, 29–54 (London: Blackwell, 2011).

neighbors. Light-transit rail networks now join the Malaysian capital with its complementary satellite cities, Petaling Jaya, Shah Alam, Sungei Buloh, and Rawang; Kuala Lumpur's cybercorridor is now almost completely built. Metropolises of lesser order that are also becoming hubs of more complex systems include Cebu in the southern Philippines and Vientiane along the Laotian shore of the Mekong River. Collectively positioned to make a difference in how regional economies are ordered and reordered, all of these centers also exhibit the characteristic qualities of adaptation to specific markets and trade routes.

Modern Southeast Asia's Cities and Concentricity

The final, vital index of the future of Southeast Asia's urban centers rotates back to the model of political and economic exchange we have already discussed. It was illustrated earlier that a hallmark feature of these kingdoms was their ability to balance economic and political tensions to the benefit of two groups: at least normatively, and as a matter of stasis, neither the center nor the periphery received more in these bargains than the other gauged was fair.[60] When this balance was upset, with one factor in the exchange suddenly looming larger and with more vitality than the driving impetus of the other (i.e., avarice on the part of the center, or political entropy on the part of the hinterland), severe strain or the dissolution of these bonds usually resulted. This dialectic took many forms in Southeast Asian history, from enforced slave-labor systems to armed revolts, or even (occasionally) to short-term wars of attrition.[61] The tale of these ongoing tensions is the history of the region, to some extent.

Parts of Southeast Asia right now face dangerous flux in terms of this dynamic. As history has unfolded, both of these driving forces, resistance-politics on the part of the periphery and an increased importance attached to economics on the part of the center, have occurred largely at the same time. Boundaries that were arbitrarily drawn by colonial powers of the twentieth century or even groupings that have existed for much greater lengths of time have been

60. Karl Hutterer, *Economic Exchange and Social Interaction in Southeast Asia: Perspectives from Prehistory, History, and Ethnography* (Ann Arbor: University of Michigan Southeast Asia Program, 1977).

61. Anthony Reid, *Slavery, Bondage, and Dependency in Southeast Asia* (St. Lucia: University of Queensland Press, 1983); Ben Kerkvliet, *The Huk Rebellion* (Berkeley: University of California Press, 1977); Paul van het Veer, *De Atjeh Oorlog* (Amsterdam: Arbeiderspers, 1969).

vigorously questioned in the past few decades. This tension is evident in land-scapes across Southeast Asia.[62] Concomitantly, the modern nation-states of the region are increasingly attempting an integration—and, more important, perhaps, an ideological unity—within their own borders that has rarely before been tried. The motivation is at least partly economic: greater unity equals greater control, and greater control spawns greater profits in the effort to maxi-mize the percentage of resources available for shipment to the world market. Where might these collisions occur with the greatest force, affecting either the evolution or devolution of urban centers in the region?

One place to look is the Thai-Burmese border. Manerplaw, a fortress city high in the dense hills overlooking the Moei River, became a symbol of all those disaffected with the brutal Burmese regime that monopolized power in Yangon (Rangoon) until only recently. Student rebels, Theravada Buddhist monks, pro–Aung San Suu Kyi forces, and fighters of other highland minori-ties (Akha, Lahu, Lisu, and Naga) all rallied to the region as holdouts from Burman cultural and political hegemony. The general area has also played host to several warlord armies in the pay and conscription of independent opium barons, men who at the same time provided a percentage of the world's supply of high-grade heroin.[63] As an agglomeration, this flashpoint of perennial in-stability both augments and detracts from future regional linkages that might be possible. The general instability provides a chance for Thai and Burmese generals to get rich in cross-border trade in illegal merchandise, but the situ-ation on Burma's borders also diminishes the amounts of legal trade reve-nues accrued to the Burmese state. If Burmese goods did not have to wind the convoluted alternate economic routes that they still—to some extent, anyway—currently do, undoubtedly the pace and flow of the exchange would stream much more heavily into the open arms of Yangon, rather than Bangkok. The present dialectic therefore has within its nature the potential to vastly increase Bangkok's efficacy as a metropole. Concomitantly, Ran-goon is being backwatered to some extent even further off the commercial grid of the region.[64]

62. For Indonesia alone, see Irena Critalis, *Bitter Dawn: East Timor, a People's Story* (London: Zed Books, 2002). For East Timor, and for Aceh and West Papua, see Daniel Dhakidae, *Aceh, Ja-karta, Papua: Akar Permasalahan dan Alternatif Proses Penyelsaian Konflik* (Jakarta: Yaprika, 2001).

63. The most detailed expose of these complicated vectors remains Alfred McCoy's *The Politics of Heroin: CIA Complicity in the Global Drug Trade* (New York: Hill Books, 1991).

64. Martin Smith, *Burma: Insurgency and the Politics of Ethnicity* (London: Zed Books, 1999).

The Indonesian archipelago is also an area of area of real importance in these calculations. Possessing perhaps the most geographically widespread history of these cross-cultural models of exchange, Indonesia is a more cohesive polity than Myanmar. Nevertheless, the present is still at a juncture of both promise and danger for the government in Jakarta. Since the Aceh Merdeka ("Free Aceh") Movement in Sumatra and the Sulawesi Rebellions of the late 1950s, the "Outer Island" challenge to Jakarta's domestic hegemony has diminished, but it has never completely disappeared. There are still whisperings in parts of the country—Maluku and Christian West Papua to be added to the aforementioned hotspots of more orthodox Islam—that the provinces should be granted a far greater degree of autonomy. East Timor has already seceded and became the independent nation of Timor-Leste. All of this comes at a time when the state doctrine of a unified and indivisible Indonesia is still sometimes questioned, causing friction in some islands where such ideas are somewhat out of sync with the unified idea of the nation. A suggestion of any comprehensive political splintering for Indonesia is unlikely. But moves toward autonomy elsewhere and the ongoing crises in the Muslim Middle East have also been heard in this part of the region, and are still in the process of being translated into local idioms that will resonate for years to come.[65] As a local imam once told me in Aceh, North Sumatra (echoing what I had heard in Fujian, in the Chinese case): "Jakarta is very far away from here. The Javanese are very far away. This place isn't called the 'verandah of Mecca' for nothing."[66]

Cambodia, finally (and most tragically) also fits into the elucidated model of exchange effecting metropolises and polities in the region. Despite reports

---

65. Theodore Friend, *Indonesian Destinies* (Cambridge, MA: Harvard University Press, 2003); Franz Magnis-Suseno, ed., *Suara dari Aceh: Identifikasi kebutuhan dan keinginan rakyat Aceh* (Jakarta: Yayasan Penguatan Partisipasi Inisiatif dan Kemitraan Masyarakat Sipil Indonesia, 2001); Zadrak Wamebu and Karlina Leksono, *Suara dari Papua: Identifikasi kebutuhan masyarakat Papua asli* (Jakarta: Yayasan Penguatan Partisipasi Inisiatif dan Kemitraan Masyarakat Sipil Indonesia, 2001). It is interesting that one of the urban areas of China least involved in the 1989 demonstrations was Guangzhou, which makes for a fascinating parallel with Indonesia. "It was as if the political pressures originating at the center—both the protests against power and the recovery of control by the power structure—ran up against the primary concern shared by all in the South of preserving the wealth attained since 1978 and not jeopardizing the development under way." See Bergere, "Tiananmen 1989" (1995).

66. Imam in Banda Aceh, North Sumatra. Author's fieldwork notes, April 1990 [translation by E. Tagliacozzo].

of significant recent growth in the capital, and investor confidence increasing, Phnom Penh will not be joining even the second-tier area centers anytime soon. Events in the past four decades have made it perfectly clear that corruption and mismanagement were attributable not only to the instability of the Khmer Rouge years, between 1975 and 1979. It is also clear that Phnom Penh's trade routes with its neighbors will continue to be suspected as outlets for large quantities of contraband. The problem lies not only in the fact that the Khmer Rouge bled the country dry for four years, before being marginalized by the invading Vietnamese in 1979.[67] At the same time, many of the ruby-mining and teak territories that could act as Phnom Penh's hard currency in building the city back into a viable contender for commerce are controlled by syndicates who have absolutely no interest in national development. Until those areas are wrested away from more or less gangsterized control, Bangkok's supremacy as the de facto hub of central mainland Southeast Asia seems safe.[68] Bangkok's potential as a true regional mart, however—in an era of true regional integration—still remains to be fulfilled. This is the double-edged sword of concentric models of exchange in an evolving modern Southeast Asia.

Conclusion

Several historical examples of the evolving lives of port cities have been examined within the confines of this chapter for a simple reason: taken as a group, they seem to at least partially whisper the tale of the future of many Southeast Asian urban centers. Models of reciprocity and exchange in politics and economics have been part of the region's urban history for at least a millennium.[69]

---

67. For some of these patterns during Khmer Rouge times, see Ben Kiernan, *The Pol Pot Regime: Race, Power, and Genocide in Cambodia under the Khmer Rouge 1975–1979* (New Haven: Yale University Press, 2002); and Andrew Mertha, *Brothers in Arms: Chinese Aid to the Khmer Rouge, 1975–1979* (Ithaca: Cornell University Press, 2014).

68. Evan Gottesman, *Cambodia after the Khmer Rouge: Inside the Politics of Nation Building* (New Haven: Yale University Press, 2003).

69. See Frank Broeze, *Brides of the Sea: Port Cities of Asia From the 16th-20th Centuries* (Kensington: New South Wales University Press, 1989); J. K. Wells and John Villiers, eds., *The Southeast Asian Port and Polity: Rise and Demise* (Singapore: Singapore University Press, 1990); and again, Frank Broeze, ed., *Gateways of Asia: Port Cities of Asia in the 13th—20th Centuries* (London: Kegan Paul International, 1997). For a general appraisal of this relationship on a theoretical, not a Southeast Asian plane, see M. Castells, *The Urban Question: A Marxist Approach* (London: Edward Arnold, 1979).

These same models—in one form or another—will almost definitely continue to be important into the future. This hypothesis should not detract, however, from the approaching realities that we are all becoming more interlinked, and that increasingly these linkages are based on a fluid, global framework that is evolving and changing all the time.

Despite this, some trends seem apparent for the future of port cities in Southeast Asia.[70] Their history as world marts and markets has positioned their basic, skeletal structures as open in character and adaptive in cadence, qualities that can only serve them in an upcoming era of frantic economic interchange.[71] Some cities within this inclusive, regional framework—notably Hong Kong, Bangkok, and Singapore—are better placed than others by virtue of geography and development to lead the pack as regional "supercities" through the twenty-first century. Yet there are elements of entropy that have been woven into the contemporary urban fabric as well, problems that could evolve to significantly rework these relationships in a very short period of time. Hong Kong's fate as the darling of two ideological camps of suitors—one socialist and bent on managing and controlling change, the other hypercapitalist and global, and determined to speed it up—could place it as a future battleground of epic proportions. Bangkok, too, has the capability (depending on events at Thailand's borders, and the kinds of governments its citizens decide to elect, including the role of the monarchy in these calculations) to grow still richer, or to spiral downward into corruption and dysfunction. Finally, Singapore, the "purest" example in some ways of a traditional Southeast Asian trading port still left in equatorial seas, will either continue its run ahead of its neighbors, or begin its own devolution as other metropolises have done before it. This eventuality hinges at least partially on economic planners in Kuala Lumpur and Jakarta deciding that it is better to encourage their own Port Kelangs and Tanjong Prioks, and take a short-term loss, rather than relying on someone else to conduct their nations' long-term business. But it is also a

70. For a fascinating meditation on the nature of the Southeast Asian city over time, see Richard O'Connor, *A Theory of Indigenous Southeast Asian Urbanism* (Singapore: ISEAS Research Monograph 38, 1983). O'Connor engages with Tonnies and the Frankfurt School on ideas of *Gemeinschaft* and *Gesellschaft*, and whether or not Western-generated models of urban theory can be applied to Southeast Asian urbanism as a whole.

71. Several interesting projections on where Southeast Asian cities may be heading into the future can be found in Y. M. Yeung and C. P. Lo, eds., *Changing Southeast Asian Cities: Readings on Urbanization* (Oxford: Oxford University Press, 1976).

political question in Singapore, given the stranglehold on power the PAP has enjoyed for so many years. The future of the region's cities will turn on many of the same processes that delivered them to the present.[72] The dictates of early-twenty-first-century globalization, therefore, will only partially ensure the pace and directions of Southeast Asia's urban evolution in the multiple futures that stretch before us.

72. For the long warp and weft of how these systems have hung together, positioning Southeast Asia as only part of much wider, "Old World" patterns, see Barry Cunliffe, *By Steppe, Desert, and Ocean: The Birth of Eurasia* (Oxford: Oxford University Press, 2015).

9

From Aden to Bombay, from Singapore to Pusan

COLONIAL CIRCUITS

The city's life flows calmly like the motion of celestial bodies . . . it acquires the inevitability of phenomena not subject to human caprice.

—ITALO CALVINO[1]

THE ADVANCE OF EUROPEAN EMPIRE in Asia has traditionally been looked at in two ways by historians. In the first instance, empires have been looked at individually, by country, so that the Portuguese project (or its Dutch, French, or British analogs) have been analyzed across the width and breadth of Asia, often as essentialized "types" of human and territorial domination. This was the historiographical bent of the study of Western adventurism in Asia for a long while.[2] A second, more recently tried-and-true method for studying empire has been through regional variants, so as to discern patterns in particular theaters of operation: the French in Indochina, for example; the Dutch imperium in the seventeen thousand islands of "greater Indonesia," or in

---

1. Italo Calvino, *Invisible Cities* (London: Harcourt, 1974), 150.

2. See, for example, Charles Boxer, *The Portuguese Seaborne Empire 1415–1825* (New York: Knopf, 1969); Matt Matsuda, *Empire of Love: Histories of France and the Pacific* (New York: Oxford University Press, 2005); Jonathan Israel, *Dutch Primacy in World Trade* (Oxford: Oxford University Press, 1989); Piers Brendon, *The Decline and Fall of the British Empire, 1781–1997* (New York: Knopf, 1998).

Bengal; the British in the Indian subcontinent.[3] Both of these historical approaches have had their merits, and there have been things to be learned by the patterns uncovered in such analyses. Yet both approaches also leave empire ghettoized at the very starting points of the examinations: focusing down on one European project or one Asian geography necessarily limits vision of the connective fibers stretched to other, nearby paradigms. Now that those historiographical basics have been laid down, and are seen to crisscross Asia both temporally and geographically, it would seem to make sense to tie some of these fibers across these systems, and also across the various projects themselves. In doing this we can see other patterns emerge, perhaps, that before were muted in appearance, even if they were always there. This is all of course to say nothing of the role of indigenous peoples of the region in these patterns, which is not the subject of this chapter (local peoples and their stories are well situated through other parts of this book). The "indigenous angle" on events is increasingly being told in the academy, thankfully, and in more and more sophisticated ways.[4]

This chapter looks at "colonial circuits" that developed astride Asia's coasts, particularly in the nineteenth century but inclusive of earlier centuries, and also extending to the first few decades of the twentieth century.[5] I examine these "circuits" (vis-à-vis intelligence; transshipment; emigration issues, and the like) regionally, from west to east, encompassing West, South, East, and Southeast Asia all into one whole. The British loom slightly larger in this discussion than their European allies and competitors because Britain did in fact

---

3. Penny Edwards, *Cambodge: The Cultivation of a Nation* (Honolulu: University of Hawai'i Press, 2007); Robert Cribb, *The Late Colonial State in Indonesia: Political and Economic Foundations of the Netherlands Indies, 1880–1942* (Leiden: KITLV Press, 1994); Om Prakash, *The Dutch East India Company and the Economy of Bengal, 1630–1720* (Princeton: Princeton University Press, 1985); John Keay, *The Honourable Company: A History of the English East India Company* (New York: HarperCollins, 1993).

4. For one of the latest and best statements toward these ends, see Tim Harper, *Underground Asia: Global Revolutionaries and the Overthrow of Europe's Empires in the East* (London: Allen Lane, 2019). See also the very interesting Kris Alexanderson, *Subversive Seas: Anticolonial Networks Across the Twentieth-Century Dutch Empire* (Cambridge: Cambridge University Press, 2019).

5. I am not the first to do this, of course; for an even broader picture, see Michael Miller, for example, *Europe and the Maritime World: A Twentieth Century History* (Cambridge: Cambridge University Press, 2012). For notions of "circuits," see Janet Abu-Lughod, *Before European Hegemony: The World System AD 1250–1350* (New York: Oxford University Press, 1991).

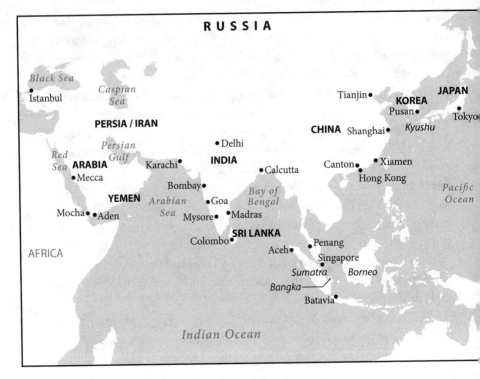

MAP 9.1. Colonial Oceanic Circuits

have this enlarged size and scope to their trans-Asian presence at this time.[6] But other imperial powers appear here too, also as component-parts of their own colonial circuits, and the larger, Western-dominated series of maritime ports that was their shared, "master-circuit" as well. The chapter stretches from the very "door" of Asia—the Bosphorus waterway separating Asia and Europe in Ottoman Turkey—through the Persian Gulf and Red Sea, to India and the subcontinent, through insular Southeast Asia and up through coastal China to Korea and Japan.[7] In all of these locales, each one connected to the

6. Though dated in many ways, one of the best ways to get a sense of both the width and breadth of the British Empire is through James/Jan Morris, *Pax Britannica Trilogy* (*Heaven's Command*; *Pax Britannica*, and *Farewell the Trumpets*), all republished by the Folio Society in London in 1993.

7. For a useful study of patterns preceding what is described here, see R. S. Lopez, "Les méthodes commerciales des marchands occidentaux en Asie du XIe au XIVe siècle," in *Sociétés et compagnies de commerce en Orient et dans l'Océan Indien*, ed. M. Mollat, 343–51.

next (and often to points further afield), I argue that clues can be found as to how the sinews of colonial connection worked across space and time. Taken as a broad template of the ports of Asia as they developed both across and between these various projects, I show how colonial "circuits" were forged, from Constantinople to Bombay, from Rangoon up to Yokohama. Far from being isolated "nodes" or "theaters" during a time of the carving up of the world, these harbors became utterly interconnected and dependent in a variety of ways.

Western Asia's Waters

The colonial circuits of Asia writ large began right at the entrance of the continent itself, in Constantinople, the bridge between Asia and Europe. In the late nineteenth century, as had been the case previously for many hundreds, if not thousands, of years, control over the city and its strategic waterway (the Bosphorus) was seen as imperative in political considerations.[8] For England, whose vast empire and influence stretched across the globe, there were few sea channels more important than this. British statesmen therefore spilled a fair bit of ink writing about ways of keeping the Bosphorus "friendly," or at least neutral, to all shipping and outside the control of potentially rival empires. In 1888 this "gateway to Asia" was discussed vis-à-vis Russian attempts to secure that country's southern borders, and London outlined scenarios whereby the Ottomans might be made to give up the waterway to Russian influence after the arrival of a hostile fleet.[9] England solicited the opinion of German engineers on where to place gun batteries astride the Bosphorus in order to avoid this, information which was then circulated between different branches of the British empire in dispatches.[10] One of these engineers, Von der Goltz Pasha, outlined how existing emplacements were basically death traps, and would

8. See, for example, G. Berchet, *La Repubblica di Venezia e la Persia*, Tornio 1865. For the wider story of British imperial considerations in the Middle East, see Priya Satia, *Spies in Arabia: The Great War and the Cultural Foundations of Britain's Covert Empire in the Middle East* (New York: Oxford University Press, 2009).

9. "Memorandum Respecting Russian Plans for 'Coup de Main' by Sea on Bosphorous, and Proposed Counter-Measures, 25 June, 1888," in *British Documents on Foreign Affairs: Reports and Papers from the Foreign Office Confidential Print Series* (hereafter BDFA), ed. Kenneth Bourne and D. Cameron Watt, Part I, series B, vol. 17, p. 88 (Lanham, Md: University Publications of America, 1985).

10. Col. Chermside to Sir W. White, 25 June 1888, in *BDFA*, Part I, series B, vol. 17, p. 87.

FIGURE 9.1. Istanbul (author's photo)

easily be taken by any real Russian aggression in the region.[11] Another engineer named Schumann concurred, and even sketched out better ways to place fortifications according to the dictates of modern warfare at the time.[12] These discussions show how seriously London regarded the situation at the doorway to Asia, and how other empires—including the Russians, but not limited to them—also kept an eye out on this ribbon of water as being of vital, international importance.

London's eye gazed farther east toward the rest of Asia in the Middle East as well. In the Persian Gulf, the British also felt the strategic shadow of the Ottomans, as reports came in to Her Majesty's spies that Constantinople was actively intriguing to separate several Persian Gulf shaykhs from England, men who already had made treaties with the British with regard to trade and local political influence. This news was difficult for London to accept, especially in places in the Gulf such as Bahrain, Qatar, and Oman, where the existing coastal commerce and the trade in pearls in particular were seen to be of no small

11. "Herbert Chermside's Remarks on Von der Goltz Pasha's Propositions, 25 June 1888," in Ibid., p. 92.

12. "Chermside's Notes on some Details of Major Schumann's Proposed System of Fortification, 25 June 1888," in Ibid., p. 93.

value.[13] Yet it was the Red Sea that was even more important in this respect, as a long lineage of colonial reportage makes clear. In the 1890s the British eyed with great alarm French movements toward taking small stretches of coast in the Red Sea, especially down toward the base of the waterway near the Bab al-mandeb (Gate of Tears) in southern Yemen, the strategic mouth of the channel opening onto the Indian Ocean. Snippets of debate in the French Chamber of Deputies were singled out for study and reproduction, as they signaled aggressive intent, it seemed, to London:

> Le mainmise sur cette position leur assuerait à jamais la porte méridionale de la mer Rouge. Cheick-Said est à nous depuis 1868; nous l'avons bel et bien acquis et payé, et occupé; en 1870, ce nous fut un réel avantage de la posséder. Je prie le Gouvernement de presser notre installation definitive sur ce point, et avant toute chose de ne pas l'abandonner à l'Angleterre qui, elle, ne nous abandonne jamais rien.[14]

> Their takeover on this location would ensure they forever hold the southern mouth of the Red Sea. Cheick-Said has been ours since 1868; we have indeed acquired it and paid for its occupation; and in 1870 it was a boon for us to possess it. I ask the regime to facilitate our permanent presence there, and above all not to allow it to England, who on their own account, never give up to us anything at all. [translation: E. Tagliacozzo]

The Ottomans had forbidden the sale of the aforementioned small coastal territories to the French, but local shaykhs had other ideas, and had professed to Paris that Constantinople had never really controlled their destinies, either politically or territorially.[15] The British, however, did not take any chances, and wrote up detailed reports of the areas in question, outlining telegraph

13. "Memorandum by Mr. Bertie on Questions with the Porte in the Persian Gulf, August 1892 to October 1893," in Ibid., p. 107. For the wider picture, see Willem Floor, *The Persian Gulf: A Political and Economic History of Five Port Cities, 1500–1730* (Washington, DC: Mage Publishers, 2006) and Pedro Machado, Steve Mullins, and Joseph Christensen, eds., *Pearls, People, and Power: Pearling and Indian Ocean Worlds* (Athens, OH: Ohio University Press, 2019).

14. For a regional overview, see Jonathan Miran, *Red Sea Citizens: Cosmopolitan Society and Cultural Change in Massawa* (Bloomington: Indiana University Press, 2009); Nancy Um, *The Merchant Houses of Mocha: Trade and Architecture in an Indian Ocean Port* (Seattle: University of Washington Press, 2009); and Roxani Margariti, *Aden and the Indian Ocean Trade: 150 Years in the Life of a Medieval Arabian Port* (Chapel Hill: University of North Carolina Press, 2007).

15. "Memorandum on Sheikh Said, 7 March 1893," in Ibid., p. 103; see also Michel Mollat [du Jourdin], "Passages français dans l'océan Indien au temps de François Ier," *Studia XI* (Lisbon, 1963), 239–248.

placements and the appearance of salt pens and industry, as well as the location of a local lighthouse.[16] Extending one's own colonial circuits and limiting those of one's rivals became of greater and greater importance as the century wore on, and less and less space presented itself to be conquered and controlled.

The Red Sea was also a locale where other powers besides the British had imperial ambitions, and set up colonial circuits of their own.[17] The Portuguese were among the earliest in this respect, engaging in trade with some Muslim potentates, even as they fought running maritime battles with others in this narrow ribbon of water.[18] The French had a long-standing interest in the area, and built up a presence—both political, in the form of consuls—and militarily, as the nineteenth century wore on. The French adventure in Egypt colored some of the aggressive, colonial thinking on these maneuvers, as France's empire in Indochina began to take shape in the third quarter of the nineteenth century, and strategic planners began to see the Red Sea more as a vital conduit to other places, perhaps, than for its own local, territorial value.[19] The Russians also got involved, setting up a political presence in the area to look after their own interests on their extended southern flank, astride their neighbor, the weakening Ottoman Empire.[20] Even the Italians also took an interest in this maritime passageway, primarily because of the growth of their own colonies in Eritrea and Somalia, and the need for an information- and supply-conduit back through the Mediterranean to the emerging Fascist metropole

16. "Sheikh Said: Memorandum in Continuation of Departmental Memorandum of 7 March 1893, 9 April 1897," in *BDFA*, Part I, series B, vol. 17, p. 162.

17. For the big picture here, see Alexis Wick, *The Red Sea: In Search of Lost Space* (Berkeley: University of California Press, 2016); Roger Daguenet, *Histoire de la Mer Rouge* (Paris: L'Harmattan, 1997); Janet Starkey, ed., *People of the Red Sea: Proceedings of the Red Sea Project II Held in the British Museum* (London: Society for Arabian Studies Monograph 3, 2005): 109–116; Nancy Um, *Shipped but Not Sold: Material Culture and the Social Order of Trade during Yemen's Age of Coffee* (Honolulu: University of Hawai'i Press, 2017); and Nancy Um, *Merchant Houses of Mocha: Trade and Architecture in an Indian Ocean Port* (Seattle: University of Washington Press, 2009).

18. For translated, contemporary Arabic-language documents on seeing this process in action, see R. B. Serjeant, *The Portuguese off the South Arabian Coast: Hadrami Chronicles, with Yemeni and European Accounts* (Beirut: Librairie du Liban, 1974).

19. See, for example, Roger Daguenet, *Histoire de la Mer Rouge* (Paris: L'Harmattan, 1997); and Roger Daguenet, *Aux origines de l'implantation français en Mer Rouge: Vie et mort d'Henri Lambert, consul de France à Aden, 1859* (Paris: L'Harmattan, 1992).

20. See Eric Tagliacozzo, *The Longest Journey: Southeast Asians and the Pilgrimage to Mecca* (New York: Oxford University Press, 2013), especially chapter 8.

of Rome.[21] A late-nineteenth-century Italian scholarly contribution summed up the importance of better understanding the region as follows:

"Donde, prima d'ogni altra cosa; il bisogno di farsi un 'idea chiara ed esalta tanto delle condizioni geo-climatiche del Hedjaz . . ."[22]

"Whence, first before all other things, we need to get a clear and exact idea as to the geo-climatic conditions of the Hijaz . . ." [translation: E. Tagliacozzo]

Yet it was the Dutch who maintained the longest and most continuous presence in the region, even if this presence was small and few in numbers on the ground. The VOC, of course, had been very active in the early modern coffee trade of the region, and had set up semipermanent "factories" and other installations in places such as Mocha, where coffee (but also other commodities) could be bought and sold.[23] Though the VOC did not have serious colonial pretensions to territory in the Yemen and Red Sea region, it did certainly see the waterway as vital—not just for its area markets, and the coasting trade with other Middle Eastern (and African) locales, but as a thoroughfare to the main Dutch colonies in the distant East Indies.[24] Though Dutch trading concerns and political representation eventually took shape in several Red Sea locales, their principal presence after a while congealed in Jeddah, which was not only a trading city in its own right, but the gateway for tens of thousands of Dutch Indies pilgrims on their way to Mecca for the annual Hajj. In Jeddah, Dutch consuls, scholars, and merchants eventually built up formidable networks over many decades, facilitating the flow of people, materiel, and information both east and west across the vast Indian Ocean.[25] The Arabian Sea

---

21. Two good period Italian-language cites here are G. B. Licata, "L'Italia nel Mar Rosson," *Boll. Sez. Fiorentina della Soc. Africana d'Italia* (March 1885): 5; and A. Mori, "Le Nostre Colonie del Mar Rosso Giudicate dalla Stanley," *Boll. Sez. Fiorentina della Soc. Africana d'Italia* (May 1886): 84.

22. E. Rossi, "Il Hedjaz, il Pellegrinaggio e il cholera," *Gior. D. Soc. Ital.* 4 (1882): 549.

23. C. G. Brouwer, *Cauwa ende comptanten: de VOC in Yemen* (Amsterdam: D'Fluyte Rarob, 1988); C. G. Brouwer, *Al-Mukha: Profile of a Yemeni Seaport as Sketched by Servants of the Dutch East India Company, 1614–1640* (Amsterdam: D'Fluyte Rarob, 1997).

24. A terrific source for looking at reprinted, centuries-old VOC Dutch-language correspondence in this vein is W. Ph. Coolhaas, ed., *Generale missiven van gouverneurs-generaal enrRaden aan heren XVII der Verenigde Oostindische Compagnie* [multivolume], ('s Gravenhage: Martinus Nijhoff, 1960).

25. Tagliacozzo, *Longest Journey*, chapter 8.

became a busy thoroughfare during this time, as an increasingly sophisticated plank of scholarly literature is making more and more clear.[26]

In South Asian Worlds

The British of course eventually found far greater expression to their imperial interests in India—the so-called jewel in the crown—than in the Middle East, with the creation of the British Raj in the centuries leading up to our own. South Asia became the seat of England's colonial circuits in Asia, and authority, directives, and control radiated outward from South Asian shores to a number of other places in what was becoming Britain's multiple spheres in Asia. Initially, the main focus of British power was concentrated in a few large cities, which eventually became the seat of presidencies—Bombay, Madras, and Calcutta being the most important, from a maritime perspective.[27] From these burgeoning cities, the talons of empire radiated outward, across the Bay of Bengal in the case of the latter two ports, and across the Arabian Sea when it came to Bombay.[28] A web of smaller port towns provided connective tissue to these extensions, so that commodities, soldiers, and supplies could be funneled along the coasts. But London's power eventually pushed into the Indian hinterland as well, and in certain places such as Bengal and Bihar the agricultural sponsorship of export crops such as jute and, especially, opium entrenched British power into the countryside.[29] A range of Indian princes were co-opted into the system to make it all work. These were collaborators of a sort, but many of them had little choice but to fall into line, while others

26. See, for example, Seema Alavi. *Muslim Cosmopolitanism in the Age of Empire* (Cambridge, MA: Harvard University Press, 2015); Johan Matthew, *Margins of the Market: Trafficking and Capitalism across the Arabian Sea* (Berkeley: University of California Press, 2016); Fahad Bishara, *A Sea of Debt: Law and Economic Life in the Western Indian Ocean* (Cambridge: Cambridge University Press, 2017); Thomas McDow, *Buying Time: Debt and Mobility in the Western Indian Ocean* (Athens, OH: Ohio University Press, 2018); Patricia Risso, "India and the Gulf: Encounters from the Mid-Sixteenth Century to the Mid-Twentieth Centuries," in *The Persian Gulf in History*, ed. Potter, Lawrence, 189–206 (New York: Palgrave Macmillan, 2009).

27. These three cities became nodes for their varying regions, both internally within Indian waters and externally to points overseas—Bombay throughout the Arabian Sea, Madras to Southeast Asia, and Calcutta to the larger Bay of Bengal trade.

28. Sunil Amrith, *Crossing the Bay of Bengal* (Cambridge: Harvard University Press, 2013; René J. Barendse, *The Arabian Seas, 1640–1700* (Armonk, New York: M. E. Sharpe, 2002).

29. See Sugata Bose, *Agrarian Bengal: Economy, Social Structure and Politics* (Cambridge: Cambridge University Press, 1986).

tried as best they could to maintain a precarious independence of action as they could. Only a few—such as the ruler of Mysore, on the Deccan Plateau in the South—chose to rebel outright.[30] British circuits stretched around and eventually through all of these local political impediments, until by the late nineteenth century nearly the entirety of what we now know as India was incorporated.

British power in these ports was nearly absolute, as it was easily understood that cities such as the ones mentioned above would become the political and commercial nodes upon which the Raj was based. Each of the ports had a ruling aristocracy among the colonizers, but then also an Indian elite, followed by large numbers of middle-class skilled workers, and an even larger pyramid base of the laboring poor. Yet each was diverse in its own way too, racially speaking, with a wide variety of Indian subethnic groups migrating into the cities, often for seasonal work, and Arabs, Armenians, Parsees, and other Asian populations also setting up shop. From this base, the international component of foreign traders along the transoceanic shipping lines also jockeyed for space, so that the ports became mini-renderings of life on the Asian seas generally.[31] Scottish engineers rubbed shoulders with Parsee shipowners, and Burmese crewmen drank tea alongside Bengali stevedores upon the crowded wharves. Information traveled both formally (via newspapers and couriers) and informally (via rumor), the latter often outrunning the more official channels of the former.[32] Ships sailed between one port and another delivering examples of both these "sanctioned" and "unsanctioned" reportage along the coasts. Trying to map all of this complexity of India's seaboard would be a daunting task, but some very good efforts have been made in these directions already.[33] What is essential is to realize that this world of the coasts was both connected to the adjoining interior, but also—sometimes in much stronger ways—to translocal geographies, across many leagues of open water. Thus Africa found representation in Bombay, for

30. A good revisionist study here is Janaki Nair, *Mysore Modern: Rethinking the Region Under Princely Rule* (Minneapolis: University of Minnesota Press, 2011).

31. See Nile Green's *Bombay Islam: The Religious Economy of the West Indian Ocean 1840–1915* (Cambridge: Cambridge University Press, 2013), a a terrific example of microstudy cosmopolitanism in one port.

32. On this fascinating dichotomy, see Christopher Bayly, *Empire and Information: Intelligence Gathering and Social Communication in India, 1780 to 1870* (Cambridge: Cambridge University Press, 2000).

33. See Indu Banga, *Ports and Their Hinterlands in India, 1700–1950* (Delhi: Manohar, 1992); and Ashin Das Gupta, *Merchants of Maritime India, 1500–1800* (Ashgate: Variorum, 1994).

example, and vice versa. British South Asia was much like this from Karachi to Calcutta, and all along the sea routes in between.[34]

Other Europeans, at least initially, fashioned their own colonial circuits in South Asia, especially in the years leading up to 1800. The Portuguese were among the first of these, and established forts at Goa and Diu, and a trading presence in a number of other places along India's outstretched coasts. Lisbon had few pretensions to conquering India, which was too vast (and their con-quistador presence too small), but the Portuguese certainly did want to trade where they could, and plunder/confiscate wealth where they might get away with that instead. These designs worked on some stretches of coast, and less well on others—the imposition of the famous *cartaz* pass was very much hit or miss, despite its fame in the scholarly literature. On the Malabar coasts, where much of the agricultural wealth was seen in the guise of spices, the Portuguese did indeed have a trading presence, but not a lasting one.[35] The Danes also built "factories" on the Indian strand and also organized trading relations, building up their own networks and piggybacking on the backs of some others in their own quest for riches.[36] But it was the French who gave the British a run for their money, again at least initially, before being outma-neuvered and outmuscled by British forces in several important battles. Paris never really saw India with the same eyes as London, though it was certainly envisioned as a trading partner of potentially some importance. It says much that the only surviving presence of French influence of any note today in this giant subcontinent is the quaint, rather sleepy port of Pondicherry, where the French built a trading fort and organized some of their commercial activities.[37] The battle for colonial supremacy in India was over by the late eighteenth century, and after that only Britain's colonial circuits held real valence, while the other powers obsolesced.

34. Sugata Bose, *A Hundred Horizons: The Indian Ocean in the Age of Global Empire* (Cambridge, MA: Harvard University Press, 2006); see also Tariq Omar Ali, *A Local History of Global Capital: Jute and Peasant Life in the Bengal Delta* (Princeton: Princeton University Press, 2018).

35. K. S. Mathew, "Trade in the Indian Ocean During the Sixteenth Century and the Portuguese," in *Studies in Maritime History*, ed. K. S. Mathew, 13–28 (Pondicherry: Pondicherry University, 1990).

36. Martin Krieger, "Danish Country Trade on the Indian Ocean in the Seventeenth and Eighteenth Centuries," in *Studies in Maritime History*, ed. Mathew, 122–29.

37. See Indrani Ray, ed., *The French East India Company and the Trade of the Indian Ocean* (Calcutta: Munshiram 1999).

One imperial power that did have a more stable, evolved interaction with South Asia than others, though, was the Dutch, and here this relationship was enacted primarily in Sri Lanka. Though the Dutch East Indies (or Indonesia) became the main focal point for Dutch colonialism in Asia, in the seventeenth and into the eighteenth century Sri Lanka was also seen as important.[38] The Dutch had a trading presence—sometimes significant, at other times only minimal—in other parts of South Asia, mostly notably on the Malabar and Coromandel coasts, where they brought spices and textiles both to Europe and to Southeast Asia as part of a giant, transoceanic carrying trade.[39] Burma also received its fair share of Dutch traders who connected its markets to Indian ones for a while, as several recent studies have shown.[40] Yet Sri Lanka became important, as the agricultural riches on offer there evolved in Dutch-controlled plantations, rather than under indigenous fiat. Cinnamon became the main export crop of Dutch Sri Lanka (known as Ceylon at that time), and by the late eighteenth century most of the world's market for this spice came from Dutch lands on that island. The population base of the island was a mixed one, comprising both Tamil and Singhalese Sri Lankans, but also Malays from Southeast Asia and some slaves from even farther away. Here, too, colonial circuits took on curious, locally adapted shapes, marrying the local and the translocal in specialized and very specific ways. Colombo became an important node in these Dutch transits, connecting Hormuz and Mocha farther west to Melaka, Batavia, and Taiwan farther to the east. These colonial circuits mirrored British ones, to some extent, but also had their own shape and their own flavor, as a reflection of both Dutch and local concerns in each place on the routes.

The Fulcrum of Southeast Asia

The creation of colonial circuits also extended to Southeast Asia, where imperial rivalries lasted far longer into the nineteenth and even twentieth centuries than in South Asia. In the island world of the Indonesian archipelago, most of this shadow-boxing was done between the British and the Dutch, with one of

---

38. Alicia Schrikker, *Dutch and British Colonial Intervention in Sri Lanka, 1780–1815: Expansion and Reform* (Leiden: Brill, 2007).

39. See some of the essays in Sanjay Subrahmanyam, ed., *Merchants, Markets, and the State in Early Modern India, 1700–1950* (Delhi: Oxford University Press, 1990).

40. Wil O. Dijk, *Seventeenth-Century Burma and the Dutch East India Company, 1634–1680* (Singapore: Singapore University Press, 2006).

the great flash points being the Aceh War of 1873–1903. As the war there be-tween the Dutch and the Acehnese progressed, Batavia erected a blockade squadron around much of Aceh to try to control the supply of arms and am-munition into the area, and the flow of commodities for export (mainly pep-per) out to the rest of the world. The British in their Malayan possessions kept a close watch on Dutch policies vis-à-vis Aceh, and sent reams of correspon-dence back to London in an effort to keep Whitehall updated on the situation, and also to press the case for British actions in defense of British interests.[41] London was particularly interested in the passage of Dutch shipping regula-tions which affected trade and commerce in the arena, and Her Majesty's dip-lomats received regular translations of Dutch decrees on this topic, usually translated from Dutch sources such as the *Amsterdamsche Handelsblad*, a Dutch trade paper published in the largest city of the Netherlands.[42] The va-garies of shipping regimes were not the only topic which interested the British, however; they also wanted to know about Dutch strategic acquisitions in and around Aceh, such as the development of a new coaling station on Pulau Weh, the island just to the north of the Acehnese capital of Banda Aceh.[43] But trans-lations of Dutch thinkers and policymakers, such as the famed orientalist Snouck Hurgronje, were also sought out, to get an idea of the strategic thinking circulating in the Netherlands as to how the Aceh War would be fought and, presumably, won by England's allies-cum-competitors in the Low Countries.[44]

The main issues in these British deliberations were not actually territorial; Aceh was well within the Dutch sphere of interest in Southeast Asia, and had been declared as such by both European powers via signed treaty in 1874. Yet the trade of the Aceh coasts was profitable, not just to British traders passing between the Indian Ocean and the South China Sea to China, but principally at Penang, one of London's two main ports in the Straits of Melaka region. Penang's official trade, as the governor of the Straits Settlements told his civil servant counterparts back in England in a missive of 1894, had been nearly destroyed by twenty years of war in the Aceh theater, since the start of hostili-ties in the early 1870s. It was true, he continued, that a robust smuggling

41. Gov. SS Sir Cecil Smith to the Marquis of Ripon, 22 February 1893, in *BDFA*, Part I, series E, vol. 29, p. 195.

42. "Extract from the *Amsterdamsche Handelsblad* of 16 December 1892, "Atjeh Shipping Regulations," in Ibid., p. 196.

43. Sir H. Rumbold to the Earl of Roseberg, 25 April 1893, no. 47, in Ibid., p. 197.

44. "Abstract of Secret Report of Dr. Snouck-Hurgronje on Acheen," in Ibid., p. 198.

commerce had evolved to fill the vacuum, but this trade did not always go into Penang's official coffers, which enriched many Asian merchants in the colony, but less so the official exchequer of the queen.[45] The Resident Councilor of Penang furthered this line of analysis by providing figures of imports into the colony from Aceh, Deli, Langkat, and other north Sumatran principalities going back to 1826, when trade had been far more robust than it was at the time of this correspondence. By contrast, returns on linen, cotton, and other staple goods for the 1880s into the 1890s showed a steady rate of decline.[46] Many letters and financial statements such as the above were circulated back to England, but with only limited effect at certain times. London replied in this instance that they were well aware of the difficulties, but that it was British government policy to support the Dutch in their efforts to subdue the Acehnese, as fellow Europeans and erstwhile allies.[47] In this a common theme of an aggressive mindset in the colonies—and far greater reticence to armed involvement in the metropole—can be seen, in this case via British concerns, but often in such dealings among other European powers as well.

If the British were on the lookout to continually maintain and expand their colonial circuits in Southeast Asia in places such as Penang and Aceh, as we have just seen, then the Dutch—their erstwhile allies and competitors in the region—were no different. Farther south in the Straits of Melaka, Dutch strategic planning focused on the rising hub of Singapore, and alternatives and complementarities that might be constructed by Batavia to both combat and feed off British influence in this arena.[48] As Singapore grew to become the most important port in Southeast Asia, the Dutch concentrated on building up docking, warehousing, and stevedoring operations in the Riau archipelago just south of the city, to take advantage of the maritime traffic passing through.[49] In places such as Belakang Padang and others, this feverish building never managed to displace Singapore, but some residual commerce did end up passing through, to the benefit of Dutch coffers.[50] Muslim sultans in the region, we know from surviving letters written in Malay, had little choice but

45. Governor Sir C. Mitchell to the Marquis of Ripon, 31 October 1894, in Ibid., 220.

46. "Minute by the Resident Councillor Penang, 10 October 1894," in Ibid., 221.

47. Foreign Office to Colonial Office, 14 December 1894, in Ibid., 226.

48. [Anon.], "Singapore's hoop op de opening der Indische kustvaart voor vreemde vlaggen," *Tijdschrijf voor Nederlandsch-Indië* I, no. 17 (1888): 29–35.

49. J. F. Niermeyer, "Barriere-Riffen en Atollen in de Oost Indiese Archipel," *Tijdschrift voor Aardrijkskundige* (1911): 877–94.

50. [Anon.], "Balakang Padang, Een Concurrent van Singapore" *Indische Gids* 2 (1902): 1295.

to acquiesce as Batavia started to survey (and eventually, to annex) these islands—the lure of profits based on the maritime transit was too great for the Dutch to ignore.[51] Batavia eventually concluded contracts with many of the indigenous potentates in the region, extending Dutch influence into the South China Sea islands and using the leverage of payments to try to enforce Dutch will in local ports.[52] Eventually, by the turn of the twentieth century, the Dutch imperial footprint ran across all of the islands of Riau, Bangka, Belitung, and Natuna/Anambas, rendering much of the region a colonial maritime preserve of sorts, as fewer and fewer territories existed to be conquered.[53]

One place that still was *terra incognita* until comparatively late in Southeast Asia, however, was Borneo—the huge, forested island at the geographic center of the region. The laying of colonial circuits was also played out here, in one of the last and least-explored tracts of terrain left in the world by the turn of the twentieth century. Europeans had been touching upon Bornean shores for centuries, even back to early Iberian explorers in the region in the sixteenth and seventeenth centuries.[54] These initial contacts had been followed by a strange, rag-tag procession of adventurers and would-be (including some actual) conquistadors from many nations, including Dutchmen, Americans, a failed Italian penal colony, and, of course, the century-long regime of the English Brooke family.[55] Yet, by the late nineteenth century, the only remaining aspirants were the British and Dutch imperial projects, as they divided up

---

51. See Arsip Nasional Indonesia, "Idzin Pembuatan Peta Baru Tentang Pulau Yang Mengililingi Sumatra," *Archief Riouw* 225, no. 9 (1889).

52. Nationaal Archief, Den Haag: Kommissorial, Raad van Nederlandsch-Indië, Advies van den Raad, 10 January 1902, Mailrapport no. 124a.

53. One of the reasons for doing this had to do with the competition felt by Chinese and Japanese shippers in the Outer Islands; see J. N. F. M. à Campo, "Een maritime BB: De rol van de Koninklijke Paketvaart Maatschappij in de integratie van de koloniale staat," in *Imperialisme in de marge: De afronding van Nederlands-Indië*, ed. J. van Goor, 123–77 (Utrecht: HES, 1985); J. N. F. M. à Campo, "De Chinese stoomvaart in de Indische archipel," *Jambatan: Tijdschrift voor de geschiedenis van Indonesië* 2, no. 2, (1984), 1–10; P. Post, "Japanese bedrijfvigheid in Indonesia, 1868–1942," PhD dissertation, (Free University of Amsterdam, 1991); and D. J. Pronk van Hoogeveen, "De KPM in na-oorlogse Jaren," *Economisch Weekblad 14e* (25 December 1948): 1001–2.

54. See Robert Nicholl, *European Sources for the History of the Sultanate of Brunei in the Sixteenth Century* (Bandar Seri Begawan: Muzium Brunei, 1895).

55. J. van Goor, "A Madman in the City of Ghosts: Nicolaas Kloek in Pontianak," in *All of One Company: The VOC in Biographical Perspective*, no author, 196–211 (Utrecht: H & S Press, 1986); also see Eric Tagliacozzo, *Secret Trades, Porous Borders: Smuggling and States along a Southeast Asian Frontier* (New Haven: Yale University Press, 2005).

the archipelago between them. Both looked to Borneo's untapped riches as a potential goldmine for minerals, timber, and the erection of profitable plantations.[56] Antimony, tin, gold, diamonds, and especially coal—in the advancing age of the steamship—all made Borneo a very worthwhile place to incorporate into growing colonial webs of influence across the equator.[57] Both the British and the Dutch did this with alacrity and with appetite, stretching the patterns seen earlier in this chapter from Aceh to Penang to the South China Sea. By the late nineteenth century, Borneo—at the very center of insular Southeast Asia—was becoming resolutely crisscrossed by imperial footprints, as both colonial projects expanded their influence even into what these men deemed to be the forested "blank spaces" of the region.

On the China Coasts

Farther north up along the stretches of the South China Sea, away from Southeast Asia and onto the China coasts, the picture of imperial aggression and the expansion of creeping colonial influence was much the same. By the nineteenth century and after the early modern era, when spices drove European interest in Southeast Asia, China began to materialize as the biggest potential prize in the ongoing contest of Western encroachment across Asia. This story, of course, is well known, and the colonial circuits that European powers were able to build upon the coasts of the Middle Kingdom are well-worn furrows in the historiography of global colonialism. Yet it was rarely an easy endeavor, and the instabilities caused by this process were ongoing over many decades. Uprisings occurred in and around the hybrid colonial/indigenous port cities with great regularity, usually being defeated (although occasionally not so in the case of the biggest rebellions, such as the Taiping and the Boxer, at least for a time), but often leaving a vast swath of destruction in their wake in places like Fuzhou and Tianjin.[58] The circulation of anti-Christian placards, leaflets, and materials were often part and parcel of these instabilities, and news of the

---

56. W. Voute, "Gound-, Diamant-, en Tin-Houdende Alluviale Gronden in de Nederlandsche Oost- en West-Indische Kolonien," *Indische Mercuur* 24, no. 7 (1901): 116–17.

57. C. J. van Schelle, "De Geologische Mijnbouwkundige Opneming van een Gedeelte van Borneo's Westkust: Rapport #1: Opmerking Omtrent het Winnen van Delfstoffen," *Jaarboek Mijnwezen* 1 (1881): 263.

58. Mr. Hansen to the Marquis of Salisbury, 4 December 1891, no. 26, in *BDFA*, Part I, Series E, vol. 23, p. 183.

distributions of these items made the rounds between the British, German, and other delegations, who often kept each other informed of events.[59] Occasionally, translated Chinese documents—such as a formal petition in Gaungxi against the spread of Catholicism, accompanied by a request for armed action against European missionaries and proponents of the religion—made their way into European files. Some of the text of these documents makes for very interesting reading, as when this particular plea intones that "the pictorial placards truly represent scenes in the churches while propagating the religion [including] Chinese and barbarian women embracing and hugging each other. Such actions are most malodorous, and wound the eyes."[60] The *London and China Telegraph* may have had it right when they boiled things down to the fact that the missionaries were in the ports by treaty, but were barely tolerated by the Chinese. This was a state of affairs that pretty much described Chinese feelings of the Western presence on China's coasts generally, at the time.[61] A range of recent scholarship has shown how the Chinese state resisted Western incursions far more than was originally posited in Western scholarship on China, looking at the kingdom's frontiers, overseas migrants, and developing navies, to name just a few examples.[62]

Christianity was not the only thing being exported from the ports. Weapons were moving, too, and this also caused major problems between the Chinese court and European powers, and particularly the British. The governor of Hong Kong, for example, had the power to periodically prohibit the export of arms from the colony to other ports along the Chinese seaboard; this was a privilege that was in fact utilized at times of instability, such as in 1892, when "secret society" activities became more intense than normally, for a time.[63] Yet the ambit of these bans was always smaller than the reality of carrying arms and ammunition along the sea-roads, which theoretically only stretched between British stations, but which actually impacted a vast network of ports stretching thousands of miles in many directions. Therefore, when the

---

59. Sir J. Welsham to the Marquis of Salisbury, 11 January 1892, in Ibid., p. 184.

60. "Tract Entitled 'Essay on the Cruel Hand,' Spring, Kwangsuh, 16th Year, 1890" (13 November 1891), in Ibid., 181.

61. Extract from the *London and China Telegraph* of 29 December 1891, in Ibid., 185.

62. This literature is vast, but see, for example, Benjamin Elman's work on the fin de siècle period, for a start.

63. "An Ordinance Enacted by the Governor of Hong Kong to Amend Ordinance #3 of 1862 (Ordinance #3 of 1894)," in Ibid., 224; "Sieh Ta-jen to the Marquis of Salisbury, 10 March 1892," in Ibid., 223.

Austro-Hungarian embassy asked the governor of Hong Kong for a permit to ship arms from Europe to Hong Kong to Shanghai on a Lloyd's steamer in 1892, a much wider circuit of cities was involved than just the latter two ports of Hong Kong and Shanghai.[64] Rifles and bullet cartridges were involved in this particular case, a seemingly simple cargo, but the range of ports called at by the steamers took in Aden, Colombo, Penang, Singapore, and Hong Kong, before Shanghai ever came into play.[65] London, which was consulted on the request by His Majesty's plenipotentiaries in Asia, pointed out that Colombo, Penang, and Singapore had no arms bans to China, but that Aden and Bombay had different rules, so that the Foreign Office would have to be involved with the request.[66] A colonial circuit that looked at first glance to be quite local in character, therefore (Hong Kong to Shanghai), turned out to be very much more translocal than that, taking in rules and regulations in British ports stretching all the way across the vast Indian Ocean.

Other powers on the outstretched Chinese strand—besides the British and Austro-Hungarians—fit these coasts into their own colonial circuits as well. Though the Dutch were considered to be only a minor European power by the late nineteenth century, they had exaggerated importance on the South China coasts because of the large numbers of Chinese laborers (or "coolies") they transported from there down to their possessions in the Dutch East Indies. Though many of these coolies passed through Singapore first as a kind of clearing center for human labor, the numbers were in the tens of thousands every year in the late nineteenth century, most of them then reshipped to various Dutch plantations and mines across the Netherlands Indies empire. Others were en route to Siam, to French Indochina, and to the British possessions in Malaya, among other destinations.[67] Dutch newspapers of the period give us a good idea of how much these economic migrants meant both to the Indies, and to South China upon their return—the *Algemeen Handlesblad* reported in February of 1890 that 1,500 returning laborers brought more than 80,000 Straits dollars back home the previous year.[68] When, in April of the same year

64. Colonial Office to Foreign Office, 19 March 1892, in Ibid., 223.

65. M. Krapf to Colonial Office, 16 March 1892, in Ibid., 223.

66. "Draft of Letter from Colonial Office to M. Krapf, March 1892," in Ibid., 224.

67. Dutch Consul, Hong Kong to Chairman of the Planter's Committee, Medan, Sumatra (27 March 1900), no. 213, Appx I, in Nationaal Archief, Den Haag, Ministerie van Buitenlandse Zaaken, 2.05.03, Doos 245, A.119 "Aanwerving."

68. See the *Algemeen Handelsblad*, 12 February 1890, clipping in Nationaal Archief, Den Haag, Ministerie van Buitenlandse Zaaken, 2.05.03, Doos 245, A.119 "Aanwerving."

(1890), the viceroy reported that all of South China's ports would finally open for coolie recruitment, the *Nieuwe Rotterdamsche Courant* trumpeted the news with great fanfare and joy.[69] The appointment of P. S. Hamel as Dutch consul in Amoy later that year showed how seriously the Dutch took this opening as a sign for expanded business.[70] Hundreds of thousands of poor Chinese laborers would now be able to be shipped down to the Indies, all to the profit of Dutch business and Dutch empire. It did not matter that the Dutch themselves knew very little about the Chinese, even in their own estimation: "Their train of thought, their internal lives, their religion, morals and customs, the ancestral practices which are the chief driving forces of all they do—all of this is still a closed book for us."[71]

Still, business needed to be served. This state of affairs was the coming together of circumstances over a number of years. Only a year prior to this, in 1889, the Dutch had been complaining vociferously to the Zongli Yamen in China that the refusal of official Chinese sponsorship on the existing labor regime left the coolie business open to all sorts of abuses.[72] Evidence for this was presented in the words of coolies themselves, many of whom spoke into judicial inquests into the coolie trade so their words were heard and translated in court. These proceedings were then assembled into a large report in 1891, which showed how enormous and inhumane the system of labor procurement had become between the coasts of South China and Southeast Asia over time. Depot dealers were interviewed, who sent men to the huge plantation complexes in northeast Sumatra.[73] The amounts of money that coolies could actually expect to earn were also tabulated, with data given by expert witnesses such as R. J. Gunn, an overseer of a coolie recruitment company active on the

---

69. *Niewe Rotterdamsche Courant*, 19 April 1890, clipping in Nationaal Archief, Den Haag, Ministerie van Buitenlandse Zaaken, 2.05.03, Doos 245, A.119 "Aanwerving."

70. Dutch Consul, Amoy, to Viceroy of Canton, 20 October 1890, no. 11687, in Nationaal Archief, Den Haag, Ministerie van Buitenlandse Zaaken, 2.05.03, Doos 245, A.119 "Aanwerving."

71. De Groot, cited in Nederburgh, "Klassen der Bevolking" (1897): 79; [translation: E. Tagliacozzo].

72. Dutch Minister and Head Consul Ferguson to Prince Zungli Yamen, Swatow, 15 August 1889, no. 270, in Nationaal Archief, Den Haag, Ministerie van Buitenlandse Zaaken, 2.05.03, Doos 245, A.119 "Aanwerving."

73. "Evidence of Tun Kua Hee, Depot Keeper, 29 October 1890," in *The Labour Commission Report*, Singapore 1891, in Nationaal Archief, Den Haag, Ministerie van Buitenlandse Zaaken, 2.05.03, Doos 245, A.119 "Aanwerving."

coasts.[74] The coolies who were transported to Borneo, it turned out, made less than the ones sent to Sumatra, a pattern which would eventually become known to workers in South China itself, and which prompted revolts on ships when it was found out that Borneo was the eventual destination.[75] Life was also considerably harder in Borneo, it turned out, so less pay also entailed more work and harsher treatment in many cases. The report even laid out a system identifying patterns of cheating in recruitment, "especially in substituting weak and infirm coolies for strong and healthy men, so that of a batch lately recruited . . . a doctor on an estate declared that fifty per cent would not live six months, even if sent to the south of France."[76] European recruiters and even medical professionals in the system may have found jest in these figures. But mortality figures of 50 percent over six months shows how brutal the system was in its entirety, connecting South China and Southeast Asia's ports in a conveyer belt of misery and death over many decades.

In Northeast Asian Seas

To the north, Japan also came into these transnational maritime considerations. The saga of Japan's entrance into this evolving world of the late nineteenth century Asian seas is a story that is already well told. This is true historically, of course, but it is also a tale writ through cultural artifacts, as in Puccini's *Madama Butterfly*, and in other social documents of the time. One of the most important components of this process of acculturation into the new international norms along the sea routes was the opening of treaty ports, both in Japan and in other places in Asia (such as China). In Japan these havens were opened in shifts, and often were designated as "special harbors of exports": Western vessels were only able to visit them under explicit conditions imposed by the Japanese government. Cereals, flour, coal, and sulfur poured out of

74. "Evidence of R. J. Gunn of Messrs. A. E. Johnston and Co., 31 October 1890," in *The Labour Commission Report*, Singapore 1891," in Nationaal Archief, Den Haag, Ministerie van Buitenlandse Zaaken, 2.05.03, Doos 245, A.119 "Aanwerving."

75. "Evidence of Mr. Romary, 1 November 1890," in *The Labour Commission Report*, Singapore 1891, in Nationaal Archief, Den Haag, Ministerie van Buitenlandse Zaaken, 2.05.03, Doos 245, A.119 "Aanwerving."

76. "Evidence of Count C. A. de Gelves d'Elsloo, Manager of the London Borneo Tobacco Co, British North Borneo, 12 November 1890," in *The Labour Commission Report*, Singapore 1891, in Nationaal Archief, Den Haag, Ministerie van Buitenlandse Zaaken, 2.05.03, Doos 245, A.119 "Aanwerving."

Shimoneseki, Moji, Muroran and Otau, for example, and some port cities specialized in trade with China (such as Naha), while others leaned toward Korea (Fushiki) and the Russian Far East (Miyazu).[77] Occasionally lists were drawn up to reflect the full range of opening ports within this scheme, alongside the numbers and tonnage of vessels calling at various treaty harbors over the course of a particular amount of time (see tables below).[78] The statistics could also be further narrowed by Western power, such as Britain's role in the newly opened ports of the Japanese coasts, while similar patterns in Japan's emerging empire (such as in Taiwan) were also tabulated.[79] All in all, a fairly good picture can be drawn for the late nineteenth century as to how these colonial circuits began to crisscross post-Meiji Japan, from Kyushu in the south to Hokkaido in the distant north of the Japanese archipelago.

In the interest of zooming in on one place in Northeast Asia, we might look at Korea during the late nineteenth century as well, and the "hermit kingdom's" dealings with Russian imperialism on its own coasts during that time. The Russians tried at this time to get access to land in and around Pusan harbor, for example, to serve as a drill ground for Russian troops, but also as a coal storage facility for the Russian Far Eastern fleet.[80] The British watched these maneuvers with some alarm—when the Russian cruiser *Mandjour* came to Pusan in 1897, for example, British correspondence on the visit picked up quickly after the event. The Russian Far Eastern fleet's flag lieutenant was on board, so this was no simple "sail-by" just looking at possible installations.[81] The Russians, in fact, said internationally that the Koreans *wanted* their military presence there in Pusan as a wedge against the Japanese, who already possessed significant influence in the country. Many Japanese had migrated to Korea by the fin de siècle period, and they were active in business and import-export across a range of cities.[82] In Pusan itself, three foreign settlements already existed—Chinese and Japanese ones, and a third which was

---

77. Sir E. Satow to the Marquess of Salisbury, 20 July 1899, no. 122, in *BDFA*, Part I, series E, vol. 6, p. 125.

78. "Official Gazette, July 13, 1899—Imperial Ordinance #342," in Ibid., 126; also Ibid, 125.

79. "British Vessels Entered at the Six Principal Ports Now Thrown Open to Foreign Commerce during the Years 1895–98," in Ibid., 129; Sir E. Satow to the Marquess of Salisbury, 1 September 1899, no. 148, in *BDFA*, Part I, series E, vol. 6, p. 147.

80. Mr. Jordan to Sir C. MacDonald, 20 April 1897, no. 35 Confidential, in *BDFA*, Part I, series E, vol. 6, p. 254.

81. Mr. J. Hunt to Mr. Jordan, 10 April 1897, in Ibid.

82. Mr. Lowther to the Marquess of Salisbury, 15 May 1897, no. 102, in Ibid., 255.

designated for all other powers.[83] Russia was clearly trying to improve on its presence "in the neighborhood." The British noted this, and then also carefully analyzed which lands the Russian were pursuing for their aims of an official Russian settlement of their own in the area.[84] Local politics and maritime commerce were often very translocal in nature, therefore. These very specific and particular constellations of trade and power had links to wider geographies and circuits along the routes.

FIGURE 9.2. Puccini's *Madama Butterfly* (cover of the first score, Leopoldo Metlicovitz)

This can be seen in wider geographies than just in Northeast Asia; Japan was also connected to the lands of Southeast Asia, far away in the distant southern ocean. British tabulations of opening Japanese treaty ports and Russian designs in Korea were both still mostly regional in character; Japan's ties with Southeast Asia were of another order, distance-wise. Here, Dutch correspondence is helpful in looking at the erection of these "colonial circuits"—again, fabricated in many cases by human hands and labor. The Dutch began to notice that undocumented Japanese migrants were showing up in the Netherlands Indies, sometimes from Japanese colonies in northeastern China and Korea, where they were legal, but then became "illegal" in Dutch eyes passing by ship to points farther south.[85] This news was published in Chinese and then in Japanese newspapers, and then sent around various levels of Dutch government in correspondence.[86] It was clear to the Dutch that American and Canadian immigration limitations pushed these Japanese migrants to other shores, and many of these laborers were heading to Southeast Asia as a result.[87]

83. Consul-General Jordan to Sir C. MacDonald, 10 September 1897, no. 70, in Ibid., 270.

84. Foreign Office to Admiralty, 14 December 1897, "Secret," in Ibid., 277.

85. Dutch Consul, Tokyo, to Minister van Buitenlandse Zaaken, 11 May 1908, no. 448/57, in Nationaal Archief, Den Haag, Ministerie van Buitenlandse Zaaken, 2.05.03, Doos 589, A.209 "Emigratie van Japanners naar Nederlandsch-Indië."

86. "Japanese Immigration," *Kobe Herald*, 27 July 1907, in Nationaal Archief, Den Haag, Ministerie van Buitenlandse Zaaken, 2.05.03, Doos 589, A.209, "Emigratie van Japanners naar Nederlandsch-Indië."

87. Minister van Kolonien to Minister van Buitelandse Zaaken, 8 January 1908, "Secret," in Nationaal Archief, Den Haag, Ministerie van Buitenlandse Zaaken, 2.05.03, Doos 589, A.209 "Emigratie van Japanners naar Nederlandsch-Indië."

TABLE 9.1. Japanese Open-Port Additions and Port Vessel/Tonnages, 1898/1899

New Japanese Open Ports by Imperial Ordinance, 1899

Port	Province
Shimizu	Suruga
Taketoyo	Owari
Yokkaichi	Ise
Shimoneseki	Nagato
Meji	Buzen
Hakata	Chikuzen
Karatsu	Hizen
Kuchinotsu	Higo
Misumi	Tsushima
Izuhara	Tsushima
Sasuna	Tsushima
Shishimi	Loochoo
Hamada	Iwami
Sakai	Hoki
Miyazu	Tango
Isuruga	Echizen
Nanao	Noto
Fushiki	Etchin
Otaru	Shiribeshi
Kushiro	Kushiro
Muroran	Iburi

Vessels and Tonnages in Japanese Ports, 1898 Returns

Place	No. of vessels	Tons
Yokkaichi	004	002,420
Shimoneseki	814	594,228
Moji	525	821,429
Hakata	038	003,980
Karatsu	062	045,802
Kuchinotsu	170	257,903
Izuhara	154	022,667
Shishimi	226	001,826
Sasuna	170	007,458
Naha	003	000,054
Hamada	015	000,346
Sagai	066	000,722
Fushiki	006	000,236
Muroran	038	047,472
Otaru	028	024,957

Sources: Official Gazette, 13 July 1899, Imperial Ordinance no. 342; and Sir E. Satow to Merquess of Salisbury, 20 July 1899, no. 122, both in *BDFA*, Part I, Series E, vol. 6, 125–26.

The governor-general in Batavia upon hearing of this then recirculated the news to various civil servants regionally in the Dutch Indies, so that local government could be on the lookout.[88] But the gaze searching for these sorts of undocumented Japanese migrants traveling along the sea routes of Asia eventually reached toward other locales as well, including Hong Kong, French Indochina, Siam, Malaya, the Philippines, and even Mexico and Peru.[89]

This state of affairs vis-à-vis illegal migrants, many of whom were seen to be possibly of "fifth column" nature, was one thing; tabulating Japanese naval strength—the official, military arm of Japan—was another. European governments kept a close eye on the erection of Japanese naval might in the turn of the century years as well. This aspect of projected Japanese presence in Northeast Asia, and eventually even further afield, also worried the various Western powers.[90] The colonial circuits of Asian trade were rendered useless if the Japanese navy ultimately controlled the sea lanes through their own burgeoning naval presence. Yet the various Europeans also kept an eye on each other's capabilities in these waters as well, each side trying to ensure that no one fell too far behind anyone else. The *Times of London* reported that Britain had a total of thirty-nine warships on the "Asia station" (China, the Indies, and Australia) in 1909, yet in a separate article in the same paper, only four of those ships on the all-important China station were shown to be real battleships, while the Indies substation had none at all.[91] The Dutch commented internally in diplomatic correspondence that few European ships in Asian waters had any real power or "punch," and this weakness was clear in how quickly the Japanese had prosecuted, fought, and won the Russo-Japanese War at sea in 1905.

88. Governor General Netherlands Indies to Heads of Regional Administration, Circulaire, "Extremely Secret," no. 407, 3 December 1907, in Nationaal Archief, Den Haag, Ministerie van Buitenlandse Zaken, 2.05.03, Doos 589, A.209 "Emigratie van Japanners naar Nederlandsch-Indië."

89. Japanese Foreign Affairs Ministry "List of Emigrants Gone Abroad, 1905/06," in Nationaal Archief, Den Haag, Ministerie van Buitenlandse Zaken, 2.05.03, Doos 589, A.209 "Emigratie van Japanners naar Nederlandsch-Indië."

90. Durch Consul Tokyo to Buitenlandse Zaken, 13 June 1910, no. 560/159; and "The Destroyer Yamakaze," *Japan Times*, 4 June 1910, in Nationaal Archief, Den Haag, Ministerie van Buitenlandse Zaken, 2.05.03, Doos 421, A.182 "Marine Begrotingen, Buitelandse 1895–1910."

91. Dutch Consul, London to Buitenlandse Zaken, 5 August 1909, no. 2257/1443; "British Warships in Far Eastern Waters," *Times of London*, 5 August 1909; Dutch Consul, London to Buitelandsae Zaken, 2 December 1909, no. 3258/2036; "Imperial Naval Defense," *Times of London*, 2 December 1909, in Nationaal Archief, Den Haag, Ministerie van Buitenlandse Zaken, 2.05.03, Doos 421, A.182, "Marine Begrotingen, Buitelandse 1895–1910."

All ships, the Dutch consul in London told the Dutch Minister for Foreign Affairs in The Hague, should have a small nucleus of men aboard who could do all necessary military tasks, so that crew could be exchanged across vessels in times of conflict.[92] This was one way to stretch thin resources in the Asia theater, where trade was a more tangible daily reality than war, but where conflagration was always just over the horizon in the late nineteenth and early twentieth centuries.

Conclusion

This chapter has sketched out a world whereby the Bosphorus was connected to Borneo, and the Sea of Japan traded down to Indonesia. I argue that west to east and north to south, Asia evolved into one large, increasingly interconnected "circuit" in numerous ways. The fiber that connected these places was trade, but trade of a specific type—commerce on the wings of empire, or perhaps more to the point, driven forward by empire in competition and collaboration with other empires. This became a global phenomenon by the late nineteenth century, the decades most traveled here, but across Asia the patterns are particularly apparent, from both regional loci and from the vantages of specific European projects spread across vast distances. The Portuguese and the Dutch may have been among the earliest attempts to fill Asia with their outstretched trade regimes, but it was really left to the British in the nineteenth century to show everyone else what the full possibilities might be, and how far empire could be connected through a kind of commerce that they, eventually, seemed to do best. Though Portuguese, Dutch, and French traders and statesmen appeared all along these Asian routes, the British ended up having more envoys and more merchants along the international maritime thoroughfares than any other power. These men traded and politicked, and they also took careful notes on the activities of others, and through these records we can get a real sense of the interconnected world they made. This Asian trading world of the late nineteenth and early twentieth centuries ultimately had many inflections in terms of language, ethnicity, and commercial bent, but it was clearly connected in ways that other, previously fashioned colonial worlds were not. This was a sort of "evolution," but an evolution that came at some price in

---

92. Dutch Consul, London to Buitelandse Zaken, 14 January 1905, #32, in Nationaal Archief, Den Haag, Ministerie van Buitenlandse Zaaken, 2.05.03, Doos 421, A.182 "Marine Begrotingen, Buitelandse 1895–1910."

terms of the weight these empires threw around on already existing denizens of the region.

We have seen that world unfold here in Ottoman Turkey and in the Persian Gulf, as well as in the narrow but ultimately crucial corridor of the Red Sea, a conduit prized by the passing ships of many nations, to say nothing of their political masters back in Europe. South Asia was also shown to be an important landscape of trade and domination, though in this arena more than most the British asserted a projection of power that none of their contemporary rivals could ever really match. Southeast Asia was different; the British were here, too, but so was everyone else—the French, the Dutch, the Portuguese, and others all looking to trade—so the patterns unfolding here appear to have been much more fragmented in nature over time. Finally, China's coasts became battlegrounds for European influence for a while, especially in the treaty ports, but they also became conduits of human labor on a scale heretofore unseen on the Asian routes. When we ultimately wind up in Korea and Japan during this time, looking at the passage of bodies but also the machinations of great powers like the Russians (and the Japanese themselves), we get an idea of how complex and intertwined these systems were, and still are to some extent a century later. Trade begat politics, and politics in turn often created the conditions for imperial control, I argue, with colonies and spheres of influence the ultimate end-product. In other chapters in this book we see how these visions combined with local actors on the ground, but here it is useful to remember that none of these unleashed energies was preordained. In fact, these processes are still with us to a degree even now, in a (supposedly) postcolonial age.

PART V

The Bounty of the Oceans

Preface: The Environmental History of Asian Seas

IN PART V, I look at environmental history as yet another window in deciphering the history of Asia's seas. The ecological wealth of Asia was sought after by many interested parties. Some of these consumers were from places such as Europe and North America, but others were from inside Asia itself, and so, intracontinental in nature. A huge spectrum of products traveled, from sea produce such as shark skins, fish maws, and pearls to other ecological products which may have been grown or harvested on land, but ultimately were transported by sea. In the Persian Gulf, for example, pearls became a huge business, and were bought and sold by a variety of Asian traders before Europeans came in and eventually started skewing the market toward their own ends. In eastern Indonesia, this same product was also plentiful, and Japanese companies eventually became leaders, first in free-diving for pearl-bearing shells, and then in trying to farm these shells later in the twentieth century. Pearls also show up in coastal China, historically, where they were scavenged by coastal populations, but also where they were bought and sold in the great ports such as Hong Kong and Canton, earmarked for China's big cities to be used in furniture, jewelry, and even in traditional medicine. This is just one product, seen in miniature. The list of Asia's ecological products goes on and on, however, and indeed both indigenous commentators (such as portmaster Zhao Ru Gua, writing in the thirteenth century) and foreign merchants (such as William Dalrymple, in his nineteenth-century compendium of Asian trade items) wrote voluminously about nature-based products of the region, and how and where they could be bought and sold. Connect the dots between these two observers, some six hundred years apart, and one can see how continual the demand was for this spectrum of commodities, as well as how natural products caught the imagination of both insiders and outsiders alike. Deerskins from Japan, edible sea cucumbers from the Philippines, birds' nests from Indonesia, seaweed from Burma, and a range of spices from India—all were transited aboard ships. These ships then traveled the world, bringing Asia's bounty to the four corners of the globe—in ever-increasing amounts—as time wore on.

Why were consumers so interested in these commodities? What drove people to pay sometimes astonishing amounts of money for rare barks, seeds, or dried animals parts, and how did these supply chains work? What cultural imperatives drove this system forward, or were the gears of the whole system purely economic in nature, so that market forces dictated supply and demand, and the results of these balances simply decided where all of these items traveled, and at what price? The answer to these interrelated questions is complex, but it would be safe to say that both culture and the market helped condition the functioning of these trades. Some commodities among Asia's natural produce were deemed to be rare and worth purchasing, even for a small mint of funds. Certain spices, such as Persian saffron, or two or three rare grades of Thai birds' nests would have fallen into this category. Pearls of some quality, or mother-of-pearl shell from parts of Eastern Indonesia would have been other commodities in this general rubric. But there were other items that circled Asia's routes which were much more common in provenance, and did not fetch high prices, but rather traveled in bulk volumes. Pepper eventually entered into this category of goods, when oversupply made the high prices of the early modern era something of a relic in the nineteenth-century world. Some spices then started to phase from being luxury products of the highest order to bulk commodities moving along long-distance commodity chains, and being sold for only median profits on high volumes of transport. The ambit of all of these trades took in wide geographies, from the pearls of the Persian Gulf and the scarlet corals of the Red Sea, to the turmeric and cumin of Malabar and Coromandel, to shark fin cargoes out in the South China Sea. All of these products headed to market, circling around Asia's coasts as they moved along the trade routes. Tastes changed and demand for certain items changed, too. Yet one thing that stayed the same for all of the centuries discussed in this book was that ships were constantly in motion, trying to meet the cultural and market requirements of a range of interested societies. This took place from the Middle East through the South Asian subcontinent, and from Southeast Asia up to China and Japan.

Chapter 10 looks at one of these complex, interconnected trades in detail: the passage of sea produce between China and Southeast Asia, from the eighteenth and nineteenth centuries. The pull of China was irresistible to Southeast Asia's marine products trade for much of the time in question in this book. State-making projects congealed around supplying these products, and vast labor regimes were organized to supply these commodities under pre-modern conditions, in industrial-size quantities. The pursuit of such items was part of the reason for the establishment of Western bases in segments of Southeast Asia, and colonial projects took off from there, eventually serving as beachheads for further, imperial designs. Parts of the region became stock-piling depots for Southeast Asian marine produce, which was then shuttled up to the South China markets (principally in Canton, but later on in Hong Kong as well) in exchange for Chinese goods. In Sulu and in Borneo, indige-nous rulers—not imperial outsiders—organized their own systems to get these good to market. This chapter shows how a range of interested Asian actors, including Chinese and Southeast Asian traders, all cooperated and competed to send the region's marine products to the Chinese market. Chap-ter 11 then shifts the locus of examination west to the Indian Ocean, and asks how the Malabar and Coromandel coasts became "spice central," both histori-cally and—to some extent—still today. This fecund region of southern India was home to a number of natural-growing spices, all sought after by the rest of the world. Pepper and turmeric as well as cumin and coriander grew here, then and now. A vast circuit of trade and exchange developed in these items, helping to fuel the opening of the world to explorers in the early modern age, as well as the transit of such items to still other places inside Asia, such as Malaysia and Singapore. Through historical data and also through con-temporary fieldwork, the outlines of this trade are laid out, to see what such patterns can tell us about trade and diaspora in the burgeoning of the modern world. Spices were not of the ocean, but eventually became more important, in value terms, than any other natural product in Asia's trades, at least for a time. Then as now, South India's spices are also sent to market almost wholly by ship. This chapter looks at that complex history, and asks how the legacy of the spice trade is still with us today, both in the regions where these items are grown and overseas.

10

Fins, Slugs, Pearls

MARINE PRODUCTS AND
SINO-SOUTHEAST ASIA

Our family has done this for generations. This generation will likely be the last.

—MERCHANT, SINGAPORE[1]

THE PARADOXICAL NATURE of "the stranger"—at once alien and uncomfortable in any given local society, but also able to use this status to further economic and even occasionally political ends, often associated with trade—was famously described by the eminent sociologist, Georg Simmel.[2] His work was adding to the foundation of others who had thought about these processes, most notably Max Weber and his interrogations of the so-called Protestant ethic, with all that this historical "ethic" supposedly signified.[3] Many contemporary scholars have seized on these ideas to study the mechanics of "stranger communities" in their own academic bailiwicks, encompassing

1. Author's fieldwork notes: Merchant interview, Nam Yong Marine Co., Singapore, October 1989 [translation: E. Tagliacozzo].

2. D. N. Levine, "Simmel at a Distance: On the History and Systematics of the Sociology of the Stranger," in *Georg Simmel. Critical Assessments*, vol. 3, ed. D. Frisby (London: Routledge, 1994), 174–89; A. Schuetz, "The Stranger: An Essay in Social Psychology," *American Journal of Psychology* 49 (1944): 499–507; Georg Simmel, "The Stranger," in *The Sociology of Georg Simmel*, ed. K. H. Wolff (New York: Free Press, 1950), 402–8.

3. M. Weber, *The Protestant Ethic and the Spirit of Capitalism*, 2nd ed. (London: George Allen and Unwin, 1976). For an early attempt to marry Weber to the study of Asian trade communities, see R. E. Kennedy, "The Protestant Ethic and the Parsis," *American Journal of Sociology* 68 (1962–63): 11–20.

Indians in East Africa, Jews in Europe, and even Armenians spread out across the Middle East.[4] Scholars of overseas Chinese communities have been no exception: some of the most important analytic writing about diasporic communities and their linkages with trade and long-distance commercial enterprises has focused on these populations. The reasons for this have been disparate, but one of the most important among them is that the Chinese— and those who conducted business with them—have often left very good records. Getting access to these records across the breadth of languages and societies that Chinese traders visited has never been easy, however.[5]

This chapter mostly examines overseas Chinese networks through a singular portal: the historical and contemporary trade in marine produce, which linked China and the many countries of Southeast Asia in an economic embrace for hundreds of years.[6] In the first third of the chapter, I note some of the theoretical, historiographical, and historical outlines for examining these communities and processes across historical time. This is done in fairly shorthand form, as I have written about these connections in more detail in other places.[7] The second two-thirds of the essay links these historical peregrinations with how the

4. For Southeast Asia, two good places to start in disentangling these patterns are Keng We Koh, "Familiar Strangers and Stranger-kings: Mobility, Diasporas, and the Foreign in the Eighteenth-Century Malay World," *Journal of Southeast Asian Studies* 48, no. 3 (2017): 390–413, and Jennifer L. Gaynor, *Intertidal History in Island Southeast Asia: Submerged Genealogy and the Legacy of Coastal Capture* (Ithaca, NY: Cornell University Press, 2016.)

5. The list is long here; for just a few of the possibilities, some of them critical and useful, others far less so, see Edgar Wickberg, "Overseas Adaptive Organizations, Past and Present," in *Reluctant Exiles? Migration from the Hong Kong and the New Overseas Chinese*, ed. Ronald Skeldon (Armonk, NY: M. E. Sharpe, 1994); Wu Wei-Peng, "Transaction Cost, Cultural Values and Chinese Business Networks: An Integrated Approach," in *Chinese Business Networks*, ed. Chan Kwok Bun (Singapore: Prentice Hall, 2000): 35–56; I-Chuan Wu-Beyens, "Hui: Chinese Business in Action," in *Chinese Business Networks*, ed. Chan Kwok Bun (Singapore: Prentice Hall, 2000): 129–51; Jamie Mackie, "The Economic Roles of Southeast Asian Chinese: Information Gaps and Research Needs," in Ibid., 234–60; Peter S. Li, "Overseas Chinese Networks: A Reassessment," in Ibid., 261–84; Sterling Seagrave, *Lords of the Rim: The Invisible Empire of the Overseas Chinese* (New York: Putnam, 1995).

6. See Roderich Ptak, *Maritime Animals in Traditional China* (Wiesbaden: Harrassowitz Verlag, 2011); and Jennifer L. Gaynor, "Maritime Ideologies and Ethnic Anomalies: Sea Space and the Structure of Subalternality in the Southeast Asian Littoral," in *Seascapes: Maritime Histories, Littoral Cultures, and Transoceanic Exchanges*, ed. Jerry H. Bentley, Renate Bridenthal, and Kären Wigen, 53–68 (Honolulu: University of Hawai'i Press, 2007).

7. Eric Tagliacozzo, "A Necklace of Fins: Marine Goods Trading in Maritime Southeast Asia, 1780–1860," *International Journal of Asian Studies* 1, no. 1 (2004): 23–48.

marine goods trade works now between China and Southeast Asia. This portion is based on published academic literature, but also significantly comprises my own oral-history interviews with these traders throughout East and Southeast Asian ports, as well as visits to collecting and transshipment sites of these commodities, too. I hope to show the broad dimensions of this commerce in both historical and contemporary terms, as a crucial connective link between China and Southeast Asia over the past several centuries. Far from being an antiquated trade in strange and often exoticized objects culled from the sea, the traffic in marine goods can be seen as an important vestige of historical transoceanic connections. These exchanges echo the past in fascinating and often melancholic ways. Yet they also show how these trades evolve into the future, as the statements of these merchants reveal when they are allowed to tell us their stories in their own words.

Histories of Marine Products and Their Commerce

A Common Orbit: Sino-Southeast Asia

Understanding of the motors and dimensions of the Chinese historical economy has advanced considerably in the past twenty to thirty years.[8] Some of these studies have focused on guild and clan associations, the famous *gongsi* that G. William Skinner and others researched in such fine detail in the 1970s and earlier.[9] Other studies have combed the *Ming Shi-lu* [Ming Veritable Records], as well as the archives of particular provinces, such as Fujian, for clues as to how commercial activities expanded in the early modern period before literally exploding in number, importance, and volume in the nineteenth century.[10] Most of these earlier studies looked at the oceans when the

8. See, in order, Marshall Sahlins, "Cosmologies of Capitalism: The Trans-Pacific Sector of the World System," in *Culture, Power, and History: A Reader in Contemporary Theory*, ed. Nicholas Dirks, Geoff Eley, and Sherry Orner, 412–55 (Princeton: Princeton University Press, 1994); Timothy Brook, *The Confusions of Pleasure: Commerce and Culture in Ming China* (Berkeley: University of California Press, 1998); and Pin-tsun Chang, "The Sea as Arable Fields: A Mercantile Outlook on the Maritime Frontier of Late Ming China," in *The Perception of Space in Traditional Chinese Sources*, ed. Angela Schottenhammer and Roderich Ptak, 17–26 (Wiesbaden: Harrassowitz Verlag, 2006).

9. For a good overview, see, for example, P. J. Golas, "Early Ching Guilds," in *The City in Late Imperial China*, ed. G. W. Skinner (Stanford: Stanford University Press, 1977), 555–80.

10. Geoffrey Wade, *The Ming Shi-lu (Veritable Records of the Ming Dynasty) as a Source for Southeast Asian History, Fourteenth to Seventeenth Centuries*, 8 vols. (Hong Kong: Hong Kong

tendrils of commerce were scrutinized as moving away from the Chinese polity, but now such research also deals with overland connections in detailed and sophisticated ways as well.[11] There has even been an effort more recently to highlight particular commodities and to follow them as "tracers" in unraveling these processes, with goods such as opium proving to be particularly useful in this regard.[12] The crux of the matter is that what used to be the province of statistics is now a historiographical field of much more nuanced dimensions, when it comes to understanding the Chinese economic world.[13]

The role of Chinese merchants in trans-Asian networks has been one of the most pressing contemporary research agendas on the nature of Chinese social and economic history. This research has built on some of the foundational work of Skinner, R. Bin Wong, Peter Purdue, and William Rowe, and now asks a range of questions on how commerce has worked in China, but particularly as one of several strands of commodity movement that became important during the last two centuries.[14] The connections with Western firms have been queried in this regard, as well as links and commercial piggybacking with Japanese business concerns.[15] Some of the research has looked at particular dialect subgroups as windows into these processes on both a micro and a

University Library Microfilms, 1996); Ng Chin-Keong, *Trade and Society: The Amoy Network on the China Coast, 1683–1735,* Singapore (Singapore University Press, 1983); Hao Yen-p'ing, *The Commercial Revolution in Nineteenth-Century China. The Rise of Sino-Western Mercantile Capital* (Berkeley: University of California Press, 1986).

11. Michael R. Godley, *The Mandarin-Capitalists from Nanyang: Overseas Chinese Enterprise in the Modernization of China, 1893–1911* (Cambridge: Cambridge University Press, 1981); Wen-Chin Chang, "Guanxi and Regulation in Networks: The Yunnanese Jade Trade Between Burma and Thailand," *Journal of Southeast Asian Studies* 35, no. 3 (2004): 479–501.

12. Zheng Yangwen, *The Social Life of Opium in China* (Cambridge: Cambridge University Press, 2005).

13. See Leonard Blussé, "Junks to Java: Chinese Shipping to the Nanyang in the Second Half of the Eighteenth Century," in *Chinese Circulations: Capital, Commodities, and Networks in Southeast Asia,* ed. Eric Tagliacozzo and Wen-Chin Chang, 221–58 (Durham: Duke University Press, 2011); and Gerrit J. Knaap and Heather Sutherland, *Monsoon Traders: Ships, Skippers and Commodities in Eighteenth-Century Makassar* (Leiden: KITLV Press, 2004).

14. See, for example, Guoting Li, *Migrating Fujianese: Ethnic, Family, and Gender Identities in an Early Modern Maritime World* (Leiden: Brill, 2015).

15. Sherman Cochran, *Encountering Chinese Networks: Western, Japanese, and Chinese Corporations in China, 1880–1937* (Berkeley: University of California Press, 2000); Peter Post, "Chinese Business Networks and Japanese Capital in Southeast Asia, 1880–1940: Some Preliminary Observations," in *Chinese Business Enterprises in Asia,* ed. Rajeswary A. Brown (London and New York: Routledge, 1995), 154–76.

macro scale, while other studies have examined how the efforts of many different actors—Chinese, French, Dutch, British, Spanish and even Persian—have combined to push and pull certain items through Asian geographies at an unprecedented scale.[16] The normative narrative of a "semi-sealed" Chinese economy as ordered by the Chinese state no longer holds. This is so as voluminous quantities of research are brought to bear on the way trading networks have expanded from China itself to other places, some of them as far away as the Americas.[17]

Chinese traders and migrants did indeed turn up in places as far afield as the "New World." But it is evident that the primary destination for both Chinese emigration and Chinese commercial expansion during this period was the Nanyang, or "South Seas" (Southeast Asia). This is particularly true for the history of marine goods procurement, but it is also true on the whole for most fields of business and endeavor, as the numbers of Chinese who eventually left for these places attest to over many years. French scholars (writing in French) have been particularly good at theorizing these connections, showing how the South China Sea acted as a fulcrum for movement and radials of contact and dispersion, even as far away as the distant island of Java.[18] English-language scholarship has also worked on these connections, either via *longue-durée* histories or through the vantages of particular institutions, such as Chinese revenue farming as a connective strand between China and Southeast Asia.[19] Japanese writers (translated into English) and Chinese scholars have also become involved, ensuring that not all attempts at explanation of these phenomena are

---

16. Wang Gungwu, "Merchants without Empire: The Hokkien Sojourning Communities," in *The Rise of Merchant Empires: Long-Distance Trade in the Early Modern World, 1350–1750*, ed. J. D. Tracy (Cambridge: Cambridge University Press, 1990), 400–21; Tagliacozzo, "A Necklace of Fins."

17. Adam McKeown, *Chinese Migrant Networks and Cultural Change: Peru, Chicago, Hawaii, 1900–1936* (Chicago: University of Chicago Press, 2001).

18. C. Salmon, "Les Marchands chinois en Asie du Sud-est," in *Marchands et hommes d'affaires asiatiques dans l'Océan Indien et la Mer de Chine 13e–20e siècles*, ed. D. Lombard and J. Aubin, 330–51 (Paris: Éditions de l'École des Hautes Études en Sciences Sociales, 1988); D. Lombard, *Le carrefour javanais: Essai d'histoire globale*, 2 Les réseaux asiatiques (Paris: Éditions de l'École des Hautes Études en Sciences Sociales, 1990).

19. Anthony Reid, ed., *Sojourners and Settlers: Histories of Southeast Asia and the Chinese* (Sydney: Allen & Unwin, 1996); John Butcher and Howard Dick, eds., *The Rise and Fall of Revenue Farming: Business Elites and the Emergence of the Modern State in Southeast Asia* (Basingstoke: Macmillan, and New York: St. Martin's Press, 1993), 193–206.

grounded solely in Western social science paradigms.[20] Taken as a whole, the collective has set up very useful parameters in helping us understand the template of historical travel. This is true regardless of our speaking about the marine products trade, or any other line of commerce that might have induced out-migration.

The Aquatic South

A destination for Chinese traders and immigrants in the so-called *Nanyang* of extended historical standing was Java. Though Java had long had contact with China, the establishment of a Dutch presence in Batavia around the turn of the seventeenth century increased the demand for Chinese merchants, artisans, and workers in far greater numbers than previously. The autocratic Jan Coen was the despot of the town, but Dutch-language scholarship shows us that Chinese *kapitans* were quickly established to look after the Chinese population, especially with regard to regulating commerce along lines of which the Dutch approved.[21] Things went fairly smoothly at first, but by the eighteenth century there were significant troubles, including massacres of these same Chinese populations.[22] When the Chinese inhabitants were not being periodically culled in such ruthless ways by the colonial overlords of the island, they were used to expand Dutch commerce in many sectors of the economy, such as petty trade, agriculture, and increasingly, the sale of chandu (retail opium).[23] Intermarriage took place on a fairly large scale with local women, and the Chinese on Java gradually phased into both a separate community

20. Shozo Fukuda, *With Sweat and Abacus: Economic Roles of the Southeast Asian Chinese on the Eve of World War II*, ed. George Hicks, trans. Les Oates (Singapore: Select Books, 1995); Qiu Liben, "The Chinese Networks in Southeast Asia: Past, Present and Future," in *Chinese Business Networks*, ed. Chan Kwok Bun (Singapore: Prentice Hall, 2000).

21. Coen, Jan Pietersz. *Bescheiden omtremt zijn bedrif in Indië*, 4 vols., ed. H. T. Colbrander (The Hague: Martinus Nijhoff, 1919–22; B. Hoetink, "Chineesche officiern te Batavia onder de Compagnie," *Bijdragen tot de Taal-, land- en Volkenkunde van Nederlandsch Indië* 78 (1922): 1–136; B. Hoetink, "Ni Hoekong: Kapitein der Chineezen te Batavia in 1740," *Bijdragen tot de Taal-, land- en Volkenkunde van Nederlandsch Indië* 74 (1918): 447–518; B. Hoetink, "So Bing Kong: Het eerste hoofd der Chineezen te Batavia (1629–1636)," *Bijdragen tot de Taal-, land- en Volkenkunde van Nederlandsch Indië* 74 (1917): 344–85.

22. J. T. Vermueulen, *De Chineezen te Batavia en de Troebelen van 1740* (Leiden: Eduard Ijdo, 1938); J. F. van Nes, "De Chinezen op Java," *Tijdshcrift voor Nederlandesh Indië* 13, no. 1 (1851): 239–54, 292–314.

23. M. van Alphen, "Iets over den orsprong en der eerste uibreiding der Chinesche Volkplanting te Batavia," *Tijdschrift voor Nederlandesch Indië* 4, no. 1 (1842): 70–100; V. B. van Gutem,

as well as a mestizo society that was mixed with the indigenes themselves.[24] Many Chinese were, in fact, scattered in the port towns and on other parts of Java's coasts, and they played a large part in the buying, selling, and transport of marine products to these larger towns. It was in these latter ports where items such as sea-products were earmarked for passage to distant destinations.

Better than almost any other historiographical tradition, Dutch-language scholarship shows us how quickly the Chinese, and Chinese marine goods traders in particular, spread into the rest of the sprawling Indies colony, out and away from the center of Dutch authority on Java.[25] Economically, this community began to serve a crucial feeder role for the Dutch via all things that the latter needed to make their colony profitable—dried fish, pearls, and fish maws among them. The most famous Chinese fishing station in the archipelago was located at Bagan Si Api-api, off the coast of north-central Sumatra, and the amounts of sea produce collected, dried, and packaged for sale here reached huge quantities by the late nineteenth and early twentieth centuries. Proximity to British-controlled Singapore, with that island's huge port and transregional shipping connections, was at least as important as Bagan Si Api-api's connections to the Dutch primate city/port of Batavia farther south and away from the mouth of the Straits of Melaka.[26] Yet Chinese appeared elsewhere as well, on the long outstretched coasts of Borneo, for example, in Sulawesi, in Eastern Indonesia, and especially in Riau, as fishers, driers, collectors and packagers of marine goods.[27] Ethnic business connections with other Chinese merchants and with Dutch colonial officials ensured that much of this

"Tina Mindering: Eeninge aanteekenigen over het Chineeshe geldshieterswesen op Java," *Koloniale Studiën* 3, no. 1 (1919): 106–50.

24. See Leonard Blussé, *Strange Company: Chinese Settlers, Mestizo Women and the Dutch in VOC Batavia* (Dordrecht and Riverton: Foris Publications, 1986); P. Carey, "Changing Javanese Perceptions of the Chinese Communities in Central Java, 1755–1825," *Indonesia* 37 (1984): 1–47.

25. Among many other sources, see Phoa Liong Gie, "De economische positie der Chineezen in Nederlandesch Indië," *Koloniale Studiën* 20, no. 5 (1936): 97–119; J. L. Vleming, *Het Chineesche zakenleven in Nederlandesch-Indië* (Weltevreden: Landsdrikkerij, 1926); Siem Bing Hoat, "Het Chineesch Kapitaal in Indonisië," *Chung Hwa Hui Tsa Chih* 8, no. 1 (1930): 7–17; Ong Eng Die, *Chinezen in Nederlansch-Indië: Sociographie van een Indonesische bevolkingsgroep* (Assen: Van Gorcum and Co., 1943).

26. The Siauw Giap, "Socio-Economic Role of the Chinese in Indonesia, 1820–1940," in *Economic Growth in Indonesia, 1820–1940*, ed. A. Maddison and G. Prince (Dordrecht: Foris, 1989), 159–83; W. J. Cator, *The Economic Position of the Chinese in the Netherlands Indies* (Oxford: Basil Blackwell, 1936).

27. M. Fernando and D. Bulbeck, *Chinese Economic Activity in Netherlands India: Selected Translations from the Dutch* (Singapore: Institute of Southeast Asian Studies, 1992).

produce reached Dutch and foreign markets quickly and fairly efficiently. Chinese communities were so important in this respect that the Dutch undertook extensive surveillance upon these populations. The reason for this of course was that the Dutch wanted their cut of the profits.[28]

A similar state of affairs existed with respect to Chinese communities and the collection of ocean produce farther north, in the waters of the British dominions of Malaya and Borneo. On Borneo, both in today's modern Malaysian states of Sarawak and Sabah, as well as in the Sultanate of Brunei, Chinese took on busy roles as the organizers and collectors of ocean produce in a variety of places.[29] The coasts of Borneo were found to be underexploited compared to many other places, so Chinese merchants and occasionally small business concerns often had their pick as to where to set up shop, drying facilities, purchase points, and other institutions to make these businesses run.[30] Revenue farming syndicates with primary interests in other products, such as opium or alcohol, sometimes helped in smoothing out some of these arrangements.[31] On the Malay Peninsula in places such as Penang, where Chinese syndicates such as the well-studied Khaw Group held economic sway, the connections between marine produce and efficient forms of Chinese business organization were even more in evidence, especially with large populations of Chinese and other ethnic laborers nearby needing to be fed.[32] The buying, sorting, packaging and eventual shipping of marine products were a crucial part of the local economy in places such as Penang. From there, England's trade interests

28. See the arguments presented in Eric Tagliacozzo, *Secret Trades, Porous Borders: Smuggling and States along a Southeast Asian Frontier, 1865–1915* (New Haven: Yale University Press, 2005).

29. Eric Tagliacozzo, "Onto the Coast and Into the Forest: Ramifications of the China Trade on the History of Northwest Borneo, 900–1900," in *Histories of the Borneo Environment*, ed. Reed Wadley (Leiden: KITLV Press, 2005), 25–60.

30. Eric Tagliacozzo, "Border-Line Legal: Chinese Communities and 'Illicit' Activity in Insular Southeast Asia," in *Maritime China and the Overseas Chinese in Transition, 1750–1850*, ed. Ng Chin Keong (Wiesbaden: Harrossowitz Verlag, 2004), 61–76.

31. Michael R. Godley, "Chinese Revenue Farm Network: The Penang Connection," in *The Rise and Fall of Revenue Farming: Business Elites and the Emergence of the Modern State in Southeast Asia*, ed. John Butcher and Howard Dick (Basingstoke: Macmillan and New York: St. Martin's Press, 1993), 89–99.

32. J. W. Cushman, "The Khaw Group: Chinese Business in the Early Twentieth-Century Penang," *Journal of Southeast Asian Studies* 17, no. 1 (1986): 58–79; see also Wong Yee Tuan, *Penang Chinese Commerce in the Nineteenth Century* (Singapore; ISEAS, 2015); and Jennifer Cushman, *Fields from the Sea: Chinese Junk Trade with Siam during the Late Eighteenth and Early Nineteenth Century* (Ithaca: Cornell University Press, 1975).

FIGURE 10.1. Turtle Shell (author's photo)

FIGURE 10.2. Pearls (author's photo)

in the region formed a large aquatic triangle, connecting Burma, Siam, Malaya and Aceh in its grasp.[33]

We see a similar state of affairs in the Philippines, first run by the Spanish and eventually (for half a century) run by the United States, though with

33. See Jos Gommans and Jacques Leider, eds., *The Maritime Frontier of Burma, Exploring Political, Cultural and Commercial Interaction in the Indian Ocean World, 1200–1800* (Leiden: KITLV Press, 2002).

FIGURE 10.3. Trepang (Edible Sea Cucumber) (author's photo)

different local permutations. Chinese had been coming to the Philippines for many centuries and often in larger numbers than in other parts of Southeast Asia, as the archipelago was closer and easier to reach using prevailing wind and current patterns of the monsoons. With more than seven thousand islands, Chinese became heavily involved in the marine produce trades of the colonial Philippines very easily, often using ships that they had originally piloted to the Philippines, first as vessels of transport and eventually as carriage containers for marine produce heading back to Fujian.[34] The ocean produce trade from the Philippines was extremely important, first for supplying cities (such as Manila and Cebu) with food, but also in mining the exceedingly plentiful waters of Sulu in the southern parts of the archipelago, where pearls, mother-of-pearl, shark fins, and fish stomachs could be procured in very large quantities. Chinese crews sailed from South China to take advantage of these riches, but they eventually also came from Singapore and other Southeast

34. See the contributions by R. Bernal, L. Diaz Trechuelo, M. C. Guerrero, and S. D. Quiason in *The Chinese in the Philippines 1570–1770*, ed. A. Felix Jr., vol. 1 (Manila: Solidaridad, 1966).

Asian ports, all in an effort to make a living off these fecund seas.[35] Though the Spanish, in particular, periodically legislated laws against Chinese over-involvement in regional trades outside of the cities, the rules often went unenforced because of Spanish weakness, and because of the outstretched geography of the islands.[36] Even into the early twentieth century and after the arrival of the Americans, Chinese involvement in these trades was main-tained. Eventually, however, other agricultural staples—often fetching very high prices on world markets, at least until the Great Depression—later diminished the role of marine products as one of the vital lines of trade in pan-Asian commerce.[37]

In sum, Chinese involvement with the marine products trade in Southeast Asia was long-lasting and fairly constant, throughout the last several centuries. We know from studies of the China coasts (and also from practical merchant tracts of that time) that Southeast Asia was an important destination for many Chinese merchants hoping to make a living off commerce such as marine com-modities.[38] Farther south, in Southeast Asian waters themselves, we know from the surviving accounts of many Western merchants and statesmen that these trades were flourishing, and in fact had been for quite some time, according to informants that these men used to gather information in the area.[39] This was clearly true throughout Southeast Asia as a region, though

35. E. Wickberg, *The Chinese in Philippine Life, 1850–1898* (New Haven: Yale University Press, 1965).

36. Benito Legarda, *After the Galleons: Foreign Trade, Economic Change and Entrepreneurship in the Nineteenth-Century Philippines* (Madison: University of Wisconsin Southeast Asia Program, 1999).

37. Wong Kwok-Chu, *The Chinese in the Philippine Economy, 1898–1941* (Manila: Ateneo de Manila Press, 1999).

38. See, in no particular order, Yen-Ping Hao, *The Commercial Revolution in Nineteenth Century China: The Rise of Sino-Western Capitalism* (Berkeley: University of California Press, 1986); W. E. Cheong, *The Hong Merchants of Canton: Chinese Merchants in Sino-Western Trade* (Richmond, Surrey: Curzon, 1997; Dilip Basu, "The Impact of Western Trade on the Hong Merchants of Canton, 1793–1842," in *The Rise and Growth of the Colonial Port Cities in Asia*, ed. Dilip Basu, 151–55 (Berkeley, Center for South and Southeast Asian Research 25, University of California Press, 1985); Randle Edwards, "Ch'ing Legal Jurisdiction over Foreigners," in *Essays on China's Legal Tradition*, ed. Jerome Cohen et al., 222–69 (Princeton: Princeton University Press, 1980); and John Phipps *A Practical Treatise on Chinese and Eastern Trade* (Calcutta: Thacker and Com., 1835).

39. For a few examples, see John Crawfurd, *Journal of an Embassy from the Governor General of India to the Courts of Siam and Cochin-China* (London: Henry Colburn 1828; Oxford

some places were more important than others as collecting centers and as the locations of far-flung diasporas who made a living out of these trades. The Sulu Sea was on such arena, with its widespread sea-procurement systems outlined in such detail by James Francis Warren, Heather Sutherland and others, all driven by Muslim sultanates in the region.[40] The Bugis diasporas based out of southwest Sulawesi, but with tendrils reaching in many different directions throughout maritime Southeast Asia, were another important locus of these trades, even though this avenue of biota-procurement was less based on a specific region (such as Sulu) and more on the networks themselves, which cross-crossed a lot of open water.[41] Finally, theorists and historians of diaspora

Historical reprints, 1967); Thomas Forrest, *A Voyage to New Guinea and the Moluccas from Balambangan: Including an Account of Maguindanao, Sooloo, and Other Islands* (London: G. Scott, 1779); D. H. Kolff, *Voyages of the Dutch Brig of War Dourga*, trans. George Windsor Earl (London: James Madden, 1840); and William Milburn, *Oriental Commerce*, vol. I (London, Black, Parry, and Co, 1813).

40. Warren, *The Sulu Zone*; Heather Sutherland, "Trepang and Wangkang: The China Trade of Eighteenth-Century Makassar," in *Authority and Enterprise among the Peoples of South Sulawesi*, ed. R. Tol, K. van Dijk, and G. Accioli (Leiden: KITLV Press, 2000); G. N. Appel, "Studies of the Taosug and Samal-Speaking Populations of Sabah and the Southern Philippines," *Borneo Research Bulletin* 1, no. 2 (1969): p. 21–22; Thomas Kiefer, *The Taosug: Violence and Law in a Philippine Muslim Society* (New York: Holt, Rinehart, and Winston, 1972), 22; Clifford Sather, "Sulu's Political Jurisdiction over the Bajau Laut Traditional States of Borneo and the Southern Philippines," *Borneo Research Bulletin* 3, no. 2 (1971): 45; and Richard Stone, "Intergroup Relations among the Taosug Samal and Badjaw of Sulu," in *The Muslim Filipinos*, ed. Peter Gowing and Robert McAmis, 90–91 (Manila: Solidaridad Publishing House, 1974); Charles Frake, "The Cultural Constructions of Rank, Identity, and Ethnic Origin in the Sulu Archipelago," in *Origins, Ancestry, and Alliance: Explorations in Austronesian Ethnography*, ed. James Fox and Clifford Sather (Publication of the Research School of Pacific and Asian Studies, Canberra, Australia National University, 1996); Peter Gowing, *Muslim Filipinos: Heritage and Horizon* (Quezon City: New Day Publishers, 1979); Alexander Spoehr, *Zamboanga and Sulu: An Archaeological Approach to Ethnic Diversity Ethnology* (Pittsburgh: Monograph 1, Dept. of Anthropology, University of Pittsburgh, 1973).

41. H. A. Mattulada, "Manusia dan Kebudayaan Bugis-Makassar dan Kaili di Sulawesi," *Antropologi Indonesia: Majalah Antropologi Sosial dan Budaya Indonesia* 15, no. 48 (Jan./Apr. 1991): 4–109; Narifumi Maeda, "Forest and the Sea among the Bugis," *Southeast Asian Studies* 30, no. 4 (1993): 420–26; Jacqueline Lineton, "Pasompe' Ugi': Bugis Migrants and Wanderers," *Archipel* 10 (1975): 173–205; Clifford Sather, "Seven Fathoms: A Bajau Laut Narrative Tale from the Semporna District of Sabah," *Brunei Museum Journal* 3, no. 3, 1975; Leonard Andaya, "The Bugis Makassar Diasporas," *JMBRAS* 68, no. 1 (1995): 119–38; and C. A. Gibson-Hill, "The Indonesian Trading Boat Reaching Singapore," *Royal Asiatic Society, Malaysian Branch* 23 (Feb. 1950).

have been helpful in showing us the filigree of these connections more generally, with the Chinese nodes just one among several which were important in these outstretched maritime frontiers.[42] Historically, all of these movements made a system, whereby sea produce from a number of locales all wound its way to the China coasts in increasing volume as the years went on.

A Contemporary Grid: The Web of Marine Products

The Chinese Center: Theory and Praxis

A remarkable picture of change and continuity appears in the transit of marine products between China and Southeast Asia, if we fast-forward to the last decades of the twentieth and the first few years of the twenty-first century. If the years spanning 1780 to 1860 were a high point of this commerce, followed by a lessening in importance of this trade as it was swamped by the much larger movement of goods in the so-called high colonial era, then the last three decades have seen a resurgence in these items, as the record-growth economies of both China and many Southeast Asian states have spun off the charts. If the worldwide Depression of the 1930s, World War II, and the early years of Southeast Asian nation-states after decolonization continued the pattern of marine goods living in the shadow of other, more important, lines of commerce since the late nineteenth century, then the explosive growth of economies in East and Southeast Asia since the 1980s has revitalized this traditional conduit of trade between the two regions in new and interesting ways. Much of this growth has been attributed to the overall dynamism of regional economies, which has encouraged a brisk flow of goods between subregions that have traditionally traded with one another for many hundreds of years. Yet it is noticeable that the passage of marine goods has become an important subrubric of this larger economic success story, begging the question as to why and

42. Chin Keong Ng, *Trade and Society: The Amoy Network on the China Coast* (Singapore: Singapore University Press, 1983); Sarasin Viraphol, *Tribute and Profit: Sino-Siamese Trade 1652–1853* (Cambridge, MA: Harvard University Press 1977); Christine Dobbin, *Asian Entrepreneurial Minorities: Conjoint Communities in the Making of the World-Economy, 1570–1940* (Richmond: Curzon, 1996); and R. Ray, "Chinese Financiers and Chetti Bankers in Southern Waters: Asian Mobile Credit During the Anglo-Dutch Competition for the Trade of the Eastern Archipelago in the Nineteenth Century," *Itinerario* 1 (1987): 209–34.

how this trade fits into a larger story of growth.[43] In the following pages I deal with this question both through social science literature on the topic and through my own interviews with Chinese marine goods merchants in various parts of China, Taiwan, and Southeast Asia itself. These approaches are added to by my own fieldwork among marine products traders and collectors, all of them in the wider Southeast Asian orbit.

There has been no lack of interest from social theorists seeking to explain the success of Chinese business re-asserting itself throughout Southeast Asia since the fall of the colonial powers at mid-century. The reasons put forward for this dynamism have been various in nature, from the importance of clan associations and language-dialect groups, to notions of *"guanxi"* and transnational networks, to an interesting thread reflecting on the nature of "Chinese capitalism" itself as a modus operandi for a range of ethnic Chinese merchants scattered throughout Southeast Asia.[44] Some of these explanations have been more sophisticated than others, but all of them point to an opinion and a worldview that Chinese business has been in a growth mode not only in "Greater China" (the PRC, Hong Kong and Taiwan, over the last twenty-five or so years), but also in Southeast Asia, a traditional field for Chinese merchant activity over the centuries (known collectively as the Nanyang).[45] Several important scholars have looked specifically at the dynamics of these interactions

43. See John Butcher, *The Closing of the Frontier: A History of the Marine Fisheries of Southeast Asia, 1850–2000* (Singapore: ISEAS, 2004).

44. See, among many other contributions, Cheng Lim Keak, "Reflections on Changing Roles of Chinese Clan Associations in Singapore," *Asian Culture* (Singapore) 14 (1990): 57–71; S. Gordon Redding, "Weak Organizations and Strong Linkages: Managerial Ideology and Chinese Family Business Networks," in *Business Networks and Economic Development in East and Southeast Asia*, ed. Gary Hamilton (Hong Kong: Center of Asian Studies, University of Hong Kong, 1991); Edmund Terence Gomez and Michael Hsiao, eds., *Chinese Enterprise, Transnationalism, and Identity* (London: Routledge, 2004); S. Gordon Redding, *The Spirit of Chinese Capitalism* (Berlin: De Gruyter, 1990); Kunio Yoshihara, "The Ethnic Chinese and Ersatz Capitalism in Southeast Asia," in *Southeast Asian Chinese and China: The Politico-economic Dimension*, ed. Leo Suryadinata (Singapore: Times Academic, 1995); and Arif Dirlik, "Critical Reflections on 'Chinese Capitalism' as Paradigm," *Identities* 3, no. 3: 1997: 303–30.

45. Rupert Hodder, *Merchant Princes of the East: Cultural Delusions, Economic Success and the Overseas Chinese in Southeast Asia* (Chichester: Wiley, 1996); better studies include Edmund Terence Gomez and Michael Hsiao, *Chinese Business in Southeast Asia: Contesting Cultural Explanations, Researching Entrepreneurship* (Richmond, Surrey: Curzon, 2001); and J. Mackie, "Changing Patterns of Chinese Big Business in Southeast Asia," in *Southeast Asian Capitalists*, ed. Ruth McVey (Ithaca: Cornell University Southeast Asia Program, 1992), 161–90.

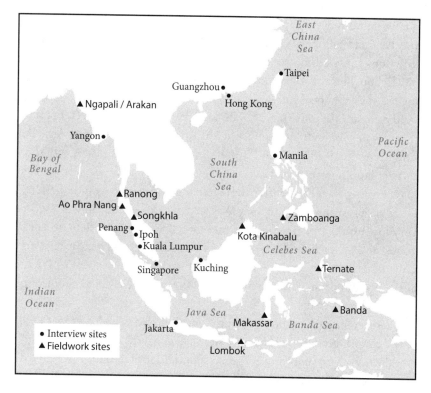

MAP 10.1. Sino-Southeast Asia

from China down to Southeast Asia itself, both historically and in the years leading up to our own time.[46] Others have concentrated more on the Southeast Asian side of things, analyzing patterns in the receiving countries of these flows rather than from the source areas of migration and merchant movement in East Asia as a whole.[47] Regardless of the approach chosen, it is clear that

46. Michael Godley, *The Mandarin Capitalists from Nanyang: Overseas Chinese Enterprise in the Modernization of China* (Cambridge: Cambridge University Press 1981); M. Freedman, *Chinese Lineage and Society: Fukien and Kwangtung*, 2nd ed. (London: The Althone Press, 1971); J. A. C. Mackie, "Changing Patterns of Chinese Big Business in Southeast Asia," in *Southeast Asian Capitalists*, ed. McVey; Rajeswary A. Brown, ed., *Chinese Business Enterprise in Asia* (London: Routledge, 1995); Yen Ching-hwang, ed., *The Ethnic Chinese in East and Southeast Asia: Business, Culture, and Politics* (Singapore: Times Academic, 2002).

47. Linda Y. C. Lim, "Chinese Economic Activity in Southeast Asia: An Introductory Review," in *The Chinese in Southeast Asia*, vol. 1: *Ethnicity and Economic Activity*, ed. Linda Y. C. Lim and L. A. Peter Gosling (Singapore: Maruzen Asia, 1983); Leo Suryadinata, ed., *Southeast Asian Chinese: The Socio-cultural Dimension* (Singapore: Times Academic Press, 1995); J. A. C. Mackie,

marine goods movements between the two spheres connect these literatures very well, and help show some of these mechanics of commerce and ethnicity in action. These business radials operate over a very large field, and tell us much about how the contours of an old commerce have managed to maintain themselves in our own era.

The coasts of Hong Kong, Taiwan, and China are the principal termini for this flow of commodities, as most products come from Southeast Asia, but sometimes from farther afield.[48] Interviews done in these places with shop owners show how truly transnational their contacts can be: owners signaled in interesting ways their entrenchment in much larger geographic systems. Some shops, such as the Kin Sang Dispensary in Kowloon, Hong Kong, are very low on the chain—they are merely bottom-rung outlets for these goods, and sell such products only in very small quantities per package, and only to local consumers. As one merchant in the dispensary said, "We are at the bottom of the market; we are the ones selling to local people, not wholesale at all."[49]

These stores are common in Hong Kong, but also in China proper itself, where comparatively low numbers of large-size concerns deal with the outside world. This was certainly true in Xiamen, Fujian (one of the most "networked" places in China), but it was also true in Guangzhou, Guangdong, and even in Ching-ping Market, where dried sea products are sold by many dozens of merchants side by side.[50] Their connections with the outside world of marine goods tend to be mediated by larger concerns that have better contacts with the government, and which can get the necessary licenses. Back in Hong Kong, and only a few blocks away from the Kin Sang Dispensary, Citiherb is a very different kind of place: gleaming and impressive, its wares are shipped

"Overseas Chinese Entrepreneurship," *Asian Pacific Economic Literature* 6, no. 1 (1992): 41–46; Victor Simpao Limlingan, *The Overseas Chinese in ASEAN: Business Strategies and Management Practices* (Manila: Vita Development Corporation, 1986).

48. For the history of how some of these trades fit into Chinese medicine, see He Bian, *Know Your Remedies: Pharmacy and Culture in Early Modern China* (Princeton: Princeton University Press, 2020).

49. Interview, Kin Sang Dispensary, Hong Kong, 4 April 2005. Author's interview notes [translation: E. Tagliacozzo].

50. Interviews were done in Xiamen, Fujian (PRC) in the spring of 2005. Fieldwork in Ching-ping Market, Guangzhou, took place in January 1990. The range of goods available in this market, in particular, was truly astounding: marine produce from the four corners of the globe could be found here, though usually from Southeast Asia (via ethnic Chinese networks).

from far and wide in the Nanyang. The fish maws alone (dried fish stomachs, used medicinally) were among the largest and best-preserved specimens that I saw anywhere in my interviews in Asia.[51] Yet even this apothecary paled in comparison to the Ho Sheng Tang Company, headquartered in Taipei, Taiwan. Ho Sheng Tang obtained its shark fins from the large fleets of Taiwanese fishing ships that comb the world's seas, and its abalone came from Mexico and California, across the vast Pacific. Its edible sea cucumber stocks not only had various grades of Southeast Asian holothurians, but even tiny, extremely expensive specimens from Japan, selling at NT$9,800 (or at US$300 per specimen).[52] Representative of a different kind of access to the outside world, compared to some of the previous shipments mentioned above, this was the high-end of end-destinations, and thus emblematic of the functioning of different altitudes of commerce.[53]

Southeast Asia's Mainland Coasts

The coasts of mainland Southeast Asia have a very long history of shipping such products north, even if marine products and dried goods come to China, Hong Kong, and Taiwan from many parts of the Nanyang. Vietnam is China's closest neighbor in Southeast Asia, and because of its long, extended coastline, fish has very often been transported to South China, frequently by ethnically Sino-Vietnamese merchants. Even fishermen themselves do this on occasion, evading customs patrols, as they know where they can land their boats to quietly unload large holds of precious fish. Observers of Vietnamese economic life have often commented on the importance of the Sino-Vietnamese community, centered on Cholon in Ho Chi Minh City, but present in large stretches of the rest of the country, too, in connecting the Chinese and Vietnamese economies.[54] It is clear that, in the realm of marine goods and dried natural products, these binding commercial sinews have been very

51. Interview, Citiherb Chinese Medicine Clinic, Hong Kong, 4 April 2005.

52. Interview, Ho Sheng Tang Company, Taipei, Taiwan, 7 January 2005.

53. See Steven W. Purcell, Yves Samyn, and Chantal Conand, *Commercially Important Sea Cucumbers of the World* (Rome: Food and Agriculture Organization of the United Nations, 2012).

54. Tsai Mauw-Kuey, *Les chinois au Sud-Vietnam* (Paris: Bibliothèque Nationale, 1986); Tranh Khanh, *The Ethnic Chinese and Economic Development in Vietnam* (Singapore: Institute of Southeast Asian Studies, 1993). I also drew on my interviews with ethnic Chinese marine goods merchants in October 2009 in Hanoi (Cua Hang 49 Marine Goods Shop) and in Ho Chi

important. In Cambodia, too, the marine industry has been vital both in feeding Cambodia's own population and as an export industry for profit, often to China. Nola Cook has studied some of these patterns over the course of the nineteenth and twentieth centuries, particularly as they related to fish and marine life coming from the Tonle Sap, Cambodia's great lake.[55] This lake is said by scientists to have the greatest density of fish in the world, and some of that density is shipped off to China every year in dried form. This is done by Chinese traders who know to come to Cambodia's markets on a seasonal basis to pick up their supplies, and by Sino-Khmer merchants who are based locally.

Across the flat plateau of the Chao Phraya River basin in Thailand, the picture is much the same. Ethnically Sino-Thai merchants are also important in this country, and help to form an economic conduit between the kingdom, which also boasts a large, extended coastline, and China, which is often a market destination for sea produce caught in both the Gulf of Thailand and in the Andaman Sea. From fieldwork done on the docks of Songkhla, on the Gulf coast in the south, it is clear that very large specimens of fish—including the shovelnose shark and various species of rays—are being sold to China for both the feeding of humans and animals alike (for the latter, some of these fish species are ground up to make animal feed).[56] This latter trade is deeply important to Chinese agro-industry, in fact.

Astride the Andaman Sea on the Indian Ocean coast of southern Thailand, somewhat different dynamics shape the sale of these commodities. In places like Ao Phra Nang, a Muslim fishing village just north of Krabi, a small resort town catering to Western travelers (as opposed to tourists, who tend to flock to Phuket and other offshore islands), much of the fishing economy is also geared toward export. Here, shellfish is collected seasonally and with the tides, mostly by women in the mudflat shallows, and then boxed and transported to

---

Minh City (Huong Xian Marine Goods Shop in Ben Thanh Market, and Lien Saigon Marine Goods Shop).

55. See Nola Cooke, "Chinese Commodity Production and Trade in Nineteenth-Century Cambodia: The Fishing Industry," paper presented to the Workshop on Chinese Traders in the Nanyang: Capital, Commodities and Networks, Academica Sinica, Taipei, Taiwan, 19 January 2007.

56. Fieldwork notes, Songkhla docks, Songkhla, South Thailand (Gulf of Thailand coast), December 1989.

collection depots for eventual resale to the Chinese market.[57] Farther north along this same coast, and at the bottom terminus of Burma, the border town of Ranong is also an important fishing and collecting center for marine exports from Thailand. Here, as opposed to Ao Nang, the industry is just that—industrial—with large, oceangoing trawlers setting out each day from Ranong's docks, the boats fishing for catch in Thai waters, international waters, and sometimes (illegally) in Burmese or Malaysian waters too. Here, too, as I have been told in interviews on the docks, a large portion of the eventual catch is dried and shipped to Hong Kong and China to meet demand.[58] Always the market for China and the Chinese-speaking world is growing; this is a constant in modern times.

In Myanmar (what used to be called Burma)—one of the world's most isolated countries for the last half-century, because of the 1962 coup that brought the Burmese military to power—traditionally sought marine goods are shuttling en masse to China, too, and only partially in officially recorded data. Here, as in the shops and dispensaries of Hong Kong, there are different kinds of concerns with different kinds of reach into the marine goods trade. Small shops, such as the one in Yangon (Rangoon) owned by U Myint Thein, have traditional roots in the trade, and have been passed on from generation to generation over time. One of U Myint Thein's parents was ethnically Burman, but one was also Yunnanese Chinese, and it was from this generation that he learned how to conduct his business in the buying and selling of items inside this pharmacopoeia. "My grandfather was from Yunnan. He taught us how to do this trade, and he built up the business. He knew many Chinese in Burma."[59]

A nearby shop, also in Yangon, had firmer roots in this commerce, and because Burma is still relatively isolated, many of the wares on view in this store were new to me, and I had not seen them in markets outside of Burma. These included items such as several species of dried fish (some black in color, others white), though there were also very expensive species of holothurians on offer here, which was surprising for a country as economically poor as

57. Fieldwork notes, Ao Phra Nang village, South Thailand (Andaman Sea coast), December 1989.

58. Fieldwork notes, Ranong docks, Ranong, South Thailand (Andaman Sea coast), December 1989.

59. Interview with U Myint Thein at his shop, Yangon, Burma, 4 January 2007. Author's interview notes [translation: E. Tagliacozzo].

Burma.[60] Fieldwork done on the Arakan coast, not too far from the Bangladesh border, also confirmed that the fishing was on a small-scale, community basis, and not just by large fishing boats owned by industrial concerns. In one village alone, I saw huge drying mats set out with fish of several different species (Commerson's anchovy [*Stolephorus commersonii*]; silver pomfret [*Pampus argenteus*]; and longfin mojarra [*Pentaprion longimanus*]), all baking in the sun.[61] When I asked a Chinese merchant in town where these small species of dried fish were heading, he told me that some were used for local consumption. He said that some were also eaten in Yangon and in other big cities of Myanmar, but that still others were en route to the Chinese market, even though that destination was a much greater distance away.

Archipelagic Worlds

What we can see on the mainland coasts of Southeast Asia with some focused research can be seen nearly everywhere else in insular Southeast Asia, where the sea is literally omnipresent, and its bounty is readily available for transport. A large literature has sprung up to study the tendrils of Chinese commerce in the contemporary Philippines, for example, where Chinese families have mixed into mestizo communities with local Filipinos for hundreds of years.[62] Some of these networks are centered on Manila, the "primate city" of the Philippines and by far its most important economic engine, but there are also important Chinese merchant interests in the provinces as well, especially in places such as Ilo-ilo in the Visayas.[63] Chinese marine goods sellers in the

60. Interview at unnamed spice/marine goods shop, also in Yangon, Burma, four streets over from U Myint Thein's apothecary/marine goods/spice store, 4 January 2007.

61. Fieldwork notes, fishing villages just north of Ngapali, Arakan State, Burma, January 2007.

62. John T. Omohondro, "Social Networks and Business Success for the Philippine Chinese," in *The Chinese in Southeast Asia,* vol. 1: *Ethnicity and Economic Activity,* ed. Linda Y. C. Lim and L. A. Peter Gosling, 65–85 (Singapore: Maruzen Asia, 1983); Arturo Pacho, "The Chinese Community in the Philippines: Status and Conditions," *Sojourn* (Singapore) (Feb. 1986): 80–3; Ellen H. Palanca, "The Economic Position of the Chinese in the Philippines," *Philippine Studies* 25 (1977): 82–8; Liao Shaolian, "Ethnic Chinese Business People and the Local Society: The Case of the Philippines," in *Chinese Business Networks,* ed. Chan Kwok Bun (Singapore: Prentice Hall, 2000).

63. J. Amyot, *The Manila Chinese: Familism in the Philippine Environment* (Quezon City: Institute of Philippine Culture, 1973); J. T. Omohundro, *Chinese Merchant families in Iloilo:*

warehouse districts of northern Manila (Binondo and Divisorio) told me of huge orders that they received for ocean produce from China, both Hong Kong and the PRC proper. Most of these merchants are Hokkien-speakers whose ancestors came to the Philippines from Fujian, and many of them still have good contacts and family scattered throughout southern China, as well as more formal business associates in Hong Kong.[64] It is a quite noticeable attribute of these Filipino-Chinese families that sons and daughters help with the business, especially because so many of them can speak good English, and this connects them to wider radials of procurement than merely the Chinese-speaking contacts allow. Because the Philippines is one of the world's largest archipelagos (with some seven thousand islands), there is no lack of maritime environment from which to find supplies for this outstretched commerce, either. Contacts of these families stretch all the way south to Zamboanga and the Sulu Sea. This is (of course) one of the most important historical fishing sources for marine products, dating back to the 1400s, and possibly earlier.[65]

What is clear for the Philippines is even clearer for Indonesia, the world's largest archipelago, and a space where marine products procurement is widely practiced. Scattered among Indonesia's more than thirteen thousand islands is a large ethnic Chinese merchant community, some of whom have been there for centuries, and others who are more recent arrivals from elsewhere in East or Southeast Asia (China, Singapore, Malaysia, etc.). Chinese merchants have been involved in the sea-products trade of this region for a very long time, and their tendrils of business and association extend far and wide.[66] It is not only Western social scientists who are interested in this phenomenon but

Commerce and Kin in a Central Philippine City (Quezon City: Ateneo de Manila University Press, and Athens, OH: Ohio University Press, 1981).

64. Interview, Inter-Asian Pacific Company, Manila, the Philippines, January 1990. The general manager of this dry-goods concern, Mr. Vicente Co Tiong Keng, gave me this information during a long interview on the premises of his shop in the warehouse districts of northern Manila.

65. Fieldwork, Zamboanga and environs, Zamboanga, Mindanao, Southern Philippines, July 2004.

66. Liem Twan Djie, *De Distribueerende Tusschenhandel der Chineezen op Java*, 2nd ed. (The Hague: Martinues Nijhoff, 1952); J. Panglaykim and I. Palmer, "The Study of Entrepreneurship in Developing Countries: The Development of One Chinese Concern in Indonesia," *Journal of Southeast Asian Studies* 1, no. 1 (1970): 85–95; L. E. Williams, "Chinese Entrepreneurs in Indonesia," *Explorations in Entrepreneurial History* 5, no. 1 (1952): 34–60; Robert Cribb, "Political Structures and Chinese Business Connections in the Malay World: A Historical Perspective," in *Chinese Business Networks*, ed. Chan Kwok Bun (Singapore: Prentice Hall, 2000).

Indonesian scholars, too—many of them of Chinese ancestry, but some of them not so—and the latter have also written about this phenomenon, sometimes in English but also in Bahasa Indonesia.[67] Fieldwork done in harvesting areas such as Lombok in Nusa Tenggara, Makassar in Sulawesi, and in Ternate and Banda in Maluku, Eastern Indonesia, shows that Chinese capital finances sea-products collecting on a grand scale, across large parts of this scattered archipelago:[68] "The Chinese have sent men to buy our sea products for many, many years. All of these trepang drying here are going to China."[69]

Jakarta is often the national collecting depot for such products, but the items can also be sent directly to Singapore, or occasionally to Hong Kong to bypass layers of middlemen.[70] The commodities are almost always harvested from the sea by local indigenes but as soon as they get to market, they go through various rungs of sorting and sale through ethnic Chinese merchants, often locally born but based progressively farther and farther from acquisition sites. This is, in fact, a broad pattern throughout Southeast Asia. If one is collecting fish maws, sea cucumbers, or mother-of-pearl, all of these items are en route through complex networks of Chinese-dominated exchange.

Having discourses with Chinese marine-goods merchants is not a problem in Malaysia. There is little of the occasional discomfort (or even downright fear) that pervades Chinese Indonesians in interviewing, and there is plenty of commercial activity in the sea-products arena here, too. Speaking to these traders throughout Malaysia's major cities is an exercise in tracking the Chinese diaspora over time, and seeing the fullest expression of its breadth, all in dealing with one product line. In Kuala Lumpur, the majority of these traders are Cantonese, in keeping with historical migration patterns to the city, while

67. Zhou, Nanjing, "Masalah Asimilasi Keturunan Tionghoa di Indonesia," *Review of Indonesian and Malaysian Affairs*, 21, no. 2 (Summer 1987): 44–66; Thung Ju Lan, "Posisi dan Pola Komunikasi Antar Budaya Antara Etnis Cina dan Masyarakat Indonesia Lainnya Pada Masa Kini: Suatu Studi Pendahuluan," *Berita Ilmu Pengetahuan dan Teknologi* 29, no. 2 (1985): 15–29; Mely Tan, *Golongan Ethnis Tinghoa di Indonesia: Suatau Masalah Pembinan Kesatuan Bangsa* (Jakarta: Gramedia, 1979).

68. The fieldwork to support this observation was done in scattered parts of Indonesia over several years, always in coastal communities: in Lombok, Nusa Tenggara, summer 2005; in Makassar, South Sulawesi, summer, 2005; in Ternate, North Maluku, spring 1990; and in Banda, Central Maluku, spring 1990.

69. Interview with trepang seller, Makassar, Sulawesi, Indonesia, July 2005. Author's fieldwork notes [translation, E. Tagliacozzo].

70. Fieldwork and interviews with sailors, Jakarta docks (Sunda Kelapa), spring 2000.

in Penang and Ipoh they are Hokkien, for the most part.[71] In Malaysian Borneo, where Chinese migrants came from different parts of China, and for different reasons, the majority are Hakka.[72] Yet, despite these varying subethnicities among the merchants, many of them seem to be buying and selling the same goods, though often along dialect lines when they can. In other cases these traders use Mandarin as a lingua franca among other ocean-products business-men scattered throughout Malaysia, in Southeast Asia, and back to East Asia itself. Quite a number of these Malaysia Chinese merchants spoke of doing their business along "traditional lines"—they do indeed use computers, faxes, and telexes in their daily transactions, but they also make use of abacuses and good tea when doing business, as their fathers before them would have done, and perhaps their fathers' fathers before that. These links to the past are inter-esting and widespread, and they also seem to be of both sentimental and utili-tarian value to many traders who are still concerned with this highly traditional line of Chinese commerce. According to studies on Chinese business in that country, this may be the case not only in the marine-products trade, but also among other product lines.[73]

The Central Radial: Singapore

The warp and weft of the traditional (and modern) Chinese marine products trade, and its connections and dissonances with its own long past, is perhaps best studied in Singapore. Then—as now—this is the central organizational axis for the commerce in marine products in Southeast Asian waters. Singa-pore has been a favored place to study the ins and outs of Chinese commerce for several reasons, not the least being that China was closed to such study for

71. For Kuala Lumpur, see interviews with Fook Hup Hsing Sdn Bhd, Tek Choon Trading Sdn. Bhd, and Tai Yik Hang Medical Hall, all completed in November 1989; in Penang, see in-terviews with Kwong Seng Hung Pte Ltd., and Soo Hup Seng Trading Co. Sdn Bhd, completed in November 1989; in Ipoh, see interview with Wing Sang Hong Sdn Bhd, also completed in November 1989.

72. For Kuching, see interviews with Syn Min Kong Sdn Bhd and Voon Ming Seng Sdn Bhd, both completed in March 1990; fieldwork done in coastal areas of Sabah, in and near Kota Kinabalu, was also useful in uncovering these patterns in 2004.

73. Edmund Terence Gomez, *Chinese Business in Malaysia: Accumulation, Accommodation and Ascendance* (Richmond, UK: Curzon Press, 1999); Edmund Terence Gomez, "In Search of Patrons: Chinese Business Networking and Malay Political Patronage in Malaysia," in *Chinese Business Networks*, ed. Chan Kwok Bun (Singapore: Prentice Hall, 2000).

a very long time, and Singaporean merchants' facilities with English meant that research could be conducted in both Chinese and English, side by side. As a result of this, the literature on Chinese commerce in Singapore is particularly rich, including several semirecent dissertations undertaken down to a level of detail that would previously have been very difficult to achieve in a mainland Chinese context.[74] Sophisticated theories of Chinese merchant behavior have sprung from Singaporean field examples, and often have been put forward as being representative in some ways of Chinese business practices as a whole across wider regional geographies.[75] There has been some truth to these assertions. Yet there has also—perhaps—been some overextension in calculating how emblematic Chinese business in this one small place may be of the larger dynamics and mechanics of Chinese commerce generally. This is true in East or Southeast Asian waters, or in thee spaces that connect them.

These patterns are very much in evidence for marine and dry-produce sellers, though they are only infrequently mentioned in the actual literature on trade and ethnicity among Chinese communities. In Singapore, the main area for these trades is scattered around South Bridge Road and its cross-streets, near Singapore's traditional Chinatown area, and north of the modern-day financial complex centered around Shenton Way.[76] Walking into these shops, in some senses, is like walking into a different time. Big burlap sacks of samples sit scattered on the floor, and on the burlap of the sacks one can see stenciled the ports of many countries—Dobo (in Aru, Eastern Indonesia); Davao (in Mindanao, the Southern Philippines); even Australia (some sea cucumbers make it all the way north from Darwin, which has a monsoon climate and is more connected to Southeast Asia's maritime rhythms than those of

74. Wolfgang Jamann, "Business Practices and Organizational Dynamics of Chinese Family-based Trading Firms in Singapore" (PhD dissertation, Department of Sociology, University of Bielefeld, 1990); Thomas Menkhoff, "Trade Routes, Trust and Trading Networks: Chinese Family-based Firms in Singapore and their External Economic Dealings," PhD dissertation (University of Bielefield, Department of Sociology, 1990).

75. Yao Souchou, "The Fetish of Relationships: Chinese Business Transactions in Singapore," *Sojourn* 2 (1987): 89–111; Cheng Lim Keak, "Chinese Clan Associations in Singapore: Social Change and Continuity," in *Southeast Asian Chinese: The Socio-Cultural Dimension*, ed. Leo Suryadinata (Singapore: Times Academic Press, 1995); Wong Siu-Lun, "Business Networks, Cultural Values and the State in Hong Kong and Singapore," in *Chinese Business Enterprises in Asia*, ed. Rajeswary A. Brown (London: Routledge, 1995).

76. See interviews completed in Singapore with Fei Fah Drug Company and Ming Tai Co. Pte Ltd., both in October 1989.

Australia). You can touch and taste specimens of the produce, even though these are company headquarters with modern communications equipment and orders coming in from (or going out to) the four corners of the world. The fact that many Chinese marine goods sellers have kept their shops in this area is important in and of itself—it is a continuity with tradition, a conscious choice though other real estate (for all intents and purposes) would now be just as good. Dialect-group preferences still manifest themselves in this community. Simply because it is so large, Singapore's Chinese population is more diverse (subethnically) than most other places in Southeast Asia, and therefore communicates such complexity as well.

An evolution to many historical patterns here is evident, however. Fifty or one hundred years ago, it was a good bet that many of these shops would have had sons involved with the business, learning the trade and helping out with day-to-day operations—this is no longer the case in most of these concerns. Most shop owners with whom I spoke lamented the fact that their sons would not follow them into their line of work, though some were glad of this, citing it as too competitive a way to make a living. Others were more philosophical— they wanted their children to receive better educations than they had, so that their lives would not be taken up with pushing odiferous, salt-caked merchandise around Asia as a means of making ends meet.[77] Singapore is still the center of these trades in Southeast Asia—it is still a collection and transshipment point for large quantities of these goods, which are collected elsewhere in Southeast Asia and eventually transited up to China, Hong Kong, and Taiwan. Yet even this competitive advantage—and link to the past—is disappearing, as ethnic Chinese concerns in various other Nanyang countries are now making their own deals with East Asia, to obtain products to market quicker and without the rising costs of Singaporean middlemen. The trade has a remorseless logic to it—the passage of marine goods must compete (like all other lines of trade) in the ferocity of today's global market.[78] Though sea cucumbers, sea horses, fish maws, pearl products, dried fish varieties, abalone, and many other commodities of the traditional trade still pass through Singapore, the days of the port city acting as the arbiter of this trade may now be numbered. Singapore has competed *too* well, in a sense, in the global economy; it has bypassed these trades in its own economic life cycle. The traders with

77. Interview with Ban Tai Loy Medical Company, Singapore, November 1989.

78. Interviews with Guan Tian Kee Spices and Dry Goods Company, and Nam Yong Marine Products, both in Singapore, October 1989.

whom I spoke over the last several decades may in fact be among the last generations to control this commerce, as it moves from Singapore into the wider stretches of the archipelago.

Conclusion

Inarguably, the global political economy in the last two to three centuries was hugely influenced by the spread of capitalism, as new modes of pursuing trade pushed to nearly every corner of the planet. These processes have been discussed within the larger structures of colonialism and existing patterns of trade, with scholars such as Philip Curtin and others showing how this happened in a variety of places, and at a variety of times, over the past several hundred years.[79] Critical to this discussion has been the role of ethnic middlemen—those who competed and later collaborated with the advancing imperial projects of the West, but who also carved out their own niches within the new parameters of commerce that came into being. These racialized networks have been visible across a number of empires and creeping colonial projects, showing that there were indeed interstitial spaces within the larger economic structures where such communities could carve their own niches of importance.[80] Chinese marine goods sellers were one among these many groups, moving from a position of early significance in the centuries before imperial rule to compradors in the nineteenth and early twentieth centuries. They were introduced yet again into new post-independence roles after the end of Pacific World War with the onset of autonomy in the region among its various new states.

79. P. D. Curtin, *Cross-Cultural Trade in World History* (Cambridge: Cambridge University Press, 1984); A. Cohen, "Cultural Strategies in the Organization of Trading Diasporas," in *The Development of Indigenous Trade and Markets in West Africa*, ed. C. Meillassoux, 266–80 (London: Oxford University Press, 1971); E. Bonadich, "A Theory of Middleman Minorities," in *Majority and Minority: The Dynamics of Racial and Ethnic Relations*, 2nd ed., ed. N. R. Yetman and C. H. Steele, 77–89 (Boston: Allyn & Bacon, 1975).

80. Z. Bader, "The Contradictions of Merchant Capital 1840–1939," in *Zanzibar under Colonial Rule*, ed. A. Sheriff and E. Ferguson (London: James Curry, 1991), 163–87; R. Robinson, "Non-European Foundations of European Imperialism: Sketch for a Theory of Collaboration," in *Studies in the Theory of Imperialism*, ed. R. Owen and B. Sutcliffe, 117–41 (London: Longman, 1972); R. McVey, "The Materialization of the Southeast Asian Entrepreneur," in *Southeast Asian Capitalists*, ed. R. McVey (Ithaca: Cornell University Southeast Asia Program, 1992), 7–34.

Though marine goods traders possess only an echo of the importance they once had in helping to prop up intraregional systems of exchange, in numerical and value terms these trades are actually larger and richer than they have ever been. This is in keeping with the growth of Asian and global markets, and also with the rising abilities of human beings to elicit the varied riches of the sea in ever-larger numbers. It is clear that some of the centuries-old ways of "doing business" in this arena are still with the Chinese marine goods sellers of East and Southeast Asia, and that some of their own specific traits and traditions as a community have been lost, or are quickly being lost right now. This has to do with the passage of time, but it also has much to do with shifting perceptions of what is important, profitable, and desirable for Chinese families and Chinese family firms, whose interests used to overlap, possibly more so than they often do today.[81] The outstretched community of Chinese marine goods traders is a very useful population to question and map some of these changes in commercial history, as this trade—like many others—tries to fit itself into the dictates of the modern commercial world.[82] Using a combined approach of historical and ethnographic methods allows us to see these changes over time and space. It also allows us to glimpse today's practitioners of these trades as part of a historical continuum of families and migrations going back centuries into the region's past.[83]

81. B. Benedict, "Family Firms and Economic Development," *Southwestern Journal of Anthropology* 24, no. 1 (1968): 1–19; A. Sen, "Economics and the Family," *Asian Development Review* 1, no. 2 (1983): 14–26.

82. Aihwa Ong, *Flexible Citizenship: The Cultural Logics of Transnationality* (Durham: Duke University Press, 1999); William G Ouchi, "Markets, Bureaucracies and Clans," *Administrative Science Quarterly* 25 (1980): 129–41.

83. See Yangwen Zhang, *China on the Sea: How the Maritime World Shaped Modern China* (Leiden: Brill, 2014); Gang Zhao, *The Qing Opening to the Ocean: Chinese Maritime Policies, 1684–1757* (Honolulu: University of Hawai'i Press, 2013); and Lin Sun, "The Economy of Empire Building: Wild Ginseng, Sable Fur, and the Multiple Trade Networks of the Early Qing Dynasty, 1583–1644"(PhD diss., Oxford University, 2018).

11

On the Docks

HOW INDIA'S SOUTHERN COASTS BECAME "SPICE CENTRAL"

We sell these spices everywhere. India is the mother of this trade.

—MALAYALAM SPICE WHOLESALER, COCHIN,
KERALA, SOUTH INDIA[1]

IN AN IMPORTANT but (to my mind) under-cited article, the great Southeast Asian historian/political scientist Ruth McVey examined what she called the "materialization" of Southeast Asian entrepreneurs in the history of the region.[2] Connecting "material" and the ethnic traders who carried commodities of all descriptions near and far in this watery domain, McVey was touching on concepts locally that were already becoming important elsewhere in the global word of trade, and across larger vistas. Indeed, pioneers such as Edna Bonacich and Ronald Robinson had already been probing into the theoretical underpinnings of middlemen minorities, in all their variate manifestations, as well as their role in the architecture of the imperial age—both concepts that became crucial in the evolution of ethnic theory in the 1980s and 1990s.[3] Other

1. Author's fieldwork notes, January 2012.

2. R. McVey, "The Materialization of the Southeast Asian Entrepreneur," in *Southeast Asian Capitalists*, ed. R. McVey, 7–34 (Ithaca: Cornell University Southeast Asia Program, 1992).

3. Edna Bonacich, "A Theory of Middleman Minorities," in *Majority and Minority: The Dynamics of Racial and Ethnics Relations*, 2nd ed., ed. N. R. Yetman and C. H. Steele, 77–89 (Boston: Allyn and Bacon, 1975); and R. Robinson, "Non-European Foundations of European Imperialism: Sketch for a Theory of Collaboration," in *Studies in the Theory of Imperialism*, ed. R. Owen and B. Sutcliffe, 117–41 (London: Longman, 1972).

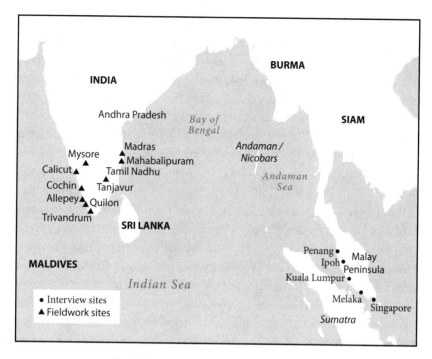

MAP 11.1. South Asian Waters: The Malabar and Coromandel Coasts

early proponents of this branch of study were also looking at what they termed "cultural strategies" in the organization of trading diasporas, as well as the ethnic contradictions of merchant capital, in places such as India and colonial East Africa.[4] Indeed, the economics of the family and the "clan" became one of the great new possibilities in the historical research of both capitalism and development, with foundational figures such as Amartya Sen and others all questioning the received wisdom of a generation of scholars, most of them reared on a steady diet of Marx and Engels in the unfolding of these questions.[5]

4. A. Cohen, "Cultural Strategies in the Organization of Trading Diasporas," in *The Development of Indigenous Trade and Markets in West Africa*, ed. C. Meillassoux, 266–80 (London: Oxford University Press, 1971); Z. Bader, "The Contradictions of Merchant Capital 1840–1939," in *Zanzibar under Colonial Rule*, ed. A. Sheriff and E. Ferguson, 163–87 (London: James Curry, 1991).

5. Amartya Sen, "Economics and the Family," *Asian Development Review* 1, no. 2 (1983): 14–26; and B. Benedict, "Family Firms and Economic Development," *Southwestern Journal of Anthropology* 24, no. 1 (1968): 1–19.

In this chapter, we examine how two places—southern India and the Malay Peninsula—have become connected by the maritime spice trade over time.[6] This work continues a trend in recent historical literature of looking at particular commodities as windows into historical processes.[7] I begin the chapter by looking at some of the wider theoretical implications of ethnicity in analyzing connections formed by traders of various groups, in this case "Chinese," "Jews," and "Indians," all encapsulated as trading communities. The second part of the chapter then pans to the historical development of India's coasts as a site for the maritime transshipment of spices, mainly in the early modern age, but also slightly prior to and after this high point of the transit. The final part of the chapter, which is also the longest, is made-up oral history interviews and fieldwork I did on the Malabar and Coromandel coasts of South India, as well as in Malaysia and Singapore, across the Bay of Bengal from these Indian locales. Some twenty interview sessions with ethnically Indian spice traders show us some of the modern legacy of the maritime spice trade, as it now takes place in our own world after the age of empire (because of these transtemporal connections, I use historical names on the map). I argue in this chapter that the transit of spices managed to connect worlds that previously were mostly (though not entirely) separate, and also managed to seed Indians on the Southeast Asian side of the eastern Indian Ocean as part of this process. Migration and commerce here were closely interlinked, in other words, both

6. I am guided in this exercise by a range of scholarship some of which has been previously cited in chapter 5; here I should also mention the helpful overview provided by Edward Alpers, *The Indian Ocean: A World History* (New York: Oxford University Press, 2014); Michael Pearson, *The World of the Indian Ocean, 1500–1800: Studies on Economic, Social, and Cultural History* (Aldershot, UK: Ashgate, 2005); and Thomas Metcalf, ed., *Imperial Connections: India in the Indian Ocean Arena, 1860–1920* (Berkeley: University of California Press, 2007).

7. One of the most important scholars to start this trend was Sidney Mintz with sugar, but the legacy of that book has been felt across a wide range of commodities, and by their accompanying historians. See Sidney W. Mintz, *Sweetness and Power: The Place of Sugar in Modern History* (New York: Penguin Books, 1985); Judith A. Carney, *Black Rice: The African Origins of Rice Cultivation in the Americas* (Cambridge: Harvard University Press, 2002); William Gervase Clarence-Smith, and Steven Topik, eds. *The Global Coffee Economy in Africa, Asia, and Latin America, 1500–1989* (New York: Cambridge University Press, 2003); Marcy Norton, *Sacred Gifts, Profane Pleasures: A History of Tobacco and Chocolate in the Atlantic World* (Ithaca: Cornell University Press, 2010); Sarah Abrevaya Stein, *Plumes: Ostrich Feathers, Jews, and a Lost World of Global Commerce* (New Haven: Yale University Press, 2010); Sven Beckert, *Empire of Cotton: A Global History* (New York: Alfred A. Knopf, 2014).

historically and today. Through conversations with many of these traders we can see these links, as they attach to longer histories of trade and movement on the wings of the spice trade in this very fluid part of the world.

Comparative Dimensions

Thinking about the role of capitalism and ethnic entrepreneurship in various cultures is instructive, because these patterns did not happen in quite the same ways everywhere, nor at the same time. In this chapter I will be looking at some of these dynamics across the Bay of Bengal and through the window of Indian traders and the spices they traded, but it is clear that the very idea of ethnicity and its connectivity with commerce is very much on the mind of the academy, in various guises. This interest, of course, has a genealogy, some of which goes back quite a while in time.[8] Some of these early ideas were then appropriated by others as they sought to use insights on so-called ethnic exceptionalisms to look at trading and ethnic communities in less-commonly researched parts of the world.[9] Yet other scholars also took this same ball and ran with it conceptually, perhaps most famously Philip Curtin in his much-lauded *Cross-Cultural Trade in World History*.[10] In that book, Curtin analyzed the role of ethnic communities in trading various commodities in different eras and across disparate geographies, and came up with a transhistorical template for what he saw. In the 1990s, then, other—sometimes less serious—attempts were made to apply these logics to the general explosion of capitalism that was being seen at the time. The result was a publishing "moment" whereby sober (and occasionally less sober) scholarship was all being produced concomitantly, all of it purporting to explain the rise of ethnic business in a hyper-capitalist world.[11]

8. M. Weber, *The Protestant Ethic and the Spirit of Capitalism*, 2nd ed. (London: George Allen & Unwin, 1976); and Stanislav Andreski, *Max Weber on Capitalism, Bureaucracy, and Religion: A Selection of Texts* (London: Allen & Unwin, 1983).

9. R. E. Kennedy, "The Protestant Ethic and the Parsis," *American Journal of Sociology* 68 (1962–63): 11–20.

10. P. D. Curtin, *Cross-Cultural Trade in World History* (Cambridge: Cambridge University Press, 1984).

11. Stewart Clegg and S. Gordon Redding, eds. *Capitalism in Contrasting Cultures* (Berlin: De Gruyter, 1990); and Joel Kotkin, *Tribes: How Race, Religion, and Identity Determine Success in the New Global Economy* (New York: Random House, 1993).

Since much of the writing on this topic started in Europe, the first group often associated with this sort of analysis was a European "ethnic" group—in this case, Jews. Jewish communities in Europe had long been seen as "ethnic outsiders" of a sort; facile at business (supposedly), handy in the role of middlemen, and used as such by various elites across the continent. Much of the ground zero of ethnic commercial analysis started with Jewish traders in different parts of Europe, and their links to the rise of capitalism during the seventeenth and eighteenth centuries. Though it took a while for it to be said, it finally came across in the more sober accounts that Jews were mostly forced into such roles by discriminatory practices elsewhere—over the holding of land, for example, but in other ways, too.[12] The literature on Jews as outsiders is voluminous, and is mostly out of the purview of this chapter. But we should note that it did not take too long for Jews to start to be compared to other groups who seemed to share some of the same attributes as mercantile minorities. This sort of comparative examination started some decades ago, but really got going in the 1990s, when (again) global capitalism was in a vigorous, expansive mode and its many attributes (including its actors grouped into communities) needed to be explained.[13] Often the first ethnic minority that was paired together with Jews for analysis in this way were the Chinese, especially when seen as outsiders in a variety of global societies.[14]

The Chinese were useful foils to European Jews because historically they spread out at least as far as the Jewish community, and they were often held

---

12. S. Z. Klausner, "Introduction," in *The Jews and Modern Capitalism*, ed. W. Sombart, xv–cxxv (New Brunswick and London: Transaction Books, 1982). See also Avner Greif's writings on this in the Maghreb, and of course Francesca Trivellato, *The Familiarity of Strangers: The Sephardic Diaspora, Livorno, and Cross-Cultural Trade in the Early Modern Period* (New Haven: Yale University Press, 2012).

13. D. S. Eitzen, "Two Minorities: The Jews of Poland and the Chinese of the Philippines," *Jewish Journal of Sociology* 10, no. 2 (1968): 221–40; and Gary G. Hamilton, "The Organizational Foundations of Western and Chinese Commerce: A Historical Perspective and Comparative Analysis," in Gary G. Hamilton, *Business Networks and Economic Development in East and Southeast Asia*, 48–65 (Hong Kong: Centre of Asian Studies, University of Hong Kong, 1991). For a more current interpretation, see Kaveh Yazdani and Dilip Menon, eds., *Capitalism: Toward a Global History* (Oxford: Oxford University Press, 2020).

14. The best modern example of this sort of scholarship is probably Daniel Chirot and Anthony Reid, eds., *Essential Outsiders: Chinese and Jews in the Modern Transformation of Southeast Asia and Central Europe* (Seattle: University of Washington Press, 1997).

with as little esteem by their "host" societies. Frequently depicted as parasitic and indeed superfluous to indigenous needs, both Chinese and Jews suffered from the same structural impediment to their welfare: the lack of a state that was willing to back them in their overseas commercial enterprises. Europeans of a variety of stripes in the age of global expansion possessed very different support than this vis-à-vis their own economic undertakings. Englishmen could count on the British crown to look after their interests in many (though not all) cases, as could the French, Dutch, Portuguese, and Spanish, among other European trading communities. The Chinese almost never could rely on Peking to back their interests when abroad, and had to develop a mode of mercantile activity that took this central political fact into everyday, economic account. Therefore, support from Chinese clan and sub-dialect associations, often known as *kongsis* in Western writing of the nineteenth and even twentieth centuries, was for more important than any macro-, political support from Chinese shores.[15] In Southeast Asia, where most Chinese merchants and indeed communities ended up, this meant dispersion patterns whereby Hokkien often followed Hokkien, Cantonese followed Cantonese, Hakka moved toward other Hakka, etc. The layout of many Chinese communities throughout Southeast Asia even now bears testament to these proclivities and these choices.[16] It is not an accident that even today we find more Teochew-speakers in Bangkok than anywhere else in Southeast Asia; more Cantonese speakers in Kuala Lumpur, and numerous Hakka-descended communities in Western Borneo. Commerce enabled migration, and migration in turn facilitated an expansion in commerce. This was the Chinese pattern, for the most part, across wide swaths of Southeast Asia's seas.[17]

If the dispersion of Chinese communities in Southeast Asia looked this way, then Indian communities in the same region shared many of these same characteristics. The figure of the Indian moneylender—long a trope in certain parts of Southeast Asia—dominated some landscapes in the same way that

15. Chan-kwok Bun and Ng Beoy Kui, "Myths and Misperceptions of Ethnic Chinese Capitalism," in *Chinese Business Networks*, ed. Chan Kwok Bun (Singapore: Prentice Hall, 2000).

16. Harry Harding, "The Concept of 'Greater China': Themes, Variations and Reservations," *China Quarterly* 136 (December 1993): 660–86.

17. Hamilton, ed., *Business Networks*; and Leo Suryadinata, ed., *Southeast Asian Chinese and China: The Politico-economic Dimension* (Singapore: Times Academic Press, 1995).

the Chinese *towkay* did in others. Though there were indeed some real differences between these groups as entrepreneurial minorities, some significant inroads have been made in the past few decades in comparing their similar functions in their respective host societies.[18] The group known as *chettiars*, especially—a caste from southeastern India that eventually became synonymous with moneylending as a profession through much of colonial Southeast Asia, at least near colonial enterprises—became almost universally despised as parasites by indigenes in large parts of the region.[19] Though Chinese merchants were found all over the "lands beneath the winds," the clearest examples of the Indian variants are often found in Burma, which was geographically closest to the British Raj, and to India itself as a site of migratory outflow.[20] There, in the frontier regions separating what we now typify as South and Southeast Asia, Indian merchant minorities connected what we presently see as separate worlds, even if these separations are mostly academic, and for area studies (academic) purposes. But in this respect Indian merchants and Chinese merchants, too, give the lie to how artificial these divisions really were, and continue to be. These commercial minorities provided the sinew of connection through their products and their migratory practices over hundreds of years. In the Indian case, they connected worlds across the Bay of Bengal that were brought together through their travels. It is to the

18. C. Dobbin, "From Middleman Minorities to Industrial Entrepreneurs: The Chinese in Java and the Parsis in Western India 1619–1939," *Itinerario* 13, no. 1 (1989): 109–32; R. K. Ray, "Chinese Financiers and Chetti Bankers in Southern Water: Asian Mobile Credit during the Anglo-Dutch Competition for the Trade of the Eastern Archipelago in the Nineteenth Century," *Itinerario* 11, no. 1 (1987): 209–34; K. A. Yambert, "Alien Traders and Ruling Elites: The Overseas Chinese in Southeast Asia and the Indians in East Africa," *Ethnic Groups* 3 (1981): 173–78.

19. W. G. Clarence Smith, "Indian Business Communities in the Western Indian Ocean in the Nineteenth Century," *Indian Ocean Review* 2, no. 4 (1989); 18–21; and H. D. Evers, "Chettiar Moneylenders in Southeast Asia," in *Marchands et hommes d'affaires asiatiques dans l'Océan Indien et la Mer de Chine 13e-20e siècles*, ed. D. Lombard and J. Aubin, 199–219 (Paris: Éditions de l'école des hautes études, 1987).

20. See M. Adas, "Immigrant Asians and the Economic Impact of European Imperialism: The Role of South Indian Chettiars in British Burma," *Journal of Asian Studies* 33, no. 3 (1974): 385–401; N. R. Chakravati, *The Indian Minority in Burma: The Rise and Decline of an Immigrant Community* (London, Oxford University Press, 1985); and R. Mahadevan, "Immigrant Entrepreneurs in Colonial Burma—An Exploratory Study of the Role of Nattukottai Chattiars of Tamil Nadu, 1880–1930," *Indian Economic and Social History Review* 15, no. 3 (1978): 329–58.

construction of those worlds historically—especially in the early modern era—
that we now turn.

Historical Dimensions

The place of spices in bringing together the world is well documented by now;
few items in transit had as much impact, and as much valence in and of themselves, as spices did in helping to fashion world history over the past five hundred years. It was of course spices that Columbus was looking for when he
"discovered" the Americas by accident, but for our purposes the voyages of a
number of other explorers—da Gama, de Albuquerque, and others—are
more pertinent. It is enough to say here that when the Portuguese (and the
Dutch, French, and English after them) spilled into the Indian Ocean in the
late fifteenth, sixteenth, and seventeenth centuries, that the spice trade was
already well under way, with India in many ways at its center. Indian spices had
traveled to the world of Mediterranean antiquity via the Persian Gulf and the
Red Sea, and Alexandria became famed throughout the Mediterranean basin
as a place to purchase Asia's spices via the European merchants of many nations.[21] Constantinople, née Istanbul, later took on this same function, with
the rise of the Ottoman world around this time. Though it seems clear that
spices from as far away as eastern Indonesia and even parts of the Sinicized
world were available in Europe at an early date, for the most part it was India's
aromatics that were prized most in this transoceanic commerce moving west.
The history of the spice trade has, in fact, become a publishing cottage industry
of sorts, with a large number of books now telling this story with various
degrees of scholarly authority.[22]

21. See, for example, Italian sources explaining some of these histories in F. Sassetti a S.E. il
Cardinale F. de' Medici in *Lettere edite e inedite di Filippo Sassetti*, raccolte e annotate da E. Marcucci (Florence, 1855): "Cochin 10 febbraio," 379–80; Francesco Sassetti, "Notizie dell'origine e
nobiltá della famiglia de' Sassetti," in *Lettere edite e inedite*, xli; and D. Catellacci, "Curiose notizie
di anonimo viaggiatore fiorentino all'Indie nel secolo XVII," *Archivio Storico Italiano* 28, no. 223
(1901): 120.

22. For just a few of these studies, see Paul Freedman, *Out of the East: Spices and the Medieval
Imagination* (New Haven: Yale University Press, 2008); Charles Corn, *The Scents of Eden: A
History of the Spice Trade* (New York: Kodansha, 1999); John Keay, *The Spice Route: A History*
(Berkeley: University of California Press, 2007), Gary Paul Nabhan, *Cumin, Camels, and Cara-
vans: A Spice Odyssey* (Berkeley: University of California Press, 2014).

India has also produced some of this scholarship itself, as Indian scholars began to write the early modern history of their own ports and regions, especially in the 1970s in the wake of independence and nation-building. Much of this story in terms of the commodities trade began in Gujarat, the arid state in Western India which was a kind of ground zero for Western-Indian interactions from the late fifteenth century onward.[23] Gujarat was not too far from Delhi, where the Mughal Empire was centered, so records on the interface between civilizations were kept from both sides, with spices and other agricultural commodities of the region forming the sinew of contact. Surat became the most important port during the early period in connecting these worlds, though it was really only replicating in some ways earlier incarnations of coastal cities (such as Bharygaza) whose histories stretched back even to Roman times.[24] The Portuguese were highly involved in this early modern trade, and eventually ports such as Diu—and Goa farther south—were incorporated into the larger web of Portuguese empire that was spinning through Asia.[25] Yet the Dutch became far more important players than the Portuguese by the late seventeenth century in funneling Gujarat's products to the rest of the world. Though the Dutch never managed to acquire much territory in India (less than the Portuguese before them, and certainly far less than the English after them), their own economic tendrils ended up having far more vitality than the Portuguese networks, and Gujarat's plants, barks, and resins traveled more often in VOC bottoms than in Iberian ones as times went on.[26]

To the south, in India, there were two other broad coastlines on the subcontinent that also played major roles in the growth and distribution of spices.[27] The Coromandel coast in southeastern India became important especially in the distribution of spices (and other commodities) to Southeast Asia,

23. For an overview of early modern patterns here, see Lakshmi Subramanian, *The Sovereign and the Pirate: Ordering Maritime Subjects in India's Western Littoral* (New Delhi: Oxford University Press, 2016).

24. B. G. Gokhale, *Surat in the Seventeenth Century: A Study of the Urban History of Pre-Modern India* (Bombay: Popular Prkashan, 1979).

25. N. Steensgaard, *The Asian Trade Revolution of the Seventeenth Century: The East India Companies and the Decline of the Caravan Trade* (Chicago: University of Chicago Press, 1974).

26. Ann Bos Radwan, *The Dutch in Western India, 1601–1632* (Calcutta, Firma KLM, 1978); H. W. van Santen, "De verenigde Oost-Indische Compagnie in Gujarat en Hindustan 1620–1660" (Leiden University, PhD thesis, 1982).

27. For an excellent study of some of these patterns, see David Ludden, *Early Capitalism and Local History in South Asia* (New York: Oxford University Press, 2005).

FIGURE 11.1. Cinnamon from Sri Lanka (author's photo)

a story that will greatly concern us here.[28] Most of the merchants here were Hindus (though there were indeed some Muslims involved in some of the trades), and these Hindu traders often came from castes that had been dealing with these specific lines of commerce for many generations. Unlike in Gujarat, there were few natural harbors of any significance on the Coromandel, so trade was much more spread out along the coast, and in fact waxed and waned with the politics of various city-states and their attendant regions over time. The monsoon evened out any natural advantages of the topography by making trade very possible and profitable at some points of the year, and next to impossible at other times, so most local merchants were in fact more or less in the same boat, with few advantages. Also unlike Gujarat, Portuguese coercion had less presence in southeastern India than in the Gulf of Cambay, too, though there were indeed Portuguese trading settlements, such as at Nagapatnam, and at Mylapore (San Thome) and on the Vellar River (Porto Novo). These factories served commerce to Southeast Asia, but also farther north up the Indian coasts to Hughli in Bengal, and eventually to Burma.[29]

28. See Geneviève Bouchon, "Le sud-ouest de l'Inde dans l'imaginaire européen au début du XVIe siècle: Du mythe à la réalité," in *Asia Maritima: Images et réalité: Bilder und Wirklichkeit 1200–1800*, ed. Denys Lombard and Roderich Ptak (Wiesbaden: Harrassowitz Verlag, 1994).

29. See, for example, Sinnappah Arasaratnam, *Maritime India in the Seventeenth Century* (Delhi: Oxford University Press, 1994), chapter 5.

FIGURE 11.2. Malabar Coast Landscape (author's photo)

Yet the locus classicus of the spice trade on the Indian subcontinent was the Malabar coast, in the southwest part of the peninsula, pointing dagger-like into the heart of the Indian Ocean.[30] This was where spices, for the most part, grew best, as rainfall coming off the nearly vertical Western Ghats—coupled with soil salinity—created conditions ripe for the production of such plants.[31] Pepper, turmeric, coriander, and other spices all grew here naturally, and with great fecundity; pepper in particular became the motor of the Indian Ocean spice trade.[32] The city-states that were active on the Malabar coast during the early modern period were cosmopolitan and diverse: Hindus, Muslims, Christians, and Jews all rubbed shoulders in the ports, and places such as Calicut and Cochin became world-famous centers for the collection, marketing, and transshipment of spices in volume. The Portuguese desperately tried to control this trade, seeing that doing so would make them rich in the global markets for these goods, as they fetched fantastic prices back in Europe, but were highly valued also elsewhere along the routes. The famed Portuguese *cartaz*, or passport, was enacted on these coasts, to try to police and compel locals into selling and transporting spices only to the Portuguese.[33] In this way a monopoly could be established. That never fully worked out, and the advent of Portuguese power in these waters has been exaggerated in early scholarship on the trade here. But it is incontrovertible that the Portuguese did have a major effect on the movement and supply of spices in the fifteenth and sixteenth centuries. By the later seventeenth century, however,

30. French scholarship has been particularly good on this region; see Geneviève Bouchon, "Mamale de Cananor," *Un adversaire de l'Inde portugaise (1507–1528)*, EPHE IV, (Geneva and Paris, 1975); Geneviève Bouchon, "L'Asie du Sud à l'époque des grandes découvertes" (London: Variorum Reprints 1987); and Claude Cahen, "Le commerce musulman dans l'Océan Indien au Moyen Age," in *Sociétés et compagnies de commerce en Orient et dans l'Océan Indien*, ed. M. Mollat (Paris: SEVPEN, 1970), 179–93.

31. The verticality of the Western Ghats needs to be seen to be believed. The incredible drop from the heights of the mountains down to the coasts allows for massive amounts of moisture to be captured by the soil. This same soil then produces spices in abundance, both in the valleys and coastal strip below, and also in the foothills of the Ghats themselves.

32. See Sebastian Prange, "Measuring by the Bushel: Reweighing the Indian Ocean Pepper Trade," *Historical Research* 84, no. 224 (May 2011): 212–35.

33. For some good background on this, see Sanjay Subrahmanyam, *The Career and Legend of Vasco da Gama* (Cambridge: Cambridge University Press, 1997); see also Geneviève Bouchon, "A Microcosm: Calicut in the Sixteenth Century," in *Asian Merchants and Businessmen in the Indian Ocean and the China Sea*, ed. Denys Lombard and Jan Aubin (Oxford: Oxford University Press, 2000).

Lisbon was a fading force in international politics, and the Dutch and others became more involved with these transit trades, carrying spices from Malabar all over the world. Some of these plants were in fact regrown successfully by the Dutch, British, and French in other tropical outposts, or even in botanical gardens back in European metropoles. By the nineteenth century spices became common enough that they no longer held the cachet (nor the cash value) that they once did, but they were still valuable enough to grow and export over long, maritime distances. It is to that story that we now turn, as colonial Indians began to move alongside these cargoes to other points in the Indian Ocean.[34]

Modern Dimensions

This second half of the chapter looks at how the transit of spice between South India and Southeast Asia looks now, through the window of interviews, mainly, in family-run spice enterprises in the latter locale. I did some twenty interviews with Indian family spice businesses in Singapore, Melaka, Kuala Lumpur, Ipoh, and Penang (in other words, in ports and towns all along the Malay Peninsula, facing the Bay of Bengal to the west). I also spoke to the Singapore Manufacturers Association and the Kuala Lumpur Indian Chamber of Commerce, who look at these spice-trade patterns from a wider, macroeconomic lens. Information gleaned from these various interviews follows below. Finally, I also did fieldwork in a number of South Asian locales on both the Coromandel and Malabar coasts, to look at how Indian spices were grown and eventually passed on for shipment to Southeast Asia across the Bay of Bengal (they also went in the other direction; see Appendix C on Yemeni herbalists, for example, who also get some of their supplies from India). I will describe that latter process only very quickly here, as much of that information is being written up for publication separately in another place. My fieldwork in South India took me from Madras south to Mahabalipuram and Tanjavur in the heart of Tamil Nadu, to Trivandrum, Quilon, Allepey, Cochin, and Calicut on the Malabar coast (I use the older spellings of all of these places here, in accord with the history of the spice trade in these spaces), where much of India's main spice belt is in operation. These travels thus passed from a very dry,

---

34. Places such as Kew Gardens outside London and the Hortus Botanicus in Leiden were crucial to these processes. The history of the spice trade in global decline, after its heyday from the fifteenth to the eighteenth centuries, has yet to be adequately told.

unforgiving landscape in parts of Tamil Nadhu to an extremely verdant and wet one in Kerala, before I eventually ended up in Mysore and then Bangalore, up on the Deccan Plateau.[35] In all of these places I was looking into the life transit of spices as a product, but also into the ways in which the growing, transport, and sale of the commodity impacted local lives and local cultural formations.

Because my focus in this chapter is on movement, both of spices themselves and of the Indian communities who ended up traveling to Southeast Asia to pursue this commerce as a livelihood, here I will give only in briefest form an idea of the South Asian fieldwork component of this research. I was able to travel very freely over two fieldwork stints in South India (in 1990 and 2012, some two decades apart) to look at the ways in which spice production was incorporated into local communities, and at the same time also into wider networks of transoceanic exchange. In places such as Madras, Mahablipuram, and Tanjavur, these patterns connect to Southeast Asia mainly through human migration. In fact, most of the Indians now living and working in the Singaporean and Malaysian cities I mention above hail from Tamil Nadu, either themselves or (more commonly) their parents, grandparents, or great-grandparents having been born there.[36] Often these genealogies stretch back several generations, as there were Indian laborers and artisans documented in some of the first British ships erecting settlements on the Malay coasts in the late eighteenth century. I have described these historical processes in greater detail elsewhere, but for our purposes here it should be clear that Tamil Nadu often contributes the human element to the Bay of Bengal spice diasporas that interest us.[37] The more material element of this exchange is often provided by Kerala (so, the Malabar coast rather than the Coromandel), as the spices themselves tend to be more from this state rather than from the southeastern part of the Indian peninsula. As I traveled up the Kerala coast talking to people, and observing the growing, bundling, and then transport of pepper, turmeric, cumin, and coriander (among other spices), it became clear that some of them

35. My interviewing of spice traders in Southeast Asia and also field site visits on South India happened courtesy of grants from the Thomas Watson Foundation (in 1990) and also the Hong Kong Institute for Social Sciences at the University of Hong Kong, 2012. I am deeply grateful to both institutions, which made these trips possible.

36. See the massive volume produced by K. Sandhu and A. Mani, *Indians in South East Asia* (Singapore: ISEAS, 1993).

37. See Tagliacozzo, *Secret Trades, Porous Borders*; the last two chapters have information pertinent here.

were heading east to Southeast Asia.[38] The vast rainfall that spills off the (at places) near-vertical Western Ghats drenches Kerala's soil with water, which is perfect in getting spice crops out of the ground. By the time I had made my way up to Mysore and Bangalore on the Deccan, and into a third microclimate where sandalwood and other aromatics then took precedence, one could visibly see the differences between the environments and the systems, all geographically close to one another on a small-scale map.[39]

It was important to undertake these travels to the sites of spice production to see how the transit starts in South India. On the other side of the Bay of Bengal, however, we can find the *destination* of some of this spice, and also of the Indian merchants who ended up coming there to facilitate this trade. It seemed important, along the lines given to us by Gayatri Spivak in her much-cited article, "Can the Subaltern Speak," to try to converse with some of these families, not least because, as Spivak tells us: "the contemporary international division of labor is a displacement of the divided field of nineteenth-century Imperialism."[40] So there is a strong connection here, across the Bay of Bengal, one that is both temporal and geographic. Much of the rest of this chapter deals with the interviews I did in the Bay of Bengal with these merchant families, but I also spent time at two institutions that help to manage the spice trade between South India and Southeast Asia, and which allow us to see larger visions of the trade. These were at the Singapore Manufacturers Association (SMA) and the Kuala Lumpur Indian Chamber of Commerce (KLICC). The former institution is important in that it shows through its records the scale of spice commerce that has made Singapore one of the world leaders in this commodity's trade. It also gives us a sense of the range of players involved.

For Indian actors in the city-state, this includes subinstitutions like the Indo Commercial Society, which was itself linked into the Bank of India, the Indian Bank, and the Indian Overseas Bank, three Indian-run financial institutions that support the spice trade. Also working through the SMA were K. Ramanlal and Co. and Ratansing and Co., Indian spice-trading concerns, as well as Latiff

---

38. I was told this numerous times during interviews, but it was also apparent from loading orders on the docks; shipments of spice were in constant motion to Southeast Asian ports, among them Singapore, Port Kelang, Penang, etc.

39. Mysore actually smells like sandalwood; so much of it is around that its scent permeates the city itself.

40. Gayatri Spivak, "Can the Subaltern Speak," in *Marxism and the Interpretation of Culture*, ed. Cary Nelson and Lawrence Grossburg (Basingstoke: Macmillan, 1988).

and Sons, who helped on the manufacturing side of the spice business. The records on Nims Pte Ltd., a joint Indo-Chinese spice concern, showed that were cross-ethnic alliances being formed to enhance profits as well. These were some of the players; what about the spices themselves? Indians in Singapore were vital in getting South Indian spices to locales further afield from the Asian tropics. From the SMA records, it became clear that Singapore was a clearinghouse of sorts, sending Indian black pepper, for example (the most valuable single spice by volume in the SMA trade) to places such as the US, Egypt, and Pakistan, the top three end destinations of this spice. White pepper (as opposed to the majority black pepper just reported on) went to Germany instead, while chilies went to Malaysia and cinnamon to Bangladesh, both presumably to make curries. Cumin was transshipped to Yemen, ginger to Pakistan, and ginseng to Hong Kong. By scrolling through the SMA's records, we can get quite a good sense of the macrodimensions of the Indian–Southeast Asian spice trade as a whole along these lines.[41]

In Malaysia, a similar but slightly more specialized function was performed by the Kuala Lumpur Indian Chamber of Commerce (KLICC). The KLICC was in fact founded in 1928 by Indian spice and textile merchants; its first president, Mr. R. E. Mohamed Kassim, was a spice mogul, and made his fortune in the trade. Officials I spoke with at the KLICC pointed out almost immediately to me that Indians had fallen behind Chinese in Malaysia in dealing with the spice trade. Indian businesses were in fact dependent on Chinese transport for their spices, and the Chinese were now dealing in toto with larger volumes. Indians, I was told, did better in the spice trade facing west from Malaysia, rather than in Southeast Asia as a whole. Toward the Middle East, Africa, and (because of Cold War ties) to the former Soviet bloc countries, Indian networks still reigned supreme when it came to spices. Singapore, in fact, was the dividing line between the two ethnic spheres: to the west of Singapore, Indian capital controlled most of the spice trade, and to the east and north of the city-state, Chinese firms had gradually become more important. Efficiency, officials said to me, was key. Malay and Indonesian spice merchants

---

41. I am grateful to the men and women of the Singapore Manufacturers Association who received me and opened many of their records to my inquiries when I was there. This repository has a huge amount of information on the day-to-day conduct of the spice trade in Southeast Asia, and with Singapore serving a central place in that trade, the information I was able to glean there was invaluable too me in sussing out broad patterns of distribution and redistribution in the region.

should be able to run these trades themselves by now, I was told, but they can't, because they have not learned "modern" business techniques of how to pool and preserve capital on a large scale. I was informed that Hindu and Muslim differences in the Indian community did not factor into competition or rivalry between these groups. The affinities were too strong, everyone being Indian, and the "enemy" (at least in terms of the spice industry) was seen to be Chinese, not a religious "other" inside one's own community. All of these observations were fascinating, especially in the self-perceptions revealed of how Indians—classically the main proprietors of the spice trade—saw themselves as basically under siege in a preserve once much more wholly their own.[42] I followed up on some of these questions with individual Indian merchant firms and their proprietors, in the interviews I turn to in the pages below.

It's helpful to get a broad sense of where these Indian merchants came from. During the interviews I always asked first about genealogies, length of time in Southeast Asia, and the like. I can go over only some of that information here, but it gives us a feeling for the composition of the traders I spoke to in these meetings. In Singapore, Mr. S. Rasoo was fairly typical; his family was comprised of Hindus originally from Negapattinam in Tamil Nadu, and his father came to Southeast Asia in 1916, and started this business in 1935.[43] K. S. Abdul Latiff's father also started his own spice business, arriving in Singapore from Gandarvakottai near Madras in the early 1940s. As was the case with Mr. Rasoo's father, Mr. Abdul Latiff's father started out as a contract laborer on a rubber plantation, and moved into the spice trade only after that.[44] T. S. Abdul Jabbar's family originally also came from Negapatinum, and he remembered hearing from his father that it took five days in a steamer to cross the Bay of Bengal to Singapore, just a couple of decades prior to his own arrival in the 1940s.[45] K. S. Mohamed Haniffa's family arrived slightly later, in the early 1950s, from Madras, while the proprietor of the Thandapani Co. owed the business to his grandfather, who had come in the 1950s from Madurai.[46] Finally, a last useful example can be found in Kirtikar Mehta, unusual among the

---

42. I am equally grateful to the Kuala Lumpur and Selangor Indian Chamber of Commerce, which (like the SMA in Singapore) opened its doors and its books to me.

43. Interview with S. Rasoo and Co., Singapore, autumn 1989.

44. Interview with Abdul Latiff and Co., Singapore.

45. Interview with Abdul Jabbar and Co., Singapore.

46. Interview with Mohamed Haniffa Co. and Thandapani Co., both in Singapore.

Singaporean Indian spice merchants in that his family came from Gujarat (Ahmedabad), and not the Tamil South. His own father had come to Singapore in 1924, and had to learn the business from his cousin and work for him; he then handed the spice concern down to his own sons, who now ran it as their own.[47]

In Malaysia many of the same patterns on arrival and genealogy were present among Indian spice merchants in the country's Indian Ocean–facing cities and ports. In Melaka, for example, H. P. Jamal Mohamed's family came from Keelayoor, about four hundred miles from Madras. His father had been a shop assistant in another Indian spice concern and learned the business there; eventually he was able to strike out on his own. But his grandfather had also been in the business in Penang roughly a century ago, though his own venture had ultimately ended in bankruptcy, so Jamal Mohamad's father had to start from scratch.[48] In Kuala Lumpur, A. K. Muthan Chettiar's father came to Malaysia doing the ghee business (clarified butter, mostly for use in Hindu temples), but eventually ended up in spices as well. His family were Hindus from Dindigul, near Madurai, and they maintained a multigenerational focus on the spice trade in their own family.[49] Also in Kuala Lumpur, P. A. Abdul Wahab's family emigrated from Tamil Nadhu to Kelang, Kuala Lumpur's port, in the 1930s. Abdul Wahab's father had built one of the biggest Indian spice concerns at the time, which eventually had branch offices in Burma, Calcutta, and Madras, among other places.[50] In Ipoh, farther north of the capital and a former tin-mining town of great importance in British Malaya, Seeni Naina Mohamed's family came from Pamban, a small island off the Tamil coast near Sri Lanka. The proprietor there told me that the island had formerly been connected to the mainland by a bridge built by the Germans in the nineteenth century. His own grandfather had come to do spices in Ipoh in 1922, though by now all of his own relatives had gotten out of the trade—he was the only one left.[51] This sort of resignation was not unique to this Ipoh shop; in Penang, men like Mohamad Yusoff, assistant manager at Eusoff and Mohamed and Sons, also professed to feeling "trapped" in a stagnating world. His own family

---

47. Interview with Kirtikhar Mehta of K. Ramanla and Co., Singapore.
48. Interview with Jamal Mohamed and Co., Melaka.
49. Interview with A. K. Muthan Chettiar and Co., Kuala Lumpur.
50. Interview with P. A. Abdul Wahab and Co., Kuala Lumpur.
51. Interview with Seeni Naina Mohamed and Co., Ipoh.

had come from Bombay, so, again, an anomaly among the South India–centered genealogies of the group. They had been in Penang since 1916, though when partition came to the subcontinent in 1948 the main part of the brain trust of the company emigrated to Karachi.[52]

These familial precedents are all interesting, and are given in brief here—I have only touched on a percentage of the interviews in the above two paragraphs, to give some sense of the genealogies across the Andaman Sea. The multigenerational nature of the businesses is one factor that stands out; many of these families were second-, third-, or even fourth-generation spice traders, for one thing. In Singapore, K. S. Abdul Latiff opined that his two adult sons, both of whom were qualified marine engineers, might come back to run this business one day. If they left their shipping companies the door would always be open for them. Abdul Latiff said that this was (in his opinion) much more rewarding than working for a huge maritime transport concern, as his own business changed day to day and was full of new challenges.[53] S. Rasoo was less sanguine—the spice business in his view was a declining one from earlier times, and his own children did not have the experiential grounding to attempt it, so he felt it "would die with him," as he put it with some sadness.[54] The Thandapani merchant house was another instance of family coming together to begin a venture, with all the brothers working together for a time, before most of them went off to do their own lines of business after that. An elder brother was now in charge, but here (as elsewhere) the initial family unit had atomized to a degree over time, as sons sought their own fortunes.[55] The Gujurati concern of K. Ramanlal run by Kirtikar and Ramesh Mehta perhaps spoke for many of these spice merchants when they told me that the first of their line who came to start this business came with almost nothing. He came to Southeast Asia to try his luck as he had no formal education in India, and couldn't get work there. It took him fifteen years to get the experience he needed to make the business a success, but the capital to really float the trading house came from elsewhere. His father had the knowledge to make things work, but not the money. Both were needed to make a go of things in the spice trade of the twentieth century.[56]

52. Interview with Mohamad Yusoff and Co., Penang.

53. Interview with K. S. Abdul Latiff and Co., Singapore.

54. Interview with S. Rasoo and Co., Singapore.

55. Interview with Thandapani and Co., Singapore.

56. Interview with Kirtikar Mehta of K. Ramanlal and Co., Singapore.

Among the Malaysian spice merchants, a number of these patterns were similar, though some were markedly different. A common theme among some of the Malaysian Indian traders was that their forebears in the business had come to Singapore first. They decamped from Bay of Bengal steamers there, and then some pushed upcountry through the Malay Peninsula to find wage work (usually but not exclusively in the rubber plantations), or to try their luck as provisioners or spice merchants serving Indian migrant communities.[57] "Distance" took up more of the discussions with these traders, as they had to deal with it more as a concept than Singaporean traders did. Sometimes five-ton lorries (trucks) were hired to ply Malaysian highways for distribution of spices coming in from India, sometimes ten-ton lorries, depending on what and how much had come in.[58] One Ipoh merchant, up in the tin-bearing hills of northern Malaysia, told me that he was constantly on the phone placing orders to wholesalers in Penang, Port Kelang, and Singapore for spices, and then after this he'd be in touch with distributors to move the commodities to more local destinations:[59] "I am on the phone all day, most days. I get in very early, before it's hot, and I'm on the phone. I leave when it's starting to cool, and I'm still on the phone."[60]

R. A. Aziz of R.A. Ahamedsah Mohamed Sultan and Co. in Penang described commissioning agents on Market Street in that same port controlling most of the flow between foreign markets and the Malay Peninsula—and almost all of these agents, he said, were South Indians.[61] Communication took place in Tamil first, and then in English, especially between South and North Indians (the former refused as a point of principle to speak Hindi with the latter). Indeed, this was a common linguistic pattern in the trade: if one could get away with doing business in Tamil one did, but it was a requisite to know English for foreign transactions, and often Malay as well for commerce conducted inside the country's borders.

What spices were being traded, and from where to where to make all of these connections work? I took pages and pages of notes over many months

57. See for example, my interview with C. A. Ramu in Melaka, though this interview was typical of a number of others.

58. Interview with A. K. Muthan Chettiar and Co., Kuala Lumpur.

59. Interview with Seemi Naina Mohamed, Ipoh.

60. Seemi Naina Mohamed, interview notes, Ipoh, Malaysia, November 1989 [translation: E. Tagliacozzo].

61. Interview with R. A. Aziz, of R.A. Ahamedsah Mohamed Sultan and Co., Penang.

of interviews, so what follows below is only a snapshot. But the easy answer is: a vast array of spices from everywhere was traveling everywhere else—Indian merchants in Southeast Asia had become middlemen par excellence, and knew how to buy cheap and sell dear throughout the ecumene of global spices. In Singapore, the array of items I was told about (and shown in sacks on the floor) gives us an idea of where these commodities were coming from, just in one shop. K. S. Mohamed Haniffa imported the following items from (predominantly) the following places: cardamom from Africa; turmeric and coriander from India; black and white pepper from Sumatra and Java, respectively; fenugreek from India; mustard from Holland; cinnamon from Indonesia; turmeric from India; "weld cardamom" from Nepal; cloves from Zanzibar and Madagascar; star anise from China; fennel seed from India and Beirut; cumin from Iran and Turkey; betel nut from Malaysia; and coriander seeds from India.[62] Most of these items I knew fairly well by then, of course, but in other shops one could find less commonly traded spices, such as elba seeds from India and bochras from Indonesia in the Thandapani shop.[63] S. Rasoo told me in his store that Indian medicinal and ayurvedic herbs like asafoetida (and many others) were also available, but only if customers requested them specially.[64] This was important, because it was clear that there were reciprocal buying arrangements with Chinese spice and medicinal shops, whereby Chinese merchants would go to the Indian shops (in this case K. S. Abdul Latiff, who told me this) and vice versa for the opposite ethnic-based items.[65] But many spices now had numerous sites where they could be grown and purchased, such as cardamom, with that same merchant telling me that he received good stocks in it from India, but it was also now available in good quantities and decent prices from Guatemala. This was confirmed to me by T. S. Abdul Jabbar of Shaik Dawood and Sons.[66]

In Malaysia, an equally bewildering array of imported and exported spices was on show, from Melaka to Kuala Lumpur to Ipoh to Penang. In Melaka I was told of distinctions in the kinds of chilies that can be bought—the China-grown ones are hotter, the Indian-grown ones are rougher, so supplies were bought according to prevailing tastes. "I can sell you whichever ones you

---

62. Interview with K. S. Mohamed Haniffa and Co., Singapore.

63. Interview with Thandapani and Co., Singapore.

64. Interview with S. Rasoo and Co., Singapore.

65. Interview with K. S. Abdul Latiff and Co., Singapore.

66. Interview with T.S. Jabbar of Shaik Dawood and Sons, Singapore.

TABLE 11.1. Singapore Manufacturer's Association Spice Statistics, 1989

Total Exports in Spices, June 1989 and January to June, 1989, in Singapore Dollars

Country	June 1989	Jan. to June 1989
Bangladesh	$2,291,000	$6,683,000
Brunei	$193,000	$1,034,000
China	n.a.	$11,000
Yemen	$121,000	$432,000
Hong Kong	$594,000	$1,798,000
India	$265,000	$10,738,000
Japan	$1,271,000	$7,057,000
S. Korea	$932,000	$3,986,000
Kuwait	$262,000	$1,141,000
Malaysia	$1,987,000	$13,734,000
Nepal	$1,084,000	$4,842,000
Pakistan	$936,000	$11,450,000
Saudi Arabia	$1,089,000	$4,927,000
Sri Lanka	$40,000	$1,053,000
Taiwan	$323,000	$2,655,000
Thailand	$75,000	$429,000

Unground Black Pepper Exports, 6/89

Country	Kgs	Prince (S$)
Australia	22,200	$103,000
Bahrain	5,000	$20,000
Bangladesh	11,000	$45,000
Belgium	20,000	$94,000
Canada	55,480	$257,000
Chile	6,000	$24,000
Colombia	3,000	$13,000
Yemen	25,000	$102,000
Denmark	12,000	$69,000

Singapore Spice Exports and Majority Importer, 6/89

1. Pepper, white	Germany
2. Other peppers	India
3. Chilies dried/ground	Malaysia
4. Cinnamon	Banglad
5. Nutmeg	Holland
6. Cardamom	Pakistan
7. Coriander	Malaysia
8. Cumin	Yemen
9. Ginger	Pakistan

Source: Statistics collected by author while working at the Singapore Manufacturer's Association archive, 1989.

want, but maybe you should stay away from the Chinese ones. You're not from here, after all."[67]

Even inside India itself, there were distinctions to be made, as with coriander coming from Ganpoor or Indur, both in North India, or turmeric coming from the farmlands around Bangalore, in the south. Traders (such H. P. Jalam Mohamed in Melaka, in this case) made sure I understood these differences, as they had to, in order to be able to understand the markets.[68] Though South India was clearly the main provenance for many of the spices coming from across the Bay of Bengal, as per some of the historical distinctions we have already noted, it was also clear that Bombay still had a powerful pull as well. Cumin, fennel, and fenugreek all came from there in large quantities, and was usually bargained for in English, given the North/South language distinction in India previously mentioned.[69] If Bombay evoked the past in these terms, and the connection to a different era in terms of trading patterns, then connections with China could also do this at times, as with the sale of star anise from Canton to the Malay Peninsula. Here, too, English was used in these transactions.[70] Even the ethnic and subethnic distinctions we have explored earlier in this chapter raised their head on occasion, as when I was told in Kuala Lumpur that asafoetida and mustard were bought solely from Indian Muslim traders by P. A. Abdul Wahab and Sons.[71] Yet, as another merchant told me, a Muslim trader in Penang, there were no real problems between Muslim and Hindu shippers across the Bay of Bengal. "Whoever gives the best price," he told me. "Most of my customers in fact are Hindus."[72]

It was this sort of openness that made conducting these interviews more often than not a real pleasure. I want to end here with two quick windows into two of these interviews, one each in Singapore and Malaysia. I can describe here just a bit more about two of these individual merchants and their shops, as well as their worldviews, at least in miniature. In Singapore, Kirtikar Mehta of K. Ramanlal (a Gujarati concern) made a big impression on me. He spoke quickly and easily about his business, and clearly knew the ins and outs of the

---

67. Interview with C. A. Ramu and Co., Melaka. Author's interview notes, Melaka, October 1989 [translation: E. Tagliacozzo].

68. Interview with H. P. Jamal Mohamed and Co., Melaka.

69. A. K. Muthan Chettiar and Sons, Kuala Lumpur.

70. Interview with Mohamed Kassim Azhar and Co., Penang.

71. Interview with P. A. Abdul Wahab and Sons, Kuala Lumpur.

72. Interview with R. A. Aziz, R.A. Ahamedsah and Co., Penang.

spice business like the back of his hand. Clocks on the wall showed off the time in San Francisco, New York, London, Durban, Bahrain, Bombay, Singapore, and Tokyo concurrently; an affectation of his business reach, perhaps (but perhaps not). Mr. Mehta himself was small, like a sparrow; he popped a white pill into his milk tea as we spoke. A painting of moonlit oceans hung over his desk, and the office was neat and tidy. At five different desks sat five different men answering phones, and Mehta himself told me he called Indonesia at least ten times per day to check on consignments. As I heard some of the haggling going on over the phone, I smiled; one of his assistants, speaking to an unknown buyer in an unknown place, said, "I can only give it to you for nine hundred, no less, by God." Two female Chinese secretaries and two Malay office helpers, one of each gender, rounded out the picture. This was a family firm, for sure, but it was also international, both in its cooperation and in its reach. As spices poured in and out of K. Ramanlal and Co.'s daily control, right before my eyes on the telex and fax machine, this small family firm was doing what it had known best for decades—since 1924, in fact. That is when the founder came to set up in Southeast Asia. A quarter century later he set out on his own, like so many Indian spice traders to the region before him.[73]

In Malaysia, high up in the hills of Ipoh, a similar scene: the musty, dark office of Seemi Nanina Mohamed and Co. smells like heaven. But the director, a small sparse man with a moustache and a Western-style business shirt atop an Indian sarong, is restless. He has been telling me that he feels bitter, and defeated. The spice business is not what it used to be. Indian teas, jasmine, and pickles adorn the walls, and the smells of honey, olive oil, and rosewater are in the air. The director wishes he could get out of this trade, frankly; he tells me as much. Ipoh is dying, its colonial best well behind it, and this might accurately describe the spice trade for Seemi Naina Mohamed, too. His sons will likely not go into the business. He offers me a beautiful little tin bottle (corkstoppered), half filled with sandalwood oil; it comes from Mysore, on the Deccan. He turns it wistfully as he hands it over to me ceremoniously. I can take it for "bladder stones," he tells me; one drop and a glass of young coconut water for ten days will set me right. The stone will break and exit through the urine. I thank him for his gift, as I finger the bottle, even though I have no kidney or "bladder stones." I'm just glad to have the tin, and his take on his decades-old involvement in this centuries-old trade. Both are precious to me.[74]

73. Interview with Kirtikar Mehta, of K. Ramanlan and Co., Singapore.
74. Interview with Seemi Naina Mohamed and Co., Ipoh.

Conclusion

I have argued above that the maritime-borne spice trade between India and Southeast Asia is the perfect vehicle, in many ways, to see how fluid market spaces were connected across large bodies of water. Though the start of spices moving between these two locales is lost in history, it is clear that by the beginning of the early modern age that there was indeed a flow of natural materiel between these two places, with spices (among a few other luxury, high-value goods like textiles) taking pride of place in the exchange. The arrival of Europeans did not start a new chapter in this sense, but quickened the dictates of an older story—spices began to be traded at an explosively accelerated pace between these two locations, but also farther afield. The Malabar and Coromandel coasts became "spice central" for a time, and—alongside Eastern Indonesia—one of the two most important places in the world for the growing and selling of such products. Pepper, coriander, turmeric, and cumin sped in the hulls of sleek sailing ships to Southeast Asian locales, and eventually to even more distant markets. The various East India Companies and later colonial-era shipping lines expedited these processes, but for a long while it was Asian merchants who were the lifeblood of the trade, including Indians in diaspora across the Bay of Bengal. By the nineteenth century and the advent of "high colonialism," these Indian merchants were nearly everywhere along the shores of this particular sea, funneling spices and other products to more and more markets. Colonial ports began to displace earlier indigenous ones, and the movement of spices became big business for all concerned, both Asians and Europeans.

By tracing some of the Indian radials in this process across the Bay of Bengal, we can see how ethnicity became a key component in the evolution of this trade. Indians of many linguistic and sublinguistic groups migrated across these waters to set up mercantile concerns, and they traded with each other, as well with other Asians and with Europeans, too, as this later group began slowly to affect market conditions. Initially, many of these commercial arrangements were non-contract based, as these various ethnic actors learned how to make the spice business work not just across space (the separated maritime geographies of the Bay of Bengal) but across ethnic divides as well.[75] Eventually, though, contractual arrangements became more and more the

---

75. For some of the typologies, see Stewart MaCaulay, "Non-Contractual Relationships in Business: A Preliminary Study," *American Sociological Review* 28 (1963): 55–69.

norm, as the sheer volume of business exploded in the eighteenth and into the nineteenth century.[76] Indians carved out a valuable and profitable niche in the spice trade, much as Chinese merchants had in the procurement, buying, and selling of marine products.[77] Historical documents and (by now) a vast weave of scholarship on the imperial advance in Asia tell us this story, but it is only by interviewing Indian family firms that we can get much of the "inside story" of how this commerce looked to Indians themselves, as they built up this trade. The descendants of these initial merchants still ply these trades now. One can almost hear the echoes of these times past in the dusty shops of the remaining storefronts, in places like Singapore, Ipoh, and Penang on the Malay Peninsula. Still connected to the Malabar and Coromandel coasts genealogically, these families are living witnesses to the age and extent of the spice trade, a commerce that at one point was the humming engine of the known world.

76. Chong Jui Choi, "Contract Enforcement across Cultures," *Organization Studies* 15, no. 5 (1994): 673–82.

77. See R. Ward and R. Jenkins, eds., *Ethnic Communities in Business: Strategies for Economic Survival* (Cambridge: Cambridge University Press, 1984).

PART VI

Technologies of the Sea

Preface: The Technological Imperative in the Maritime History of Asia

THE FINAL RUBRIC of this book deals with technologies of the sea. Though commerce and trade were likely behind many of the maritime circuits detailed in this book, and power and the desire to rule were also important, none of these instincts could have been acted upon without specific technologies to make these journeys possible. Technologies of the sea affected mercantile exchange and also the projection of power; these technologies additionally made certain things possible and others impossible, depending on the date of particular implementations. Thus the role of the opening of the Suez Canal in 1869 was fundamental to a range of issues: travel times to the colonies, and the dissemination of information; the peopling of plantations, via the rise of the great steamship companies; and the quickening of the European impulse to build empires, to name just a few. All became increasingly viable through the opening of Suez. We can look for similar issues elsewhere, too, such as port design and harbor construction, as well as the erection of weather stations and maritime governmental bureaus. Knowledge accompanied the pursuit of technology, and technology in turn facilitated the acquisition of more know-how to achieve specific tasks. By the late decades of the nineteenth century, there was no longer any doubt as to who possessed the lion's share of data and facility in dealing with the sea. The West in this was paramount; indigenous Asian powers could only look on in envy as more and more sophisticated ships showed up off their own coastlines. This was a far cry from the sixteenth and seventeenth centuries, for example, when the playing field of maritime technology was far more even. Though the traditional historiographical literature has presented the advent of the West in Asian waters as cataclysmic in nature, replete with technological superiority from the start, this trope was not in fact true. Dominion in technological matters for the most part took quite some time to be achieved. As an operating set of factors, this superiority really only deeply affected the nature and pace of aggression and conquest after the initial period of "contact" between civilizations.

It is tempting to think otherwise, but accommodations were made right from the start when it came to technologies of the sea. One of the first of these accommodations was cooperation in the field of piloting; European ships could not (and did not) sail blindly into most of Asia's waters; rather, they went with Asian pilots at the helms of their ships, guiding their way into indigenous harbors. This sort of knowledge of the sea was invaluable, and the West was sure to make use of it in first approaches to local societies. Technologies such as cantilevered fishing nets (in Cochin, South India) and in ship designs (among both "dhows" in the Indian Ocean, and "junks" in the South China Sea, not to mention among "prahus" in Southeast Asian waters) often incorporated European designs. This process sometimes created hybrid ships, vessels which then traded in Asian waters, often crewed by men from both Asia and Europe, but who were doing different sets of tasks. The ships themselves, though, were not ontologically Asian or European, but curious admixtures of the two. The same thing can be said for knowledge of wind systems, monsoons, and currents, as the seafaring traditions of distant places started to mingle in these waters. The technologies of sail design, for example, changed over time, and gradually over the centuries oceangoing ships became slimmer and also of deeper draft, riding lower and lower in the water, to achieve better stability in rough seas. Kettle-bottomed boats were also commissioned, however, for better use in inlets and shallow bays, often where the majority of trading with local peoples took place. The technology of seafaring was often the point of the spear where indigenous and Western conceptions of science met, as this particular branch of knowledge was so vital to both sets of people. Because of this, we often have very good data on this aspect of the meeting of cultures in the past several hundred years, both on the high seas and in the ports, which were the normative "ground zeros" of contact between parties in Asian seas.

Chapter 12 takes lighthouses as a case study in the power of developing technologies in Asian waters. Much like Foucault's famous example of the prison as panopticon, lighthouses achieved essentially the same thing: as circular structures, all was laid bare around them in an effort by the colonial state to help "see" its many subjects. This was an important project, as—especially at night—Asian ships traded in all sorts of directions, many of them operating outside the desires and proscriptive pathways of the colonial state. Lighthouses were built to protect shipping, for sure, but they were also constructed as platform towers, with men sometimes spending months at a time in tours upon the structures. Eventually, the grandest designs—spread throughout insular Southeast Asia, and particularly in the Dutch East Indies, the world's largest archipelago—became huge fortresses of surveillance upon local populations. As lighting technologies evolved over the late nineteenth and into the early twentieth century, the lighting apparatuses themselves became ornate and increasingly powerful, showcasing panoptic (and then dioptric and finally holophotal) uses of light. The politics of lighting also became ornate and complicated, with the British and Dutch both sharing and competing in the process of illuminating their combined seas. Chapter 13 continues this discussion, but in the guise of maps, rather than via towers of light. Sea mapping was one of the most important technologies of knowledge in the premodern world; those who could map the sea had the power (ultimately) to understand its implications and possibilities better than other parties. Hydrographic institutes were set up in the colonies, though back in metropolitan Europe larger, more complete bureaus were also staffed, responsible for keeping the data of Asian conquests all in one place. As Asia's seas were mapped down to increasingly fine detail, the imperial project made use of these projections of space, and followed up on using such acquired knowledge. Foucault would have understood this paradigm yet again, only this time outside the panopticon: knowledge begat power, and power in turn funneled more knowledge back to the center. These last two chapters of the book show how intertwined these processes were on the ground, as the premodern world of Asian maritime trade gradually gave way to something increasingly "modern" and familiar to our own eyes.

12

Foucault's Other Panopticon, or Lighting Colonial Southeast Asia

It's like sitting amongst lighthouses. Each lighthouse is giving you a bearing on lost spaces of time.[1]

THE HISTORY of technology as it has pertained to the imperial project has been an evolving subdiscipline in historical monographs over the past twenty to twenty-five years.[2] The evidence for this is geographically broad, in places such as the French Caribbean, where historians have studied the activities of missionary naturalists, medical administrators, economic botanists, and meteorologists, as well as their combined contribution to the expansion of regional Gallic influence.[3] Perhaps this attention has been even more salient for British India, however, where a number of studies have examined museums, World's Fairs, archaeology, Ganges River steamers, and even (though far more rarely) local resistance against these projects, all under the purview of the

---

1. Veronica Strang, et al., eds., *From the Lighthouse: Interdisciplinary Reflections on Light* (London: Routledge, 2018), 158.

2. In Southeast Asia alone, a number of classics have been spun out along this theme in the scholarly literature of the past few decades; see work in prisons, epidemiology, and plantations, as three cases in point: Peter Zinoman, *The Colonial Bastille: A History of Imprisonment in Vietnam 1862–01940* (Berkeley: University of California Press, 2001); Warwick Anderson, *Colonial Pathologies* (Durham: Duke University Press, 2006); and Ann Stoler, *Capitalism and Confrontation on Sumatra's Plantation Belt, 1870–1979* (Ann Arbor: University of Michigan Press, 1985).

3. See, for example, James E. McClellan, *Colonialism and Science: Saint Domingue in the Old Regime* (Baltimore: Johns Hopkins University Press, 1992.)

expanding British Raj.[4] Science, technology, and imperial relationships stretch back even into studies of the ancient Mediterranean, where more recent writers have looked at the impact of sciences of the body and of the stars on the health, breadth, and reach of the Roman empire and its far-flung dependencies.[5]

Yet the locus classicus of examinations targeting technology, empire, and science is still the nineteenth century, when the vast majority of the earth's surface came under European domination in the space of less than a century. Despite it being true that a decent-size industry has developed out of studying these changes and patterns in the early modern era, when the age of European overseas expansion really began, it has still been the nineteenth century which has caught the attention of most chroniclers of imperial technology.[6] Daniel Headrick's books were among the first to explore these connections on the global stage, but Michael Adas has also looked at these patterns writ large, from India and China to technology and the African slave trade.[7] Recent interest in technology has reinvigorated arguments about the nature of European imperialism that stretch back to the time of Marx and Engel, and have absorbed many of modern history's seminal thinkers (including John Atkinson Hobson, Vladimir Lenin, Hannah Arendt, John Gallagher and Ronald Robinson, and Eric Hobsbawm).[8] Yet, as at least one historian has pointed out, while many

4. Examples of scholarship on science and the Raj abound; see Zaheer Baber, *The Science of Empire: Scientific Knowledge, Civilization, and Colonial Rule in India* (Albany: SUNY Press, 1996); Satpal Sangwan, *Science, Technology and Colonisation: An Indian Experience 1757–1857* (Delhi, 1991), especially plates following page 102; Deepak Kumar, *Science and the Raj, 1857–1905* (Delhi, 1995) 180–227.

5. Tamsyn Barton, *Power and Knowledge: Astrology, Physiognomics, and Medicine under the Roman Empire* (Ann Arbor, 1994), 27–94, 95–132, 133–168; for some interesting applications of technology on the reach of the Roman imperium, see *Roman Frontier Studies: Papers Presented to the Sixteenth Congress of Roman Frontier Studies* (Oxford, 1995).

6. Two of the best books available on these processes in the early modern era are Carlo Cipolla, *Guns, Sails, and Empires: Technological Innovation and the Early Phases of European Expansion 1400–1700* (New York, 1965), 90 and passim; and Geoffrey Parker, *The Military Revolution, Military Innovation and the Rise of the West, 1500–1800* (Cambridge, 1990).

7. See Daniel Headrick, *The Tools of Empire: Technology and European Imperialism in the Nineteenth Century* (New York, 1981); Daniel Headrick, *The Tentacles of Progress: Technology Transfer in the Age of Imperialism, 1850–1940* (New York, 1988); and Michael Adas, *Machines as the Measure of Men: Science, Technology, and Ideologies of Western Dominance* (Ithaca, 1989.)

8. See J. A. Hobson, *Imperialism: A Study* (London, 1902), 224–34; V. I. Lenin, *Imperialism: The Highest Stage of Capitalism* (New York, 1939), 88–92, 123–27; Hannah Arendt, *The Origins*

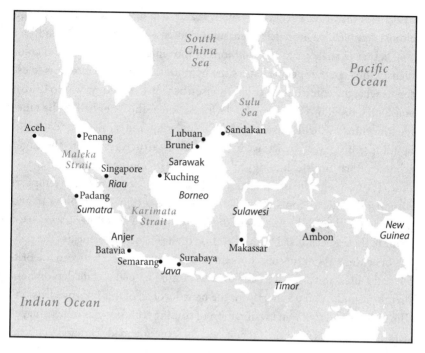

MAP 12.1. An Arena of Lights

of the general trends of science and empire have been fleshed out, "there are still difficulties in pinpointing when a version of a tool had become sufficiently diffused and effective to institute change in behavior and relationships."[9] The history of lighthouses, beacons, and buoys in European expansion makes an interesting case in point.[10] Although strangely underrepresented in the literature on science and imperialism, their spread has an important story to tell us about the nature of the imperial project. And this has been particularly the

---

of Totalitarianism (Cleveland, OH: World Publishing, 1958), 124–27, 147–55; J. Gallagher and R. Robinson, "The Imperialism of Free Trade," *Economic History Review* 1, no. 1 (1953); Eric Hobsbawm, *The Age of Empire 1875–1914* (New York: Pantheon, 1987).

9. Robert Kubicek, "British Expansion, Empire, and Technological Change," in *The Oxford History of the British Empire*, vol. III: *The Nineteenth Century*, ed. Andrew Porter, 247–69 (Oxford: Oxford University Press, 1999).

10. For some very early avatars, see K. Booth, "The Roman Pharos at Dover Castle," *English Heritage Historical Review* 2, (2007): 9–22; and Doris Behrens-Abouseif, "The Islamic History of the Lighthouse of Alexandria," *Muqarnas* 23 (2006): 1–14.

case in Southeast Asia, where lighthouses and such maritime tools have been almost completely ignored as a measurable force of imperialism's spread.[11]

Chapter 12 analyzes local evolutions of movement, technology, and colonialism through the specific lens of the lighthouse. Broadly, it attempts to estimate what the contribution of lighthouses, beacons, and buoys was to British and Dutch programs of colonial state-formation in the latter half of the nineteenth century. The first quarter of the chapter lays out a brief foundation of lighthouse history, as well as asking where these structures fit into the larger scheme of maritime technology and expansion in Southeast Asia during this time. The next segment of the chapter delves into the geographic and temporal dispersion of these "tools of empire." Why were certain geographies lit and others ignored until the passing of the new century? What criteria were used to make these decisions? The third section of the chapter interrogates the politics of lighting, as internecine cooperation and competition (between the British and Dutch and also internally in both camps) helped dictate deployment on the ground. Who was to pay for the benefits of all of this improved vision? The chapter ends with an examination of shifting technologies of lighting, as new developments in lenses, fueling, and construction made certain structures quickly obsolete. It is argued here that lighthouses acted as both symbols and structures of power, and played a crucial role in the Western advance in the region, setting out grids and avenues of imperial vision in a huge, maritime space. Instead of being confronted by a darkened maze of islands, as had been the case in 1860, the British and Dutch transformed this domain by 1910 into a "lit archipelago." This was an arena that was capable of being surveilled now into the twentieth century, in increasingly vigorous ways.

Geography and the Imperial Advance in the Island World

A vast assembly of Dutch and English officials spent a large amount of ink while writing on their respective colonial forward movements. This literature certainly included material on the role of science in the extension of imperial gains. English-language dimensions of this writing are not surprising, given

---

11. The only treatment of a colonial lighthouse in Southeast Asia that I am aware of is Nicholas Tarling, "The First Pharos of the Seas: The Construction of the Horsburgh Lighthouse on Pedra Branca," *Journal of the Malay Branch of the Royal Asiatic Society* 67, no. 1 (1994): 1–8. For lights on the coast of China, see Robert Bickers, "Infrastructural Globalisation: The Chinese Maritime Customs and the Lighting of the China Coast, 1860s–1930s," *Historical Journal* 56, no. 2 (2013): 431–58.

the vast extent of territory that fell to the British empire. The Dutch also have a vibrant publishing industry of their own, however, which continues to focus on its own imperial and geographical past. It is from the union of these studies that we can start to get an idea of how lighthouses and lighting apparatuses fit into the general schema of maritime expansion in the region. Though significant sections of the Indies, for example, were still terra incognita to Europeans inland (and upland) even until the end of the nineteenth century, large parts of the coasts and seas of the colony were being charted by the 1870s and 1880s.[12] This was an active policy, decided upon by central planners in the Dutch and British Southeast Asian colonial capitals of Batavia and Singapore, and was part of a larger program which included research in astronomy, geophysics, and medicine in the region.[13] Expeditions were being sent out in all directions as the Dutch imperium expanded in particular, and many of these journeys were concerned with the principles and modalities of mapping.[14] It should not surprise us that the larger project of surveying in the Indies (see the next chapter) was often bound together with branches of the Dutch military, which was gaining an ever-higher profile in the "Outer Islands" of the Indies (Sumatra, Borneo, and New Guinea) as Batavia's servants charted the vast extremities of the colony.[15]

12. For a good overview, see John Butcher and Robert Elson, *Sovereignty and the Sea: How Indonesia Became an Archipelagic State* (Singapore: National University of Singapore Press, 2017). See, for example, the blank interior spaces of late-nineteenth-century Jambi (Sumatra), except for the density of villages all along Jambi's river, in P. G. E. I. J. van der Velde, "Van Koloniale Lobby naar Koloniale Hobby: Het Koninklijk Nederlands Aardrijkskundig Genootschap en Nederlands-Indië, 1873–1914," *Geografisch Tijdschrift* 22, no. 3 (1988): 215.

13. For a glimpse of this larger scientific milieu in the Indies, for example, see Lewis Pyenson, *Empire of Reason: Exact Sciences in Indonesia, 1840–1940* (Leiden: E. J. Brill, 1989.)

14. See John Butcher, "A Note on the Self-Governing Realms of the Netherlands Indies in the Late 1800s," *BTLV* 164, no. 1 (2008): 1–12. For a period overview of cartography, see *De Topographische Dienst in Nederlandsch-Indië: Eenige Gegevens Omtrent Geschiedenis, Organisatie en Werkwijze* (Amsterdam, 1913), 1–15; for contemporary analyses of hydrography, see Christiaan Biezen, "'De Waardigheid van een Koloniale Mogendheid': De Hydrografische Dienst en de Kartering van de Indische Archipel tussen 1874 en 1894," *Tijdschrift voor Zeegeschiedenis* 18, no. 2 (Sept. 1999), especially 23–34, and the museum catalogue *Catalogus van de Tentoonstelling 'Met Lood en Lijn'* (Rotterdam, Maritime Museum, 1974), especially 78–81, which gives short mapping histories of three areas as examples of hydrography in the Indies (the Sunda Strait, Riouw Strait, and the southern coast of New Guinea.)

15. H. W. van den Doel, "De Ontwikkeling van het Militaire Bestuur in Nederlands-Indië: De Officier-Civiel Gezaghebber, 1880–1942," *Mededeelingen van de Sectie Militaire Geschiedenis* 12 (1989): 27–50.

The rise of steam-shipping in the outstretched islands of maritime Southeast Asia also added fuel to the unfolding of these processes. The momentous effects of the opening of Suez in 1869 on ports like Singapore are well known, as shipping distances were cut and steam power brought the colonies ever closer to metropolitan markets. Less well known is how the rise of steam galvanized Dutch expansion in the Indies, leading to the growth of massive shipyards like Onrust off Batavia, and the Surabaya Harbor works, both of which serviced generations of steamers as they traded in the dispersed ports of the archipelago.[16] Indeed, with very limited resources in the "Outer Islands," Batavia eventually decided on a partnership arrangement with steam shipping services in the Indies, financing (and in turn being financed by) private concerns to the benefit of both business and empire in the region. The NISM (Nederlandsch-Indische Stoomvaart Maatschappij) and, after it, the KPM (Koninklijke Paketvaart Maatschappij) both received exclusive contracts for government passenger and cargo shipping, which facilitated Dutch incursions into the maritime periphery.[17] While different branches of the Dutch marine forces vied and jockeyed for scarce funds from The Hague, Batavia decided that the best way to maximize resources was to link its own interests with the private sector's.[18] Maritime infrastructure in the archipelago developed under these circumstances, therefore, and lighthouses were very much the children of this dual public and private fiscal parentage.

The spread of lighthouses as a functional tool for building empire was a pan-archipelago development. For this reason, the more common locus of nation-states as a framework for analysis has been thrown out in favor of a wider, more inclusive geography, which reveals larger maritime spatial patterns as they unfolded. Although a start has been made toward this kind of supranational historiography in other parts of the world, Southeast Asia has lagged behind this evolving geographical paradigm until recently, though there are

16. The Surabaya Marine establishment in East Java undertook repairs, provided laying-up facilities, and equipped vessels with boilers and other equipment, while also looking after pilotage and buoying needs on a pan-Indies scale (some of this was also done by local harbor departments.) After 1891 Tanjung Priok (near Batavia) also had a large dry-dock company. See *Twentieth Century Impressions of Netherlands India: Its History, People, Commerce, Industries, and Resources*, ed. Arnold Wright and Oliver T. Breakspear (London, 1909), 281.

17. See J. N. F. M. à Campo's monumental study of the KPM, *Koninklijke Paketvaart Maatschappij: Stoomvaart en Staatsvorming in de Indonesische Archipel 1888–1914* (Hilversum: Verloren, 1992).

18. G. Teitler, "The Netherlands Indies: An Outline of Its Military History," *Revue Internationale d'Histoire Militaire* 58 (1984): 138.

signs the shift in vantage is now catching on.[19] The long, interwoven history of the British and the Dutch in these seas, allies and enemies for almost three hundred years by the time of this narrative, and the very nature of their playing field (a maritime one), seem to make this shift in perspective a prudent one.[20] Java-centric histories of the Indies were almost the rule until fairly recently, but following these recent developments analysis is focused not on land-based empires but on the seas which separated these two powers.[21] The Straits of Melaka and the South China Sea (which bisected British Malaya, the Straits Settlements, Sarawak, and the British North Borneo Company from all of the Dutch dominions) assume pride of place in this chapter, therefore: these were the maritime conduits that formed the crucial "terrain" that needed to be lit, at least from the perspective of area states.[22]

Favored Coasts, Crucial Passages: Lighting a Dim Archipelago, 1860–1910

One would have to search hard to find an arena whose maritime traffic expanded as quickly as Southeast Asia's did in the fin de siècle period. English-language seaman's guides to navigation of the intricate waterways of the area

19. One of the best theoretical works to come out which challenges tendencies to amalgamate geographies into comfortable (but not necessarily applicable) categories is Martin Lewis and Kären Wigen, *The Myth of Continents: A Critique of Metageography* (Berkeley: University of California Press, 1997).

20. See especially J. A. de Moor, "'A Very Unpleasant Relationship': Trade and Strategy in the Eastern Seas: Anglo-Dutch Relations in the Nineteenth Century from a Colonial Perspective," in *Navies and Armies: The Anglo-Dutch Relationship in War and Peace*, ed. G. J. A. Raven and N. A. M. Rodger (Edinburgh: Donald and Co., 1990.)

21. For critiques of these Java-centered histories, see J. Thomas Lindblad, "Between Singapore and Batavia: The Outer Islands in the Southeast Asian Economy in the Nineteenth Century," in *Kapitaal, Ondernemerschap en Beleid: Studies over Economie en Politiek in Nederland, Europa en Azië van 1500 tot Heden,* edited by C. A. Davids, W. Fritschy, and L. A. van der Valk, 528–30 (Amsterdam: NEHA, 1996); Howard Dick, "Indonesian Economic History Inside Out," *RIMA* 27 (1993): 1–12; and C. van Dijk, "Java, Indonesia, and Southeast Asia: How Important Is the Java Sea?," in *Looking in Odd Mirrors: The Java Sea,* ed. Vincent Houben, Hendrik Meier, and Willem van der Molen, 289–301 (Leiden, Culturen van Zuidoost–Asië en Oceanië, 1992).

22. See John Roger Owen. "Give Me a light? The Development and Regulation of Ships' Navigation Lights up to the Mid-1960s" *International Journal of Maritime History* 25, 1, (2013): 173–203; R. Williams. "Nightspaces: Darkness, Deterritorialisation and Social Control" *Space and Culture* 11/4, (2008): 514–532; and Tim Edensor. "Reconnecting with Darkness: Gloomy Landscapes, Lightless Places" *Social and Cultural Geography* 14 (4) 2013: 446–465.

were published often, outlining the winds, storms, and currents of the region for the merchantmen of many nations.[23] Selling nautical charts became a large publishing industry on its own, with ever-smaller-scale maps becoming available.[24] Yet one of the best ways to see how important nautical advances were to people in the region is through Malay-language newspapers of the period. Shipping insurers from Britain, Hong Kong, Holland, and New Zealand all advertised their services in these pages (and their longevity "in the business") to eager Southeast Asian clients.

> Kita, nama yang tersebut dibawah ini, sudah menjadi agents sebab company yang tersebut diatas, bulih trima insurance laut mengikut harga yang ada jalan sekarang.[25]

> We, the below-mentioned, have become agents because the above-named company is allowed to sell maritime-insurance at current market prices. [translation: E. Tagliacozzo]

These insurers, foreign and local, showed off their capital and premium payments in an effort to attract the most business possible from merchants in the region.[26] The result was an overall shipping milieu where Asians as well as Europeans were highly involved in area commerce; vessels ran west to Suez and the Indian Ocean, north to China and Japan, and even south to the expanding ports of British Australia.

23. See, for example, W. H. Rosser and J. F. Imray, *Indian Ocean Directory: The Seaman's Guide to the Navigation of the Indian Ocean, China Sea, and West Pacific Ocean* (London, n.d.)

24. See charts no. 119 to 135, titled "East India Archipelago," each of which gives detailed sailing instructions for small sections of the Indies archipelago, in *Catalogue of the Latest and Most Approved Charts, Pilots', and Navigation Books Sold or Purchased by James Imray and Sons* (London, 1866.)

25. See the advertisements of the Ocean Marine Insurance Co., London (founded 1859), the Batavia Sea and Fire Insurance Co. (founded 1845), the Jardine Matheson Co. (of Hong Kong), and the Southern British Fire and Marine Insurance Co. (of New Zealand), in *Bintang Timor*, no. 3 (4 July 1894):1; *Bintang Timor*, no. 1 (2 July 1894):1; and *Bintang Timor*, no. 34 (10 August 1894): 1. The Borneo Co., for example, acted as local agents in Singapore for the Ocean Marine Shipping Co. of London.

26. The Canton Insurance Co., for which Jardine and Matheson (Hong Kong) were agents, advertised to their Malay customers that they had reserves of $2 million; the Borneo Company, local agents for the Ocean Marine Insurance Company of London (see n. 22 above), made sure their Malay clients knew that the company had 1 million pounds sterling in reserve. See *Bintang Timor*, no. 1 (2 July 1894):1; no. 3 (4 July 1894):1.

Alongside the rising number of ships came a rising number of disasters, Indonesian historians tell us, writing in their own language. This was so as more and more ships foundered on the many hidden dangers of the region's seas.[27] One of the first steamers in the Dutch Indies, the *Willem I*, met this fate on its inaugural run in the archipelago; grounding off Ambon in 1837, the crew was stranded and then attacked by pirates from Mindanao, before gaining their freedom through a ransom of cash, opium, and precious linen. British ships foundered on unseen rocks and reefs as well, such as the Singapore-registered *Giang Ann*, which went down in the Thousand Islands, not far from Batavia, the Indies capital.[28] Though accidents involving ships continued to be fairly common, involving leaks, fires, and other mishaps, even in port, it was the dangers while at sea which were the most dangerous:[29]

Seorang kuli Jawa bernama Amir telah mati ditimpa oleh subutir peti besar pada masa memunggati barang didalam sebuah kapal api bernama "De Klerk" di Tanjong Periok itu.

A Javanese laborer named Amir was killed by the fall of a large crate, while unloading goods in a steamship named *De Klerk* in Tanjong Priok harbor. [translation: E. Tagliacozzo]

Kapal api "Nam Yong" yang disangkakan sudah tengglam itu telah sampai disini smalam pagi dengan slamatnya. Khabarnya apabila didapati kapal itu ada bochor Captain Nicol larikan kapal itu ka suatu teluk dekat pulau

---

27. For a sense of the shipping milieu from Indonesian maritime historians themselves, see S. T. Sulistiyono, "Liberalisasi pelayaran dan perdagangan di Indonesia 1816–1870," *Lembaran Sastra* 19 (1996): 31–44; M. Adi, "Mengisi kekurangan ruangan kapal," *Suluh Nautika* 9, nos. 1–2 (Jan./Feb. 1959): 8–9; D. Soelaiman, "Selayang pandang pelayaran di Indonesia," *Suluh Nautika* 9, no. 3, (1959): 40–43; Dewan Pimpinan Pusat INSA, *Melangkah Laju Menerjang Gelomban: Striding along Scouring Seas* (Jakarta: Dewan Pimpinan Pusat INSA, 1984); Dewan Redaksi Puspindo, *Sejarah pelayaran niaga di Indonesia Jilid 1: Pra sejarah hingga 17 Agustus 1945* (Jakarta: Yayasan Puspindo, 1990); S. T. Sulistiyono, *Sektor maritim dalam era mekanisasi dan liberalisasi: Posisi armada perahu layar pribumi dalam pelayaran antarpulau di Indonesia, 1879–1911* (Yogyakarta: Laporan penelitian dalam rangka / Summer Course in Indonesian Economic History, 1996).

28. F. C. Backer Dirks, *De Gouvernements marine in het voormalige Nederlands-Indië in haar verschillende tijdsperioden geschetst; III. 1861–1949* (Weesp: De Boer Maritiem, 1985), 40–41; Governor Straits Settlements to Colonial Office (hereafter, CO), 25 February 1890, in CO 273/165.

29. See *Utusan Malayu*, no. 182 (9 January 1909):1; *Bintang Timor*, no. 37 (13 August 1894): 2.

Soreto itu, supaya iya bulih menampalkan bochornya itu. Setlah ditampal-
kannya blayarlah iya ka Singapura.

The steamship *Nam Yong*, which was thought to have sunk, arrived here
safely last night. It is reported that when it was found the ship had a leak,
that Captain Nicol brought the ship to the bay near the island of Soreto, so
that he could patch the leak. After this was done, it sailed on to Singapore.
[Translation: E. Tagliacozzo]

This was true outside the large ports, like the Batavia incident mentioned
above, but it was also true in smaller locales, such as British Labuan, where
ships such as the German steamer *Triton* went down in 1897.[30] In the truly
"peripheral" coasts of the region, like the long, outstretched shores of British
Borneo, accidents were even more frequent. Even as late as 1913 a British merchant captain called the lighting situation on these coasts a "standing disgrace,"
and asked how such a state of affairs could come about when fees were charged
by area British administrations to keep shipping safe.[31]

Improved night-time vision of this arena's fraught maritime environment
was thus viewed by both colonial powers as a crucial, imperial act, to be undertaken in the interest of shipping generally, and empire more specifically.
"Advanced" colonial states did not want to be viewed as "deficient" in this regard; the monetary losses would be substantial but the loss in face would have
been even more damaging to many Europeans of the time. Yet, especially in
the early years under discussion here, resources were scarce and the reach of
these states was limited. The Gouvernements Marine (GM, the Dutch sub-
bureau charged with lighting, beaconing, and buoying, about which more in
a moment) found itself unable to service all of these lighting stations and apparatus on a regular basis. Though it was responsible for delivering food, fuel,
and repairs to the various lights, beacons, and buoys already constructed in
the Indies, the GM was also responsible for many other tasks. These included
fighting "pirates" in local Indies waters, cruising against "smugglers," undertaking hydrographical measurements, helping ships in distress, and transporting
administrative officials and supplies, among other chores. After 1873, with the

30. Gov. Labuan to CO, 20 May 1897, in CO 144/71. A British steamer of 2,000 tons (the
Howick Hall) tried to help the 1,000-ton *Triton* but ran aground on the same rocks herself. A
listing of all ships which wrecked themselves on rocks, shoals, or other dangers in Southeast
Asia during our time frame would take many pages.

31. Captain E. Wrightson's letter to the Imperial Merchant Service Guild, n.d, in CO 531/5.

start of the four-decades-long Aceh War in North Sumatra, these duties also included GM ships being co-opted into the Indies fleet, to serve on war station in the perilous seas off Aceh. Matters were also not helped by the fact that many of the old beacons put in use by the GM in years past were swept away by the sea, or that the first steamer drafted into service specifically for these duties (in 1870), was so broken down that it was almost useless, and quickly had to be replaced.[32] In the late 1860s and early 1870s, Singapore saw similar hyper-extension, a state of affairs commented upon frequently by area civil servants.[33]

The amalgamation of all of these factors over time—rising maritime traffic, the loss of shipwrecks and by extension of precious nautical resources in state programs of expansion—brought about amendments to the organizational structure of lighting, beaconing, and buoying, especially in the Dutch Indies. Though the archipelago's first lights had been erected at Anjer, in the Sunda Straits, in 1851, with other lights soon following on the north coast of Java, an Inspectorship of Lighting, Beaconing, and Pilotage was not erected until 1854. P. F. Uhlenbeck was named as the Indies' first inspector; his jurisdiction was split between the Department of the Interior and the Royal Dutch Navy. Soon after, in 1859, a decision was taken by the government to erect fifty more lights throughout the archipelago, to be placed in strategic maritime locations which would be paid for over the next twenty-five years. In 1861 the Gouvernements Marine was created, while in 1867 a reshuffling in organization brought the whole responsibility for lighting over to the Marine Department. In the 1880s and 1890s, these reorganizations continued, with the Lighting, Beaconing, and Pilotage service alternately being subsumed under the Gouvernements Marine, and sometimes gaining its independence as a separate entity under the larger Department of Marine. What is most important for our purposes here is the recognition that lighting had finally come of age in the Indies; Batavia had finally decided, by 1860, that the lighting of the Indies' dim seas was to be a new imperial priority.[34]

32. Backer Dirks, *De Gouvernements marine*, 155, 211, 314; H. E. van Berckel, "Zeehavens en Kustverlichting in de Koloniën: Oost Indië," *Gedenkboek Koninklijk Instituut Ingenieurs* (1847–97): 307–8.

33. See Board of Trade to CO, 10 November 1871, in CO 273/52; Governor Straits Settlements (hereafter, Gov SS) to CO, 30 May 1873, in CO 273/66; Gov SS to CO, 22 September 1880, in CO 273/104.

34. "Bebakening," *ENI* 1 (1917): 213; "Kustverlichting," *ENI* 2 (1917): 494; Backer Dirks, *De Gouvernements marine*, 284–95.

Of course, things put out in planning diagrams and the building of structures in real time and space were different. The process of lighting maritime Southeast Asia, split between British and Dutch spheres, took much of the next fifty years. We can glance at this process temporally and spatially in three blocks, the first of which comprises the years 1860–80. During these twenty years, the foundations of maritime lighting were laid in the archipelago; islands and shoals, important waterways, approaches to major ports, and unseen rocks all received the initial attentions of these states. The British and Dutch competed to make Singapore and Batavia, respectively, as attractive as possible to passing shipping, and one of the ways to do this was through lighting. In British waters in the 1860s, these lights consisted of a tower, ninety-five feet high, called the Horsburgh, near Singapore, as well as several other installations at Melaka and in the immediate vicinity of Singapore, some of which were lightships.[35] Dutch lights were more limited until slightly later; Batavia had its own lighthouse, as did the Bangka Strait, in addition to Anjer and other northern Javanese coastal lights which we have mentioned previously.[36] The 1870s saw a massive program of expansion, however, especially in Dutch waters: literally dozens of lights began to go into operation, as lighthouses, lightships, and beacons were scattered throughout the western half of the archipelago.[37]

35. The Horsburgh was visible for fifteen miles, and was built on a summit of rock; the British side of the Straits also had three fixed bright lights (one called the Raffles, another on Government Hill in Singapore, and a third on St. Paul Hill in Melaka), as well as a lightship in the Strait of Melaka. See Alexander Findlay, *A Description and List of the Lighthouses of the World* (London: R. H. Laurie, 1861), 106.

36. See J. E. de Meijier, "Zeehavens en Kustverlichting in Nederlandsch-Indië," *Gedenkboek Koninklijk Instituut Ingenieurs* (1847–97): 304; James Imray, *The Lights and Tides of the World* (1866), 83–84. The light at Anjer mentioned here was destroyed in the eruption of Krakatoa; see Simone Jacquemard, *L'éruption du Krakatoa; ou des chambres inconnues dans la maison* (Paris: Éditions du Seuil, 1969); Tek Hoay Kwee, *Drama dari Kratatau* (Batavia: Typ. Druk. Hoa Siang In Kok, 1929); King Hoo Liem, *Meledaknja Goenoeng Keloet: Menoeroet tjatetan jang dikompoel*. Sourabaya: (S. n., 1929); Zam Nuldyn, *Cerita purba: Dewi Krakatau* (Jakarta: Penerbit Firma Hasmar, 1976); Muhammad, Saleh, *Syair Lampung dan Anyer dan Tanjung Karang naik air laut* (Singapore: Penerbit Haji Sa[h]id, 1886).

37. One of the best sources for this spread of the state's technology is the *Tijdschrift voor het Zeewezen* [Nautical Journal], which chronicles in enormous detail the individual construction of these lights. Lights were going up, of various intensities and constructions, in Makassar, Java, Borneo, Aceh, Madura, and many other places; see notices of these examples in *Tijdschrift voor het Zeewezen* (1871): 125; (1872): 90; (1873): 274; (1875): 230; and (1879): 83. This is only a very small sampling; the entire spread of Dutch lighting in the Indies can be seen in this periodical.

Segments of Sumatra, the South China Sea islands, and Borneo's sea-passages were lit during this time, constructing a ring around the Indies' aquatic borders, in opposition to British possessions to the north.

By the decades of the 1880s and 1890s, such frenetic development on each side of the Strait was commonplace. Where major harbors, dangerous geographic anomalies, and international waterways were lit as a first order of policy in previous decades, larger swaths of maritime terrain were now also beaconed as both states extended their reach. The *Straits Settlements Blue Books* give figures for when and how these new lights were built (as well as the costs for crew salaries, lamp oil, rations, and maintenance), from Penang south to the environs of Singapore, and Singapore north to Labuan off the Bornean mainland.[38] *Indische Staatsbladen* and the *Regeerings Almanak voor Nederlandsch Indië* also give the official notice of this spread, as coastal Borneo, Sulawesi, Riau and even the far-flung Natuna/Anambas archipelago were charted and then lit. Here, too, the human dimension of these tools of empire can be seen down to extraordinary detail, as the names and stationing duties of several generations of lighthouse men are recorded for the entirety of the period.[39] The quickened tempo of Dutch lighting at this time was performed in concert with the expansion and modernization of the Indies fleet, which was seen (by policy makers and the Dutch reading public alike) as too small and ineffective in the event of an attack on the outstretched Indies. Engineering, empirism, and even the encouragement of European geographical societies pushed these structures farther and farther to the periphery, as lighthouses took on the symbolism of state power, in scattered, architectural form.[40]

38. See Straits Settlements Blue Books (hereafter, *SSBB*) 1883, W2; *SSBB* 1887–8, 1–2; *SSBB* 1899, W2–3; and *SSBB* 1910, V2–3, for overviews on all of the above details; in 1883 the cost of maintaining British lights in the Straits was $22,501; by 1910 it was almost twice this amount ($38,997). New lights were built during this period at Muka Head, Pulau Rimau, Tanjong Hantu, in Penang Harbor, at Pulau Undang, Pulau Pisang, and at the Sultan Shoal off Singapore.

39. The legal/administrative history of lighting in the Indies can be gleaned from the assembled *Staatsbladen* produced in the *Regeerings Almanak voor Nederlandsch-Indië*, 1890 (1); 1900 (31), and 1910 (1); these chronicle government decisions about which parts of the Indies needed to be lit, in what order and by what priorities, etc.

40. See "Onze Zeemacht in den Archipel," *Tijdschrift voor Nederlandsch-Indië* (hereafter *TNI*) (1890) 1: 146–151; "De Indische Marine," *TNI* (1902): 695–707; for the role of Dutch geographical societies in this expansion, see *Catalogus, Koloniaal-Aardrijkskundige Tentoonstelling ter Gelegenheid van het Veertigjarig Bestaan van het Koninklijk Nederlandsch Aardrijkskundig Genootschap* (Amsterdam, 1913), which has contributions on cartography, hydrography, oceanography, and geology, among other subjects.

Into the early 1900s, all of these tools—lights, beacons, and buoys—had become fairly common across maritime Southeast Asia. Where in previous years all available resources (both British and Dutch) had been directed toward lighting crucial stretches of water for clearly delineated purposes, by 1900 an *afronding* (Dutch, "rounding off") was taking place, as Singapore and Batavia tried to light remaining spaces which were still opaque. Parts of the eastern half of the Indies began to be buoyed and lit during this time, including parts of Nusa Tenggara, Maluku, and some of the outstretched coasts of Irian Jaya.[41] On the British side of the Strait, larger tracts of Borneo's coastline came under increased lighting as well, though by no means all of it (as Captain Wrightson's earlier disparaging comment from 1913 will attest).[42] The lighting of vital passages, shoals, and harbors of the western archipelago continued to expand, as both colonial regimes recognized that more beacons and buoys meant a better government presence in a variety of places along the frontier. By the years around 1900, the western archipelago (Straits of Melaka, South China Sea, and western half of the Java Sea) was thick with lit passages, which pushed commerce and indeed physical motion itself into avenues that were legible to both colonial regimes.[43]

Can we attribute all of this lighting to state-sanctioned expansion? While it is tempting to find concrete policy of this concrete building, both British and Dutch, the answer is probably no. Here again, Malay-language newspapers help us see the larger picture. The rise of local Chinese shipping concerns between Sumatra and Singapore, for example, helped give impetus to more light-construction in the Straits of Melaka, for the sake of general trade.[44] Increasing private (some of it indigenous) participation in the prosperity of the vast ocean steamship lines also helped pave the way for more lights.[45] Big business, such as the Labuan Coalfields Company, pestered the Colonial

---

41. The term is Jurriaan van Goor's; see his essay "Imperialisme in de Marge?," in his *Imperialisme in de Marge: De Afronding van Nederlands-Indië* (Utrecht, 1986.); "Bebakening," *ENI* 1 (1917): 213; "Kustverlichting," *ENI* 2 (1918): 495.

42. Imperial Merchant Service Guild to CO, 24 June 1913, in CO 531/5; for a Dutch analog of only uncertain "progress" and dissastisfaction, also after 1900, see "De Uitbreiding der Indische Kustverlichting," *Indische Gids* 2 (1903): 1772.

43. C. H. De Groeje, *De Kustverlichting in Nederlandsch-Indië* (Batavia, 1913), 4–8.

44. See, for example, the itinerary of local Chinese steamers in *Bintang Timor*, 10 August (1894), 34: 4.

45. Shipping movements of the "P & O" line, for example, were reported daily by the Malay press for its interested readers, some of whom had cargo on board; see *Bintang Timor*, 26 October 1894, 100:1.

Office in London for better lights, buoys, and beacons as well, to better protect its investments in notoriously dangerous seas. Other large business concerns on both the British and Dutch sides of the Strait followed suit. Yet the hand of the state is evident in most places, and certainly pushed the pace of lighting and buoying, even if both Singapore and Batavia were affected by other developments and considerations. We can see this in the concomitant rise of lights and the petroleum industry in Sumatra and Borneo, as oil poured forth from Belawan Deli, Palembang, and the western Makassar Strait. We can also see it in the appearance of lights along evolving shipping routes, which took Indies agricultural exports (via relatively underused sea passages) to Australia and Japan.[46] Imperial footprints were also evident in the increase of surveillance lighting over smaller and smaller vessels in the ports themselves:

Sebuah perahu Bugis telah dipungut oleh seorang pegawai shahbandar didalam pelabohan pada hari Thalasa dahulu. Perahu ini telah karim dudok dengan layar dan muatannya buah buah nenas.[47]

A Bugis ship was caught by the portmaster in the harbor on Tuesday. The vessel was sitting bountifully with its sail, and was caught with its cargo of pineapples. [Translation: E. Tagliacozzo]

This also happened in programs to ensure that these lights were standardized, as much as was feasible. This was practiced throughout the width and breadth of the Netherlands Indies as a colony.[48] In all ways, we can see a promulgated program of "seeing like a state" in all of the senses that James Scott's work has implied, albeit here in a very specific way.[49]

46. Board of Trade to CO, 12 January 1900, no. 16518, in CO 144/74; British North Borneo Co. Headquarters to CO, 15 April 1903; Labuan Coalfields Co. to British North Borneo Co. Headquarters, 30 March 1903; Government Pilot of Labuan to Labuan Coalfields Co., 4 Oct 1903, and Labuan Coalfields Co. to British North Borneo Co. Headquarters, 20 November 1903, all in CO 144/77; same author to same recipient, 20 September 1904, CO 144/78; "Kustverlichting," *ENI* 2 (1918): 495.

47. This surveillance even captured the activities of small Bugis craft carrying very prosaic cargoes (like pineapples) in Singapore harbor; see *Utusan Malayu* 1 (22 December 1908), 175.

48. See ARA, 1902, MR no. 210.

49. This kind of centralized attempt at uniformity, regardless (and often in spite of) the vagaries and demands of local conditions, is discussed brilliantly in James Scott, *Seeing like a State: How Certain Schemes to Improve the Human Condition Have Failed* (New Haven: Yale University Press, 1998.)

Lighting and Its Political Implications

Because Batavia and Singapore shared an enormous, extended liquid frontier, negotiations and occasional strife were part and parcel of colonial coexistence in the region.[50] Perhaps chief among these was the fact that each colony's oceanic policies significantly affected the other's; lights built on one side of the Straits of Melaka, for example, acted as beacons for shipping passing through the waterway regardless of the vessel's final destination. Active discussions (and downright squabbles) were constantly taking place across this international divide, therefore. Yet another political reality rested on the fact that the Straits Settlements was only part of a larger colonial enterprise in the region; the British presence included the Federated (and later Unfederated) Malay States, the "White Raja" of Sarawak's lands and seas in Borneo, as well as those of Sarawak's northern neighbor's, the British North Borneo Company. These divisions often clouded policy decisions, too. Finally, complicating the picture still further were attempts at centralization and control by the metropoles in London and the Hague, who often saw lighting as part of empire-wide plans for shipping lanes and grand strategy.[51] Even within the two colonies there were often countervailing political forces at work; in the Indies this took the form of late attempts at lighthouse uniformity (which we have just mentioned), while at the same time decentralization impulses divided regional jurisdiction over these very same installations.[52]

One of the most important conflicts played out over lighting, however, was the one contested internally between the British colonies and London. The

---

50. We might think of this outstretched domain as a "waterworld". For the implications of studying lighthouses as part of this world, part natural and part constructed, see Kirsten Hastrup. and Hastrup, Frida, eds. *Waterworlds: Anthropology and Fluid Environments*. New York: Berghahn Books, 2015, and John A. Love. *A Natural History of Lighthouses*. Dunbeath: Whittles Publishing, 2015.

51. See the discussions in the "Report from the Royal Commission on the Condition and Management of Lights, Buoys, and Beacons with Minutes of Evidence and Appendices," *British Parliamentary Papers*, Sessions 1861, vol. 5: *Shipping Safety*, 631–51.

52. In addition to the uniformity discussions (see n. 51), see ARA, Commander of the Marine to Gov Gen NEI, 24 Jan 1899, no. 895, in MR no. 159, for attempts at decentralization in Sumatra's East Coast and Southeastern Borneo. Decentralization was a government program initiated by Batavia and The Hague around the turn of the twentieth century. The Dutch Indies had grown enormously in size and complexity by this time, and it was felt that better governance would be achieved by devolving some power and decision-making to regional administrations.

needs (and desires) of the Straits Settlements in its relationship with London can serve as an example here. In the early 1870s the Straits Settlements continually petitioned the Colonial Office in London for new buoys to mark out harbor channels, even offering to pay for part of the experimental costs of getting new and high-technology buoys out to Southeast Asia. The same process happened again in 1901, this time with beacons, as the Straits government tried to pit two colonial agencies against each other (the crown agents and the Colonial Office) to make sure Penang got new beacons at a good price.[53] Paying for new equipment and installations was always a source of friction between London and the Straits. When the Master Attendant of the latter suggested new lights for Pulau Pisang, for example, Trinity House demurred and sent a new gas buoy instead, citing costs. This happened again and again in the correspondence between the two government entities, over lightships on Formosa Bank in 1887, or new lanterns for the Raffles lights in 1904.[54] The idea that general British interests should be served never seemed to enter into the discussion; both London and Singapore kept track of what mattered to each of them most, as the often acerbic nature of their correspondence suggests.

The relationship of British Sarawak with both Singapore and London was even more incendiary on the subject of lighting. In 1907 a long series of letters passed between Charles Brooke and various colonial administrators, both in London and Singapore; as a semi-independent "raja," Brooke was under little compunction to do anything the British asked of him. When Brooke wanted to demolish the Brooketon lighthouse in Muara, the Colonial Office begged him to think of Labuan's trade, which would suffer; "we had better avoid expropriation if we possibly can. There will be a difficulty about price and we shall annoy Sir Brooke and start him on further intrigues."[55] A British naval officer was sent to Borneo to assess the impact of Brooketon's closing, and he

---

53. See Governor Straits to CO, 20 April 1871, no. 93, in CO 273/46; Governor Straits to CO, 19 September 1873, no. 277, in CO 273/69; and Master Attendant, Singapore Harbour to CO, 11 Jan 1876, no. 14, in CO 273/83; The crown agents wrote to the Colonial Office that the Straits were writing to each London agency separately, and comparing prices; see Crown Agents to CO, 18 July 1901, in CO 273/276.

54. Trinity House to CO, 10 January 1887, no. 4204/86, in CO 273/149; Trinity House to CO, 11 February 1887, no. 271, in CO 273/149; Report by the Colonial Engineer on the Proposals of the Trinity House Engineer in Chief, 17 Aug 1904, no. 267, in CO 273/300.

55. Colonial Office to Charles Brooke, 9 January 1907, and Colonial Office Jacket, 8 January 1907, Telegram, both in CO 531/1.

recommended immediate construction of a new light (nearby, but offshore), if the raja demolished the existing structure. Charles Brooke eventually decided not to destroy the light; evidently he thought his influence would wane on that part of the Borneo coast if he razed the structure (the lighthouse was actually positioned on Brunei soil, but administered by Sarawak, because land claims in the area were still uncertain). He used this forbearance to full advantage in dealing with London, however. Anarchy might descend if he withdrew his presence from this part of the coast, Brooke stated, and "it is not my wish to part with any of (the) rights ceded to me by His Highness the Sultan of Brunei."[56] Lighthouse construction (and destruction) was used as a bargaining tool, therefore, in regional politics; a card to be played in helping (or hurting) other people's trade in neighboring waters.

Such changes in local politics in Sarawak were also visible in North Borneo as well. Labuan, London's small island outpost off the coast, was seen as a strategic way station along the China routes in the middle third of the nineteenth century; the dangers of piracy in these waters also made the island a Colonial Office priority, as Labuan was thought to have "some queer neighbors."[57] By the turn of the twentieth century, however, Labuan's importance had diminished, and Whitehall was kept busy full-time turning away requests by the North Borneo Co. to better light her shores. The Colonial Office felt that the Company should be responsible for these duties; the Company, trying to stretch its profits as far as possible, attempted whenever possible to get London to do her work for her. By 1907, however, even London was acknowledging that huge stretches of North Borneo's coasts were precariously underlit, and that this had all kinds of implications for regional security, as well as losses of shipping.[58] One colonial official summed up the mood at Whitehall admirably when he said that adequate lighting of North Borneo "would

56. H. Grants-Dalton, Captain and Senior Naval Officer, Straits of Malacca Division, to High Commissioner, Straits Settlements, 4 January 1907, in CO 531/1; Sir Charles Brooke to Lord Elgin, 11 January 1907; Sir Charles Brooke to Secretary of Colonial Office, 11 January 1907, both in CO 531/1.

57. The term was the Colonial Office's; piracy, the sultan of Brunei, and intrigues in the southern Philippines (between Sulu, the Spanish, Germany, and the United States) all were seen to make the area highly unstable. See Governor Labuan to CO, 20 March 1877, no. 32, and CO Jacket, 20 March 1877, both in CO 144/48.

58. British North Borneo Co. Headquarters to CO, 26 October 1899, and CO Jacket, 26 October 1899, both in CO 144/73; see also Admiralty to CO, 15 October 1907, M8148, and the Report of the HMS Cadmus on Sandakan Harbor and Marudu Bay, both in CO 531/1.

be desirable, but there is not enough money to do things that are only desirable."[59] The Company paid for some lighting in the following years, and the Colonial Office for other sections of the Borneo coast, but no one seemed to be fully satisfied with the solution. Matters had devolved sufficiently in 1913 that the Company even approached the American Philippines to do some of Borneo's lighting on contract, sending waves of protest and incredulity through the Colonial Office at the very thought of such an offer.[60]

A large part of this politics of lighting rested on the fact that lighthouses and their attendant maintenance costs were so expensive. In 1859, as mentioned, Batavia decided on a massive building program for lighthouses, beacons, and buoys in the Indies; 6.5 million guilders were set aside for the next twenty-five years, in an effort to build ten first-class, eighteen second-class, and ten third-class lighthouses, as well as twelve port-lights. Though some modifications were later made on these grandiose plans, by 1897 there were more than thirty lighthouses and beacons in the Indies, and more than that number of port-lights.[61] An examination of *Ministerie van Marine* archives data on light-construction shows why so much money was needed; around 1870, for example, iron light-towers were being built in the Bali Straits, stone foundations were being laid for other lights in the Java Sea, and more lighting was being planned for Batavia, in the tiny "Thousand Islands" archipelago.[62] By the 1880s, these construction plans were even more developed. Semarang was getting a new lighthouse, as was the southwest corner of Sumatra; coral reefs were being lit, and Bangka's channels were also being illuminated.[63] Though the costs of lighting the Indies were rising enormously in absolute terms, Dutch planners obviously thought the price was one well worth paying, as huge stretches of the islands were quickly being illuminated.[64]

59. Colonial Office Jacket, 10 May 1907, in CO 531/1.

60. See U.S. Dept. of State to British Ambassador, Washington, 3 March 1913; Foreign Office to CO, 22 April 1913, no. 13174/13; Colonial Office to British North Borneo Co. Headquarters, 26 April 1913, all in CO 531/5.

61. J. E. de Meijier, "Zeehavens en Kustverlichting," *Gedenkboek Koninklijk Instituut Ingenieurs* (1897): 304.

62. See ARA, Ministerie van Marine, Plaatsinglijst van Archiefbescheiden Afkomstig van de Vierde Afdeling: Bijlage 3, Specificatie van Pll nos. 321–32, no. 321/2.10, 2.11, 6.9.

63. Ibid., Bijlage 3, Specificatie van Pll nos. 321–332, no. 322/8.2, 8.11, 8.16; no. 323/12.7. These are just a few of the many light-constructions of this period, scattered throughout the archipelago.

64. This process could also work against the colonial state, however. An account in the National Archives of Indonesia (Arsip Nasional, Jakarta) tells of local pirates learning that a new

In the Straits Settlements the money needed (and allocated) for lighting, beaconing, and buoying British Southeast Asia was ever-increasing. In 1867, for example, the Cape Rachado Light was allocated $1,344 per year, with the Horsburgh light receiving $3,024 and the Raffles Lighthouse $900; all of the Straits lights together received $7,520. These funds were spent on salaries of the lightkeepers, transport to and from the lights, as well as maintenance, gas, and oil costs for each of the installations. By 1883, however, the total of nine Straits lights were annually costing the Singapore administration $22,501, which increased to $38,997 by 1910.[65] Yet this huge outlay of investment and materiel also paid for itself in the form of lights dues, which the Straits increasingly charged to passing shipping as a service rendered in area waters. In 1883, Singapore made $34,987 in this way; the following year, revenues climbed to $37,377.[66] Salaries, by the turn of the century, were costing the Straits government about $15,000 per annum, while oil and stores ran almost $5,000 per year, and rations for the lightkeepers over $7,500. While some money was recouped in the form of lights dues, building new lighthouses could be extremely expensive. While small or older lights could run only about $3–5,000 for total construction costs, the larger and newer installations were closer to the $50,000 range by the turn of the twentieth century.[67]

If lighting the archipelago was so expensive, therefore, it seems only natural that there would be both cooperation and competition between Singapore and Batavia on these matters. For the British, much of the equation rested on a feeling that Batavia insufficiently lit her own Indies waters; this was a problem for Singapore (and even London) as well, as so many English vessels passed through these same seas. The English solution was to disparage Dutch

---

light off the coast of South Sumatra was an ideal place to wait for passing prey; corsairs knew that shipping would make for the light to guide their passage, and the pirates could then come upon them unawares. See ARNAS, Maandrapport der Residentie Banka 1871 (Banka no. 97/5: July). The fact that area ports began to be better and better lit was also no guarantee for passing ships' safety; the much larger volume of ships, like moths around a flame, also attracted piracy and predation, even in places like Singapore. See the court case *The King vs. Chia Kuek Chin and Others* in *Straits Settlements Legal Reports* 13 (1915): 1, which outlines the parameters of an attack off Singapore as late as 1909. Most piracy was pushed to increasingly remote, interstitial spaces of state power by the turn of the twentieth century, however.

65. See Gov. Ord's dispatch in CO 273/13, 178ff; and CO 273/13/927 ff.224ff; also SSBB, 1883, p. W2; SSBB, 1910, V2.

66. *Straits Settlements Legislative Council Proceedings*, 1885, C141.

67. SSBB, 1899, W2.

FIGURE 12.1. The Panopticon: Karimata Strait, 1909
(KITLV Collection, Leiden, Netherlands)

"ineptitude" privately and to publicly coax Batavia into better lighting their shared international waterways. The British envoy in The Hague asked the Dutch minister for the colonies to improve the lighting situation at the Willem lighthouse, Pulau Bras, as well as at Diamondpoint (both in North Sumatra); privately, the Board of Trade in London wondered whether it wouldn't just be easier to have Singapore pay for these improvements herself. "We need not hint, at present, even to the Foreign Office, that the Straits Government should pay for part of this improved lighting," the Board of Trade said; first London wanted to see if the Dutch would make the improvements on their own bill.[68] Yet the Board of Trade also took an active part in less Machiavellian orchestrations as well, notifying British vessels when other lighting installations in the Indies were found to be deficient, or even downright dangerous. A situation of this nature happened in the Sunda Straits in 1883, for example, when the Krakatoa volcano exploded and the resulting conflagration destroyed all Dutch beacons and lights anywhere near the site of the devastation.[69]

Official thinking in the Dutch sphere on this issue was not the same. The Dutch needed the British lights on the other side of the Straits of Melaka for the safety of their own international shipping as well, so goodwill between these two colonial states was also an important factor in Dutch planning

68. See British Envoy, Den Haag to Foreign Office (hereafter FO), 25 November 1893, no. 79, in CO 273/192; Board of Trade to CO, 2 August 1893, no. 5707; Board of Trade Cover, 1 November 1893; and Board of Trade to CO, 1 November 1893, no. 417775, all in CO 273/191.

69. Board of Trade to CO, 30 August 1883, no. 6531; CO to Board of Trade, 31 August 1883, both in CO 273/124.

circles. Much of the Indies' exports were carried in English-owned bottoms, so there was often a natural symbiosis between these regimes in arrangements regarding colonial lighting. Yet many Dutchmen also felt that their own imperial project depended too heavily on English power and technology, and this seems to have been true especially in the maritime realm. Dutch authors periodically took to print in order to air their grievances on this issue, decrying the willingness of Batavia to depend on English lights, beacons, and hydrographic surveys, instead of undertaking their own. Some of this invective may have been employment related; the venom of men who saw contracts for such projects being held out to English firms or the Straits government, rather than to local Dutch concerns. Yet a significant portion of these complaints also seems to have been genuinely nationalistic in character, lamenting the fact that the Indies could not perform all of the duties incumbent upon a "real" imperial power (a situation we will see replicated in our next chapter, on hydrography).[70] Therefore, while each of these colonial regimes counted on the other's abilities to light their shared maritime frontier, the reasoning and rationales behind these concordances appear to have been quite at odds. London and its dependences saw themselves as "stuck" with the Dutch and their insufficient abilities vis-à-vis lighthouses. Batavia, meanwhile, saw themselves as marginalized by both the demands and the technological acumen of their neighbors to the north in the Straits.

The Technics of an Imperial Archipelago

One last component of colonial lighting as part of the colonial project needs to be discussed, and that is the technology itself behind this aspect of empire building. How were lighthouses, beacons, and buoys of the region constructed, how did their lenses work, and what was the science behind various installations? Certainly, as the technologies of such instruments improved over the course of the second half of the nineteenth century, these "tools of empire" became ever more valuable to Singapore and Batavia in monitoring and

---

70. For examples of Dutch writings on the shared seas between themselves and the British, and comparative appraisals of their abilities, see "Havenbedrijf in Indië," *Indische Gids* (hereafter, *IG*) 2 (1907): 1244–46; and I. S. G. Gramberg, "Internationale Vuurtorens," *De Economist* 1 (1882): 17–30; see also "De Indische Hydrographie," *IG* 6 (1882): 12–39; "Engeland's Hydrographische Opnemingen in Onze Kolonien," *IG* 2 (1891): 2013–15; and "Naschrift van de Redactie," *IG* 2 (1898): 1219.

channeling movements along their shared maritime frontier. Technology, in this sense, was crucial to the maturation of empire. Improvements in lighting apparatus meant that these states bettered their abilities to cordon, mark, and see the waters of a vast colonial archipelago. This last section of the chapter examines some of the changes that took place in specific technologies of lighting and buoys, as well as how these tools were bent toward the evolution of a more totalizing imperial project.

The structure and physicality of lighthouses in colonial Southeast Asia was extremely variable. Depending on the soil and/or bedrock of a given area, as well as on the local winds and seas, various designs and constructions could be implemented. Sandy and loose soils beneath these structures gave rise to screw-pile designs, for example; long, spear-like legs which caught the firmament with curved blades, making it harder for the light or beacon to be overturned. In areas of high winds or seas, where a massive structure would only attract more (not less) of nature's energy and brute force, iron-legged structures were also developed, which reduced surface area and weight while also making such structures easier to transport.[71] These structures, in the words of the theorist Roland Barthes, consisted of "empty centers"—a notion that Barthes used to great effect in describing the "empty" palace grounds in central Tokyo, paradoxically the most condensed and crowded city on earth: "Modernity is therefore built around an opaque ring . . . Whose own center is no more than an evaporated notion."[72]

We can think of many of these Indies lighthouses in the same way vis-à-vis Barthes's notion of the empty center; they were constructed mostly of air. In still other areas stone foundations were used, with many lights built on promontories, or along wide stretches of unmarked coast.[73] All of these geologies and topographies were found in the outstretched lands and seas of insular Southeast Asia. Lightships were also used extensively as stationary, moored hulks marking dangers with a light attached to the skeleton of a ship. The higher the construction of the light, the farther off it could be seen by mariners,

71. Findlay, *Description and List*, 5; see also the line drawings in *British Parliamentary Papers*, Sessions 1845, vol. 4: *Shipping Safety*, "Reports from Select Committees on Lighthouses, with Minutes of Evidence" (Shannon, 1970): 693.

72. Roland Barthes, *Empire of Signs* (New York: Hill and Wang, 1983), 32.

73. See ARA, Ministerie van Marine, Plaatsinglijst van Archiefbeschieden Afkomstig van de Vierde Afdeling: Bijlage 3, Specificatie van Pll nos. 321–32, no. 321/2.11 for Boompjeseiland; no. 323/10.6 for Edam Island; no. 323/11.6 for Tandjong Berikat, the first two in the Java Sea, the third in the waters off Bangka.

sometimes for dozens of miles.[74] The technologies behind all of these structures changed over time, as scientists and engineers continually found ways to reduce torque and strengthen the foundations of these objects.

The mechanics of lighting, fueling, and lenses also changed over time. The earliest lights and beacons in the region were oil-lit, a method both dangerous (because of the possibility of fire) and difficult to maintain, especially in the many out-of-the-way places of this vast archipelago. Gas lights followed, and this method was especially adopted after natural gas and petroleum was found in large quantities in the Indies, especially in northern Sumatra.[75] However, the main technological breakthrough was in mirrors and lenses, as the science of optics advanced internationally, and was applied locally in both British and Dutch waters. Catoptric systems of lighting were developed using reflection and mirrors; this kind of light gave off fixed, revolving, flashing or intermittent light, always by reflection through a central bank of mirrors. Polished copper was shaped into a geometrically perfect parabola to capture the beams; the light could then be concentrated and emanated in a single direction. Copper was used because it was relatively malleable, and resistant to corrosion in the harsh tropical climate of Southeast Asia. Eventually, more than a single lamp could be inserted inside the parabola, giving off larger and larger amounts of light. Up to twelve might be used on a single panel, which could then be rotated in different directions.[76] As Figure 12.2 shows, placing a light source at the focus of a parabolic reflector meant that all of the rays of light emerged parallel to one another. A single very bright beam was emitted, which was vital in shining illumination over the vast aqueous spaces of the archipelago.[77]

74. Findlay, *Description and List*, 7–8, for British lightships; ARA, Ministerie van Marine, Plaatsinglijst van Archiefbeschieden Afkomstig van de Vierde Afdeling: Bijlage 3, Specificatie van Pll nos. 321–32, no. 321/8.14 discusses a lightship being delivered for the Ministerie van Kolonien in The Hague, 1884; see also the table provided in Imray, *Lights and Tides*, xix.

75. "Kustverlichting," *ENI* 2 (1918): 495–96.

76. See Wolffe, *Brandy, Balloons, and Lamps*.

77. For more on the science of lighting, see Brian Bowers, *Lengthening the Day: A History of Lighting Technology* (Oxford: Oxford University Press, 1998); Sean Cubitt, "Electric Light and Electricity," *Theory, Culture and Society* 30, no. 7/8 (2013): 309–23; Tim Edensor, "Reconnecting with Darkness: Gloomy Landscapes, Lightless Places," *Social and Cultural Geography* 14, no. 4 (2013): 446–65; Tim Edensor, "Light Design and Atmosphere," *Journal of Visual Communication* 14, no. 3 (2015): 331–50; and Andrew Parker, "On the Origin of Optics," *Optics and Laster Technology* 43 (2011): 323–29.

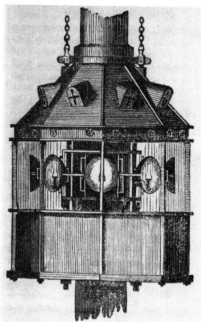

FIGURE 12.2. Screw-Pile Lights and Dioptric Lenses (Alexander Findlay, *A Description and List of the Lighthouses of the World* [London, 1861], 5, 24)

Relying rather on refracted light and lenses, dioptric systems were also utilized. In this case as well, the nature and quality of the light given off could be varied, depending on local conditions and requirements. Luminous flux was organized through a sequence of refractions, which then gave off a single, solid beam of light. Prisms, concentrators, and co-linearizers were all utilized to tighten the beam so that the light would be as densely packed as possible.[78] A later improvement was also made in the development of holophotal light for lighthouse and beacon use, which used the range of the light spectrum (through azimuthal condensing) more effectively than either of the two earlier systems.[79] This was particularly important in the tropics, because during the monsoons fog and heavy rains hung over much of maritime Southeast Asia.

78. "Dioptric" in *Webster's Unabridged Dictionary* (G. and C. Merriam Co, 1913), 415.

79. See Thomas Stevenson, *Lighthouse Illumination; Being a Description of the Holophotal System and of Azimuthal Condensing and Other New Forms of Lighthouse Apparatus* (Edinburgh, 1871); also Findlay, *Description and List*, 13–18, 19–24, 25–27; Imray, *Lights and Tides*, xvi–xvii.

Finally, after the turn of the twentieth century, electrical light was also being experimented with in lighthouses, though the Dutch seem to have lagged behind the British in implementing it in the Indies.[80] In 1912, Swedish engineer Nils Gustaf Dalén won a Nobel Prize in Physics for his invention of an automatic solar valve that regulated gaslight, which led to the spread of unmanned lighthouses on a grand scale. This development spread throughout the Indies after this time.

The technology of buoys also changed after the turn of the century, switching from small, often troublesome tools to massive, much more efficient ones, all of which began to ring these archipelagic seas. The use of iron in buoy construction made these devices much less susceptible to breaking away in Southeast Asia's heavy tropical storms; a strong chain link connected the surface float with a heavy impediment on the sea floor. The buoy itself could be fashioned in any one of a number of ways; red and black were used to mark off different sides of a channel depending on direction; green buoys signaled a dangerous wreck underneath the waves; top markers were stenciled in with numbers, to guide traffic along officially desired routes.[81] Following these directions, of course, implied moving under the vision of the state; vessels could be "herded" in this sense into channels where they were "safe," but also visible to the ruling regime. Despite rising costs, therefore, the British and the Dutch eagerly marked off the sea with these tools, all in an effort to direct the passing of traffic. Buoys were constantly on order in Penang, for example, to service the island's channel with the Malay mainland; this involved a good amount of negotiating with London, especially over who would pay the cost.[82] In the Dutch Indies, buoys were also ordered regularly, and were sent out to the colony (and later constructed locally) to map out area seas.[83] The *Tijdschrift voor het Zeewezen* gives a minute accounting of this process, as buoys appeared in many far-flung channels, from Pontianak to Palembang to southwest Sulawesi.[84] By the fin de siècle period, the colonial powers had graphed

---

80. "Kustverlichting," *ENI* 2 (1918): 497.

81. See the different kinds of buoys (mooring, can, "nun," wreck, iron spherical, and "monster") produced in James Imray, *Lights and Tides* (1866), xxii; "Bebakening," *ENI* 1 (1917): 212.

82. Gov. Straits to CO, 19 September 1873, no. 277, in CO 273/69; see also Board of Trade to CO, 18 July 1871, no. 2780, and I. N. Douglass to Robin Allen, Esq., 11 July 1871, in CO 273/52.

83. ARA, Ministerie van Marine, Plaatsinglijst van Archiefbeschieden Afkomstig van de Vierde Afdeling: Bijlage 3, Specificatie van Pll nos. 321–32, no. 329/25.1.

84. "Pontianak-Rivier," *TvhZ* (1875): 236; "Tonen Gelegd voor de Monding van de Soensang," Palembang," *TvhZ* (1878): 210–11; "Bakens op de Reede van Makassar," *TvhZ* (1880): 308.

significant stretches of archipelagic space through these devices, and then moved shipping along the resultant grids accordingly.

In this very broad maritime arena, harbor improvements were another important part of advancing state maritime technologies. As many area ports grew in size and importance during the second half of the nineteenth century, they became bustling, chaotic commercial centers, places where even the state itself (at the very center of government power) had trouble seeing all activity that was occurring. Harbor-improvement schemes allowed Batavia and Singapore the chance to try to gain control over runaway growth by altering the physical dimensions of the harbor into desired shapes and forms. This happened in very small ports, such as on the coast of Selangor in the early 1890s, but also in much larger harbors, such as Penang's, which received a large number of new beacons and lights around the turn of the century. Even Singapore was continually undergoing these massive "face-lifts," designed to render the port more functional and workable to the state.[85] Port buoys were troublesome and unreliable in the Indies until the mid-nineteenth century, but this too began to change by our time frame, when attempts at stricter supervision were instituted at the end of the century. In 1871 the roads of Batavia, for example, received no less than forty-two new (or repaired) lighting or buoying installations over the course of that year. Especially with the construction of Tanjung Priok between 1877 and 1885, this program of expansion and development continued over the next few decades.[86]

This examination of lights, beacons, and buoys in insular Southeast Asia, and their relationship to colonial state-formation can be concluded with two glances at particular cases of lighting, both of them in the Straits of Melaka. The first concerns the eastern approaches to Singapore around the turn of the twentieth century. Private suggestions had been made to the Straits government that a light was urgently needed here, as many vessels sailed from Singapore all the way to Hong Kong without seeing a lighthouse or beacon for 1,300

85. See *Papers Relating to the Protected Malay States: Reports for 1890*, "Selangor," 47; "Penang Harbour Improvements," *SSLCP* C (1899): 341; "Correspondence Regarding a Light-Ship for Penang Harbour," *SSLCP* C (1901): 79–80; "Penang Harbour Improvements," *SSLCP* C (1902): 35; "Singapore Harbour Improvements," *SSLCP* C (1902): 43; "Report on the Blasting Operations Carried Out in 1902 upon Sunken Rocks at the Mouth of the Singapore River," *SSLCP* C (1903): 131–32.

86. Meijier, "Zeehavens," 304; "Kustverlichting," *ENI* 2 (1918): 497; "Reede van Batavia," *TvhZ* (1871): 222–24; ARA, Ministerie van Marine, Plaatsinglijst van Archiefbeschieden Afkomstig van de Vierde Afdeling: Bijlage 3, Specificatie van Pll nos. 321–32, no. 322/8.1

nautical miles.[87] Yet this project, on a small island called Pulau Alor, proved a complicated undertaking. For one thing, the island was owned by the sultan of Johor, so nothing could be done without the sultan's express permission. Diplomacy thus complicated matters of lighting, a problem not encountered on the Formosa shoal on the other side of the Straits. The sultan ultimately gave his consent to the establishment of an English light-structure on this island, but refused to pay the costs.[88] The other problem with the Pulau Aor light was that it had the misfortune of being proposed at the same time as a much larger lighting project. The lighthouse at Fort Canning, one of the most important lights in the Straits, was in the process of being scheduled for modernization and a refitting at century's end. Most resources and administrative attention went to its repairs and upgrades which were significant and expensive.[89] Pulau Aor eventually got a small iron light structure, but the eastern approaches to Singapore, as well as the waters bordering on Johor (Singapore's northern neighbor) were given secondary priority.[90] The balance of international diplomacy and the designs of the metropolitan center were crucial in lighting, therefore, alongside the designs and wishes of serving civil servants..

In Dutch waters, across the Straits of Melaka, the complex of debates around lights and lighting was no less complex. The importance of these structures—especially in a theater of war like Aceh—were even more apparent to officials, who understood very clearly that these installations were to help facilitate trade, but also to keep any eye on local movements. One of the first constructions attempted by the Dutch after a beachhead had been established in Aceh was a lighthouse; it was stationed on Pulao Bras off the coast. The tower took much longer to build than anticipated because of sickness and evacuations from the war, but the first stones were set in 1874, and the light came on the next year. In 1876 the structure withstood its first serious earthquake;

---

87. An official complaint came from Captain Symons of the *Paramatta*. See Deputy of the Officer Administering the Government, Straits, to Sultan of Johore, 20 February 1900, in *SSLCP* (1900): C258.

88. See Sultan of Johore to Gov. Straits, 25 April, 1900, in *SSLCP*, App. C (1900): 258–59.

89. Detailed examinations of many witnesses (mostly sea captains) about this project are produced, along with much official correspondence, in "Minutes of the Committee to Report on the Fort Canning Light," *SSLCP* (1900), App. C5–16; and "Correspondence Regarding Proposed New Light for Fort Canning," in *SSLCP*, App. C (1900): 252–58.

90. "Report of the Committee," 3 January 1900, no. 3, in *SSLCP* (1900): C3–4.

towering at 160 meters high, it was visible for 32 miles.[91] Later in 1876 a second light was added to the installation, to warn the Dutch of any potential sea dangers from the northwest. Further lights followed on the outstretched east coast of Aceh, and this area, along with Pulau Weh at the extreme northern corner of Sumatra, ultimately became among the best-lit areas in all of the Indies.[92] This should hardly surprise us. Situated alongside a wide, shallow strait, this arena provided all of the attributes and conditions which marked lighting in Southeast Asia for the entirety of our period. Ships passed by in great numbers, and trade was always increasing. Indigenous people, usually thought to be unable to adequately light area waters themselves, had to be helped toward modern navigation, it was thought by Europeans. And another colonial power, in this case the British, sat just over the horizon with their own imposing structures facing south. The lighthouses of these two regimes examined each other silently until the decades of decolonization in the 1940s and '50s. Alternately allies, and sometimes even enemies, both attempted continuous illumination across their mutually shared domain.

Conclusion

The evolution of coast lighting in maritime Southeast Asia and the rise of state optics in colonial times offer salient instruction about the pace and nature of evolving imperial control in this part of the world. Much like other technologies of colonial governance, lighthouses sprang up in increasing numbers as state concerns grew over maritime safety and navigational movement.[93] The first lights were positioned in places of the greatest importance to these regimes: outside major harbors, on busy shipping routes, and near points of danger, like wrecks or submerged reefs. Yet they gradually came to dot much

91. H. E. van Berckel, "De Bebakening en Kustverlichting," *Gedenkboek Koninklijke Instituut Ingenieurs* (1847–97): 309–10.

92. "Poeloe Bras," *TvhZ* (1876): 247; "Kustverlichting," *ENI* 2 (1918): 495; "Poeloe-Weh," *Indische Mercuur* 44 (5 November 1901): 820.

93. Here similarities with the colonial prison, the other imposing structure of colonial vision and coercion, are manifest. Zinoman points out that French naval officers almost immediately drew up plans for prisons after taking parts of southern Vietnam in 1862; by 1865, there were already two enormous penitentiaries in the colony. See Peter Zinoman on the history of the modern prison in Peter Zinoman, *The Colonial Bastille: A History of Imprisonment in Vietnam 1862–1940* (Berkeley: University of California Press, 2001).

of the region's seascape, as Batavia and Singapore increasingly lit their shared archipelago for the burgeoning traffic of the twentieth century. By 1910 the busiest local harbors were illuminated by these administrations, as were many of the most distant maritime frontiers of this enormous island world. Far-flung geographies and difficult terrain could still thwart the European colonial advance in the early twentieth century, though this state of affairs would not last long. The ocean, however, had mostly been mastered by the West by this time, and it was exactly technologies of maritime control that helped allow such small numbers of men to eventually dominate one of the world's largest archipelagoes.

Building imperial lighthouses as part of this dialectic was usually a contested phenomenon, I have argued, and was not simply dictated from above by a "monolithic" state.[94] A range of different actors had different interests in this arena, and these programs only sometimes converged when it came to lighting. The fragmented nature of British authority in the region, for example, made it difficult to coordinate lighting policy, as the Straits Settlements, British North Borneo, and Sarawak rarely agreed on who was responsible for lights, and who would pay their costs. Metropolitan policies from London and The Hague also often ran counter to local colonial interests when it came to lighting, sometimes for reasons of funding, and sometimes because of disputes over which spaces required these installations first. Finally, international diplomacy was contentious as well, both between the British and the Dutch, and between these European regimes and local elites. Southeast Asians understood that the grafting of these technologies onto local seascapes had significant power implications. The sultan of Johor used his leverage to obtain revenue from Singapore in exchange for his permission to station a British lighthouse on his soil. Conversely, across the Strait in North Sumatra, the Acehnese lost their sultanate to the Dutch, and this was partially achieved through the military navigational support provided by Batavia's massive

---

94. Lighthouses were and are powerful symbols and structures of state power, but their history—especially in the colonies—shows that their imposition was far from completely coordinated. In this sense, they provide interesting foils to literature on the maturing colonial state in Southeast Asia. To take one example from many, John Furnivall's portrayal of British rule in Burma implies a much more orderly and coherent process than we have seen in the British and Dutch (often) fumbling efforts to construct lighthouses and buoys in insular Southeast Asia. See John Furnivall, *The Fashioning of Leviathan: The Beginnings of British Rule in Burma*, ed. Gehan Wijeyewardene (Canberra: Economic History of Southeast Asia Project and the Thai-Yunnan Project, 1991).

lighthouse on Pulau Bras. In both cases, the imposition of lights as crucial "tools of empire" helped signal the maintenance of indigenous authority or its demise. The substantial, sometimes towering presence of lighthouses went some way in laying out who would be able to dominate in the new power hierarchies of "high colonialism," albeit as second-tier vassals, and who would give up authority to ever more insistent colonial governments.

At the fin de siècle, the powers of Dutch and British statecraft in Southeast Asia were more vital and substantial than they had ever been in the region. This was more discernible in the oceanic realm than in many other fields of imperial interest (the "unpacified uplands" of Borneo and Sumatra, for example), and the expansion of lights, beacons, and buoys was one reason why. These devices not only allowed trade and shipping to be afforded relatively safer navigational passage at different places along the frontier; they also allowed commerce and movement to be channeled into discernible, regulated avenues for the state.[95] Shipping that sailed outside prescribed pathways could increasingly be nudged toward sanctioned routes; the state was able to dictate the flow and direction of mercantile activity as never before. Beacons, marked buoys, and strategically placed lighthouses ensured that this would be so. Equipped with new technologies of lighting that allowed this regulation to be carried out ever larger geographies, Batavia and Singapore slowly illuminated maritime Southeast Asia in larger and larger swaths. All spaces of imperial navigational "blindness" did not disappear at once, or at the same rate in the various far-flung parts of the world's largest archipelago. Yet by the early twentieth century, unlike much of the century previously, many of insular Southeast Asia's thousands of islands were lit by the optical tools of the two principal colonial regimes. Hegemony, in this case, went hand in hand with the technologies that enabled it. A seascape of dozens of lighthouses outstretched to the margins of the horizons meant greater navigational security for many, yet it also signified a vista of a more fraught and surveillance-filled world.[96]

---

95. Here the best analogy to other instruments of coercion is not the prison but the fingerprint; the emerging "science" of dactyloscopy allowed the state to channel and index moving subjects.

96. See, for example, Chris Otter, *The Victorian Eye: A Political History of Light and Vision in Britain, 1800–1900* (University of Chicago Press, 2008), and A. Miller, "The Lighthouse Top I See: Lighthouses as Instruments and Manifestations of State Building in the Early Republic," *Building and Landscapes: Journal of Vernacular Architecture Forum* 17, no. 11 (2010): 13–14.

13

Of Maps and Men

HYDROGRAPHY AND EMPIRE

Laut menjadi pantai, pantai menjadi laut. [The sea becomes the shore, the shore becomes the sea.]

—INDONESIAN SEAMAN'S PROVERB[1]

LITERATURE ON COLONIAL cartography has never been as occupied with the sea as it has been on mapping done on land.[2] Valid rationales abound for this. Almost nine-tenths of the globe's land surface came to be controlled by the West on the eve of World War I, and historians no doubt felt they had their hands full in trying to explain these terra firma conquests alone. Land was the "ground zero" of cultural contact; surely the terrestrial realm was the best place to formulate interpretations of domination. Yet these processes of conquest and incorporation were also very important by sea, and epistemological translations of "space" into maps also took place in this realm.[3] This happened globally, but it especially happened in archipelagic settings, such as were found in island Southeast Asia (the area currently comprised by Indonesia,

---

1. Translation: E. Tagliacozzo.

2. See, for example, Jeremy W. Crampton. "Maps as Social Constructions: Power, Communication and Visualization," *Progress in Human Geography* 25, no. 2 (2001): 235–52; and Jeremy W. Crampton and John Krygier, "An Introduction to Critical Cartography," *ACME: An International E-Journal for Critical Geographies* 4, no. 1 (2006): 11–33.

3. See Dava Sobel, *Longitude* (New York: Penguin, 1995) for a general overview; and John Noble Wilford, *The Mapmakers* (New York: Vintage, 1982), especially 128–60.

Malaysia, Singapore, Brunei, and the Philippines).[4] Here a "rounding off" of sorts took place, as Europeans hydrographically cordoned off empires that were separated by open sea. Colonial powers eyed each other warily in these arenas, competing and sometimes also cooperating in the maritime division of the world. Contemporary historians have begun to peer at these mapping processes as well, looking at piracy as a form of resistance against the expanding colonial state; Japanese maritime surveying as a precursor to later armed aggression in Southeast Asia; and other such themes.[5] The academy is now burrowing back into the archives to analyze the sea once more as a complex site of cultural exchange.[6] The new lines of research that result bring together

4. For some of the global manifestations of these historical processes, encompassing Hawaii, Canada, and East Africa, see Simo Laurila, *Islands Rise from the Sea: Essays on Exploration, Navigation, and Mapping in Hawaii* (New York: Vantage Press, 1989); Stanley Fillmore, *The Chartmakers: The History of Nautical Surveying in Canada* (Toronto: Canadian Hydrographic Service, 1983); US Mississippi River Commission, *Comprehensive Hydrography of the Mississippi River and its Principal Tributaries from 1871 to 1942* (Vicksburg, MS: Mississippi River Commission, 1942); Edmond Burrows, *Captain Owen of the African Survey: The Hydrographic Surveys of Admiral WFW Owen on the Coast of Africa and the Great Lakes of Canada* (Rotterdam: A. A. Balkema, 1979); C. G. C. Martin, *Maps and Surveys of Malawi: A History of Cartography and the Land Survey Profession, Exploration Methods of David Livingstone on Lake Nyassa, Hydrographic Survey and International Boundaries* (Rotterdam: A. A. Balkema, 1980). For Southeast Asia, especially colonial Indonesia, see Christiaan Biezen, "'De Waardigehid van een Koloniale Mogendheid': De Hydrografische Dienst en de Kartering van de Indische Archipel tussen 1874 en 1894," *Tijsdchrift voor het Zeegeschiedenis* 18, no. 2 (1999): 23–38.

5. See John Butcher and Robert Elson, *Sovereignty and the Sea: How Indonesia Became an Archipelagic State* (Singapore: National University of Singapore Press, 2017); Eric Tagliacozzo, "'Kettle on a Slow Boil': Batavia's Threat Perceptions in the Indies' Outer Islands," *Journal of Southeast Asian Studies* 31, no. 1 (2000): 70–100; J. L. Anderson, "Piracy in the Eastern Seas, 1750–1856: Some Economic Implications," in *Pirates and Privateers: New Perspectives on the War on Trade in the Eighteenth and Nineteenth Centuries*, ed. David Starkey, E. S. van Eyck van Heslinga, and J. A. de Moor (Exeter: University of Exeter Press, 1997); Ghislaine Loyre, "Living and Working Conditions in Philippine Pirate Communities," in *Pirates and Privateers*, ed. Starkey, Van Eyck van Heslinga, and Moor; Kunio Katayama, "The Japanese Maritime Surveys of Southeast Asian Waters before the First World War" *Institute of Economic Research Working Paper* 85 (Kobe University of Commerce, 1985).

6. In Indonesian waters, see H. M. van Aken, "Dutch Oceanographic Research in Indonesia in Colonial Times," *Oceanography* 18, no. 4 (2005): 30–41; and J. I. Pariwono, A. G. Ilahude, and M. Hutomo, "Progress in Oceanography of the Indonesian Seas: A Historical Perspective," *Oceanography* 18, no. 4 (2005): 42–49. More generally, see, for example, Peter Linebaugh and Marcus Rediker, *The Many-Headed Hydra: Sailors, Slaves, Commoners, and the Hidden History of the Revolutionary Atlantic* (Boston: Beacon Press, 2000).

science, colonialism, and the imperial interface, and examine their collective confluence across a range of local possibilities.

Chapter 13 adds to this growing scholarship by analyzing the imbricated roles of hydrography, technology, and coercion in late-nineteenth-century Southeast Asia.[7] At issue here are predominantly the waters of what is now termed Malaysia, Singapore, and Indonesia, which stretched from North Sumatra east to West Papua, and from Timor north to Mindanao. In this vast maritime domain, the size of the continental United States, improvements in hydrographic knowledge went hand in hand with the advancing imperial presence. Though the evolution of sea maps was partially conditioned by expanding trade (metropoles, after all, knew that greater hydrographic knowledge equaled fewer marine disasters, and hence more revenue), crucially, I argue, this evolution was usually linked to colonial expansion as well. As James Scott has asked, "How did the state gradually get a handle on its subjects and their environment? Suddenly (many) processes . . . seemed comprehensible as attempts at legibility and simplification. In each case, officials took exceptionally complex, illegible, and local practices . . . and created a standard grid whereby it could be centrally recorded and monitored."[8]

We will view the above interrelationships in three sections. First, we will examine how a "seepage" of vessels, autochthonous and otherwise, crossed the evolving spheres of British and Dutch maritime space, continuing freewheeling patterns of trade and shipping which area regimes now eyed very warily, including cartographically. Second, we will analyze how both colonial powers began to explore and map these marine domains, using hydrography as a tool in order to better understand the limits and dimensions of their emerging empires. Finally, we will see how this advancing knowledge was applied to statecraft and coercion, as the English and Dutch imperial projects marked off Southeast Asia's maritime environment into domains that each controlled, though always in part only.[9]

7. For an analog with India, see Matthew Edney, "The Ideologies and Practices of Mapping and Imperialism," in *Social History of Science in Colonial India*, ed. S. Irfan Habib and Dhruv Raina, 25–68. New Delhi: Oxford University Press, 2007.

8. James Scott, *Seeing like a State: How Certain Schemes to Improve the Human Condition Have Failed* (New Haven: Yale University Press, 1992), 2.

9. For the link between power and praxis in mapping, see Chris Perkins, "Cartography—Cultures of Mapping: Power in Practice," *Progress in Human Geography* 28, no. 3 (2004): 381–91.

MAP 13.1. Hydrographic Waters

Without these simultaneous advances in marine mapping, colonial consolidation could only have happened with great difficulty in Southeast Asia. Though the history of cartography has traditionally been a land-based avenue of inquiry, as discussed above, in this part of the world the sea and knowledge *of* the sea were crucial in building an imperial project. Insular Southeast Asia's topography dictated this equation from the start. With its thousands of far-flung islands, broad but shallow seas, and extensive interior river systems, coercion and the projection of imperial power were made possible only through maritime means. Yet local marine environments were not immediately receptive arenas for European political maneuvers; they needed to be mapped and understood by those who hoped to use them for their own purposes. The processes of tabulating, indexing, and surveying local waters, therefore, became of crucial importance to both of these colonial states. This involved the physical layout of the sea bottom and any structures and formations therein, but also understanding and describing currents, tides, and attributes of the sea across large geographies. How did the British and Dutch envision these vast maritime spaces in the mid-nineteenth century, as opposed to the years around the fin de siècle? How central was hydrography to cooperating and competing imperial projects in this part of the world? In Central Asia in the late nineteenth century, Imperial Russia, Britain, and China raced to map the huge spaces of the high steppe.[10] In much of Africa during this same period, colonial powers struggled to chart the interior worlds of the rain forest belt, across the vast equatorial center of that continent.[11] In Southeast Asia, however, the contested terrain—whether politically or intellectually conceived—was largely maritime in its essence. Such a theater made sure that a highly unusual set of circumstances ruled locally, and this in turn assisted the manner in which power, knowledge, and politics came together in the fading years of the nineteenth century.[12]

Surveillance and the "Seepage" of Indigenous Movement

Southeast Asia as a maritime arena was on the verge of huge changes by the fin-de-siècle period. The exceedingly open maritime trading cadence of the region, which has been discussed by many historians through different lenses, was starting to significantly change by this time.[13] In the early decades of the

10. Peter Hopkirk, *The Great Game: The Struggle for Empire in Central Asia* (New York: Kodansha International, 1992).

11. See Samuel Nelson, *Colonialism in the Congo Basin, 1880–1940* (Athens, OH: Ohio University Center for International Studies, 1994); for some of the primary sources here, see Barbara Harlow and Mia Carter, *Imperialism and Orientalism: A Documentary Sourcebook* (Malden: Blackwell, 1999).

12. See Stuart Elden, "Contingent Sovereignty, Territorial Integrity and the Sanctity of Borders," *SAIS Review* 26, no. 1 (2006): 11–24.

13. The fullest explication of these centuries immediately prior to our period can be found in Anthony Reid, *Southeast Asia in the Age of Commerce, 1450 to 1680*, 2 vols. (New Haven: Yale University Press, 1988 and 1993). French-language scholarship has also been particularly good on this theme, especially via Denys Lombard; see Denys Lombard, *Le sultanat d'Atjéh au temps d'Iskandar Muda (1607–1636)*, Publications de l'École française d'Extrême-Orient, vol. 61 (Paris: École française d'Extrême-Orient, 1967); Denys Lombard, "Voyageurs français dans l'Archipel insulindien, XVIIe, XVIIIe et XIXe siècles," *Archipel* 1 (1971): 141–68; Denys Lombard, "L'horizon insulindien et son importance pour une compréhension globale," in *L'islam de la*

century, the first paper manifestation of this change was felt through the Anglo-Dutch Treaty of 1824, which divided the Straits of Melaka not geographically, but rather into northern and southern "spheres of influence." The British inherited sway over lands and seas north of this imaginary line, while the Dutch were free to expand outward from their base in Java to the southern reaches of the insular world. Though there were practical ramifications to this agreement (most notably the swapping of Dutch Melaka on the Malay peninsula for British Bengkulu in West Sumatra), the abilities of England and the Netherlands to police the entirety of this maritime frontier was still quite limited. As we can see from Western transcriptions and translations of early Malay maps, European were still coming to terms not only with the topography of this part of the world but also with terminologies. In the linguistic renderings of one such early local map, pride of place was given mainly to hydrographic terms (in addition to place-names, which I do not include here):

Ayer	= stream	padang	= plain
Bakau	= mangrove	perenggan	= frontier
Batu	= stone	pulau	= island
Benua	= mainland	selat	= channel
Besar	= large	sunggai	= river
Beting	= shoal	tanah	= territory
Gunong	= mountain	tanjong	= promontory
Kechil	= small	tasik	= harbor[14]

Over the next several decades, these policing abilities started to slowly grow, however, and the imposition of a new treaty in 1871 started to concretize what had existed mostly in name a half century earlier. The Treaty of 1871 gave Batavia a free hand at expansion in the remaining indigenous areas of Sumatra, in exchange for guaranteed British commercial privileges south of the original Straits dividing line. Aggression and expanding influence proceeded quickly

---

seconde expansion: Actes du Colloque organisé au Collège de France en mars 1981 (Paris: Association pour l'Avancement des Études Islamiques, 1983), 207–26; reedited in Archipel 29 (1985): 35–52. See also French translations of Indonesian historians writing on this general theme; A. B. Lapian, "Le rôle des orang laut dans l'histoire de Riau," Archipel 18 (1979): 215–22; Dg Tapala La Side, "L'expansion du royaume de Goa et sa politique maritime aux XVIe et XVIIe siècles," Archipel 10 (1975): 159–72.

14. From R. H. Phillimore, "An Early Map of the Malay Peninsula," Imago Mundi 13 (1956): 175–79, at 178.

after this in both Malay and "Indonesian" waters. In 1873 the Dutch attacked Aceh, the last remaining sultanate of any size in the Indies, and in 1874 England's own "Forward Movement" started, with the Pangkor Engagement of that year. In 1878 North Borneo was annexed by the British North Borneo Company, and by 1896 British influence over half of the Malay Peninsula was unchallenged. By the fin de siècle period, both European powers marshalled colonies in the region that appear strikingly similar to the post-independence avatars of Malaysia and Indonesia in our own time.

Yet building these empires was one thing; maintaining them was something else entirely, in terms of frontier formation.[15] This was apparent nearly everywhere along the emerging Anglo-Dutch divide in the region. In the Straits of Melaka, Sultan Taha of Jambi's men were continually able to cross the maritime boundary, bringing back food and weapons from Singapore to feed Taha's highland resistance project against the Dutch.[16] These supply journeys were successful enough by the 1880s that the Dutch consul in Penang asked Batavia to require oaths from passing traders, stating that they were not carrying any contraband bound for the resistance forces in Sumatra.[17] Dutch attempts to concretize the imaginary line across the Straits eventually led to a chorus of outrage from merchants under the British flag, however, as the latter saw their economic opportunities being undercut by any stricter imposition of the frontier.[18] By the years approaching the turn of the twentieth century, when Dutch naval patrols were becoming better able to police the Straits against trade movements crossing these shallow waters, this outrage had reached beyond the local authorities and was even heard back in Europe. London's official policy by this time, however, was to let the Dutch subdue the indigenous sultanates of Sumatra, even if this meant a temporary decline in trade for England's own merchants in the Straits.[19] The oceanic boundary between states, thus, gradually became ossified, and this state of affairs was at least partially due to

15. Eric Tagliacozzo, *Secret Trades, Porous Borders: Smuggling and States along a Southeast Asian Frontier, 1865–1915* (New Haven: Yale University Press, 2005).

16. Algemeene Rijksarchief (Dutch State Archives, The Hague, hereafter, ARA), Dutch Consul, Singapore to Gov. Gen. NEI, 26 December 1885, no. 974 in 1885, MR no. 802; see Elsbeth Locher-Scholten, *Sumatraans sultanaat en koloniale staat: De relatie Djambi-Batavia (1830–1907) en het Nederlandse imperialisme* (Leiden: KITLV Uitgeverij, 1994).

17. ARA, Dutch Consul, Penang to Gov. Gen. NEI, 29 March 1887, no. 125, in 1887, MR no. 289.

18. ARA, 1894, MR no. 298.

19. See the plea by the Penang Chamber of Commerce to the English authorities, 18 August 1893, in PRO/FO Confidential Print Series no. 6584/16(i).

England's desire to maintain existing trade realities and opportunities in the archipelago.

This was true not only in the Straits of Melaka, however. The huge, landed presence of Borneo also meant that there was a huge amount of "trade seepage" across nominally separate spheres, at least until the turn of the twentieth century. We have already noted that the treaties of 1824 and 1871 set the diplomatic parameters of the Anglo-Dutch frontier in Southeast Asia, drawing a fixed line between the two evolving colonial projects. Yet the small historiography that presently exists on the border regions shows us clearly that these lines were transgressed in a variety of ways, including by way of rivers that cut across this huge forest wilderness. James Warren has shown, for example, how the historical Captain Lingard (who would later become famous in Joseph Conrad's novels) bartered opium, salt, and guns into the interior of East Borneo, mostly via his travels up several local rivers. Lingard set off a "seepage effect" of movement and trade from the North Borneo Company's expanding dominions, as indigenous merchants headed south into Batavia's sphere.[20] Warren has also shown how Bugis trade settlements in Eastern Borneo overlapped Tausug forts in the interior, connecting outstretched networks of alliance, competition, and commerce across the emerging frontier.[21] Working on the opposite side of the border in British Sarawak, Daniel Chew has brought to light the boundary-crossing activities of interior Chinese traders, who fled outstanding debts to more prominent Chinese merchants downriver, and disappeared silently across the Dutch frontier.[22] A variety of scholars have illuminated how difficult it was for Batavia to halt these diffusions in the fin de siècle period, as the Dutch weren't entirely certain where the boundary between empires began, and where it ended.[23]

20. James Francis Warren, "Joseph Conrad's Fiction as Southeast Asian History," in James Francis Warren, *At the Edge of Southeast Asian History: Essays by James Frances Warren* (Quezon City: New Day Publishers, 1987), 12.

21. James Francis Warren, *The Sulu Zone: The Dynamics of External Trade, Slavery, and Ethnicity in the Transformation of a Southeast Asian Maritime State* (Singapore: Singapore University Press, 1981), 83–84.

22. Daniel Chew, *Chinese Pioneers on the Sarawak Frontier (1841–1941)* (Singapore: Oxford University Press, 1990), 115–17.

23. Reed Wadley, "Warfare, Pacification, and Environment: Population Dynamics in the West Borneo Borderlands (1823–1934)," *Moussons* 1 (2000): 41–66; G. J. Resink, "De Archipel voor Joseph Conrad," *BTLV* (1959): ii; F. C. Backer Dirks, *De Gouvernements marine in het*

The explosion of maritime commerce in the region pointed to two opposing trends.[24] Oceanic trade could be useful as an engine of growth and coercion by the state if harnessed, but it could also be used by those who wished to trade outside of the state's vision. By the 1880s and 1890s, therefore, a renewed effort was made on the part of the colonial state to try to control these processes, and to bend maritime growth toward the state's own ends. In the Dutch East Indies, the KPM (Koninklijke Paketvaart Maatschappij, Dutch Colonial Packet Service) was given its inaugural contract in 1891, with orders from Batavia to expand shipping links to the rest of the archipelago.[25] Joop à Campo has shown how KPM expansion slowly snaked up Borneo's rivers, and toward some of the more distant coasts of the Indies, binding the archipelago into a grid over the next several decades.[26] The Dutch used the KPM, and a series of exclusionary shipping rules called the *scheepvaartregelingen*, to try to monopolize trade and shipping patterns throughout their maritime empire in Southeast Asia. Yet, even as the marine transport arm of the colonial state expanded, British, French, Chinese, and indigenous Southeast Asian shipping continued to ply Batavia's archipelago. Sailing and steam craft under these flags were continuing to run a huge breadth of trade goods of all sorts across the frontier.[27]

Many of these commodities were moving beyond legal circuits of exchange, and this played on the minds of Dutch civil servants, both in the Indies and in Holland. Without the taxes accrued from trade, it was difficult to build the empire, let alone pay for the soldiers who maintained it. Yet there were also politics involved in these matters as well. Pointing to Dutch complaints about the levels of smuggling across the Straits, a British envoy in the Indies

voormalige Nederlands-Indië in haar verschillende tijdsperioden geschetst; III. 1861–1949 (Weesp: De Boer Maritiem, 1985), 173.

24. Chiang Hai Ding, *A History of Straits Settlements Foreign Trade, 1870–1915* (Singapore: Memoirs of the National Museum, 6, 1978), 136, 139.

25. ARA, 1888, MR no. 461. The KPM was only the latest incarnation of steam-shipping services in the Dutch East Indies. Two companies, the first called Cores de Vries, and the second the NISM (Nederlandsch-Indische Stoomvaart Maatschappij/Dutch-Indies Steamship Company), had preceded it. Neither of these two companies, however, was charged with helping Batavia conquer and maintain its East Indian possessions to the degree that the KPM was from its very beginnings (indeed, the NISM, despite its name, was British-owned).

26. The KPM's reach, by 1902, stretched all the way to Merauke in Dutch New Guinea; see ARA 1902, MR no. 402. Also see the maps reproduced in à Campo, *Koninklijke Paketvaart Maatschappij*, 697–99.

27. H. La Chapelle, "Bijdrage tot de Kennis van het Stoomvaartverkeer in den Indischen Archipel," *De Economist* (1885) 2, 689–90.

80

Rif Samuel, Zuidoostelijk van Zuid Pageh-eiland, Sumatra, W. kust. — Volgens bekendmaking is door den Gezagvoerder van het N. I. schip Samuel, ZO. lijk van Zuid Pageh-eiland, een rif gezien, kenbaar aan verkleuring van water, op de peiling:

Mongo-eiland NW., Zuidhoek van Zuid Pageh ZW. t. W. ½ W.

Ligging ongeveer: 3° 16′ Z. Br., 100° 32′ 30″ O. L.

—

Onderzoek naar reven NO. van Bangka. — Volgens bekendmaking van den Kommandant der Zeemacht te Batavia, is door Zr. Ms. Opnemingsvaartuig Hydrograaf, een nauwkeurig onderzoek ingesteld naar de reven NO. van Bangka, waaromtrent het navolgende wordt medegedeeld:

A. De volgende reven bestaan niet:

1.	Columbia-rif	op 2° 21′	Z.Br.	en	106° 46′ 30″	O.L.
2.	Rif	» 2° 11′	»	»	106° 51′	»
3.	Rif	» 1° 42′	»	»	106° 14′	»
4.	Aeteon-rif	» 1° 40′	»	»	106° 36′	»
5.	Branding gezien	» 2° 4′	»	»	106° 34′	»
6.	Scheveningen-rif	» 1° 19′ 30″	»	»	106° 40′	»
7.	Catharina-rif	» 1° 30′	»	»	107° 1′ 30″	»
8.	Pratt-rots	» 1° 31′ 30″	»	»	107° 23′	»
9.	Atwick-rots	» 1° 48′ 30″	»	»	107° 31′	»
10.	Lawrick-rif	» 1° 52′ 30″	»	»	107° 1′	»

B. De volgende reeds bekende reven werden gevonden en nader bepaald:

1. Sittard-rif op 2° 10′ 30″ Z. Br. en 106° 44″ O. L., gevonden op 2° 11′ 32″ Z. Br. en 106° 44′ 42″ O. L., is steil en 700 m. groot. De minste diepte bedraagt 2,7 m. (1½ vad.) en rondom staat 21,6 à 32,4 m. (12 à 18 vadem).

2. Rif op 2° 1′ 30″ Z. Br. en 106° 31′ O. L., gevonden op 2° 2′ 5″ Z. Br. en 106° 30′ 46″ O. L., is steil en 500 m. groot. De minste diepte bedraagt 3,2 m. (1¾ vadem), en rondom staat 18 à 22,2 m. (10 à 14 vadem).

81

3. Rif op 2° 5′ Z. Br. en 106° 31′ O. L, gevonden op 2° 4′ 30″ Z. Br. en 106° 30′ 55″ O. L., is steil en 150 m. groot. De minste diepte bedraagt 3,6 m. (2 vadem), en rondom staat 18 à 23,4 m. (10 à 13 vadem).

4. Rif op 2° 2′ Z. Br. en 106° 36′ O. L., gevonden op 2° 1′ 47″ Z. Br. en 106° 36′ 56″ O. L., is steil en in de richting ZW. en NO. 500 m groot. De minste diepte bedraagt 8,1 m. (4½ vadem), en rondom staat 25,2 à 28,8 m. (14 à 16 vadem).

5. Rif op 1° 57′ Z. Br. en 106° 24′ O. L. (Palmer-reven), gevonden op 1° 57′ 54″ Z. Br. en 106° 21′ 52″ O. L., is steil en 500 m. groot. De minste diepte bedraagt 2,2 m. (1¼ vadem), en rondom staat 18 à 23,4 m. (10 à 13 vad.)

6. Rif op 1° 57′ 30″ Z. Br. en 106° 25′ O. L. (Palmer-reven), gevonden op 1° 58′ 10″ Z. Br. en 106° 22′ 42″ O. L., is steil en 400 m. groot. De minste diepte bedraagt 2,7 m. (2½ vad.) en rondom staat 18 à 23,4 m. (10 à 13 vad.)

7. Iwan-rif op 1° 40′ Z. Br. en 106° 16′ O. L., gevonden op 1° 40′ 10″ Z. Br. en 106° 17′ 32″ O. L., is steil en 350 m. groot. De minste diepte bedraagt 3,2 m. (1¾ vad.) en rondom staat 25,2 à 27 m. (14 à 15 vadem).

8. Severn-rif op 1° 40′ Z. Br. en 106° 28′ O. L., gevonden op 1° 37′ 10″ Z. Br. en 106° 30′ 22″ O. L., is steil en 400 m. groot. De minste diepte bedraagt 3,2 m. (1¾ vadem), en rondom staat 30,6 à 32,4 m. (17 à 18 vadem).

9. Wild Pigeon-rif op 1° 11′ 30″ Z. Br. en 106° 40′ 30″ O. L., gevonden op 1° 12′ 12″ Z. Br. en 106° 41′ 45″, bestaat uit twee reven, op 100 m. afstand van elkander, en ieder 100 m. groot. De minste diepte op het eene rif bedraagt 5,4 m. (3 vad.), en op het andere 2,2 m. (1¼ vadem); tusschen de beïde reven staat 25,2 m. (14 vad.) en rondom 30,6 à 36 m. (17 à 20 vadem).

10. Celestial-reven. Een rif op 1° 15′ 30″ Z. Br. en 106° 46′ 30″ O. L., gevonden op 1° 12′ 20″ Z. Br. en 106° 46′ 40″ O. L, is in de richting WNW. en OZO. 100 m. lang en 30 m. breed. De minste diepte bedraagt 3,2 m. (1¾ vadem).

(1880) 6

FIGURE 13.1. Colonial Dutch Reef Notices (*Tijdschrift voor het Zeewezen* [*Dutch Seaman's Journal*], 1880, p. 801)

suggested that many Dutchmen stood to lose money if the business of steam shipping was conducted in a completely evenhanded way. The *scheepvaartregelingen* limited certain forms of foreign participation in these carrying trades; indeed, Batavia explicitly pointed to the fact that too much trade fell outside of legal channels in explaining their imposition.[28] The control of maritime trade and movement therefore became a serious policy concern for the Dutch, and this was especially so in regard to merchant shipping emanating from the

28. British Consul, Oleh Oleh to Gov. SS, 29 June 1883, no. 296, in "Traffic in Contraband," vol. 11 in PRO/FO/220/Oleh-Oleh Consulate (1882–85).

'neighboring British possessions. By the turn of the twentieth century, the maritime expansion of the two colonial states had reached the entire width of what we today call Malaysia and Indonesia, and the need to tabulate, understand, and define these marine spaces had become crucial, especially for Batavia. The volume of steamships outpaced sailing craft in Singapore's harbor statistics only two years after the Suez Canal opened in 1869, yet the increasing numbers of junks and prahus also meant that the routes were choked with a variety of different vessels.[29] European colonial governments, but especially Batavia, came to the conclusion that it was better to understand the nature and scale of local oceans as well as this could be accomplished.

Mapping and Exploring the Ocean

An important manner in which the British and Dutch changed *longue-durée* shipping patterns (themselves variable, but identifiable in certain broad contours) was through the mapping and exploration of the nautical frontier.[30] This occurred in numerous locales, yet we can focus our vision for now on the maze of islands in the southernmost reaches of the South China Sea. Indigenous polities on some of these islands had been known to the Dutch for a long time, and many of these peoples had significant contacts with larger Malay politics and trade in the region. Scholars have shown this for Bangka in the seventeenth and eighteenth centuries, and for Riau in the eighteenth and nineteenth centuries, in the maritime area just south of Singapore.[31] Other scholars have worked on the gradual incorporation of these islands into the regional web of trade and alliances through mining and the Chinese presence, both of

29. See George Bogaars, "The Effect of the Opening of the Suez Canal on the Trade and Development of Singapore," *Journal of the Malay Branch of the Royal Asiatic Society* 28, no. 1 (1955): 104, 117. For the "motorization" of these vessels, see B. Nur, "Bitjara tentang perahu: Bagaimana cara pembinaan dan motorisasi perahu lajar?," *Dunia Maritim* 21, no. 9 (1971): 15–28.

30. Much of the science, as well as the bureaucratic organization of hydrography in the Dutch Indies, has been described in Backer Dirks, *De Gouvernements marine*, 269–75.

31. Barbara Watson Andaya, *To Live as Brothers: Southeast Sumatra in the Seventeenth and Eighteenth Centuries* (Honolulu: University of Hawai'i Press, 1993); Carl Trocki, *Prince of Pirates: The Temenggongs and the Development of Johor and Singapore 1784–1885* (Singapore: Singapore University Press, 1979); Barbara Watson Andaya, "Recreating a Vision: Daratan and Kepulaunan in Historical Context," *Bijdragen tot de Taal-, Land-, en Volkenkunde* 153, no. 4 (1997): 483–508.

which only grew in the nineteenth century.[32] Bangka and Belitung were especially important centers for trade and production well before mid-century,
making explorations there essentially a matter of filling in spaces already
known to the Dutch.[33] Yet the island groups of Anambas, Natuna, and Tambelan, all in the lower reaches of the South China Sea, were much more distant
from the international shipping crossroads, and received only scant attention
from Batavia until later. Dutch East Indies planners understood that these
archipelagoes were a multi-ethnic amalgam of Chinese, Bugis, Malays, and
Orang Laut, but they knew fairly little about day-to-day realities there, including those involving cross-cultural contact and commerce.[34]

Leading up to the turn of the twentieth century, however, this ignorance of
the South China Sea island groups was beginning to be altered by policy and
by fiat. Ship captains' notations on the geography of the islands started to be
compiled and collated. New bays and creeks were noted, depth charts in fathoms presented, and drinking-water sources pointed out, rendering the islands
more transparent to traders and statesmen alike.[35] Exploratory expeditions
conducted between 1894 and 1896 were especially instructive, showing that
earlier maps of the area contained islands that did not exist, or that were simply
drawn in the wrong place, to the detriment of travelers. Though this information was compiled by Dutchmen, the source of these reports was potentially
problematic. Most of the corrections came from English Admiralty charts,
which had been completed a few years earlier in the area, and had produced
excellent maps. Though these charts had been done with the permission of

32. Mary Somers Heidhues, *Bangka Tin and Mentok Pepper: Chinese Settlement on an Indonesian Island* (Singapore: ISEAS, 1992); Ng Chin Keong, "The Chinese in Riau: A Community
on an Unstable and Restrictive Frontier," unpublished paper, Singapore, Institute of Humanities
and Social Sciences, Nanyang University, 1976.

33. See, for example, H. M. Lange *Het Eiland Banka en zijn aangelegenheden* ('s Hertogenbosch [Den Bosch], 1850); P. van Dest, *Banka Beschreven in Reistochten* (Amsterdam, 1865); and
Cornelis de Groot, *Herinneringen aan Blitong: Historisch, Lithologisch, Mineralogisch, Geographisch, Geologisch, en Mijnbouwkundig* (The Hague, 1887). The same was true for seascapes along
the Madura coast; see F. A. S. Tjiptoatmodjo, "Kota-kota pantai di sekiatr selat Madura (Abad
ke-17 sampai medio abad ke-19)." PhD thesis (Yogyakarta: Gadjah Mada University, 1983).

34. R. C. Kroesen, "Aantekenningen over de Anambas-, Natuna-, en Tambelan Eilanden,"
TBG 21 (1875): 235 and passim; A. L. van Hasselt, "De Poelau Toedjoeh," *TAG* 15 (1898):
21–22.

35. [Anon.], "Chineesche Zee: Enkele Mededeelingen Omtrent de Anambas, Natoena, en
Tambelan-Eilanden," *Mededeelingen op Zeevaartkundig Gebied over Nederlandsch Oost-Indië* 4
(1 Aug. 1896): 1–2.

TABLE 13.1. Hydrographic Mapping of the Dutch East Indies

Maritime Surveying by Period, Region, and Ship

1858–65	Banka Strait	Pylades
1865–10	Banka North coast	Pylades + Stavoren
1871–79	Banka East coast	Stavoren + Hydrograaf
1880–11	Billiton	Hydrograaf
1881–84	Karimata Strait	Hydrograaf
1884–90	South Java Sea	Hydrograaf
1890–92	SE Borneo coast	Banda
1892–	Makassar Strait	Banda
1883–91	South Java Sea	Blommendal + M. v. Carnbee
1890–96	East Coast Sumatra	Blommendal + M. v. Carnbee
1894–	Riau/Lingga Archipelago	Blommendal + M. v. Carnbee

Hydrographic Dutch East Indies Survey Ships

Pylades	1858–68	steamship
Stavoren	1868–73	steamship
Hydrograaf	1874–90	steamship
Banda	1890–99	steamship
Blommendal	1883–99	sail-ship
Melville van Carnbee	1883–99	sail-ship

Details on the Surveying of Reefs and Atolls in Indies Waters

Tjdschrift voor het Zeewezen

1871: 135–40, 273 .	1876: 256, 463–64
1872: 100–1, 431	1877: 221, 360–61
1873: 213, 339–40	1878: 98, 100–1, 198, 212, 321, 331
1874: no data available	1879: 9, 82–83, 168, 236
1875: 78–79, 241	1880: 66, 76–77, 80–84, 315

Source: The author's surveying of the journal *Tijdschrift voor het Zeewezen* and also Christiaan Biezen, "De waardigheid van een koloniale mogendheid: De hydrografische Dienst en de kartering van de Indische Archipel tussen 1874 an 1894," *Tijdschrift voor Zeegeschiedenis*, 18, no. 2, 1999: 23–36, appendix (p. 37).

Batavia, Dutch hydrographers stated that Dutch explorers should have been the ones to make these measurements, as the islands (after all) were inside the sphere of influence of the Netherlands East Indies.[36] The vocabulary lists of area peoples, photographs of local coastal topography, and ethnographic notes that followed brought Dutch knowledge of the northern parts of the archipelago to a new degree of sophistication.[37] In these same years at the turn

36. On the evolving international law of territorial waters, and its effect on maritime Southeast Asia, see Gerke Teitler, *Ambivalente en Aarzeeling: Het Belied van Nederland en Nederlands-Indië ten Aanzien van hun Kustwateren, 1870–1962* (Assen: Van Gorcum, 1994), 37–54.

37. Hasselt, "De Poelau Toedjoeh," 25–26.

of the twentieth century, in fact, more general directives started to come down from Batavia, asking administrators of far-flung groups to send as much of this kind of data as possible to the capital. Vital data, pertaining to area seas but also otherwise, could therefore be gathered, filed, and studied through the various administrative arms of the Indies government.[38]

After the fin de siècle, the surveying of the archipelago became more and more important to the colonial state. Mining interests took the lead in new surveying operations and expeditions, mapping Bangka down to minute detail. Belitung, and even the tiny islands off Belitung's coasts, quickly followed after 1894.[39] The waters around Blakang Padang, facing Singapore in the Riau archipelago, were also extensively surveyed at this time, according to Indonesian historiography.[40] Though formerly the island had been seen by Batavia as a useless scrap of land (with few natural resources and a small population), by the turn of the century Dutch planners were seeing Blakang Padang as a complementary port for Singapore, with coal sheds, docking complexes, and a series of interconnected lighthouses.[41] This sort of maritime exploration, with a systematic program of "development" attached to it, was the last stage of the European discovery process along the length of the Anglo-Dutch frontier. Even reefs and atolls along the maritime boundaries of Malaya and the Indies, from Aceh eastward to Sulawesi and Sulu, began to be explored by oceanographers in the decades leading up to the turn of the twentieth century.[42] Some

38. These directives had been issued for some time already, but were particularly important around this time. See ARA, Directeur van Onderwijs, Eeredienst, en Nijverheid to Gov. Gen. NEI, 21 March 1890, no. 2597, in 1890, MR no. 254.

39. The extensive surveying of Bangka began even earlier, in the 1870s. See ARA, 1894, MR no. 535; and H. Zondervan, "Bijdrage tot de kennis der Eilanden Bangka en Blitong," *TAG* 17 (1900):. 519.

40. See D. Sutedja, *Buku himpunan pemulihan hubungan Indonesia Singapura. Himpunan peraturan-peraturan anglkutan laut* (Jakarta: Departement Perhubungan Laut, 1967).

41. "Balakang Padang, Een concurrent van Singapore," *IG* 2 (1902): 1295.

42. J. F. Niermeyer, "Barriere riffen en atollen in de Oost Indische Archipel," *TAG* (1911):877; "Straat Makassar," in *Mededeelingen op Zeevaartkundig Gebied over Nederlandsch Oost-Indië* 6 (1 May 1907); Sydney Hickson, *A Naturalist in North Celebes* (London: John Murray, 1889), 188–89; and P. C. Coops, "Nederlandsch Indies zeekaarten," *Nederlandsche Zeewezen* 3 (1904): 129. See also Adrian Lapian, *Orang Laut-Bajak Laut-Raja Laut: Sejarah Kawasan Laut Sulawesi Abad XIX* (Yogyakarta: Disertasi pada Universitas Gadjah Mada, 1987). The reporting of reefs, atolls, and submerged rocks became an important subset of Western navigational literature by the later years of the nineteenth century. The notices presented here describe a series of ten reefs northeast of Bangka island, along the sea routes between Singapore and Batavia. For further

of this interest was purely scientific, or was fueled by the emerging nationalist impulse to mark off the boundaries of the archipelago with Dutch and British flags. Yet a significant portion of it was also economic and utilitarian, as exploration was bent to the service of the state to locate new resources and wealth. Mapping the sea became the policy *and* business of the colonial state, and increasingly it was difficult to separate the two paradigms. When the Dutch military was added into this equation, the "military industrial complex" of mapping at the time becomes perfectly clear.

This process is visible at Labuan, off the coast of Borneo, and also at Aceh, off Sumatra's Indian Ocean north coast. No serious maps existed of Labuan's topography even thirty years after the colony's founding in the 1840s: the island was hydrographically surveyed as part of the sea routes leading to China, but not in its own local detail and context, an omission which limited British imperial vision in Western Borneo's waters.[43] This situation would remain almost unchanged until the turn of the twentieth century, when government officials and businessmen alike complained that local hydrographical inadequacies were actually impeding trade and policing alike.[44] The crucial importance of the hydrographic project to Dutch expansion can be seen best in Aceh, where sea mapping was a matter of life and death for the invading Dutch armies. Reconnaissance voyages by the Dutch marine started triangulations of the coasts, while other ships steamed up Aceh's rivers to map interior waterways where resistance forces hid.[45] Both of these missions—coastal and riverine—were crucial to European military expansion in Aceh. Batavia's forces couldn't maintain a concerted presence onshore for the first ten months of the war, so reconnaissance information had to be gathered by other means, contemporary Indonesian historians tell us.[46] Mapping the sea and mapping

descriptions across the length of the archipelago in the 1870s, see *Tijdschrift voor het Zeewezen*: 1871: 135–40 (Java Sea); 1872: 100–1 (Melaka Strait); 1873: 339–40 (Natuna and Buton); 1874: 306 (Makassar Strait); 1875: 78, 241 (East Coast Sulawesi and Northeast Borneo); 1876: 463 (Aceh); 1877: 221, 360 (West Coast Sumatra, Lampung); 1878, p. 98, 100 (West Borneo, Sulu Sea); and 1879, p. 79 (North Sulawesi).

43. Surveyor General R. Howard, Labuan, to Col. Secretary, Labuan, 6 May 1873, in CO 144/40.

44. See Government Pilot of Labuan to Labuan Coalfields Co., 4 October 1903; Labuan Coalfields Co. to BNB Co. HQ, London, 20 November 1903, both in CO 144/77.

45. Kruijt, *Twee Jaren Blokkade*, 169, 189.

46. See H. Mohammad Said, *Aceh Sepanjang Abad*, vol. 1 (Medan: P. T. Harian Waspada, 1981): 675–753; *Perang Kolonial Belanda di Aceh* (Banda Aceh: Pusat Dokumentasi dan Informasi Aceh, 1997): 87–104.

coastlines from the sea, therefore, was one of the most important steps in imperial processes of subjugation in Southeast Asia. This happened early in some regional arenas, as in Aceh, though these protocols took longer in other European island outposts, like Labuan. The combined requirements of politics and finances often helped decide which areas would be surveyed by ships, and for what reasons.

A final glimpse of these exigencies can be found in and around the significant maritime cities of the archipelago. Important harbors often received cartographic attention at an early date because of their value to colonial trade; this is very evident in the 1870s and 1880s, though records for soundings go back even to the early seventeenth century.[47] By the end of the nineteenth century, as frontier areas became a priority and increasingly were hydrographically mapped (such as Labuan, Aceh, and the South China Sea Islands, all of which we have discussed above), the major ports of Southeast Asia were once again revisited, in order to perfect these states' knowledge locally. We can see these improvements especially on the English side of the Straits. In July 1899, Penang received permission to undertake extensive maritime surveying of her harbor, while two years later Melaka began to prepare for similar improvements.[48] In 1902, Singapore itself, the seat of British power in the region, started to carry out blasting operations at the mouth of the Singapore River, in order to better the shipping channel leading into one of the world's busiest ports.[49] These kinds of activities also took place on banks and coral outcroppings just outside of these centers, as with the Ajax Shoal just outside of Singapore.[50] Britain and the Netherlands were slowly ensuring that the totality of their realms were being brought into the oceanic view of the state. Such an ability to see also revitalized commerce, policing, and colonial control, however, from the seas of metropolitan Europe all the way out to Southeast Asia itself.

47. See *Straits Times*, 9 October 1875; *Singapore Daily Times*, 2 May 1879; and *Singapore Daily Times*, 9 May 1882.

48. "Penang Harbour Improvements," *Straits Settlements Legislative Council Proceedings* (hereafter, *SSLCP*), 1899, C341; Messrs. Coode, Son and Matthews to Gov. SS, 23 December 1901, in *SSLCP*, 1902, C32.

49. "Report on the Blasting Operations Carried Out in 1902 Upon Sunken Rocks at the Mouth of the Singapore River," *SSLCP*, 1903, C131.

50. "Survey of the Ajax Shoal," *SSLCP*, 1885, C135.

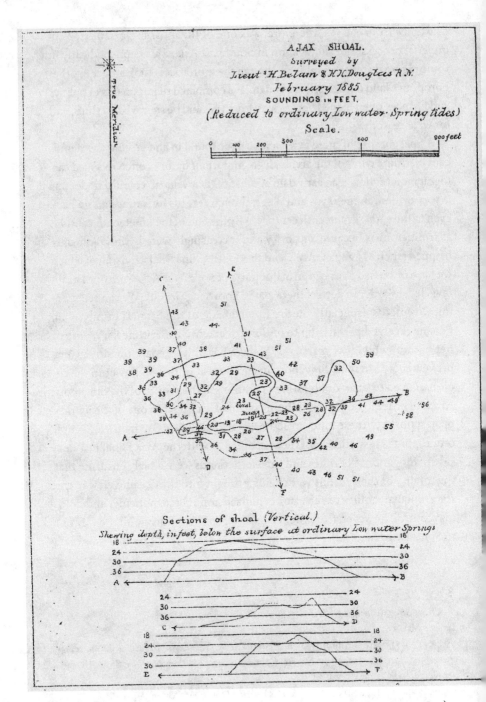

FIGURE 13.2. The Ajax Shoal (Straits Settlements Legislative Proceedings, 1885, p. C135)

The Wider World and Science of the Sea

In the 1900s and 1910s, hydrographic mapping in this part of the world became an increasingly more sophisticated and international science, even compared with only a half century earlier. Such development happened principally because of several interrelated factors. First and foremost, as we have seen, were the combined imperatives of imperial coercion and imperial business, both of which pushed hydrography forward as a necessary tool for the colonial state. Other reasons for cartographic evolution can be traced to the science's expanding popular interest and to national pride. Imperial cartographers attended international congresses with their data on Southeast Asia's seas, and presses back in Europe picked up on their discoveries as well, fanning the new knowledge out to a wider reading public.[51] Even as early as the 1870s Batavia was beginning to give out its maritime notices to the British across the Straits, data which then appeared as warnings and notifications in regional English newspapers.[52] By the same token, funds were made available by the Dutch Ministry of Marine to translate English-language soundings and sightings, so that Dutch mariners would also have up-to-date charts of the region.[53] A third and final factor for expansion can be found in the contentious nature of the maritime frontier itself. As both the British and Dutch jockeyed over where their frontier would eventually be laid, accurate hydrographic readings became more of a priority to international diplomacy. These shifting importances can be glimpsed in maritime maps from the time, especially in arenas anywhere near international borders.[54]

Naturally, concourse of some sort—an existing line of communication—concerning hydrography was necessary between these colonial powers and the very small polities that abutted their shared frontier. Yet, as European power was still comparatively underdeveloped until late in the nineteenth

51. C. M. Kan, "Geographical Progress in the Dutch East Indies 1883–1903," *Report of the Eighth International Geographic Congress* (1904/5): 715; W. B. Oort, "Hoe een Kaart tot Stand Komt," *Onze Eeuw* 4 (1909): 363–65.

52. See *Penang Guardian and Mercantile Advertiser*, 23 October 1873, p. 4. British interest in Indies discoveries was very widespread; see also *Singapore Free Press*, 28 June 1860, 27 September 1860, and 3 September 1863, as well as *Straits Times*, 14, 15, and 16 August, 1883; 19 March 1884; and 15 April 1885.

53. ARA, 1871, MR no. 464.

54. For a time-sensitive comparison on hydrographic evolution, see the two British maps of Darvel and St. Lucia Bays in East Borneo, approximately thirty years apart on both sides of 1900. Both can be found in CO 874/998.

century, especially hydrographically, complex arrangements were formulated to bind these relationships.[55] In Jambi, for example, the sultan was made responsible by contract for the safety of shipwrecked Dutch seamen, as these latter men occasionally washed up on Jambi's shores.[56] The sultan of Gunung Tabur in East Borneo was punished for his involvement in sponsoring piracy, meanwhile, as cartographers and traders sometimes disappeared off his shores, apparently at the connivance of the ruler himself.[57] In Riau, surviving Indonesian-language letters also show how mapping expeditions were forced upon local rulers, who increasingly had little say as to whether their domains should be surveyed or not.[58] Both Batavia and Singapore were required, in fact, by treaty to send copies of all agreements signed with local potentates to each other, so that their metropolitan capitals could appraise the nature of contacts along the border.[59] This did not stop both sides from maneuvering within these obligations, however, as each often responded late (or sometimes not at all) over new contracts that had been closed. Indigenous area rulers also paid close attention to the evasive possibilities of this complicated system, often attempting to pit one Western entity against another in an attempt to guarantee their own tenuous freedoms.[60]

55. Britain's Asia-stationed ships were often described as being "leaky" or in "dilapidated condition," while steam launches were desperately sought after by Singapore to keep an eye on illegal trading in local waters. See PRO/Admiralty, Vice Admiral Shadwell to Secretary of the Admiralty, 16 April 1872, no. 98, in no. 125/China Station Corrospondence/no. 21; Gov. SS to CO, 8 Jan 1873, no. 2, in CO 273/65; Gov SS to CO, 14 Jan 1875, no. 15, in CO 273/79; Gov SS to CO, 16 July 1881, no. 260, and CO to SS, 20 August 1881, both in CO 273/109.

56. "Overeenkomsten met Inlandsche Vorsten: Djambi, " IG 1 (1882): 540; ARA, 1872, MR no. 170. For examples of the kinds of contracts concluded between Europeans and Southeast Asian states, see PRO, Dutch Consul, London to FO, 20 August 1909, and FO to British Consul, The Hague, 26 August 1909, both in FO/Netherlands Files, "Treaties Concluded between Holland and Native Princes of the Eastern Archipelago" (no. 31583).

57. ARA, 1872, MR no. 73, 229; "Overeenkomsten met Inlandsche Vorsten: Pontianak," IG 1 (1882): 549. Penalties for the protection for pirates were also mentioned in Dutch/Riau contracts going all the way back to 1818; see the contract dated 26 November, Article 10 in *Surat-Surat Perdjandjian Antara Kesultanan Riau dengan Pemerintahan (2) V.O.C. dan Hindia-Belanda 1784–1909* (Jakarta: Arsip Nasional Indonesia, 1970), 43.

58. Arsip Nasional Indonesia (Indonesian State Archives, hereafter ANRI), "Idzin Pembuatan Peta Baru Tentang Pulau Yang Mengililingi Sumatra," in Archief Riouw [Jakarta Repository], no. 225/9 (1889).

59. FO to CO, 29 September 1871, in CO 273/53.

60. See the complaint of the sultan of Sulu to the British in Labuan, in which an alliance is sought with the English to counteract the growing influence of Spain: Gov. Labuan to CO, 15 August 1871, no. 33, in CO 144/34.

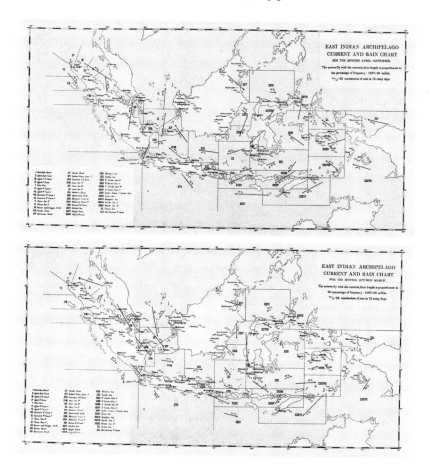

FIGURE 13.3. Dutch Hydrography in the Netherlands Indies (J. P. van der Strok, *Wind and Weather, Currents, Tides, and Tidal Streams in the East Indian Archipelago* [Batavia: Government Printing Office, 1897])

England's maritime data gradually accrued, and as this happened, London's claims on archipelago lands and seas became more forceful. This induced The Hague to follow suit, though this process happened only fitfully, however. A diplomatic incident in 1909, in which the Dutch envoy to London seemed himself not to know the nature of Dutch maritime claims in Eastern Borneo, acted as an alarm for The Hague to acquaint all of her foreign service personnel with the Indies' "true boundaries."[61] The Dutch ambassador, Baron Gericke, was confused as to the extent of Dutch coastal territory in East Borneo when

61. See ARA, Minister for the Colonies to Minister for Foreign Affairs, 15 July 1909, no. I/14735; Ministry for Foreign Affairs Circulaire 26 November 1909, no. I/23629, all in

an offshore piratical act there necessitated Anglo-Dutch naval cooperation in 1909. In private correspondence between the Dutch ministers for the colonies and foreign affairs after this, both stressed the importance of having Dutch envoys be familiar with the outlines of Dutch authority in the Indies. Atlases, maps, and charts were sent shortly thereafter to Dutch representatives in a variety of world capitals, including Berlin, London, Tokyo, Peking, Paris, Constantinople, St. Petersburg, and Washington. This information on the nature and exact location of the maritime frontier was shared across the Anglo-Dutch border as well. As early as 1891, in fact, Batavia had ordered the Resident of Western Borneo to send maps of the frontier, as well as soundings of the local river systems, to Charles Brooke, the raja of neighboring Sarawak. The processes of cartographic and hydrographic surveying were thus vital to the playing out of area politics, and were often employed in colonial negotiations in the region.

Despite this, both powers' abilities to discern the outlines of the sea in this arena were still uneven. Major international waterways, such as the eastern half of the Makassar Strait, and even much of the maritime route between Singapore and Java, were still inadequately surveyed and dangerous to passing maritime traffic by the turn of the twentieth century.[62] In British waters, according to local accounts, the approach to Labuan remained "neither safe nor easy" as late as 1900, with rocks and low shoals imperiling navigation.[63] Europeans in parts of maritime Southeast Asia simply still could not see properly, and ships which sailed through their dominions, in turn, were often invisible to the state. To make matters worse from the state's point of view, shifting politics often made fixing these situations extremely difficult. The different administrative entities in British waters—the Straits government, the British North Borneo Company, the raja of Sarawak and the Federated Malay States—constantly quarreled over who should incur the costs for necessary hydrographic improvements.[64] This becomes abundantly clear in the correspondence that went back and forth between these various centers, much of which concerned who would pay for what in terms of hydrographic mapping. In an atmosphere such

MvBZ/A/277/A.134) also ARA, First Government Secretary, Batavia, to Resident West Borneo, 20 February 1891, no. 405, in 1891, MR no. 158.

62. "De Uitbreiding der Indische Kustverlichting," *IG* 2 (1903): 1772.

63. Board of Trade to CO, 12 January 1900, no. 16518, in CO 144/74.

64. For just a few examples, see Charles Brooke to CO, 11 January 1907, in CO 531/1; Trinity House to CO, 10 January 1887, no. 42204/86, in CO 273/149; BNB Co. HQ to CO, 26 October 1899, in CO 144/73.

as this, it was not wholly difficult for "smugglers," "pirates," and "rebels" (or any other actors defined as "transgressive" by these colonial states) to sail through the region without much interference at all. Although there were indeed areas where British surveillance was excellent there still existed long stretches of coast which were virtually unwatched even after the end of the nineteenth century.

The fact that an "arms race" of sorts had begun in this fin de siècle period between colonial rivals helped push the pace of hydrographic surveying along. The pace of technological advances in world naval capabilities acted as a catalyst in Dutch maritime policy circles around this time. By the time of the Sino-Japanese War in 1895, dispatches were being sent out to Dutch envoys around the globe to find out how much the major powers were spending on their respective naval forces, and what form these overhauls took. These appeals went out to Dutch ambassadors in Europe, but they also were sent to The Hague's envoys in the rest of the world, to see how non-European states were integrating nautical changes into their navies.[65] From the Dutch envoy in Paris, Batavia learned that French fleet expansion was imminent, with the improvement of colonial ports especially targeted for immediate action.[66] From the Dutch representative in Berlin, further information was received about German naval capabilities in the Pacific, which was important to Batavia because of Berlin's expanding interests in shipping in the area.[67] Yet it was the obvious inadequacy of the Indies' marine in comparison to English naval strength in the Straits which really alarmed the Dutch. English armor-plate experiments, steam-engine trials, and shallow-draft-hull constructions were quickly making Dutch ships obsolete in the archipelago. This state of affairs was disagreeable even while amity existed between the two powers, but it was judged to be downright dangerous for the longer term.[68] Western military intelligence came in that Japan was constructing vessels of even greater technological sophistication than Britain's after the fin de siècle, these fears were broadened even further, as Batavia understood that their own presence in Southeast Asia was

---

65. See, for example, ARA, MvBZ Circulaire to the Dutch Envoys in London, Paris, Berlin, and Washington, 1 Feb 1895, no. 1097.

66. ARA, Dutch Consul, Paris, to MvBZ, 14 Feb 1900, no. 125/60, in MvBZ/A/421/A.182.

67. ARA, Dutch Consul, Berlin, to MvBZ, 3 August 1904; 22 May 1903; 5 April 1902; 6 July 1899; 17 June 1898; 13 July 1897, and 30 November 1896, all in MvBZ/A/421/A.182.

68. "The Navy Estimates," *Times of London*, 3 March 1897, enclosed in ARA, Dutch Consul, London, to MvBZ, 5 March 1897, no. 113, in MvBZ/A/421/A.182.

archaic in comparison to the Indies' near neighbors.[69] Such developments assisted in pouring more funds, and more attention, into Holland's surveying of the Indies' colonial waters. If Dutch Indonesia was to become a maritime battlefield, officials in the Netherlands felt, then Holland would at least know the parameters of these seas more thoroughly than any other Western regime.

Conclusion

Lewis Mumford has said in his landmark study *Technics and Civilization* that "as a practical instrument, the machine has enormously complicated the (human) environment." The author continued by comparing the "cobblestones of the old-fashioned street, set directly into the earth, with the cave of cables, pipes, and subway systems that run under the asphalt," in laying out his idea of how machines have altered not only our lives but human surroundings at the same time.[70] Certainly there must be some truth to Mumford's assertion, but the cord between science and the natural world runs in the opposite direction as well. Machines, while complicating human interactions with our surroundings, simplified the environment as well. Epistemologically useful tools such as hydrographic surveying vessels rendered nature legible and malleable to state-makers everywhere. As a means toward empire building, they were particularly valuable to the state, since it was the state that most controlled machines, and used them for its own purposes.[71] I argue here that this is what happened in maritime Southeast Asia in the second half of the nineteenth century. Colonial regimes, in this case the British in Malaya and the Dutch in the Netherlands East Indies, respectively, used science and its machines to gain power over the environment, and over local peoples living in this environment at the same time.[72] Though these processes have certainly

69. "The Destroyer Yamakaze," *The Japan Times*, 4 June 1910, enclosed under ARA, Dutch Consul, Tokyo, to MvBZ, 13 June 1910, no. 560/159, in MvBZ/A/421/A.182.

70. See Lewis Mumford, *Technics and Civilization* (New York, Harcourt, Brace, and World, 1963); both quotes can be found on p. 357.

71. For a longer elucidation of this argument, see Jacob Christian, Tom Conley (trans.), and Edward H. Dahl (ed.), *The Sovereign Map: Theoretical Approaches in Cartography throughout History* (Chicago: University of Chicago Press, 2006).

72. The majority of governments making use of these technologies in late nineteenth century were colonial; for the American/Philippine example, see *Report of the Philippine Commission to the President*, 31 January 1900 (Washington, DC: US Gov't Printing Office, 1900–1901), 3:157–200. Siam, the only regional polity which escaped conquest and domination, also began to

been undertaken on land, structures of colonial governance required an ease with these machines and ideas in the ocean, too. Mapping of the sea ensured that Western empires could refigure some of the fluid maritime realities of Southeast Asian contact across cultures, and reorder by force local worlds into templates much more fitting for imperial hegemony.[73] As Adri Lapian, the great Indonesian historian of the seas, has said by way of comparison:

> Dalam hubungan ini historigrafi tentang "bajak laut Moro" mempunyai paralel dengan penilaian masyarakat Eropa Barat (Kristen) terhadap apa yang mereka sebut "Korsario Barbar" di Laut Tengeh yang berasal dari pantai Afrika Utara.[74]

> In this context historiography about "Moro piracy" has parallels with the Western (Christian) appraisal toward what they called the "Barbary corsairs" in the Mediterranean, coming from the north coast of Africa. [Translation: E. Tagliacozzo]

The evolution of this process occurred over many years, however, and certainly in haphazard ways.[75] Few "turning points" suggest themselves in this process, few moments when sea maps decisively swung the pendulum of colonial control irredeemably toward the West.[76] In North Sumatra, hydrography was used from the initial Dutch assault, figuring prominently in the

---

experiment with hydrography at this time; see Luang Joldhan Brudhikrai, "Development of Hydrographic Work in Siam From the Beginning up to the Present," *International Hydrographic Review* 24 (1947).

73. Of course, these processes are also utilized in our own time as well, as states try to use hydrographic mapping to lay claims to islands, reefs, and resource-rich sea beds in a variety of locations around the world. For a discussion of contemporary events, see G. Francalanci and T. Scovazzi, *Lines in the Sea* (Dordrecht: Martinus Nijhoff, 1994); Dorinda Dallmeyer and Louis DeVorsey, *Rights to Oceanic Resources: Deciding and Drawing Maritime Boundaries* (Dordrecht: Martinus Nijhoff, 1989).

74. Adrian Lapian, *Orang Laut, Bajak Laut, Raja Laut* (Jakarta: Kounitas Bambu, 2009): 227.

75. For the *longue durée* of some of these maritime processes, see S. Soempeno, *Buku sejarah pelayaran Indonesia* (Jakarta: Pustaka Maritim, 1975); B. Nur, "Mengenal potensi rakyat di bidang angkutan laut, Part XVI," *Dunia Maritim* 20, no. 3 (1970): 19–21; B. Nur, "Mengenal potensi rakyat di bidang angkutan laut, Part XI," *Dunia Maritim* 19, no. 7 (1969): 17–19; and S. T. Sulistiyono, "Politik kolonial terhadap pelabuhan di Hindia Belanda," *Lembaran Sastra* 18 (1995): 86–100.

76. For the notion of "turning points" in technological processes, especially in how machines have been applied to human history, see D. S. L. Cardwell, *Turning Points in Western Technology: A Study of Technology, Science, and History* (New York: Neale Watson, 1972), esp. 140–95.

campaign to overrun the Malay world's last real challenge to Western control. By contrast in Labuan, hydrography was employed locally only at the very end of the nineteenth century, and used only to situate the colony along Britain's larger imperial maritime routes. Far-flung frontiers, theaters of war, and outlying commercial ports saw these technologies applied at different paces, therefore. Yet hydrography allowed both colonial states to gradually see their marine environments better than they once had, and to translate this knowledge into allocations of manpower, materiel, and surveillance that furthered imperial policies.[77] In the mid-nineteenth century, Western conceptions of maritime space were rather inadequate, and praxis ensuring the control of these arenas was quite impossible to enact. By 1900, however, the cartography of this huge island domain was extensively in process, and the ramifications of these actions, most notably in the theater of geopolitical control, were deeply ingrained in the region.[78]

77. To understand the tail end of this time period, particularly in the less "tamed" eastern archipelago, see the wonderful new book by Heather Sutherland, *Seaways and Gatekeepers: Trade and Society in the Eastern Archipelagos of Southeast Asia, c. 1600–1906* (Singapore: National University of Singapore Press, 2021).

78. For two cogent theoretical meditations on these processes, see Mark Monmonier, "Cartography: Distortions, World-views and Creative Solutions," *Progress in Human Geography* 29, no. 2 (2005): 217–24; and Joe Painter, "Cartographic Anxiety and the Search for Regionality," *Environment and Planning A* 40 (2008): 342–61.

14

If China Rules the Waves

One thousand years ago, this was the center of the world.

—CHINESE MUSLIM GRAVEYARD ATTENDANT,
GUANGZHOU, CHINA[1]

A FEW YEARS AGO, China unveiled to the world its latest military armament—a huge aircraft carrier, festooned with flags and uniformed men at attention in one of its northern harbors. The aircraft carrier looked quite impressive in the file photos. Yet, on further inspection, it seemed rather less so than at first glance. The dramatic, sweeping curve of the flight deck sat on top of an old (but refurbished) hull. The carrier had been bought secondhand from the Ukrainian navy, when the latter no longer had the funds to keep the vessel in operation.[2] Despite this genealogy, the ship was paraded before the world's media. Pronouncements started almost immediately about projections of Chinese power, and the erection of a blue-water navy capable of moving away from the nation's shores. With several island disputes as background context— the Senkaku/Diaoyu with Japan, the Spratlys and Paracels in the South China Sea with a host of Southeast Asian nations—the unveiling of the ship seemed like an expression of intent.[3] Already on at least some of the South China Sea

---

1. Author's fieldwork notes, January 1990 [translation: E. Tagliacozzo].

2. See http://www.bbc.com/news/world-asia-pacific-13017882, accessed 15 July 2015; the *Liaoning* was launched in September 2012. China recently finished its second aircraft carrier, the *Shandong,* which was wholly fabricated domestically. China's maritime forces recently became the single largest navy in the world.

3. Monique Chemillier-Gendreau, *Sovereignty over the Paracel and Spratly Islands* (Leiden: Springer, 2000); see also Tim Liao, Kimie Hara, and Krista Wiegand, eds., *The China-Japan Border Dispute: Islands of Contention in Multidisciplinary Perspective* (London: Ashgate, 2015).

disputed atolls, work had begun to expand essentially low-tide reefs into actual islets; sand was being dredged to extend the spits of land, and real islands were being made, replete with fluttering red Chinese flags.[4] China trumpeted the extent of its claims in Asian waters, essentially marking off nearly all the seas within any reach at all of its shores as being quintessentially—and crucially, historically—"Chinese." The inevitable clamor of objections from a range of interested parties, stretching from Tokyo south to Jakarta, and from Manila east to Washington, quickly followed. How would these claims be met? What was the fate of Asian seas going to be if Beijing became a new, territorial power with maritime hegemony as part of its aims?[5] In short, what would happen if—in the lines of the old song, focusing this time not on Britannia but on a power far, far away—China ruled the waves?

It is worth noting that from an historical viewpoint, this was not the first time a huge Chinese ship was pointing outward toward Asia from mainland China's shores. Nearly six hundred years earlier, the flagship of Admiral Zheng He's fleet stood at anchor, waiting to join an expedition of nearly thirty thousand souls on scores of ships heading down to Southeast Asia. The principal mission of this fleet was rather simple: to fly the Chinese flag, and to let it be known among the vassal states of Asia's trade routes that ethnically Han China was back in business as a world power. This overture came at the beginning of the Ming Dynasty, as we have previously seen in this book, and after a nearly century-long interstice of Steppes-rule in China that had interrupted the flow of Han Chinese dynastic history. When Zheng He's fleets first traveled down to Southeast Asia between 1405 and 1433 (all seven of the great expeditions touched upon Southeast Asia, in one place or another), one can only imagine what local powers must have thought upon seeing these ships on their morning horizons.[6] The previous night, all had gone to sleep with empty skies looking out to sea. By dawn, reality had changed, and conceptions of power had

4. See "China Building Great Wall of Sand in South China Sea," April 1, 2015; http://www.bbc.com/news/world-asia-32126840; accessed 15 July 2015.

5. For some of the historical baggage here, see Shih-Shan Henry Tsai, *Maritime Taiwan: Historical Encounters with the East and the West* (Armonk: M. E. Sharpe, 2009); and Tonio Andrade, *Lost Colony: The Untold Story of China's First Great Victory over the West* (Princeton: Princeton University Press, 2013). A new statement of where things stand can be found in Geoffrey Gresh, *To Rule Eurasia's Waves: The New Great Power Competition at Sea* (New Haven: Yale University Press, 2020).

6. The most arresting single study is still Louise Levathes, *When China Ruled the Seas: The Treasure Fleet of the Dragon Throne, 1405–1433* (New York: Oxford University Press, 1994).

changed, too, for the string of polities along the maritime routes. China had long existed as a faraway possibility, and as a place to pay tribute. It had little local valence, though, except perhaps in the commodities that came from the Middle Kingdom, and the occasional traders who came with them, carrying them in their ships.[7] But what was nebulous before was now clear—the arrival of Zheng He's fleets showed the rest of maritime Asia that there was an existing power that was far beyond them in politics, dominion, and sophistication. Indeed, China professed to need nothing from the region in the trade that trickled between the two places; the voyages were at least partially symbolic, and had fairly little to do with the transit of actual things. Still, a few items did remain from the visits, such as some large bronze bells and also some huge iron anchors, as well as some temples which were endowed to worship the departing admiral. Some of these things—real or conjured up much later than the expeditions themselves—can still be found in the region.[8] Yet it is difficult to disaggregate fact from fiction as to which items are genuine, and which merely serve to fuel the wheels of the tourist trade. "Zheng He is everywhere and nowhere," a Chinese scholar of maritime history told me in Chinese when we met at an academic event. "It is more about what he represents than where he really went."[9]

One item did certainly travel on these ships, however, as we have previously seen in chapter 2. This was a giraffe; a beautiful and (presumably) very healthy beast, as it made it all the way from the Horn of Africa back across the Indian Ocean, up through Southeast Asia, and to the Chinese court, all in one lifetime. There, as we have seen through the painter and calligrapher Shen Du, the giraffe was immortalized in pigment in the year 1415, being held by a retainer who

---

7. John Miksic, "Before and after Zheng He: Comparing Some Southeast Asian Archaeological Sites of the Fourteenth and Fifteenth Centuries," in *Southeast Asia in the Fifteenth Century: The China Factor*, ed. Geoff Wade and Sun Laichen, 384–408 (Singapore: NUS Press, 2010).

8. In passing through parts of Southeast Asia, you can find detritus here and there, all with a provenance supposedly dating back to the great admiral's missions. It would be a minor miracle if all of these identifications were true; some of them almost certainly aren't. But some likely are, as it makes good sense that anchors, bells, and the like—all heavy and made out of metals that could withstand the tropical climate—might make it through the years. There are certainly temples to be found in Java and other places where effigies of Sam Po Keng (Zheng He) can still be found.

9. Given the political climate, this was a rather courageous thing to say to a foreigner. I have kept his identity anonymous here as a result.

MAP 14.1. Competing Claims in the South China Sea

looks up admiringly at the beast's head.[10] As with the case of huge fleets appearing on morning horizons, when previously these vistas were clear, we can only imagine what the passerby of Nanjing thought in first seeing this scene. The giraffe was paraded through the streets of the capital before being brought to the court for the emperor to have a closer look. It was declared to be a *qi-lin*,

10. See Leavathes, *When China Ruled the Seas*, for more on this painting.

a magical beast whose existence had finally been proven from the Chinese zoological pantheon.[11] As an expression of the possibilities of both the Chinese state and the Asian maritime routes it had mastered, it was a symbol that all in attendance understood. China indeed ruled the waves. The emperor could bring all of the earth's objects—even objects that were only rumored to exist but had never been seen by any living person's eyes—to the capital for inspection. The giraffe, in fact, was the routes made corporeal; the fullest expression in flesh, sinew, and blood of the nautical pathways that tied together vast tracks of the known world. And it was transportable, a movable cypher of the power of commerce and connection that was made possible by China's trade. The Chinese portmaster Zhao Ru Gua had already written some two centuries earlier about the wares of the far-western Indian Ocean, and what sorts of commodities might be found there.[12] But this was a piece of the most distant parts of the trade routes now on the Chinese doorstep, and the fact that it was alive and breathing—preserved against all odds on routes thousands upon thousands of miles long—made its appearance all the more remarkable. This was the power of trade.[13] This was the power of being able to control the routes and slipways of the maritime nexus that made being a subject of the world's most dynamic country completely worthwhile.

This book has argued for a vision of Asia's oceanic history focused less on the power and politics described above, and more on the notion of conjoined seas—the mingling of waters connecting the Middle East to Japan, with all of the maritime realms and possibilities in between. The routes connecting these places made a world. These sea-lanes and their transit literally fashioned a history of conversations that lasted some twenty centuries in duration, with the legacy of the last five hundred years or so particularly important, and still with us today. The maritime trade routes between Aden and Tokyo, I have argued, helped condition the parameters of what we think of as our contemporary, day-to-day realities.[14] Coffee spilled out of these networks, indigenous to

11. See my chapter 2 above for more on this identification. The poem written by Shen Du to commemorate the beast's passage to the court must surely rank as one of the great moments of cross-cultural contact in world history.

12. Frederick Hirth and W. W. Rockhill, *Chau Ju Kua: His Work on the Chinese and Arab Trade in the 12th and 13th Centuries, Entitled Chu Fan Chï* (New York: Paragon Book Reprint Co., 1966).

13. Steven Topik and Kenneth Pomeranz, *The World That Trade Created: Society, Culture, and the World Economy, 1400 to the Present* (New York: Routledge, 2012).

14. See Kennon Brazeale, ed., *From Japan to Arabia: Ayutthaya's Maritime Relations* (Bangkok: Toyota Thailand Foundation, 1999).

Ethiopia but eventually grown and exported by Yemenis on the Red Sea corridor, until the beans washed ashore literally everywhere the trade routes could take them.[15] Spices were also crucial in the history of Asia's seas, drawing travelers from very far afield through their siren song, and eventually contributing to the laying of vast, far-flung empires in the region. Chinese and Indian laborers also moved with these pathways, and were spun down to Southeast Asia and west to Africa, as well as outside these circuits as time wore on.[16] Their descendants still live in diaspora in these outstretched regions, from the Swahili coasts all the way east to Japan.

In addition to the flows of people that we have seen in this book, technologies and ideas, languages and biota—all took flight on the routes and passed from one place to another, and then again to further locales after that. One of the few things that we can say for sure about these transits is that they were continually evolving, never static; opportunities presented themselves constantly—and then when they did—the pathways changed.[17] Religions began in one place and then seeded others; we have seen this with the faiths of India early on in this story, and with Islam and Christianity almost a millennium later. Ports sprang up to receive influences, where before there had only been quiet coastlines. The histories of consumption and demography gradually changed, for thousands at a time and then (ultimately) for millions of people. This book looks at these processes over time and asks through the different windows presented how these connections changed the face of the region. Though hindsight is often twenty-twenty, as the saying goes, the only surety we have in looking at these vast patterns is that history could certainly have unfolded differently. Hinduism could have dominated in diaspora moving

15. See Julien Berthaud, "L'origine et la distribution des caféiers dans le monde," in *Le Commerce du café avant l'ère des plantations coloniales,* ed. Michel Tuchscherer (Cairo: Institut Français d'Archéologie Orientale, 2001); and Ernestine Carreira, "Les français et le commerce du café dans l'Océan Indien au XVIIIe siècle," in *Le Commerce du café,* ed. Tuchscherer. For the geopolitics surrounding this process, see Giancarlo Casale, *The Ottoman Age of Exploration* (New York: Oxford University Press, 2010).

16. Philip Kuhn, *Chinese among Others: Emigration in Modern Times* (Lanham, MD: Rowman & Littlefield, 2009); Lynn Pan, *Sons of the Yellow Emperor: A History of the Chinese Diaspora* (New York: Kodansha International, 1994); Wang Gungwu, *China and the Chinese Overseas* (Singapore: Times Academic Press, 1991).

17. For a useful discussion on the "possibilities," see Giancarlo Casale, Carla Rahn Phillips, and Lisa Norling, "Introduction to 'The Social History of the Sea,'" *Journal of Early Modern History* 14, nos. 1–2 (2010 Special Issue): 1–7.

east, instead of Theravada Buddhism; spices could have been marginal moving to the west, instead of being central to the genesis and unfolding of empires.[18] Thinking across these vast ocean pathways "from Asia to the Mediterranean" allows us to see some of these possibilities.[19] The fact that things turned out as they did on the elongated maritime arc of Asia is testament to the fact that history is always unexpected. It is unexpected in its pathways, and also in its eventual outcomes.

———

The Zheng He fleets, though considerably older than the hybrid Sino-Ukrainian aircraft carrier, were also not the first time that power and commerce moved along Asia's sea routes en masse. Zhao Ru Gua, in his remarkable compendium of the trade routes titled *Zhu Fan Zhi*, written in 1225 CE, had spoken of the products of Africa two hundred years before the Zheng He expeditions ever set sail. Yet it was a series of sea voyages later in that same century, culminating in two expeditions in the years 1274 and 1281 CE, that show us the beginnings of how commerce and power entwined on these routes in ways that had been impossible before. It was in those two years that the Mongols, freshly installed as the conquerors of the Chinese empire, sent vast fleets to occupy feudal Japan, a major trading partner of medieval China. The fleet of the first invasion of 1274 sent 8,000 Korean soldiers and 15,000 Mongol and/or Chinese soldiers on nearly 1,000 ships. The second invasion of 1281 was even larger, with 900 ships transporting 40,000 Yuan troops from

18. For an interesting approach to imagining how history might not have followed the course it did, see the essays compiled in Robert Cowley, ed., *What If? The World's Foremost Military Historians Imagine What Might Have Been* (New York: Berkeley Publishing, 2000).

19. On this same notion, see, for example, François Gipouloux, *The Asian Mediterranean: Port Cities and Trading Networks in China, Japan and Southeast Asia, 13th–21st Century*, trans. Jonathan Hall and Dianna Martin (Cheltenham, UK: Edward Elgar, 2011); Angela Schottenhammer, ed., *The East Asian 'Mediterranean': Maritime Crossroads of Culture, Commerce, and Human Migration* (Wiesbaden: Harrassowitz Verlag, 2008); Sanjay Subrahmanyam, "Notes of Circulation and Asymmetry in Two Mediterraneans, c. 1400–1800," in *From the Mediterranean to the China Sea: Miscellaneous Notes*, ed. Claude Guillot, Denys Lombard, and Roderich Ptak: 21–43 (Wiesbaden: Harrassowitz Verlag,1998); Heather Sutherland, "Southeast Asian History and the Mediterranean Analogy," *Journal of Southeast Asian Studies* 34, no. 1 (2003): 1–20; John E. Wills, "Maritime Asia 1500–1800: The Interactive Emergence of European Domination," *American Historical Review* 98, no. 1 (1993): 83–105.

Korea, and a further 3,500 ships carrying 100,000 troops from South China. Both fleets foundered off the coasts of Japan, caught in battle—but more so by enormous typhoons, the so-called "kamikazes" of Japanese lore. Both fleets limped home (or disappeared) as only shadows of themselves, and neither made much of a dent in either the trade or the political autonomy of Japan. This did not fully dissuade the Mongols from trying again; another invasion fleet in 1293 traveled even farther, landing on Java with 20–30,000 troops and helping to eventually supplant the indigenous Singhasari Empire.[20] The lesson is the same in all cases, however: perspicacious rulers along the sea routes understood that trade led to increased power, but that over the horizon even more intimidating polities might exist, eager to increase their own market share.[21] Medieval Asia's routes existed as a continuum of contact and trade, but it was also a dog-eat-dog world, and one where the biggest potential threat on the horizon was usually Chinese.

Yet in the early modern era this began to change. If the Chinese (and the Mongols as a Chinese dynasty themselves, known as the Yuan, 1279–1368 CE) dominated the patterns of the South China Sea, by the sixteenth century a new power was extant which challenged some of these earlier assumptions of commerce and coercion. The Portuguese sailed into the Indian Ocean toward the end of the fifteenth century, but through the sixteenth century had become a new policing force of sorts in parts of this outstretched sea. Less interested in a formalized tribute system than the Chinese, and more interested in taxing the proceeds of trade on a case-by-case basis, the Portuguese Estado da Índia imposed a quasi-passport system called the *cartaz* which levied fines on any and all shipping moving outside of Lisbon's own designs.[22] As we have seen previously in this book, the *cartaz* system never functioned perfectly, and plenty of ships were able to escape its exactions, either through diplomacy, negligence, or outright graft in relations between the Portuguese and regional

20. T. T. Allsen, *Culture and Conquest in Mongol Eurasia* (Cambridge: Cambridge University Press, 2001).

21. For a relatively new interpretation of these fleets, see James Delgado, *Khublai Khan's Lost Fleet* (Berkeley: University of California Press, 2010). For the larger context of China and its medieval international contexts, see two excellent studies: Hyunhee Park, *Mapping the Chinese and Islamic Worlds: Cross-Cultural Exchange in Pre-Modern Asia* (Cambridge: Cambridge University Press, 2012); and John Chaffee, *Muslim Merchants of Pre-Modern China: The Hisory of a Maritime Asian Trade Diaspora, 750–1400* (Cambridge: Cambridge University Press, 2018).

22. See Anthony Disney, *A History of Portugal and the Portuguese Empire*, 2 vols. (Cambridge: Cambridge University Press, 2009), esp. vol. 2.

Asian rulers. But plenty more did indeed have to pay the tax, and the Portuguese were able to alter and ultimately to disrupt for a time some existing maritime trade patterns along India's coasts, and sometimes farther afield, particularly in the Persian Gulf and the Arabian Sea.[23] Lisbon's ability to project its power was—in the end—not sufficient to do this for long. There were simply not enough Portuguese ships or the conquistadors to run and staff them, and the Indian Ocean was a vast arena for trade, too large for sustained policing of this sort, at this particular point of time. But the dictates of a policy were laid down, and were shown to to be effective enough in places that others took notice. The germination of an idea on how to deal with the realities of Asia's trade routes, and its fantastic possibilities, was put forth for others to improve.

This idea—monopoly, or as close to a monopoly as one can forge—was adopted by the Dutch when their own ships came into the arena of Asian trade in the seventeenth century. The Dutch also wished to profit from the dynamism of Asia's trade routes, and they signaled their intent at this being a marriage of commerce and coercion in the middle decades of that same century. It was then, in the famous "spice islands" of Eastern Indonesia that the VOC pursued a policy not just of attempted monopoly, but of outright murder on those trying to evade their proscriptions.[24] English merchants were among the first, and most famous, executed via this line of reasoning, but certainly many more Asian traders suffered this fate over time than their European counterparts. The latter just assume more weight in the existing (almost wholly European) records of the time. If Dutch policies were less draconian in other parts of the archipelago—less murder, but the same amount of attempted monopoly on items such as tin ore and other valuable products—then the intent was still clear.[25] Asia's maritime trade routes were there to be exploited, but commerce was only part of the equation, and force would be used when

23. See Jean-Louis Bacque-Grammont and Anne Kroell, *Mamlouks, ottomans et portugais en Mer Rouge: L'Affaire de Djedda en 1517* (Paris: Le Caire, 1988); R. B. Serjeant, *The Portuguese off the South Arabian Coast: Hadrami Chronicles; With Yemeni and European Accounts* (Beirut, Librairie du Liban, 1974); and Michel Lesure, "Une document ottoman de 1525 sur l'Inde portugaise et les pays de la Mer Rouge," *Mare Luso-Indicum* 3 (1976): 137–60.

24. On the Amboina and Banda massacres, see Charles Corn, *The Scents of Eden: A Narrative of the Spice Trade* (New York: Kodansha International, 1998).

25. See Locher-Scholten, *Sumatraans sultanaat en koloniale staat*; and Barbara Watson Andaya, *To Live as Brothers: Southeast Sumatra in the Seventeenth and Eighteenth Centuries* (Honolulu: University of Hawai'i Press, 1993).

necessary. As the Dutch project gradually petered out over the course of the eighteenth century, their fellow northern Europeans, the English, began to take on a greater valence in the conduct of business in these seas. First in India but increasingly in other places along the routes as well, English ships began to call at more and more harbors, and with greater and greater frequency. After a time, well into the nineteenth century, Britain became the signal power of the nautical pathways skirting the continent, and London's political dictates were carried with the ships, often (but not always) marrying policy and trade together. It is not an accident, as have seen in chapter 5, that English became a lingua franca of commerce in many societies across the Indian Ocean, from Cape Town up to Kenya and Tanzania, and from Pakistan, Bangladesh, India, Sri Lanka, and Burma down to Malaysia, Singapore, and ultimately to distant Australia. English trade bound these societies together into a kind of maritime propinquity, and the commercial routes that connected them were plied by more English ships than by those of any other nation (ergo Lloyd's, the P & O, etc.)[26]

Only in the first few decades of the twentieth century did this state of affairs begin to be challenged in Asian waters. Since 1868 and the Meiji Reforms, Japan became bent on becoming a "modern power," and followed through with great ruthlessness and precision on making good this aim.[27] State industry and large-scale commerce were joined together in this effort, and large companies—and also many smaller ones—began to expand their business interests into the rest of Asia. Initially many of these concerns were fairly modest—small-scale pearlers in Eastern Indonesia; timber merchants prospecting in what is now Malaysia; Japanese labor traffickers into the Philippines.[28] But eventually tramp-steamer companies held significant trade interests on the maritime routes between Japan and Southeast Asia, and also plied

26. See Keay, *The Honourable Company*, for a good summary of the power of the English East India Company in doing this. Of course, after the time of the company, this trend was continued both by the Crown and by private English steam-shipping and insurance companies, including the P & O, Lloyd's, etc. For a localized look at these processes in one place later on in the period, see Tim Harper, "Singapore, 1915, and the Birth of the Asian Underground," *Modern Asian Studies* 47 (2013): 1782–1811.

27. Mikiso Hane, *Peasants, Rebels, and Outcasts: The Underside of Modern Japan (1800–1940)* (New York: Pantheon Books, 1982).

28. C. Fasseur, "Cornerstone and Stumbling Block: Racial Classification and the Late Colonial State in Indonesia," in *The Late Colonial State in Indonesia: Political and Economic Foundations of the Netherlands Indies 1880–1942*, edited by Robert Cribb, 31–57 (Leiden: KITLV Press,

to and from the median ports of China, connecting the northern and southern geographies of Asia just mentioned.[29] Commerce between Japan and Asia flourished through this "connective tissue" of the sea routes. Japan began to build up its navy, too, partially to protect is overseas investments in Taiwan and elsewhere, but also for other, more ideologically driven reasons at home. Within a few short decades Japanese sea power was superior to almost anything in Asian waters, and was in fact comparable to a number of European navies. Tokyo proved this in the Tsushima Straits in 1905 when Russia's fleet was annihilated, shortly after making the huge, transcontinental journey from European waters. Further Japanese expansion followed this victory, to Manchuria, to Korea, and eventually, by mid-century, to the rest of Asia, which could no longer count on Western ships for any real protection. The maritime trade routes of Asia were "reoriented" (to reuse Andre Gunder Frank's phrase from the introduction of this book) to now point to Japan. Only after cataclysmic war and destruction was this pattern of half a century of building stopped, and the routes restored to their more international, capitalist character.[30] Those are the routes that we have now inherited today as twenty-first-century humans: open, sprawling, and running in many directions, and through the harbors of many ports. It is a long history and a complex one. But it is one whose evolution makes sense within the ambit of a much longer history of contact and exchange, even if, as Ann Stoler elegantly reminds us, we still sit in "the political life of imperial debris, the longevity of structures of dominance, and the uneven pace with which people can extricate themselves from the colonial order of things."[31]

———

This book has been less about attempted domination of these routes, and more about chronicling the life of the maritime pathways of Asia over time. It is a

1994); and Motoe Terami-Wada, "Karayuki-san of Manila 1880–1920," *Philippine Studies* 34 (1986),: 287–316.

29. Peter Post, "Japan and the Integration of the Netherlands East Indies into the World Economy, 1868–1942," *Review of Indonesian and Malaysian Affairs* 27, nos. 1–2 (1993): 134–65. More locally, see Tim Harper, *The End of Empire and the Making of Malaya* (Cambridge: Cambridge University Press, 1999).

30. For more on this writ large, see Clive Schofield, *The Maritime Political Boundaries of the World* (Leiden: Martinus Nijhoff, 2005).

31. Ann Stoler, "Imperial Debris: Reflections on Ruin and Ruination," *Cultural Anthropology* 23, no. 2 (2008): 191–219, at 193.

peek through different kinds of windows at what these routes were like, from the early modern age into the imperial one, and then spilling briefly into our own times. Part I of the book chronicled maritime connections, but did so through very different kinds of approaches. After the introduction, chapter 2 took on the entirety of the maritime circuits, linking China in the "far east" with the westernmost extremities of the Indian Ocean, washing ashore in East Africa. This history is a long one, but one that is also little understood, and it needs to be marked off in DNA strands and pottery shards, as much as it is written through texts and chronicles. The passage of time saw real connections being made between these two opposite poles of the routes. But contact was episodic, and only in selected moments was there "florescence" of this trade, such as when Zheng He's fleets came to the Horn of Africa, or when Africans showed up as merchants and/or mercenaries in Canton. Chapter 3 starts from an altogether different locus—the coasts of a single polity, in this case maritime Vietnam. By examining the trade of this one political entity over time, we have been able to look at the intricate web that the Vietnamese spun in order to connect themselves to wider oceanic economies in the early modern Age. This connection was not sustained, nor was it altogether vital; internal, domestic concerns were usually deemed to be more important in Vietnam. But it was intermittently important in connecting Vietnam both to China and to Southeast Asia for certain periods of time. From those connections, Vietnam opened itself to the world, but only grudgingly for the most part, at least in Confucian times. To some extent, as chapter 4 clearly shows, this recalcitrance is still with us today, though fast disappearing.

Part II of the book focused down on bodies of water, and did so through examinations of the two largest "internal seas" in Asia: the South China Sea and the Indian Ocean, both seen as a system. Chapter 4, as stated above, looked at Vietnam but also at the other societies of the South China Sea, to see how their histories could be linked through patterns of smuggling. Historically these patterns have been very noticeable in this particular body of water. Though smuggling has happened nearly everywhere in human history, the opportunities for this sort of high-risk, high-reward commerce has been pronounced in the South China Sea over many centuries. This chapter looked at these tendencies over the *longue durée*, but then also examined the propensities for the pursuit of regional maritime contraband today, in our own time. If smuggling is one way to conceptualize the South China Sea as a body of water into an internal system, then the Indian Ocean, as seen through chapter 5, also had its possibilities in this respect. The Indian Ocean saw trade on an oceanwide basis earlier than many other places, but it was not a real system of sorts until some of these patterns started to happen with greater frequency, as K. N. Chaudhuri and others have shown. Yet, once the outlines of a large-scale commerce did take shape, this body of water congealed around trade as few other coastlines have in recorded human history. From Cape Town to Perth, radials stretched themselves across the horizon, driven by the ships of many nations. Chapter 5 focused on how the British, of all of these projects, became the most successful, especially as the early modern era wound into the Imperial Age in the eighteenth and nineteenth centuries. New "centers" and new "margins" were created, but Britain bound together these evolving geographies through its trade, and through its seeding of regional relationships on a continent-wide scale.

Part III looked at "religion on the tides" and asked what the relationship of belief was to all of these developments. Chapter 6 did this through the movement of Hindu/Buddhism from South to Southeast Asia in the centuries before the early modern era began. These two religions, seen as harbingers of the old world of India, came to the "new" world of Southeast Asia through traders, primarily. But they also came through men of the faith, some of whom may have come ashore in the wake of invading armed incursions such as those of the Dravidian (South Indian) Cholas. Though what we now call holistically "Hindu/Buddhism" came overseas to many parts of Southeast Asia, it only really stuck on the mainland, principally in the rice-basin corridors of the great rivers (the Irrawaddy, the Chao Phraya, the Mekong). After a journey across the Bay of Bengal by sea, most of the rest of this transit of ideas likely proceeded by land, as cultural and religious notions traveled between these individual kingdoms. The Kra Isthmus and its environs in early Siam was probably a particularly important transit point for this to happen, and this place is given special attention here. Chapter 7 then moves out to sea, as it were, and lands in Zamboanga, a port at the very end of the southern Philippines, but also within sight of the geographic extremes of modern-day Malaysia and Indonesia. In Zamboanga, a Spanish port town of some antiquity, Islam and Christianity engaged in a centuries-long conversation, which was only sometimes peaceful in nature. Astride the wide basin of the Sulu Sea, Zamboanga was near the heart of important trade routes, and the rise of several sultanates in the area meant that Islam was a daily, vital force in this region. Yet Christianity was, too, as this was the endpoint of the Hispanized imperial project in Asia as well. Through historical records and also through oral history interviews, this dialogue is brought out here, as the two concepts sought to contend with one another in this port, which still feels in some ways like the end of the world.

If Zamboanga has been important regionally, then it is just one of many cities that deserves this designation along the outstretched arc of Asia's trade routes. Part IV took on urbanism as part of this conversation, looking at cities and the sea as its central inquiry. Chapter 8 does this regionally, examining the morphogenesis of port cities in "the lands beneath the winds," on a pan–Southeast Asian basis. It takes in both the world of insular Southeast Asia, which is often described by social scientists as a single, predominantly Austronesian-speaking entity, but it also looks at the coasts of mainland Southeast Asia as part of this story. As such, it entwines worlds that other historians of the region—most notably Anthony Reid and Victor Lieberman, in both of their pathbreaking studies—have often seen as vaguely separate spheres. This chapter, as is the case with chapter 4 on smuggling in the South China Sea, avails itself of both historical and more contemporary approaches, looking at the rise of cities over time, including in our own, contemporary world. Chapter 9 changes register again, looking at the concept of cities across an even wider, more inclusive geography. The "colonial circuits" start in Istanbul, the doorway of Asia, and wind their way through the Middle East, through South, Southeast, and East Asia, before landing finally in colonial Korea, in the port of Pusan. This chapter asks how colonial circuits have been forged and maintained across the width and breadth of Asia's routes, connected by sea the entire time across astonishingly vast tracts of open water. Though the British project is given center stage here, Dutch, French, and Japanese colonial circuits are also interrogated. We take for granted that influence and communication can be exerted across space very easily in our own era, but this was not so for long periods of time. This chapter shows how that feat was accomplished historically, forging a unity to the Asian routes as empires sought to bind what they had won into single, interconnected grids.

Part V brought the level of vision down to an ecological level, tying together the marine produce of Sino-Southeast Asian commerce with the spices of South India, items that helped launch the so-called European Age of Discovery. Both classes of products helped to transform the maritime trade routes of Asia from vital, centuries-old arteries of trade into more vestigial lines of commerce, which nevertheless have held vitality over long periods of time. Chapter 10 looks at the fins, slugs, and pearls of East and Southeast Asia that accomplished this task in the South China Sea, and the coastlines both north and south of that body of water that were connected as a result of these items' transit. Bruno Latour might call these sea biota "quasi-objects": he sees these sorts of "once-alive," but now nonliving commodities, as "much more social, much more fabricated, much more collective than the 'hard' parts of nature . . . (yet) they are much more real, non-human and objective (than we think)."[32]

This history is an old one, though records for marine produce trading are often hard to find, and the evidence itself has long ago disappeared with the ravages of time in a tropical climate. Yet from the mid-eighteenth to the later decades of the nineteenth century, this commerce was of extreme importance in Asian waters, funneling goods to Canton via indigenous sultanates who built their power on the acquisition of such items. This, in turn, attracted the notice of Europeans, who began to pursue the export of these commodities in their own attempts to pry open the vast Chinese economy. I examine these transits both historically and ethnographically, traveling between collection sites and the merchant shops still selling these objects, to try to piece together the story of their passage. Chapter 11 then looks farther west to pursue a similar story: the exit of spices from South India's coasts into transnational and transregional circuits of exchange. Indian spices such as pepper, turmeric, and cumin brought visitors to the country's shores from an early age, but it was only in the early modern period that the transport of these odiferous seeds, barks, and woods began to occur on a more voluminous basis. Some of this transit was to the west, and helped to seed classical antiquity with ideas of the "Orient," ideas that stayed in the Western imagination for many centuries after that. Yet some of this transit also pushed east to places like the Malay Peninsula, where generations of Indian traders ended up migrating to continue the conduct of this trade even into our own time. Through historical records and also through interviews and fieldwork both in South and Southeast Asia, the passage of spices is examined here as well, as perhaps the single most important of all the ecological trades of Asia that induced vessels to sail overseas.

Finally, Part VI looked at technologies of the sea, and the technological imperative generally in the unfolding of the maritime history of Asia. No study of the history of this theme would be complete without a nod toward technology, as technology made the vessels run, and also told sailors, speculators, and insurance agents where to send the ships in the first place. Chapter 12 analyzes the role of lighthouses, beacons, and buoys in that story, "tools of empire"

---

32. Bruno Latour, *We Have Never Been Modern* (Cambridge: Cambridge University Press, 1993), 55.

(to borrow a phrase) that enabled the visible and outright conquests of Asia to happen on a continent-wide basis. Yet the lights made this visibility possible; prior to the erection of lighthouses throughout insular Southeast Asia, for example, expanding colonial projects had little or no idea where their subjects sailed at night, and to what ends. These new tools helped to surveille captive populations, and in fact as instruments they have much in common with Foucault's much more famous example of the panoptic prison as methods for controlling those "who need to be controlled." Western powers used these lights to herd channels of indigenous maritime activity toward the state's own ends. Chapter 13 looks at another formidable tool, the hydrographic map, as a further instrument of control by the West over "the rest." Hydrographic mapping was perhaps the single most important innovation in the early conquest of Asia's maritime routes, because the knowledge won could be continually improved, and was, in fact, repeatedly over time. Maps allowed for space to be translated into action in the imperial sense. Europeans ships got to know the region's seas at least as well as Asians themselves, who for long periods of time had a decided advantage in "local knowledge" during encounters. Both in war and in commerce, the West eventually caught up to these local levels of knowledge, and then were able to dictate new terms to these relationships as their own sense of the sea grew over time. Foucault's equally famous paradigm of power and knowledge applies in both of these cases, therefore. Chapter 14, the conclusion, wraps up this book by asking again on a *longue durée* basis what these patterns might mean, both historically and also in our own time. If the specter of China as a reemerging power on these routes comes to pass, what will be the result? How will China impact these maritime conduits in all of the ways we have described above? Does history give us any clues in this respect? And how much can we rely on past patterns as substrate for future events?

―――――

In much of Asia, the sea was considered to be free for a long time before anyone had the notion that political will could be enacted in forcible ways upon its surface. Historians have pointed to the penning of *Mare Liberum* by the Dutch jurist Hugo Grotius in 1609 as the start date for some of these ideas in an international legal context.[33] But the reality of things is that this notion—that

33. Martine Julia van Ittersum, *Profit and Principle: Hugo Grotius, Natural Rights Theories, and the Rise of Dutch Power in the East Indies, 1595–1615* (Leiden: Brill, 2006).

anyone could trade by sea, and had the freedom to do this without hindrance—
existed in this part of the world for a long time before this. Though there was
a continuum of "showing force" on the high seas, as we have seen with both
the Mongols and the Ming well prior to Grotius's pronouncement in that year,
it was really the arrival of the Portuguese that signaled the start of the *mare
clausum* idea, in many respects. Through this some seas were deemed to be
enforceable spaces of transit, with armed naval force and primitive "passports"
enforcing the evolution of the surveilled movement. The ability to back up this
rhetoric did not happen all at once. As far as we know, many Asian rulers
looked for ways around the new evolving realities of trade on the routes, which
were (in fact) still viable for quite some time, at least in places. But the West
in piecemeal but ultimately collective fashion began to study the routes and
the seas that connected Asia's ports. Year by year more and more data were
collected, more and more bodies of water were better known, and—crucially—
all of the information was archived, with the express idea of using this knowledge for economic (and, increasingly, political) ends. The monsoons were
charted and their timetables penned; the flow of currents connecting many
shores were written down, and the development of longitude as a science
helped this process along.[34] The routes became more and more knowable as a
connective entity, and more and more foreigners were seeking to profit from
this knowledge. The world became a smaller place over the course of the centuries after the "age of contact" and the "quickening" I mentioned in my introduction.[35] The gradual untangling of Asia's sea routes as something to be known
and studied was one important reason why this happened.

These same maritime pathways today still exist, though in altered forms.
Some large ships still do make the end-to-end run of the routes, connecting
the oil refineries of the Persian Gulf (or the aquatic channel to Europe of the
Red Sea) with the huge, populous markets of East Asia, especially China,
Korea, and Japan. Oil tankers and car carriers often sail those circuits now,
though you can find almost any kind of commodity on the large container
ships. But I would posit that it is on the smaller, more regional legs of the
routes that one can still hear best the murmur of these old trades. Some years
ago, in the westernmost part of the Indian Ocean, not too far from where

34. Dava Sobel, *Longitude: The True Story of a Lone Genius Who Solved the Greatest Scientific
Problem of His Day* (New York: Penguin, 1995).

35. Tim Harper and Sunil Amrith, eds., *Sites of Asian Interaction: Ideas, Networks, and Mobility* (Cambridge: Cambridge University Press, 2014).

Zheng He's fleets came ashore looking for a giraffe, I took ship from Zanzibar in Tanzania to Mombasa in Kenya overnight. The old corrugated steamer was overloaded with local people and their wares, and in the middle of the night the vessel began listing dangerously to its port side, with far too much weight on board. We could see the twinkle of lights on the distant shore to the west. But we were a long way from the coast, and I was eyeing dubiously the currents, the depth of the water, and the distance from shore, all for an unforeseen swim in the dark. There are plenty of sharks in those waters, too. The ship made it to port the next morning, but a number of ferries have gone down on this route, and they still do (even recently), often with scores or even hundreds of passengers lost when that happens.[36] That night, staring out at the farthest western horizons of trade in the Indian Ocean, I wondered how often this must have occurred: those on deck looking out to sea and feeling how small their chances were against anything that nature might throw at them. For centuries people have sailed these routes, to move some mangrove poles here and some ivory bangles there, but always with the depths calling out for more souls. They litter the bottom.[37] Making a living sailing these seas off the sea channels has always been a grim business. The romance of the routes, in truth, is for those who do not make a living off plying back and forth across these circuits of commerce, likely every working day of their adult lives.

All the way across the Indian Ocean, and even across most of the Java Sea, I had similar thoughts on another night, and on another ship—again in the dark. I took a Bugis *prahu-pinisi*, an old schooner replete with huge sails and a giant, sloping bow, from Makassar in Sulawesi to Surabaya in Java. The Bugis were sometimes piratical in centuries past; it's from their name that the West received the epithet *bogeyman*, as in "the bogeyman is going to get you." Bugis crews sailed most of Indonesia's waters historically, and they still do. It has been estimated that if the world ran out of oil, that Indonesia's economy would still continue to run longer than most others, because there are still so many

---

36. I took this journey up the East African coast in 1990, mostly in native dhows, but then again in 2012. In that latter year, another Zanzibar ferry sank with great loss of life; see "Tanzania Ferry Sinks Off Zanzibar," 19 July 2012, http://www.bbc.com/news/world-18896985, accessed 15 July 2015.

37. Abdul Sheriff, *Slaves, Spices, and Ivory: Integration of an East African Commercial Empire into the World Economy, 1770–1873* (Athens, OH: Ohio University Press, 1987). On the possibilities of combining ethnography and history, see Andrew Willford and Eric Tagliacozzo, eds., *Clio/Anthropos: Exploring the Boundaries between History and Anthropology* (Palo Alto: Stanford University Press, 2009).

large Bugis ships that could transport commodities on wind power alone. Sleeping on a sack of salt out on the deck that night, somewhere between Sulawesi and Java, I wondered how long people had been sailing these routes, and what they had hoped to find. The ancestors of the Bugis voyaged as far as northern Australia, finding edible sea cucumbers (*trepang*) in shallow, local waters to send on to the Chinese in Canton. Aboriginal Australians marked their arrival in cave paintings near Darwin, where it is now thought that the Bugis ships must have been coming seasonally for at least three to four hundred years.[38] Here again, the power of the routes in action is palpable, as is their echo. Those black-sailed ships that plied the trade winds crisscrossed the known world, and in fact opened up new realms, predating Cook's voyages to Australia by at least a century, if not significantly more. The fruits of the journeys wound up far to the north, eaten at rich merchant tables somewhere in the Pearl River estuary. Canton's lights glistened in the dark as those sea cucumbers were consumed. Do trade routes have enduring secrets? Did the Chinese know how far those holothurians had traveled so that they could be eaten in a tonic of soup? It is difficult to be sure. Yet, as we have seen with the medieval portmaster Zhao Ru Gua, if anything the Chinese thirst for knowledge about the routes was every bit as voracious, at least episodically, as that of Europeans, the latter only coming to Asia many centuries later.[39]

So will China rule the seas, as we asked at the beginning of this chapter? Will the many centuries of Asia's sea routes culminate in a near future where China again becomes—as in the days of the eunuch Admiral Zheng He— master of these oceans, flying a flag of power that all witness from shore in awe, and also possibly in dread? It is impossible to know, and these are the moments when I am glad to be a historian, and not in a more presentist discipline. But history perhaps again gives us some clues. Rather than looking for the big footprint of power on the routes, designed in the form of an aircraft carrier, perhaps it is better to seek out the small. The epigrapher Wolfgang Frank has chronicled an astonishing array of old inscriptions—there are literally thousands of them—that the Chinese have left across the width and breadth of the Malay world, in temples, caves, and on posts, often in the middle of nowhere.

---

38. See MacKnight, Charles Cambell. 1976. *The Voyage to Marege: Macassan Trepangers in Northern Australia* (Carlton: Melbourne University Press); and Christian Pelras, *The Bugis* (Oxford: Blackwell, 1996).

39. Hirth and Rockhill, *Chau Ju Kua*, 1966. Australia is not mentioned in Zhao Ru Gua's account of the Asian maritime trade routes.

They chronicle the passing of the Chinese historically, all of them traveling the routes.[40] We know from other scholarship—some of it even focusing on Papua New Guinea, and the islands technically outside what is considered to be Southeast Asia, and what is now classified in the realm of Oceania instead—that the Chinese passed this way, too. They traded for shells and coconuts on distant shores, and on even more remote atolls.[41] There are few records of their passing, and the chronicles of their trips are far and few between.

But the DNA does not lie, and we know from those clues among others that such far-flung approaches were also a part of this story. Asia's sea routes stretched from the far shores of East Africa all the way to the mid-Pacific. The routes continually changed, but what did *not* change was the desire and the ability for such intrepid traders to travel. The footfall was quiet, but the legacy of transit is still with us, in bloodlines as well as in diaspora, in colonies as well as in trade connections. The best evidence, in fact, may be on a rounded hill in Melaka, which once was *the* major center of trade in monsoon Asia, and likely one of the largest ports in the world in the sixteenth century. There, within plain sight of the port, is Bukit Cina, or China Hill, home to one of the largest graveyards in the world of Chinese people outside of China. It is an eerie, wonderful place, the air filled with nostalgia, and the sound of small bells tinkling in the wind.[42] That same wind blew these voyagers here over the centuries, and some of the graves date back to the Ming. There, more than perhaps any other place, the aura of Asia's maritime routes can be felt—in all that was carried, and all that was left behind.

40. Wolfgang Frank and Chen Tieh Fan, *Chinese Epigraphic Materials in Malaysia*, 3 vols. (Kuala Lumpur: University of Malaya Press, 1982–87).

41. See David Wu, *The Chinese in Papua New Guinea, 1880–1980* (Hong Kong: Hong Kong University Press, 1982); and Eric Tagliacozzo, "Navigating Communities: Distance, Place, and Race in Maritime Southeast Asia," *Asian Ethnicity* (Routledge) 10, no. 2 (2009): 97–120.

42. Bukit Cina is not a place without complications; it is a site rife with the memory-politics of ethnicity in contemporary Southeast Asia.

LIST OF APPENDIX DOCUMENTS

Appendix A: Base Chronologies for Asia's Seas

This appendix lays out some base chronologies for both the Indian Ocean and the South China Sea, and the states and proto-state polities which ring them.

Appendix B: Written-Down Oral Histories of the Swahili Coasts

Oral History fragments of the indigenous histories of Kilwa Kisiwani, Lindi, and Dar es Salaam, showing local notions of trade, politics, and society in this maritime locale.

Appendix C: Fieldwork Excerpt: An Arab Herbalist, Central Souk, Sana'a, Yemen

A fieldwork excerpt of an interview with an Arab traditional herbalist, done in the markets of Sana'a, in highland Yemen astride the Red Sea routes. His main connections were with India.

Appendix D: Indian Spice Traders in India and Malaysia

A fieldwork excerpt and an interview excerpt, each dealing with Indians and the spices they produce (and trade) in Indian Ocean networks, across the Bay of Bengal.

Appendix E: Dutch East Indies Regulations with Local Maritime States

Dutch and Malay interpretations of statecraft and politics in the Dutch East Indies (Indonesia), as well as the establishment of marine lights in this region.

Appendix F: Chinese Marine Goods Traders in East and Southeast Asia

Interview fragments with Chinese marine traders in Yangon, Taipei, and Hong Kong, and a longer fragment of an interview with a marine goods merchant in Singapore.

Appendix G: Chinese Marine Products Newspaper Clipping, Taipei, Taiwan

Newspaper cutout from a Taiwanese daily about marine products being sold in Taiwan, their provenances, prices, etc.

Base Chronologies for Asia's Seas

Western Seas

Western Indian Ocean

MIDDLE EAST/ARABIAN SEA

Founding of Abbasid Dynasty, 750 CE
Founding of Baghdad, 762
Ghaznavid Dynasty founded, 977
First sight of Mongols in Persia, 1220
Sack of Baghdad, 1258
Mamluk Sultanate, 1250–1517
Portuguese on Persian coast, 1508
Safavid Empire, 1501–1736
VOC enters into pact with Shah Abbas, 1623
Portuguese evicted from Gulf by EI Co., 1650
French East India Co. established, 1664
Ottoman Empire, 1517–1923
Suez Canal opens, 1869
Telegraph links Persia, India, Europe, 1898
Persia enters League of Nations, 1920

EAST AFRICAN COAST

Islam reaches Shanga, 780 CE
Muslim dynasty in Kilwa, 1050
Swahili coastal society develops after this
Cheng He expeditions, first half 15th century

South Asian Subcontinent

EARLY DEVELOPMENTS

Early Hinduism develops, 900 BCE
Buddhism born, India/Nepal, 500 BCE
Gupta Empire, 320–500 CE
Hun invasions, 455–528
Rajput Dynasties, 650–1335
Arab armies take Sindh, 711
Mahmud of Ghazni's raids, 997–1027
Delhi Sultanate, 1192–1526
Vijayanagar Empire, 1336–1646
Portuguese arrival in India, 1498
Mughal Empire, 1526–1858
Dutch trade established, 1609
English trade established, 1612
French trade established, 1674
Growth of European coastal trade

BRITISH INDIA

EI Co. annexes first Bombay land, 1615
Anglo-French War in India, 1748
Battle of Plassey, 1757
EI Co. defeats Tippu Sultan, 1792

EAST AFRICAN COAST

Ethiopian coffee cultivated in Yemen, 1450
Portuguese in Zanzibar, 1503
Muslim Somalis versus Christian Ethiopia, 1530
Omani fleet destroys Portuguese Mombasa
And Zanzibar, 1698
Zanzibar becomes Omani Empire center, 1837
UK consul ends Zanzibari slave trade, 1873
The Mahdi Revolt in Sudan, 1883
Italians in Eritrea, 1885
Zanzibar becomes UK protectorate, 1890
German East African protectorate, 1891
Kenya becomes UK protectorate, 1895

BRITISH INDIA

Mutiny at Vellore, 1806
First Indian War of Independence, 1857
Last Mughal emperor deposed, 1858
Crushing of the Great Revolt, 1858
End of Company rule in India, 1858
End of Mughal rule in India, 1858
Start of the British Raj, 1858
Mahatma Gandhi born in Gujarat, 1869
Queen Victoria, Empress of India, 1877
Indian National Congress formed, 1885
Victoria's Diamond Jubilee, 1897
Start of Europe's Great War, 1914

**Adapted/expanded from OxfordReference.com (East Africa);
AsiaforEducators.columbia.edu (Indian subcontinent); *Encyclopaedia Iranica*.

Eastern Seas

WESTERN MAINLAND SOUTHEAST ASIA

Pyu Era, c. 200–840
Pagan, c. 950–1300
Ava Period, 1365–1555
Independent Ra-manya Polity, c. 1300–1539
First Toungoo Dynasty, c. 1486–1599
Restored Toungoo, 1597–1752
Kon-baung Dynasty, 1752–1885
Anglo-Burmese Wars, 1824, 1852, 1888

CENTRAL MAINLAND SOUTHEAST ASIA

Funan, c. 200–600
Dvaravati Period, c. 550–900
Pre-Angkorian Cambodia, c. 600–800
Angkor, 802/889–c. 1440
Early Ayudhya Period, 1351–1569
Late Ayudhya Period, 1569–1767

JAPAN

Heian-centered Polity, 900–1280
Late Kamakura to Ashikaga, 1280–1467
Warring States/Reunification 1467–1603
Tokugawa Shogunate, 1603–1854
Meiji Restoration, 1868

CHINA

T'ang Dynasty, 618–907
Song Dynasty, 960–1279
Yuan Dynasty, 1279–1368
Ming Dynasty, 1368–1644
Ch'ing Dynasty, 1644–1911
Republic and War Period, 1912–49

ISLAND SOUTHEAST ASIA

Srivijaya Polity, 7th–12th centuries
"Charter Era," 650–1350/1500

CENTRAL MAINLAND
SOUTHEAST ASIA

Taksin, 1767–1782
Chakri Dynasty, 1782–present
Modern Thai state, 1932 onward

EASTERN MAINLAND
SOUTHEAST ASIA

Chinese Imperial Period, 43–938
Ly Dynasty, 1009–1225
Tran Dynasty, 1225–1400
Ming Occupation, 1407–27
Lê Dynasty, 1428–1788
Mac Period at Thăng Long, 1527–92
Trịnh Period, 1592–1786
Southern Nguyễn, c. 1600–1802
Tây Sơn Era, 1771–1802
Nguyễn Dynasty, 1802–1945
French period, 1859 onward

ISLAND SOUTHEAST ASIA

Majapahit Kingdom, 1293—c. 1500
"Charter Era" collapses, 1300–1500
European Interventions, 1511–1660
Magellanic Voyages, 1519–22
Turn of the 17th c., Dutch arrival, NEI
VOC Rule, Indonesia, to 1799/1800
Cultivation System, 1830–70
"Liberal Period," 1870–1900
"Ethical Period," 1900 onward
1786 UK arrival, Penang
1819 UK arrival, Singapore
1825–30 Java War; 1873–1903 Aceh War
1824, 1874 division of Melaka Straits
1898–1900 Spanish American War, PI
1900–45, American period, PI

**Adapted/expanded from various parts of Lieberman, *Strange Parallels: Southeast Asia in Global Context, 800–1830*, vols. 1 and 2 (Cambridge: Cambridge University Press, 2003).

Written-Down Oral Histories
of the Swahili Coasts

The Ancient History of Kilwa Kisiwani

Then there ruled Sultan Isufu bin Sultan Hassan. The people agreed with him because of the strength of his rule, and paid dues on grain. Their occupations were fishing, farming, and trade. The occupation from which they derived great profit (was) . . . the slave trade. And the Frenchman was there, as we have said above. This sultan dwelt in the ancient fort in the Shangani quarter and enlarged it. . . . Then there came to Kisiwani Sayyid Ali bin Sefu al-Busaidi: he came from Muscat. He went to the ruler, and the ruler gave him the prison which is near the present-day market, and he dwelt there. This Sayyid Ali bin Sefu came in force, with his ships and men and goods. This was the beginning of the time of Said bin Sultan. There was great friendship between him and Sultan Isufu. Said bin Sultan sent his own man to Kisiwani, an Arab called Marhun bin Ali, who came and settled in Kisiwani. . . . Said bin Sultan was on excellent terms with the people and the ruler. He began a custom of sending very year two rolls of cloth, and giving them to the ruler and to the Wamalindi, and this was done every year. The reason for these presents from Said bin Sultan was that there were disturbances on the coast, so that the caravan could not set out. . . .

The Ancient History of Lindi

If a merchant comes to the country; he is not permitted to trade until he has paid a sultan something like forty reals, which he gives to town elders. This is an ancient custom. In the merchant is a native of the town, he pays nothing. . . .

If a man has come to the country and gained much wealth, and then wishes to return to his home, the sultan says, "You cannot go until you have divided your wealth among us, because you have got this wealth in my country." The Makonde are their neighbors, and they put plugs in their upper lips, shaping them with a piece of wood. It is similar to a Persian real and placed in the upper lip. This is considered beautiful among them.

The Ancient History of Dar es Salaam

At that time the Arabs left Muscat and came to settle in Zanzibar: one of them was called Said bin Sultan. He came with his vessel and disembarked at Zanzibar: when he saw the original inhabitants, the Hadimi and the Tumbatu, he fought them, and beat them. They had not the strength to make war against him. After he had conquered Zanzibar, he settled and built large stone houses. . . . Then Said sent word to Muscat, and many Arabs came. After the Arab had settled in Zanzibar, there came Europeans—Englishmen—and asked the Arab for a large house. He gave it to them, and the Englishman settled down. Later he said, "I wish to display my own flag." The Sultan of Zanzibar answered, "You have my permission, but the flag will be at my orders."

All from G. S. P. Freeman-Grenville, *The East African Coast: Select Documents from the First to the Earlier Nineteenth Century* (Oxford: Clarendon Press, 1962), 223, 232, 233.

Fieldwork Excerpt from Sana'a

AN ARAB HERBALIST

LATE-NIGHT CONVERSATION with an herbalist in the souk; we spoke for roughly 40 minutes, with the help of a translator. His glass jars were filled with various remedies and natural items used for healing, which included frankincense, myrrh, all sorts of other gum resins indigenous to the southern and eastern Arab Peninsula, as well as small weights and scales and bins of larger dried goods, some of which I could see and ascertain, and some of them which were unknown to me entirely. He had several glass jars filled with bright blue (raw) arsenic, and I bought a little of this wrapped in the day's Yemeni newspaper, just to bring home. There were also piles of cardamoms (green), cloves (brown), chilies (red), and ginger (tan) scattered in the shop, which was narrow and cramped, with each wall lined entirely with these products, and little to no room to sit, except for the merchant himself. He is worried that the art of these medicines is dying, and he has photos up of his teachers (old men) and their teachers (now dead men). It's clear he cares about the longevity of this trade and its disappearance from the earth. My translator says he is a very decent man and well known in the souk for being honest and trustworthy; he knows his remedies and people trust him. He has been selling his knowledge and the medicines in the market for many, many years.

See also Gisho Honda, Wataru Miki, and Saito Mitsuko, *Herb Drugs and Herbalists in Syria and North Yemen* (Tokyo: Institute for the Study of Languages and Cultures of Asia and Africa, 1990).

Indian Spice Traders in India and Malaysia

Fieldwork Excerpt, Small Towns in the Western Ghats, Kerala, Malabar Coast (1990)

The vertical drop here in the Ghats is extremely steep; you can fall down these mountains and you would not stop until you hit the plains, then the sea. Very dense, wet climate, with the spices being grown in very humid conditions. The moisture in the air is palpable and is conditioned by the ghats themselves, and the air blowing in from the sea, which is not far away. The verticality of this landscape also allows for the moisture to constantly be recycled, and it permeates the soil, which is red-brown and very rich. Spices grow so well here because the natural environmental conditions are just perfect. The labor force works in these hills and is able to get the spices out in large quantities because the roads pass through the mountains; the lorries can then transport the spices to the go-downs on the coasts. From there they head to Cochin and Trivandrum and then out to sea, to places like Malaysia and Singapore and the Indian diaspora communities there, but also of course to many other places.

Interview Extract with Seeni Naina Mohamed & Co., Ipoh, Malaysia (3 November 1989)

"Our family originally comes from the Ramnad District, in Tamil Nadu. We are a Muslim family; our grandfather came to Malaysia in 1922. He worked in the spice trade in India for another man there, but then started his own business here. All of my brothers are now out of this trade, though everyone participated in it when they were younger; now one is a professor, one is an

Regd. Buss. Cert. No. 10543
Telegram : "NAINAMCO"
Telephone No. ~~3128~~
Post Box No. 26

TRADE

MARK

M   № 000893

60 JALAN SULTAN ISKANDAR
(Hugh Low Street) Ipoh

Bought of

30 000 IPOH..........................19......

SEENI NAINA MOHAMED & CO.

(ESTABLISHED 1932)

Menjual Barang Barang Runcit

GENERAL MERCHANTS, WHOLESALE AND RETAIL DEALERS.

சீனி நெய்னு முகம்மது அன் கம்பெனி

பலசரக்கு வியாபாரம்

accountant, one is a lawyer and one is a doctor. This job is monotonous and also very time-consuming; there is little time away from it." He thinks his sons would rather not do this job for a living; the world is getting modernized, and very competitive. There is a lot of competition with Chinese merchants at the moment. In Ipoh the Chinese have the upper hand in business. He does roughly 80 percent retail and 20 percent wholesale for the entirety of his business. In addition to many of the spices in burlap sacks that I recognize (see notes for provenances of his coriander; fenugreek; saffron; turmeric; cumin, cardamom; white and black pepper, etc.), he has asafoetida, for medicinal purposes. Gives me small tin of Mysore sandalwood oil at end of interview.

Dutch East Indies Regulations with Local Maritime States

THE BEGINNING AND THE END (AND COAST-LIGHTING IN BETWEEN)

Later Nineteenth Century

Het Sultanaat blijft als leen afgestaan aan Sultan Abdoelrachman Maadlam Sjah onder uitdrukkelijke voorwaarde van stipte en trouwe nakoming der in dit contract omschreven verplichtingen.

SEE *SURAT-SURAT PERDJANDJIAN ANTARA KESULTANAN RIAU DENGAN PEMERINTAHAN (2) V.O.C. DAN HINDIA-BELANDA 1784–1909* (JAKARTA: ARSIP NASIONAL INDONESIA, 1970), 239–40.

The Lingga Riau Sultanate remains as a loan to the Sri Paduka Tuan Sultan 'Adulrrahman Ma'azhzham Sjah with resolute understanding from the Sri Paduka Tuan Sultan that he will follow the stipulations set in this treaty loyally and in full.

Turn of the Century

Het hier in station behoorende raderstoomschip "Singkawang" deed gedurende den verdagstijd enkele reizen naar Indragiri tot het overvoeren van Gouvernements passagiers, gelden, en goederen, en naar ZuidOosthoek van Lingga ten einde de gemeenschap met het aldaar in aanbouw zijnde

kustlichtetablissement te onderhouden . . . In de maand December werd
nog twee malen het kustlicht op Tandjong-Djong bezocht. . . .

VERRICHTINGEN EN BEWEGINGEN DER STOOMSCHAPEN VAN DE
GOUVERNMENTS MARINE, ATJEH, 1897, VIERDE KWARTAL,
REPRODUCED IN F. C. BACKER DIRKS, DE GOUVERNMENTS
MARINE, 317 (WEESP: DE BOER MARITIEM, 1985).

The in-station steamship *Singkawang* during its last few trips to Indragiri
transported government passengers, cash, and commodities, and to the
southeast corner of Lingga, a crew for the building there of the coast-
lighting establishment. . . . In December, the coast-light on Tanjong Jong
was also sought. . . .

Early Twentieth Century

. . . Maka tuan Sultan diberhentikan dari pangkatnya itu sebab banjak kali
melanggar Politik Contract; beberapa kali djuga diberi nasehat oleh Sri
Paduka Governeur Generaal Betawi dan Sri Padoeka Toean Besar Resident
Tanjoeng Pinang. Maka itu dengan tiada Tuan Sultan mengindahkan atau
mengingatkan perdjandjian yang akan mengubahkan apa-apa jang tiada
patut itu. Dan tiada sekali-kali akan melanggar Polotik Contract lagi dan
mesurat segala perintah dan aturan Sri Padoeka Governeur dan wakilnya. . . .

SEE TENGKU AHMAD ABUBAKAR AND HASAN JUNUS, SEKELUMIT
KESAN PENINGGALAN SEJARAH RIAU (ASMAR RAS, 1972)

. . . The Sultan [of Riau-Lingga] hereby loses his title due to the numerous
occasions whereby he has rebelled against the political contract; he has
been counseled of this repeatedly by the Governor General of Batavia and
the Resident of Tanjung Pinang. [This is] in consequence of the Sultan
ignoring or breaking the agreement as it should be. There will never be a
breaking of the political contract again in the writing down of all law and
order of the Governor and his representatives. . . .

—*translations by E. Tagliacozzo*

Chinese Marine Goods Traders in East and Southeast Asia

Interview Excerpt: Yangon

species of holothurian on sale here; one is on-cured, yellow in color; the other is the more usual, smoky-white variety. But both versions are rare and not found in other parts of Southeast Asia that I have seen. The dried version is 10,000 *kyat* for one piece; it's heavy, and she lets me hold it, it's about the size of my hand. There are species here which are not making it out to the larger int'l markets; this is what a closed Burma means.

Interview Excerpt: Taipei

Lee Xing Shun's shop in Taipei has a wild, huge assortment of marine products. His father came to Taiwan from Fujian in 1946, so, during the middle of the Chinese Civil War. There are many grades of trepang, but also packaged turtle shell, a whole hawks-bill turtle on the wall next to a whole deer head, with a rack of antlers. Deer tails are in the glass cabinet; many large ginseng bundles sit behind the glass too. The largest shark fins I have ever seen are also behind that glass; very pricey.

中醫診療所 中醫全科門診
CHINESE MEDICINE CLINIC

千草城
CITIHERB

內婦兒科　跌打骨傷專科
針灸拔罐　皮膚頑疾專科

27 NAM KOK ROAD, G/F.,
KOWLOON CITY, H.K.
香港 九龍城 南角道27號 地下
TEL 電話: 27188228, 27188229
FAX 傳真: 27188810

營業時間
星期一至六　　上午9時至下午9時
星期日及假日　上午10時至下午9時

中醫師駐診時間
星期一至六　　上午9時至下午8時半
星期日及假日　上午10時至下午8時半

專營: 燕窩·蔘茸·海味·健康食品

健生中西药房
KIN SANG DISPENSARY

本藥房由政府註冊藥劑師主理
(精配藥方)

九龍九龍城衙前圍圍道35號地下 (漢賓酒樓側)
G/F., 35 NGA TSIN WAI ROAD, KOWLOON CITY, KOWLOON.
TEL:2382 3040, 2382 3060 FAX: 2382 3061

Interview Excerpt: Hong Kong

Great conversation with Elsa, who gives me a black resinous tonic to help my blood, she says, and also to clear up my red eyes. They have giant *lizhe* mushrooms, beautifully set out and polished. The deer antlers are cut and shaved to thin slices, for immediate use in medicinal form. The fish maws (stomachs) are the largest I have ever seen; they are woven in texture and yellow in color. Edible birds' nests from marine caves in the corner.

Interview Excerpt: Hong Kong

This is a much smaller shop; much more retail here, and less wholesale. Much of the merchandise is already in prepared form, so, for taking medicinally right away. But even here, you can see how the materials find their way from the sea and into the stomachs and circulatory systems of humans, all the way at the end of the commodity chain. Mandarin is in short supply here; Cantonese would have been far better. But the one guy I talk to is friendly enough, and shows me the marine goods they do have.

—*translations by E. Tagliacozzo*

dial 161 Directory assistance; Nat'l Museum
ask for Museum Director; for tour

NAM YONG MARINE PRODUCTS
#45, N. CANAL ROAD, SING 0105

1. 你的家庭是从什么地方来的

Canton

南荣海真私人有限公司
Nam Yong Marine Products (Pte) Ltd.
新加坡怒干拿律門牌四十五號
No. 45, NORTH CANAL ROAD,
SINGAPORE 0105.

劉 選 彬
LOW SWAN PIANG

TEL: 5337286
5358938
RES: 2257250

couldn't exact addr. b/c there are
many of the same businesses in this area
N. Canal Road / S. Bridge Road intersection

2. 你做这个生意做多久了?

dad at age 17 came here
came as coolie
become his own boss at 42   Company started 1951   } 38 years total

这是你家的祖传的生意吗?

no. Grandfather was Guangdong farmer

已经有几代了?

∅   [2]

3. 你家移民来这儿多久了?

2.

4. 你在东南亚的别的国家有没有亲戚朋友? yes. Malaysia
Penang. (Relatives)

他們也做香料的生意吗?

no. not in marine products.

Chinese:
marine products,
medicine (abacus)

Indian:
food.

1

5. 你的家庭是直接移民到这儿来的吗?

directly from Canton → Singapore

还是先到过别的地方?

那些地方?

你在开始你的生意的时候,你的家庭在经济上给了
你帮助吗? *No. Money saved from being coolie.*
Married & had children

你们移民的路线跟你们的亲戚有关系吗?

all dad's relatives stay in China. 1 brother, but
he died in China.

跟你们的生意,也有关系吗?

No.

6. 你们的香料是在那儿採购的?

这些香料的产地在那儿?

back page 没有

7. 种香料的人是那种人? *back page*

2

8. 你想把你的生意传给你的后代吗?

Yes. Definitely. Can't learn from books, only experience.

你要你的后代继续做你的生意吗?

15 years old.
Gets to be his own boss; kept in family
(yes)

9. 你觉得你的生意对在东南亚发担中华文化有贡献吗?

Yes. Because majority of items eaten by chinese.

10. 阿拉伯跟印度的商人在东南亚有很大的影响力, 这对你有竞争的压力吗?

No trust Indian/Arab vs. chinese
Marine Products Association
22 Companies in Singapore & Guild

那个压力比较大?

11. 你知不知道他们卖什么样的香料? Indians more food: from Indonesia + India.

他们卖的跟你们卖的差不多吗? Entirely different markets.

3

Chinese Marine Products
Newspaper Clipping, Taipei, Taiwan

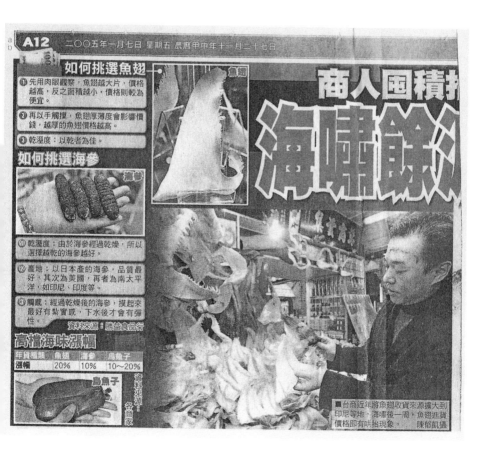

BIBLIOGRAPHY

Fieldwork Locales

Fieldwork and interviewing for this book was conducted in the following places:

- Brunei
- Hong Kong
- Japan
- Oman
- Singapore
- Thailand
- Burma
- India
- Kenya
- Philippines
- Taiwan
- Vietnam
- China
- Indonesia
- Malaysia
- Qatar
- Tanzania
- Yemen

Libraries and Repositories Consulted

I. Europe

UNITED KINGDOM

- Greenwich Maritime Museum, Greenwich
- Cambridge University Library, Cambridge
- India Office, British Library (IOL), London
- Public Records Office (PRO), Kew, Surrey

NETHERLANDS

- National Maritime Museums, Amsterdam and Rotterdam
- Koninklijke Instituut voor de Tropen, Amsterdam (Royal Institute of the Tropics)
- Koninklijke Instituut voor Taal-, Land-en Volkenkunde, Leiden (KITLV)

- Koninklijke Bibliotheek, Den Haag (Royal Library, The Hague)
- Nationaal Archief, Den Haag (National Archives, Netherlands)

FRANCE

- Bibliothèque Nationale de France, Paris (National Library of France)
- Bibliothèque SciencesPo, Paris (Library of the University of SciencePo)

ITALY

- Istituto Italiano per l'Africa e l'Oriente, Roma (Italian Institute of Africa and Asia)

II. Middle East

QATAR

- Museum of Islamic Art, Doha

OMAN

- Bait Zubair Museum, Muscat

YEMEN

- Centre Français des Études Yemenites, Sana'a
- American Institute for Yemeni Studies, Sana'a
- National Library of Yemen, Aden

III. Asia

JAPAN

- Kyoto University Library, Kyoto
- Osaka Ethnology Museum, Osaka
- Dejima Museum, Nagasaki

TAIWAN

- Academia Sinica Library, Taipei

HONG KONG

- Hong Kong University Library, Hong Kong

SINGAPORE

- Singapore National History Archives, Singapore
- National University of Singapore Library, Singapore

MALAYSIA

- Perpustakaan Negara Malaysia, Kuala Lumpur (National Library of Malaysia)
- Universitas Islam Antarabangsa Library, Gombak
- Arkib Negara Malaysia, Kuala Lumpur (National Archives of Malaysia)

INDONESIA

- Museum Bahari, Sunda Kelapa (Jakarta)
- Perpustakaan Negara Indonesia, Jakarta (National Library of Indonesia)
- Arsip Nasional Republik Indonesia, Jakarta (National Archives of Indonesia)

Sources Cited

Abbreviations Used

ANRI	Arsip Nasional Republik Indonesia, Jakarta
ARA	Algemeen Rijksarchief (now Nationaal Archief), The Hague
BEFEO	*Bulletin de l'École Française d'Extrême-Orient*
BTLV	Bijdragen tot de Taal-, Land-, en Volkenkunde (or BKI)
CO	Colonial Office Files (London)
ENI	Encyclopaedie van Nederlandsch-Indië
FO	Foreign Office Files (London)
IG	*Indische Gids, De*
ISEAS	Institute for Southeast Asian Studies
JESHO	*Journal of the Social and Economic History of the Orient*
JMBRAS	*Journal of the Malay Branch of the Royal Asiatic Society*
JSEAS	*Journal of Southeast Asian Studies*
MR	Mailrapporten, Nederlandsch Oost-Indië
RIMA	*Review of Indonesian and Malay Affairs*
SOAS	School of Oriental and African Studies
SSBB	Straits Settlements Blue Books
SSLCP	Straits Settlements Legislative Council Proceedings
TAG	*Tijdschrift van het Koninklijk Aardrijkskundig Genootschap*
TBG	*Tijdschrift voor Indische Taal-, Land-, en Volkenkunde*
TNI	*Tijdschrift voor Nederlandsch-Indië*
TvhZ	*Tijdschrift voor het Zeewezen*

Abdullah, Makmun, Nangsari Ahmad, F. A. Soetjipto, and Mardanas Safwan. *Kota Palembang sebagai "kota dagang dan industri."* Jakarta: Departemen Pendidikan dan Kebudayaan, Direktorat Sejarah dan Nilai Tradisional, Proyek Inventarisasi dan Dokumentasi Sejarah Nasional, 1985.

Abeydeera, Ananda. "Anatomy of an Occupation: The Attempts of the French to Establish a Trading Settlement on the Eastern Coast of Sri Lanka in 1672." In Giorgio Borsa, *Trade and Politics in the Indian Ocean*. Delhi: Manohar, 1990.

Abinales, Patricio. *Making Mindanao: Cotabato and Davao in the Formation of the Philippine Nation State*. Honolulu: University of Hawai'i Press, 2000.

———. *Orthodoxy and History in the Muslim-Mindanao Narrative*. Quezon City: Ateneo de Manila Press, 2010.

Abu-Lughod, Janet. *Before European Hegemony: The World System AD 1250–1350*. New York: Oxford University Press, 1991.

Abubakar, Tengku Ahmad, and Hasan Junus. *Sekelumit kesan peninggalan sejarah Riau*. Asmar Ras, 1972.

Adams, John, and Nancy Hancock. "Land and Economy in Traditional Vietnam." *JSEAS* 1, no. 2 (1970).

Adas, M. "Immigrant Asians and the Economic Impact of European Imperialism: The Role of South Indian Chettiars in British Burma." *Journal of Asian Studies* 33, no. 3 (1974): 385–401.

Adas, Michael. *The Burma Delta: Economic Development and Social Change on an Asian Rice Frontier, 1852–1941.* Madison: University of Wisconsin Press, 1974.

———. *Machines as the Measure of Men: Science, Technology, and Ideologies of Western Dominance.* Ithaca: Cornell University Press, 1989.

Adelaar, Alexander. "The Indonesian Migrations to Madagascar: Making Sense of the Multidisciplinary Evidence." In *Austronesian Diaspora and the Ethnogenesis of People in Indonesian Archipelago: Proceedings of the International Symposium,* edited by Truman Simanjuntak, Ingrid H. E. Pojoh, and Muhammad Hisyam. Jakarta: LIPI Press, 2006.

Adelaar, K. Alexander. "Borneo as a Cross-Roads for Comparative Austronesian Linguistics." In *The Austronesians: Historical and Comparative Perspectives,* edited by Peter Bellwood, James Fox, and Darrell Tryon, 75–95. Canberra: Department of Anthropology, Research School of Pacific and Asian Studies, Australian National University, 1995.

Adhyatman, Sumarah. *Keramik kuna yang diketemukan di Indonesia: Berbagai pengunaan dan tempat asal.* Jakarta: Himpunan Keramik Indonesia, 1981.

Adi, M. "Mengisi kekurangan ruangan kapal." *Suluh Nautika* 9, nos. 1–2 (January/ February, 1959): 8–9.

Aken, H. M. van. "Dutch Oceanographic Research in Indonesia in Colonial Times." *Oceanography* 18, no. 4 (2005): 30–41.

Alavi, Seema. *Muslim Cosmopolitanism in the Age of Empire.* Cambridge: Harvard University Press, 2015.

Alexanderson, Kris. *Subversive Seas: Anticolonial Networks across the Twentieth-Century Dutch Empire.* Cambridge: Cambridge University Press, 2019.

Ali, Tariq Omar. *A Local History of Global Capital: Jute and Peasant Life in the Bengal Delta.* Princeton: Princeton University Press, 2018.

Alkatiri, Zeffry. *Dari Batavia sampai Jakarta, 1619–1999: Peristiwa sejarah dan kebudayaan Betawi-Jakarta dalam sajak.* Magelang: IndonesiaTera, 2001.

Allsen, T. T. *Culture and Conquest in Mongol Eurasia.* Cambridge: Cambridge University Press, 2001.

Alpers, Edward. *The Indian Ocean in World History.* New York: Oxford University Press, 2014.

———. *Ivory and Slaves: The Changing Pattern of International Trade in East Central Africa to the Later Nineteenth Century.* Berkeley: University of California Press, 1975.

Alphen, M. van. "Iets over den oorsprong en der eerste uitbreiding der chinesche volkplanting te Batavia." *Tiderschrift voor Nederlandesch Indië* 4, no. 1 (1842): 70–100.

Amrith, Sunil. *Crossing the Bay of Bengal: The Furies of Nature and the Fortunes of Migrants.* Cambridge: Harvard University Press, 2013.

———. *Unruly Waters: How Rains, Rivers, Coasts, and Seas Have Shaped Asia's History.* New York: Basic Books, 2018.

Amyot, J. *The Manila Chinese: Familism in the Philippine Environment.* Quezon City: Institute of Philippine Culture, 1973.

Andaya, Barbara Watson. "Cash-Cropping and Upstream/Downstream Tensions: The Case of Jambi in the 17th and 18th-Centuries." In *Southeast Asia in the Early Modern Era,* edited by Anthony Reid. Ithaca: Cornell University Press, 1993.

———. *The Flaming Womb: Repositioning Women in Early Modern Southeast Asia*. Honolulu: University of Hawai'i Press, 2006.

———. "Oceans Unbounded: Traversing Asia Across 'Area Studies.'" *The Asia-Pacific Journal* 5, no. 4 (2007), https://apjjf.org/-Barbara-Watson-Andaya/2410/article.html.

———. "Recreating a Vision: Daratan and Kepulaunan in Historical Context." *Bijdragen Tot- de Taal-, Land-, en Volkenkunde* 153, no. 4 (1997), 483–508.

———. *To Live As Brothers: Southeast Sumatra in the Seventeenth and Eighteenth Centuries*. Honolulu: University of Hawai'i Press, 1993.

———, ed. *Other Pasts: Women, Gender and History in Early Modern Southeast Asia*. Honolulu: University of Hawai'i Press, 2000.

Andaya, Leonard. "The Bugis Makassar Diasporas." *JMBRAS* 68, no. 1 (1995): 119–38.

———. "A History of Trade in the Sea of Melayu." *Itinerario* 1, no. 24 (2000): 87–110.

———. *The Kingdom of Johor, 1641–1728: A Study of Economic and Political Developments in the Straits of Malacca*. Kuala Lumpur: Oxford University Press, 1975.

———. *Leaves from the Same Tree: Trade and Ethnicity in the Straits of Melaka*. Honolulu: University of Hawai'i Press, 2008.

———. *The World of Maluku: Eastern Indonesia in the Early Modern Period*. Honolulu: University of Hawai'i Press, 1993.

Anderson, Benedict. *Imagined Communities: Reflections on the Origins and Spread of Nationalism*. London: Verso, 2006.

Anderson, Clare. *Convicts in the Indian Ocean: Transportation from South Asia to Mauritius, 1815–1853*. London: Palgrave, 2000.

———. *Subaltern Lives: Biographies of Colonialism in the Indian Ocean World, 1790–1920*. Cambridge: Cambridge University Press, 2012.

Anderson, Jamie. "Slipping through Holes: The Late Tenth and Early Eleventh Century Sino-Vietnamese Coastal Frontier as a Subaltern Trade Network." In *The Tongking Gulf through History*, edited by Nola Cooke, Tana Li, and Jamie Anderson, 87–100. Philadelphia: University of Pennsylvania Press, 2011.

Anderson, J. L. "Piracy in the Eastern Seas, 1750–1856: Some Economic Implications." In *Pirates and Privateers: New Perspectives on the War on Trade in the Eighteenth and Nineteenth Centuries*, edited by David Starkey, E. S. van Eyck van Heslinga, and J. A. de Moor. Exeter: University of Exeter Press, 1997.

Anderson, John. "Piracy and World History: An Economic Perspective on Maritime Predation." In *Bandits at Sea*, edited by C. R. Pennell, 82–105. New York: New York University Press, 1991.

Anderson, Warwick. *Colonial Pathologies*. Durham: Duke University Press, 2006.

Andrade, Tonio. "The Company's Chinese Pirates: How the Dutch East India Company Tried to Lead a Coalition of Pirates to War against China, 1621–1662." *Journal of World History* 15, no. 4 (2004): 415–44.

———. *The Gunpowder Age: China, Military Innovation, and the Rise of the West in World History*. Princeton: Princeton University Press, 2016.

———. *Lost Colony: The Untold Story of China's First Great Victory over the West*. Princeton: Princeton University Press, 2013.

Andreski, Stanislav. *Max Weber on Capitalism, Bureaucracy, and Religion: A Selection of Texts*. London: Allen & Unwin, 1983.

Ang, Claudine. *Poetic Transformations: Eighteenth Century Cultural Projects on the Mekong Plains.* Cambridge, MA: Harvard East Asia Monographs, 2019.

[Anon.] "Agreement between the Nabob Nudjum-ul-Dowlah and the Company, 12 August 1765." In *Imperialism and Orientalism: A Documentary Sourcebook,* edited by Barbara Harlow and Mia Carter. Oxford: Wiley, 1999.

[Anon.] *Autonomy and Peace Review.* Cotabato: Institute for Autonomy and Governance in Collaboration with the Konrad-Adenauer Stiftung, 2001.

[Anon.] "Bakens op de reede van Makassar." *TvhZ* (1880): 308.

[Anon.] "Balakang Padang, een concurrent van Singapore." *IG* 2 (1902): 1295.

[Anon.] "Bebakening." *ENI* I (1917): 213.

[Anon.] *Catalogue of the Latest and Most Approved Charts, Pilots', and Navigation Books Sold or Purchased by James Imray and Sons.* London, 1866.

[Anon.] *Catalogus van de tentoonstelling "met lood enlLijn."* Rotterdam, 1974.

[Anon.] *De Topographische Dienst in Nederlandsch-Indië: Eenige gegevens omtrent geschiedenis, organisatie en werkwijze.* Amsterdam, 1913.

[Anon.] "Chineesche Zee: Enkele mededeelingen omtrent de Anambas, Natoena, en Tambelan-Eilanden." *Mededeelingen op zeevaartkundig gebied over Nederlandsch Oost-Indië* 4, (1 August 1896): 1–2.

[Anon.] "De Indische Hydrographie." *IG* 6 (1882): 12–39.

[Anon.] "De Indische Marine." *TNI* (1902): 695–707. For the role of Dutch geographical societies in this expansion, see *Catalogus, Koloniaal-Aardrijkskundige tentoonstelling ter gelegenheid van het veertigjarig bestaan van het Koninklijk Nederlandsch Aardrijkskundig Genootschap.* Amsterdam, 1913.

[Anon.] "De Uitbreiding der Indische Kustverlichting." *Indische Gids* 2 (1903): 1772.

[Anon.] "De Cheribonsche havenplannen." *Indisch Bouwkundig Tijdschrift* (15 August 1917): 256–66.

[Anon.] "De haverwerken te Tanjung Priok." *Tijdschrift voor Nederlandsch—Indië* II (1877): 278–87.

[Anon.] "De nieuwe haven van Cheribon." *Weekblad voor Indië* 5 (1919): 408–9.

[Anon.] "Departement der Burgerlijke Openbare Weken." *Nederlandsch-Indiche Havens Deel I.* Batavia: Departement der Burgerlijke Openbare Werken, 1920.

[Anon.] "Dioptric" in *Webster's Unabridged Dictionary* (G and C Merriam Co., 1913), 415.

[Anon.] "Engeland's Hydrographische Opnemingen in Onze Koloniën." *IG* 2 (1891): 2013–15.

[Anon.] "Havenbedrijf in Indië." *Indische Gids* 2 (1907): 1244–46.

[Anon.] *Historical and Statistical Abstracts of the Colony of Hong Kong 1841–1930,* 3rd ed. Hong Kong: Norohna and Co., Government Printers, 1932.

[Anon.] "Kustverlichting." *ENI* II (1917): 494.

[Anon.] "Naschrift van de redactie." *Indische Gids* 2 (1898): 1219.

[Anon.] "Onze zeemacht in den archipel." *Tijdschrift voor Nederlandsch-Indië* 1 (1890): 146–51.

[Anon.] "Overeenkomsten met inlandsche vorsten: Djambi." *Indische Gids* 1 (1882): 540.

[Anon.] "Overeenkomsten met inlandsche vorsten: Pontianak." *Indische Gids* 1 (1882): 549.

[Anon.] *Perang kolonial Belanda di Aceh.* Banda Aceh: Pusat Dokumentasi dan Informasi Aceh, 1997.

[Anon.] "Poeloe Bras." *TvhZ* (1876): 247.

[Anon.] "Poeloe-Weh." *Indische Mercuur* 44 (5 November 1901): 820.

[Anon.] "Pontianak-Rivier." *TvhZ* 236 (1875).

[Anon.] "Presiden tak pernah kirim peace feelers: Mungkin tukang-tukang catut yang ke Kuala Lampur." *Sinar Harapan* (2 February 1966).

[Anon.] "Produce Shipped by the Japanese from the Netherlands Indies." *Economic Review of Indonesia* 1, no. 4 (1947): 25–27.

[Anon.] "Reede van Batavia." *TvhZ* (1871): 222–24.

[Anon.] *Report of the Philippine Commission to the President, January 31, 1900.* Washington, DC: US Gov't Printing Office, 1900–1901), 3:157–200.

[Anon.] "Report from the Royal Commission on the Condition and Management of Lights, Buoys, and Beacons with Minutes of Evidence and Appendices." *British Parliamentary Papers*, Sessions 1861, Volume 5: *Shipping Safety*, 631–51.

[Anon.] *Roman Frontier Studies: Papers Presented to the Sixteenth Congress of Roman Frontier Studies.* Oxford, 1995.

[Anon.] *Selected Documents and Studies for the Conference on the Tripoli Agreement: Problems and Prospects.* Quezon City: International Studies Institute of the Philippines, 1985.

[Anon.] "Singapore's hoop op de opening der Indische kustvaart voor vreemde vlaggen." *Tijdschrijf voor Nederlandsch-Indië* 1, no. 17 (1888): 29–35.

[Anon.] "Straat Makassar." *Mededeelingen op zeevaartkundig gebied over Nederlandsch Oost-Indië* 6 (1 May 1907).

[Anon.] "The Ancient History of Dar es-Salaam." In *The East African Coast: Select Documents from the First to the Earlier Nineteenth Century*, edited by G. S. P. Freeman-Grenville, 233–37. Oxford: Oxford University Press, 1962.

[Anon.] *The East India Pilot, Or Oriental Navigator: A Complete Collection of Charts, Maps, and Plans for the Navigation of the Indian and China Seas.* London: Robert Sayer and John Bennett (1783?), 64 and 91.

[Anon.] "Tonen gelegd voor de monding van de soensang, Palembang." *TvhZ* (1878): 210–11.

[Anon.] *Tijdschrift voor het Zeewezen* (1871), 135–40 (Java Sea); (1872), 100–1 (Melaka Strait); (1873), 339–40 (Natuna and Buton); (1874), 306 (Makassar Strait); (1875), 78, 241 (East Coast Sulawesi and Northeast Borneo); (1876), 463 (Aceh); (1877), 221, 360 (West Coast Sumatra, Lampung); (1878), 98, 100 (West Borneo, Sulu Sea); and (1879), 79 (North Sulawesi).

Antony, Robert. *Like Froth Floating on the Sea: The World of Pirates and Seafarers in Late Imperial China.* Berkeley: Institute for East Asian Studies, 2003.

———. *Unruly People: Crime, Community and State in Late Imperial South China.* Hong Kong: Hong Kong University Press, 2016.

———, ed. *Elusive Pirates, Pervasive Smugglers: Violence and Clandestine Trade in the Greater China Seas.* Hong Kong: Hong Kong University Press, 2010.

Antunes, Luis Frederico Dias. "The Trade Activities of the Banyans in Mozambique: Private Indian Dynamics in the Portuguese State Economy, 1686–1777." In *Mariners, Merchants, and Oceans: Studies in Maritime History*, edited by K. S. Mathew, 301–32. Delhi: Manohar, 1995.

Aoyagi, Yoji. "Production and Trade of Champa Ceramics in the Fifteenth Century." In *Commerce et navigation en Asie du Sud-est (XIV–XIX siècles)*, edited by Nguyễn Thế Anh and Yoshiaki Ishizawa, 91–100. Paris: L'Harmattan, 1999.

Appadurai, Arjun, ed. *The Social Life of Things.* Cambridge: Cambridge University Press, 1986.

Appel, G. N. "Studies of the Taosug- and Samal-Speaking Populations of Sabah and the South-ern Philippines." *Borneo Research Bulletin* 1, no. 2 (1969): 21–22.

Aquino, Benigno. "From Negotiations to Consensus-Building: The New Parameters for Peace." In *Compilation of Government Pronouncements and Relevant Documents on Peace and Development for Mindanao*, 17–21. Manila: Office of the Press Secretary, 1988.

———. "The Historical Background of the Moro Problem in the Southern Philippines." In *Compilation of Government Pronouncements and Relevant Documents on Peace and Development for Mindanao*, 1–16. Manila: Office of the Press Secretary, 1988.

Aquino, Corazon. "Responsibility to Preserve Unity." In *Compilation of Government Pronouncements and Relevant Documents on Peace and Development for Mindanao*, 26–28. Manila: Office of the Press Secretary, 1988.

———. "ROCC: The Start of a New Kind of Political Involvement." In *Compilation of Government Pronouncements and Relevant Documents on Peace and Development for Mindanao*, 22–25. Manila: Office of the Press Secretary, 1988.

Arasaratnam, S. *Maritime India in the Seventeenth Century.* Delhi: Oxford University Press, 1994.

———. *Maritime Trade, Society and European Influence in Southern Asia, 1600–1800.* Ashgate: Variorum, 1995.

———. "Slave Trade in the Indian Ocean in the Seventeenth Century." In *Mariners, Merchants, and Oceans: Studies in Maritime History*, edited by K. S. Mathew, 195–208. Delhi: Manohar, 1995.

———. "Weavers, Merchants, and Company: The Handloom Industry in South-Eastern India 1750–1790." In *Merchants, Markets, and the State in Early Modern India*, edited by Sanjay Subrahmanyam, 190–214. Delhi: Oxford University Press, 1990.

Arendt, Hannah. *The Origins of Totalitarianism.* Cleveland, OH: World Publishing, 1958.

Arifin-Cabo, Pressia, Joel Dizon, and Khomenie Mentawel. *Dar-ul Salam: A Vision of Peace for Mindanao.* Cotabato: Kadtuntaya Foundation, 2008.

Armitage, David, Alison Bashford, and Sujit Sivasundaram, eds. *Oceanic Histories.* New York: Cambridge University Press, 2017.

Arokiasawang, Celine. *Tamil Influences in Malaysia, Indonesia, and the Philippines.* Manila: no publisher; Xerox typescript, Cornell University Library, 2000.

Arrighi, Giovanni, Takeshi Hamashita, and Mark Selden. "Introduction: The Rise of East Asia in Regional and World Historical Perspective." In *The Resurgence of East Asia: 500, 150 and 50 Year Perspectives*, edited by Giovanni Arrighi, Takeshi Hamashita, and Mark Selden, 1–16. London and New York: Routledge, 2003.

Asad, Talal. "Anthropological Conceptions of Religion: Reflections on Geertz." *Man* 18, no. 2 (1983): 237–59.

Askarai, Syed Hasan. "Mughal Naval Weakness and Aurangzeb's Attitude towards the Traders and Pirates on the Western Coast." *Journal of Indian Ocean Studies* 2, no. 3 (1995): 236–42.

Aslanian, Sebouh. *From the Indian Ocean to the Mediterranean: The Global Trade Networks of Armenian Merchants from New Julfa.* Berkeley: University of California Press, 2011.

Assavairulkaharn, Prapod. *Ascending of the Theravada Buddhism in Southeast Asia.* Bangkok: Silkworm, 1984.

Atwell, William S. "Ming China and the Emerging World Economy, c.1470–1650." In *The Cambridge History of China*, 1–33. Volume 8: *The Ming Dynasty, 1368–1644, Part 2*, edited by Denis Twitchett and Frederick Mote, 376–416. Cambridge: Cambridge University Press, 1998.

Atwell, William. "Notes on Silver, Foreign Trade, and the Late Ming Economy." *Ch'ing Shih Wen-t'i* 3 (1977), 1–33.

Aubin, Jean. "Merchants in the Red Sea and the Persian Gulf at the Turn of the Fifteenth and Sixteenth Centuries." In *Asian Merchants and Businessmen in the Indian Ocean and the China Sea*, edited by Denys Lombard and Jan Aubin, 79–86. Oxford: Oxford University Press, 2000.

Baber, Zaheer. *The Science of Empire: Scientific Knowledge, Civilization, and Colonial Rule in India*. Albany: SUNY Press, 1996.

Backer Dirks, F. C. *De Gouvernements marine in het voormalige Nederlands-Indië in haar verschillende tijdsperioden geschetst; III. 1861–1949*. Weesp: De Boer Maritiem, 1985.

Bacque-Grammont, Jean-Louis, and Anne Kroell. *Mamlouks, ottomans et portugais en Mer Rouge: L'Affaire de Djedda en 1517*. Paris: Le Caire, 1988.

Bader, Z. "The Contradictions of Merchant Capital 1840–1939." In *Zanzibar under Colonial Rule*, edited by A. Sheriff and E. Ferguson, 163–87. London: James Curry, 1991.

Bailey, Warren, and Lan Truong. "Opium and Empire: Some Evidence from Colonial-Era Asian Stock and Commodity Markets." *Journal of Southeast Asian Studies* 32 (2001): 173–94.

Bailyn, Bernard. *The Ideological Origins of the American Revolution*. Cambridge: Harvard University Press, 1967.

———. *The Peopling of British North America*. New York: Vintage Press, 1988.

———. *Voyagers to the West: A Passage in the Peopling of America on the Eve of the Revolution*. New York: Vintage Press, 1988.

Baker, Chris, and Pasuk Phongpaichit. *A History of Ayutthaya: Siam in the Early Modern World*. Cambridge: Cambridge University Press, 2017.

———. "Protection and Power in Siam: From Khun Chang Khun Phaen to the Buddhist Amulet." *Southeast Asian Studies* 2, no. 2 (2013): 215–42.

Baladouni, Vahe, and Margaret Makepeace, eds. *Armenian Merchants of the Early Seventeenth and Early Eighteenth Centuries*. Philadelphia: American Philosophical Society, 1998.

Banerjee, Kum Kum. "Grain Traders and the East India Company: Patna and Its Hinterland in the Late Eighteenth and Early Nineteenth Centuries." In *Merchants, Markets, and the State in Early Modern India*, edited by Sanjay Subrahmanyam, 163–89. Delhi: Oxford University Press, 1990.

Banga, Indu. *Ports and Their Hinterlands in India, 1700–1950*. Delhi: Manohar, 1992.

Banner, Stuart. *Possessing the Pacific: Lands, Settlers, and Indigenous People from Australia to Alaska*. Cambridge: Harvard University Press, 2007.

Barendse, René J. *The Arabian Seas: The Indian Ocean World of the Seventeenth Century*. Armonk, NY: M. E. Sharpe, 2002.

———. "Reflections on the Arabian Seas in the Eighteenth Century." *Itinerario* 25, no. 1 (2000): 25–50.

Barthes, Roland. *Empire of Signs*. New York: Hill and Wang, 1983.

Baron, Samuel. "A Description of the Kingdom of Tonqueen." In *A Collection of the Best and Most Interesting Voyages and Travels in All Parts of the World*, edited by John Pinkerton (London, 1811).

Barrow, John. *A Voyage to Cochin China*. Kuala Lumpur: Oxford University Press, 1975; orig. 1806.

Barton, Tamsyn. *Power and Knowledge: Astrology, Physiognomics, and Medicine under the Roman Empire*. Ann Arbor: University of Michigan Press, 1994.

Bassi, Ernesto. *An Aqueous Territory: Sailor Geographies and New Granada's Transimperial Greater Caribbean World*. Durham: Duke University Press, 2016.

Bastin, John. "The Changing Balance of the Southeast Asian Pepper Trade." In *Spices in the Indian Ocean World*, edited by M. N. Pearson, 283–316. Ashgate: Variorum, 1996.

Basu, Dilip. "The Impact of Western Trade on the Hong Merchants of Canton, 1793–1842." In *The Rise and Growth of the Colonial Port Cities in Asia*, edited by Dilip Basu, 151–55. Berkeley, Center for South and Southeast Asian Research 25, University of California Press, 1985.

Bautista, Julius, ed. *The Spirit of Things: Materiality and Religious Diversity in Southeast Asia.* Ithaca, NY: Cornell University Southeast Asia Program, 2012.

Bayly, Christopher. *Empire and Information: Intelligence Gathering and Social Communication in India, 1780 to 1870.* Cambridge: Cambridge University Press, 2000.

Beckert, Sven. *Empire of Cotton: A Global History.* New York: Alfred A. Knopf, 2014.

Behrens-Abouseif, Doris. "The Islamic History of the Lighthouse of Alexandria." *Muqarnas* 23 (2006): 1–14.

Bellina, Berenice. *Khao Sam Kaeo: An Early Port-City Between the Indian Ocean and the South China Sea.* Paris: EFEO, 2017.

Bellwood, Peter. *Prehistory of the Indo-Malaysian Archipelago.* Honolulu: University of Hawai'i Press, 1997.

Benedict, B. "Family Firms and Economic Development." *Southwestern Journal of Anthropology* 24, no. 1 (1968): 1–19.

Bengzon, Alfredo, "Each of Us Is Really a Peace Commissioner." In *Compilation of Government Pronouncements and Relevant Documents on Peace and Development for Mindanao*, 34–38. Manila: Office of the Press Secretary, 1988.

———. "Now That We Have Freedom, Let Us Seek Peace." In *Compilation of Government Pronouncements and Relevant Documents on Peace and Development for Mindanao*, 29–33. Manila: Office of the Press Secretary, 1988.

Bentley, Jerry H. "Sea and Ocean Basins as Frameworks of Historical Analysis." *Geographical Review* 89, no. 2 (April 1999): 215–24.

Bentley, Jerry, Renate Bridenthal, and Kären Wigen, eds. *Seascapes: Maritime Histories, Littoral Cultures, and Transoceanic Exchanges.* Honolulu: University of Hawai'i Press, 2007.

Benton, Lauren, and Nathan Perl-Rosenthal, eds. *A World at Sea: Maritime Practices and Global History.* Philadelphia: University of Pennsylvania Press, 2020.

Benton, Ted, "Adam Smith and the Limits to Growth." In *Adam Smith's Wealth of Nations: New Interdisciplinary Essays*, edited by Stephen Copley and Kathryn Sutherland, 144–170. Manchester: Manchester University Press, 1995.

Berchet, G. *Le antiche ambasciate giapponesi in Italia: Saggio storico con documenti.* Venice, M. Visentini, 1877.

———. *La Repubblica di Venezia e la Persia.* Turin: G. B. Paravia, 1865.

Berckel, H. E. van. "De Bebakening en Kustverlichting," *Gedenkboek Koninklijke Instituut Ingenieurs* (1847–97): 309–310.

———. "Zeehavens en kustverlichting in de kolonien: Oost Indie." *Gedenkboek Koninklijk Instituut Ingenieurs* (1847–97): 307–8.

Bernal, R., L. Diaz Trechuelo, M. C. Guerrero, and S. D. Quiason. "The Chinese Colony in Manila, 1570–1770." In *The Chinese in the Philippines 1570–1770.* Volume 1, edited by A. Felix Jr. Manila: Solidaridad Publishing House, 1966.

Bernier, Ronald. "Review of *Hindu Gods of Peninsular Siam* by Stanley O'Connor." *Journal of Asian Studies* 33, no. 4 (1974): 732–33.

Berthaud, Julien. "L'origine et la distribution des caféiers dans le monde." In *Le Commerce du café avant l'ère des plantations coloniales: Espaces, réseaux, sociétés (XVe-XIXe siècle)*, edited by Michel Tuchscherer. Cairo: Institut Français d'Archéologie Orientale, 2001.

Bhacker, M. Reda. *Trade and Empire in Muscat and Zanzibar: Roots of British Domination.* London: Routledge, 1992.

Bian, He. *Know Your Remedies: Pharmacy and Culture in Early Modern China.* Princeton: Princeton University Press, 2020.

Bickers, Robert. "Infrastructural Globalisation: The Chinese Maritime Customs and the Lighting of the China Coast, 1860s—1930s." *Historical Journal* 56, no. 2 (2013): 431–58.

Biezen, Christiaan. "'De waardigehid van een koloniale mogendheid': De hydrografische dienst en de kartering van de Indische Archipel tussen 1874 en 1894." *Tijsdchrift voor het Zeegeschiedenis* 18, no. 2 (1999): 23–38.

Bishara, Fahad. "The Many Voyages of Fateh-Al-Khayr: Unfurling the Gulf in the Age of Oceanic History." *International Journal of Middle East Studies* 52, no. 3 (2020): 397–412.

———. *A Sea of Debt: Law and Economic Life in the Western Indian Ocean, 1780–1850.* New York: Cambridge University Press, 2017.

Blackburn, Anne. "Localizing Lineage: Importing Higher Ordination in Theravadin South and Southeast Asia." In *Constituting Communities: Theravada Buddhism and the Religious Cultures of South and Southeast Asia*, edited by John Holt, Jonathan Walters, and Jacob Kinnard, chapter 7. Albany: State University of New York Press, 2003.

Blench, Roger. "Was There an Austroasiatic Presence in Island Southeast Asia Prior to the Austronesian Expansion?" *Bulletin of the Indo-Pacific Prehistory Association* 30 (2010): 133–44.

Bloom, P. A. F. *Onze nationale scheepvaart op and in Oost-Indië.* Nijmegen: Schippers, 1912.

Blussé, Leonard. "The Chinese Century: The Eighteenth Century in the China Sea Region." *Archipel* 58 (1999): 107–30.

———. "Chinese Trade to Batavia during the Days of the VOC." *Archipel* 18 (1979): 195–213.

———. "Junks to Java: Chinese Shipping to the Nanyang in the Second Half of the Eighteenth Century." In *Chinese Circulations: Capital, Commodities, and Networks in Southeast Asia*, edited by Eric Tagliacozzo and Wen-Chin Chang, 221–58. Durham: Duke University Press, 2011.

———. "No Boats to China: The Dutch East India Company and the Changing Pattern of the China Sea Trade, 1635–1690." *Modern Asian Studies* 30, no. 1 (1996): 51–76.

———. *Strange Company: Chinese Settlers, Mestizo Women, and the Dutch in VOC Batavia.* Leiden: Foris, 1986.

———. "The Vicissitudes of Maritime Trade: Letters from the Ocean Hang Merchant, Li Kunhe, to the Dutch Authorities in Batavia (1803–9)." In *Sojourners and Settlers: Histories of Southeast Asia and the Chinese*, edited by Anthony Reid. St. Leonards, Aust.: Allen & Unwin, 1996.

———. *Visible Cities.* Cambridge: Harvard University Press, 2008.

Blust, Robert. "The Prehistory of the Austronesian-Speaking Peoples: A View from Language." *Journal of World Prehistory* 9, no. 4 (1995): 453–510.

Bogaars, G. "The Effect of the Opening of the Suez Canal on the Trade and Development of Singapore." *JMBRAS* 28, no. 1, 1955.

Bois, Paul, Pierre Boyer, and Yves J. Saint-Martin. *L'Ancre et la Croix du Sud: La marine française dans l'expansion coloniale en Afrique noire et dans l'Océan indien, de 1815 à 1900.* Vincennes: Service Historique de la Marine, 1998.

Bonacich, Edna. "A Theory of Middleman Minorities." In *Majority and Minority: The Dynamics of Racial and Ethnics Relations,* 2nd ed., edited by N. R. Yetman and C. H. Steele, 77–89. Boston: Allyn & Bacon, 1975.

Boncompagni-Ludovisi, F. *Le prime due ambasciate dei giapponesi a Roma (1585–1615).* Rome: Forzani e Comp., Tipografi del Senato, 1904.

Boomgaard, Peter, ed. *A World of Water: Rain, Rivers, and Seas in Southeast Asian Histories.* Leiden: KITLV Press, 2007.

Booth, K. "The Roman Pharos at Dover Castle." *English Heritage Historical Review* 2 (2007): 9–22.

Bopearachichi, Osmand, ed. *Origin, Evolution, and Circulation of Foreign Coins in the Indian Ocean.* Delhi: Manohar, 1988.

Borges, Charles. "Intercultural Movements in the Indian Ocean Region: Churchmen, Travelers, and Chroniclers in Voyage and in Action." In *Indian Ocean and Cultural Interaction, 1400–1800,* edited by K. S. Mathew, 21–34. (Pondicherry: Pondicherry University, 1996).

Borofsky, Robert, ed. *Remembrance of Pacific Pasts: An Invitation to Remake History.* Honolulu: University of Hawai'i Press, 2000.

Borri, Christopher. "An Account of Cochin-China." In *A Collection of the Best and Most Interesting Voyages and Travels in All Part of the World.* Volume XI, edited by John Pinkerton. London: Longman, Hurst, Rees, and Orme, 1811.

Borscheid, Peter, and Niels Viggo Haueter. "Institutional Transfer: The Beginnings of Insurance in Southeast Asia. *Business History Review* 89, no. 2 (2015).

Bose, Sugata. *A Hundred Horizons: The Indian Ocean in the Age of Global Empire.* Cambridge, MA: Harvard University Press, 2006.

———. *Peasant Labour and Colonial Capital: Rural Bengal Since 1770.* Cambridge: Cambridge University Press, 1993.

———, ed. *South Asia and World Capitalism.* Oxford: Oxford University Press, 1991.

Bouchon, Geneviève. "L'Asie du Sud à l'époque des grandes découvertes." London: Variorum Reprints, 1987.

———. *Mamale de Cananor: Un adversaire de l'Inde portugaise (1507–1528).* Geneva and Paris: Droz, Hautes études islamiques et orientales d'histoire comparée, École Pratique des Hautes Études, IVe Section, 1975.

———. "A Microcosm: Calicut in the Sixteenth Century." In *Asian Merchants and Businessmen in the Indian Ocean and the China Sea,* edited by Denys Lombard and Jan Aubin, 78–87. Oxford: Oxford University Press, 2000.

———. "Les Musulmans de Kerala à l'époque de la découverte portugaise." *Mare Luso-Indicum* II, 3–59. Geneva and Paris, 1973.

———. "Le sud-ouest de l'Inde dans l'imaginaire européen au début du XVIe siècle: Du mythe à la réalité." in *Asia Maritima: Images et réalité: Bilder und Wirklichkeit 1200–1800,* edited by Denys Lombard and Roderich Ptak. Wiesbaden: Harrassowitz Verlag, 1994.

Bowers, Brian. *Lengthening the Day: A History of Lighting Technology.* Oxford: Oxford University Press, 1998.

Boxer, Charles. *The Portuguese Seaborne Empire 1415–1825*. New York: Knopf, 1969.

Boxer, C. R. *South China in the 16th Century*. London: Crown Press, 1953.

Braudel, Fernand. *The Mediterranean and the Mediterranean World in the Age of Phillip II*. 2 volumes. Berkeley: University of California Press Reprints, 1996.

Brazeale, Kennon, ed. *From Japan to Arabia: Ayutthaya's Maritime Relations*. Bangkok: Toyota Thailand Foundation, 1999.

Brendon, Piers. *The Decline and Fall of the British Empire, 1781–1997*. New York: Knopf, 1998.

Brennig, Joseph. "Textile Producers and Production in Late Seventeenth Century Coromandel." In *Merchants, Markets, and the State in Early Modern India*, edited by Sanjay Subrahmanyam, 66–89. Delhi: Oxford University Press, 1990.

British Documents on Foreign Affairs: Reports and Papers from the Foreign Office Confidential Print, multivolume. Washington, D.C.: University Press of America, 1995.

British Parliamentary Papers. Sessions 1845. Volume 4: *Shipping Safety*, "Reports from Select Committees on Lighthouses, with Minutes of Evidence." Shannon, 1970.

Broeze, F. J. A. "From Imperialism to Independence: The Decline and Re-emergence of Asian Shipping." *The Great Circle [Journal of the Australian Association for Maritime History]* 9, no. 2 (1987): 70–89.

———. "The Merchant Fleet of Java 1820–1850: A Preliminary Survey." *Archipel* 18, (1979): 251–69.

Broeze, Frank. *Brides of the Sea: Port Cities of Asia From the 16th–20th Centuries*. Kensington: New South Wales University Press, 1989.

———, ed. *Gateways of Asia: Port Cities of Asia in the 13th–20th Centuries*. London: Kegan Paul International, 1997.

Bronson, Bennet. "Exchange at the Upstream and Downstream Ends: Notes toward a Functional Model of the Coastal States in Southeast Asia." In *Economic Exchange and Social Interaction in Southeast Asia: Perspectives from Prehistory, History, and Ethnography*, edited by K. L. Hutterer, 39–52. Ann Arbor: University of Michigan Southeast Asia Program, 1977.

———. "Export Porcelain in Economic Perspective: The Asian Ceramic Trade in the 17th Century." In *Ancient Ceramic Kiln Technology in Asia*, edited by Ho Chumei. Hong Kong: University of Hong Kong, 1990.

Brook, Timothy. *The Confusions of Pleasure: Commerce and Culture in Ming China*. Berkeley: University of California Press, 1998.

Brook, Timothy, and Bob Tadashi Wakabayashi, eds. *Opium Regimes: China, Britain, and Japan, 1839–1952*. Berkeley: University of California Press, 2000.

Brouwer, C. G. *Al-Mukha: Profile of a Yemeni Seaport as Sketched by Servants of the Dutch East India Company, 1614–1640*. Amsterdam: D'Fluyte Rarob, 1997.

———. *Cauwa ende Comptanten: De VOC in Yemen*. Amsterdam: D'Fluyte Rarob, 1988.

Brown, Edward. *A Seaman's Narrative of His Adventures during a Captivity among Chinese Pirates on the Coast of Cochin China*. London: Charles Westerton, 1861.

Brown, Ian. *The Elite and the Economy in Siam, 1890–1920*. Oxford: Oxford University Press, 1988.

Brown, Rajeswary A., ed. *Chinese Business Enterprise in Asia*. London and New York: Routledge, 1995.

Brown, Roxanna. *The Ceramics of South-East Asia: Their Dating and Identification*. Singapore: Oxford University Press, 1988.

―――. "A Ming Gap? Data from Southeast Asian Shipwreck Cargoes." In *Southeast Asia in the Fifteenth Century: The China Factor*, edited by Geoff Wade and Sun Laichen, eds., 359–83. Singapore: NUS Press, 2010.

Brudhikrai, Luang Joldhan. "Development of Hydrographic Work in Siam from the Beginning up to the Present." *International Hydrographic Review* 24 (1947): 48–53.

Buch, W. J. M. "La Compagnie des Indes Néerlandaises et l'Indochine." *BEFEO* 36–37 (1936–37): 121–237.

―――. *De Oost-Indische Compagine en Quinam: De betrekkingen der Nederlanders met Annam in de XVIIᵉ eeuw.* (Amsterdam and Paris, 1929).

Bun, Chan-kwok and Ng Beoy Kui. "Myths and Misperceptions of Ethnic Chinese Capitalism." In *Chinese Business Networks*, edited by Chan Kwok Bun. Singapore: Prentice Hall, 2000.

Burrows, Edmond. *Captain Owen of the African Survey: The Hydrographic Surveys of Admiral WFW Owen on the Coast of Africa and the Great Lakes of Canada.* Rotterdam: AA Balkema, 1979.

Burton, R. F. *The Lake Regions of Central Africa.* Volume I. London, 1860.

―――. *Zanzibar: City, Island and Coast.* Volume II. London: Tinsely, 1872.

Buschmann, Rainer F., Edward R. Slack Jr., and James B. Tueller. *Navigating the Spanish Lake: The Pacific in the Iberian World, 1521–1898.* Honolulu: University of Hawai'i Press, 2014.

Butcher, John. *The Closing of the Frontier: A History of the Marine Fisheries of Southeast Asia, 1850–2000.* Singapore; ISEAS, 2004.

―――. "A Note on the Self-Governing Realms of the Netherlands Indies in the Late 1800s." *BTLV* 164, no. 1 (2008): 1–12.

Butcher, John, and Robert Elson. *Sovereignty and the Sea: How Indonesia Became an Archipelagic State.* Singapore: National University of Singapore Press, 2017.

Butcher, John, and Howard Dick, eds. *The Rise and Fall of Revenue Farming: Business Elites and the Emergence of the Modern State in Southeast Asia.* Basingstoke: Macmillan and New York: St. Martin's Press, 1993.

Cahen, Claude. "Le commerce musulman dans l'Océan Indien au Moyen Age." In *Sociétés et compagnies de commerce en Orient et dans l'Océan Indien*, edited by M. Mollat, 179–93. Paris: SEVPEN, 1970.

Calmard, Jean. "The Iranian Merchants: Formation and Rise of a Pressure Group between the Sixteenth and Nineteenth Centuries." in *Asian Merchants and Businessmen in the Indian Ocean and the China Sea*, edited by Denys Lombard and Jan Aubin, 87–104. Oxford: Oxford University Press, 2000.

Calvino, Italo. *Invisible Cities.* London: Harcourt, 1974.

Campbell, Gwyn. *Africa and the Indian Ocean World from Early Times to Circa 1900.* Cambridge: Cambridge University Press, 2019.

―――, ed. *The Structure of Slavery in Indian Ocean Africa and Asia.* Portland: Frank Cass Publishers, 2004.

Campo, J. N. F. M. à. "The Accommodation of Dutch, British and German Maritime Interest in Indonesia, 1890–1910." *International Journal of Maritime History* 4, no. 1 (1992): 1–41.

―――. "De Chinese stoomvaart in de Indische archipel." *Jambatan: Tijdschrift voor de geschiedenis van Indonesië* 2, no. 2 (1984):1–10.

———. *Koninklijke Paketvaart Maatschappij: Stoomvaart en staatsvorming in de Indonesische archipel 1888–1914.* Hilversum: Verloren, 1992.

———. "Indonesia as Maritime State." Paper presented at the First International Conference on Indonesian Maritime History: The Java Sea Region in an Age of Transition 1870–1970, Semarang, 1–4 December (1999).

———. "Een maritime BB: De rol van de Koninklijke Paketvaart Maatschappij in de integratie van de koloniale staat." In *Imperialisme in de marge: De afronding van Nederlands-Indië,* edited by J. van Goor, 123–77. Utrecht: HES, 1985.

———. "Perahu Shipping in Indonesia 1870–1914." *Review of Indonesian and Malaysian Affairs* 27 (1993): 33–60.

———. "Steam Navigation and State Formation." In *The Late Colonial State in Indonesia: Political and Economic Foundations of the Netherlands Indies 1880–1942,* edited by Robert Cribb, 11–29. Leiden: KITLV Press, 1994.

Cañizares-Esguerra, Jorge, and Erik R. Seeman, eds. *The Atlantic in Global History, 1500–2000,* 2nd ed. New York: Routledge, 2018.

Capelli, Cristian, et al. "A Predominantly Indigenous Paternal Heritage for the Austronesian-Speaking Peoples of Insular Southeast Asia and Oceania." *American Journal of Human Genetics* 68, no. 2 (2001): 432–43.

Cardwell, D. S. L. *Turning Points in Western Technology: A Study of Technology, Science, and History.* New York: Neale Watson 1972.

Carey, Peter. "Changing Javanese Perceptions of the Chinese Communities in Central Java, 1755–1825." *Indonesia* 37 (1984): 1–47.

Carioti, Patrizia. "The Zhengs' Maritime Power in the International Context of the Seventeenth Century Far Eastern Seas: The Rise of a 'Centralized Piratical Organization' and Its Gradual Development into an Informal State." *Ming Qing Yanjiu* 5, no. 1 (1996): 29–67.

Carney, Judith A. *Black Rice: The African Origins of Rice Cultivation in the Americas.* Cambridge: Harvard University Press, 2002.

Carreira, Ernestine. "Les français et le commerce du café dans l'Océan Indien au XVIIIe siècle." In *Le Commerce du café avant l'ère des plantations coloniales: Espaces, réseaux, sociétés (XVe-XIXe siècle),* edited by Michel Tuchscherer, 333–37. Cairo: Institut Français d'Archéologie Orientale, 2001.

Cartier, Michel. "The Chinese Perspective on Trade in the Indian Ocean." In *Asian Merchants and Businessmen in the Indian Ocean and the China Sea,* edited by Denys Lombard and Jan Aubin, 121–24. Oxford: Oxford University Press, 2000.

———. "La vision chinoise des étrangers: Réflexions sur la constitution d'une pensée anthropologique." In *Asia Maritima: Images et réalité: Bilder und Wirklichkeit 1200–1800,* edited by Denys Lombard and Roderich Ptak, 63–77. Wiesbaden: Harrassowitz Verlag, 1994.

———. "La vision chinoise du monde: Taiwan dans la littérature géographique ancienne." In *Appréciation par l'Europe de la tradition chinoise: À partir du XVIIe siècle; Actes du IIIe Colloque international de sinologie, 11–14 septembre 1980,* Centre de recherches interdisciplinaire de Chantilly (CERIC), 1–12. Paris, 1983.

Cartwright, David E. "Tonkin Tides Revisited." *The Royal Society* 57, no. 2 (2003), https://doi.org/10.1098/rsnr.2003.0201.

Casale, Giancarlo. *The Ottoman Age of Exploration.* New York: Oxford University Press, 2010.

Casale, Giancarlo, Carla Rahn Phillips, and Lisa Norling. "Introduction to 'The Social History of the Sea.'" *Journal of Early Modern History* 14, nos. 1–2 (Special Issue, 2010): 1–7.

Casino, Eric. *Mindanao Statecraft and Ecology: Moros, Lumads, and Settlers across the Lowland-Highland Continuum*. Cotabato: Notre Dame University, 2000.

Castells, M. *The Urban Question: A Marxist Approach*. London: Edward Arnold, 1979.

Castillo, Gelia. *Beyond Manila: Philippine Rural Problems in Perspective*. Ottawa: International Development Research Center, 1980.

Catellacci, D. "Curiose notizie di anonimo viaggiatore fiorentino all'Indie nel secolo XVII." *Archivio Storico Italiano* 28, no. 223 (1901) 120–29.

Cator, W. J. *The Economic Position of the Chinese in the Netherlands Indies*. Oxford: Basil Blackwell, 1936.

Catz, Rebecca D., trans. and ed. *The Travels of Mendes Pinto / Fernão Mendes Pinto*. Chicago: University of Chicago Press, 1989.

Cense, A. A. "Makassarsche-Boeginese paruwvaart op Noord-Australië." *Bijdragen tot de Taal-Land-en Volkenkunde* 108 (1952): 248–65.

Chaffee, John. *Muslim Merchants of Pre-Modern China: The History of a Maritime Asian Trade Diaspora, 750–1400*. Cambridge: Cambridge University Press, 2018.

Chaiklin, Martha. *Cultural Commerce and Dutch Commercial Culture: The Influence of European Material Culture on Japan, 1700–1850*. Leiden: CNWS, 2003.

Chaiklin, Martha, Philip Gooding, and Gwyn Campbell, eds. *Animal Trade Histories in the Indian Ocean World*. London: Palgrave Series in the Indian Ocean World, 2020.

Chakravati, N. R. *The Indian Minority in Burma: The Rise and Decline of an Immigrant Community*. London: Oxford University Press, 1985.

Chandra, Savitri. "Sea and Seafaring as Reflected in Hindi Literary Works During the 15th to 18th Centuries." In *Mariners, Merchants, and Oceans: Studies in Maritime History*, edited by K. S. Mathew, 84–91. Pondicherry: Pondicherry University, 1990.

Chang, David A. *The World and All the Things upon It: Native Hawaiian Geographies of Exploration*. Minneapolis: University of Minnesota Press, 2016.

Chang, Kuei-sheng. "The Ming Maritime Enterprise and China's Knowledge of Africa prior to the Age of Great Discoveries." *Terrae Incognitae* 3, no. 1 (1971): 33–44.

Chang, Pin-tsun. "Maritime China in Historical Perspective." *International Journal of Maritime History* 4, no. 2 (1992): 239–55.

———. "The Sea as Arable Fields: A Mercantile Outlook on the Maritime Frontier of Late Ming China." In *The Perception of Space in Traditional Chinese Sources*, edited by Angela Schottenhammer and Roderich Ptak, 17–26. Wiesbaden: Harrassowitz Verlag, 2006.

Chang Wen-Chin. "Guanxi and Regulation in Networks: The Yunnanese Jade Trade Between Burma and Thailand." *Journal of Southeast Asian Studies* 35, no. 3 (2004): 479–501.

Chappell, David A. *Double Ghosts: Oceanian Voyagers on Euroamerican Ships*. New York: M. E. Sharpe, 1997.

Chapelle, H. M. La. "Bijdrage tot de kennis van het stoomvaartverkeer in den Indischen Archipel." *De Economist* 2 (1885): 689–90.

Chaudhuri, K. N. *Trade and Civilisation in the Indian Ocean: An Economic History from the Rise of Islam to 1750*. Cambridge: Cambridge University Press, 1985.

Chemillier-Gendreau, Monique. *Sovereignty over the Paracel and Spratly Islands*. Leiden: Springer, 2000.

Chen Dasheng and Denys Lombard. "Foreign Merchants in Maritime Trade in Quanzhou ('Zaitun'): Thirteenth and Fourteenth Centuries." In *Asian Merchants and Businessmen in the Indian Ocean and South China Sea*, edited by Denys Lombard and Jan Aubin, 19–24. Oxford; Oxford University Press, 2000.

Cheng Lim Keak. "Chinese Clan Associations in Singapore: Social Change and Continuity." In *Southeast Asian Chinese: The Socio-Cultural Dimension*, edited by Leo Suryadinata, 67–77. Singapore: Times Academic Press, 1995.

———. "Reflections on Changing Roles of Chinese Clan Associations in Singapore." *Asian Culture* (Singapore) 14 (1990): 57–71.

Cheong, W. E. *The Hong Merchants of Canton: Chinese Merchants in Sino-Western Trade*. Richmond, Surrey: Curzon, 1997.

Chew, Daniel. *Chinese Pioneers on the Sarawak Frontier (1841–1941)*. Singapore: Oxford University Press, 1990).

Chew, Ernest, and Edwin Lee, eds. *A History of Singapore*. Singapore: Oxford University Press, 1991.

Chiang, Hai Ding. *A History of Straits Settlements Trade (1870–1915)*. Singapore: Memoirs of the National Museum, 1978.

Chin, James K. "Merchants, Smugglers, and Pirates: Multinational Clandestine Trade on the South China Coast, 1520–50." In *Elusive Pirates, Pervasive Smugglers: Violence and Clandestine Trade in the Greater China Seas*, edited by Robert J. Antony, 43–57. Hong Kong: Hong Kong University Press, 2010.

Chin, James Kong. "The Junk Trade between South China and Nguyen Vietnam in the Late Eighteenth and Early Nineteenth Centuries." In *Water Frontier: Commerce and the Chinese in the Lower Mekong Region, 1750–1880*, edited by Nola Cooke and Tana Li, 53–70. Lanham: Rowman & Littlefield, 2004.

Chirapravati, Pattaratorn. *The Votive Tablets in Thailand: Origins, Styles, and Usages*. Oxford: Oxford University Press, 1999.

Chirot, Daniel, and Anthony Reid, eds. *Essential Outsiders: Chinese and Jews in the Modern Transformation of Southeast Asia and Central Europe*. Seattle: University of Washington Press, 1997.

Chittick, Neville. *Kilwa: An Islamic Trading City on the East African Coast*. Nairobi: British Institute in Eastern Africa, 1974.

Choi, Byung Wook. "The Nguyen Dynasty's Policy toward Chinese on the Water Frontier in the First Half of the Nineteenth Century." In *Water Frontier: Commerce and the Chinese in the Lower Mekong Region, 1750–1880*, edited by Nola Cooke and Tana Li, 85–100. Lanham: Rowman & Littlefield, 2004.

Choi, Chong Jui. "Contract Enforcement across Cultures." *Organization Studies* 15, no. 5 (1994): 673–82.

Chouvy, Pierre-Arnoud. *An Atlas of Trafficking in Southeast Asia: The Illegal Trade in Arms, Drugs, People, Counterfeit Goods, and Natural Resources in Mainland Southeast Asia*. London: Bloomsbury, 2013.

Chua Beng Huat. "Singapore as Model: Planning Innovations, Knowledge Experts." In *Worlding Cities: Asian Experiments and the Art of Being Global*, edited by Ananya Roy and Aihwa Ong, 29–54. London: Blackwell, 2011.

Chutintaranond, Sunait. "Mergui and Tenasserim as Leading Port Cities in the Context of Autonomous History." In *Port Cities and Trade in Western Southeast Asia* [Anon.], 1–14. Bangkok: Institute of Asian Studies, Chulalongkorn University, 1998.

Cipolla, Carlo. *Guns, Sails, and Empires: Technological Innovation and the Early Phases of European Expansion 1400–1700*. New York: Pantheon, 1965.

Clark, Hugh R. "Frontier Discourse and China's Maritime Frontier: China's Frontiers and the Encounter with the Sea through Early Imperial History." *Journal of World History* 20, no. 1 (2009): 1–33.

Clegg, Stewart, and S. Gordon Redding, eds. *Capitalism in Contrasting Cultures*. Berlin: De Gruyter, 1990.

Clements, John. *Coxinga and the Fall of the Ming Dynasty*. Phoenix Mill: Sutton Publishing, 2005).

Clulow, Adam. *The Company and the Shogun: The Dutch Encounters with Tokugawa Japan*. New York: Columbia University, 2013.

Coates, W. H. *The Old Country Trade of the East Indies*. London: Imray, Laurie, Nurie, and Wilson, 1911.

Cochran, Sherman. *Encountering Chinese Networks: Western, Japanese, and Chinese Corporations in China, 1880–1937*. Berkeley: University of California Press, 2000.

Coedes, Georges. *The Indianized States of Southeast Asia*. Honolulu: East-West Press, 1968.

Coen, Jan Pietersz. *Bescheiden omtremt zijn bedrif in Indië*. 4 volumes, edited by H. T. Colbrander. The Hague: Martinus Nijhoff, 1919–22.

Cohen, A. "Cultural Strategies in the Organization of Trading Diasporas." In *The Development of Indigenous Trade and Markets in West Africa*, edited by C. Meillassoux, 266–80. London: Oxford University Press, 1971.

Condominas, Georges. *We Have Eaten the Forest: The Story of a Montagnard Village in the Central Highlands of Vietnam*. New York: Hill & Wang, 1977.

Conrad, Joseph. *An Outcast of the Islands*. Oxford, Oxford University Press Reprints, 1992.

Cook, Kealani. *Return to Kahiki: Native Hawaiians in Oceania*. New York: Cambridge University Press, 2018.

Cooke, Nola. "Chinese Commodity Production and Trade in Nineteenth-Century Cambodia: The Fishing Industry." Paper presented to the Workshop on Chinese Traders in the Nanyang: Capital, Commodities and Networks, 19 Jan. 2007. Taipei, Taiwan: Academica Sinica:.

Cooke, Nola, and Tana Li, eds. *Water Frontier: Commerce and the Chinese in the Lower Mekong Region, 1750–1880*. Lanham: Rowman & Littlefield, 2004.

Coolhaas, W. Ph., ed. *Generale missiven van gouverneurs-generaal en raden aan heren XVII der Verenigde Oostindische Compagnie* [multivolume]. 's–Gravenhage: Martinus Nijhoff, 1960.

Cooper, Frederick. *From Slaves to Squatters: Plantation Labor and Agriculture in Zanzibar and Coastal Kenya, 1890–1925*. New Haven: Yale University Press, 1980.

Coops, P. C. "Nederlandsch Indies zeekaarten." *Nederlandsche Zeewezen* 3 (1904).

Corn, Charles. *The Scents of Eden: A History of the Spice Trade*. New York: Kodansha, 1999.

Cort, Louise Allison. "Vietnamese Ceramics in Japanese Contexts." In *Vietnamese Ceramics, A Separate Tradition*, edited by John Stevenson and John Guy. Michigan: Art Media Resources, 1994; repr. Chicago: Art Media Resources, 1997.

Cowley, Robert, ed. *What If? The World's Foremost Military Historians Imagine What Might Have Been*. New York: Berkley Publishing, 2000.

Crampton, Jeremy W. "Maps as Social Constructions: Power, Communication and Visualization." *Progress in Human Geography* 25, no. 2 (2001): 235–52.

Crampton, Jeremy W., and John Krygier. "An Introduction to Critical Cartography." *ACME: An International E-Journal for Critical Geographies* 4, no. 1 (2006): 11–33.

Crawfurd, John. *History of the Indian Archipelago.* Volume III. London: Cass, 1820; repr. 1967.

———. *Journal of an Embassy from the Governor General of India to the Courts of Siam and Cochin-China.* London: Henry Colburn, 1828; Oxford Historical Reprints, 1967.

Cribb, Robert. *The Late Colonial State in Indonesia: Political and Economic Foundations of the Netherlands Indies, 1880–1942.* Leiden: KITLV Press, 1994.

———. "Political Structures and Chinese Business Connections in the Malay World: A Historical Perspective." In *Chinese Business Networks,* edited by Chan Kwok Bun. Singapore: Prentice Hall, 2000.

Cristalis, Irena. *Bitter Dawn: East Timor, a People's Story.* London: Zed Books, 2002.

Cubitt, Sean. "Electric Light and Electricity." *Theory, Culture and Society* 30, nos. 7/8 (2013): 309–23.

Cunliffe, Barry. *By Steppe, Desert, and Ocean: The Birth of Eurasia.* Oxford: Oxford University Press, 2015.

Curtin, P. D. *Cross-Cultural Trade in World History.* Cambridge: Cambridge University Press, 1984.

Cushman, Jennifer. *Fields from the Sea: Chinese Junk Trade with Siam during the Late 18th and Early 19th Centuries.* Ithaca: Cornell University Southeast Asia Program, 1993.

Cushman, J. W. "The Khaw Group: Chinese Business in the Early Twentieth-Century Penang." *Journal of Southeast Asian Studies* 17, no. 1 (1986): 58–79.

Daguenet, Roger. *Histoire de la Mer Rouge.* Paris: L'Harmattan, 1997.

———. *Aux origines de l'implantation français en Mer Rouge: Vie et mort d'Henri Lambert, consul de France à Aden, 1859.* Paris: L'Harmattan, 1992.

Dallmeyer, Dorinda, and Louis DeVorsey. *Rights to Oceanic Resources: Deciding and Drawing Maritime Boundaries.* Dordrecht: Martinus Nijhoff, 1989.

Dalrymple, Alexander. "An Account of Some Nautical Curiosities at Sooloo." In *Historical Collection of Several Voyages and Discoveries in the South Pacific Ocean.* Volume I, edited by Alexander Dalrymple, 1–14. London: Ale, 1770.

———. *Oriental Repertory.* Volume II. London: George Bigg, 1808.

———. *A Plan for Extending the Commerce of this Kingdom, and of the East-India-Company.* London (Printed for the Author), 1769.

Damais, Louis-Charles. "L'épigraphie musulmane dans le sud-est asiatique." *Befeo* 54 (1968): 567–604.

———. "Études d'épigraphie indonésienne III." *Befeo* 46 (1952): 1–105.

———. "Études sino-indonésiennes I: Quelques titres javanais de l'époque des Song." *Befeo* 50 (1960): 1–29.

———. "Études sino-indonésiennes III: La transcription chinoise *Ho-ling* comme désignation de Java." *Befeo* 52 (1964): 93–141.

Dars, J. "Les jonques chinoises de haute mer sous les Song et les Yuan." *Archipel* 18 (1979): 41–56.

Das Gupta, Ashin. *Merchants of Maritime India: Collected Studies, 1500–1800.* Ashgate: Variorum, 1994.

Datta, Rajat. "Merchants and Peasants: A Study of the Structure of Local Trade in Grain in Late Eighteenth Century Bengal." In *Merchants, Markets, and the State in Early Modern India,* edited by Sanjay Subrahmanyam, 139–62. Delhi: Oxford University Press, 1990.

Day, Tony. *Fluid Iron: State Formation in Southeast Asia*. Honolulu: University of Hawai'i Press, 2002.

De Goeje, C. H. *De Kustverlichting in Nederlandsch-Indië*. Batavia, 1913.

de Souza, Philip. *Seafaring and Civilization: Maritime Perspectives on World History*. London: Profile Books, 2001.

Defrémery, C., and B. R. Sanguinetti. *Les voyages d'Ibn Batoutah*. Volume II. Paris: Société arabic, 1854.

Deshima Dagregisters. Volumes XI (1641–50) and XII (1651–60), edited by Cynthia Viallé and Leonard Blussé. Leiden: Intercontinenta 23 & 25, 2001 & 2005.

Delgado, James. *Khublai Khan's Lost Fleet*. Berkeley: University of California Press, 2010.

D'Elia, Pasquale M. *Galileo in Cina: Relazioni attraverso il Collegio Romano tra Galileo e i gesuiti scienziati missionari in Cina (1610–1640)*. Rome: Serie Facultatis Missologicae, Sectio A, no. 1, 1947.

D'Elia, P. M., ed. *Fonti Ricciane: Documenti originali concernenti Matteo Ricci e la storia delle prime relazioni tra l'Europa e la Cina (1579–1615)*. Volume I. Rome: Librerio dello Stato, 1942.

Dening, Greg. *Islands and Beaches: Discourse on a Silent Land; Marquesas 1774–1880*. Chicago: Dorsey Press, 1980.

Dest, P. van. *Banka beschreven in reistochten*. Amsterdam, 1865.

Dewan Pimpinan Pusat INSA. *Melangkah Laju Menerjang Gelombang: Striding along Scouring the Seas*. Jakarta, 1984.

Dewan Redaksi Puspindo. *Sejarah pelayaran niaga di Indonesia Jilid 1: Pra sejarah hingga 17 Agustus 1945*. Jakarta: Yayasan Puspindo, 1990.

Dg Tapala La Side. "L'expansion du royaume de Goa et sa politique maritime aux XVIe et XVIIe siècles." *Archipel* 10 (1975): 159–72.

Dhakidae, Daniel. *Aceh, Jakarta, Papua: Akar permasalahan dan alternatif proses penyelsaian konflik*. Jakarta: Yaprika, 2001.

Dhiravat na Pombejra. "Ayutthaya at the End of the Seventeenth Century: Was There a Shift to Isolation?" In *Southeast Asia in the Early Modern Era: Trade, Power, and Belief*, edited by Anthony Reid, 250–72. Ithaca: Cornell University Press, 1993.

———. "Port, Palace, and Profit: An Overview of Siamese Crown Trade and the European Presence in Siam in the Seventeenth Century." In [Anon.], *Port Cities and Trade in Western Southeast Asia*, 65–84. Bangkok: Institute of Asian Studies, Chulalongkorn University, 1998.

Dick, Howard. "Indonesian Economic History Inside Out." *RIMA* 27 (1993): 1–12.

———. "Japan's Economic Expansion in the Netherlands Indies between the First and Second World Wars." *Journal of Southeast Asian Studies* 20, no. 2 (1989): 244–72.

Dijk, C. van. "Java, Indonesia, and Southeast Asia: How Important Is the Java Sea?" In *Looking in Odd Mirrors: The Java Sea*, edited by Vincent Houben, Hendrik Meier, and Willem van der Molen, 289–301. Leiden: Culturen van Zuidoost–Asië en Oceanië, 1992.

Dijk, L. C. D. van. *Neerlands vroegste betrekkingen met Borneo, den Solo Archipel, Cambodja, Siam en Cochinchina*. Amsterdam: J. H. Scheltema, 1862.

Dijk, Wil O. *Seventeenth-Century Burma and the Dutch East India Company, 1634–1680*. Singapore: Singapore University Press, 2006.

Ding, Chiang Hai. *A History of Straits Settlements Foreign Trade, 1870–1915*. Singapore: Memoirs of the National Museum 6, 1978.

Dinh, Khac Thuan. "Contribution à l'histoire de la Dynastie des Mac au Viet Nam." PhD dissertation, Université de Paris, 2002.

Dirlik, Arif. "Critical Reflections on 'Chinese Capitalism' as Paradigm." *Identities* 3, no. 3 (1997): 303–30.

Disney, Anthony. *A History of Portugal and the Portuguese Empire.* 2 volumes, especially volume 2. Cambridge: Cambridge University Press, 2009.

Dixon, J. M. "Voyage of the Dutch Ship 'Groll' from Hirado to Tongking." *Transactions of the Asiatic Society of Japan* XI (Yokohama, 1883): 180–216.

Dobbin, C. "From Middleman Minorities to Industrial Entrepreneurs: The Chinese in Java and the Parsis in Western India 1619–1939." *Itinerario* 13, no. 1 (1989): 109–32.

Dobbin, Christine. *Asian Entrepreneurial Minorities: Conjoint Communities in the Making of the World-Economy, 1570–1940.* London: Curzon, 1996.

Doel, H. W. van den. "De ontwikkeling van het militaire bestuur in Nederlands-Indië: De Officier-Civiel Gezaghebber, 1880–1942." *Mededeelingen van de Sectie Militaire Geschiedenis* 12 (1989): 27–50.

Donohue, Mark, and Tim Denham. "Farming and Language in Island Southeast Asia: Reframing Austronesian History. *Current Anthropology* 51–52 (2010): 223–56.

Dreyer, Edward J. *Zheng He: China and the Oceans in the Early Ming Dynasty, 1405–1433.* New York: Pearson Longman, 2007.

Dutton, George. *The Tay Son Uprising: Society and Rebellion in Eighteenth-Century Vietnam.* Honolulu: University of Hawai'i Press, 2006.

———. *A Vietnamese Moses: Philippe Binh and the Geographies of Early Modern Capitalism.* Berkeley: University of California Press, 2016.

Dy, Al Tyrone B., ed. *SWS Surveybook of Muslim Values, Attitudes, and Opinions, 1995–2000.* Manila: Social Weather Stations, 2000.

Dyke, Paul van. *The Canton Trade: Life and Enterprise on the China Coast, 1700–1845.* Hong Kong: Hong Kong University Press, 2007.

———. *Merchants of Canton and Macao: Politics and Strategies in Eighteenth Century Chinese Trade.* Hong Kong: Hong Kong University Press, 2011.

Ebing, Ewald. *Batavia-Jakarta, 1600–2000: A Bibliography.* Leiden: KITLV Press, 2000.

Edensor, Tim. *From Light to Dark: Daylight, Illumination and Gloom.* Minneapolis: Minnesota University Press, 2017.

———. "Light Design and Atmosphere." *Journal of Visual Communication* 14, no. 3 (2015): 331–50.

———. "Reconnecting with Darkness: Gloomy Landscapes, Lightless Places." *Social and Cultural Geography* 14, no. 4 (2013): 446–65.

Edney, Matthew. "The Ideologies and Practices of Mapping and Imperialism." In *Social History of Science in Colonial India,* edited by S. Irfan Habib and Dhruv Raina, 25–68. New Delhi: Oxford University Press, 2007.

Edwards, Penny. *Cambodge: The Cultivation of a Nation.* Honolulu: University of Hawai'i Press, 2007.

Edwards, Randle. "Ch'ing Legal Jurisdiction over Foreigners." In *Essays on China's Legal Tradition,* edited by Jerome Cohen, Fu-Mei Chang Chin, and R. Randle Edwards, 222–69. Princeton, Princeton University Press, 1980.

Eitzen, D. S. "Two Minorities: The Jews of Poland and the Chinese of the Philippines." *Jewish Journal of Sociology* 10, no. 2 (1968): 221–40.

Elden, Stuart. "Contingent Sovereignty, Territorial Integrity and the Sanctity of Borders." *SAIS Review* 26, no. 1 (2006): 11–24.

Elkin, Jennifer. "Observations of Marine Animals in the Coastal Waters of Western Brunei Darussalam." *Brunei Museum Journal* 7, no. 4 (1992): 74–80.

Ellen, Roy. "Environmental Perturbation, Inter-Island Trade, and the Relocation of Production along the Banda Arc; or, Why Central Places Remain Central." In *Human Ecology of Health and Survival in Asia and the South Pacific*, edited by Tsuguyoshi Suzuki and Ryutaro Ohtsuka, 35–62. Tokyo: University of Tokyo Press, 1987.

———. *On the Edge of the Banda Zone: Past and Present in the Social Organization of a Moluccan Trading Network.* Honolulu: University of Hawai'i Press, 2003.

Emmerson, Donald. "Security and Community in Southeast Asia: Will the Real ASEAN Please Stand Up?" In *International Relations of the Asia-Pacific.* Stanford, CA: Shorenstein Asia-Pacific Research Center, 2005.

Esherick, Joseph. *The Origins of the Boxer Rebellion.* Berkeley: University of California Press, 1987.

Evers, H. D. "Chettiar Moneylenders in Southeast Asia." In *Marchands et hommes d'affaires asiatiques dans l'Océan Indien et la Mer de Chine 13e–20e siècles*, edited by D. Lombard and J. Aubin, 199–219. Paris, Éditions de l'École des Hautes Études en Sciences Sociales, 1987.

Evers, Hans-Dieter, and Rudiger Korff. *Southeast Asian Urbanism: The Meaning and Power of Social Space.* Singapore: ISEAS, 2000.

Fasseur, C. "Cornerstone and Stumbling Block: Racial Classification and the Late Colonial State in Indonesia." In *The Late Colonial State in Indonesia: Political and Economic Foundations of the Netherlands Indies 1880–1942*, edited by Robert Cribb, 31–57. Leiden: KITLV Press, 1994.

Fawaz, Leila Tarazi, and C. A. Bayly, eds. *Modernity and Culture: From the Mediterranean to the Indian Ocean.* New York: Columbia University Press, 2002.

Feener, Michael, and Terenjit Sevea, eds. *Islamic Connections: Muslim Societies in South and Southeast Asia.* Singapore: SIEAS Press, 2009.

Fernández-Armesto, Felipe. "Maritime History and World History." In *Maritime History as World History*, edited by Daniel Finamore, 7–24. Gainesville: University Press of Florida, 2004.

Fernando, M. R., and David Bulbeck. *Chinese Economic Activity in Netherlands India: Selected Translations from the Dutch.* Singapore: ISEAS, 1992.

Ferrand, Gabriel. *Essai de phonétique comparée du malaise et des dialectes malgaches.* Paris: Paul Guenther, 1909.

———. "Madagascar et les îles Uâq-uâq." *Journal Asiatique* 10, no. 3 (1904): 489–509.

———."Les voyages des Javanais à Madagascar." *Journal Asiatique* 10, no. 15 (1910): 281–330.

Filesi, Teobaldo. "I viaggi dei Cinesi in Africa nel medioevo." *Africa: Rivista trimestrale di studi e documentazione dell'Istituto italiano per l'Africa e l'Oriente* 16, no. 6 (1961): 275–88.

Fillmore, Stanley. *The Chartmakers: The History of Nautical Surveying in Canada.* Toronto: Canadian Hydrographic Service, 1983.

Finamore, Daniel, ed. *Maritime History as World History.* Gainesville: University Press of Florida, 2004.

Findlay, Alexander. *A Description and List of the Lighthouses of the World.* London: R. H. Laurie, 1861.

Floor, Willem. *The Persian Gulf: A Political and Economic History of Five Port Cities, 1500–1730.* Washington, DC: Mage Publishers, 2006.

Flynn, Thomas. "Foucault and the Eclipse of Vision." In *Modernity and the Hegemony of Vision,* edited by David Michael Levin, 273–86. Berkeley: University of California Press, 1993.

Ford, James. "Buddhist Materiality: A Cultural History of Objects in Japanese Buddhism." *Journal of Japanese Studies* 35, no. 2 (2009): 368–73.

Ford, Michele, Lenore Lyons, and Willem van Schendel, eds. *Labour Migrations and Human Trafficking in Southeast Asia: Critical Perspectives.* London: Routledge, 2014.

Forest, Alain. "L'Asie du sud-est continentale vue de la mer." In *Commerce et navigation en Asie du Sud-est (XIVe–XIXe siècles),* edited by Nguyễn Thế Anh and Yoshiaki Ishizawa, 7–30. Paris: L'Harmattan, 1999.

———. *Les missionaires français au Tonkin et au Siam, XVIIe–XVIIIe siècles: Analyse comparée d'un relatif succès et d'un total échec.* Volume 2: *Histoires du Tonkin.* Paris: l'Harmattan, 1998.

Forrest, Thomas. *A Voyage to New Guinea and the Moluccas from Balambangan: Including an Account of Magindano, Sooloo, and Other Islands.* London: G. Scott, 1779.

Fox, Robert. "The Catalangan Excavations." *Philippine Studies* 7, no. 3 (1959): 325–90.

Frake, Charles. "The Cultural Constructions of Rank, Identity, and Ethnic Origin in the Sulu Archipelago." In *Origins, Ancestry, and Alliance: Explorations in Austronesian Ethnography,* edited by James Fox and Clifford Sather. Canberra, Australia: National University Publication of the Research School of Pacific and Asian Studies, 1996.

Francalanci, G., and T. Scovazzi. *Lines in the Sea.* Dordrecht: Martinus Nijhoff, 1994.

Francis, E. "Timor in 1831." *TNI* 1, no. 1 (1838): 353–69.

Frank, Andre Gunder. *ReOrient: Global Economy in the Asian Age.* Berkeley: University of California Press, 1998.

Frank, Wolfgang, and Chen Tieh Fan. *Chinese Epigraphic Matrials in Malaysia.* 3 volumes. Kuala Lumpur: University of Malaya Press, 1982–87.

Frassen, Chris van. "Ternate, de Molukken and de Indonesische Archipel." 2 volumes. PhD thesis. Leiden University, 1987.

Freedman, Paul. *Out of the East: Spices and the Medieval Imagination.* New Haven: Yale University Press, 2008.

Freeman-Grenville, G. S. P. *The East African Coast: Select Documents from the First to the Earlier Nineteenth Century.* Oxford: Clarendon Press, 1962.

Friend, Theodore. *Indonesian Destinies.* Cambridge: Harvard University Press, 2003.

Fry, Howard. *Alexander Dalrymple and the Expansion of British Trade.* London: Cass, for the Royal Commonwealth Society Imperial Studies 29, 1970.

Fu, Shen. *Fu Sheng Liu Chi: Six Records of a Floating Life.* Translated and with Introduction by Chiang Su-hui and Leonard Pratt. Harmondsworth, Middlesex: Penguin Books, 1983.

Fuller, Dorian, Nicole Boivin, Tom Hodgervorst, and Robin Allaby. "Across the Indian Ocean: The Prehistoric Movement of Plants and Animals." *Antiquity* (June 2011): 544–58.

Fukuda, Shozo. *With Sweat and Abacus: Economic Roles of the Southeast Asian Chinese on the Eve of World War II.* Edited by George Hicks; translated by Les Oates. Singapore: Select Books, 1995.

Furber, Holden. *Private Fortunes and Company Profits in the India Trade in the 18th Century.* Aldershot: Variorum, 1997.

Furnivall, John. *The Fashioning of Leviathan: The Beginnings of British Rule in Burma*, edited by Gehan Wijeyewardene. Canberra: Department of Anthropology, Research School of Pacific Studies, ANU, 1991.

Gaastra, Femme. *Bewind en beleid bij de VOC, 1672–1702*. Amsterdam: Walburg, 1989.

———. *The Dutch East India Company, Expansion and Decline*. Zutphen: Walburg Pers, 2003.

———. "Geld tegen goederen: Een structurele verandering in het Nederlands-Aziatisch handelsverkeer." *Bijdragen en mededelingen betreffende de geschiedenis der Nederlanden* 91, no. 2 (1976): 249–72.

Gallagher, J., and R. Robinson. "The Imperialism of Free Trade." *Economic History Review* 1, no. 1 (1953): 1–15.

Gaynor, Jennifer. *Intertidal History in Island Southeast Asia: Submerged Genealogy and the Legacy of Coastal Capture*. Ithaca: Cornell University Press, 2016.

———. "Maritime Ideologies and Ethnic Anomalies: Sea Space and the Structure of Subalternality in the Southeast Asian Littoral." In *Seascapes: Maritime Histories, Littoral Cultures, and Transoceanic Exchanges*, edited by Jerry H. Bentley, Renate Bridenthal, and Kären Wigen, 53–68. Honolulu: University of Hawai'i Press, 2007.

Geertz, Clifford, *Agricultural Involution*. Berkeley: University of California Press, 1963.

Gerritsen, Anne. "From Long-Distance Trade to the Global Lives of Things: Writing the History of Early Modern Trade and Material Culture." *Journal of Early Modern History* 20, no. 6 (2016): 526–44.

Gibson-Hill, C. A. "The Indonesian Trading Boat Reaching Singapore." *Royal Asiatic Society, Malaysian Branch* 23 (February 1950).

Ghosh, Durba. *Sex and the Family in Colonial India: The Making of Empire*. New York: Cambridge University Press, 2006.

Gilbert, Erik. *Dhows and the Colonial Economy of Zanzibar, 1860–1970*. Athens, OH: Ohio University Press, 2004.

Gilroy, Paul. *The Black Atlantic: Modernity and Double Consciousness*. Cambridge: Harvard University Press, 1993.

Gipouloux, François. *The Asian Mediterranean: Port Cities and Trading Networks in China, Japan and Southeast Asia, 13th–21st Century*. Translated by Jonathan Hall and Dianna Martin. Cheltenham, UK: Edward Elgar, 2011.

Giraldez, Arturo. *The Age of Trade: The Manila Galleons and the Dawn of the Global Economy*. Lanham: Rowman & Littlefield, 2015.

Glassman, Jonathan. *Feasts and Riot: Revelry, Rebellion, and Popular Consciousness on the Swahili Coast, 1856–1888*. London: Heinemann, 1995.

Godley, Michael R. "Chinese Revenue Farm Network: The Penang Connection." In *The Rise and Fall of Revenue Farming: Business Elites and the Emergence of the Modern State in Southeast Asia*, edited by John Butcher and Howard Dick, 89–99. Basingstoke: Macmillan and New York: St. Martin's Press, 1993.

Godley, Michael R. *The Mandarin-Capitalists from Nanyang: Overseas Chinese Enterprise in the Modernization of China, 1893–1911*. Cambridge: Cambridge University Press, 1981.

Gokhale, B. G. *Surat in the Seventeenth Century: A Study of the Urban History of Pre-Modern India*. Bombay: Popular Prakashan, 1979.

Gomez, Edmund Terence. *Chinese Business in Malaysia: Accumulation, Accommodation and Ascendance.* Richmond, UK: Curzon Press, 1999.

———. "In Search of Patrons: Chinese Business Networking and Malay Political Patronage in Malaysia." In *Chinese Business Networks,* edited by Chan Kwok Bun. Singapore: Prentice Hall, 2000.

Gomez, Edmund Terence, and Michael Hsiao. *Chinese Business in Southeast Asia: Contesting Cultural Explanations, Researching Entrepreneurship.* Richmond, Surrey: Curzon, 2001.

———, eds. *Chinese Enterprise, Trans-nationalism, and Identity.* London: Routledge, 2004.

Gommans, Jos, and Jacques Leider, eds. *The Maritime Frontier of Burma, Exploring Political, Cultural and Commercial Interaction in the Indian Ocean World, 1200–1800.* Leiden: KITLV Press, 2002.

Gonschor, Lorenz. *A Power in the World: The Hawaiian Kingdom in Oceania.* Honolulu: University of Hawai'i Press, 2019.

Goor, J. van. "A Madman in the City of Ghosts: Nicolaas Kloek in Pontianak." In *All of One Company: The VOC in Biographical Perspective* (no author), 196–211. Utrecht: H & S Press, 1986.

Goor, Jurriaan van. "Imperialisme in de Marge?" In Jurriaan van Goor, *Imperialisme in de marge: De afronding van Nederlands-Indië.* Utrecht, 1986.

Gordon, Stewart. *When Asia Was the World.* Philadelphia: Da Capo, 2008.

Goscha, Christopher E. "La présence vietnamienne au royaume du Siam du XVIIème siècle: Vers une perspective péninsulaire." In *Guerre et paix en Asie du sud-est,* 211–43. Paris: L'Harmattan, 1998.

Gosling, Betty, *Sukothai: Its History, Culture, and Art.* Oxford: Oxford University Press, 1991.

Gottesman, Evan. *Cambodia after the Khmer Rouge: Inside the Politics of Nation Building.* New Haven: Yale University Press, 2003.

Gowing, Peter. *Mandate in Moroland: The American Government of Muslim Filipinos, 1899–1920.* Dillliman: University of the Philippines Press, 1977.

———. *Muslim Filipinos: Heritage and Horizon.* Quezon City: New Day Publishers, 1979.

Gowing, Peter, and Robert McAmis, eds. *The Muslim Filipinos.* Manila: Solidaridad Publishing, 1974.

Grahn, Lance, *The Political Economy of Smuggling: Regional Informal Economies in Early Bourbon New Granada.* Boulder, CO: Westview Press, 1997.

Gramberg, I. S. G. "Internationale Vuurtorens." *De Economist* 1 (1882): 17–30.

Gray, Sir John. *The British in Mombasa, 1824–1826.* London: Macmillan, 1957.

Green, Jeremy. "Maritime Aspects of History and Archaeology in the Indian Ocean, Southeast and East Asia." In *The Role of Universities and Research Institutes in Marine Archaeology: Proceedings of the Third Indian Conference of Marine Archaeology,* edited by S. R. Rao. Goa: National Institute of Oceanography, 1994.

Green, Jeremy, Rosemary Harper, and Sayann Prishanchittara. *The Excavation of the Ko Kradat Wrecksite Thailand, 1979–1980.* Perth: Special Publication of the Department of Maritime Archaeology, Western Australian Museum, 1981.

Green, Nile. *Bombay Islam: The Religious Economy of the West Indian Ocean 1840–1915.* Cambridge: Cambridge University Press, 2013.

Greene, Jack P., and Philip D. Morgan, eds. *Atlantic History: A Critical Appraisal*. New York: Oxford University Press, 2009.

Gregori, F. A. A. "Aantekeningen en beschouwingen betrekkelijk de zeerovers en hunn rooverijen in den Indischen Archipel, alsmede aangaande magindanao en de Soolo-Archipel." *TNI* 7, no. 2 (1845): 139–69.

Greif, Avner. *Institutions and the Path to the Modern Economy: Lessons from Medieval Trade*. Cambridge: Cambridge University Press, 2006.

Greif, Avner, Paul Milgrom, and Barry R. Weingast. "Coordination, Commitment, and Enforcement: The Case of the Merchant Guild." *Journal of Political Economy* 102, no. 4 (1994): 745–76.

Gresh, Geoffrey. *To Rule Eurasia's Waves: The New Great Power Competition at Sea*. New Haven: Yale University Press, 2020.

Griffith, Robert and Carol Thomas, eds. *The City-State in Five Cultures*. Santa Barbara: ABC-Clio, 1981.

Griffiths, Arlo. "Written Traces of the Buddhist Past: Mantras and Dharais in Indonesian Inscriptions." *Bulletin of the School of Oriental and African Studies* 77, no. 1 (2014): 137–94.

Grijns, Kees, and Peter J. M. Nas. *Jakarta-Batavia: Socio-Cultural Essays*. Leiden: KITLV Press, 2000.

Groot, Cornelis de. *Herinneringen aan Blitong: Historisch, lithologisch, mineralogisch, geographisch, geologisch, en Mijnbouwkundig*. The Hague: H. L. Smits, 1887.

Groslier, B. Ph. "Angkor et le Cambodge au XVI siècle." *Annales du Musée Guimet*. Paris: PUF, 1958.

———. "La céramique chinoise en Asie du Sud-est: Quelques points de méthode." *Archipel* 21 (1981): 93–121.

Grosset-Grange, H. "Les procédés arabes de navigation en Océan Indien au moment des grandes découvertes." In *Sociétés et compagnies de commerce en Orient et dans l'Océan Indien*, edited by M. Mollat, 227–46. Paris: SEVPEN, 1970.

Guida, Donatella. *Immagini del Nanyang: Realtà e stereotipi nella storiografia cinese verso la fine della dinastia Ming*. Naples: Istituto Universitario Orientale di Napoli, 1991.

Guillain, M., *Documents sur l'histoire, la geographie et le commerce de l'Afrique orientale*. Volume I. Paris, 1856.

Gunawan, Restu, I. Z. Leirissa, and Shalfiyanta. *Ternate Sebagai bandar Jalur Sutra*. Jakarta: Departemen Pendidikan dan Kebudayaan, Direktorat Sejarah dan Nilai Tradisional, Proyek Inventarisasi dan Dokumentasi Sejarah Nasional, 1999.

Gunn, Geoffrey. *History without Borders: The Making of an Asian World Region, 1000–1800*. Hong Kong: Hong Kong University Press, 2011.

———. *Overcoming Ptolemy: The Making of an Asian World Region*. Lexington: Rowman and Littlefield, 2018.

Gupta, Ashin Das. "India and the Indian Ocean in the Eighteenth Century." In *India and the Indian Ocean 1500–1800*, edited by Ashin Das Gupta and M. N. Pearson, 131–61. Calcutta: Oxford University Press, 1987.

———. *Merchants of Maritime India, 1500–1800*. Ashgate: Variorum, 1994.

———. "The Merchants of Surat, 1700–1750." In *Elites in South Asia*, edited by Edmund Leach and S. N. Mukherjee, 201–22. Cambridge: Cambridge University Press, 1970.

Gutem, V. B. van. "Tina Mindering: Eeninge aanteekenigen over het Chineeshe geldshieterswesen op Java." *Koloniale Studiën* 3, no. 1 (1919): 106–50.

Guy, John. "The Intan Shipwreck: A Tenth Century Cargo in Southeast Asian Waters." In *Song Ceramics: Art History, Archaeology and Technology*, edited by S. Pearson, 171–192. London: Percival David Foundation, 2004.

———. *Lost Kingdoms: Hindu-Buddhist Sculpture of Early Southeast Asia*. New York and New Haven: Metropolitan Museum of Art and Yale University Press, 2018).

———. "Vietnamese Ceramics from the Hoi An Excavation: The Cu Lau Cham Ship Cargo." *Orientations* 31, no. 7 (Sept. 2000): 125–28.

———. "Vietnamese Ceramics in International Trade." In *Vietnamese Ceramics, A Separate Tradition*, edited by John Stevenson and John Guy, 47–61. Michigan: Art Media Resources, 1994; repr. Chicago: Art Media Resources, 1997.

Haan, F. de. *Oud Batavia*. Volume I. Batavia: Kolff, 1922.

Haellquist, Karl, ed. *Asian Trade Routes: Continental and Maritime*. London: Curzon Press, 1991.

Hall, Kenneth. *A History of Early Southeast Asia: Maritime Trade and Societal Development, 100–1500*. Lanham: Rowman & Littlefield, 2011.

———. *Maritime Trade and State Development in Early Southeast Asia*. Honolulu: University of Hawai'i Press, 1985.

Hall, Kenneth, and John Whitmore, eds. *Explorations in Early Southeast Asian History: The Origins of Southeast Asian Statecraft*. Ann Arbor: University of Michigan, Center for South and Southeast Asian Studies, 1976.

Hall, Kenneth R. "Multi-Dimensional Networking: Fifteenth-Century Indian Ocean Maritime Diaspora in Southeast Asian Perspective." *JESHO* 49, no. 4 (2006): 454–81.

Hall, Richard. *Empires of the Monsoon: A History of the Indian Ocean and Its Invaders*. London: Harper Collins, 1996.

Hamashita, Takeshi. *China, East Asia, and the Global Economy: Regional and Historical Perspectives*. New York: Routledge, 2013.

———. "The Intra-regional System in East Asia in Modern Times." In *Network Power: Japan and Asia*, edited by Peter J. Katzenstein and Takashi Shiraishi, 113–35. Ithaca, NY: Cornell University Press, 1997.

———. "The Tribute Trade System and Modern Asia." Translated by Neil Burton and Christian Daniels. In Hamashita Takeshi, *China, East Asia and the Global Economy: Regional and Historical Perspectives*, edited by Linda Grove and Mark Selden, 12–26. London and New York: Routledge, 2008.

Hamilton, Gary. "The Organizational Foundations of Western and Chinese Commerce: A Historical Perspective and Comparative Analysis." In *Business Networks and Economic Development in East and Southeast Asia*, 48–65. Hong Kong: Centre of Asian Studies, University of Hong Kong, 1991.

———, ed. *Business Networks and Economic Development in East and Southeast Asia*. Hong Kong: Centre of Asian Studies, University of Hong Kong, 1991.

Hane, Mikiso. *Peasants, Rebels, and Outcasts: The Underside of Modern Japan (1800–1940)*. New York, Pantheon Books, 1982.

Hansen, Valerie. *The Open Empire: A History of China to 1600*. New York: Norton, 2000.

Hao, Yen-Ping. *The Commercial Revolution in Nineteenth Century China: The Rise of Sino-Western Capitalism*. Berkeley: University of California Press, 1986.

Harding, Harry. "The Concept of "Greater China: Themes, Variations and Reservations." *China Quarterly* 136 (December, 1993): 660–86.

Harlow, Barbara, and Mia Carter. *Imperialism and Orientalism: A Documentary Sourcebook*. Malden: Blackwell, 1999.

Harvey, Simon. *Smuggling: Seven Centuries of Contraband*. London: Reaktion Books, 2016.

Harms, Erik. *Luxury and Rubble: Civility and Dispossession in the New Saigon*. Berkeley: University of California Press, 2016.

———. *Saigon's Edge: On the Margins of Ho Chi Minh City*. Minneapolis: University of Minneapolis Press, 2011.

Harper, Tim. *The End of Empire and the Making of Malaya*. Cambridge: Cambridge University Press, 1999.

———. "Singapore, 1915, and the Birth of the Asian Underground." *Modern Asian Studies* 47 (2013): 1782–1811.

———. *Underground Asia: Global Revolutionaries and the Overthrow of Europe's Empires in the East*. London: Allen Lane, 2019)

Harper, Tim, and Sunil Amrith, eds. *Sites of Asian Interaction: Ideas, Networks, and Mobility*. Cambridge: Cambridge University Press, 2014.

Harrison, Barbara. *Pusaka: Heirloom Jars of Borneo*. Singapore: Oxford University Press, 1986.

Hasselt, A. L. van. "De Poelau Toedjoeh." *TAG* 15 (1898), 21–22.

Hastrup, Kirsten, and Hastrup, Frida, eds. *Waterworlds: Anthropology and Fluid Environments*. New York: Berghahn Books, 2015.

Hau'ofa, Epeli. "Our Sea of Islands," *The Contemporary Pacific* 6, no. 1 (1994): 148–61.

———. *We Are the Ocean: Selected Works*. Honolulu: University of Hawai'i Press, 2008.

Hawksley, Humphrey. *Asian Waters: The Struggle over the South China Sea and the Strategy of Chinese Expansion*. New York: Abrams, 2018.

Headrick, Daniel. *The Tentacles of Progress: Technology Transfer in the Age of Imperialism, 1850–1940*. New York, 1988.

———. *The Tools of Empire: Technology and European Imperialism in the Nineteenth Century*. New York, 1981.

Heidhues, Mary Somers. *Bangka Tin and Mentok Pepper: Chinese Settlement on an Indonesian Island*. Singapore: ISEAS, 1992.

Hellyer, Robert. *Defining Engagement: Japan and Global Contexts, 1640–1868*. Cambridge: Harvard University Asia Center, 2009.

Heng, Derek. *Sino-Malay Trade and Diplomacy from the Tenth through the Fourteenth Century*. Athens, OH: Ohio University Southeast Asian Studies, 2009.

———. "Trans-Regionalism and Economic Co-dependency in the South China Sea: The Case of China and the Malay Region (Tenth to Fourteenth Centuries AD)." *International History Review* 35, no. 3 (2013): 486–510.

Hickey, Gerald. *Sons of the Mountains: Ethnohistory of the Vietnamese Central Highlands to 1954*. New Haven: Yale University Press, 1982.

Hickson, Sydney. *A Naturalist in North Celebes*. London: John Murray, 1889.

Higham, Charles, and Rachanie Thosarat. *Early Thailand: From Prehistory to Sukothai*. Bangkok: River Books, 2012.

———. *Prehistoric Thailand: From Early Settlement to Sukothai*. Bangkok: River Books, 1998.

Hill, Ann Maxwell. *Merchants and Migrants: Ethnicity and Trade Among Yunnanese in Southeast Asia*. New Haven: Yale University Southeast Asia Studies, 1998.

Hill, Catherine, et al. "A Mitochondrial Stratigraphy for Island Southeast Asia." *American Journal of Human Genetics* 80–81 (2007): 29–43.

Hirth, Frederick, and W. W. Rockhill. *Chau Ju Kua: His Work on the Chinese and Arab Trade in the 12th and 13th Centuries, Entitled Chu Fan Chï*. New York: Paragon Book Reprint Co., 1966.

Hobsbawm, Eric. *The Age of Empire 1875–1914*. New York: Pantheon, 1987.

Hobson, J. A. *Imperialism: A Study*. London, 1902.

Hoevell, W. R. van. "Laboean, Serawak, de Noordoostkust van Borneo en de Sulthan van Soeloe." *Tijdschrift voor Nederlandsche Indie* 11, part 1 (1849): 66–83.

Ho, Engseng. "Empire through Diasporic Eyes: A View from the Other Boat." *Comparative Studies in Society and History* 46, no. 2 (2004): 210–46.

———. *The Graves of Tarim: Genealogy and Mobility across the Indian Ocean*. Berkeley: University of California Press, 2006.

Hodder, Rupert. *Merchant Princes of the East: Cultural Delusions, Economic Success and the Overseas Chinese in Southeast Asia*. Chichester: Wiley, 1996.

Hoetink, B. "Chineesche officiern te Batavia onder de compagnie." *Bijdragen tot de Taal-, land- en Volkenkunde van Nederlandsch Indië* 78 (1922): 1–136.

———. "Ni Hoekong: Kapitein der Chineezen te Batavia in 1740." *Bijdragen tot de Taal-, land- en Volkenkunde van Nederlandsch Indië* 74 (1918): 447–518.

———. "So Bing Kong: Het eerste hoofd der Chineezen te Batavia (1629–1636)." *Bijdragen tot de Taal-,land- en Volkenkunde van Nederlandsch Indië* 74 (1917): 344–85.

Hofmeyer, Isabel. "The Complicating Sea: The Indian Ocean as Method." *Comparative Studies of South Asia, Africa and the Middle East* 32, no. 3 (2012): 584–90.

Hopkirk, Peter. *The Great Game: The Struggle for Empire in Central Asia*. New York: Kodansha International, 1992.

Hopper, Matthew. *Globalization and Slavery in Arabia in the Age of Empire*. New Haven: Yale University Press, 2015.

Horton, Mark. *Shanga*. London: British Institute in Eastern Africa, 1996.

Horton, Mark, and John Middleton. *The Swahili: The Social Landscape of a Mercantile Society*. Oxford: Blackwell, 2000.

Howe, K. R. *Nature, Culture and History: The "Knowing" of Oceania*. Honolulu: University of Hawai'i Press, 2000.

Howitz, Pensak C. *Ceramics from the Sea: Evidence from the Kho Kradad Shipwreck Excavated in 1979*. Bangkok: Archaeology Division of Silpakorn University, 1979.

Hull, Terence, Endang Sulistyaningsih, and Gavin Jones, eds. *Pelacuran di Indonesia: Sejarah dan perkembangannya*. Jakarta: Pusat Sinar Harapan, 1997.

Hurles, M. E., B. C. Sykes, M. A. Jobling, and P. Forster. "The Dual Origin of the Malagasy in Island Southeast Asia and East Africa: Evidence from Maternal and Paternal Lineages." *American Journal of Human Genetics* 76 (2005): 894–901.

Hutterer, K. L. *Economic Exchange and Social Interaction in Southeast Asia: Perspectives from Prehistory, History, and Ethnography*. Ann Arbor: University of Michigan Southeast Asia Program, 1977.

Igler, David. *The Great Ocean: Pacific Worlds from Captain Cook to the Gold Rush*. New York: Oxford University Press, 2013.

Iioka, Naoko. "The Trading Environment and the Failure of Tongking's Mid-Seventeenth Century Commercial Resurgence." In *The Tongking Gulf through History*, edited by Nola Cooke, Tana Li, and Jamie Anderson, 117–32. Philadelphia: University of Pennsylvania Press, 2011.

Ileto, Reynaldo. *Magindanao, 1860–1888: The Career of Datu Utto of Buayan*. Manila: Anvil, 2007.

———. *Pasyon and Revolution: Popular Movements in the Philippines, 1840–1910*. Manila: Ateneo de Manila Press, 1997.

Insoll, Timothy. *The Archaeology of Islam in Sub-Saharan Africa*. Cambridge: Cambridge University Press, 2003.

Ishii, Yoneo, ed. *The Junk Trade from Southeast Asia: Translations from the Tosen Fusetsu-gaki, 1674–1723*. Canberra: Research School of Pacific and Asian Studies, Australian National University; Singapore: ISEAS, 1998.

Israel, Jonathan. *Dutch Primacy in World Trade*. Oxford: Oxford University Press, 1989.

Iwao, Seichii. "Japanese Foreign Trade in the 16th and 17th centuries." *Acta Asiatica* 30, 1976.

Jacob, Christian, Tom Conley (trans.), and Edward H. Dahl (ed.). *The Sovereign Map: Theoretical Approaches in Cartography throughout History*. Chicago: University of Chicago Press, 2006.

Jacob, H. K. s'. "De VOC en de Malabarkust in de 17de eeuw." In *De VOC in Azië*, edited by M. A. P. Meilink-Roelofsz, 85–99. Bussum: Uniebok, 1976.

Jacobs, Els M. *Koopman in Azië: De handel van de Vernigde Oost-Indische Companie tijdens de 18de eeuw*. Zutphen: Walburg Pers, 2000.

Jacquemard, Simone. *L'éruption du Krakatoa, ou des chambres inconnues dans la maison*. Paris: Éditions du Seuil, 1969.

Jacques, Roland. *Les missionnaires portugais et les débuts de l'Église catholique au Viêt-nam*. 2 volumes. Reichstett-France: Dinh Huóng Túng Thu, 2004.

Jamann, Wolfgang. "Business Practices and Organizational Dynamics of Chinese Family-based Trading Firms in Singapore." PhD dissertation, Department of Sociology, University of Bielefield, 1990.

Jansen, A. J. F. "Aantekeningen omtrent Sollok en de Solloksche Zeerovers." *Tijdschrift voor Indische Taal-, Land-, en Volkenkunde* 7 (1858): 212–39.

Jennings, John. *The Opium Empire: Japanese Imperialism and Drug Trafficking in Asia, 1895–1945*. Westport: Praeger, 1997.

Jones, A. M. *Africa and Indonesia: The Evidence of the Xylophone and Other Musical and Cultural Factors*. Leiden: Brill, 1964.

Jorg, Christian, and Michael Flecker. *Porcelain from the Vung Tau Wreck*. London: Sun GTree Publishing, 2001.

Julia van Ittersum, Martine. *Profit and Principle: Hugo Grotius, Natural Rights Theories, and the Rise of Dutch Power in the East Indies, 1595–1615*. Leiden: Brill, 2006.

Junker, Laura Lee. *Raiding, Trading and Feasting: The Political Economy of Philippine Chiefdoms.* Honolulu: University of Hawai'i Press, 1999.

Kaempfer, Englebert. *The History of Japan, together with a Description of the Kingdom of Siam.* Richmond, Surrey: Curzon Press, 1906; repr. 1993.

Kan, C. M. "Geographical Progress in the Dutch East Indies 1883–1903." *Report of the Eighth International Geographic Congress* (1904/5).

Kang, David C. *East Asia before the West: Five Centuries of Trade and Tribute.* New York: Columbia University Press, 2010.

Kangying, Li. *The Ming Maritime Trade Policy in Transition, 1368 to 1567.* Wiesbaden: Harrassowitz Verlag, 2010.

Kaplan, Robert. *Asia's Cauldron: The South China Sea and the End of a Stable Pacific.* New York: Random House, 2014.

Karafet, Tatiana M., et al. "Major East-West Division Underlines Y Chromosome Stratification Across Indonesia." *Molecular Biology and Evolution* 27–28 (2010): 1833–44.

Katayama, Kunio. "The Japanese Maritime Surveys of Southeast Asian Waters before the First World War." *Institute of Economic Research Working Paper* no. 85, Kobe University of Commerce, 1985.

Katz, Claudio J. "Karl Marx on the Transition from Feudalism to Capitalism." *Theory and Society* 22 (1993).

Kausar, Kabir, editor and compiler. *Secret Correspondence of Tipu Sultan.* New Delhi 1980, 253–65.

Keay, John. *The Honourable Company: A History of the English East India Company.* New York: HarperCollins, 1993.

———. *The Spice Route: A History.* Berkeley: University of California Press, 2007.

Kemp, P. H. van der. *Het Nederlandsch-Indisch bestuur van 1817 op 1818 over de Molukken, Sumatra, Banka, Billiton, en de Lampongs.* 's-Gravenhage: M. Nijhoff, 1917.

Kendall, Laurel. "Popular Religion and the Sacred Life of Material Goods in Contemporary Vietnam." *Asian Ethnology* 67, no. 2 (2008): 177–99.

Kennedy, R. E. "The Protestant Ethic and the Parsis." *American Journal of Sociology* 68 (1962–63): 11–20.

Kerkvliet, Ben. *The Huk Rebellion.* Berkeley: University of California Press, 1977.

Khan, Iftikhar Ahmad. "Merchant Shipping in the Arabian Sea—First Half of the 19th Century." *Journal of Indian Ocean Studies* 7, nos. 2/3 (2000): 163–73.

Khin, Maung Myunt. "Pegu as an Urban Commercial Centre for the Mon and Myanmar Kingdoms of Lower Myanmar." In [Anon.], *Port Cities and Trade in Western Southeast Asia.* Bangkok: Institute of Asian Studies, Chulalongkorn University, 1998, pp. 15–36.

Khoo, Kay Kim. "Melaka: Persepsi Tentang Sejarah dan Masyarakatnya." In *Esei-Esei Budaya dan Sejarah Melaka,* edited by Omar Farouk Bajunid. Kuala Lumpur: Siri Minggu Kesenian Asrama Za'ba, 1989.

Kiefer, Thomas. *The Taosug: Violence and Law in a Philippine Muslim Society.* New York: Holt, Rinehart, and Winston, 1972.

Kiernan, Ben. *The Pol Pot Regime: Race, Power, and Genocide in Cambodia under the Khmer Rouge 1975–1979.* New Haven: Yale University Press, 2002.

Kim, Diana. *Empires of Vice: The Rise of Opium Prohibition across Southeast Asia.* Princeton: Princeton University Press, 2020.

Kitiarsa, Pattana. *Mediums, Monks, and Amulets: Thai Popular Buddhism Today.* Chiang Mai: Silkworm Books, 2012.

Klausner, S. Z. "Introduction." In Werner Sombart, *The Jews and Modern Capitalism*, xv–cxxv. New Brunswick and London: Transaction Books, 1982.

Klein, Beernhard, and Gesa Mackenthun, eds. *Sea Changes: Historicizing the Ocean.* New York: Routledge, 2004.

Klein, P. W. "De Tonkinees-Japanse zijdehandel van de Vereenigde Oost-indische Compagine en het inter-Aziatische verkeer in de 17e eeuw." In *Bewogen en bewegen: De historicus in het spanningsveld tussen economie and cultuur*, edited by W. Frijhoff and M. Hiemstra. Tilburg: Gianotten, 1986.

Knaap, Gerrit. *Shallow Waters, Rising Tide: Shipping and Trade in Java Around 1775.* Leiden: KITLV Press, 1996.

Knaap, Gerrit J., and Heather Sutherland. *Monsoon Traders: Ships, Skippers and Commodities in Eighteenth-Century Makassar.* Leiden: KITLV Press, 2004.

Kniphorst, J. H. P. E. "Historische Schets van den Zeerof in den Oost-Indischen Archipel." *Tijdschrift Zeewezen* 1, 2, 3 (1876).

Koh, Keng We. "Familiar Strangers and Stranger-kings: Mobility, Diasporas, and the Foreign in the Eighteenth-Century Malay World." *Journal of Southeast Asian Studies* 48, no. 3 (2017): 390–413.

Kotkin, Joel. *Tribes: How Race, Religion, and Identity Determine Success in the New Global Economy.* New York: Random House, 1993.

Krairiksh, Piriya. "Review Article: Re-Visioning Buddhist Art in Thailand." *Journal of Southeast Asian Studies* 45, no. 1: 113–18.

Krieger, Martin. "Danish Country Trade on the Indian Ocean in the 17th and 18th Centuries." In *Indian Ocean and Cultural Interaction, 1400–1800*, edited by K. S. Mathew, 122–29. Pondicherry: Pondicherry University, 1996.

Kritz, M. M., and C. B. Keely. "Introduction." In *Global Trends in Migration: Theory and Research on International Migration Movements*, edited by M. M. Kritz and C. B. Keely. Staten Island: Center for Migration Studies, 1981.

Kroesen, R. C. "Aantekenningen over de Anambas-, Natuna-, en Tambelan Eilanden." *TBG* 21 (1875): 235.

Kuo, Hue-Ying. "Charting China in the Thirteenth-Century World: The First English Translation of *Zhu Fan Zhi* and Its Recipients in China in the 1930s." In *Global Patterns of Scientific Exchange, 1000–1800 C.E.*, edited by Patrick Manning and Abigail Own. Pittsburgh: University of Pittsburgh Press, 2018): 93–116.

Kubicek, Robert. "British Expansion, Empire, and Technological Change." In *The Oxford History of the British Empire: III, The Nineteenth Century*, edited by Andrew Porter, 247–69. Oxford: Oxford University Press, 1999.

———. "The Role of Shallow-Draft Steamboats in the Expansion of the British Empire, 1820–1914." *International Journal of Maritime History* VI (June 1994): 86–106.

Kuhn, Philip. *Chinese among Others: Emigration in Modern Times.* Lanham, MD.: Rowman and Littlefield, 2009.

Kumar, Ann. "'The Single Most Astonishing Fact of Human Geography': Indonesia's Far West Colony." *Indonesia* 92 (2011): 59–95.

Kumar, Deepak. *Science and the Raj, 1857–1905*. Delhi, Oxford University Press, 1995), 180–227.

Kwee, Hui Kian. *The Political Economy of Java's Northeast Coast, 1740–1800*. Leiden: Brill, 2006.

Kwee, Tek Hoay. *Drama dari Kratatau*. Batavia: Typ. Druk. Hoa Siang In Kok, 1929.

La Chapelle, H. "Bijdrage tot de kennis van het stoomvaartverkeer in den Indischen Archipel." *De Economist* 2 (1885): 689–90.

Ladwig, Patrice. "Haunting the State: Rumours, Spectral Apparitions and the Longing for Buddhist Charisma in Laos." *Asian Studies Review* 37, no. 4 (2013): 509–26.

Laffan, Michael. *Islamic Nationhood and Colonial Indonesia: The Umma below the Winds*. London: Routledge, 2003.

———. *The Makings of Indonesian Islam: Orientalism and the Narration of a Sufi Past*. Princeton: Princeton University Press, 2011.

Lafont, Pierre-Bernard, ed. *Les frontières du Vietnam: Histoires et frontières de la péninsule indochinoise*. Volume 1 of *Histoire des frontières de la péninsule indochinoise*. Collection recherches asiatiques. Paris: Éditions l'Harmattan, 1989.

Lakshmi Labh, Vijay. "Some Aspects of Piracy in the Indian Ocean during the Early Modern Period." *Journal of Indian Ocean Studies* 2, no. 3 (1995): 259–69.

Lamb, A. *The Mandarin Road to Old Hué: Narratives of Anglo-Vietnamese Diplomacy from the 17th Century to the Eve of the Trench Conquest*. London: Chatto & Windus, 1970.

Lamb, Alastair. "British Missions to Cochin China 1778–1882." *JMBRAS* 34, nos. 3, 4 (1961): 1–248.

Landes, David. *The Wealth and Poverty of Nations: Why Some Are So Rich, and Some So Poor*. New York: W. W. Norton and Co, 1998.

Lange, H. M. *Het Eiland Banka en zijn aangelegenheden*. 's Hertogenbosch [Den Bosch], 1850).

Lapian, A. B. "Le rôle des *orang laut* dans l'histoire de Riau." *Archipel* 18 (1979): 215–22.

Lapian, Adrian. "Laut Sulawesi: The Celebs Sea, from Center to Peripheries." *Moussons* 7 (2004): 3–16.

———. *Orang Laut, Bajak Laut, Raja Laut*. Jakarta: Kounitas Bambu, 2009: 227.

Latour, Bruno. *We Have Never Been Modern*. Cambridge: Cambridge University Press, 1993.

Larson, Pier Martin. *Ocean of Letters: Language and Creolization in an Indian Ocean Diaspora*. Cambridge: Cambridge University Press, 2009.

Latham, R. E. *The Travels of Marco Polo*. New York: Penguin Books, 1958.

Laurila, Simo. *Islands Rise from the Sea: Essays on Exploration, Navigation, and Mapping in Hawaii*. New York: Vantage Press, 1989.

Law, Lisa. *Sex Work in Southeast Asia: A Place of Desire in a Time of AIDS*. New York: Routledge, 2000.

Leach, Edmund. *Political Systems of Highland Burma: A Study of Kachin Social Structure*. Cambridge, MA: Harvard University Press, 1954.

Leaf, Michael. "New Urban Frontiers: Periurbanization and Retentionalization in Southeast Asia." In *The Design of Frontier Spaces: Control and Ambiguity*, edited by Carolyn S. Loeb and Andreas Loescher, 193–212. Burlington: Ashgate, 2015.

———. "Periurban Asia: A Commentary on Becoming Urban." *Pacific Affairs* 84, no. 3: 525–34.

———. "A Tale of Two Villages: Globalization and Peri-Urban Change in China and Vietnam." *Cities* 19, no. 1: 23–32.

Le Blanc, Charles, and Rémi Mathieu. "L'inquiétante étrangeté." In *Mythe et philosophie à l'aube de la Chine impériale: Études sur le Huainan zi*, edited by Charles Le Blanc and Rémi Mathieu, 15–26. Montreal and Paris, 1992.

———. "Voir à ce propos Rémi Mathieu." *Étude sur la mythologie et l'ethnologie de la Chine ancienne: Traduction annotée du Shanhaijng*. Paris, Diffusion de Boccard, 1983.

Legarda, Benito, *After the Galleons: Foreign Trade, Economic Change and Entrepreneurship in the Nineteenth-Century Philippines*. Madison: University of Wisconsin Southeast Asia Program, 1999)

Lenin, V. I. *Imperialism: The Highest Stage of Capitalism*. New York, International Publishers, 1969.

Lesure, Michel. "Une document ottoman de 1525 sur l'inde portugaise et les pays de la Mer Rouge." *Mare Luso-Indicum* 3 (1976): 137–60.

Leur, J. C. van. *Indonesian Trade and Society: Essays in Asian Social and Economic History*. The Hague: W. van Hoeve, 1955.

Levathes, Louise. *When China Ruled the Seas: The Treasure Fleet of the Dragon Throne, 1405–1433*. New York: Oxford University Press, 1994.

Levine, D. N. "Simmel at a Distance: On the History and Systematics of the Sociology of the Stranger." In *Georg Simmel. Critical Assessments*. Volume 3, edited by D. Frisby, 174–89. London and New York: Routledge, 1994).

Lewis, Dianne. *Jan Compagnie in the Straits of Malacca*. Columbus: Ohio University Press, 1995.

Lewis, Martin. "Dividing the Ocean Sea." *Geographical Review* 89, no. 2 (April 1999): 188–214.

Lewis, Martin, and Kären Wigen. *The Myth of Continents: A Critique of Metageography*. Berkeley: University of California Press, 1997.

Lewis, Su Lin. *Cities in Motion: Urban Life and Cosmopolitanism in Southeast Asia, 1920–1940*. Cambridge: Cambridge University Press, 2016.

Li Guoting. *Migrating Fujianese: Ethnic, Family, and Gender Identities in an Early Modern Maritime World*. Leiden: Brill, 2015.

Li, Peter S. "Overseas Chinese Networks: A Reassessment." In *Chinese Business Networks*, edited by Chan Kwok Bun. Singapore: Prentice Hall, 2000.

Li Tana. "An Alternative Vietnam? The Nguyễn Kingdom in the Seventeenth and Eighteenth Centuries." *Journal of Southeast Asian Studies* 29, no. 1 (1998): 111–21.

———. "The Late-Eighteenth and Early-Nineteenth-Century Mekong Delta in the Regional Trade System." In *Water Frontier: Commerce and the Chinese in the Lower Mekong Region, 1750–1880*, edited by Nola Cooke and Tana Li, 71–84. Lanham, MD: Rowman & Littlefield, 2004.

———. *Nguyễn Cochinchina: Southern Vietnam in the Seventeenth and Eighteenth Centuries*. (Ithaca: SEAP, 1998).

———. "A View from the Sea: Perspectives on the Northern and Central Vietnam Coast." *Journal of Southeast Asian Studies* 37, no. 1 (2006): 83–102.

Li, Tana, and Anthony Reid, eds. *Southern Vietnam under the Nguyen: Documents on the Economic History of Cochin China (Dang Trong), 1602–1777*. Singapore: ISEAS, 1993.

Li, Tania. "Marginality, Power, and Production: Analyzing Upland Transformations." In *Transforming the Indonesian Uplands: Marginality, Power, and Production*, edited by Tania Li, 1–44. Amsterdam: Harwood Academic Publishers, 1999.

Liao Shaolian. "Ethnic Chinese Business People and the Local Society: The Case of the Philippines." *Chinese Business Networks*, edited by Chan Kwok Bun. Singapore: Prentice Hall, 2000.

Liao, Tim, Kimie Hara, and Krista Wiegand, eds. *The China-Japan Border Dispute: Islands of Contention in Multidisciplinary Perspective*. London: Ashgate, 2015.

Licata, G. B. "L'Italia nel Mar Rosso." *Boll. Sez. Fiorentina della Soc. Africana d'Italia* (March 1885):1–11.

Lieberman, Victor. *Strange Parallels: Southeast Asia in Global Context, 800–1830*. Volume 1: *Integration on the Mainland*. Cambridge: Cambridge University Press, 2003.

———. "Was the Seventeenth Century a Watershed in Burmese History?" In *Southeast Asia in the Early Modern Era: Trade, Power, and Belief*, edited by Anthony Reid, 214–49. Ithaca: Cornell University Press, 1993.

Liem, Khing Hoo. *Meledaknja Goenoeng Keloet: Menoeroet tjatetan jang dikompoel*. Sourabaya: Hahn and Co., 1929.

Lim, Lin Leam. *The Sex Sector: The Economic and Social Bases of Prostitution in Southeast Asia*. Geneva: International Labour Office, 1998.

Lim, Linda Y. C. "Chinese Economic Activity in Southeast Asia: An Introductory Review." In *The Chinese in Southeast Asia*. Volume 1: *Ethnicity and Economic Activity*, edited by Linda Y. C. Lim and L. A. Peter Gosling, 1–29. Singapore: Maruzen Asia, 1983.

Limlingan, Victor Sampao. *The Overseas Chinese in ASEAN: Business Strategies and Management Practices*. Manila: Vita Development Corporation, 1986.

Lin Yu-ju and Madeleine Zelin, eds. *Merchant Communities in Asia, 1600–1980*. Brookfield: Pickering and Chatto, 2015.

Lindblad, J. Thomas. "Between Singapore and Batavia: The Outer Islands in the Southeast Asian Economy in the Nineteenth Century." In *Kapitaal, ondernemerschap en beleid: Studies over economie en politiek in Nederland, Europa en Azië van 1500 tot heden*, edited by C. A. Davids, W. Fritschy, and L. A. van der Valk, 528–30. Amsterdam: NEHA, 1996.

Linebaugh, Peter, and Marcus Reddiker. *The Many-Headed Hydra: Sailors, Slaves, Commoners, and the Hidden History of the Revolutionary Atlantic*. Boston: Beacon Press, 2000.

Lineton, Jacqueline. "Pasompe 'Ugi': Bugis Migrants and Wanderers." *Archipel* 10 (1975): 173–205.

Lintner, Bertil. *Cross-Border Drug Trade in the Golden Triangle*. Durham: International Boundaries Research Unit, 1991.

Lipson, Mark, Po-Ru Loh, Nick Patterson, Priya Moorjani, Ying-Chin Ko, Mark Stoneking, Bonnie Berger, and David Reich. "Reconstructing Austronesian Population History in Island Southeast Asia." *Nature Communications* 5, no. 4689 (2014); https://doi.org/10.1038/ncomms5689.

Locher-Scholten, Elsbeth. *Sumatraans sultanaat en koloniale staat: De relatie Djambi-Batavia (1830–1907) en het Nederlandse imperialisme*. Leiden: KITLV Uitgeverij, 1994.

Loh, Wei Leng. "Visitors to the Straits Port of Penang: British Travel Narratives as Resources for Maritime History. In *Memory and Knowledge of the Sea in Southeast Asia*, edited by Danny Wong Tze Ken, 23–32. Kuala Lumpur: Institute of Ocean and Earth Sciences, University of Malaya, 2008.

Lombard, Denys, *Le carrefour javanais: Essai d'histoire globale*. Paris: Édition de l'École des Hautes Études en Sciences Sociales, 1990.

———. "L'horizon insulindien et son importance pour une compréhension globale." *L'Islam de la seconde expansion: Actes du Colloque organisé au Collège de France en mars 1981*, 207–26. Paris: Association pour l'avancement des études islamiques 1983; reedited in *Archipel* 29 (1985): 35–52.

———. *Le sultanat d'Atjéh au temps d'Iskandar Muda (1607–1636)*. Volume 61 of Publications de l'École française d'Extrême-Orient. Paris : École française d'Extrême-Orient, 1967.

———. "Voyageurs français dans l'Archipel insulindien, XVIIe, XVIIIe et XIXe siècles." *Archipel* 1 (1971): 141–68.

Lombard, Denys, and Jean Aubin, eds. *Marchands et hommes d'affaires asiatiques dans l'Océan Indien et la Mer de Chine (13e–20e siècles)*. Paris: Éditions de l'École des Hautes Études en Sciences Sociales, 1988.

Lopez, R. S. "Les méthodes commerciales des marchands occidentaux en Asie du XIe au XIVe siècle." In *Sociétés et compagnies de commerce en Orient et dans l'Océan Indien: Actes du 8e colloque international d'histoire maritime, Beirut, 1966*, edited by M. Mollat. Paris: SEVPEN, 1970.

Lorenzon, David. "Who Invented Hinduism?" *Comparative Studies in Society and History* 41, no. 4 (1999): 630–59.

Louis Forbes, Vivian. *The Maritime Boundaries of the Indian Ocean Region*. Singapore: Singapore University Press, 1995.

Love, John A. *A Natural History of Lighthouses*. Dunbeath: Whittles Publishing, 2015.

Loyre, Ghislaine. "Living and Working Conditions in Philippine Pirate Communities." In *Pirates and Privateers: New Perspectives on the War on Trade in the Eighteenth and Nineteenth Centuries*, edited by David Starkey, E. S. van Eyck van Heslinga, and J. A. de Moor. Exeter: University of Exeter Press, 1997.

Lubeigt, Guy. "Ancient Transpeninsular Trade Roads and Rivalries over the Tenasserim Coasts." In *Commerce et navigation en Asie du sud-est (XIVe–XIXe siècles)*, edited by Nguyễn Thế Anh and Yoshiaki Ishizawa, 47–76. Paris: L'Harmattan, 1999.

Ludden, David, *Early Capitalism and Local History in South Asia*. New York: Oxford University Press, 2005.

MaCaulay, Stewart. "Non-Contractual Relationships in Business: A Preliminary Study." *American Sociological Review* 28 (1963): 55–69.

Macdonald, Charles. "Le culte de la baleine, une exception Vietnamienne?" *Aseanie* 12 (2003): 123–36.

Machado, Pedro, Steve Mullins, and Joseph Christensen, eds. *Pearls, People, and Power: Pearling and Indian Ocean Worlds*. Athens, OH: Ohio University Press, 2019.

Mackie, J. "Changing Patterns of Chinese Big Business in Southeast Asia." In *Southeast Asian Capitalists*, edited by R. McVey. Ithaca, Cornell University Southeast Asia Program, 1992, 161–90.

Mackie, J. A. C. "Overseas Chinese Entrepreneurship." *Asian Pacific Economic Literature* 6 (1): (1992): 41–46.

Mackie, Jamie. "The Economic Roles of Southeast Asian Chinese: Information Gaps and Research Needs." In *Chinese Business Networks*, edited by Chan Kwok Bun. Singapore: Prentice Hall, 2000.

MacKnight, Charles Campbell. *The Voyage to Marege: Macassan Trepangers in Northern Australia*. Carlton: Melbourne University Press, 1976.

Maeda, Narifumi. "Forest and the Sea among the Bugis." *Southeast Asian Studies* 30, no. 4 (1993): 420–26.

Magnis-Suseno, Franz, ed. *Suara dari Aceh: Identifikasi kebutuhan dan keinginan rakyat Aceh.* Jakarta: Yayasan Penguatan Partisipasi Inisiatif dan Kemitraan Masyarakat Sipil Indonesia, 2001.

Mahadevan, R. "Immigrant Entrepreneurs in Colonial Burma—An Exploratory Study of the Role of Nattukottai Chattiars of Tamil Nadu, 1880–1930." *Indian Economic and Social History Review* 15 (1978): 329–58.

Mahmud, Zaharah binti Haji. "The Malay Concept of Tanah Air: The Geographer's Perspective." In *Memory and Knowledge of the Sea in Southeast Asia*, edited by Danny Wong Tze Ken, 5–14. Kuala Lumpur: Institute of Ocean and Earth Sciences, University of Malaya, 2008.

Majul, Cesar Adib. *Muslims in the Philippines.* Quezon City: University of the Philippines Press, 1973.

Malinowski, Branislaw. *Argonauts of the Western Pacific.* London: Routledge & Kegan Paul, 1922.

Manguin, Pierre-Yves. "Brunei Trade with Macao at the Turn of the 19th Century. À propos of a 1819 Letter from Sultan Khan Zul Alam." *Brunei Museum Journal* 6, no. 3, (1987): 16–25.

———. "New Ships for New Networks: Trends in Shipbuilding in the South China Sea in the Fifteenth and Sixteenth Centuries." In *Southeast Asia in the Fifteenth Century: The China Factor*, edited by Geoff Wade and Sun Laichen, 333–58. Singapore: NUS Press, 2010.

———. *Les Nguyễn, Macau et la Portugal: Aspects politiques et commerciaux d'une relation privilégiée en Mer de Chine, 1773–1802.* Paris: École française d'Extrême-Orient, 1984.

———. *Les portugais sur les côtes du Viêt-Nam et du Campā: Étude sur les routes maritimes et les relations commerciales, d'après les sources portugaises (XVIe, XVIIe, XVIIIe siècles).* Paris: EFEO, 1972.

———. "Trading Ships of the South China Sea: Shipbuilding Techniques and Their Role in the Development of Asian Trade Networks." *Journal of the Economic and Social History of the Orient* 36: 253–80.

Mantienne, Frédéric. "Indochinese Societies and European Traders: Different Worlds of Trade?" In *Commerce et navigation en Asie du sud-est (XIVe–XIXe siècles)*, edited by Nguyễn Thế Anh and Yoshiaki Ishizawa, 113–26. Paris: L'Harmattan, 1999.

Mardsen, Richard. *The Nature of Capital: Marx after Foucault.* London: Routledge, 1999.

Margariti, Roxani. *Aden and the Indian Ocean Trade: 150 Years in the Life of a Medieval Arabian Port.* Chapel Hill: University of North Carolina Press, 2007.

Marsh, Zoe, ed. *East Africa through Contemporary Records.* Cambridge: Cambridge University Press, 1961.

Marshall, P. J. "Private Trade in the Indian Ocean Before 1800." In *India and the Indian Ocean 1500–1800*, edited by Ashin Das Gupta and M. N. Pearson, 276–300. Calcutta: Oxford University Press, 1987.

———. *Trade and Conquest: Studies on the Rise of British Dominance in India.* Aldershot: Variorum, 1993.

Marston, John. "Death, Memory and Building: The Non-Cremation of a Cambodian Monk." *Journal of Southeast Asian Studies* 37, no. 3 (2006): 491–505.

Martin, C. G. C. *Maps and Surveys of Malawi: A History of Cartography and the Land Survey Profession, Exploration Methods of David Livingstone on Lake Nyassa, Hydrographic Survey and International Boundaries.* Rotterdam: A. A. Balkema, 1980.

Martin, Esmond Bradley. *Cargoes of the East: The Ports, Trade, and Culture of the Arabian Seas and Western Indian Ocean.* London: Elm Tree Books, 1978.

Martinez, Julia, and Adrian Vickers. *The Pearl Frontier: Indonesian Labor and Indigenous Encounters in Australia's Northern Trading Network.* Honolulu: University of Hawai'i Press, 2015.

Marx, Karl. *Capital.* Volume III. Edited by Friedrich Engels. New York: International Publishers, 1976.

Matsukata Fuyoko, "From the Threat of Roman Catholicism to the Shadow of Western Imperialism." In *Large and Broad: The Dutch Impact on Early Modern Asia,* edited by Yoko Nagazumi, 130–46. Tokyo: Toyo Bunko, 2010.

Masuzawa, Tomoko. *The Invention of World Religions.* Chicago: University of Chicago Press, 2005.

Mathew, K. S. "Trade in the Indian Ocean during the Sixteenth Century and the Portuguese." In *Studies in Maritime History,* edited by K. S. Mathew, 13–28. Pondicherry: Pondicherry University, 1990.

Matsuda, Matt, *Empire of Love: Histories of France and the Pacific.* New York: Oxford University Press, 2005.

———. *Pacific Worlds: A History of Seas, Peoples, and Cultures.* New York: Cambridge University Press, 2012.

Matthew, Johan. *Margins of the Market: Trafficking and Capitalism across the Arabian Sea.* Berkeley: University of California Press, 2016.

Mattulada, H. A. "Manusia dan Kebudayaan Bugis-Makassar dan Kaili di Sulawesi." In *Antropologi Indonesia: Majalah Antropologi Sosial dan Budaya Indonesia* 15, no. 48 (Jan./Apr. 1991): 4–109.

May, Glenn, *The Battle for Batangas: A Philippine Province at War.* New Haven: Yale University Press, 1991.

Maybon, C. B. "Une factorerie anglaise au Tonkin au XVIIe siècle (1672–1697)." *BEFEO* 10 (1910).

Mazru'I, Shaikh al-Amin bin 'Ali al. *The History of the Mazru'i Dynasty.* London: Oxford University Press, 1995.

McCargo, Duncan. "The Politics of Buddhist Identity in Thailand's Deep South: The Demise of Civil Religion." *Journal of Southeast Asian Studies* 40, no. 1 (2009): 11–32.

McClellan, James E. *Colonialism and Science: Saint Domingue in the Old Regime.* Baltimore: Johns Hopkins University Press, 1992.

McCoy, Alfred. *The Politics of Heroin: CIA Complicity in the Global Drug Trade.* New York: Hill Books, 1991.

McCrindle, J. W. *The Christian Topography of Cosmas, an Egyptian Monk.* London: Hakluyt Society, 1897.

McDaniel, Justin. "This Hindu Holy Man Is a Thai Buddhist." *South East Asia Research* 20, no. 2: 2013: 191–209.

McDermott, James. "The Buddhist Saints of the Forest and the Cult of the Amulets: A Study in Charisma, Hagiography, Sectarianism, and Millennial Buddhism by Stanley Tambiah." *Journal of the American Oriental Society* 106, no. 2 (1986): 350.

McDougall, Walter. *Let the Sea Make a Noise: A History of the North Pacific from Magellan to MacArthur.* New York: Harper Perennial, 1993.

McDow, Thomas. *Buying Time: Debt and Mobility in the Western Indian Ocean.* Athens, OH: Ohio University Press, 2018.

McGee, T. G. *The Southeast Asian City: A Social Geography of the Primate Cities of Southeast Asia.* London: Bell, 1967.

McGee, T. G., and Ira Robinson, eds. *The Mega-Urban Regions of Southeast Asia.* Vancouver: UBC Press, 1995.

McHale, Thomas, and Mary McHale, eds. *The Journal of Nathaniel Bowditch in Manila, 1796.* New Haven: Yale University Southeast Asian Studies, 1962.

McKeown, Adam. *Chinese Migrant Networks and Cultural Change: Peru, Chicago, Hawaii, 1900–1936.* Chicago: University of Chicago Press, 2001.

McPherson, Kenneth. *The Indian Ocean: A History of People and the Sea.* Delhi: Oxford University Press, 1993.

McPherson, Kenneth. "Maritime Communities: An Overview." In *Cross Currents and Community Networks: The History of the the Indian Ocean World,* edited by Himanshu Prabha Ray and Edward Alpers, 34–49. New Delhi: Oxford University Press, 2007.

McVey, Ruth. "The Materialization of the Southeast Asian Entrepreneur. In *Southeast Asian Capitalists,* edited by Ruth McVey, 7–34. Ithaca, Cornell University Southeast Asia Program, 1992.

Meijer, J. E. de. "Zeehavens en kustverlichting in Nederlandsch-Indië." *Gedenkboek Koninklijk Instituut Ingenieurs* (1847–97).

Menkhoff, Thomas. "Trade Routes, Trust and Trading Networks: Chinese Family-Based Firms in Singapore and their External Economic Dealings." PhD dissertation. University of Bielefield, Department of Sociology, 1990.

Mertha, Andrew. *Brothers in Arms: Chinese Aid to the Khmer Rouge, 1975–1979.* Ithaca: Cornell University Press, 2014.

Metcalf, Thomas, ed. *Imperial Connections: India in the Indian Ocean Arena, 1860–1920.* Berkeley: University of California Press, 2007.

Meyer, Kathryn, and Terry Parssinen. *Webs of Smoke: Smugglers, Warlords, Spies, and the History of the International Drug Trade.* Lanham, MD: Rowman & Littlefield Publishers, 1998.

Mijer, P. "Geschiedenis der Nederlandsche O.I. bezitingen onder de Fransche heerschappij." *TNI* 2, no. 2 (1839): 229–427.

Mikhail, Alain. *God's Shadow: Sultan Selim, His Ottoman Empire, and the Making of the Modern World.* New York: W. W. Norton, 2020.

Miksic, John. "Before and after Zheng He: Comparing Some Southeast Asian Archaeological Sites of the Fourteenth and Fifteenth Centuries." In *Southeast Asia in the Fifteenth Century: The China Factor,* edited by Geoff Wade and Sun Laichen, 384–408. Singapore: NUS Press, 2010.

Milburn, William. *Oriental Commerce.* 2 volumes. London: Black and Parry Co., 1813.

Miller, A. "The Lighthouse Top I See: Lighthouses as Instruments and Manifestations of State Building in the Early Republic." *Building and Landscapes: Journal of Vernacular Architecture Forum* 17, no. 11 (2010): 13–14.

Miller, Michael. *Europe and the Maritime World: A Twentieth-Century History.* Cambridge: Cambridge University Press, 2012.

Mills, J. V. G.. trans. *Ying-yai Sheng-lan: The Overall Survey of the Ocean's Shores, by Ma Huan.* London: Haklyut Society, 1970.

Ming, Hanneke. "Barracks-Concubinage in the Indies, 1887–1920." *Indonesia* 35 (1983): 65–93.

Mintz, Sidney W. *Sweetness and Power: The Place of Sugar in Modern History.* New York: Penguin Books, 1985.

Miran, Jonathan. *Red Sea Citizens: Cosmopolitan Society and Cultural Change in Massawa.* Bloomington: Indiana University Press, 2009.

Mizushima, Tsukaya, George Souza, and Dennis Flynn, eds. *Hinterlands and Commodities: Place, Space, Time and the Political Economic Development of Asia over the Long Eighteenth Century.* Leiden: Brill, 2015.

Mollat [du Jourdin], Michel. "Les contacts historiques de l'Afrique et de Madagascar avec l'Asie du sud et du sud-est: Le rôle de l'Océan indien." *Archipel* 21 (1981): 35–54.

———. "Passages français dans l'Océan indien au temps de Francois Ier," *Studia XI* (Lisbon, 1963): 239–48.

Monmonier, Mark. "Cartography: Distortions, World-views and Creative Solutions." *Progress in Human Geography* 29, no. 2 (2005): 217–24.

Montella, Andrea. "Chinese Porcelain as a Symbol of Power on the East African Coast from the 14th Century Onward." *Ming Qing Yanjiu* 20, 1, 2016: 74–93.

Moor, J. A. de. "'A Very Unpleasant Relationship': Trade and Strategy in the Eastern Seas, Anglo-Dutch Relations in the Nineteenth Century from a Colonial Perspective." In *Navies and Armies: The Anglo-Dutch Relationship in War and Peace 1688–1988*, edited by G. J. A. Raven and N. A. M. Rodger, 46–69. Edinburgh: Donald and Co., 1990.

Moosvi, Shireen. "The Gujarat Ports and Their Hinterland: The Economic Relationship." In *Ports and Their Hinterlands in India, 1700–1950*, edited by Indu Banga, 121–30. Delhi: Manohar, 1992.

Mori, A. "Le Nostre Colonie del Mar Rosso Giudicate dalla Stanley." *Boll. Sez. Fiorentina della Soc. Africana d'Italia* (May 1886).

Morris, James/Jan. *Pax Britannica Trilogy: Heaven's Command; Pax Britannica; Farewell the Trumpets.* London: Folio Society: 1993.

Mudimbe, V. Y. *The Invention of Africa.* Bloomington: Indiana University Press, 1988.

Murakami, Ei. "Trade and Crisis: China's Hinterlands in the Eighteenth Century." In *Place, Space, Time and the Political Development of Asia over the Long Eighteenth Century*, edited by Tsukusa Mizushima, George Bryan Souza, and Dennis Flynn, 215–34. Leiden: Brill, 2015.

Mukmin, Mohamed Jamil bin. *Melaka pusat penyebaran Islam di nusantara.* Kuala Lumpur: Nurin Enterprise, 1994.

Muller, H. P. N. *De Oost-Indische Compagnie in Cambodja en Laos.* The Hague: Martinus Nijhoff, 1917.

Mullins, Steve. "Vrijbuiters! Australian Pearl-Shellers and Colonial Order in the Late Nineteenth-Century Moluccas." *The Mariner's Mirror* 96, no. 1 (2010): 26–41.

Mumford, Lewis. *The City in History.* New York: Harcourt, Brace, Jovanovich, 1961; repr. 1989).

———. *Technics and Civilization.* New York, Harcourt, Brace, and World, 1963.

Mungello, David E. *The Great Encounter of China and the West, 1500–1800.* Lanham, MD: Rowman & Littlefield Publishers, 1999.

Munoz, Paul Michel. *Early Kingdoms of the Indonesian Archipelago and the Malay Peninsula.* Paris: Éditions Didier Millet, 2006.

Murray, Dian. *Conflict and Coexistence: The Sino-Vietnamese Maritime Boundaries in Historical Perspective.* Madison: Center for Southeast Asian Studies, University of Wisconsin, 1988.

————. *Pirates of the South China Coast (1790–1810)*. Stanford: Stanford University Press, 1987.

Nabhan, Gary Paul. *Cumin, Camels, and Caravans: A Spice Odyssey*. Berkeley: University of California Press, 2014.

Nair, Janaki. *Mysore Modern: Rethinking the Region under Princely Rule*. Minneapolis: University of Minnesota Press, 2011.

Naulleau, Gérard. "Islam and Trade: The Case of Some Merchant Families from the Gulf." In *Asian Merchants and Businessmen in the Indian Ocean and the China Sea*, edited by Denys Lombard and Jan Aubin, 297–309. Oxford: Oxford University Press, 2000.

Nazery, Khalid, Margaret Anf, and Zuliati Md. Joni. "The Importance of the Maritime Sector in Socio-Economic Development: A Southeast Asian Perspective." In *Maritime Social and Economic Developments in Southeast Asia*, edited by Hanizah Idris, Tan Wan Hin, and Mohammad Raduan Mohd. Ariff, 9–30. Kuala Lumpur: Institute of Ocean and Earth Sciences, University of Malaya, 2008.

Needham, Joseph, ed. *Science and Civilisation in China*. Volume IV, part III. Cambridge: Cambridge University Press, 1971.

Nelson, Samuel. *Colonialism in the Congo Basin, 1880–1940*. Athens, OH: Ohio University Center for International Studies, 1994.

Nes, J. F. van. "De Chinezen op Java." *Tijdschrift loor Nederlandesh Indië* 13, no. 1 (1851): 239–54, 292–314.

Ng, Chin Keong. "The Chinese in Riau: A Community on an Unstable and Restrictive Frontier." Unpublished paper. Singapore: Institute of Humanities and Social Sciences, Nanyang University, 1976.

————. *Trade and Society: The Amoy Network on the China Coast*. Singapore: Singapore University Press, 1983.

Nguyễn Long Kerry. "Vietnamese Ceramic Trade to the Philippines in the Seventeenth Century." *Journal of Southeast Asian Studies* 30, no. 1 (1999): 1–21.

Nguyen Quoc Thanh. *Le culte de la baleine: Un héritage multiculturel du Vietnam maritime*. Aix: Presses Universitaires de Provence, 2017.

————. "The Whaler Cult in Central Vietnam: A Multicultural Heritage in Southeast Asia." In *Memory and Knowledge of the Sea in Southeast Asia*, edited by Danny Wong Tze Ken, 77–95. Kuala Lumpur: Institute of Ocean and Earth Sciences, University of Malaya, 2008.

Nguyễn Thế Anh. "Ambivalence and Ambiguity: Traditional Vietnam's Incorporation of External Cultural and Technical Contributions." *East Asian Science* 40, no. 4 (2003): 94–113.

————. "From Indra to Maitreya: Buddhist Influence in Vietnamese Political Thought." *Journal of Southeast Asian Studies*, 33, no. 2 (2002): 225–41.

————. "Trade Relations between Vietnam and the Countries of the Southern Seas in the First Half of the Nineteenth Century." In *Commerce et navigation en Asie du sud-est (XIVe–XIXe siècles)*, edited by Nguyễn Thế Anh and Yoshiaki Ishizawa, 171–85. Paris: L'Harmattan, 1999.

Nguyễn Thế Anh and Yoshiaki Ishizawa, eds. *Commerce et navigation en Asie du sud-est (XIVe–XIXe siècles)*. Paris: L'Harmattan, 1999.

Nguyễn Thúa Hy, *Economic History of Hanoi in the 17th, 18th and 19th Centuries*. Hanoi: ST Publisher, 2002.

Nicholl, Robert. *European Sources for the History of the Sultanate of Brunei in the Sixteenth Century*. Bandar Seri Begawan: Muzium Brunei, 1895.

Nicholls, C. S. *The Swahili Coast: Politics, Diplomacy, and Trade on the East African Littoral, 1798–1856*. London: Allen & Unwin, 1971.

Niermeyer, J. F. "Barriere-riffen en atollen in de Oost Indiese Archipel." *Tijdschrift voor Aardrijkskundige* (1911): 877–94.

Niu Junkai and Li Qingxin. "Chinese 'Political Pirates' in the Seventeenth-Century Gulf of Tongking." In *The Tongking Gulf through History*, edited by Nola Cooke, Tana Li, and Jamie Anderson, 133–42. Philadelphia; University of Pennsylvania Press, 2011.

Noonsuk, Wannasarn. "Archaeology and Cultural Geography of Tambralinga in Peninsular Siam." PhD thesis. Cornell University, History of Art Department, 2012.

Nordin, Mardiana. "Undang-Undang Laut Melaka: A Note on Malay Maritime Law in the Fifteenth Century." In *Memory and Knowledge of the Sea in Southeast Asia*, edited by Danny Wong Tze Ken, 15–22. Kuala Lumpur: Institute of Ocean and Earth Sciences, University of Malaya, 2008.

Norton, Marcy. *Sacred Gifts, Profane Pleasures: A History of Tobacco and Chocolate in the Atlantic World*. Ithaca: Cornell University Press, 2010.

Nuldyn, Zam. *Cerita purba: Dewi Krakatau*. Jakarta: Penerbit Firma Hasmar, 1976.

Nur, B. "Bitjara tentang perahu: Bagaimana cara pembinaan dan motorisasi perahu lajar?" *Dunia Maritim* 21, no. 9 (1971), 15–28.

———. "Mengenal potensi rakyat di bidang angkutan laut Part XI." *Dunia Maritim* 19, no. 7 (1969): 17–19.

———. "Mengenal potensi rakyat di bidang angkutan laut Part XVI." *Dunia Maritim* 20, no. 3 (1970): 19–21.

Nurcahyani, Lisyawati. *Kota Pontianak sebagai bandar dagang di jalur sutra*. Jakarta: Departemen Pendidikan dan Kebudayaan, Direktorat Sejarah dan Nilai Tradisional, Proyek Inventarisasi dan Dokumentasi Sejarah Nasional, 1999.

Obeyesekere, Gananath. *The Apotheosis of Captain Cook: European Mythmaking in the Pacific*. Princeton: Princeton University Press, 1992.

O'Connor, Richard. *A Theory of Indigenous Southeast Asian Urbanism*. Singapore: ISEAS Research Monograph 38, 1983.

O'Connor, Stanley. *Hindu Gods of Peninsular Siam*. Ascona, Switzerland: Artibus Asiae Publishers, 1972.

———, ed. *The Archaeology of Peninsular Siam*. Bangkok: The Siam Society, 1986.

Ohorella, G. A., ed. *Ternate sebagai bandar di jalur Sutra: Kumpulan makalah diskusi*. Jakarta: Departemen Pendidikan dan Kebudayaan, Direktorat Sejarah dan Nilai Tradisional, Proyek Inventarisasi dan Dokumentasi Sejarah Nasional, 1997.

Oki, Akira. "The River Trade in Central and South Sumatra in the Nineteenth Century." In *Environment, Agriculture, and Society in the Malay World*, edited by Tsuyoshi Kato, Muchtar Lufti, and Narafumi Maeda, 3–48. Kyoto: Center for Southeast Asian Studies, 1986.

Omohundro, John T. *Chinese Merchant Families in Iloilo: Commerce and Kin in a Central Philippine City*. Quezon City: Ateneo de Manila University Press, and Athens, OH: Ohio University Press, 1981.

———. "Social Networks and Business Success for the Philippine Chinese." In *The Chinese in Southeast Asia. Volume 1: Ethnicity and Economic Activity*, edited by Linda Y. C. Lim and L. A. Peter Gosling, 65–85. Singapore: Maruzen Asia, 1983.

Ong, Aiwha. *Flexible Citizenship: The Cultural Logics of Transnationality.* Durham: Duke University Press, 1999.

Ong Eng Die. *Chinezen in Nederlansch-Indië: Sociographie van een Indonesische bevolkingsgroep.* Assen: Van Gorcum and Co., 1943.

Oonk, Gijsbert. *The Karimjee Jiwanjee Family, Merchant Princes of East Africa, 1800–2000.* Amsterdam: Pallas, 2009.

Oort, W. B. "Hoe een Kaart tot Stand Komt." *Onze Eeuw* 4 (1909): 363–65.

Ota, Atsushi. *Changes of Regime and Social Dynamics in West Java Society, State, and the Outer World of Banten, 1750–1830.* Leiden: Brill, 2006.

Otter, Chris. *The Victorian Eye: A Political History of Light and Vision in Britain, 1800–1900.* Chicago: University of Chicago Press, 2008.

Ouchi, William G. "Markets, Bureaucracies and Clans." *Administrative Science Quarterly* 25 (1980): 129–41.

Owen, John Roger. "Give Me a Light? The Development and Regulation of Ships' Navigation Lights up to the Mid-1960s." *International Journal of Maritime History* 25, no. 1 (2013): 173–203.

Pacho, Arturo. "The Chinese Community in the Philippines: Status and Conditions." *Sojourn* (Singapore; Feb. 1986): 80–83.

Padrón, Ricardo. *The Indies of the Setting Sun: How Early Modern Spain Mapped the Far East as the Transpacific West.* Chicago: University of Chicago Press, 2020.

Paine, Lincoln. *The Sea and Civilization: A Maritime History of the World.* New York: Alfred Knopf, 2013.

Painter, Joe. "Cartographic Anxiety and the Search for Regionality." *Environment and Planning A* 40 (2008): 342–61.

Palanca, Ellen H. "The Economic Position of the Chinese in the Philippines." *Philippine Studies* 25 (1977): 82–88.

Pan, Lynn. *Sons of the Yellow Emperor: A History of the Chinese Diaspora.* New York: Kodansha International, 1994.

Panglaykim, J., and I. Palmer. "The Study of Entrepreneurship in Developing Countries: The Development of One Chinese Concern in Indonesia." *Journal of Southeast Asian Studies* 1, no. 1 (1970): 85–95.

Park, Hyunhee. *Mapping the Chinese and Islamic Worlds: Cross-Cultural Exchange in Pre-Modern Asia.* Cambridge: Cambridge University Press, 2012.

Pariwono, J. I., A. G. Ilahude, and M. Hutomo. "Progress in Oceanography of the Indonesian Seas: A Historical Perspective." *Oceanography* 18, no. 4 (2005): 42–49.

Parker, Andrew. "On the Origin of Optics." *Optics and Laser Technology* 43 (2011): 323–29.

Parker, Geoffrey. *The Military Revolution: Military Innovation and the Rise of the West, 1500–1800.* Cambridge: Cambridge University Press, 1996.

Parkinson, C. Northcote. *Trade in the Eastern Seas (1793–1813).* Cambridge: Cambridge University Press, 1937.

Pearson, Michael. *The Indian Ocean.* New York: Routledge, 2003.

———. *Port Cities and Intruders: The Swahili Coast, India, and Portugal in the Early Modern Era.* Baltimore: Johns Hopkins University Press, 1998.

———. "Studying the Indian Ocean World: Problems and Opportunities." In *Cross Currents and Community Networks: The History of the the Indian Ocean World,* edited by Himanshu Prabha Ray and Edward Alpers, 15–33. New Delhi: Oxford University Press, 2007.

———, ed. *Trade, Circulation, and Flow in the Indian Ocean World*. London: Palgrave Series in the Indian Ocean World, 2015.

———. *The World of the Indian Ocean, 1500–1800: Studies on Economic, Social, and Cultural History*. Aldershot, UK: Ashgate, 2005.

Pearson, M. N. "India and the Indian Ocean in the Sixteenth Century." In *India and the Indian Ocean 1500–1800*, edited by Ashin Das Gupta and M. N. Pearson, 71–93. Calcutta: Oxford University Press, 1987.

———. "Indians in East Africa: The Early Modern Period." In *Politics and Trade in the Indian Ocean World*, edited by R. Mukherjee and L. Subramanian, 227–49. Delhi: Oxford University Press, 1998.

———. *Spices in the Indian Ocean World*. Ashgate: Variorum, 1996.

Pelras, Christian. *The Bugis*. Oxford: Blackwell, 1996.

Perkins, Chris. "Cartography—Cultures of Mapping: Power in Practice." *Progress in Human Geography* 28, no. 3 (2004): 381–91.

Pham, Charlotte. "The Vietnamese Coastline: A Maritime Cultural Landscape." In *The Sea, Identity and History: From the Bay of Bengal to the South China Sea*, edited by Satish Chandra and Himanshu Prabha Ray, 137–67. Delhi: Society for Indian Ocean Studies, 2013.

Phillimore, R. H. "An Early Map of the Malay Peninsula." *Imago Mundi* 13 (1956): 175–79.

Phipps, John. *A Practical Treatise on Chinese and Eastern Trade*. Calcutta: Thacker and Com., 1835.

Phoa Liong Gie. "De economische positie der Chineezen in Nederlandesch Indië." *Koloniale Studiën* 20, no. 5 (1936): 97–119.

Phongpaichit, Pasuk, and Chris Baker. *Thailand: Economy and Politics*. Kuala Lumpur: Oxford University Press, 1995.

Pigafetta, Antonio. "The First Voyage Round the World," and "De Moluccis Insulis." In *The Philippine Islands*, edited by Emma Blair and James Robertson, 33:211 and passim; and 1:328, respectively. Cleveland: Arthur H. Clark, 1903.

Pinto, Mendes. *The Travels of Mendes Pinto*. Translated by Rebecca Catz. Chicago: University of Chicago Press, 1990.

Plas, C. C. van der. *Tonkin 1644/45, Journal van de Reis van Anthonio Brouckhorst*. Amsterdam: Koninklijk Instituut voor de Trompen, Mededeling No. CXVII, 1995.

Po, Ronald. *The Blue Frontier: Maritime Vision and Power in the Qing Empire*. Cambridge: Cambridge University Press, 2018.

Poillard, Elizabeth Ann. "Indian Spices and Roman 'Magic' in Imperial and Late Antique Indomediterranean." *Journal of World History* 24, no. 1 (2013): 1–23.

Pointon, A. G. *The Bombay-Burma Trading Corporation*. Southampton: Milbrook Press, 1964.

Polo, Marco. *The Travels of Marco Polo*. Edited and revised from William Marsden's translation by Manuel Komroff. New York: Modern Library, 2001.

Pombejra, Dhiravat na. "Ayutthaya at the End of the Seventeenth Century: Was There a Shift to Isolation?" In *Southeast Asia in the Early Modern Era: Trade, Power, and Belief*, edited by Anthony Reid, 250–72. Ithaca: Cornell University Press, 1993.

Pomeranz, Kenneth. *The Great Divergence: Europe, China, and the Making of the Modern World Economy*. Princeton: Princeton University Press, 2000.

Post, P. "Japanese bedrijfvigheid in Indonesia, 1868–1942." PhD dissertation. Amsterdam: Free University of Amsterdam, 1991.

Post, Peter. "Chinese Business Networks and Japanese Capital in Southeast Asia, 1880–1940: Some Preliminary Observations." In *Chinese Business Enterprises in Asia*, edited by Rajeswary A. Brown. London and New York: Routledge, 1995.

———. "Japan and the Integration of the Netherlands East Indies into the World Economy, 1868–1942." *Review of Indonesian and Malaysan Affairs* 27, nos. 1–2 (1993): 134–65.

Prakash, Om. *The Dutch East India Company and the Economy of Bengal, 1630–1720*. Princeton: Princeton University Press, 1985.

———. *The Dutch Factories in India, 1617–1623*. Delhi: Munshiram Manoharlal, 1984.

———. "European Corporate Enterprises and the Politics of Trade in India, 1600–1800." In *Politics and Trade in the Indian Ocean World*, edited by R. Mukherjee and L. Subramanian, 165–82. Delhi: Oxford University Press, 1998.

———. *Precious Metals and Commerce: The Dutch East India Company and the Indian Ocean Trade*. Ashgate: Variorum, 1994.

———, ed. *European Commercial Expansion in Early Modern Asia*. Aldershot: Variorum, 1997.

Prange, Sebastian. "Measuring by the Bushel: Reweighing the Indian Ocean Pepper Trade." *Historical Research* 84, no. 224 (May 2011): 212–35.

Prescott, J. R. V. *Political Frontiers and Political Boundaries*. London: Allen and Unwin, 1987.

Prestholdt, Jeremy. *Domesticating the World: African Consumerism and the Genealogies of Globalization*. Berkeley: University of California Press, 2008.

Preston, P. W. *Pacific Asia in the Global System: An Introduction*. Oxford: Blackwell, 1998.

Prince, G. "Dutch Economic Policy in Indonesia." In *Economic Growth in Indonesia, 1820–1940*, edited by A. Madison and G. Prince, 203–26. Dordrecht and Providence: Foris, 1989.

Pronk van Hoogeveen, D. J. "De KPM in na-oorlogse Jaren." *Economisch Weekblad* 14e (25 December, 1948): 1001–2.

Ptak, Roderich. "China and the Trade in Tortoise-Shell." In *China's Seaborne Trade with South and Southeast Asia*, edited by Roderich Ptak. (Abingdon: Variorum, 1999).

———. *Maritime Animals in Traditional China*. Wiesbaden: Harrassowitz Verlag, 2011.

———. "Ming Maritime Trade to Southeast Asia, 1368–1567: Visions of a 'System.'" In *From the Mediterranean to the China Sea: Miscellaneous Notes*, edited by Claude Guillot, Denys Lombard, and Roderich Ptak, 157–91. Wiesbaden: Harrassowitz Verlag, 1998.

———. "Notes on the Word 'Shanhu' and Chinese Coral Imports from Maritime Asia, 1250–1600." In *China's Seaborne Trade with South and Southeast Asia (1200–1750)*, edited by Roderich Ptak. Abingdon: Variorum, 1999.

Puangthong Rungwasdisab. "Siam and the Control of the Trans-Mekong Trading Networks." In *Water Frontier: Commerce and the Chinese in the Lower Mekong Region, 1750–1880*, edited by Nola Cooke and Tana Li, 101–18. New York: Rowman & Littlefield, 2004.

Purcell, Steven W., Yves Samyn, and Chantal Conand. *Commercially Important Sea Cucumbers of the World*. Rome: Food and Agriculture Organization of the United Nations, 2012.

Pye, Michael. *The Edge of the World: A Cultural History of the North Sea and the Transformation of Europe*. New York: Pegasus Books, 2014.

Pyenson, Lewis. *Empire of Reason: Exact Sciences in Indonesia, 1840–1940*. Leiden: E. J. Brill, 1989.

Qasim, S. Z. "Concepts of Tides, Navigation and Trade in Ancient India." *Journal of Indian Ocean Studies* 8, nos. 1/2 (2000): 97–102.

Qasim, S. Zahoor. "The Indian Ocean and Cyclones." *Journal of Indian Ocean Studies* 1, no. 2 (1994): 30–40.

————. "The Indian Ocean and Mangroves." *Journal of Indian Ocean Studies* 2, no. 1 (1994) 1–10.

Qin, Dashu. "Archaeological Investigations of Chinese Ceramics Excavated from Kenya." In *Ancient Silk Trade Routes: Selected Works from Symposium on Cross-Cultural Exchanges and Their Legacies in Asia*, edited by Qin Dashu and Jian Yuan, chapter 4. Singapore: World Scientific Publishing, 2015.

Qiu Liben. "The Chinese Networks in Southeast Asia: Past, Present and Future." In *Chinese Business Networks*, edited by Chan Kwok Bun. Singapore: Prentice Hall, 2000.

Radwan, Ann Bos. *The Dutch in Western India, 1601–1632*. Calcutta: Firma KLM, 1978.

Raffles, Sir Thomas Stamford. *History of Java*. London: Murray, 1830–31.

Ragionamenti di Francesco Carletti fiorentino sopra le cose da lui vedute ne'suoi viaggi si dell'Indie Occidentali, e Orientali come d'altri paesi. All'Illustriss. Sig. Marchese Cosimo da Castiglione gentiluomo della Camera del Serenissimo Granduca di Toscana. Part II: *Ragionamenti . . . sopra le cose da lui vedute ne' suoi viaggi dell'Indie Orientali, e d'altri paesi*. Florence, 1701.

Rao, S. R., ed. *Recent Advances in Marine Archaeology: Proceedings of the Second Indian Conference on Marine Archaeology of the Indian Ocean*. Goa: National Institute of Oceanography, 1991.

Rao, T. S. S., and Ray Griffiths. *Understanding the Indian Ocean: Perspectives on Oceanography*. Paris: UNESCO, 1998.

Ray, Aniruddha. "Cambay and Its Hinterland: The Early Eighteenth Century." In *Ports and Their Hinterlands in India, 1700–1950*, edited by Indu Banga, 131–52. Delhi: Manohar, 1992.

Ray, Haraprasad. "Sino-Indian Historical Relations: Quilon and China." *Journal of Indian Ocean Studies* 8, nos. 1/2 (2000): 116–28.

Ray, Himanshu Prabha. "Crossing the Seas: Connecting Maritime Spaces in Colonial India." In *Cross Currents and Community Networks: The History of the the Indian Ocean World*, edited by Himanshu Prabha Ray and Edward Alpers, 50–78. New Delhi: Oxford University Press, 2007.

————. "Far-Flung Fabrics—Indian Textiles in Ancient Maritime Trade." In *Textiles in Indian Ocean Societies*, edited by Ruth Barnes, 17–37. New York: Routledge, 2005.

Ray, Indrani, ed. *The French East India Company and the Trade of the Indian Ocean*. Calcutta: Munshiram, 1999.

Ray, R. "Chinese Financiers and Chetti Bankers in Southern Waters: Asian Mobile Credit during the Anglo-Dutch Competition for the Trade of the Eastern Archipelago in the Nineteenth Century." *Itinerario* 1 (1987): 209–34.

Redding, S. Gordon. *The Spirit of Chinese Capitalism*. Berlin: De Gruyter, 1990.

————. "Weak Organizations and Strong Linkages: Managerial Ideology and Chinese Family Business Networks. In *Business Networks and Economic Development in East and Southeast Asia*, edited by Gary Hamilton. Hong Kong: Center of Asian Studies, University of Hong Kong, 1991.

Rediker, Marcus. *Between the Devil and the Deep Blue Sea: Merchant Seamen, Pirates, and the Anglo-American Maritime World, 1700–1750*. Cambridge: Cambridge University Press, 1989.

Rediker, Marcus, and Peter Linebaugh. *The Many-Headed Hydra: Sailors, Slaves, Commoners, and the Hidden History of the Revolutionary Atlantic*. New York: Beacon Press, 2013.

Reid, Anthony. "Aceh between Two Worlds: An Intersection of Southeast Asia and the Indian Ocean." In *Cross Currents and Community Networks: The History of the the Indian Ocean World*, edited by Himanshu Prabha Ray and Edward Alpers, 100–22. New Delhi: Oxford University Press, 2007.

———. *Charting the Shape of Early Modern Southeast Asian History.* Chiang Mai: Silkworm, 1999.

———. "The End of Dutch Relations with the Nguyen State, 1651–2: Excerpts Translated by Anthony Reid." In *Southern Vietnam under the Nguyen: Documents on the Economic History of Cochin China (Dang Trong), 1602–1777,* edited by Tana Li and Anthony Reid. Singapore: ISEAS, 1993.

———. "Europe and Southeast Asia: The Military Balance." *James Cook University of North Queensland, Occasional Paper #16.* Townsville: Queensland University Press, 1982.

———. "Hybrid Identities in the Fifteenth-Century Straits." In *Southeast Asia in the Fifteenth Century: The China Factor,* edited by Geoff Wade and Sun Laichen, 307–32. Singapore: NUS Press, 2010.

———. "Islamization and Christianization in Southeast Asia: The Critical Phase, 1550–1650." In *Southeast Asia in the Early Modern Era: Trade, Power, and Belief,* edited by Anthony Reid, 151–79. Ithaca: Cornell University Press, 1993.

———. *Slavery, Bondage, and Dependency in Southeast Asia.* St. Lucia: University of Queensland Press, 1983.

———. *Southeast Asia in the Age of Commerce 1450–1680.* Volume I: *The Lands below the Winds.* Volume II: *Expansion and Crisis.* New Haven: Yale University Press, 1988, 1993.

———. "The Structure of Cities in Southeast Asia, 15th to 17th Centuries." *Journal of Southeast Asian Studies* 11 (1980): 235–50.

———. "The Unthreatening Alternative: Chinese Shipping in Southeast Asia 1567–1842." *RIMA* 27, nos. 1–2 (1993): 13–32.

———, ed. *Sojourners and Settlers: Histories of Southeast Asia and the Chinese.* Sydney: Allen & Unwin, 1996.

Reid, Daniel. *Chinese Herbal Medicine.* London, Thornsons Publishing Group, 1987.

Reinaud, M. *Géographie d'Aboul-feda.* Paris, 1848.

Resink, G. J. "De Archipel voor Joseph Conrad." *BTLV* (1959): ii.

Ricci, Ronit. *Islam Translated: Literature, Conversion and the Arabic Cosmopolis of South and Southeast Asia.* Chicago: University of Chicago Press, 2011.

Risso, Patricia. "India and the Gulf: Encounters from the Mid-Sixteenth Century to the Mid-Twentieth Centuries." In *The Persian Gulf in History,* edited by Lawrence Potter, 189–206. New York: Palgrave Macmillan, 2009.

———. *Merchants and Faith: Muslim Commerce and Culture in the Indian Ocean.* Boulder: Westview, 1995.

———. *Oman and Muscat: An Early Modern History.* New York: St. Martin's Press, 1986.

Robinson, R. "Non-European Foundations of European Imperialism: Sketch for a Theory of Collaboration." In *Studies in the Theory of Imperialism,* edited by R. Owen and B. Sutcliffe, 117–41. London: Longman, 1972.

Rodriguez, Noelle. *Zamboanga: A World between Worlds, Cradle of an Emerging Civilization.* Pasig City: Fundación Santiago, 2003.

Rosaldo, Renato. *Ilongot Headhunting.* Palo Alto: Stanford University Press, 1980.

Rosario-Braid, Florangel, ed. *Muslim and Christian Cultures: In Search of Commonalities.* Manila: Asian Institute of Journalism and Communication, 2002.

Rose di Meglio, Rita. "Il commercio arabo con la Cina dal X secolo all'avvento dei Mongoli." *Ann. Ist. Univ. Orient* (Naples, 1965): 137–75.

———. "Il commercio arabo con la Cina dalla Gahiliyya al X secolo." *Annali del Instituto Universitario Orientale* (Naples, 1964): 523–52.

Rosser, W. H., and J. F. Imray. *Indian Ocean Directory: The Seaman's Guide to the Navigation of the Indian Ocean, China Sea, and West Pacific Ocean.* London: n.d.

Roszko, Edyta. "Fishers and Territorial Anxieties in China and Vietnam: Narratives of the South China Sea beyond the Frame of the Nation." *Cross-Currents: East Asian History and Culture Review* 21 (2016): 19–46.

———."Geographies of Connection and Disconnection: Narratives of Seafaring in Ly Son." In *Connected and Disconnected in Vietnam: Remaking Social Relationships in a Post-Socialist Nation,* edited by Philip Taylor, 347–77. Canberra: Australian National University Press, 2016.

Rowe, William. *Hankow.* 2 volumes. Stanford: Stanford University Press, 1984; repr. 1989.

Russell, Susan, ed. *Ritual, Power, and Economy: Upland-Lowland Contrasts in Mainland Southeast Asia.* DeKalb: Center for Southeast Asian Studies, 1989.

Russell-Wood, A. J. R. "The Expansion of Europe Revisited: The European Impact on World History and Global Interaction, 1450–1800." *Itinerario* 23, no. 1 (1994): 89–94.

Sahai, Baldeo. *Indian Shipping: A Historical Survey.* Delhi: Ministry of Information, 1996.

Sahlins, Marshall. "Cosmologies of Capitalism: The Trans-Pacific Sector of the World System." In *Culture, Power, and History: A Reader in Contemporary Theory,* edited by Nicholas Dirks, Geoff Eley, and Sherry Orner, 412–55. Princeton: Princeton University Press, 1994.

———. *How "Natives" Think: About Captain Cook, for Example.* Chicago: The University of Chicago Press, 1995.

———. *Islands of History.* Chicago: The University of Chicago Press, 1985.

Said, H. Mohammad. *Aceh sepanjang abad.* Volume I. Medan: P. T. Harian Waspada, 1981.

Saleeby, Najeeb. *The History of Sulu.* Manila: Filipiniana Book Guild, 1963.

Saleh, Muhammad. *Syair Lampung dan Anyer dan Tanjung Karang naik air laut.* Singapore: Penerbit Haji Sa[h]id, 1886.

Salmon, Claudine. "Les marchands chinois en Asie du Sud-est. In *Marchands et hommes d'affaires asiatiques dans l'Océan Indien et la Mer de Chine 13e–20e siècles,* edited by D. Lombard and J. Aubin, 330–51. Paris: Éditions de l'École des Hautes Études en Sciences Sociales, 1988.

———. "Regards de quelques voyageurs chinois sur le Viêtnam du XVIIe siècle." In *Asia Maritima: Images et réalité: Bilder und Wirklichkeit 1200–1800,* edited by Denys Lombard and Roderich Ptak, 117–46. Wiesbaden: Harrassowitz Verlag, 1994.

San Nyein U. "Trans Peninsular Trade and Cross Regional Warfare between the Maritime Kingdoms of Ayudhya and Pegu in mid-16th–mid-17th century." In [Anon.], *Port Cities and Trade in Western Southeast Asia,* 55–64. Bangkok: Institute of Asian Studies, Chulalongkorn University, 1998.

Sandhu, K., and A. Mani. *Indians in South East Asia.* Singapore: ISEAS, 1993.

Sandhu, Kernial, and A. Mani, eds. *Indian Communities in Southeast Asia.* Singapore: ISEAS/ Times Academic Press, 1993.

Sandhu, Kernial Singh, and Paul Wheatley, eds. *Melaka: The Transformations of a Malay Capital, c. 1400–1980.* Kuala Lumpur: Oxford University Press, 1983.

Sangwan, Satpal. *Science, Technology and Colonisation: An Indian Experience 1757–1857.* Delhi: Anamika Parakashan, 1991.

Santen, H. W. van. *De vedernegide Oost-Indische Compagnie in Gujarat en Hindustan 1620–1660.* PhD thesis. Leiden: Leiden University, 1982.

Santos, M. *The Shared Space: The Two Circuits of the Urban Economy Underdevelopment Concept.* London: Methuen, 1979.

Sardesai, R. S. *British Trade and Expansion in Southeast Asia (1830–1914).* New Delhi: Allied Publishers, 1977.

Sartori, Andrew. *Bengal in Global Concept History: Culturalism in the Age of Capital.* Chicago: University of Chicago Press, 2008.

Sassetti, F[rancesco], a S.E. il Cardinale F. de'Medici. *Lettere edite e inedite di Filippo Sassetti,* raccolte e annotate da E. Marcucci. Florence: 1855.

Sather, Clifford. *The Bajau Laut: Adaptation, History, and Fate in a Maritime Fishing Society of South-Eastern Sabah.* Kuala Lumpur: Oxford University Press, 1997.

———. "Seven Fathoms: A Bajau Laut Narrative Tale from the Semporna District of Sabah." *Brunei Museum Journal* 3, no. 3 (1975): 30.

Satia, Priya. *Spies in Arabia: The Great War and the Cultural Foundations of Britain's Covert Empire in the Middle East.* New York: Oxford University Press, 2009.

Scammell, G. V. "European Exiles, Renegades and Outlaws and the Maritime Economy of Asia, c. 1500–1750." *Modern Asian Studies* 26, no. 4 (1992): 641–61.

Schaeffer, Edward. *The Golden Peaches of Samarkand.* Berkeley: University of California Press, 1967.

Schelle, C. J. van. "De geologische mijnbouwkundige opneming van een gedeelte van Borneo's westkust: Rapport #1: Opmerking Omtrent het Winnen van Delfstoffen" *Jaarboek Mijnwezen* 1 (1881): 260–63.

Schober, Juliane, and Steven Collins, eds. *Theravada Encounters with Modernity.* London: Routledge, 2019.

Schofield, Clive. *The Maritime Political Boundaries of the World.* Leiden: Martinus Nijhoff, 2005.

Scholten, C. *De Munten van de Nederlandsche gebiedsdeelen overzee, 1601–1948.* Amsterdam: J. Schulman, 1951.

Schottenhammer, Angela. "The 'China Seas' in World History: A General Outline of the Role of Chinese and East Asian Maritime Space from Its Origin to c. 1800." *Journal of Marine and Island Culture* 1: 2012: 63–89.

———. *Early Global Interconnectivity in the Indian Ocean World.* London. Palgrave Series in the Indian Ocean World, 2019.

———, ed. *The East Asian 'Mediterranean': Maritime Crossroads of Culture, Commerce, and Human Migration.* Wiesbaden: Harrassowitz Verlag, 2008.

Schrikker, Alicia. *Dutch and British Colonial Intervention in Sri Lanka, 1780–1815: Expansion and Reform.* Leiden: Brill, 2007.

Schuetz, A. "The Stranger: An Essay in Social Psychology." *American Journal of Psychology* 49 (1944): 499–507.

Schurhammer, G. O. "Il contributo dei missionary cattolici nei secoli XVI e XVII alla conoscenza del Giappone." In *Le missioni cattoliche e la cultura dell'Orient: Conferenze "Massimo Piccinini,"* 115–17. Rome: Istituto italiano per il Medio ed Estremo Oriente, 1943.

Schurz, William. *The Manila Galleon.* New York: Historical Reprints, 1939.

Schwarz, E. H. L. "The Chinese Connection with Africa." *Journal of Bengal Branch, Royal Asiatic Society, Letters* 4 (1938): 175–93.

Scott, James. *Seeing like a State: How Certain Schemes to Improve the Human Condition Have Failed.* New Haven: Yale University Press, 1998.

———. *Weapons of the Weak: Everyday Forms of Peasant Resistance.* New Haven: Yale University Press, 1985.

Scott, Julius S. *The Common Wind: Afro-American Currents in the Age of the Haitian Revolution.* New York: Verso, 2020.

Seagrave, Sterling. *Lords of the Rim: The Invisible Empire of the Overseas Chinese.* New York: Putnam, 1995.

Seetah, Krish, ed. *Connecting Continents: Archaeology and History in the Indian Ocean World.* Athens, OH: Ohio University Press, 2018.

Seidensticker, Edward. *Low City, High City: Tokyo from Edo to the Earthquake; How the Shogun's Ancient Capital Became a Great Modern City, 1867–1923.* Cambridge, MA: Harvard University Press, 1991.

Sejarah Daerah Bengkulu. Jakarta: Departemen Penilitian dan Pencatatan, Kebudayaan Daerah, Departemen Pendidikan dan Kebudayaan, n.d.

Sen, Amartya. "Economics and the Family." *Asian Development Review* 1, no. 2 (1983): 14–26.

Sen, Tansen. "The Impact of Zheng He's Expeditions on Indian Ocean Interactions." *Bulletin of the School of Oriental and African Studies,* 79, no. 3 (2016): 609–36.

———. "Maritime Interactions between China and India: Coastal India and the Ascendancy of Chinese Maritime Power in the Indian Ocean." *Journal of Central Eurasian Studies* 2 (2011): 41–82.

———. "Changing Regimes: Two Episodes of Chinese Military Interventions in Medieval South Asia." In *Asian Encounters: Exploring Connected Histories,* edited by Upinder Singh and Parul Dhar, 62–85. New Delhi: Oxford University Press, 2014.

———. "Diplomacy, Trade, and the Quest for the Buddha's Tooth: The Yongle Emperor and Ming China's South Asian Frontier." In *Ming China: Courts and Contacts, 1400–1450,* edited by Craig Clunas, Jessica Harrison-Hall and Luk Yu-Ping, 26–36. London: British Museum, 2016.

———. "The Formation of Chinese Maritime Networks to Southern Asia, 1200–1450." *Journal of the Social and Economic History of the Orient* 49, no. 4 (2006): 421–53.

———, ed. *Buddhism across Asia: Networks of Material, Cultural and Intellectual Exchange.* Singapore: ISEAS, 2014.

———. *Buddhism, Diplomacy, and Trade: The Realignment of Sino-Indian Relations, 600–1400.* Honolulu: University of Hawai'i Press, 2003.

Serjeant, R. B. *The Portuguese off the South Arabian Coast: Hadrami Chronicles; With Yemeni and European Accounts.* Beirut: Librairie du Liban, 1974.

Shen, John. "New Thoughts on the Use of Chinese Documents in the Reconstruction of Early Swahili History." *History in Africa* 22 (1995): 349–58.

Sheriff, Abdul. *Dhow Cultures of the Indian Ocean: Cosmopolitanism, Commerce, and Islam.* New York: Columbia University Press, 2010.

———. "The Persian Gulf and the Swahili Coast: A History of Acculturation over the Longue Durée." In *The Persian Gulf in History,* edited by Lawrence Potter, 173–88. New York: Palgrave Macmillan, 2009.

———. *Slaves, Spices, and Ivory in Zanzibar: The Integration of an East African Commercial Enterprise into the World Economy 1770–1873.* Athens, OH: Ohio University Press, 1987.

Sherry, Frank. *Pacific Passions: The European Struggle for Power in the Great Ocean in the Age of Exploration.* New York: William Morrow, 1994.

Sheth, V. S. "Dynamics of Indian Diaspora in East and South Africa." *Journal of Indian Ocean Studies* 8, no. 3 (2000): 217–27.

Shimada, Ryuto."Hinterlands and Port Cities in Southeast Asia's Economic Development in the Eighteenth Century." In *Hinterlands and Commodities: Place, Space, Time and the Political Economic Development of Asia over the Long Eighteenth Century*, edited by Tsukasa Mizushima, George Bryan Souza, and Dennis Flynn, 197–214. Leiden: Brill, 2015.

———. *The Intra-Asian Trade in Japanese Copper by the Dutch East India Company during the Eighteenth Century*. Leiden: Brill, 2005.

Shin, Chia Lin. "The Development of Marine Transport." *South-East Asian Transport: Issues in Development*. In T.R. Leinbach & Chia Lin Sien, 197–232. Singapore, Oxford, and New York: Oxford University Press, 1965.

Shiro, Momoki."Dai Viet and the South China Sea Trade: From the Tenth to the Fifteenth Century." *Crossroads: An Interdisciplinary Journal of Southeast Asian Studies* 12, no. 1 (1998): 1–34.

———. "Was Dai Viet a Rival of Ryukyu within the Tributary Trade System of the Ming during the Early Le Period, 1428–1527?" In *Commerce et navigation en Asie du sud-est (XIVe–XIXe siècles)*, edited by Nguyễn Thế Anh and Yoshiaki Ishizawa, 101–12. Paris: L'Harmattan, 1999.

Siem Bing Hoat. "Het Chineesch Kapitaal in Indonisië." *Chung Hwa Hui Tsa Chi*, 8, no. 1 (1930): 7–17.

Simmel, G. "The Stranger." In *The Sociology of Georg Simmel*, edited by K. H. Wolff, 402–8. New York: The Free Press, 1950.

Singh, Dilbagh, and Ashok Rajshirke. "The Merchant Communities in Surat: Trade, Trade Practices, and Institutions in the Late Eighteenth Century." In *Ports and their Hinterlands in India, 1700–1950*, edited by Indu Banga, 181–98. Delhi: Manohar, 1992.

Siu, Helen, and Mike McGovern. "China-Africa Encounters: Historical Legacies and Contemporary Realities." *Annual Review of Anthropology* 46 (2017): 337–55.

Sivasundaram, Sujit. *Waves across the South: A New History of Revolution and Empire*. Chicago: University of Chicago Press, 2020.

Skilling, Peter. "Traces of the Dharma: Preliminary Reports on Some Ye Dhamma and Ye Dharma Inscription from Mainland Southeast Asia." *Bulletin de l'École française d'Extrême-Orient* 90–91 (2003/4): 273–87.

Skilling, Peter, Jason A. Carbine, Claudio Cicuzza, and Santi Pakdeekham. *How Theravada Is Theravada? Exploring Buddhist Identities*. Seattle: University of Washington Press, 2012.

Skinner, William. *Chinese Society in Thailand*. Ithaca: Cornell University Press, 1957.

———. "Creolized Chinese Societies in Southeast Asia." In *Sojourners and Settlers: Histories of Southeast Asia and the Chinese*, edited by Anthony Reid, 51–93. Honolulu: University of Hawai'i Press, 2001.

———. *Marketing and Social Structure in Rural China*. Tucson: University of Arizona Press, 1965.

———, ed. *The City in Late Imperial China*. Stanford: Stanford University Press, 1977.

Skrobanek, Siriporn. *The Traffic in Women: Human Realities of the International Sex Trade*. New York: Zed Books, 1997.

Smith, Adam. *An Inquiry into the Nature and Causes of the Wealth of Nations*. Volume I. Clarendon: Oxford University Press, 1976.

Smith, Clarence, and William Gervase. "Indian Business Communities in the Western Indian Ocean in the Nineteenth Century." *Indian Ocean Review* 2, no. 4 (1989); 18–21.

Smith, Clarence, William Gervase, and Steven Topik, eds. *The Global Coffee Economy in Africa, Asia, and Latin America, 1500–1989*. New York: Cambridge University Press, 2003.

Smith, Martin. *Burma: Insurgency and the Politics of Ethnicity*. London: Zed Books, 1999.

Smitka, Michael. *The Japanese Economy in the Tokugawa Era, 1600–1868*. New York: Garland Publishers, 1998.

Snow, Philip. *The Star Raft: China's Encounter with Africa*. New York: Weidenfeld and Nicholson, 1988.

Sobel, Dava. *Longitude: The True Story of a Lone Genius Who Solved the Greatest Scientific Problem of His Day*. New York: Penguin, 1995.

Soelaiman, D. "Selayang pandang pelayaran di Indonesia." *Suluh Nautika* 9, no. 3 (1959): 40–43.

Soempeno, S. *Buku sejarah pelayaran Indonesia*. Jakarta: Pustaka Maritim, 1975.

Sofwan, Mardanas, Taher Ishaq, Asnan Gusti, and Syafrizal. *Sejarah Kota Padang*. Jakarta: Departemen Pendidikan dan Kebudayaan, Direktorat Sejarah dan Nilai Tradisional, Proyek Inventarisasi dan Dokumentasi Sejarah Nasional, 1987.

Souza, George B. *The Survival of Empire: Portuguese Trade and Society in China and the South China Sea 1930–1754*. Cambridge: Cambridge University Press, 1986.

Spence, Jonathan. *The Memory Palace of Matteo Ricci*. New York: Penguin Books, 1985.

Spence, Jonathan, and John Wills, eds. *From Ming to Ch'ing: Conquest, Region, and Continuity in 17th-Century China*. New Haven: Yale University Press, 1979.

Spillet, Peter. *A Feasibility Study of the Construction and Sailing of a Traditional Makassar Prahu From Sulawesi to N. Australia*. Printed by the Historical Office of the N. Territory (Winnellie) Australia, n.d.

Spivak, Gayatri. "Can the Subaltern Speak?" In *Marxism and the Interpretation of Culture*, edited by Cary Nelson and Lawrence Grossburg, 271–313. Basingstoke: Macmillan, 1988.

Spoehr, Alexander. *Zamboanga and Sulu: An Archaeological Approach to Ethnic Diversity Ethnology*. Monograph 1. Pittsburgh: University of Pittsburgh, Dept. of Anthropology, 1973.

Spyers, Patricia. *The Memory of Trade*. Durham: Duke University Press, 2000.

Sriwijaya dalam perspektif arkeologi dan sejarah. Palembang: Pemerintah Daerah Tingkat I Sumatera Selatan, 1993.

Starkey, Janet, ed. *People of the Red Sea: Proceedings of the Red Sea Project II Held in the British Museum*. London: Society for Arabian Studies Monograph 3, 2005.

Steensgaard, N. *The Asian Trade Revolution of the Seventeenth Century: The East India Companies and the Decline of the Caravan Trade*. Chicago: University of Chicago Press, 1974.

Stein, Sarah Abrevaya. *Plumes: Ostrich Feathers, Jews, and a Lost World of Global Commerce*. New Haven: Yale University Press, 2010.

Steinberg, Philip E. *The Social Construction of the Ocean*. New York: Cambridge University Press, 2001.

Stern, Philip. *The Company-State: Corporate Sovereignty and the Early Modern Foundations of the British Empire in India*. New York: Oxford University Press, 2011.

Stern, Tom. *Nur Misuari: An Authorized Biography*. Manila: Anvil Publishing, 2012.

Steur, J. *Herstel of Ondergang: De Voorstellen tot Redres van de VOC, 1740–1795*. Utrecht: H & S Publishers, 1984).

Steurs, F. V. A. de. "Losse Aantekeningen over de Nagel-Kultuur in de Molukko's." *TNI* 4, no. 2 (1842): 458–64.

Stevens, Harm. *De VOC in bedrijf, 1602–1799*. Amsterdam: Walburg Press, 1998.

Stevenson, John. "The Evolution of Vietnamese Ceramics." In *Vietnamese Ceramics: A Separate Tradition*, edited by John Stevenson and John Guy, 22–45. Michigan: Art Media Recourses, 1994; repr. Chicago: Art Media Resources, 1997.

Stevenson, Thomas. *Lighthouse Illumination; Being a Description of the Holophotal System and of Azimuthal Condensing and Other New Forms of Lighthouse Apparatus*. Edinburgh, 1871.

Stoler, Ann. *Capitalism and Confrontation in Sumatra's Plantation Belt 1870–1979*. New Haven: Yale University Press, 1986.

———. "Imperial Debris: Reflections on Ruin and Ruination." *Cultural Anthropology* 23, no. 2 (2008): 191–219.

Studnicki-Gizbert, Daviken. *A Nation upon the Ocean Sea: Portugal's Atlantic Diaspora and the Crisis of the Spanish Empire, 1492–1640*. New York: Oxford University Press, 2007.

Subrahmanyam, Sanjay. *The Career and Legend of Vasco da Gama*. Cambridge: Cambridge University Press, 1997.

———. "Notes of Circulation and Asymmetry in Two Mediterraneans, c. 1400–1800." In *From the Mediterranean to the China Sea: Miscellaneous Notes*, edited by Claude Guillot, Denys Lombard, and Roderich Ptak, 21–43. Wiesbaden: Harrassowitz Verlag, 1998.

———. *The Political Economy of Commerce: Southern India, 1500–1650*. Cambridge Cambridge University Press, 1990.

———. "Profit at the Apostle's Feet: The Portuguese Settlement of Mylapur in the Sixteenth Century." In *Improvising Empire: Portuguese Trade and Settlement in the Bay of Bengal*, edited by Sanjay Subrahmanyam, 47–67. Delhi: Oxford University Press, 1990.

———, ed. *Merchants, Markets, and the State in Early Modern India, 1700–1950* (Delhi: Oxford University Press, 1990).

Subrahmanyam, Sanjay, and C. A. Bayly. "Portfolio Capitalists and the Political Economy of Early Modern India." In *Merchants, Markets, and the State in Early Modern India* Sanjay Subrahmanyam, 242–65. Delhi: Oxford University Press, 1990.

Subramanian, Lakshmi. *The Sovereign and the Pirate: Ordering Maritime Subjects in India's Western Littoral*. New Delhi: Oxford University Press, 2016.

———. "Western India in the Eighteenth Century: Ports, Inland Towns, and States." In *Ports and Their Hinterlands in India, 1700–1950*, edited by Indu Banga, 153–80. Delhi: Manohar, 1992.

Sulistiyono, S. T. "Liberalisasi pelayaran dan perdagangan di Indonesia 1816–1870." *Lembaran Sastra* 19 (1996): 31–44.

———. "Perkembangan pelabuhan Cirebon dan pengaruhnya terhadap kehidupan sosial ekonomi masyarakat kota Cirebon 1859–1930." MA thesis. Yogyakarta: Gajah Mada University, 1994.

———. "Politik kolonial terhadap pelabuhan di Hindia Belanda." *Lembaran Sastra* 18 (1995): 86–100.

———. *Sektor maritim dalam era mekanisasi dan liberalisasi: Posisi armada perahu layar pribumi dalam pelayaran antarpulau di Indonesia, 1879–1911*. Yogyakarta: Laporan penelitian dalam rangka / Summer Course in Indonesian Economic History, 1996.

Sun, Lin. "The Economy of Empire Building: Wild Ginseng, Sable Fur, and the Multiple Trade Networks of the Early Qing Dynasty, 1583–1644." PhD dissertation, Oxford University, 2018.

Surat-Surat Perdjandjian Antara Kesultanan Riau dengan Pemerintahan. Volume 2: *V.O.C. dan Hindia-Belanda 1784–1909.* Jakarta: Arsip Nasional Indonesia, 1970.

Suryadinata, Leo, ed. *Southeast Asian Chinese: The Socio-cultural Dimension.* Singapore: Times Academic Press, 1995.

Susilowati, Endang. "The Impact of Modernization on Tradiditonal Perahu Fleet in Banjarmasin, South Kalimantan in the Twentieth Century." In *Maritime Social and Economic Developments in Southeast Asia,* edited by Hanizah Idris, Tan Wan Hin, and Mohammad Raduan Mohd. Ariff, 61–76. Kuala Lumpur: Institute of Ocean and Earth Sciences, University of Malaya, 2008.

Sutedja, D. *Buku himpunan pemulihan hubungan Indonesia Singapura: Himpunan peraturan-peraturan anglkutan laut.* Jakarta: Departement Perhubungan Laut, 1967.

Sutherland, Heather. *Seaways and Gatekeepers: Trade and Society in the Eastern Archipelagos of Southeast Asia, c. 1600–1906.* Singapore: National University of Singapore Press, 2021.

———. "Southeast Asian History and the Mediterranean Analogy." *Journal of Southeast Asian Studies* 34.1 (2003): 1–20.

———. "Trepang and Wangkang: The China Trade of Eighteenth-Century Makassar." In *Authority and Enterprise among the Peoples of South Sulawesi,* edited by R. Tol, K. van Dijk, and G. Accioli: 451–72. Leiden: KITLV Press, 2000.

Sutherland, Heather, and Gerrit Knaap. *Monsoon Traders: Ships, Skippers and Commodities in Eighteenth-Century Makassar.* Leiden: Brill, 2004.

Synthetic Drugs in East and Southeast Asia: Latest Developments and Challenges, 2021. New York: United Nations Office on Drugs and Crime, 2021.

Syper, Patricia. *The Memory of Trade: Modernity's Entanglements on an Eastern Indonesian Island.* Durham: Duke University Press, 2000.

Tacchi, P., and S. I. Venturi. *Alcune lettere del P. Antonio Rubino.* Turin: D.C.D.G., 1901.

Tagliacozzo, Eric. "Border-Line Legal: Chinese Communities and 'Illicit' Activity in Insular Southeast Asia." In *Maritime China and the Overseas Chinese in Transition, 1750–1850,* edited by Ng Chin Keong, 61–76. Wiesbaden: Harassowitz Verlag, 2004.

———. "The Dutch in Indian Ocean History." In *The Cambridge History of the Indian Ocean.* Volume II, edited by Seema Alavi, Sunil Amrith, and Eric Tagliacozzo. Cambridge: Cambridge University Press, forthcoming.

———. "'Kettle on a Slow Boil': Batavia's Threat Perceptions in the Indies' Outer Islands." *Journal of Southeast Asian Studies* 31, no. 1 (2000): 70–100.

———. *The Longest Journey: Southeast Asians and the Pilgrimage to Mecca.* New York: Oxford University Press, 2013.

———. "Navigating Communities: Distance, Place, and Race in Maritime Southeast Asia." In *Asian Ethnicity* 10, no. 2 (2009): 97–120.

———. "A Necklace of Fins: Marine Goods Trading in Maritime Southeast Asia, 1780–1860." *International Journal of Asian Studies* 1, no. 1 (2004): 23–48.

———. "Onto the Coast and into the Forest: Ramifications of the China Trade on the History of Northwest Borneo, 900–1900." In *Histories of the Borneo Environment,* edited by Reed Wadley, 25–60. Leiden: KITLV Press, 2005.

——. *Secret Trades, Porous Borders: Smuggling and States along a Southeast Asian Frontier.* New Haven: Yale University Press, 2005.

——. "The South China Sea." In *Oceanic Histories*, edited by David Armitage, Alison Bashford, and Sujit Sivasundaram, 113–33. Cambridge: Cambridge University Press, 2018.

Tan, Mely. *Golongan ethnis Tinghoa di Indonesia: Suatau masalah pembinan kesatuan bangsa.* Jakarta: Gramedia, 1979.

Tarling, Nicholas. "The First Pharos of the Seas: The Construction of the Horsburgh Lighthouse on Pedra Branca." *Journal of the Malay Branch of the Royal Asiatic Society* 67, no. 1 (1994): 1–8.

——. *Imperial Britain in Southeast Asia.* Kuala Lumpur: Oxford University Press, 1975.

Taylor, Keith W. "The Literati Revival in Seventeenth-Century Vietnam." *Journal of Southeast Asian Studies* 18, no. 1 (1997): 1–23.

——. "Regional Conflicts among the Viêt People between the 13th and 19th Centuries." In *Guerre et paix en Asie du sud-est*, edited by Nguyên Thê Anh and Alain Forest, 109–33. Paris: L'Harmattan, 1998.

Teitler, G. "The Netherlands Indies: An Outline of Its Military History." *Revue Internationale d'Histoire Militaire* 58 (1984): 138.

Teitler, Gerke. *Ambivalente en aarzeeling: Het belied van Nederland en Nederlands-Indië ten aanzien van hun kustwateren, 1870–1962.* Assen: Van Gorcum, 1994.

Ter Weil, Barend. "Early Ayyuthaya and Foreign Trade: Some Questions." In *Commerce et navigation en Asie du sud-est (XIVe–XIXe siècles)*, edited by Nguyên Thê Anh and Yoshiaki Ishizawa, 77–90. Paris: L'Harmattan, 1999.

Terami-Wada, Motoe. "Karayuki-san of Manila 1880–1920." *Philippine Studies* 34 (1986): 287–316.

Tesfay, Netsanet. *Impact of Livelihood Recovery Initiatives on Reducing Vulnerability to Human Trafficking and Illegal Recruitment: Lessons from Typhoon Haiyan.* Geneva: International Organization for Migration and International Labour Organization, 2015.

Thai, Philip. *China's War on Smuggling: Law, Economic Life, and the Making of the Modern State.* New York: Columbia University Press, 2018.

The Siauw Giap. "Socio-Economic Role of the Chinese in Indonesia, 1820–1940." In *Economic Growth in Indonesia, 1820–1940*, edited by A. Maddison and G. Prince, 159–83. Dordrecht and Providence: Foris, 1989.

Thomas, Nicholas. *Islanders: The Pacific in the Age of Empire.* New Haven: Yale University Press, 2010.

Thomaz, L. F. F. R. "Les portugais dans les mers de l'Archipel au XVIe siècle." *Archipel* 18 (1979): 105–25.

Thornton, John. *Africa and Africans in the Making of the Atlantic World, 1400–1800.* 2nd ed. New York: Cambridge University Press, 1998.

Thung Ju Lan. "Posisi dan pola komunikasi antar budaya antara etnis Cina dan masyarakat Indonesia lainnya pada masa kini: Suatu studi pendahuluan." *Berita Ilmu Pengetahuan dan Teknologi* 29, no. 2 (1985): 15–29.

Tijdschrift voor het Zeewezen (1871): 125; (1872): 90; (1873): 274; (1875): 230; (1879): 83.

Tirumalai, R. "A Ship Song of the Late 18th Century in Tamil." In *Studies in Maritime History*, edited by K. S. Mathew, 159–64. Pondicherry: Pondicherry University Press, 1990.

Tjiptoatmodjo, F. A. S. "Kota-kota pantai di sekiatr selat Madura (Abad ke-17 sampai medio abad ke-19)." PhD dissertation. Yogyakarta: Gadjah Mada University, 1983.

Toby, Ronald. *State and Diplomacy in Early Modern Japan: Asia in the Development of the Tokugawa Bakufu.* Princeton: Princeton University Press, 1984.

Topik, Steven, and Kenneth Pomeranz. *The World That Trade Created: Society, Culture, and the World Economy, 1400 to the Present.* New York: Routledge, 2012.

Trainor, Kevin. *Relics, Ritual, and Representation.* Cambridge: Cambridge University Press, 1997.

Tran, Nhung. *Familial Properties: Gender, State, and Society in Early Modern Vietnam, 1463–1778.* Honolulu: University of Hawai'i Press, 2018.

Tran, Nhung Tuyet, and Anthony J. S. Reid, eds. *Việt Nam: Borderless Histories.* Madison: University of Wisconsin Press, 2006.

Tranh, Khanh. *The Ethnic Chinese and Economic Development in Vietnam.* Singapore: Institute of Southeast Asian Studies, 1993.

Travers, Robert. *Ideology and Empire in Eighteenth-Century India.* Cambridge: Cambridge University Press, 2009.

Tremml-Werner, Birgit. *Spain, China and Japan in Manila, 1571–1644: Local Comparisons and Global Connections.* Amsterdam: University of Amsterdam Press, 2015.

Trivellato, Francesca. *The Familiarity of Strangers: The Sephardic Diaspora, Livorno, and Cross-Cultural Trade in the Early Modern Period.* New Haven: Yale University Press, 2012.

Trocki, Carl. *Opium, Empire, and the Global Political Economy: A Study of the Asian Opium Trade.* New York: Routledge, 1999.

Truong, Thanh-Dam. *Sex, Money, and Morality: Prostitution and Tourism in Southeast Asia.* London: Zed Books, 1990.

Truong-Vinh-Ky, P. J. B. *Voyage to Tonking in the Year 1876.* Translated by P. J. Honey. London: School of African and African Studies, 1982.

Truong, Van Mon. "The Raja Praong Ritual: A Memory of the Sea in Cham-Malay Relations." In *Water Frontier: Commerce and the Chinese in the Lower Mekong Region, 1750–1880,* edited by Nola Cooke and Tana Li, 97–111. Lanham, MD: Rowman & Littlefield, 2004.

Tsai Mauw-Kuey. *Les chinois au Sud-Vietnam.* Paris, Bibliothèque Nationale, 1986.

Tsukaya Mizushima, George Souza, and Dennis Flynn, eds. *Hinterlands and Commodities: Place, Space, Time and the Political Economic Development of Asia over the Long Eighteenth Century.* Leiden: Brill, 2015

Tuấn, Hoàng Anh. *Silk for Silver: Dutch-Vietnamese Relations, 1637–1700.* Leiden: Brill, 2007.

Tsai, Shih-Shan Henry. *Maritime Taiwan: Historical Encounters with the East and the West.* Armonk: M. E. Sharpe, 2009.

Tucci, G. "Antichi ambasciatori giapponesi patrizi romani." *Asiatica* 6 (1940): 157–65.

———. "Pionieri italiani in India." *Asiatica* 2 (1936): 3–11.

———. "Pionieri italiani in India." In *Forme dello spirito asiatico,* edited by G. Tucci, 30–49. Milan and Messina, 1940.

———. "Del supposto architetto del Taj e di altri italiani alla Corte dei Mogul." *Nuova Antologia* 271 (1930): 77–90.

Tuck, Patrick. *French Colonial Missionaries and the Politics of Imperialism in Vietnam, 1857–1914: A Documentary Survey.* Liverpool University Press, 1987.

Turton, Andrew. "Ethnography of Embassy: Anthropological Readings of Records of Diplomatic Encounters between Britain and Tai States in the Early Nineteenth Century." *South East Asia Research* 5, no. 2 (1997): 175–205.

Um, Nancy. *The Merchant Houses of Mocha: Trade and Architecture in an Indian Ocean Port*. Seattle: University of Washington Press, 2009.

———. *Shipped but Not Sold: Material Culture and the Social Order of Trade During Yemen's Age of Coffee*. Honolulu: University of Hawai'i Press, 2017.

US Mississippi River Commission. *Comprehensive Hydrography of the Mississippi River and Its Principal Tributaries from 1871 to 1942*. Vicksburg, MS: Mississippi River Commission, 1942.

Van den Berg, N. P. *Munt-crediet—en bankwezen, Hadel en scheepvaart in Nederlandsch-Indië: Historisch-statishtisch bijdragen*. The Hague: Nijhoff, 1907.

Van Dyke, Paul. *Americans and Macao: Trade, Smuggling and Diplomacy on the South China Coast*. Hong Kong: Hong Kong University Press, 2012.

Veer, Paul van het. *De Atjeh Oorlog*. Amsterdam: Arbeiderspers, 1969.

Velde, P. G. E. I. J. van der. "Van koloniale lobby naar koloniale hobby: Het Koninklijk Nederlands Aardrijkskundig Genootschap en Nederlands-Indië, 1873–1914." *Geografisch Tijdschrift* 22, no. 3 (1988): 215.

Vermueulen, J. T. *De Chineezen te Batavia en de troebelen van 1740*. Leiden: Eduard Ijdo, 1938.

Verschuer, Charlotte von. *Across the Perilous Sea: Japanese Trade with China and Korea from the Seventh to the Sixteenth Centuries*. Translated by Kristen Lee Hunter. Ithaca, NY: Cornell University Press, 2006.

Villiers, J. "Makassar: The Rise and Fall of an East Indonesian Maritime Trading State, 1512–1669." In *The Southeast Asian Port and Polity: Rise and Demise*, edited by J. Kathirithamby-Wells and J. Villiers. Singapore: Singapore University Press.

Vink, Markus. "Indian Ocean Studies and the New Thalassology." *Journal of Global History* 2 (2007): 41–62.

Viraphol, Sarasin. *Tribute and Profit: Sino-Siamese Trade 1652–1853*. Cambridge, MA: Harvard University Press, 1977.

Vleet, Jeremias van. "Description of the Kingdom of Siam." Translated by L. F. van Ravenswaay. *Journal of the Siam Society* 7, no. 1 (1910): 1–105.

Vleming, J. L. *Het Chineesche zakenleven in Nederlandesch-Indië*. Weltevreden: Landsdrikkerij, 1926.

Vosmer, Tom. "Maritime Archaeology, Ethnography and History in the Indian Ocean: An Emerging Partnership." In *Archaeology of Seafaring*, edited by Himanshu Prabha Ray, 65–79. Delhi: Pragati Publishers, 1999.

Voute, W., "Gound-, diamant-, en tin-houdende alluviale gronden in de Nederlandsche Oost- en West-Indische kolonien." *Indische Mercuur* 24, no. 7 (1901): 116–17.

Vu Duong Luan and Nola Cooke. "Chinese Merchants and Mariners in Nineteenth-Century Tongking." In *The Tongking Gulf through History* Nola Cooke, Tana Li, and Jamie Anderson, 143–59. Philadelphia: University of Pennsylvania Press, 2011.

Vuuren, L. van. "De prauwvaart van Celebes." *Koloniale Studiën* 1 (1917): 329–39.

Wade, G. P. "Borneo-Related Illustrations in a Chinese Work." *Brunei Museum Journal* 6, no. 3 (1987): 1–3.

Wade, Geoff. "A Maritime Route in the Vietnamese Text 'Xiem-la-quoc lo-trinh tap-luc' (1810)." In *Commerce et navigation en Asie du Sud-est (XIVe–XIXe siècles)*, edited by Nguyễn Thế Anh and Yoshiaki Ishizawa, 137–70. Paris: L'Harmattan, 1999.

———. "Southeast Asia in the Fifteenth Century." In *Southeast Asia in the Fifteenth Century: The China Factor*, edited by Geoff Wade and Sun Laichen, 3–42. Singapore: NUS Press, 2010.

———. "Engaging the South: Ming China and Southeast Asia in the Fifteenth Century." *JESHO* 51 (2008): 578–638.

———. "Ming China's Violence against Neighboring Polities and Its Representation in Chinese Historiography." In *Asian Encounters: Exploring Connected Histories*, edited by Upinder Singh and Parul Dhar, 20–41. New Delhi: Oxford University Press, 2014.

———. *Southeast Asia in the Ming Shi-lu: An Open Access Resource*. Singapore: Asia Research Institute and the Singapore E-Press, National University of Singapore; http://epress.nus.edu.sg/msl.

———. "The Southern Chinese Borders in History." In *Where China Meets Southeast Asia: Social and Cultural Change in the Border Regions*, edited by G. Evans, C. Hutton, and K. E. Kuah, 28–50. Singapore; ISEAS Press, 2000.

———. "The Zheng He Voyages: A Reassessment." *Journal of the Malaysian Branch of the Royal Asiatic Society* 78, no. 1 (2005): 37–58.

Wadley, Reed. "Warfare, Pacification, and Environment: Population Dynamics in the West Borneo Borderlands (1823–1934)." *Moussons* 1 (2000): 41–66.

Wake, Christopher. "The Myth of Zheng He's Great Treasure Ships." *International Journal of Maritime History* 16, no. 1 (2004): 59–75.

Wakeman, Frederic. *The Great Enterprise*. Berkeley: University of California Press, 1985).

Waley-Cohen, Joanna. *The Sextants of Beijing: Global Currents in Chinese History*. New York: W. W. Norton, 1999.

Waley, Arthur. *The Opium War through Chinese Eyes*. London: Allen & Unwin, 1958.

Wamebu, Zadrak, and Karlina Leksono. *Suara dari Papua: Identifikasi kebutuhan masyarakat Papua asli*. Jakarta: Yayasan Penguatan Partisipasi Inisiatif dan Kemitraan Masyarakat Sipil Indonesia, 2001.

Wang Gungwu. *China and the Chinese Overseas*. Singapore: Times Academic Press, 1991.

———. "The China Seas: Becoming an Enlarged Mediterranean." In *The East Asian 'Mediterranean': Maritime Crossroads of Culture, Commerce and Human Migration*, edited by Angela Schottenhammer, 7–22. Wiesbaden: Harrassowitz Verlag, 2008.

———. "Merchants without Empire: The Hokkien Sojourning Communities." In *The Rise of Merchant Empires. Long-Distance Trade in the Early Modern World, 1350–1750*, ed. J. D. Tracy, 400–21. Cambridge: Cambridge University Press, 1990.

Ward, Kerry. *Networks of Empire: Forced Migration in the Dutch East India Company*. New York: Cambridge University Press, 2009.

Ward, R., and R. Jenkins, eds. *Ethnic Communities in Business: Strategies for Economic Survival*. Cambridge, Cambridge University Press, 1984.

Ward, W. E. F., and L. W. White. *East Africa: A Century of Change 1870–1970*. New York: Africana Publishing Corporation, 1972.

Warren, James Francis. *Ah Ku and Karayuki-san: Prostitution in Singapore (1880–1940.)* Singapore: Oxford University Press, 1993.

———. "Joseph Conrad's Fiction as Southeast Asian History." In *At the Edge of Southeast Asian History: Essays by James Frances Warren*, edited by James Francis Warren, 1–15} Quezon City: New Day Publishers, 1987.

———. *The Sulu Zone: The Dynamics of External Trade, Slavery, and Ethnicity in the Transformation of a Southeast Asian Maritime State*. Singapore: Singapore University Press, 1981.

Watson, Bruce. *Foundation for Empire: English Trade in India 1659–1760*. New Delhi: Vikas, 1980.

———. "Indian Merchants and English Private Interests: 1659–1760." In *India and the Indian Ocean 1500–1800*, edited by Ashin Das Gupta and M. N. Pearson, 301–16. Calcutta: Oxford University Press, 1987.

Weaver, Jace. *The Red Atlantic: American Indigenes and the Making of the Modern World, 1000–1927*. Chapel Hill: The University of North Carolina Press, 2014.

Weber, Max. *The Protestant Ethic and the Spirit of Capitalism*, 2nd ed. London: George Allen & Unwin, 1976.

Weber, Nicholas. "The Vietnamese Annexation of Panduranga (Champa) and the End of a Maritime Kingdom." In *Memory and Knowledge of the Sea in Southeast Asia*, edited by Danny Wong Tze Ken, 65–76. Kuala Lumpur: Institute of Ocean and Earth Sciences, University of Malaya, 2008.

Webster, Anthony. *Gentleman Capitalists: British Imperialism in South East Asia 1770–1890*. London: Tasuris, 1998.

Weddik, A. L. "De Notenmuskaat-Kultuur op Java." *TNI* 2, no. 2 (1839): 589–600.

———. "Proeve over de Teelt van den Kruidnagelboom op Java." *TNI* 3, no. 1 (1840): 413–18.

Wells, J. K., and John Villiers, eds. *The Southeast Asian Port and Polity: Rise and Demise*. Singapore: Singapore University Press, 1990.

Welsh, Frank. *A Borrowed Place: The History of Hong Kong*. New York: Kodansha, 1993.

Wheatley, Paul. "Analecta Sino-Africana Recensa." In *East Africa and the Orient*, edited by H. Neville Chittick and Robert Rotberg, 76–114. New York: Africana Publishers, 1975.

———. *The Golden Chersonese: Studies in the Historical Geography of the Malay Peninsula Before AD 1500*. Kuala Lumpur, University of Malaya Press, 1961.

———. *Nagara and Commandary: Origins of the Southeast Asian Urban Traditions*. Chicago: University of Chicago Press, 1983.

———, ed. *Melaka: Transformation of a Malay Capital 1400–1980*. 2 volumes. Kuala Lumpur: Oxford University Press, 1983.

Wheeler, Charles. "One Region, Two Histories: Cham Precedents in the History of Hoi An Region." In *Việt Nam: Borderless Histories*, edited by Nhung Tuyet Tran and Anthony J. S. Reid, 163–93. Madison: University of Wisconsin Press 2006.

———. "Placing the 'Chinese Pirates' of the Gulf of Tonking at the End of the Eighteenth Century." In *Asia Inside Out: Connected Places*, edited by Eric Tagliacozzo, Helen F. Siu, and Peter C. Perdue, 30–63. Cambridge, MA: Harvard University Press, 2015.

———. "Re-thinking the Sea in Vietnamese History: The Littoral Integration of Thuận-Quảng, Seventeenth–Eighteenth Centuries." *Journal of Southeast Asian Studies* 17, no. 1 (Feb. 2006): 123–53.

White, John. *A Voyage to Cochin China*. Kuala Lumpur: Oxford University Press 1972; orig. 1824).

Whitmore, John. "Vietnam and the Monetary Flow of Asia, 13–18th Centuries." In *Precious Metals in the Later Medieval and Early Modern Worlds*, edited by J. F. Richards, 363–96. Durham: Carolina Academic Press, 1983.

Wick, Alexis. *The Red Sea: In Search of Lost Space*. Berkeley: University of California Press, 2016.

Wickberg, Edgar. *The Chinese in Philippine Life, 1850–1898*. New Haven and London: Yale University Press, 1965.

———. "Overseas Adaptive Organizations, Past and Present." In *Reluctant Exiles? Migration from the Hong Kong and the New Overseas Chinese*, edited by Ronald Skeldon, 68–86. Armonk, NY: M. E. Sharpe, 1994.

Wigen, Kären. "Oceans of History." *American Historical Review* 111, no. 3 (2006): 717–21.

Williams, L .E. "Chinese Entrepreneurs in Indonesia." *Explorations in Entrepreneurial History* 5, no. 1 (1952): 34–60.

Williams, R. "Nightspaces: Darkness, Deterritorialisation and Social Control." *Space and Culture* 11, no. 4 (2008): 514–32.

Wild, John Peter, and Felicity Wild. "Rome and India: Early Indian Cotton Textiles from Berenike, Red Sea Coast of Egypt." In *Textiles in Indian Ocean Societies*, edited by Ruth Barnes, 11–16. New York: Routledge, 2005.

Wilford, John Noble. *The Mapmakers*. New York: Vintage, 1982.

Willford, Andrew, and Eric Tagliacozzo, eds. *Clio/Anthropos: Exploring the Boundaries between History and Anthropology*. Palo Alto: Stanford University Press, 2009.

Wills, John. *Embassies and Illusions: Dutch and Portuguese Envoys to K'ang-hsi, 1666–1687*. Cambridge, MA: Harvard University East Asian Studies, 1984.

———. "Maritime Asia 1500–1800: The Interactive Emergence of European Domination." *American Historical Review* 98, no. 1 (1993): 83–105.

———. *Pepper, Guns, and Parleys*. Cambridge, MA: Harvard University Press 1974.

Winichakul, Thongchai. *Siam Mapped*. Honolulu: University of Hawai'i Press, 1994.

Winter, C. F. "Verbod Tegen het Gebruik van Amfioen." *TNI* 3, no. 2 (1840): 588.

Wolf, Eric. *Europe and the People without History*. Berkeley: University of California Press, 1982.

Wolff, John. *Brandy, Balloons, and Lamps: Ami Argand*. Carbondale, IL: Southern Illinois University Press, 1999.

Wolters, O. W., *Early Indonesian Commerce: A Study of the Origins of Srivijaya*. Ithaca: Cornell University Press, 1967.

Wong Kwok-Chu. *The Chinese in the Philippine Economy, 1898–1941*. Manila: Ateneo de Manila Press, 1999.

Wong Siu-Lun. "Business Networks, Cultural Values and the State in Hong Kong and Singapore. In *Chinese Business Enterprises in Asia*, edited by Rajeswary A. Brown. London and New York: Routledge, 1995.

Wong Yee Tuan. *Penang Chinese Commerce in the Nineteenth Century*. Singapore: ISEAS, 2015.

Woodside, Alexander. *Vietnam and the Chinese Model*. Cambridge, MA: Harvard University Press, 1971.

Woodward, Hiram. *The Art and Architecture of Thailand from Prehistoric Times through the Thirteenth Century*. Leiden: Brill, 2003.

Wray, William D. "The Seventeenth-century Japanese Diaspora: Questions of Boundary and Policy." In *Diaspora Entrepreneurial Networks: Four Centuries of History*, edited by Ina Baghdiantz McCabe, Gelina Harlaftis, and Ioanna Pepelasis Minoglu, 73–93. Oxford and New York: Berg, 2005.

Wright, Arnold, and Oliver T. Breakspear, eds. *Twentieth Century Impressions of Netherlands India: Its History, People, Commerce, Industries, and Resources*. London, 1909.

Wu, David. *The Chinese in Papua New Guinea, 1880–1980*. Hong Kong: Hong Kong University Press, 1982.

Wu Wei-Peng. "Transaction Cost, Cultural Values and Chinese Business Networks: An Integrated Approach." In *Chinese Business Networks*, edited by Chan Kwok Bun. Singapore: Prentice Hall, 2000.

Wu-Beyens, I-Chuan. "Hui: Chinese Business in Action." In *Chinese Business Networks*, edited by Chan Kwok Bun. Singapore: Prentice Hall, 2000.

Wyatt, Don. *The Blacks of Premodern China*. Philadelphia: University of Pennsylvania Press, 2010.

Xing Hang and Tonio Andrade, eds. *Sea Rovers, Silver, and Samurai: Maritime East Asia in Global History, 1550–1700*. Honolulu: University of Hawai'i Press, 2016.

Xing Hang. *Conflict and Commerce in Maritime East Asia: The Zheng Family and the Shaping of the Modern World, 1620–1720*. Cambridge: Cambridge University Press, 2016.

Yao, Souchou. "The Fetish of Relationships: Chinese Business Transactions in Singapore." *Sojourn* 2 (1987): 89–111.

Yen, Ching-hwang, ed. *The Ethnic Chinese in East and Southeast Asia: Business, Culture, and Politics*. Singapore: Times Academic Press, 2002.

Yambert, K. A. "Alien Traders and Ruling Elites: The Overseas Chinese in Southeast Asia and the Indians in East Africa." *Ethnic Groups* 3 (1981): 173–78.

Yang, Pao-yun. *Contribution à l'histoire de la principauté des Nguyên au Vietnam méridional (1600–1775)*. Geneva: Éditions Olizane, 1992.

Yegar, Moshe. *Between Integration and Succession: The Muslim Communities of the Southern Philippines, Southern Thailand, and Western Burma/Myanmar*. Lanham, MD: Lexington Books, 2002.

Yen Ching-hwang, ed. *The Ethnic Chinese in East and Southeast Asia: Business, Culture, and Politics*. Singapore: Times Academic Press, 2002.

Yeung, Y. M., and C. P. Lo, eds. *Changing Southeast Asian Cities: Readings on Urbanization*. Oxford: Oxford University Press, 1976.

Ylvisaker, Marguerite. *Lamu in the Nineteenth Century: Land, Trade, and Politics*. Boston: Boston University African Studies Association, 1979.

Yoshihara Kunio. "The Ethnic Chinese and Ersatz Capitalism in Southeast Asia." In *Southeast Asian Chinese and China: The Politico-economic Dimension*, edited by Leo Suryadinata. Singapore: Times Academic Press, 1995.

Yu-ju, Lin, and Madeleine Zelin, eds. *Merchant Communities in Asia, 1600–1800*. London: Routledge, 2016.

Zainol, Salina Binti Haji. "Hubungan perdagangan antara Aceh, Sumatera Timur dan pulaua Pinang, 1819–1871." MA thesis. Kuala Lumpur: Universiti Malaya, 1995.

Zeeman, J. H. *De Kustvaart in Nederlandsch-Indië, beschouwd in verband met het Londensch Tractaat van 17 Maart 1824*. Amsterdam: J. H. de Bussy, 1936.

Zelin, Madeleine. "Economic Freedom in Late Imperial China." In *Realms of Freedom in Modern China*, edited by William Kirby, 57–83. Palo Alto: Stanford University Press, 2004.

Zhang, Yangwen. *China on the Sea: How the Maritime World Shaped Modern China*. Leiden: Brill, 2014.

———. *The Social Life of Opium in China*. Cambridge: Cambridge University Press, 2005.

Zhao Bing. "La céramique chinoise importée en Afrique orientale (IXe-XVIe siècles): Un cas de changement de valeur marchande et symbolique dans le commerce global." https://doi.org/10.4000/afriques.1836

———. "Global Trade and Swahili Cosmopolitan Material Culture: Chinese-style Ceramic Shards from Sanje ya Kati and Songo Mnara (Kilwa, Tanzania)." *Journal of World History* 23, no. 1 (2012): 41–85.

Zhao, Gang. *The Qing Opening to the Ocean: Chinese Maritime Policies, 1684–1757.* Honolulu: University of Hawai'i Press, 2013.

Zhou, Nanjing. "Masalah asimilasi keturunan Tionghoa di Indonesia." *RIMA* 21, no. 2 (Summer 1987): 44–66.

Zinoman, Peter. *The Colonial Bastille: A History of Imprisonment in Vietnam 1862–1940.* Berkeley: University of California Press, 2001.

Zuhdi, Susanto. *Cilacap (1830–1942): Bangkit dan runtuhnya suatu pelabuhan di Jawa.* Jakarta: KPG, 2002.

———, ed. *Cirebon sebagai bandar jalur sutra.* Jakarta: Departemen Pendidikan dan Kebudayaan, Direktorat Sejarah dan Nilai Tradisional, Proyek Inventarisasi dan Dokumentasi Sejarah Nasional, 1996.

INDEX

Abdul, K. S., 298
Abdul Jabbar, T. S., 298, 302
Abdul Latiff, K. S., 300, 302
Abdul Wahab, P. A., 299
Abinales, Patricio (Jojo), 182
Abu al-Fida, 34
Abubakar, Carmen, 183
Abu-Lughod, Janet, 5
Abu al-Mashasin, 34
Abu Sayyaf, 176
acacia trees, 30
accidents, 321–22
Aceh, 32, 151, 340–41, 350, 358
Aceh Merdeka ("Free Aceh") Movement, 220
Aceh War, 236
adaptation, evolution and, 205–6
Africa, 25–26, 28, 47–49. *See also specific locations*
African-Asian connections, 26–31
Age of Commerce, 111
Age of Mercantilism, 108
Ahmed bin Said, 133
aircraft carrier, of China, 369
Ajax Shoal, 360
alcohol, 87, 88, 109
Alexandria, Egypt, 289
Alonto, Abul Kahyr, 176
Ambon, Maluku, Indonesia, 321
Amoy (Xiamen), China, 83, 85
Amrith, Sunil, 9, 13, 150
amulets, 157–64, 165–66
Anambas, Indonesia, 355
"Ancient History of Dar es Salaam," 128
"Ancient History of Kilwa Kisiwani," 128

Andaman Sea, 75, 142, 272
Andaya, Barbara Watson, 11
Andaya, Leonard, 11
Angkor Wat, 152
Anglo-Dutch competition, 112, 119
Anglo-Dutch Treaty, 112, 349
animals, voyages of, 44, 45
Anjer, Indonesia, 323, 324
Ao Phra Nang, 272–73
Appadurai, Arjun, 34
Aquino, Benigno, 175, 178
Aquino, Corazon, 177, 178–79
Arab geographers, 22
Arabian Sea, 75, 231–32
Arakan, Burma, 114
Arena of Lights, 315
argonauts, 31
Argonauts of the Western Pacific (Malinowski), 31
Arifin-Cabo, Pressia, 181
armaments, 135
ARMM Organic Act, 177
Asia: colonial oceanic circuits of, 226; ecological products within, 251; map of, 3; northeast seas of, 243–48; sea route effects within, 3–4; water geography of, 75; western waters of, 227–32, 391. *See also specific locations*
astronomy, 39–40
Australia, 31n16, 387
"Ave Maria" (Vietnam), 59
Axum (Eritrea), 34
Ayutthaya, 154–55, 203
Aziz, R. A., 301

Bab al-mandeb (Gate of Tears), 229

Bagan civilization, 152

Bagan Si Api-api, 261

Bagomoyo port, 132

Bahrain, 228–29

Bailyn, Bernard, 6, 7

Baker, Chris, 158

Bali Straits, 331

Bamboo gang, 97

Banda Sea, 75

bang, work of, 83

Bangka, 354–55, 357

Bangka Straits, 86, 324

Bangkok, Thailand, 196, 217, 222

Bangsamoro Land, 176

banians, 133, 134–35

Bank of India, 296

Baptista, Julius, 164

Barendse, René, 13

Barrow, John, 65

Barthes, Roland, 335

Basilan, 184–85, 189–90

Batak people, 207

Batam, Indonesia, 101

Batavia: Aceh War and, 236; agreement
    requirements of, 362; Anglo-Dutch Treaty
    and, 349; Dutch and, 237–38, 260, 317;
    harbor-improvement schemes of, 339;
    lighthouses/lighting within, 324, 331, 332,
    334–35, 343; maritime notices of, 361;
    political conflict of, 328; smuggling within,
    81; steam-shipping and, 318

Batavia/Jakarta, 204–5

Batina, 135

Bay of Bengal, 75, 118, 142–43, 146–47, 148, 152

Beijing, China, 202–3, 214

Belawan Deli, 327

Belitung, Indonesia, 354–55, 357

Bengal, India, 114, 124n61, 151, 232

Bengkulu, Indonesia, 125

Benyon, Richard, 126n71

Bihar, India, 232

BIMP-EAGA development triangle, 92

binary authority, 212–13, 214–15

blackbirding, 136

The Blacks of Premodern China (Wyatt), 47–48

Blakang Padang, 357

Blockade Runners (Dutch), 90, 91

Bombay, 232, 233–34, 304

Bonacich, Edna, 282

borax, 66

Borneo: accidents near, 322; British presence
    within, 328; Brooketon lighthouse and,
    329–30; Chinese porcelain in, 109;
    Chinese within, 261; colonial circuits
    within, 238–39; coolies to, 243; East
    Borneo, 362, 363–64; European presence
    within, 238–39; Gunung Tabur, sultan of,
    362; lighthouses/lighting within, 325;
    North Borneo, 87, 330–31, 350; trade
    seepage within, 351

Bose, Sugata, 150

Bosphorus, 227

Bowring Treaty, 116n38

Braudel, Fernand, 6, 7, 150

bride-price, negotiations of, 38–39

Britain/British: aggressive mindset of, 237;
    Anglo-Dutch Treaty and, 349; antislavery
    campaign of, 130–31, 130n86; "Asia station"
    warships of, 247; battles of, 122; Borneo
    and, 238–39; capitalism control by, 138–39;
    clove industry and, 136; Constantinople
    and, 227, 229–30; control shift by, 137;
    diplomacy of, 114; dominion viewpoint of,
    114, 122, 123–24; Forward Movement of,
    350; greed of, 126; hydrography by, 354–60;
    Indian control by, 232–33; within Indonesia,
    235–36; internal conflicts of, 328–29;
    lighthouse/lighting authority of, 342;
    monopoly system of, 378; policies of, 123;
    power and politics of, 122; Red Sea and,
    229; within Southeast Asia, 112, 328; spice
    trade and, 110–11; trade lobbying by, 115

British India, 109, 128, 391–92

British North Borneo Company, 328, 350, 364

bronze, 109

Brooke, Charles, 329–30, 364

Brooketon lighthouse, 329–30

Brown, Edward, 68

Brown, Roxanna, 155–56

Brunei, 97, 101

Buddhism: amulet of protection within, 157–58; Hinduism and, 159; Indian Ocean and, 106; as instructive, 145–46; locations of, 155; movement of, 141, 142, 159; origin of, 159; relics of, 160; women in, 155. *See also specific countries*

Bugi people, 31n16, 386–87

Bukit Cina (China Hill), 388

buoys, 338

Burdawan, India, 151

Burma: Bagan civilization in, 152; Britain and, 114–15; marine product trade within, 273; merchants within, 288; smuggling statistics of, 95; Thailand and, 219; Theravada Buddhism in, 118, 141; trading within, 207–8

Busaidi, Sayyid Ali bin Sefu al-, 395

Calcutta, India, 232

Calicut, India, 117

Calvino, Italo, 224

Cambay, India, 119n49

Cambodia, 93, 95, 97, 141, 220–21, 272

Campbell, Gwyn, 48

Campo, Joop à, 352

Canning Award, 130

Canton, China, 59–60

Cape Delgado, 131

Cape Rachado Light, 332

Capital (Marx), 105, 137

capitalism, 71, 128, 138–39, 280

cardamom, 66

Carpenter, Frank, 175

cartaz system, 376–77

Catholicism, 141, 167–68, 240

catoptric systems of lighting, 336

catty, 67

celadons, 36

ceramics, 34–37, 155–56, 161

Ceram Sea, 75

Chaiya, 161

chandu, 89

Changsha painted wares, 36

Chaudhuri, K. N., 12, 105, 150

Chavacano language, 170

Chavez, Juan de, 170

Chen Chen-kong, 171

Chengwimbe (slave), 136

Chettiar, A. K. Muthan, 299

chettiars, 288

Chetties, Tamil, 126n71

Chew, Daniel, 351

chiles, 302–3

China/Chinese: Africa as compared to, 25–26; African roles within, 48–49, 50; Africans toward, 47–49; base chronologies for, 392; binary authority within, 212–13; Buddhism in, 141; within Cambodia, 272; Catholicism and, 240; colonial influence within, 239–43; commodities traded by, 66; copper cash from, 60; drug smuggling in, 97; Dutch within, 241–43; East African texts/knowledge of, 38–47; as ethnic outsiders, 286–87; exotica goods of, 60; fragmentation within, 213; human trafficking from, 100; within Indonesia, 275–76; influence of, 149; Islam in, 141; within Java, 260–61, 262; magnetism of, 149; within Malaysia, 276–77; map of, 28; marine product industry within, 270, 403–7, 409; merchant role of, 258, 259; military armament of, 369; Ming/Ch'ing transition within, 62, 64; pearl industry within, 251; within the Philippines, 264–65, 274–75; porcelains of, 37, 109; power of, 373, 387–88; ship building within, 41; shipping complications within, 83; within Singapore, 277–80; smuggling and, 86–87, 95; within Southeast Asia, 268–74, 287; tagging efforts within, 94; trading by, 63–64; traditional polity within, 214; urban history of, 200; Vietnam trade with, 61, 70–71; weapons trade within, 240–41; women within, 68

China Hill (Bukit Cina), 388

Chinese Central Planning, 213

Ch'ing, 85

Ching-hsing Chi [Record of Travels], 38

Chola empire, 151, 159

Christians/Christianity, 1, 106, 142, 175

Christian West Papua, 220

cinnamon, 66, 291

cities, challenges, competition, and evolution of, 210–11, 215–18. *See also specific cities*

Citiherb (Hong Kong), 270–71

climate change, 75

Clive, leadership of, 124

clothing, trading of, 66

clove industry, 130, 131, 131–32n90, 131n89, 136

Coates, W. H., 83

cocaine, 95

Cochin, India, 117

Cocks, Richard, 56–57

Coen, Jan, 260

coffee trade, 231, 373–74

Cola Empire, 165

colonial oceanic circuits, 226, 235–39

commerce, language of, 67

commodities trade: of China, 63–64; of ecological products, 251–52; illegal transit of, 94; of Japan, 63; in Southeast Asia, 63, 108–9; within Vietnam, 60. *See also specific items*

Confucianization, 58

conquistadors, religion transfer by, 141

Constantinople, 227–28, 229–30, 289

constellations, bearings from, 39–40

consulates, 192

contrabanding: country traders, European within, 81, 83; deals within, 85–86; of drugs, 88–91, 96–97; economy and, 102; of firearms, 86; human trafficking within, 97–101; items within, 87; on junks, 83; of narcotics, 87, 96–97; of opium, 81, 83, 86, 88–91, 96; photo of, 98; politics and, 102; source of, 97; South China Sea history of, 81–91; South China Sea present of, 92–101; of spirits, 87; statistics of, 95; tagging for, 93–94

Cook, Kealani, 8

Cook, Nola, 272

coolies, recruiting of, 241–43

copper, 61–62, 336

copper cash, 67

Cores de Vries, 352n25

Coromandel coast, 283, 290–91

Cotabato, 175

cotton industry, 115, 124n61, 135

country traders, European, as smugglers, 81, 83

Coxinga, 49, 50, 51

Crawford, John, 65, 83

Cross-Cultural Trade in World History (Curtin), 285

Crossing the Bay of Bengal (Amrith), 150

currency, 58, 61, 67

Curtin, Philip, 285

Dalén, Nils Gustaf, 338

dammar, 66

Danish/Danes, 234

Dar es Salaam, 396

Dar-ul Salam (Arifin-Cabo, Dizon, and Mantawel), 181

Day, Tony, 200

Dayak people, 207

Deccan Plateau, 161

decentralization, 328n52

decolonization, effects of, 96

De Klerk (ship), 321

Delhi, India, 201, 203

Demak, 203

dependence, process of, 122

Deshima (Dejima), 1–2

dhows, 30

Diamondpoint lighthouse, 333

dioptric lenses, 337

diplomacy, 114

Dizon, Joel, 181

drugs, 66, 88–91, 95, 96–97

drums, archaeology of, 162

Du, Shen, 371–72

dual functionality, 212

Dunsun, 153

Dusun jars, 36

Dutch Blockade Runners, 90, 91
Dutch East India Company (VOC), 231
Dutch East Indies, 241–43, 354–60, 401
Dutch Indies, 328n52, 338
Dutch/Netherlands: aggressive mindset of, 237; Anglo-Dutch Treaty and, 349; within Batavia, 237–38, 260, 317; Borneo and, 238–39; within China, 241–43; exploration methods of, 317; Gouvernements Marine (GM), 322–23; hydrography by, 354–60, 361; hydrography of, 363; within India, 290; within Indonesia, 235–36; Japan and, 245; within Java, 261–62; lighthouses and, 333–34, 343; maritime policy of, 365; monopoly system of, 377–78; political interest within, 231; production control of, 138; publishing industry of, 317; scheepvaartregelingen use by, 352–53; slavery and, 241–43; within South Asia, 235; spice industry and, 294; spice trade and, 110; trading of, 62; within Vietnam, 57–58
Dutch Reef Notices, 353
Dvaravati civilization, 153
dwifungsi, 212

East Africa: armament imports to, 135; Asia and, 26–27; base chronologies for, 391–92; British presence within, 132; ceramics in, 36; Chinese texts/knowledge on, 38–47; fluctuations within, 135; Indians within, 135; Indonesian seafarers to, 27; industry types within, 135; map of, 34; Portuguese presence within, 128–29; poverty within, 136–37; slavery in, 130–31, 136; urbanization of, 31–32; warfare and turmoil within, 128. *See also specific locations*
East Asia, 76, 403–4. *See also specific locations*
East Borneo, 362, 363–64
East India Company, 123, 138
East Indies, 112
East Timor, 220
ecological products, 251–52
economy, 55–61, 102

ecstasy, 95
Edo (Tokyo), Japan, 202
Egypt, 230
Ellen, Roy, 11
Engels, Friedrich, 129
environmental history, of Asian seas, 251–53
Eritrea (Axum), 34
ethnic middlemen, 280

Faifo (Hội An), Vietnam, 56, 63, 64, 71
Faria, Dom Antonio da, 56
farming, revenue, Chinese, 259
Federated Malay States (FMS), 91, 328, 364
Ferrer, Raymundo, 181
Final Peace Agreement, 177
firearms, smuggling of, 86
fish, as marine product trade, 2–3, 271, 272–74
fishing, technology in, 310
Forbidden City, 202–3
Fort Canning, 340
Fort Jesus, Mombasa, 129
Foucault, Michel, 105
14K gang, 97
France/French, 57, 65, 72, 138, 230, 234
Frank, Andre Gunder, 9
Franklin (ship), 66–67
free trade, 114
French Chamber of Deputies, 229
Froberville, Barthélémy Huet de, 29
Fujian, China, 64, 83, 85, 213, 214

Gaddafi, Muammar, 177
Gate of Tears (Bab al-mandeb), 229
gems, 115
genetics, within Madagascar, 27
Gericke, Baron, 363–64
Germany, 114
Ghats, 399
Gia-long (Nguyễn Ánh), Emperor, 65, 66–67, 71
Giang Ann (ship), 321
Gilroy, Paul, 7
giraffe, 44, 45, 371–73
globalization, 92

Global Positioning Systems (GPS), 93
gold, 60, 66
Golden Triangle, 96
gold mining industry, 32
Gouvernements Marine (GM), 322–23
Gowing, Peter, 172
Great China Bazaar, 67
Gresik, Indonesia, 203
Grotius, Hugo, 384, 385
Guangdong, China, 83, 213, 214
Guangzhou, China, 84, 85, 270
guanxi (networks or connections), 209–10
Gujarati, 119, 290
Gulf of Thailand, 142, 162, 217, 272, 347
Gulf Sultanate, 135
gum copal, 134
Gunn, R. J., 242–43
Gunung Tabur, sultan of, 362

The Hague, 248, 328, 328n52, 342, 363
Hall, Kenneth, 148
Hamashita, Takeshi, 9–10
Hamel, P. S., 242
Hangzhou, China, 201
Haniffa, K. S. Mohamed, 298, 302
Hanoi, Vietnam, 214
Hashim, Salamet, 176
Hau'ofa, Epeli, 8
Hawai'i, United States, 28
herbalist, personal story of, 397–98
heroin, 95
Hindu Gods of Peninsular Siam (O'Connor),
    159–60
Hinduism/Hindus, 151, 158–59, 160, 291
Hoàng Anh Tuấn, 62, 63
Ho Chi Minh City (Saigon), Vietnam, 67,
    71–72, 215–16, 271
Hội An, Vietnam, 56, 63, 64, 71
holophotal light, 337
holothurians, 273–74
Hong Kong, China, 97, 196, 215, 222, 240–41,
    270, 404
Honshu, Japan, 62
Hooghly, India, 151

Horsburgh light, 332
Horton, Mark, 36
Ho Sheng Tang Company (Taipei, Taiwan),
    271
Houtman, Cornelis de, 29
Houtman, Frederick de, 29
Howrah, India, 151
human trafficking, 97–101
A Hundred Horizons (Bose), 150
Hurgronje, Snouck, 236
hybrid ships, 310
hydrography/hydrographic waters: agree-
    ments within, 362; conflicts regarding,
    364–65; importance of, 364; map of, 347;
    process of, 354–60; role of, 368; technology
    within, 361; terms of, 349

Ibn Battuta, 34, 191–92
India/Indians: British within, 123, 124–25,
    232–33; Buddhism in, 141, 146, 151, 160;
    chettiars, 288; Chola empire within, 159;
    commodity specialization of, 117–18;
    competition within, 125; Coromandel
    coast of, 290; dependence within, 122;
    Dutch within, 290; as emissaries, 133;
    English greed within, 126; Europeans
    within, 64–65, 117, 119–20, 121; fleets of,
    120–21; forts within, 152; Hinduism in,
    158–59, 160; influence of, 149, 152; Islam
    in, 141; London Board of Control and, 123;
    moneylender of, 287–88; Muslim Indian
    shippers within, 125; Mussalmans and, 122;
    Ottoman Sultans and, 122; Portuguese
    within, 291; private trading within, 126;
    within Singapore, 297; spice industry
    within, 289, 296–305, 399–400; stevedore
    in, 120; textile shipments to, 109; trading
    by, 118–19, 126, 129–30; urban history of,
    200; Zanzibar, 133. See also specific locations
Indian Ocean: Arena of Lights, 315; base
    chronologies for, 391; capitalism control
    within, 138–39; colonial oceanic circuits
    within, 226; eastern rim of, 108–16; gift
    variations within, 150; hydrographic

waters within, 347; Islam around, 141; linking themes within, 103–4; location of, 75; map of, 106; monsoon patterns within, 35; northern rim of, 116–27; personal story of, 385–86; piracy in, 113; ports around, 191; religion and, 106, 118; South China Sea connection to, 153; spice industry within, 110–11, 289; study centers for, 13; trade routes within, 21; Western commercial concerns within, 138; western rim of, 127–37. *See also* India; Southeast Asia

Indian Overseas Bank, 296

Indian Portuguese, 67

Indicopleustes, Cosmas, 32, 34

indigenous movement, surveillance and seepage of, 348–54

indigo, 66

Indische Staatsbladen, 325

Indochina, 230

Indo Commercial Society, 296

Indonesia: bridge concept for, 92–93; British power within, 235–36; Buddhism in, 146; China within, 275–76; drug smuggling to, 96–97; Dutch power within, 235–36; Islam in, 118; Malagasy language within, 28; marine product trade within, 275–76; pearl industry within, 251; polity of, 220; seafarers to East Africa from, 27; smuggling statistics of, 95; tagging efforts within, 94; trade routes within, 21

Indonesian New Guinea (West Papua), 101

Inspectorship of Lighting, Beaconing, and Pilotage, 323

intermarriage, 260–61

Iqbal, Mohagher, 181

Iranun people, 173–74

Irian Jaya, 326

iron, 109, 109n19, 338

Islam/Muslims, 32, 106, 118, 141, 142, 143, 176–81, 177, 184–85. *See also specific locations*

Istanbul, Turkey, 228

Isufu bin Sultan Hassan, 395

Italy, 230–31

ivory, 66, 132–33, 134

Jakarta, Indonesia, 211, 222, 276

Jambi, Sumatra, 203, 362

Japan: base chronologies for, 392; Buddhism in, 141, 146; competition by, 114; connections of, 245; Dutch and, 245; East India Company within, 56; exports from, 243–44; human trafficking from, 100; invasion of, 375–76; maritime influence of, 243–44; as modern power, 378–79; Mongols within, 375; narcotics legislation of, 91; pearl industry within, 251; ports of, 246; power of, 247; smuggling statistics of, 95; trading by, 63; urban history of, 200; Vietnam trade with, 61–62

Java, 32, 109n19, 260–67, 323, 376

Java Sea, 75, 331, 347, 386–87

Jeddah, Saudi Arabia, 231

Jesuits, 186, 186n42

Jews, 286

Johor, sultan of, 342

Joint Ceasefire Ground Rules, 177

junks, smuggling on, 83

Kaempfer, Engelbert, 29

Kassim, R. E. Mohamed, 297

Kedah, Malaysia, 153

kettle-bottomed boats, 310

Khmer empire, 152

Khmer Rouge, 221

Kilwa Kisiwani, Tanzania, 32, 136, 395

Kilwa Kivinge port, 132

Kim Eng Seng (ship), 113

Kin Sang Dispensary (Kowloon, Hong Kong), 270

Kizimbani, Zanzibar, 131

knowledge production, of the trade routes, 22

kofiyya, 135

Koh Kradad (ship), 157

Ko Khram (ship), 156

Koninklijke Pakevaart Maatschappij (KPM), 318, 352

Korea, 21, 141, 244–45

Ko Si Chang III (ship), 156

Ko Si Chung II (ship), 156, 157

Kota Kinabalu, 27
Kowloon, Hong Kong, 270
Kra Isthmus, 153, 154, 158, 164
K. Ramanlal and Co., 296, 300, 304–5
Kreutz, William, 185–86
Kuala Lumpur, Malaysia, 94, 217–18, 222, 276–77, 299
Kuala Lumpur Indian Chamber of Commerce (KLICC), 297
Kudarat, Sultan, 169–70
kunlun, 48
Kyoto, Japan, 201

Labuan, 87, 330, 358, 364, 368
Labuan Coalfields Company, 326–27
Laichen, Sun, 149
Lamu, Kenya, 32
Lanao, Philippines, 175
Langkasuka, 153, 154
Laos, 93, 95, 141, 146
Lapian, Pak Adrian, 195, 367
Latiff, Abdul, 298
Latiff and Sons, 296–97
Lê Dynasty, 54
lenses, lighthouse, 336–38
Lewis, Dianne, 11, 112
Lewis, Su Lin, 200
Libya, 177
Lieberman, Victor, 11, 199–200
lighthouses/lighting: in Anjer, 323; buoys and, 338; catoptric systems of, 336; designs of, 335–36; dioptric lenses, 337; expenses regarding, 331, 332; features of, 324, 325; by Gouvernements Marine (GM), 322–23; overview of, 310–11; photo of, 333; political implications of, 328–34; Screw-Pile lights, 337; symbolism of, 325, 342n94; technology changes within, 336–38; variability of, 335
lightships, 335
Lindi, 395–96
Lingard, Captain, 351
liquor, 87, 88
Lombard, Denys, 11

London Board of Control, 123
Longquan ceramics, 36
Lucman, Haroun al-Rashid, 178

Macao, 64
Macartney Mission, 65
Macau, China, 97
Madagascar, 27, 28
Madama Butterfly (Puccini), 244, 245
Madras, India, 126n71, 232
Maguindanao Sultanate, 170–71, 172
Ma Huan, 42–44, 192
Majapahit, 208
Majul, Cesar, 171
Makassar Strait, 327, 364
Malabar, India, 125, 283, 292, 293–94
Malagasy language, 28–31
Malay Peninsula, 112, 113, 118, 155, 160, 350
Malaysia: bridge concept for, 92–93; Chinese within, 276–77; contrabanding protection within, 93; drug smuggling to, 97; foreign laborers and, 97; hydrography of, 359; Japanese presence within, 378; law enforcement cooperation of, 93; Malagasy language within, 28–29; marine product trade within, 276–77; photo of, 98; prostitution within, 101; smuggling statistics of, 95; spice industry within, 297–98, 299, 301, 302, 304, 305, 399–400; trading within, 92
Malay States, 70
Malay tribal people, 48
Malindi, Kenya, 32
Malinowski, Bronislaw, 31
Maluku, 141, 220, 326
Manchu Qing, 49
Mandalay, Burma, 203
Mandarin, 67
Manerplaw, Burma, 219
Manila, Philippines, 175, 189, 203, 211, 274–75
Manila galleons, religion transfer by, 141
Mantawel, Khomenie, 181
mapping, 344–45, 347–48, 354–60. See also hydrography/hydrographic waters

Marcos, Ferdinand, 177, 178
Mare Liberum (Grotius), 384
Mariano, Luis, 29
marijuana, 95
marine product industry: history of, 257–67; photo of, 263, 264; trading of, 145, 403–7, 409; web of, 267–80
Marsden, William, 29, 31
Marshall, P. J., 123–24
Martaban jars, 36
Martin, Esmond Bradley, 136
Marx, Karl, 103, 105, 108, 117, 129, 137
Matrah, Oman, 135
Matsuda, Matt, 8
McVey, Ruth, 282
Mehta, Kirtikar, 304–5
Meiji Reforms, 378
Mekong Delta, 214
Melaka: connection with, 32; conquest of, 109; global reputation of, 215; harbor improvements within, 359; history of, 205–6; lighthouses/lighting within, 324; Madagascar's people from, 29; spice industry within, 299, 302, 304
Melaka Strait. *See* Straits of Melaka
Melaka Sultanate, 215
metals/precious metals, 58, 60, 61–62, 109, 109n19. *See also specific metals*
methamphetamine, 95
Middle East, 34, 125, 130–31, 136, 141, 391. *See also specific locations*
Midnapur, India, 151
Mindanao, Philippines, 141, 169, 170, 173, 174, 175
Ming Dynasty, 39, 156, 370
Ming Promulgation, 61–62
Ming Shi, 39
Minh-Mạng, 71
mining industry, 32, 60–61, 71
Mishima, Yukio, 1
Misuari, Nur, 176, 177–78
Mocha, Yemen, 119n49
Mogadishu, Somalia, 32
Mohamed, H. P. Jamal, 299
Mohamed, Seeni Naina, 299

Mombasa, Kenya, 32, 129
moneylender, Indian, 287–88
Mongkut, King, 116
Mongols, 375, 376
monopoly coercion, 206
monsoons, 21–22, 35, 117, 385
Moresby Treaty, 131
Moro Islamic Liberation Front (MILF), 176
Moro Kurier (periodical), 180
Moro National Liberation Front (MNLF), 176, 177
mosques, ceramics within, 36
Mozambique, 141
Muara, Brunei, 329–30
Mudimbe, V. Y., 137
Mughals, 118–19
multicultural exchange, 117
Mumford, Lewis, 366
Murray, Dian, 10
Muscat, Oman, 119n49, 133–34
Muslim Indian shippers, 125
Muslims/Islam, 32, 106, 118, 141, 142, 143, 176–81, 177, 184–85. *See also specific locations*
Mussalmans, 122
mustard, trading of, 66
Myanmar, 273
Mysore, India, 233

Nagasaki, Japan, 1, 202
Nakhon Si Thammarat, Thailand, 211
Nam Yong (ship), 322
Napoleonic Wars, 112
Narayan, Adiappa, 126n71
narcotics, 87, 95, 96–97
Natuna/Anambas, 325, 355
Nawab of Bengal, 122
Nederlandsch-Indsche Stoomvart Maatschappij (NISM), 318, 352n25
Needham, Joseph, 40
Nepal, 146, 159
Netherlands Indies, 363
networks (*guanxi*), 209–10
Nguyễn Dynasty, 54–56, 58, 62, 64
Nims Pte Ltd., 297

Noonsuk, Wannasarn, 162
North Borneo, 87, 330–31, 350. *See also* Borneo
North Korea, 95
North Sumatra, 342, 367–68
Nudjum-ul-Dowlah, Nabob, 124
Nusa Tenggara, 326

O'Connor, Stanley, 159–60, 163
oil, 385
Okinawa, Japan, 61
Oman, 2, 130, 133, 135, 228–29
Omani Arabs, 128
Omani station (Zanzibar), 129
Onrust shipyard, 318
opium, 81, 83, 86, 88–91, 96
Orang Laut, 172–73
Organization of Islamic Cooperation
    (OIC), 176
Ottomans, 229
Ottoman Sultans, 122
Oudh, India, 123–24, 124n61
Oxenden, George, 126n71

Pacific Ocean, 7, 315
Pakistanis, drug smuggling by, 97
Palembang, Indonesia, 327
Pangani port, 132
Pangkor Engagement, 350
Panopticon lighthouse, 333
Panpan, 153
Parak, Bhinji, 126n71
Parameswara (prince), 205
Pate Island, 32
pearl industry, 251, 263
Pearson, Michael, 150
Pemba, Mozambique, 32, 131, 131–32n90, 135
Penang, Malaysia, 98, 114, 125, 236–37, 338, 339, 359
pepper/pepper industry, 110, 252, 297, 303
Periplus of the Erythraean Sea (Ptolemy), 32
Pershing, John, 175
Persia, 34, 141
Persian Gulf, 75, 251, 385
Philippines: Catholicism within, 141; Chinese
    porcelain in, 109; Chinese within, 264–65,

274–75; conflict within, 176–81; contra-
    banding protection within, 93; drug
    smuggling to, 96–97; foreign laborers
    and, 97; international influences within,
    263–64; Japanese presence within, 378;
    Malagasy language within, 29; marine
    product trade within, 264–65; peace
    agreements of, 177; political hierarchy
    within, 178; publishing industry within,
    180–81; smuggling statistics of, 95; Spanish
    within, 170; United States and, 174
Phnom Penh, Cambodia, 221
Phongpaichit, Pasuk, 158
piloting, technology in, 310
Pinto, Mendes, 67–68
piracy, 67–68, 113, 321
Polaris (star), 39
polar seas, history of, 8–9
politics, contrabanding and, 102
Polo, Marco, 34, 191
Pondicherry, India, 234
porcelain. *See* ceramics
porcelain, trading of, 37, 66, 109
portmaster (shahbandar), office of, 192,
    201
ports, 191, 192, 339. *See also specific locations*
Portugal/Portuguese: within India, 291; pass
    system of, 118, 376–77; Red Sea trade by,
    230; within South Asia, 234; spice industry
    and, 290, 293–94; within Vietnam, 57, 58;
    writings from, 148
Portuguese Expulsion, 62
poverty, 136–37
Prasae Rayong (ship), 156, 157
Pritcher's Current, 22, 31
prostitution, 99–101, 111
Ptolemy, 32
Puccini, Giacomo, 244, 245
Pulangi River, 170
Pulao Condore, 65
Pulau Aor, Indonesia, 340
Pulau Bras lighthouse, 333, 340–41, 343
Pulau Weh, 236, 341
Pusan, South Korea, 244–45

Qatar, 228–29
Qin Dashu, 37
Qingping Market (Guangzhou), 84, 85

R. A. Ahamedsah Mohamed Sultan and
    Co., 301
Raffles Lighthouse, 332
Rajas, 113, 118
Ramos, Fidel, 177
Rampley, W. J., 136
Ranariddh, Norodom, 97
Rang Kwien (ship), 156, 157
Rangoon (Yangon), 204–5, 219, 273–74
Ranong, Burma, 273
Rasoo, S., 298, 302
Ratansing and Co., 296
Rediker, Marcus, 7
Red Sea, 75, 229, 230–31
Regeerings Almanak voor Nederlandsch Indië,
    325
Reid, Anthony, 11, 108, 151, 154–55, 199
Reland, Adriaan, 29
religion, 106, 118, 141–43, 145, 165, 374. See
    also specific religions
ReOrient (Frank), 9
revenue farming, 259
rhinoceros horn, 66
Riau, 261, 325, 362
rice, 66
Robinson, Ronald, 282
Rodriguez, Noelle, 182
Roszko, Edyta, 71
Russia, 230, 244
Russian Far Eastern fleet, 244
Russo-Japanese War, 247, 365

Sabah, Malaysia (Borneo), 27
Said bin Sultan, 395, 396
Saigon (Ho Chi Minh City), Vietnam, 67,
    71–72, 215–16, 271
sails, technology in, 310
Sarawak, Malaysia, 329, 330
Sawankhalok/Si Satchanalai, 34
scheepvaartregelingen, 352–53

Schell, Orville, 212–13
Scott, John, 124
Screw-Pile lights, 337
Seaman's Narrative of His Adventures during
    a Captivity among Chinese Pirates on the
    Coasts of Cochin-China (Brown), 68
Sea of Japan, 75
secret societies (Chinese), 87
Seemi Nanima Mohamed and Co., 305
seepage effect, 351
Selangor, 339
Semarang, Java, 211, 331
sepecks, 67
shellfish, 272–73
Shen Du, 44
Shenzhen, China, 213, 215
shipwrecks, 156, 157
Siam: archaeology within, 163–64; Britain
    and, 115–16; Buddhism in, 142, 158, 159–60;
    ceramics from, 34; Chinese within, 70;
    connections within, 163; as ground zero
    for contact, 152–57; Hinduism in, 159–60;
    Indian influence within, 153; Theravada
    Buddhism in, 118; trading within, 116,
    116n38, 148, 207–8
silk, 66
silver, 60, 62
Simmel, Georg, 255
Singapore: agreement requirements of, 362;
    British Sarawak and, 329; China within,
    277–80; Dutch within, 237; as economic
    and political center, 204–5; harbor improve-
    ments within, 339, 359; painting of harbor
    of, 204; Indians within, 297; influence of,
    196, 217; law enforcement cooperation of,
    93; lighthouses/lighting within, 324, 332,
    333, 334–35, 342, 343; marine product trade
    within, 277–80; origin of, 114; overview of,
    216–17; political conflict of, 328; prostitution
    within, 101; significance of, 222; smug-
    gling and, 86, 95; spice industry within,
    297, 300, 302, 303, 304–5; trading within, 92
Singapore-Batam-Johor Bahru Growth
    Triangle, 196

Singhasari Empire, 376

Sino-Southeast Asia, 257–60, 269

Sino-Vietnamese border, 94

Sivite temple, 159

Skinner, G. William, 257

slavery: in East Africa, 130–31, 136; as economic arrangement, 131n87; legislation regarding, 134; in Maguindanao, 170; to the Netherlands empires, 241–43; in Southeast Asia, 172–73; in West Africa, 136; in Zanzibar, 130–31, 134, 136

Smith, Adam, 104–5, 108, 117, 128, 137

Snow, Philip, 38

The Social Life of Things (Appadurai), 34

Sofala, Mozambique, 32

Somalia, 141

Song Dynasty, 38, 149

South Asia: base chronologies for, 391; British power within, 232–34; Danes within, 234; Dutch within, 235; French within, 234; map of, 283; Portuguese power within, 234; significance of, 248. *See also specific locations*

South China Sea: analysis of, 76; Arena of Lights, 315; Chinese presence within, 259, 369–70; commerce within, 60; connective project concepts for, 92–93; European control of, 81; exploration within, 355; functions of, 79; human trafficking within, 97–101; hydrographic waters within, 347; Indian Ocean connection to, 153; map of, 82, 372; prostitution and, 99–101; sharing examples within, 149–50; shipping expansion within, 81; smuggling history of, 81–91; smuggling present of, 92–101

Southeast Asia: archaeology within, 155–56; archipelagic worlds, marine product trade within, 274–77; base chronologies for, 392–93; British presence within, 112, 328; Chinese marine goods traders within, 268–74, 403–4; Chinese within, 259, 287; colonial circuits within, 235–39; concentricity of, 218–21; cultural changes within, 111; economic and political exchange within, 206–8, 212–15; economy of, 108–9; European arrival to, 109–10; evolution and adaptation/competition within, 205–6, 215–18; fulcrum of, 235–39; global cadence of, 209–11; human migration within, 295; hydrography within, 344–45; ideological unity within, 219; Indian influence within, 150–51; lighthouses/lighting within, 319–27, 341–43; mainland coast marine product industry within, 271–74; as middle ground, 51; military dimension within, 109–10; monarch power within, 110; political and religious systems in, 152; ports within, 195–96, 197; prostitution in, 111; religion within, 142; resistance-politics within, 218–19; slaving/raiding expeditions in, 172–73; social arenas of, 111; South China Sea and, 76, 150; spice trade in, 110–11; steam-shipping within, 318; technology studies within, 313n2; topography of, 347; trading within, 63, 108–9, 209–10; transitions within, 108; trans-regional cadence within, 200–202; travel routes to, 148; urban overview of, 198–200, 201, 208–9, 210–11. *See also specific locations*

Southeast Asia and the Ming Shi-lu (Wade), 45–46

Southeast Asia in the Age of Commerce (Reid), 11, 199

South Korea, 95

Spain, 170, 173

Spanish Manila, 60

spice industry: in Bombay, 304; historical dimensions of, 289–94; in India, 290–94, 304, 399–400; institutions supporting, 296–97; in Malaysia, 297–98, 299, 301, 302, 304, 305, 399–400; in Melaka, 302, 304; modern dimensions of, 294–305; overview of, 110, 145, 374; photo of, 291; significance of, 252; in Singapore, 300, 302, 303, 304–5

Spice Islands (Maluku), 208

spirits, smuggling of, 87, 88
Sri Lanka, 141, 161, 235
Srivijaya Empire, 162, 165
state-building, limits of, 96
stevedore, 120
stoneware, 36
Straights Settlements Blue Books, 325
Straits of Melaka: Anglo-Dutch competition within, 112; Anglo-Dutch Treaty and, 349; bridge concept for, 92–93; British presence within, 112; lighthouses/lighting within, 326, 328, 333–34, 339–41; location of, 75; Singapore and, 196; Srivjaya Empire in, 162; supply journeys within, 350; trading to, 148
Straits Settlements, 328, 329, 332
Strange Parallels (Lieberman), 199–200
stranger communities, 255–56
Suez Canal, 309, 318
Sukhothai, Siam, 34, 152
Sulawesi, Indonesia, 261, 325
Sulawesi Rebellion, 220
Sulu basin, 172, 174, 175
Sulu Sea, 75, 83, 168, 266, 315
Sulu Sultanate, 170, 172–73, 174
The Sulu Zone (Warren), 172
Sumatra, 220, 243, 325, 331, 350
Sumba, 141
Sunda Shelf, 75
Sunda Strait, 347
Sur, Oman, 2
Surabaya Harbor, 318
Surabaya Marine, 318n16
Surat, India, 119n49, 121, 125
Sutherland, Heather, 266
Suzhou, China, 201
Swahili Coast, 30
Swahili language, 32

tagging, 93–94
Taiwan, 64, 95, 270
Tambelan, 355
Tambiah, Stanley, 158
Tambralinga, 154, 162

Tamil people, 48
Tandjoeng Tedoeng, 86
T'ang Dynasty, 38, 161
Tansen Sen, 46
Tân Sơn Rebellion, 65, 71
Tanzania, 131
Tarling, Nicholas, 113
Tausug people, 173–74
taxes, 132
Technics and Civilization (Mumford), 366
technology, 309–11, 313–14, 320, 335, 361, 374
textiles, trading of, 109
Thailand: amulet significance within, 157–64; Burma and, 219; foreign laborers and, 97; marine product trade within, 272; shipwrecks near, 156; smuggling statistics of, 95; Theravada Buddhism in, 141; vessel photo from, 99; votive significance within, 157–64
Thandapani Co., 298
Theravada Buddhism, 118, 141, 159
Thousand Islands, 321, 331
Timmanna, Beri, 126n71
tin, 112
tobacco, 109
Tokyo, Japan, 91
Tonle Sap, Cambodia, 272
Trade and Civilisation in the Indian Ocean (Chaudhuri), 12
Treaty of Paris, 65
Trengganu, sultan of, 113–14
trepang (sea cucumber), 264
Trịnh polity, 54–55, 57, 58, 62–63
Tripoli Agreement, 177
Triton (ship), 322
Tsushima Straits, 379
Tuban, Java, 203
turtle shell, 263
typhoons, 376

Uhlenback, P. F., 323
U Myint Thein, 273
Unfederated Malay States, 328
United States, 114, 174

Unyamwezi, 132
Utto, Datu, 174

Venkatapati, Khrishnama, 126n71
vermilion, 66
vessels: blockade runners (Dutch), 90,
    91; building of, 41; European bottoms,
    119–20; illustration of, 42; of India, 120–21;
    Koh Kradad, 157; *Ko Khram*, 156; *Ko Si
    Chang III*, 156; *Ko Si Chung II*, 156, 157;
    Orang Laut, 172–73; *Prasae Rayong*, 156,
    157; *Rang Kwien*, 156, 157; technology in,
    310; of Thailand, 99; *Triton*, 322; turtle
    ships (Korea), 141; *Willem I*, 321
Vietnam: "Ave Maria," 59; binary authority
    within, 214–15; Buddhism in, 146; capital-
    ism and, 71; ceramics from, 34; China
    trade with, 61, 70–71; commodities traded
    within, 66; Dutch within, 57–58; economy
    within, 55–61; ethnic miniorities in court
    of, 69; Europeans within, 56–57, 64–65,
    67–71; French within, 57, 72; gold trade
    of, 60; Japan trade with, 61–62; kingdoms
    within, 152; law enforcement cooperation
    of, 93; linkages within, 61–67; marine
    product trade within, 271; maritime trade
    orbit of, 54; merchant characteristics
    within, 69; mining industry within, 60–61,
    71; missionaries to, 58; piracy within,
    67–68; Portuguese within, 57, 58; precious
    metals within, 58; silver trade of, 60, 62;
    smuggling statistics of, 95; topography
    photo of, 70; trade closing by, 72; trading
    fleets in, 69; women within, 68–69
Vietnam War, 216
Viraphol, Sarasin, 85
Vishnu, 160
Visnaivite temple, 159
VOC (Dutch East India Company), 231
Von der Goltz Pasha, 227–28
votives, 157–64, 165–66

Wade, Geoff, 45–46, 149
Wadi, Julkipli, 183

Wallerstein, Immanuel, 106
Waq-Waqs, 31
Warren, James Francis, 11, 172, 266, 351
Wat Arun (Bangkok), 36
Wazir of Oudh, 122
weapons, trading of, 86, 240–41
weather, cycles of, 21–22
weaving, 135
Weber, Max, 255
West Africa, slavery in, 136
White, John, 65, 66–67, 68
whitewares, 36–37
Willem I (ship), 321
Willem lighthouse, 333
Winter, Edward, 126n71
Wolf, Eric, 104, 114, 135
women: Age of Commerce and, 111; within
    Buddhism, 155; within China, 68; human
    trafficking of, 99–101; within Vietnam,
    68–69
Wood, General Leonard, 174–75
wood, trading of, 66
Woodward, Hiram, 160–61
Wu-Bei-Zhi [Notes on Military Preparedness],
    39, 43
Wyatt, Don, 47–48

Xiamen (Amoy), Fujian, China, 83, 85,
    270
Xing-cha Sheng-lag [The Triumphant Vision
    of the Starry Raft], 39

Yemen, 21
Ying-yai Shen-lan, 39
Yokohama, Japan, 202
Yuan Dynasty, 149
Yunnan, China, 114–15
Yu-yang Tsa-tsu [Assorted Dishes from
    Yu-yang], 38

Zamboanga, Mindanao: bombing in,
    168n2, 185; Catholicism within, 167–68;
    Chavacano language within, 170; conflict
    within, 176–81; demographics of, 187n43;

features of, 143, 167, 188–89; history of, 169–76; Islam within, 143, 167–68, 171–72, 189; Jesuits within, 186; location of, 167, 189; personal experience within, 181–88; photo of, 173; slave escape to, 170, 173; Spanish within, 170, 185n40
Zamorins, 118
Zanzibar: British dependence by, 130, 134; British India and, 128; cloves within, 130, 131; Indians within, 133–34; ivory trade within, 132–33; *kofiyya* in, 135; Omani station at, 129; Oman split from, 130; rise of, 127; slavery in, 130–31, 134, 136; structural changes of, 127–28, 129, 130; taxes within, 132; trading within, 129
Zhao Bing, 37
Zhao Ru Gua, 25, 38, 373, 375
Zhejiang, China, 83
Zheng He, 41, 42, 51, 156, 192, 370–71
Zhu Fan Zhi [Gazetteer of Foreigners] (Gua), 38, 375
Zhuhai, China, 213